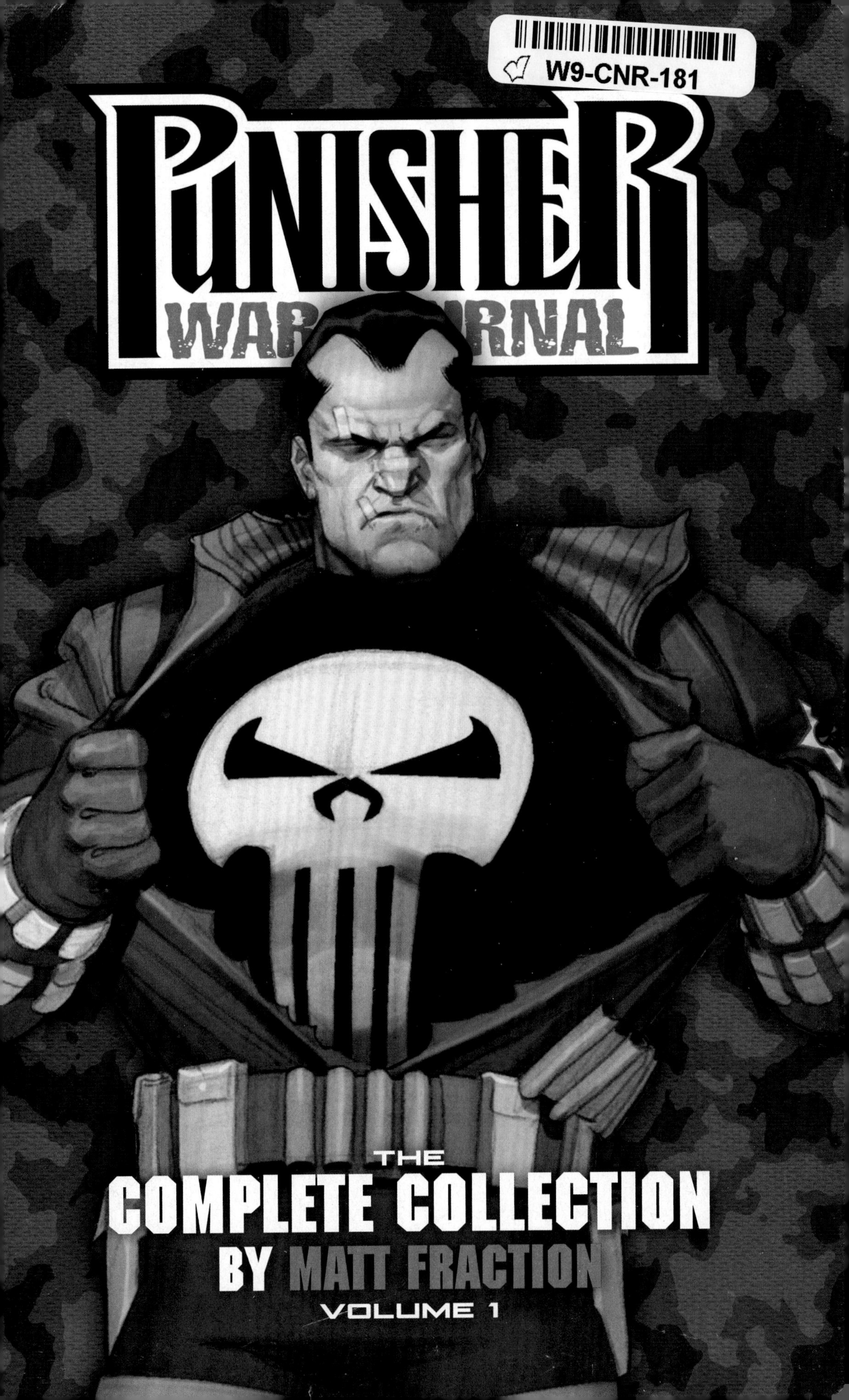
PUNISHER
THE
COMPLETE COLLECTION
BY MATT FRACTION
VOLUME 1

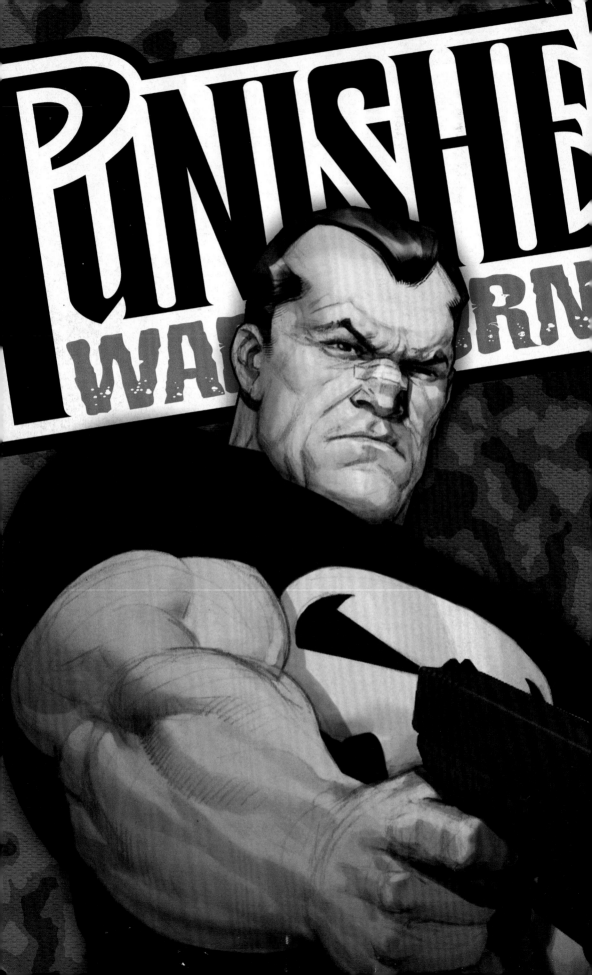

THE COMPLETE COLLECTION

MATT FRACTION
WRITER

ISSUES #1-3

ARIEL OLIVETTI
ARTIST

DEAN WHITE
COLOR ARTIST

ISSUES #4

MIKE DEODATO JR.
ARTIST

RAIN BEREDO
COLORIST

ISSUES #5-10 & #12

ARIEL OLIVETTI
ARTIST & COLORIST

ISSUE #11

LEANDRO FERNÁNDEZ
PENCILER

FRANCISCO PARONZINI
INKER

VAL STAPLES
COLORIST

ISSUE #1 BLACK-&-WHITE EDITION

ARIEL OLIVETTI
ARTIST

VC'S JOE CARAMAGNA [#1-11 & #1 B&W edition] & RUS WOOTON [#12]
LETTERERS

ARIEL OLIVETTI & JASON KEITH [#1]
ARIEL OLIVETTI [#2-3, #5-12 & #1 B&W edition]
MIKE DEODATO JR. & RAIN BEREDO [#4]
COVER ART

MICHAEL O'CONNOR & AUBREY SITTERSON
ASSISTANT EDITORS

WARREN SIMONS
EDITOR, ASSISTING

AXEL ALONSO & AUBREY SITTERSON
EDITORS

AXEL ALONSO
EXECUTIVE EDITOR

COLLECTION EDITOR MARK D. BEAZLEY ■ ASSISTANT EDITOR CAITLIN O'CONNELL
ASSOCIATE MANAGING EDITOR KATERI WOODY ■ ASSOCIATE MANAGER, DIGITAL ASSETS JOE HOCHSTEIN
SENIOR EDITOR, SPECIAL PROJECTS JENNIFER GRUNWALD ■ VP PRODUCTION & SPECIAL PROJECTS JEFF YOUNGQUIST
RESEARCH & LAYOUT JEPH YORK ■ BOOK DESIGNER JAY BOWEN ■ SVP PRINT, SALES & MARKETING DAVID GABRIEL

EDITOR IN CHIEF C.B. CEBULSKI ■ CHIEF CREATIVE OFFICER JOE QUESADA
PRESIDENT DAN BUCKLEY ■ EXECUTIVE PRODUCER ALAN FINE

PUNISHER WAR JOURNAL BY MATT FRACTION: THE COMPLETE COLLECTION VOL. 1. Contains material originally published in magazine form as PUNISHER WAR JOURNAL #1-12 and #1 B&W EDITION. First printing 2018. ISBN 978-1-302-91642-8. Published by MARVEL WORLDWIDE, INC., a subsidiary of MARVEL ENTERTAINMENT, LLC. OFFICE OF PUBLICATION: 135 West 50th Street, New York, NY 10020. **Printed in Canada.** DAN BUCKLEY, President, Marvel Entertainment; JOHN NEE, Publisher; JOE QUESADA, Chief Creative Officer; TOM BREVOORT, SVP of Publishing; DAVID BOGART, SVP of Business Affairs & Operations, Publishing & Partnership; DAVID GABRIEL, SVP of Sales & Marketing, Publishing; JEFF YOUNGQUIST, VP of Production & Special Projects; DAN CARR, Executive Director of Publishing Technology; ALEX MORALES, Director of Publishing Operations; DAN EDINGTON, Managing Editor; SUSAN CRESPI, Production Manager; STAN LEE, Chairman Emeritus. For information regarding advertising in Marvel Comics or on Marvel.

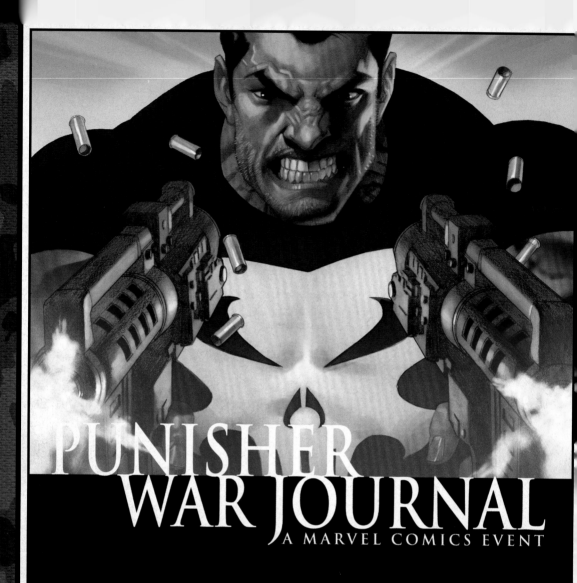

PUNISHER
WAR JOURNAL
A MARVEL COMICS EVENT

CIVIL
WAR

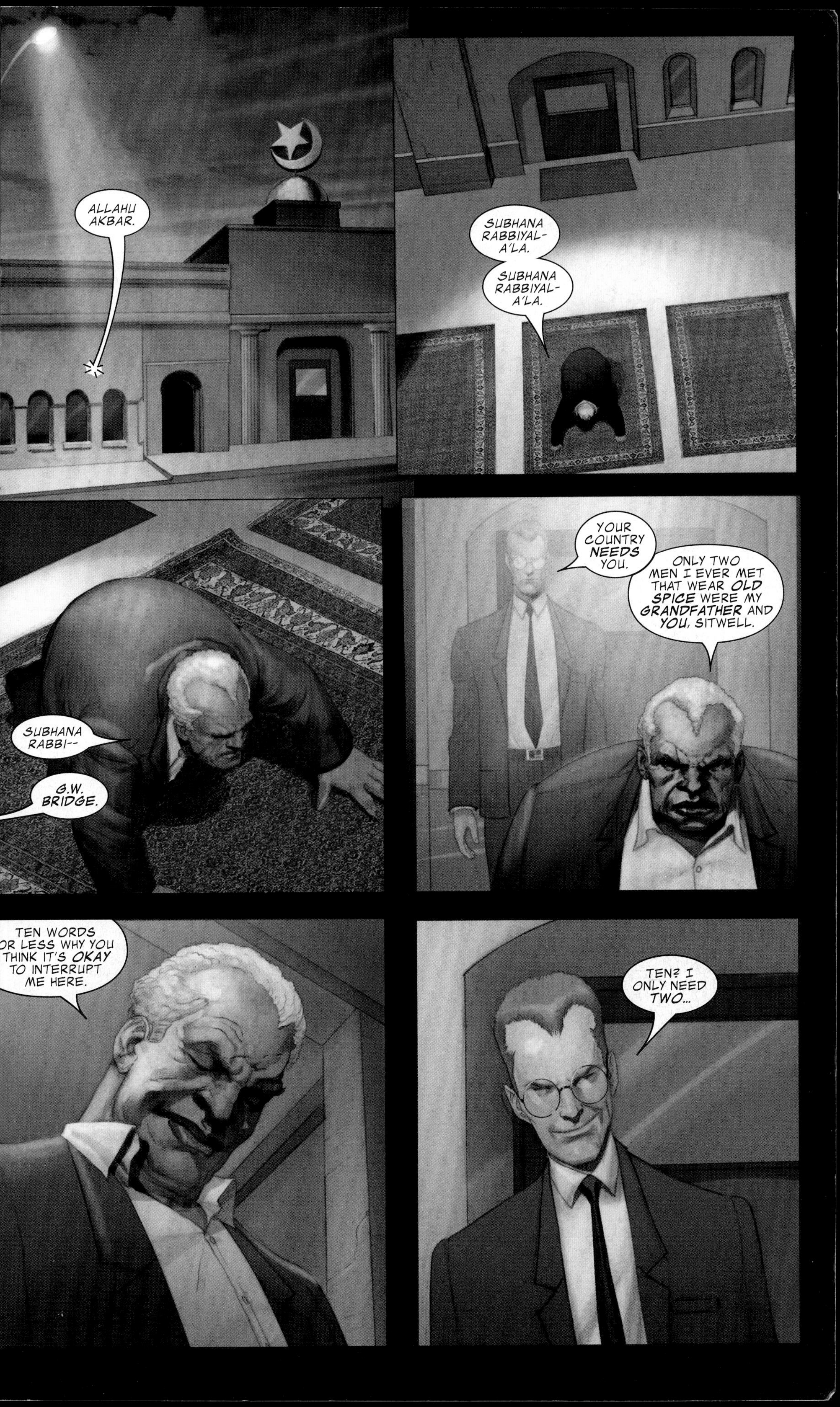
ALLAHU AKBAR.
SUBHANA RABBIYAL-A'LA.
SUBHANA RABBIYAL-A'LA.
SUBHANA RABBI--
G.W. BRIDGE.
YOUR COUNTRY NEEDS YOU.
ONLY TWO MEN I EVER MET THAT WEAR OLD SPICE WERE MY GRANDFATHER AND YOU, SITWELL.
TEN WORDS OR LESS WHY YOU THINK IT'S OKAY TO INTERRUPT ME HERE.
TEN? I ONLY NEED TWO...

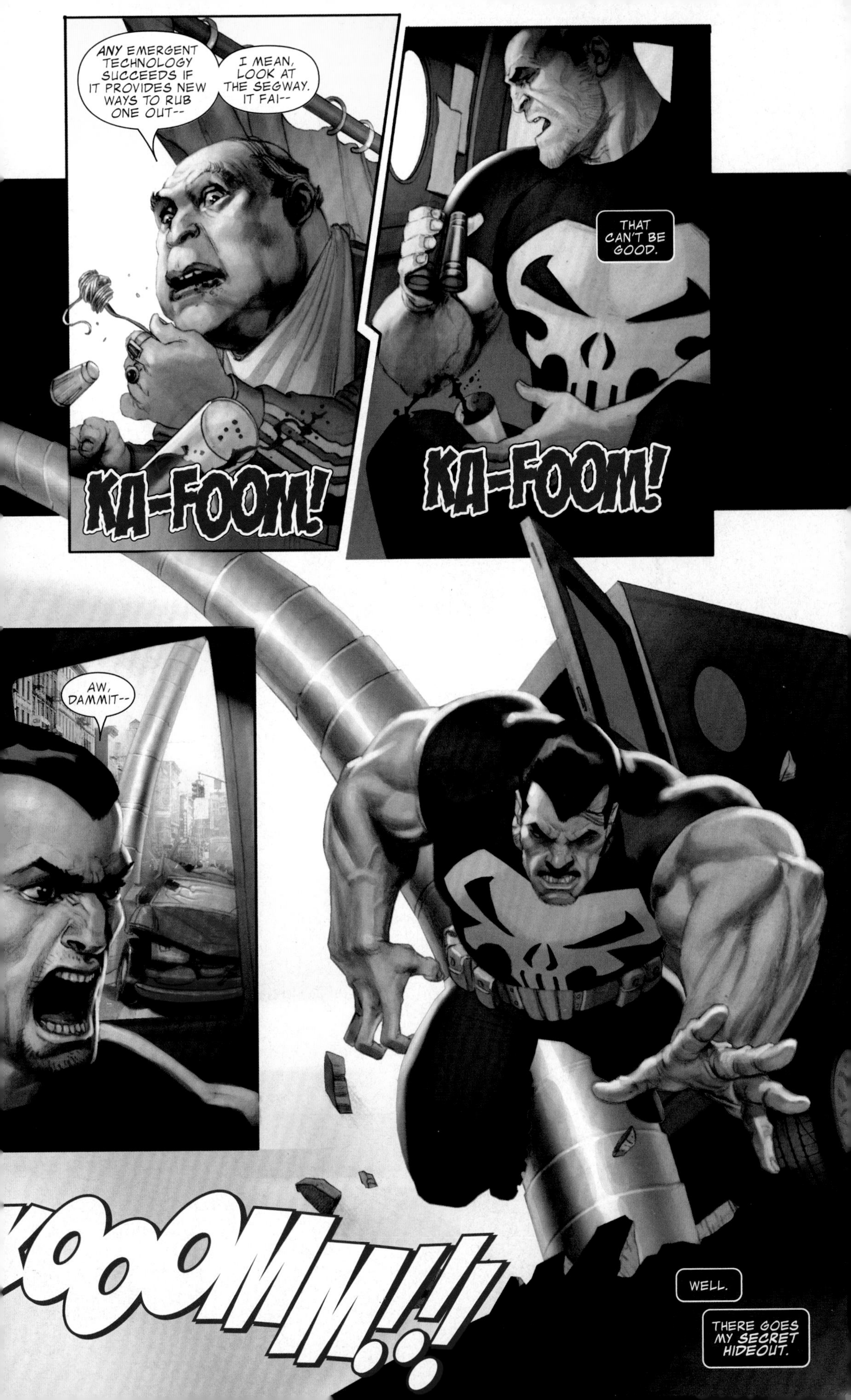
ANY EMERGENT TECHNOLOGY SUCCEEDS IF IT PROVIDES NEW WAYS TO RUB ONE OUT--
I MEAN, LOOK AT THE SEGWAY. IT FAI--
KA-FOOM!
THAT CAN'T BE GOOD.
KA-FOOM!
AW, DAMMIT--
KOOOMM!!!
WELL.
THERE GOES MY SECRET HIDEOUT.

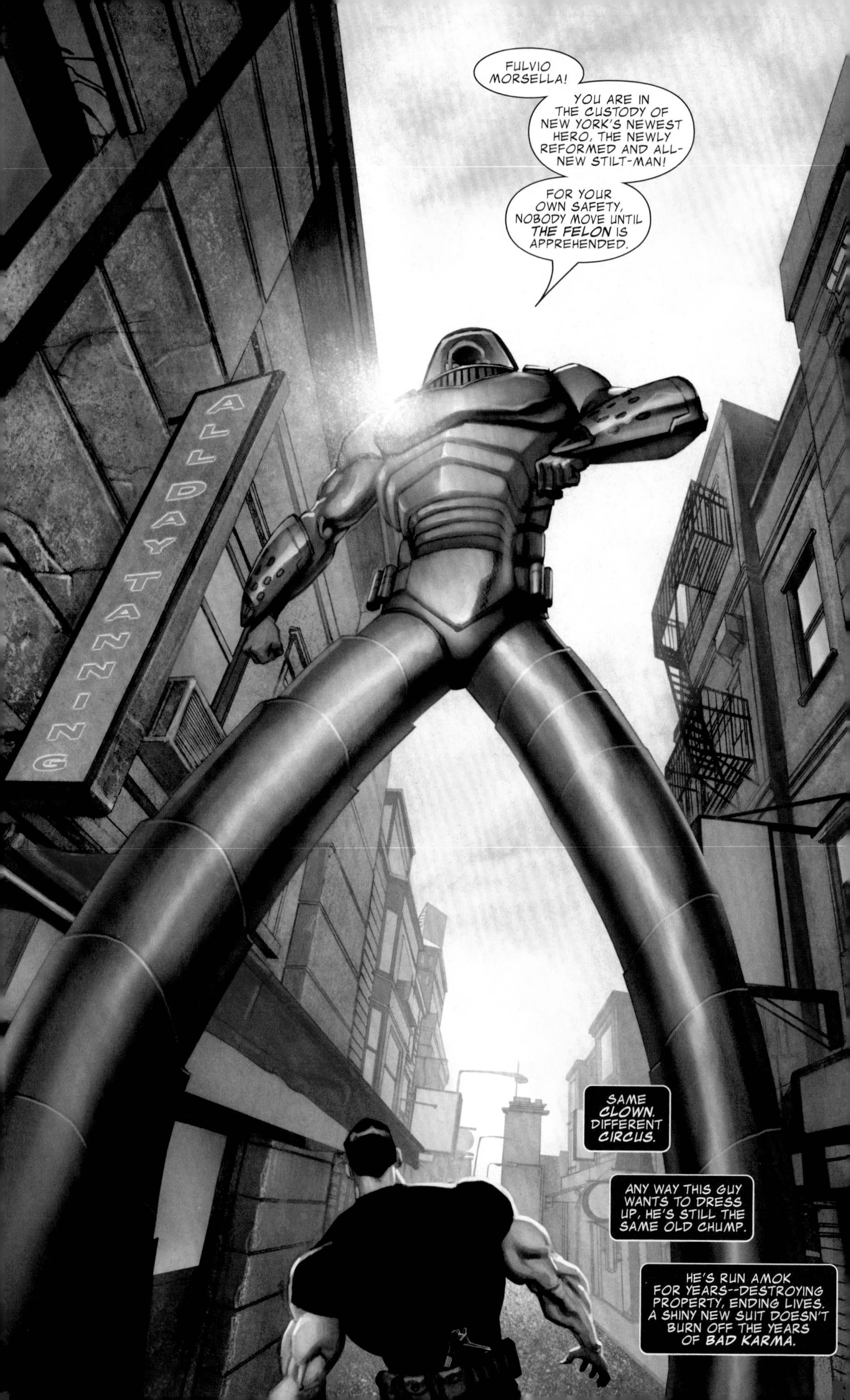
FULVIO MORSELLA!
YOU ARE IN THE CUSTODY OF NEW YORK'S NEWEST HERO, THE NEWLY REFORMED AND ALL-NEW STILT-MAN!
FOR YOUR OWN SAFETY, NOBODY MOVE UNTIL *THE FELON* IS APPREHENDED.
ALL DAY TANNING
SAME *CLOWN*. DIFFERENT *CIRCUS*.
ANY WAY THIS GUY WANTS TO DRESS UP, HE'S STILL THE SAME OLD CHUMP.
HE'S RUN AMOK FOR YEARS--DESTROYING PROPERTY, ENDING LIVES. A SHINY NEW SUIT DOESN'T BURN OFF THE YEARS OF *BAD KARMA*.

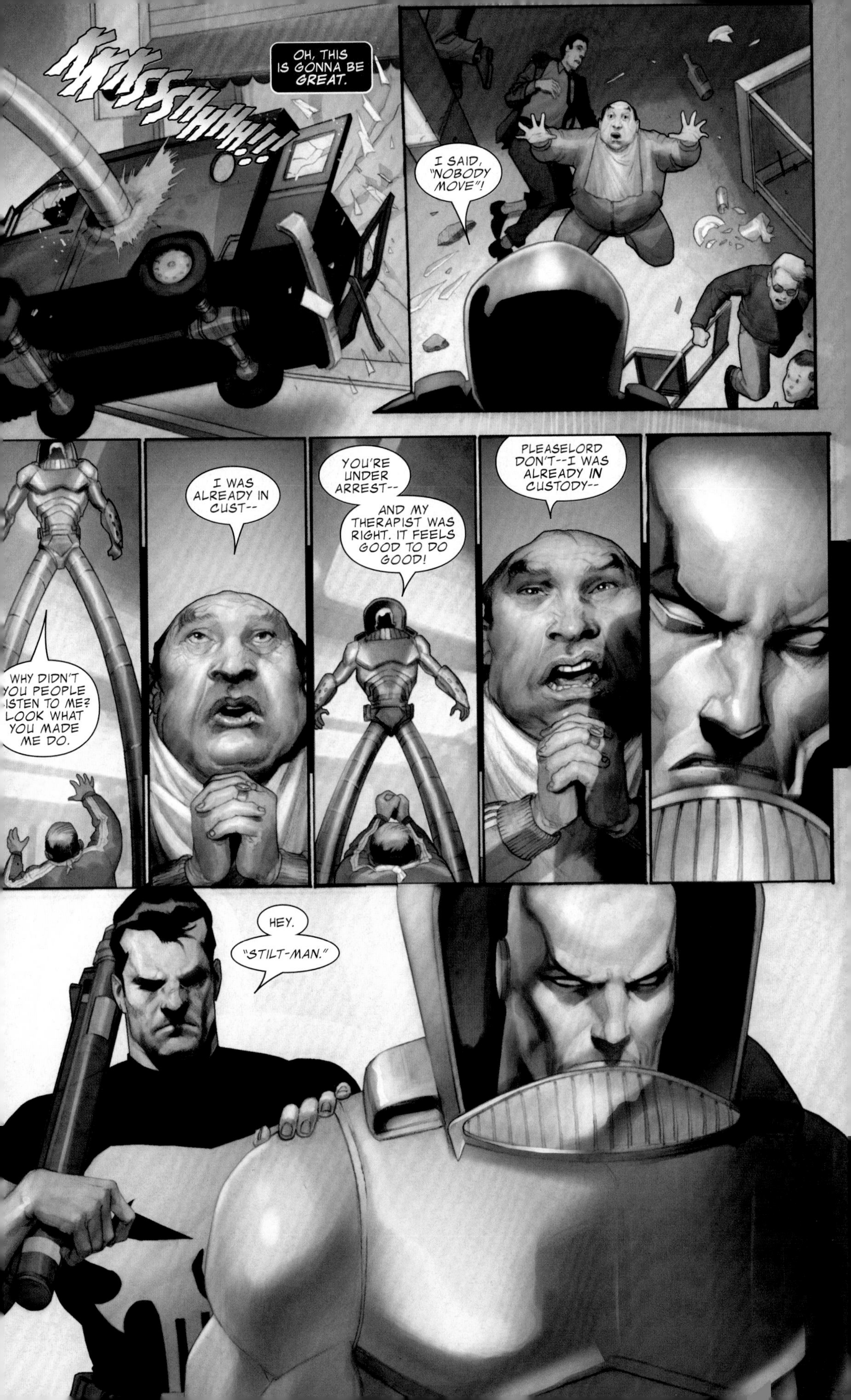
KKKSSHHHH!!!
OH, THIS IS GONNA BE GREAT.
I SAID, "NOBODY MOVE"!
WHY DIDN'T YOU PEOPLE LISTEN TO ME? LOOK WHAT YOU MADE ME DO.
I WAS ALREADY IN CUST--
YOU'RE UNDER ARREST--
AND MY THERAPIST WAS RIGHT. IT FEELS GOOD TO DO GOOD!
PLEASELORD DON'T--I WAS ALREADY IN CUSTODY--
HEY.
"STILT-MAN."

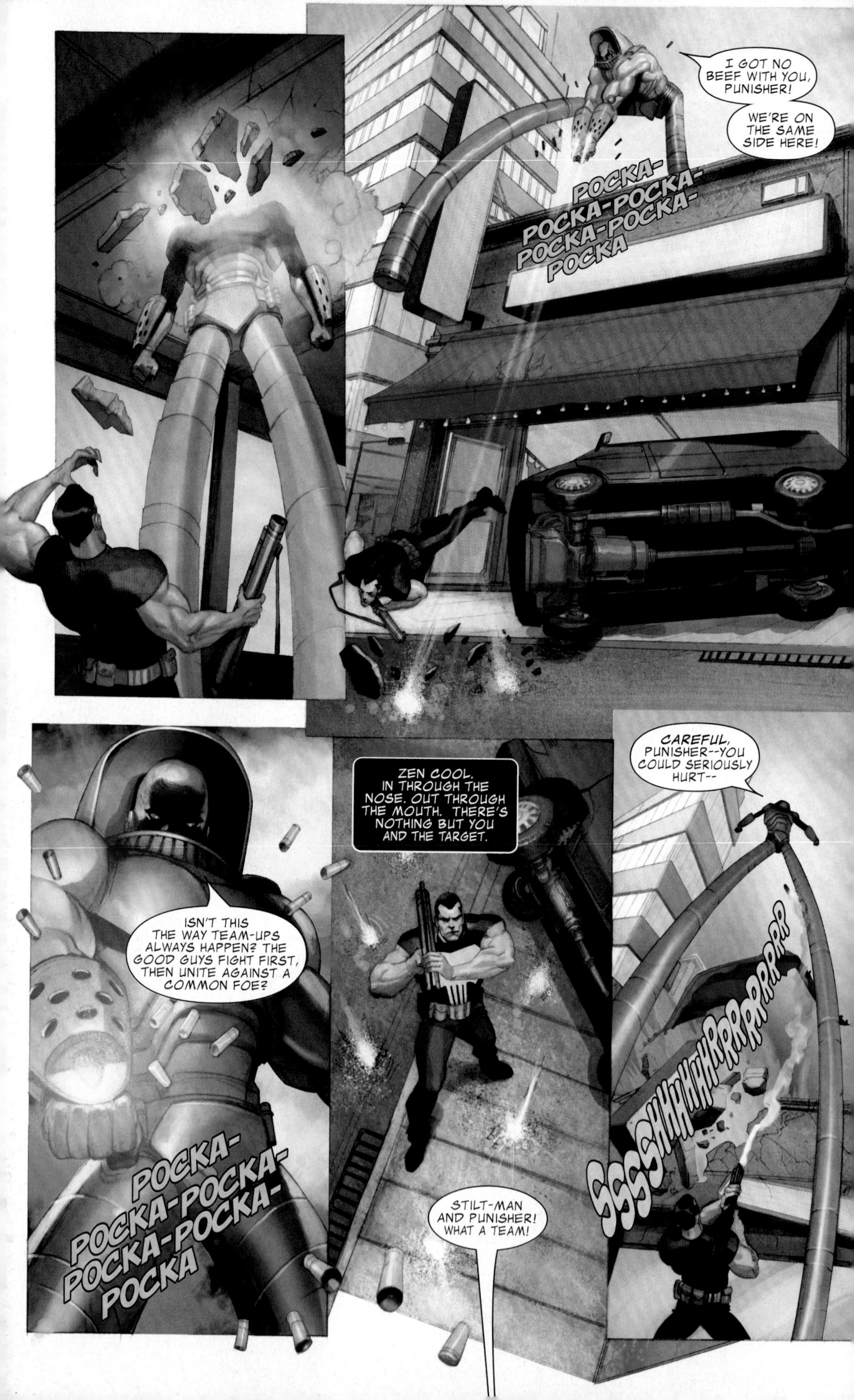
I GOT NO BEEF WITH YOU, PUNISHER!
WE'RE ON THE SAME SIDE HERE!
POCKA-POCKA-POCKA-POCKA-POCKA-POCKA
ISN'T THIS THE WAY TEAM-UPS ALWAYS HAPPEN? THE GOOD GUYS FIGHT FIRST, THEN UNITE AGAINST A COMMON FOE?
POCKA-POCKA-POCKA-POCKA-POCKA-POCKA
ZEN COOL. IN THROUGH THE NOSE. OUT THROUGH THE MOUTH. THERE'S NOTHING BUT YOU AND THE TARGET.
STILT-MAN AND PUNISHER! WHAT A TEAM!
CAREFUL, PUNISHER--YOU COULD SERIOUSLY HURT--
SSSSHHHHHHRRRRRRRRR

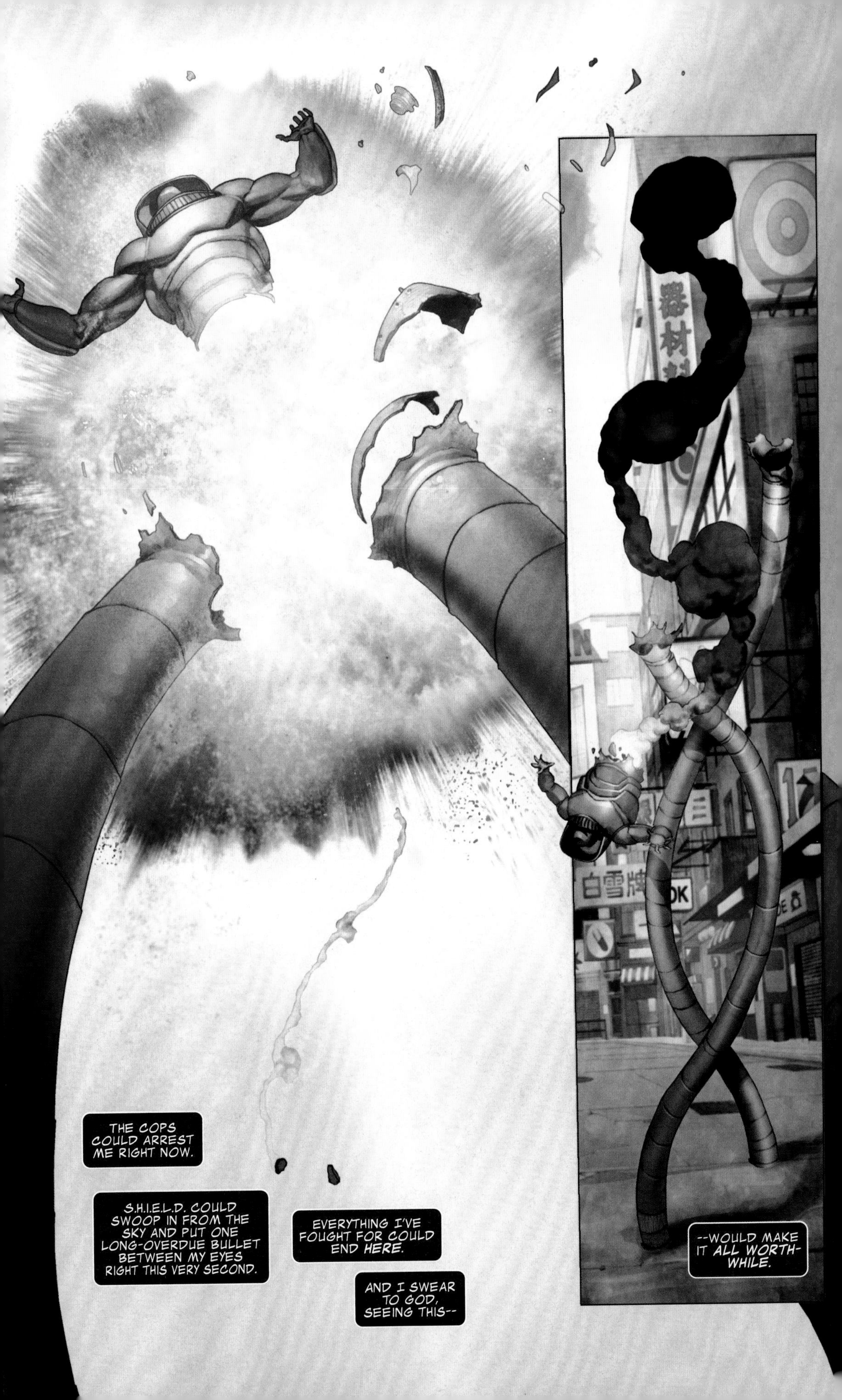
THE COPS COULD ARREST ME RIGHT NOW.
S.H.I.E.L.D. COULD SWOOP IN FROM THE SKY AND PUT ONE LONG-OVERDUE BULLET BETWEEN MY EYES RIGHT THIS VERY SECOND.
EVERYTHING I'VE FOUGHT FOR COULD END HERE.
AND I SWEAR TO GOD, SEEING THIS--
--WOULD MAKE IT ALL WORTH-WHILE.

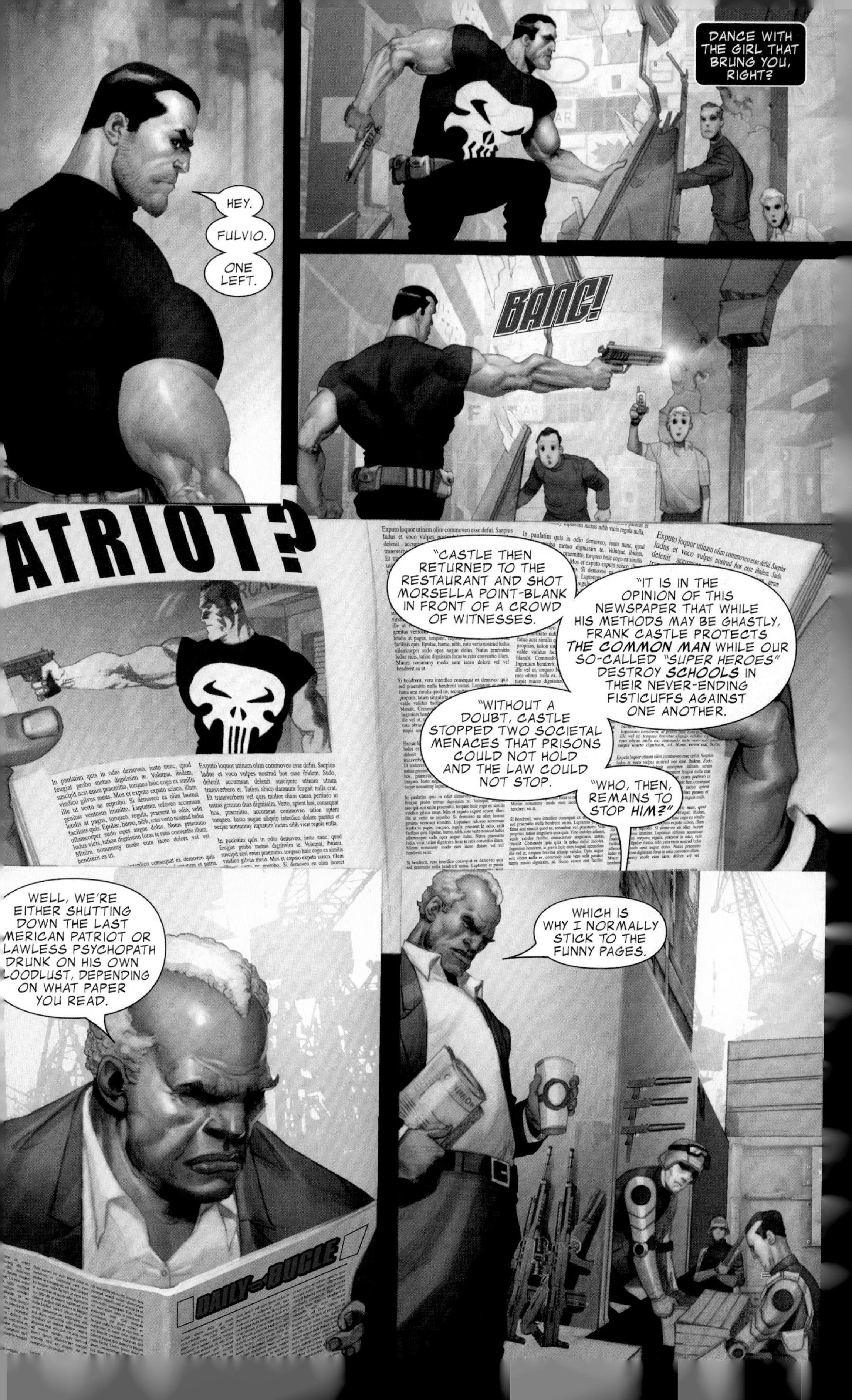
HEY.
FULVIO.
ONE LEFT.
DANCE WITH THE GIRL THAT BRUNG YOU, RIGHT?
BANG!
ATRIOT?
"CASTLE THEN RETURNED TO THE RESTAURANT AND SHOT MORSELLA POINT-BLANK IN FRONT OF A CROWD OF WITNESSES.
"IT IS IN THE OPINION OF THIS NEWSPAPER THAT WHILE HIS METHODS MAY BE GHASTLY, FRANK CASTLE PROTECTS THE COMMON MAN WHILE OUR SO-CALLED "SUPER HEROES" DESTROY SCHOOLS IN THEIR NEVER-ENDING FISTICUFFS AGAINST ONE ANOTHER.
"WITHOUT A DOUBT, CASTLE STOPPED TWO SOCIETAL MENACES THAT PRISONS COULD NOT HOLD AND THE LAW COULD NOT STOP.
"WHO, THEN, REMAINS TO STOP HIM?"
WELL, WE'RE EITHER SHUTTING DOWN THE LAST MERICAN PATRIOT OR LAWLESS PSYCHOPATH DRUNK ON HIS OWN LOODLUST, DEPENDING ON WHAT PAPER YOU READ.
DAILY BUGLE
WHICH IS WHY I NORMALLY STICK TO THE FUNNY PAGES.

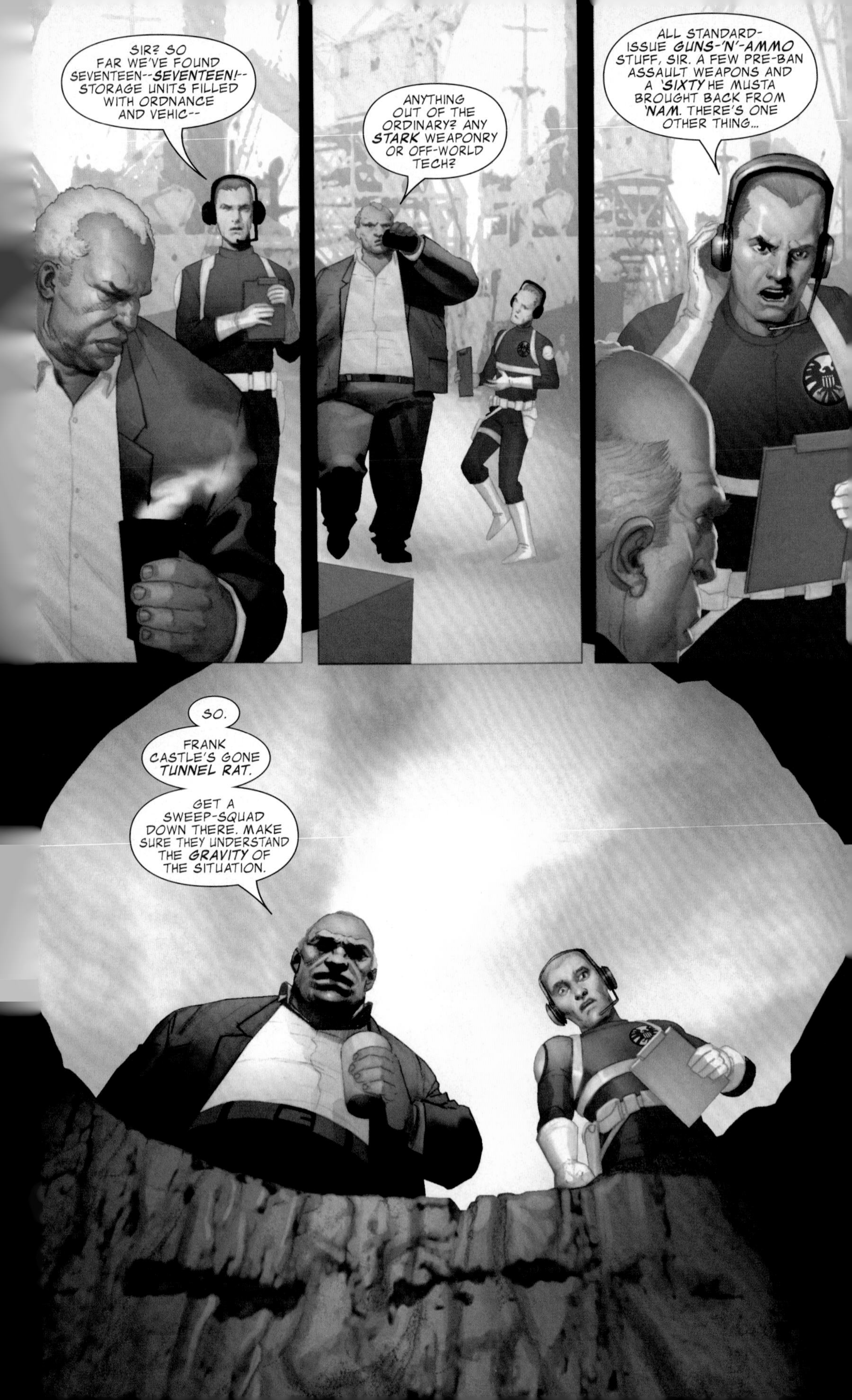
SIR? SO FAR WE'VE FOUND SEVENTEEN--SEVENTEEN!--STORAGE UNITS FILLED WITH ORDNANCE AND VEHIC--
ANYTHING OUT OF THE ORDINARY? ANY STARK WEAPONRY OR OFF-WORLD TECH?
ALL STANDARD-ISSUE GUNS-'N'-AMMO STUFF, SIR. A FEW PRE-BAN ASSAULT WEAPONS AND A 'SIXTY HE MUSTA BROUGHT BACK FROM 'NAM. THERE'S ONE OTHER THING...
SO.
FRANK CASTLE'S GONE TUNNEL RAT.
GET A SWEEP-SQUAD DOWN THERE. MAKE SURE THEY UNDERSTAND THE GRAVITY OF THE SITUATION.

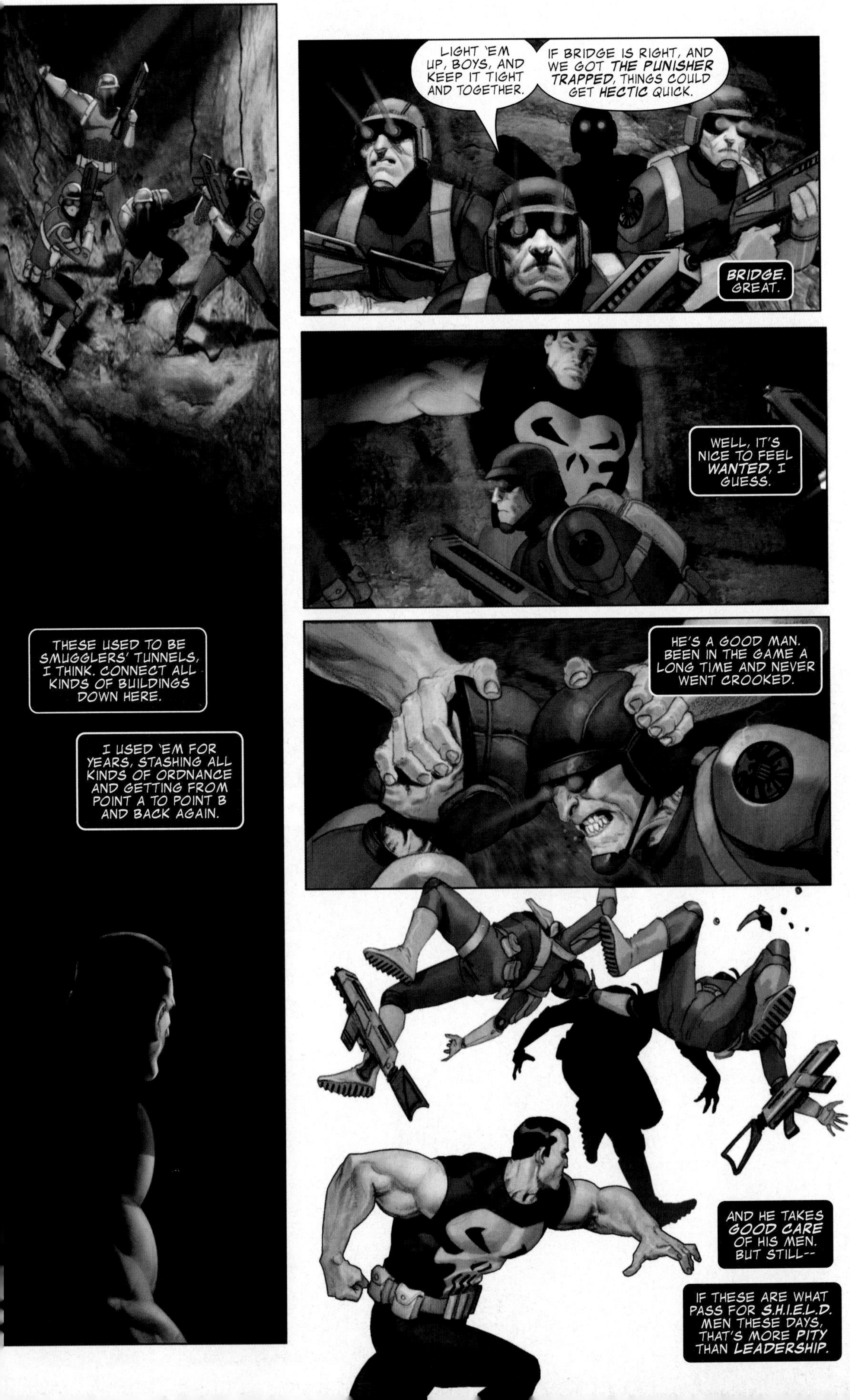
LIGHT 'EM UP, BOYS, AND KEEP IT TIGHT AND TOGETHER.
IF BRIDGE IS RIGHT, AND WE GOT THE PUNISHER TRAPPED, THINGS COULD GET HECTIC QUICK.
BRIDGE. GREAT.
WELL, IT'S NICE TO FEEL WANTED, I GUESS.
THESE USED TO BE SMUGGLERS' TUNNELS, I THINK. CONNECT ALL KINDS OF BUILDINGS DOWN HERE.
I USED 'EM FOR YEARS, STASHING ALL KINDS OF ORDNANCE AND GETTING FROM POINT A TO POINT B AND BACK AGAIN.
HE'S A GOOD MAN. BEEN IN THE GAME A LONG TIME AND NEVER WENT CROOKED.
AND HE TAKES GOOD CARE OF HIS MEN. BUT STILL--
IF THESE ARE WHAT PASS FOR S.H.I.E.L.D. MEN THESE DAYS, THAT'S MORE PITY THAN LEADERSHIP.

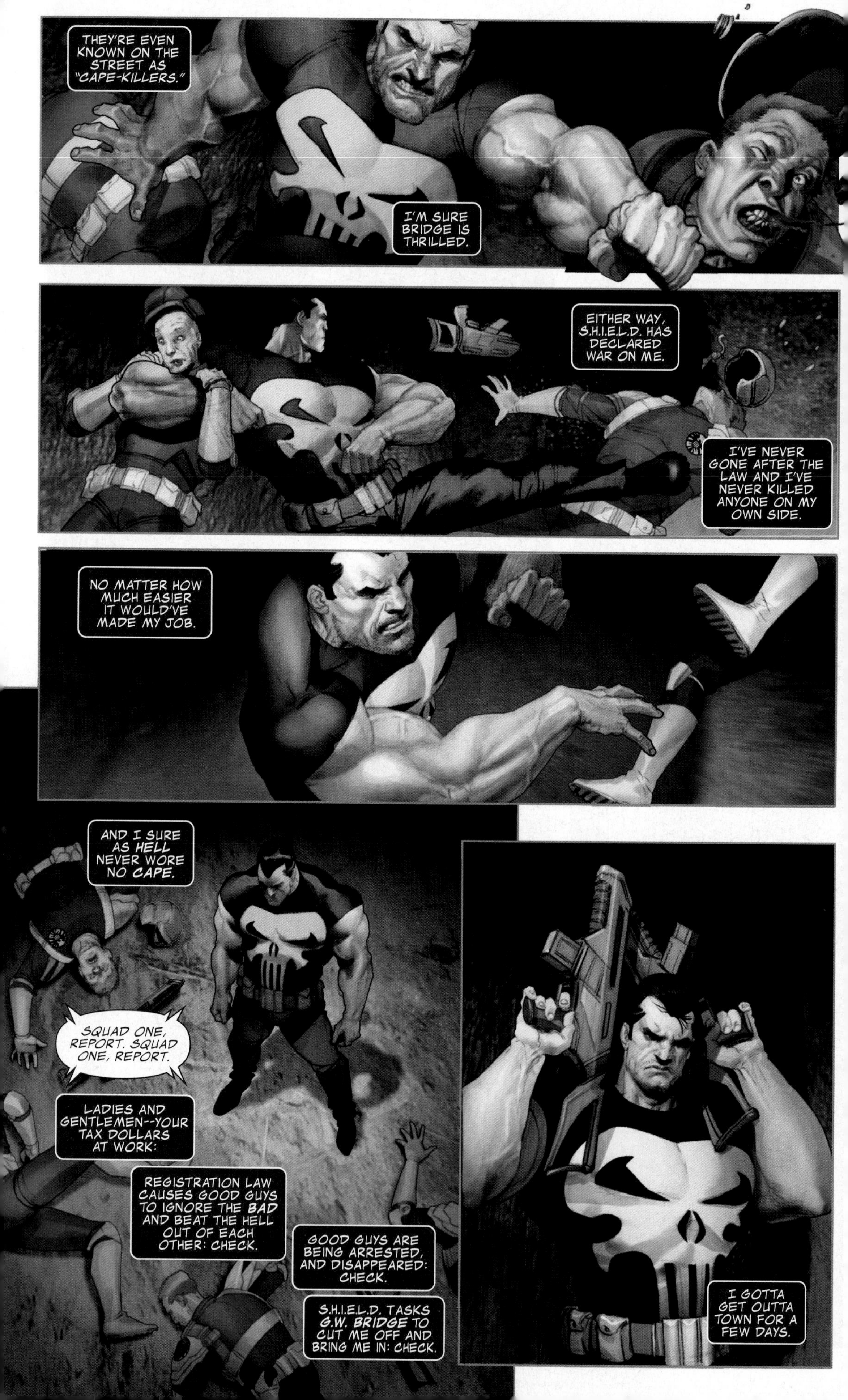

THEY'RE EVEN KNOWN ON THE STREET AS "CAPE-KILLERS."
I'M SURE BRIDGE IS THRILLED.
EITHER WAY, S.H.I.E.L.D. HAS DECLARED WAR ON ME.
I'VE NEVER GONE AFTER THE LAW AND I'VE NEVER KILLED ANYONE ON MY OWN SIDE.
NO MATTER HOW MUCH EASIER IT WOULD'VE MADE MY JOB.
AND I SURE AS HELL NEVER WORE NO CAPE.
SQUAD ONE, REPORT. SQUAD ONE, REPORT.
LADIES AND GENTLEMEN--YOUR TAX DOLLARS AT WORK:
REGISTRATION LAW CAUSES GOOD GUYS TO IGNORE THE BAD AND BEAT THE HELL OUT OF EACH OTHER: CHECK.
GOOD GUYS ARE BEING ARRESTED, AND DISAPPEARED: CHECK.
S.H.I.E.L.D. TASKS G.W. BRIDGE TO CUT ME OFF AND BRING ME IN: CHECK.
I GOTTA GET OUTTA TOWN FOR A FEW DAYS.

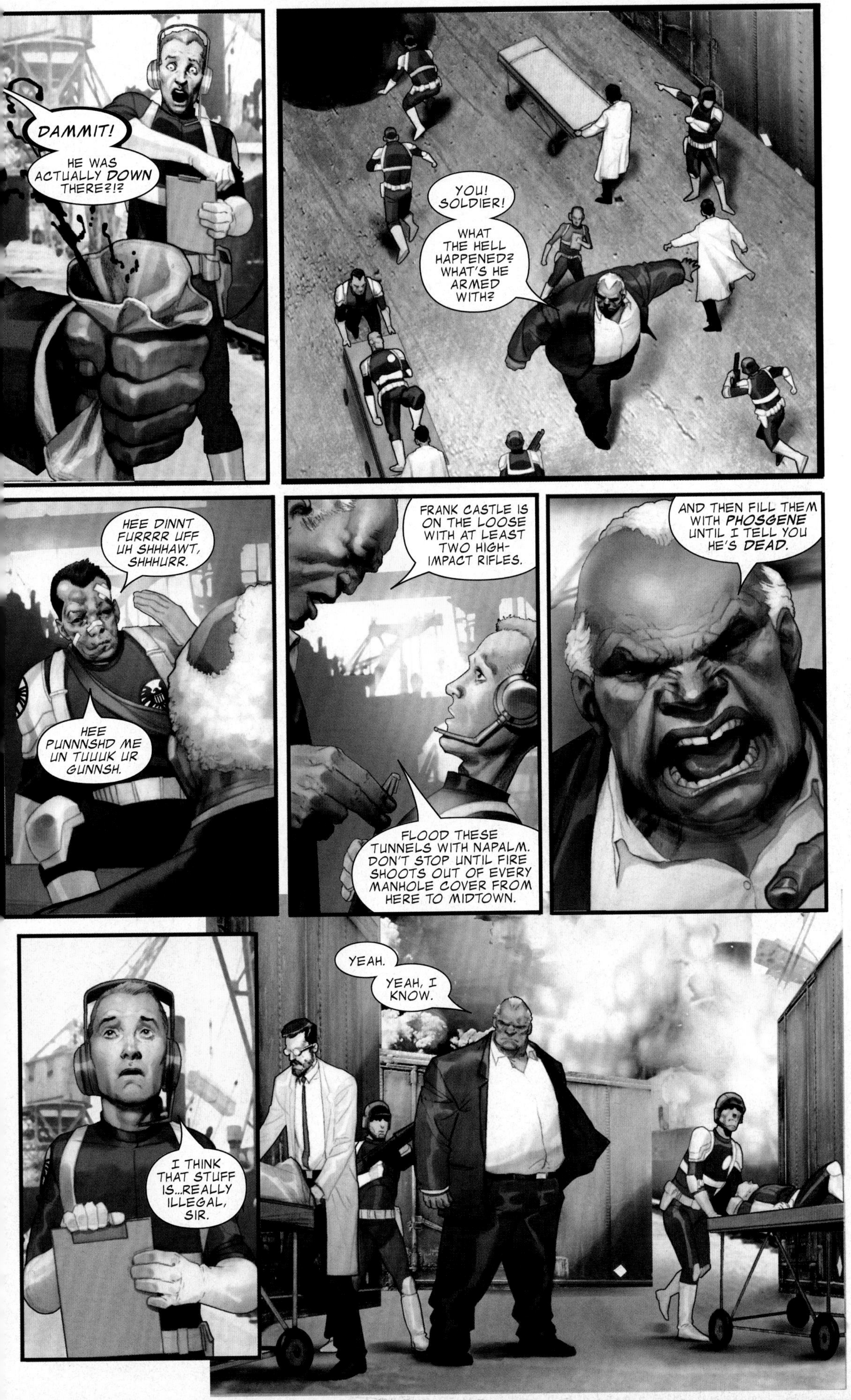
DAMMIT!
HE WAS ACTUALLY DOWN THERE?!?
YOU! SOLDIER!
WHAT THE HELL HAPPENED? WHAT'S HE ARMED WITH?
HEE DINNT FURRRR UFF UH SHHHAWT, SHHHURR.
HEE PUNNNSHD ME UN TUUUK UR GUNNSH.
FRANK CASTLE IS ON THE LOOSE WITH AT LEAST TWO HIGH-IMPACT RIFLES.
FLOOD THESE TUNNELS WITH NAPALM. DON'T STOP UNTIL FIRE SHOOTS OUT OF EVERY MANHOLE COVER FROM HERE TO MIDTOWN.
AND THEN FILL THEM WITH PHOSGENE UNTIL I TELL YOU HE'S DEAD.
I THINK THAT STUFF IS...REALLY ILLEGAL, SIR.
YEAH.
YEAH, I KNOW.

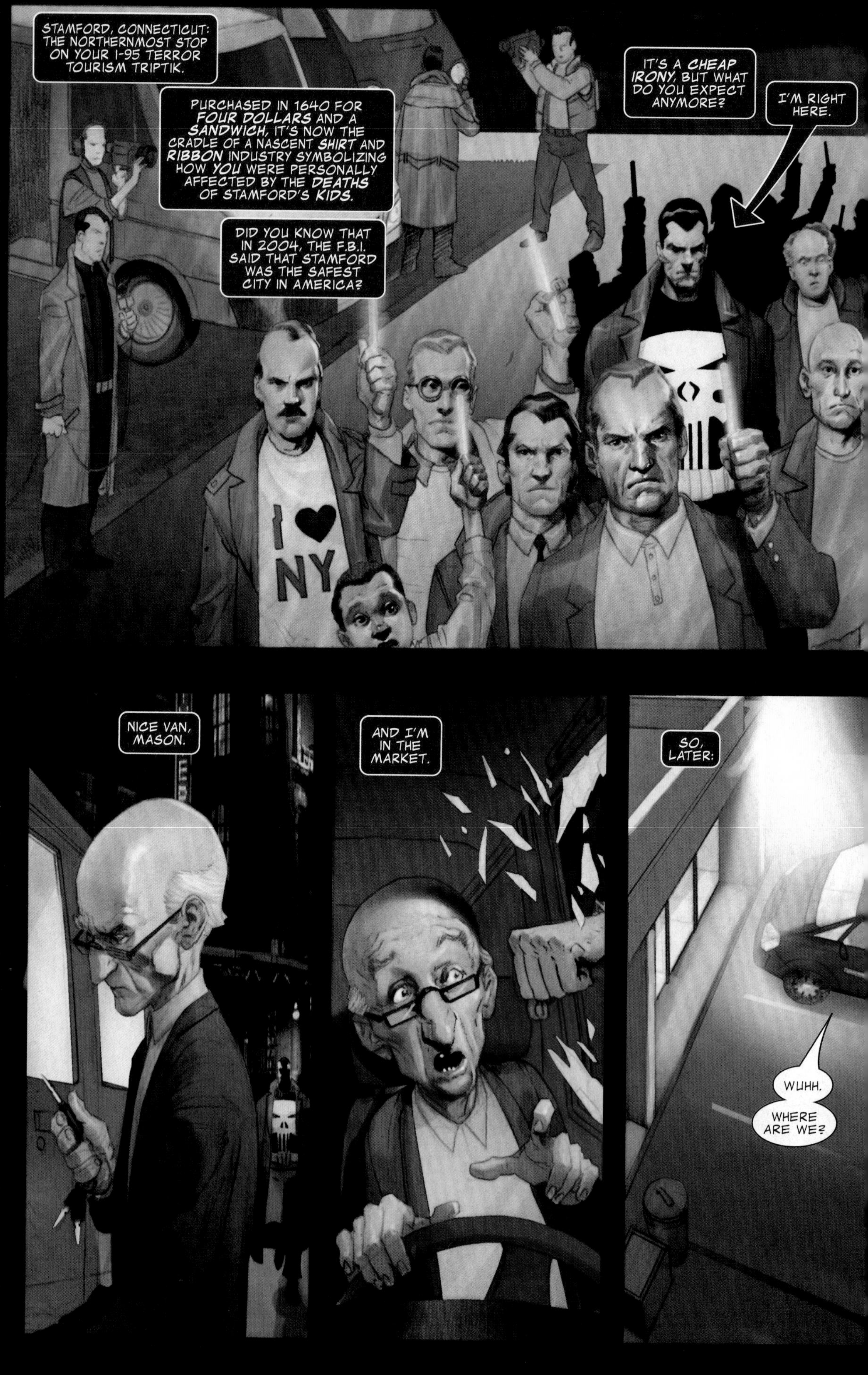

STAMFORD, CONNECTICUT: THE NORTHERNMOST STOP ON YOUR I-95 TERROR TOURISM TRIPTIK.
PURCHASED IN 1640 FOR FOUR DOLLARS AND A SANDWICH, IT'S NOW THE CRADLE OF A NASCENT SHIRT AND RIBBON INDUSTRY SYMBOLIZING HOW YOU WERE PERSONALLY AFFECTED BY THE DEATHS OF STAMFORD'S KIDS.
DID YOU KNOW THAT IN 2004, THE F.B.I. SAID THAT STAMFORD WAS THE SAFEST CITY IN AMERICA?
IT'S A CHEAP IRONY, BUT WHAT DO YOU EXPECT ANYMORE?
I'M RIGHT HERE.
I ♥ NY
NICE VAN, MASON.
AND I'M IN THE MARKET.
SO, LATER:
WUHH.
WHERE ARE WE?

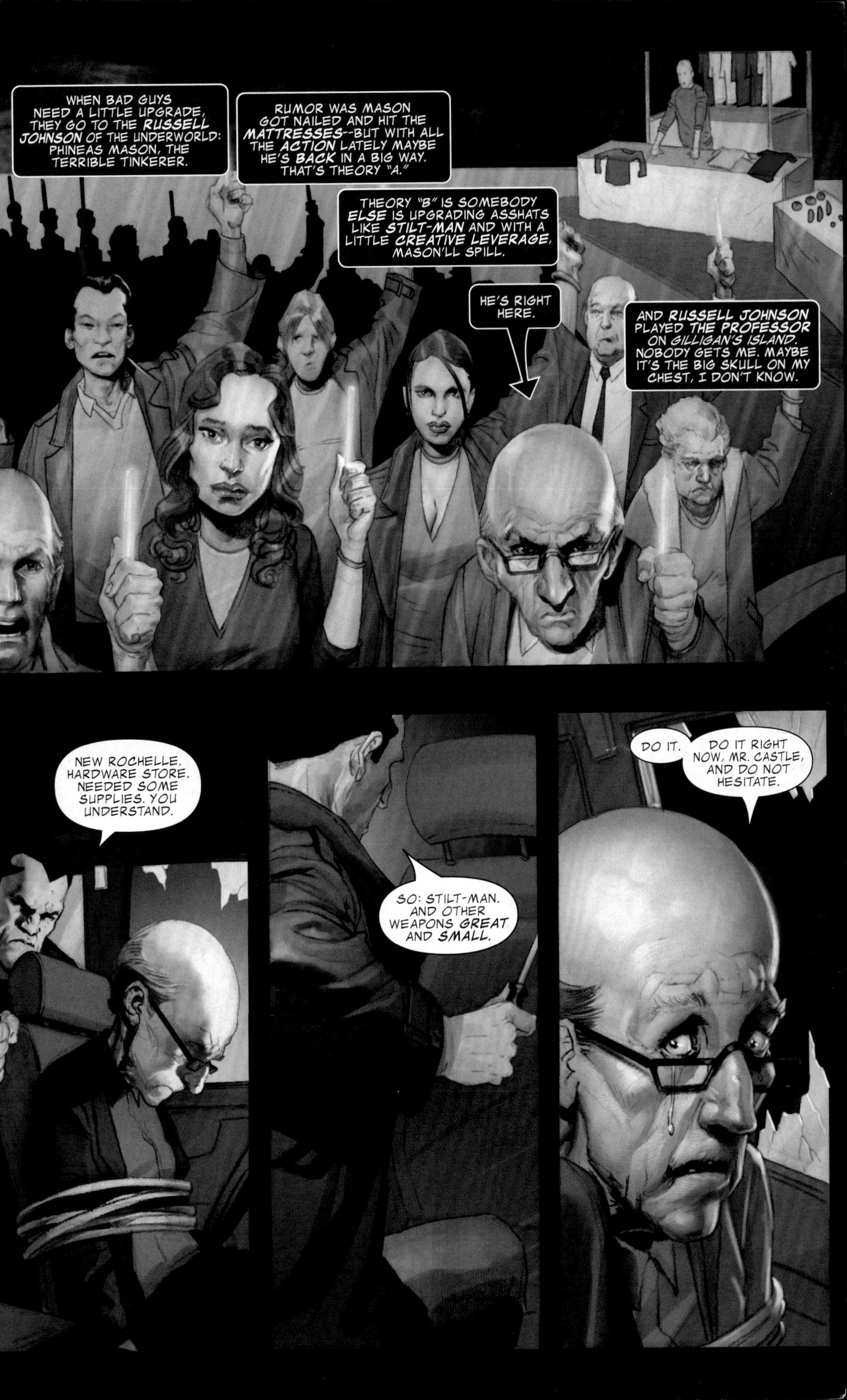

WHEN BAD GUYS NEED A LITTLE UPGRADE, THEY GO TO THE RUSSELL JOHNSON OF THE UNDERWORLD: PHINEAS MASON, THE TERRIBLE TINKERER.
RUMOR WAS MASON GOT NAILED AND HIT THE MATTRESSES--BUT WITH ALL THE ACTION LATELY MAYBE HE'S BACK IN A BIG WAY. THAT'S THEORY "A."
THEORY "B" IS SOMEBODY ELSE IS UPGRADING ASSHATS LIKE STILT-MAN AND WITH A LITTLE CREATIVE LEVERAGE, MASON'LL SPILL.
HE'S RIGHT HERE.
AND RUSSELL JOHNSON PLAYED THE PROFESSOR ON GILLIGAN'S ISLAND. NOBODY GETS ME. MAYBE IT'S THE BIG SKULL ON MY CHEST, I DON'T KNOW.
NEW ROCHELLE. HARDWARE STORE. NEEDED SOME SUPPLIES. YOU UNDERSTAND.
SO: STILT-MAN. AND OTHER WEAPONS GREAT AND SMALL.
DO IT.
DO IT RIGHT NOW, MR. CASTLE, AND DO NOT HESITATE.

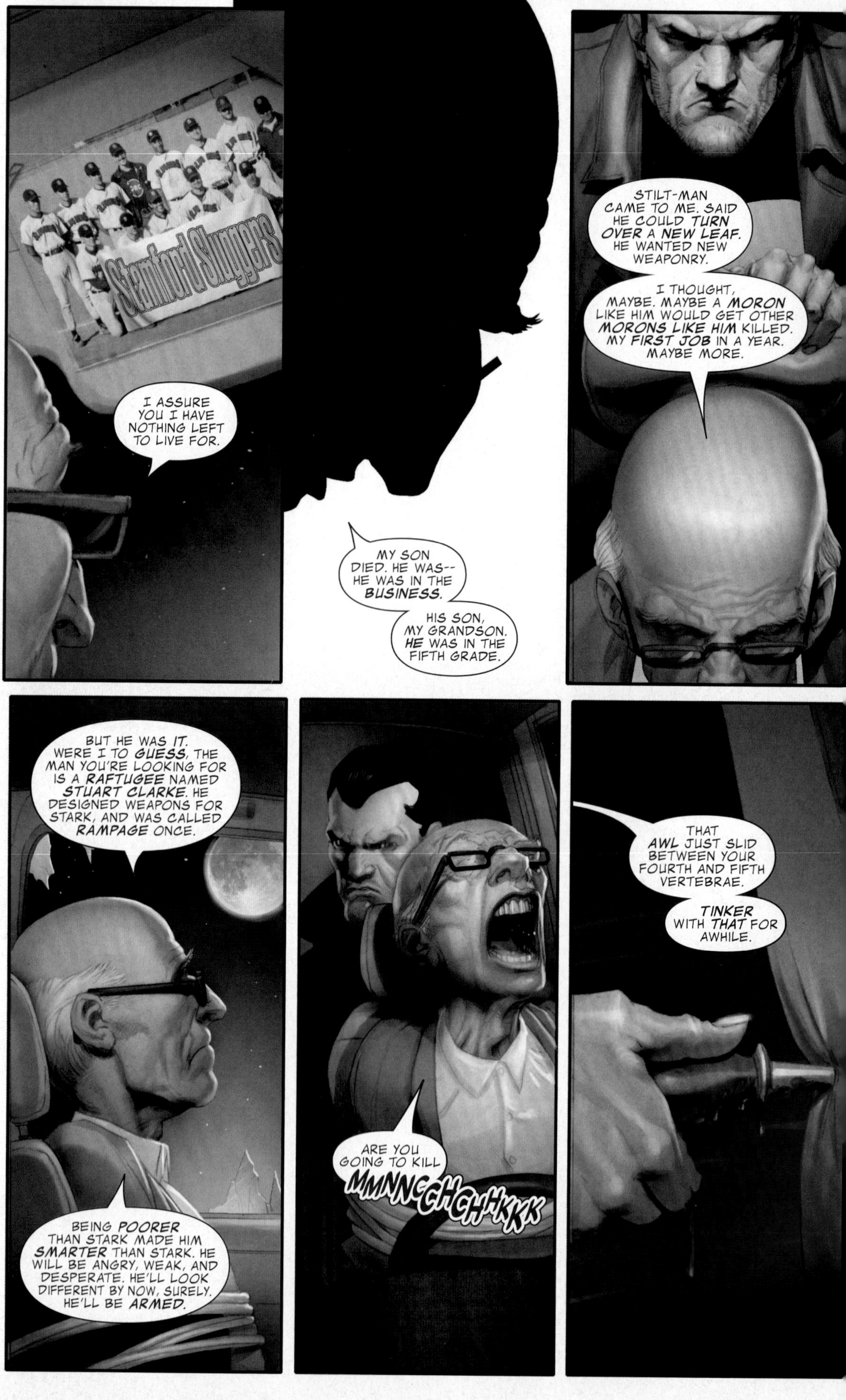
Stamford Sluggers
I ASSURE YOU I HAVE NOTHING LEFT TO LIVE FOR.
MY SON DIED. HE WAS-- HE WAS IN THE BUSINESS.
HIS SON, MY GRANDSON. HE WAS IN THE FIFTH GRADE.
STILT-MAN CAME TO ME. SAID HE COULD TURN OVER A NEW LEAF. HE WANTED NEW WEAPONRY.
I THOUGHT, MAYBE. MAYBE A MORON LIKE HIM WOULD GET OTHER MORONS LIKE HIM KILLED. MY FIRST JOB IN A YEAR. MAYBE MORE.
BUT HE WAS IT. WERE I TO GUESS, THE MAN YOU'RE LOOKING FOR IS A RAFTUGEE NAMED STUART CLARKE. HE DESIGNED WEAPONS FOR STARK, AND WAS CALLED RAMPAGE ONCE.
BEING POORER THAN STARK MADE HIM SMARTER THAN STARK. HE WILL BE ANGRY, WEAK, AND DESPERATE. HE'LL LOOK DIFFERENT BY NOW, SURELY. HE'LL BE ARMED.
ARE YOU GOING TO KILL
MMNNCHCHHKKK
THAT AWL JUST SLID BETWEEN YOUR FOURTH AND FIFTH VERTEBRAE.
TINKER WITH THAT FOR AWHILE.

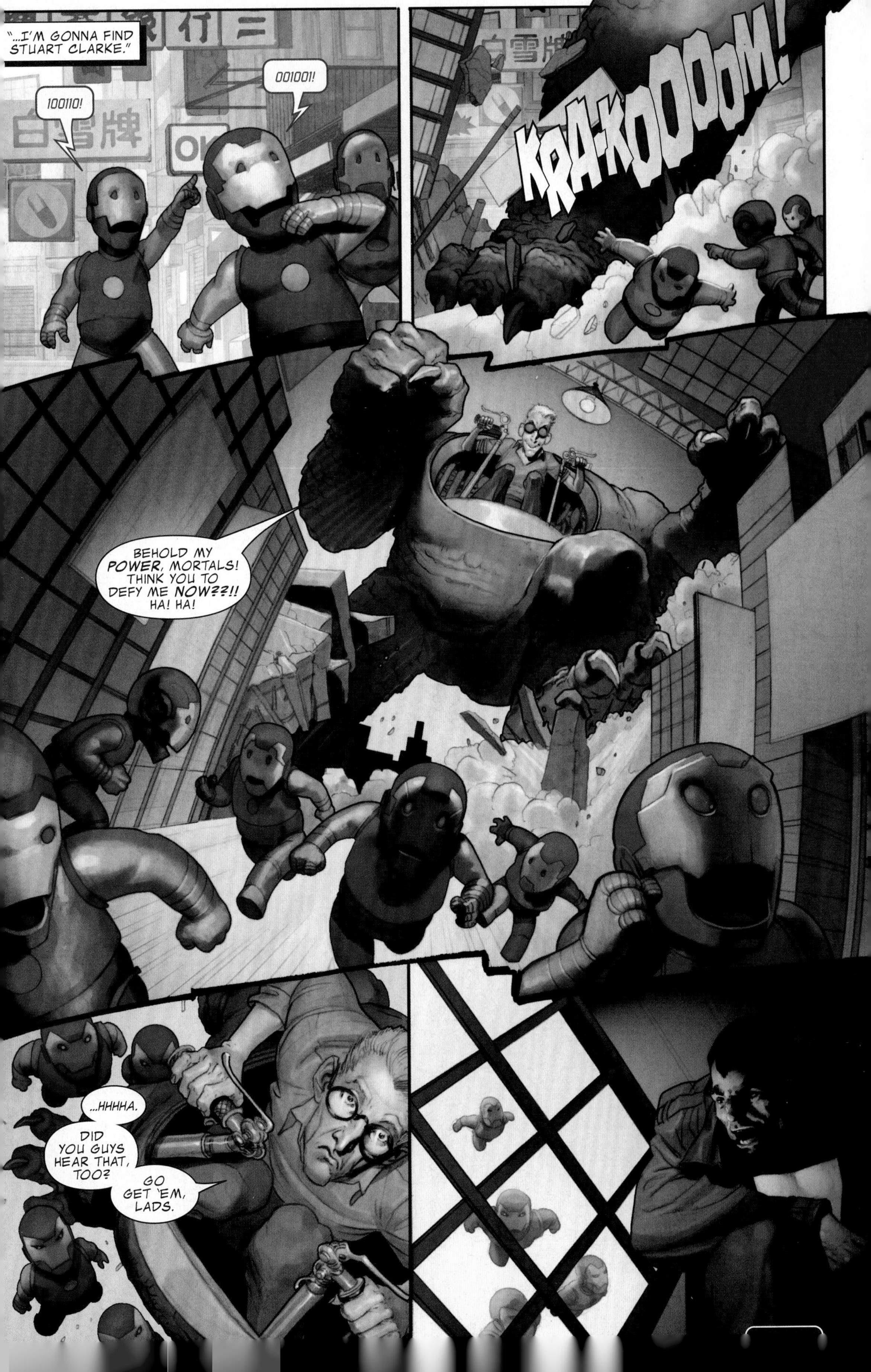

"...I'M GONNA FIND STUART CLARKE."
100110!
001001!
KRA-KOOOOM!
BEHOLD MY POWER, MORTALS! THINK YOU TO DEFY ME NOW??!! HA! HA!
...HHHHA.
DID YOU GUYS HEAR THAT, TOO?
GO GET 'EM, LADS.

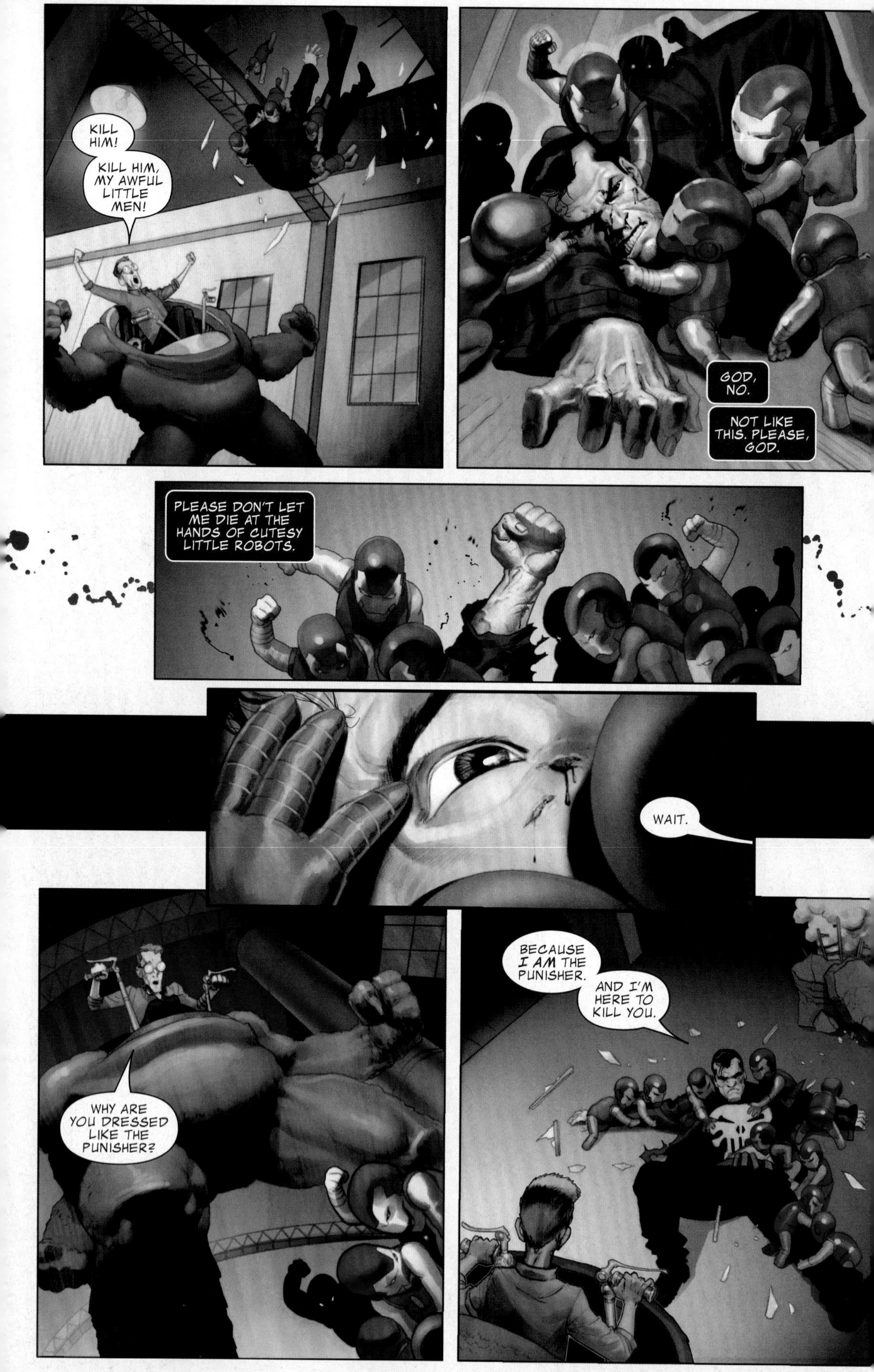
KILL HIM!
KILL HIM, MY AWFUL LITTLE MEN!
GOD, NO.
NOT LIKE THIS. PLEASE, GOD.
PLEASE DON'T LET ME DIE AT THE HANDS OF CUTESY LITTLE ROBOTS.
WAIT.
WHY ARE YOU DRESSED LIKE THE PUNISHER?
BECAUSE *I AM* THE PUNISHER.
AND I'M HERE TO KILL YOU.

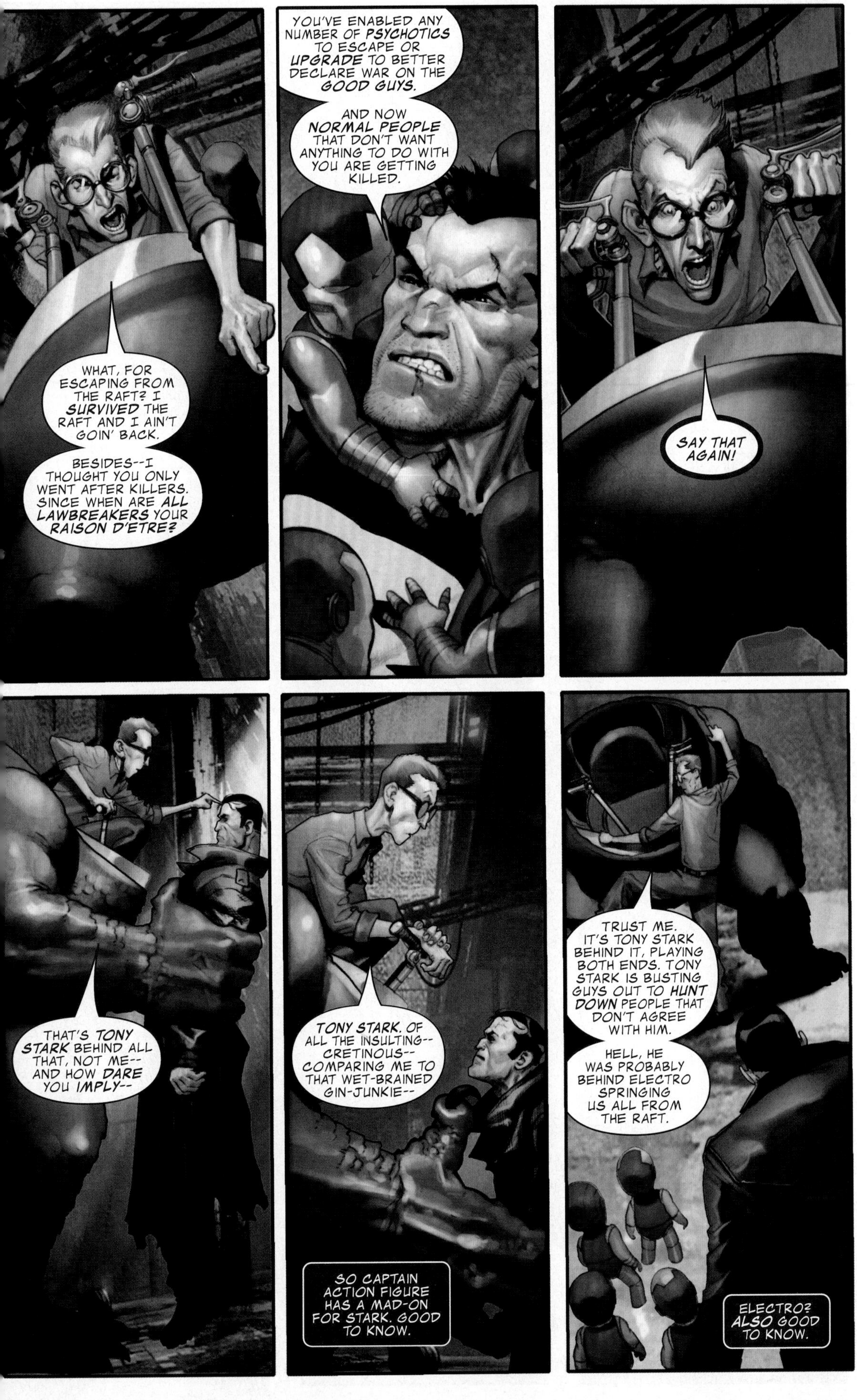

WHAT, FOR ESCAPING FROM THE RAFT? I SURVIVED THE RAFT AND I AIN'T GOIN' BACK.
BESIDES--I THOUGHT YOU ONLY WENT AFTER KILLERS. SINCE WHEN ARE ALL LAWBREAKERS YOUR RAISON D'ETRE?
YOU'VE ENABLED ANY NUMBER OF PSYCHOTICS TO ESCAPE OR UPGRADE TO BETTER DECLARE WAR ON THE GOOD GUYS.
AND NOW NORMAL PEOPLE THAT DON'T WANT ANYTHING TO DO WITH YOU ARE GETTING KILLED.
SAY THAT AGAIN!
THAT'S TONY STARK BEHIND ALL THAT, NOT ME-- AND HOW DARE YOU IMPLY--
TONY STARK. OF ALL THE INSULTING-- CRETINOUS-- COMPARING ME TO THAT WET-BRAINED GIN-JUNKIE--
SO CAPTAIN ACTION FIGURE HAS A MAD-ON FOR STARK. GOOD TO KNOW.
TRUST ME. IT'S TONY STARK BEHIND IT, PLAYING BOTH ENDS. TONY STARK IS BUSTING GUYS OUT TO HUNT DOWN PEOPLE THAT DON'T AGREE WITH HIM.
HELL, HE WAS PROBABLY BEHIND ELECTRO SPRINGING US ALL FROM THE RAFT.
ELECTRO? ALSO GOOD TO KNOW.

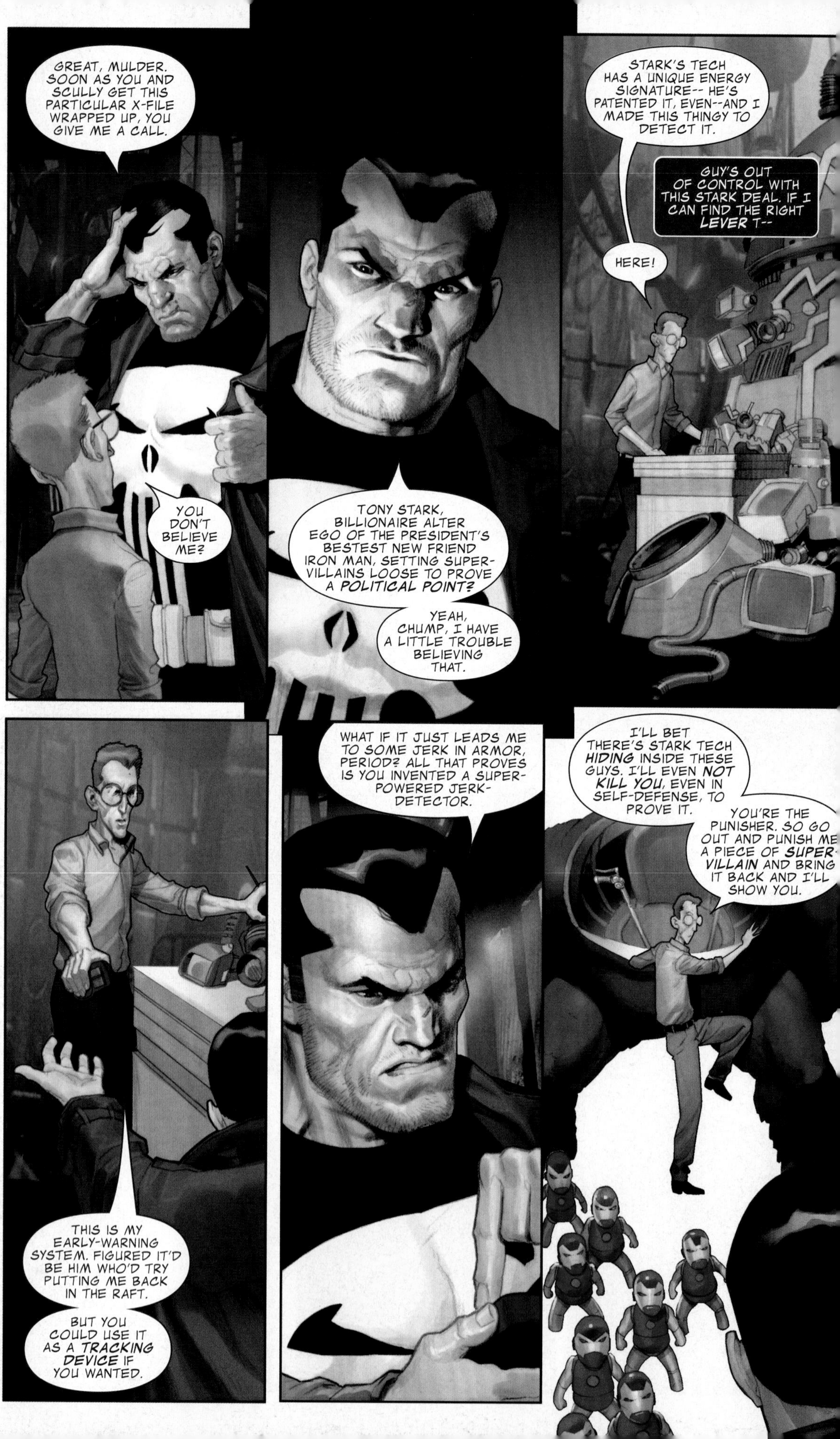
GREAT, MULDER. SOON AS YOU AND SCULLY GET THIS PARTICULAR X-FILE WRAPPED UP, YOU GIVE ME A CALL.
YOU DON'T BELIEVE ME?
TONY STARK, BILLIONAIRE ALTER EGO OF THE PRESIDENT'S BESTEST NEW FRIEND IRON MAN, SETTING SUPER-VILLAINS LOOSE TO PROVE A POLITICAL POINT?
YEAH, CHUMP, I HAVE A LITTLE TROUBLE BELIEVING THAT.
STARK'S TECH HAS A UNIQUE ENERGY SIGNATURE-- HE'S PATENTED IT, EVEN--AND I MADE THIS THINGY TO DETECT IT.
GUY'S OUT OF CONTROL WITH THIS STARK DEAL. IF I CAN FIND THE RIGHT LEVER T--
HERE!
THIS IS MY EARLY-WARNING SYSTEM. FIGURED IT'D BE HIM WHO'D TRY PUTTING ME BACK IN THE RAFT.
BUT YOU COULD USE IT AS A TRACKING DEVICE IF YOU WANTED.
WHAT IF IT JUST LEADS ME TO SOME JERK IN ARMOR, PERIOD? ALL THAT PROVES IS YOU INVENTED A SUPER-POWERED JERK-DETECTOR.
I'LL BET THERE'S STARK TECH HIDING INSIDE THESE GUYS. I'LL EVEN NOT KILL YOU, EVEN IN SELF-DEFENSE, TO PROVE IT.
YOU'RE THE PUNISHER. SO GO OUT AND PUNISH ME A PIECE OF SUPER-VILLAIN AND BRING IT BACK AND I'LL SHOW YOU.

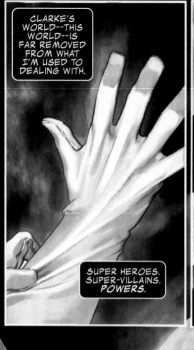

CLARKE'S WORLD—THIS WORLD—IS FAR REMOVED FROM WHAT I'M USED TO DEALING WITH.

SUPER HEROES. SUPER-VILLAINS. POWERS.

I MEAN, DID YOU SEE THAT GUY? WITH HIS FIN-FANG-FEET AND LITTLE IRON MAN TOYS?

THESE GUYS, THE SUPER-POWERS—THAT TWEAKED BLOOD GETS INTO THE BRAIN AND ALL THAT POWER MAKES 'EM BELIEVE THEY HAVE THE RIGHT TO TELL ANYONE HOW TO LIVE.

AND PEOPLE SAY I'M CRAZY.

I'M THE SANEST GUY THIS TOWN HAS EVER SEEN.

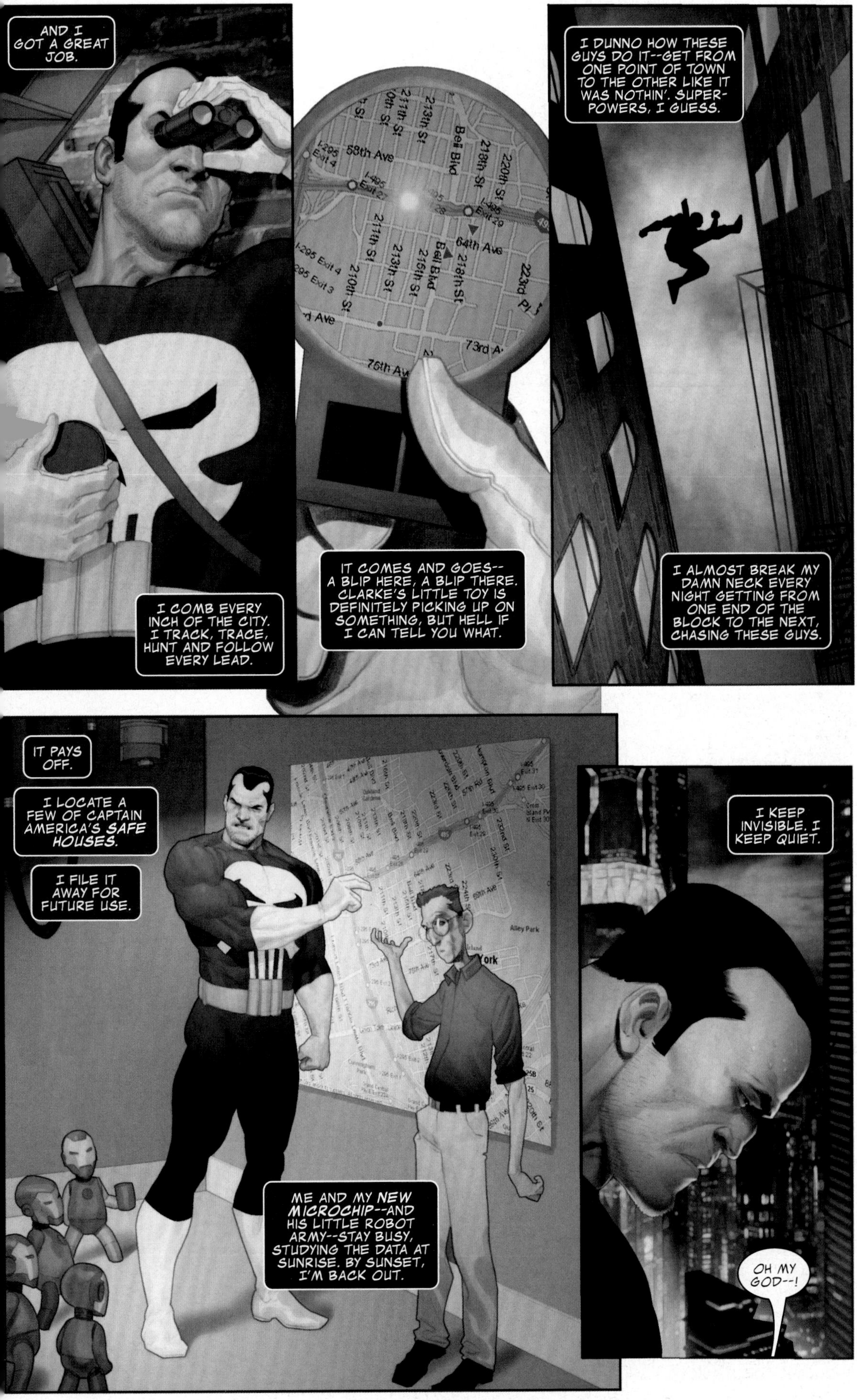
AND I GOT A GREAT JOB.
I COMB EVERY INCH OF THE CITY. I TRACK, TRACE, HUNT AND FOLLOW EVERY LEAD.
IT COMES AND GOES-- A BLIP HERE, A BLIP THERE. CLARKE'S LITTLE TOY IS DEFINITELY PICKING UP ON SOMETHING, BUT HELL IF I CAN TELL YOU WHAT.
I DUNNO HOW THESE GUYS DO IT--GET FROM ONE POINT OF TOWN TO THE OTHER LIKE IT WAS NOTHIN'. SUPER-POWERS, I GUESS.
I ALMOST BREAK MY DAMN NECK EVERY NIGHT GETTING FROM ONE END OF THE BLOCK TO THE NEXT, CHASING THESE GUYS.
IT PAYS OFF.
I LOCATE A FEW OF CAPTAIN AMERICA'S SAFE HOUSES.
I FILE IT AWAY FOR FUTURE USE.
ME AND MY NEW MICROCHIP--AND HIS LITTLE ROBOT ARMY--STAY BUSY, STUDYING THE DATA AT SUNRISE. BY SUNSET, I'M BACK OUT.
I KEEP INVISIBLE. I KEEP QUIET.
OH MY GOD--!

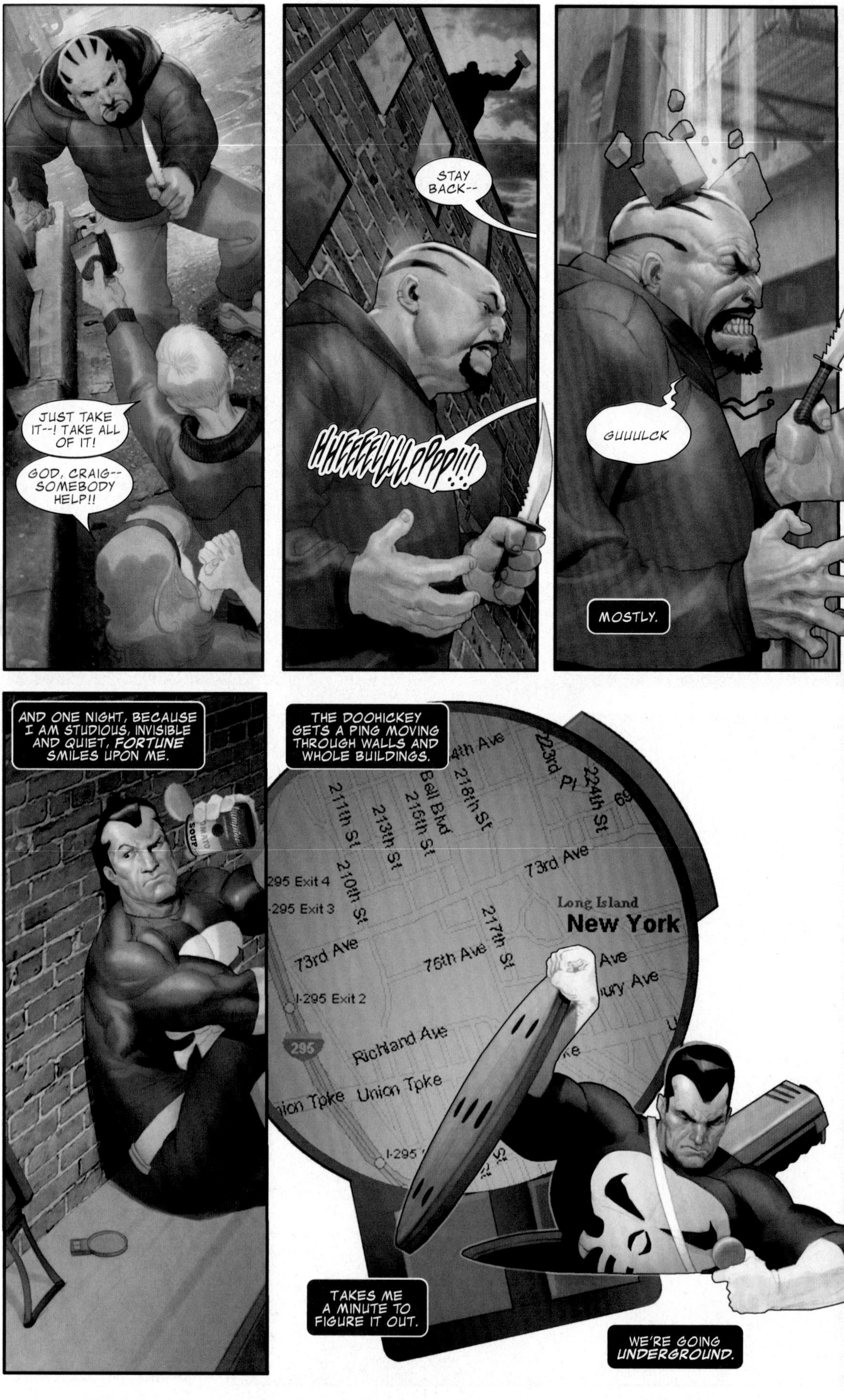
JUST TAKE IT--! TAKE ALL OF IT!
GOD, CRAIG-- SOMEBODY HELP!!
STAY BACK--
HHEEEELLLLPPPP!!!
GUUULCK
MOSTLY.
AND ONE NIGHT, BECAUSE I AM STUDIOUS, INVISIBLE AND QUIET, FORTUNE SMILES UPON ME.
THE DOOHICKEY GETS A PING MOVING THROUGH WALLS AND WHOLE BUILDINGS.
SOUP
211th St
213th St
Bell Blvd
216th St
218th St
223rd Pl
224th St
73rd Ave
295 Exit 4
I-295 Exit 3
210th St
217th St
Long Island
New York
73rd Ave
75th Ave
I-295 Exit 2
295
Richland Ave
Union Tpke
TAKES ME A MINUTE TO FIGURE IT OUT.
WE'RE GOING UNDERGROUND.

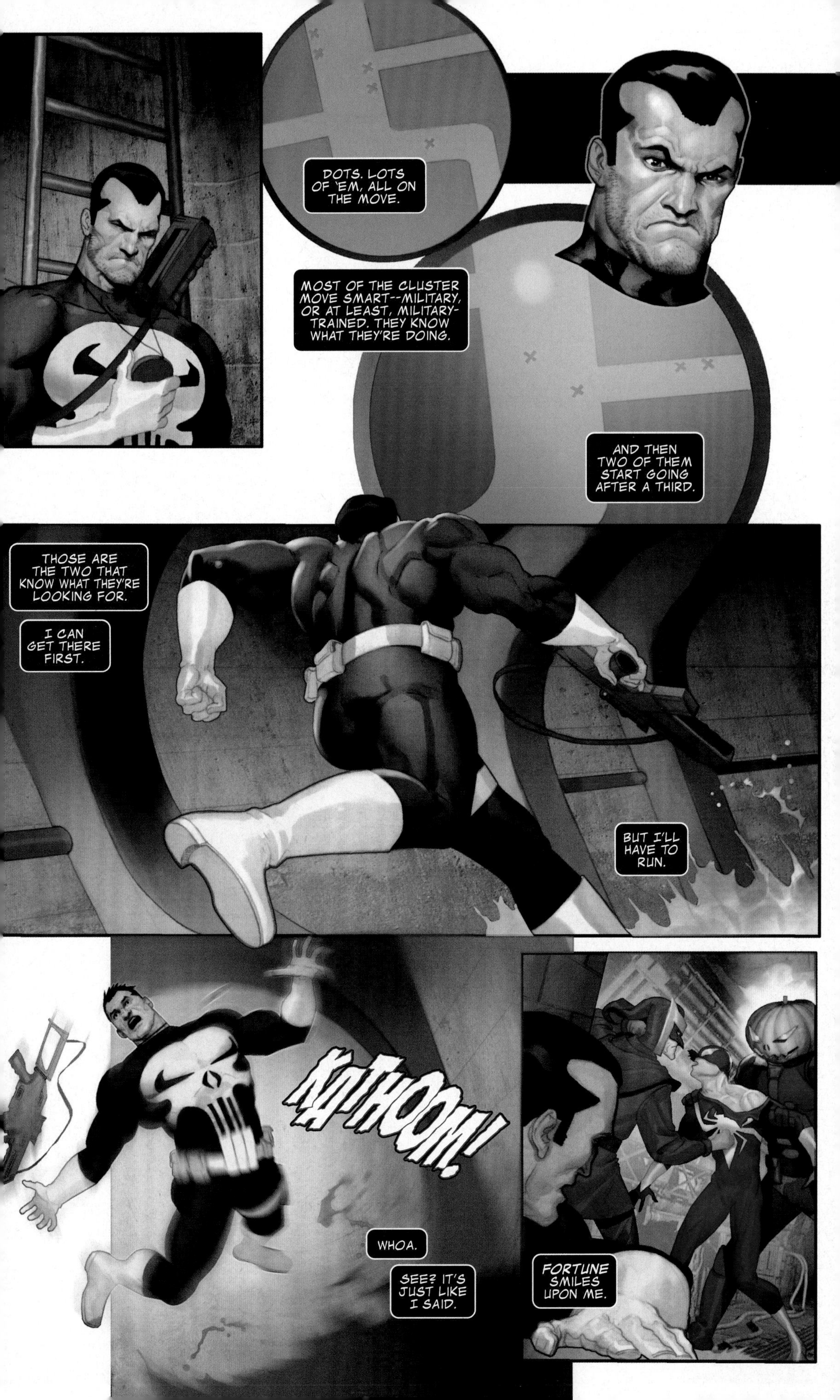
DOTS. LOTS OF 'EM, ALL ON THE MOVE.
MOST OF THE CLUSTER MOVE SMART--MILITARY, OR AT LEAST, MILITARY-TRAINED. THEY KNOW WHAT THEY'RE DOING.
AND THEN TWO OF THEM START GOING AFTER A THIRD.
THOSE ARE THE TWO THAT KNOW WHAT THEY'RE LOOKING FOR.
I CAN GET THERE FIRST.
BUT I'LL HAVE TO RUN.
KATHOOM!
WHOA.
SEE? IT'S JUST LIKE I SAID.
FORTUNE SMILES UPON ME.

I KNOW I PROBABLY SHOULDN'T BE SURPRISED.

I KNOW, I KNOW.

IT'S ONE OF THOSE MOMENTS IN MY LIFE WHERE I REALIZE EVERYTHING'S ABOUT TO CHANGE.

THE GENIE'S ABOUT TO COME OUT OF THE BOTTLE.

...

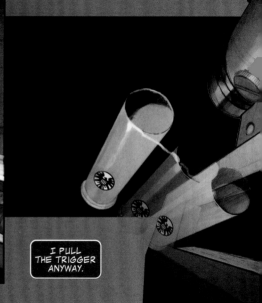

I PULL THE TRIGGER ANYWAY.

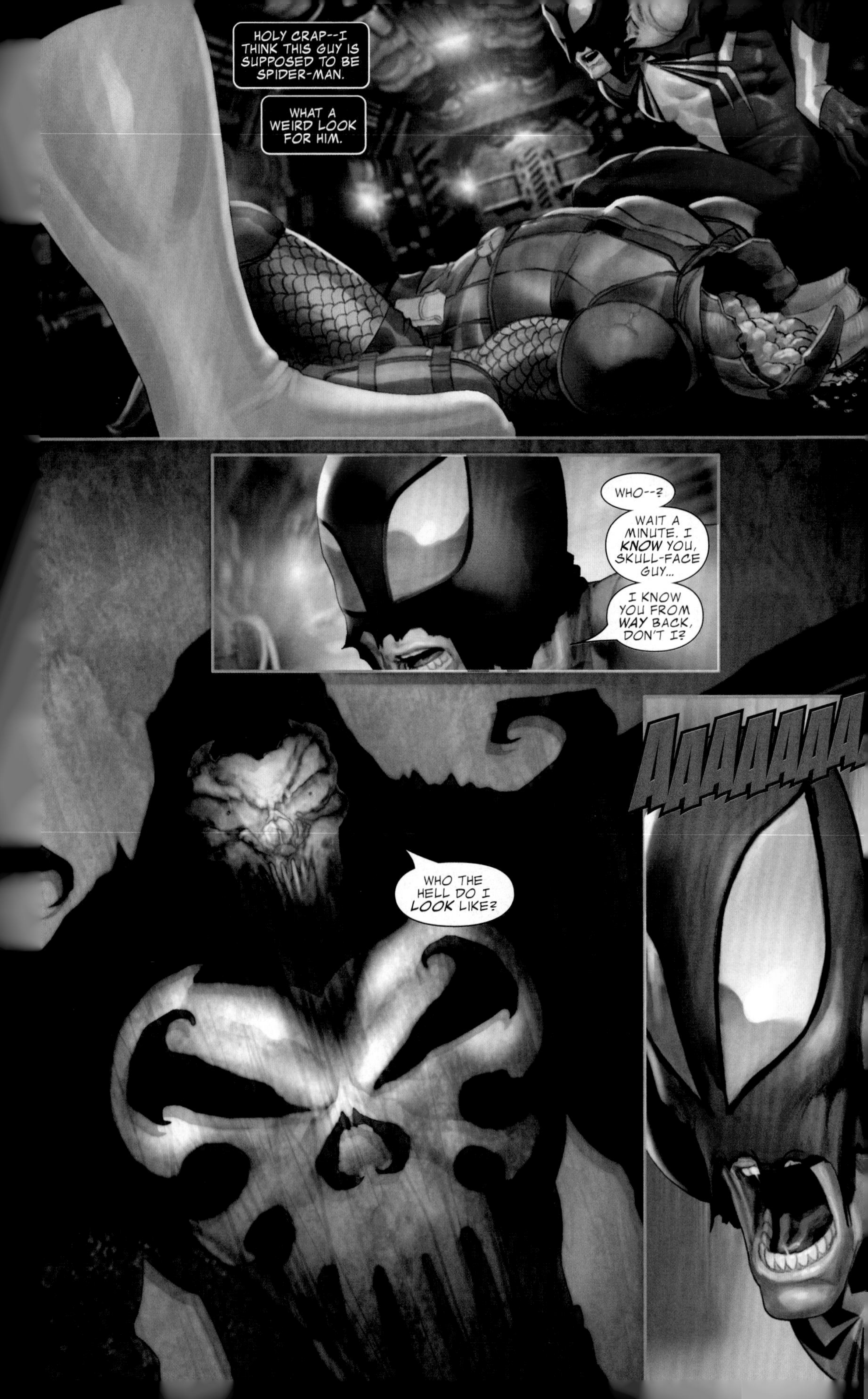
HOLY CRAP--I THINK THIS GUY IS SUPPOSED TO BE SPIDER-MAN.
WHAT A WEIRD LOOK FOR HIM.
WHO--?
WAIT A MINUTE. I KNOW YOU, SKULL-FACE GUY...
I KNOW YOU FROM WAY BACK, DON'T I?
WHO THE HELL DO I LOOK LIKE?
AAAAAAA

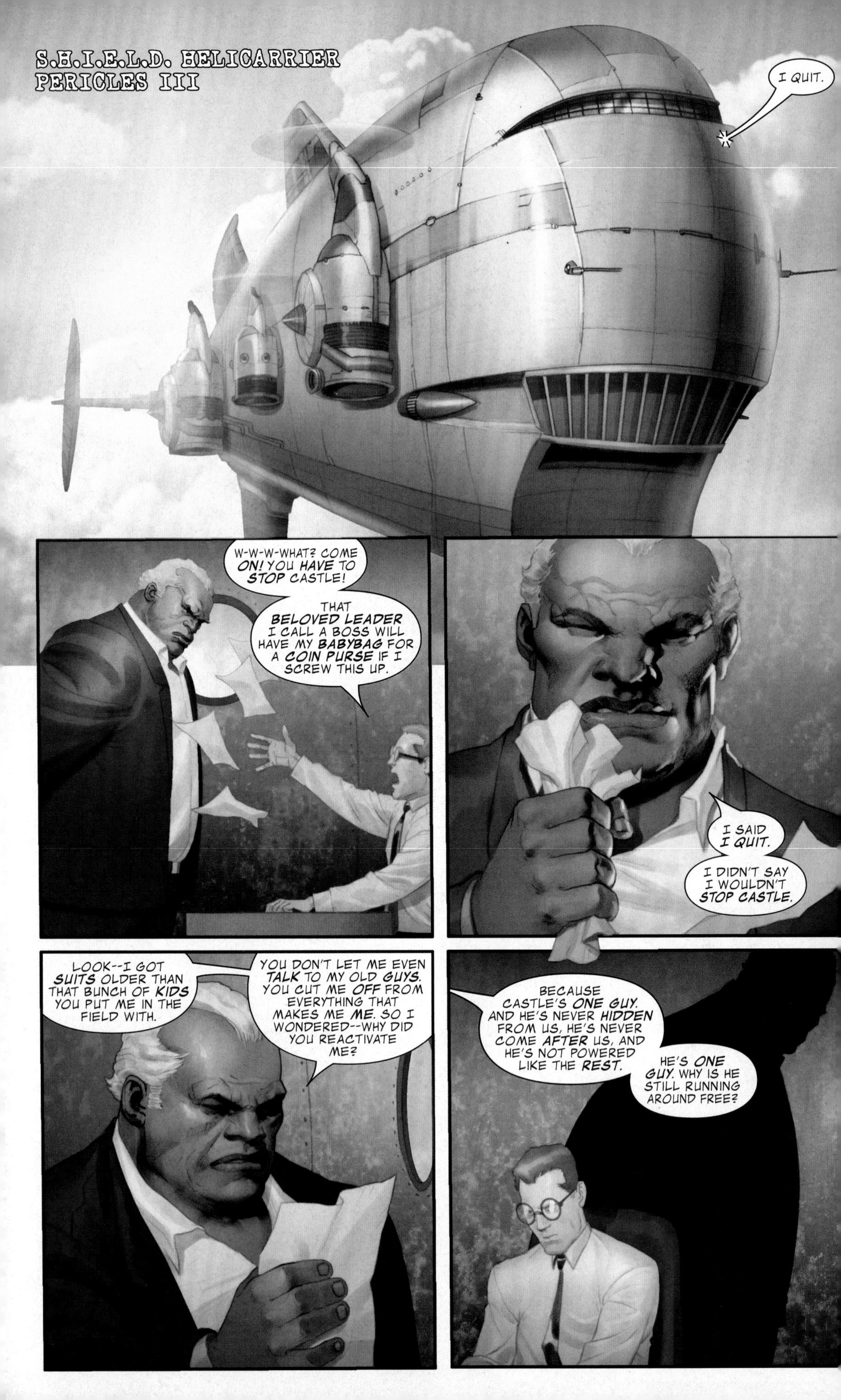

S.H.I.E.L.D. HELICARRIER
PERICLES III
I QUIT.
W-W-W-WHAT? COME ON! YOU HAVE TO STOP CASTLE!
THAT BELOVED LEADER I CALL A BOSS WILL HAVE MY BABYBAG FOR A COIN PURSE IF I SCREW THIS UP.
I SAID I QUIT.
I DIDN'T SAY I WOULDN'T STOP CASTLE.
LOOK--I GOT SUITS OLDER THAN THAT BUNCH OF KIDS YOU PUT ME IN THE FIELD WITH.
YOU DON'T LET ME EVEN TALK TO MY OLD GUYS. YOU CUT ME OFF FROM EVERYTHING THAT MAKES ME ME. SO I WONDERED--WHY DID YOU REACTIVATE ME?
BECAUSE CASTLE'S ONE GUY. AND HE'S NEVER HIDDEN FROM US, HE'S NEVER COME AFTER US, AND HE'S NOT POWERED LIKE THE REST.
HE'S ONE GUY. WHY IS HE STILL RUNNING AROUND FREE?

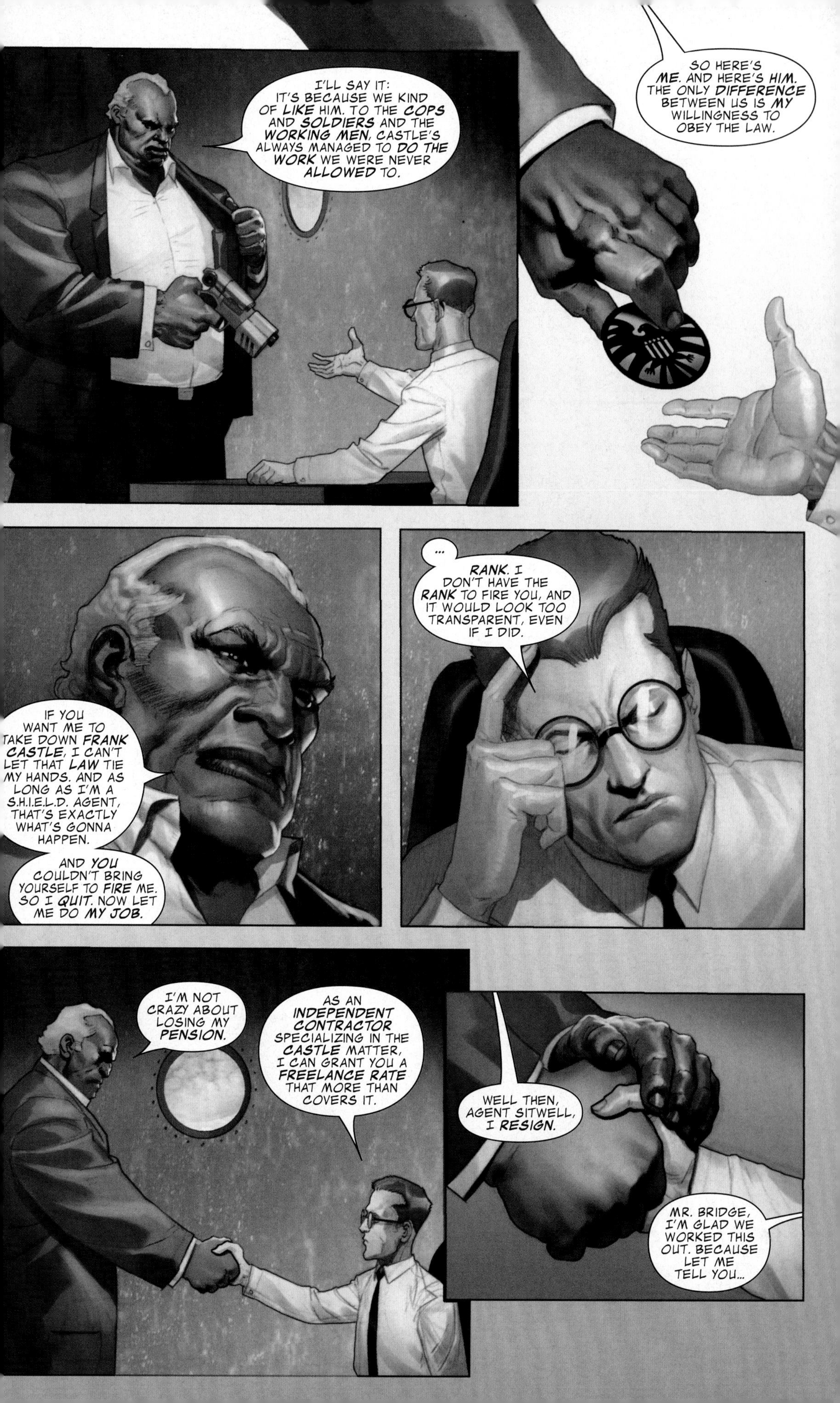
I'LL SAY IT: IT'S BECAUSE WE KIND OF LIKE HIM. TO THE COPS AND SOLDIERS AND THE WORKING MEN, CASTLE'S ALWAYS MANAGED TO DO THE WORK WE WERE NEVER ALLOWED TO.
SO HERE'S ME. AND HERE'S HIM. THE ONLY DIFFERENCE BETWEEN US IS MY WILLINGNESS TO OBEY THE LAW.
IF YOU WANT ME TO TAKE DOWN FRANK CASTLE, I CAN'T LET THAT LAW TIE MY HANDS. AND AS LONG AS I'M A S.H.I.E.L.D. AGENT, THAT'S EXACTLY WHAT'S GONNA HAPPEN.
AND YOU COULDN'T BRING YOURSELF TO FIRE ME. SO I QUIT. NOW LET ME DO MY JOB.
...
RANK. I DON'T HAVE THE RANK TO FIRE YOU, AND IT WOULD LOOK TOO TRANSPARENT, EVEN IF I DID.
I'M NOT CRAZY ABOUT LOSING MY PENSION.
AS AN INDEPENDENT CONTRACTOR SPECIALIZING IN THE CASTLE MATTER, I CAN GRANT YOU A FREELANCE RATE THAT MORE THAN COVERS IT.
WELL THEN, AGENT SITWELL, I RESIGN.
MR. BRIDGE, I'M GLAD WE WORKED THIS OUT. BECAUSE LET ME TELL YOU...

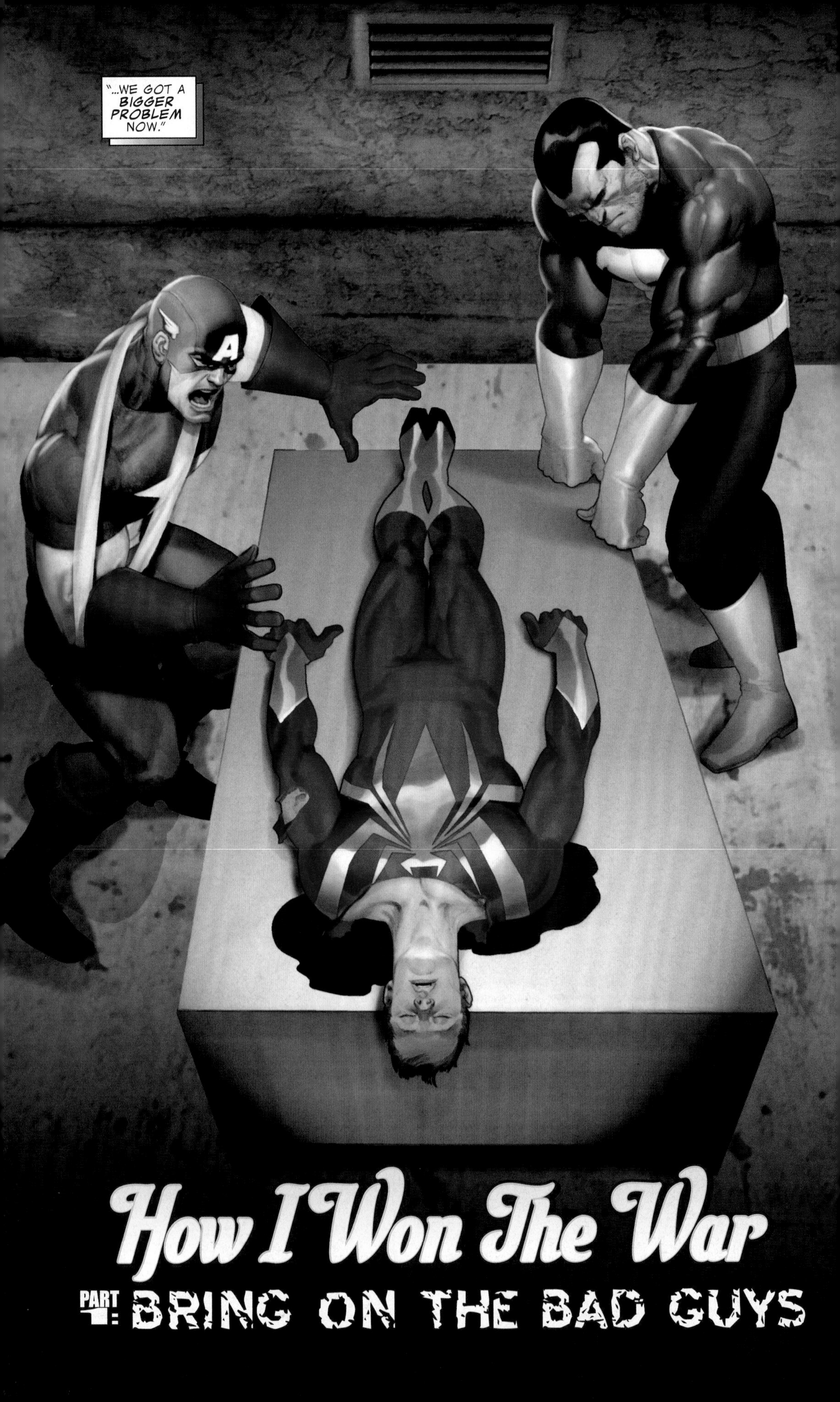
"...WE GOT A BIGGER PROBLEM NOW."
How I Won The War
PART 1: BRING ON THE BAD GUYS

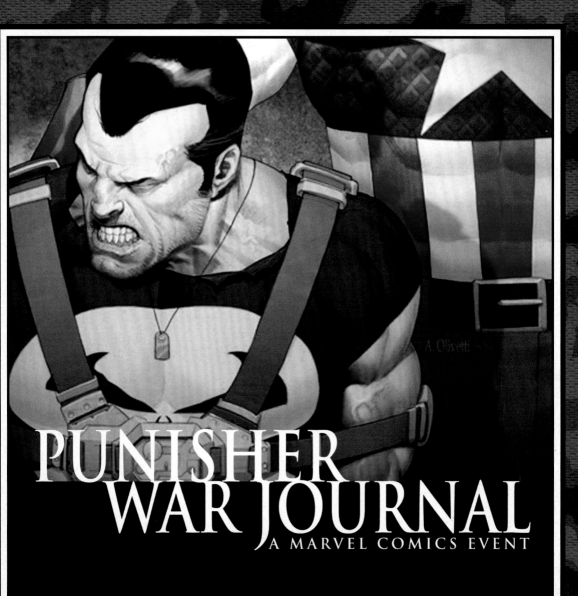

PUNISHER
WAR JOURNAL
A MARVEL COMICS EVENT

CIVIL
WAR

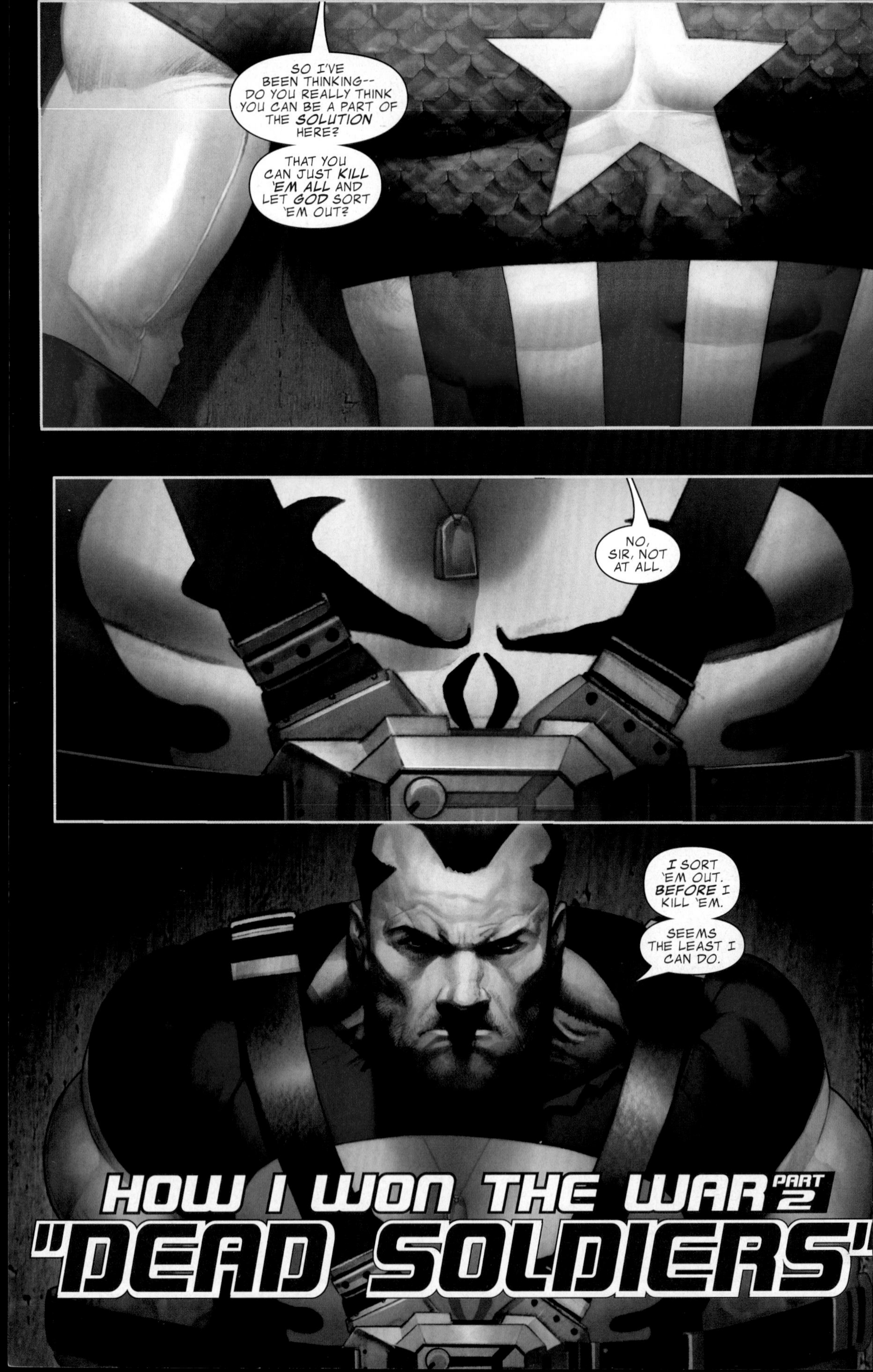
SO I'VE BEEN THINKING-- DO YOU REALLY THINK YOU CAN BE A PART OF THE SOLUTION HERE?
THAT YOU CAN JUST KILL 'EM ALL AND LET GOD SORT 'EM OUT?
NO, SIR, NOT AT ALL.
I SORT 'EM OUT. BEFORE I KILL 'EM.
SEEMS THE LEAST I CAN DO.
HOW I WON THE WAR PART 2
"DEAD SOLDIERS"

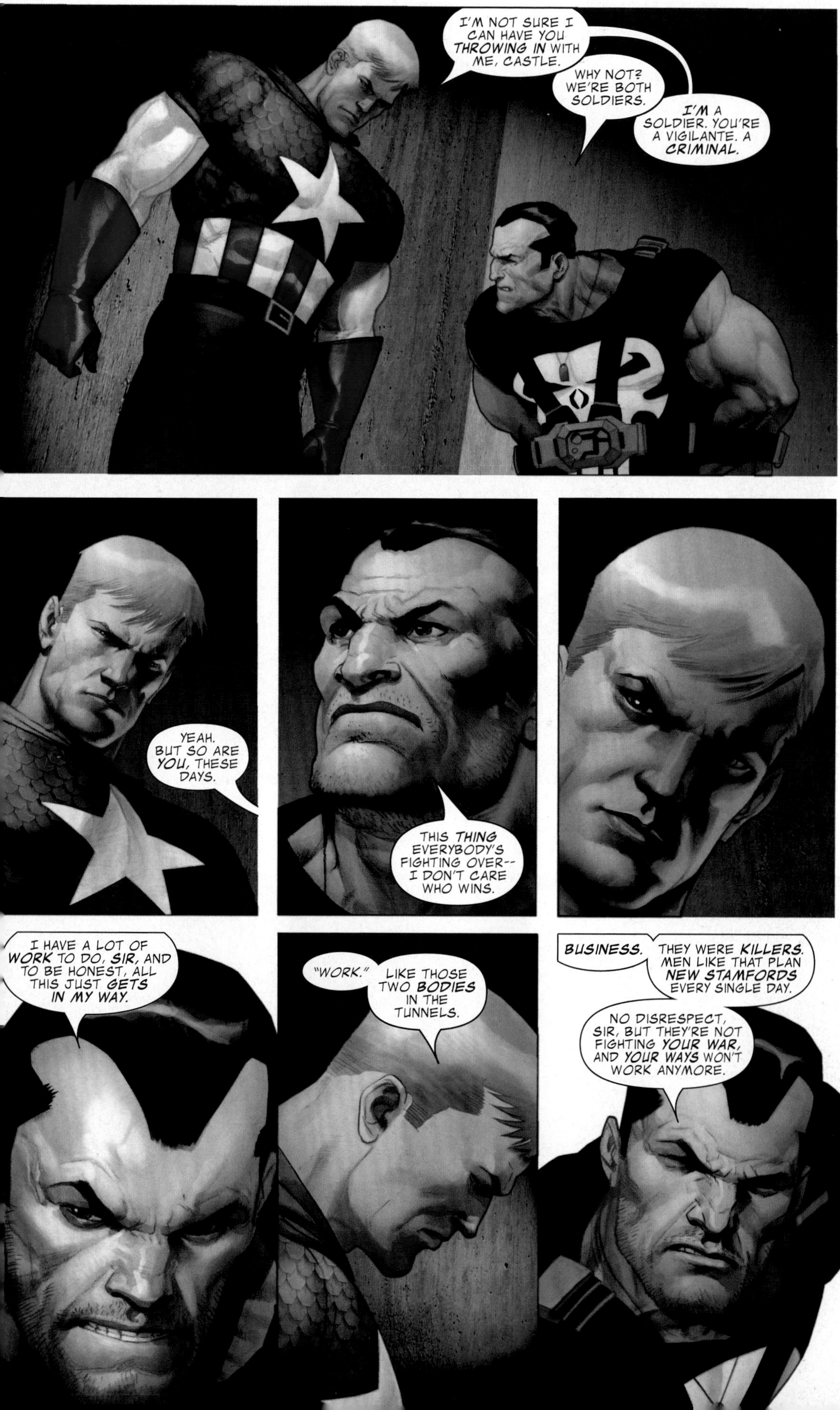
I'M NOT SURE I CAN HAVE YOU THROWING IN WITH ME, CASTLE.
WHY NOT? WE'RE BOTH SOLDIERS.
I'M A SOLDIER. YOU'RE A VIGILANTE. A CRIMINAL.
YEAH. BUT SO ARE YOU, THESE DAYS.
THIS THING EVERYBODY'S FIGHTING OVER-- I DON'T CARE WHO WINS.
I HAVE A LOT OF WORK TO DO, SIR, AND TO BE HONEST, ALL THIS JUST GETS IN MY WAY.
"WORK."
LIKE THOSE TWO BODIES IN THE TUNNELS.
BUSINESS.
THEY WERE KILLERS. MEN LIKE THAT PLAN NEW STAMFORDS EVERY SINGLE DAY.
NO DISRESPECT, SIR, BUT THEY'RE NOT FIGHTING YOUR WAR, AND YOUR WAYS WON'T WORK ANYMORE.

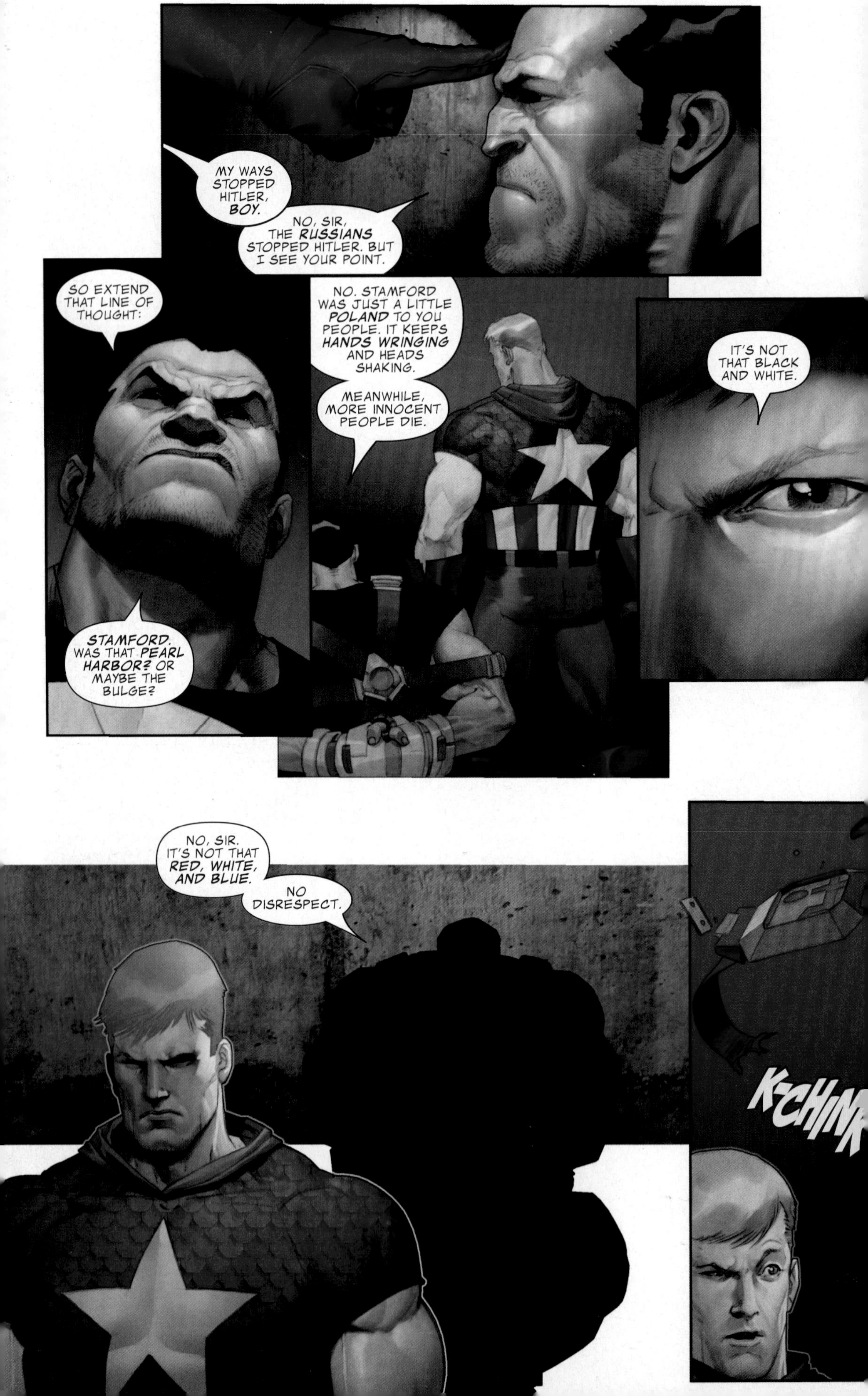

MY WAYS STOPPED HITLER, BOY.
NO, SIR, THE RUSSIANS STOPPED HITLER. BUT I SEE YOUR POINT.
SO EXTEND THAT LINE OF THOUGHT:
STAMFORD. WAS THAT PEARL HARBOR? OR MAYBE THE BULGE?
NO. STAMFORD WAS JUST A LITTLE POLAND TO YOU PEOPLE. IT KEEPS HANDS WRINGING AND HEADS SHAKING.
MEANWHILE, MORE INNOCENT PEOPLE DIE.
IT'S NOT THAT BLACK AND WHITE.
NO, SIR. IT'S NOT THAT RED, WHITE, AND BLUE.
NO DISRESPECT.
K-CHINK

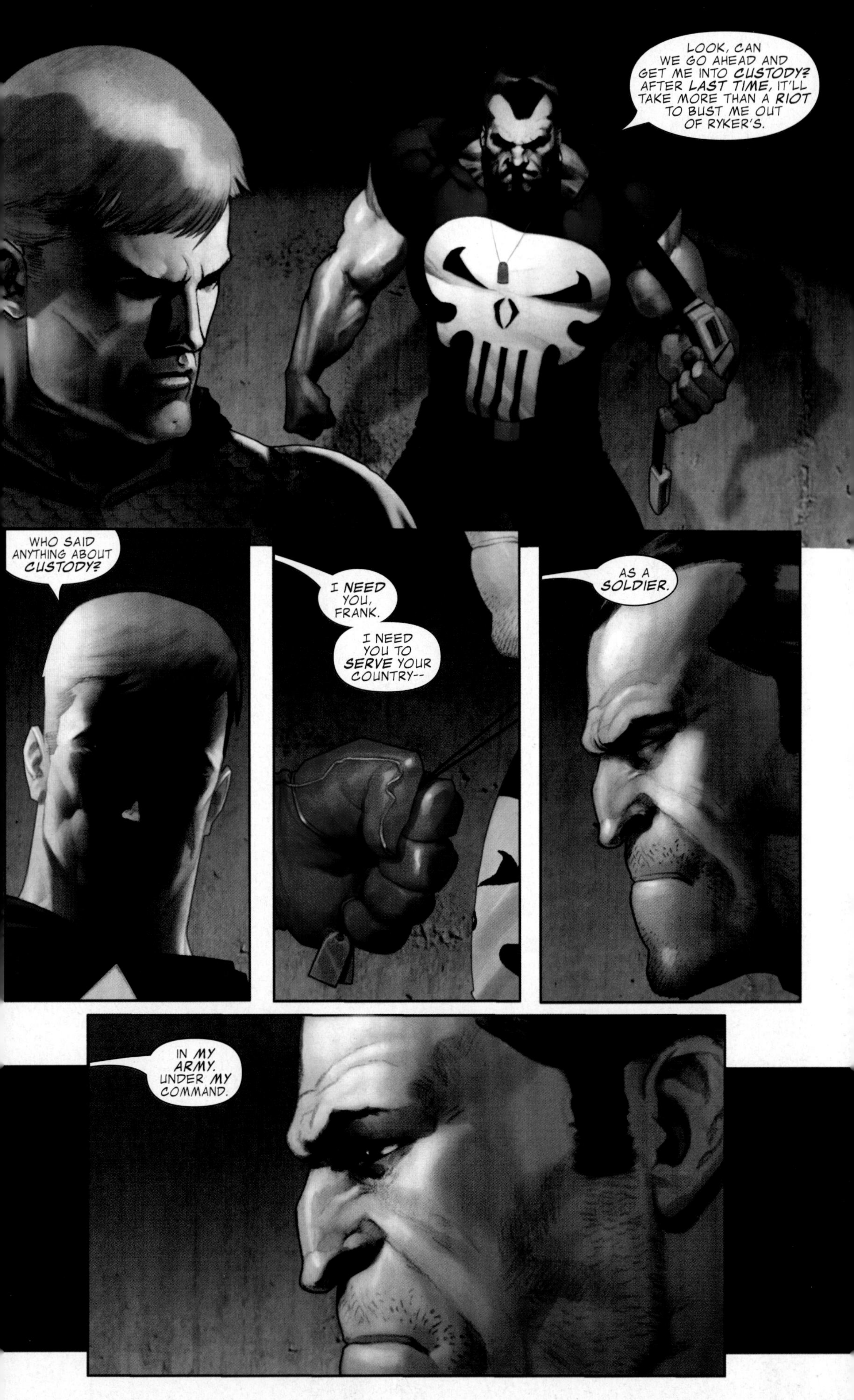
LOOK, CAN WE GO AHEAD AND GET ME INTO CUSTODY? AFTER LAST TIME, IT'LL TAKE MORE THAN A RIOT TO BUST ME OUT OF RYKER'S.
WHO SAID ANYTHING ABOUT CUSTODY?
I NEED YOU, FRANK.
I NEED YOU TO SERVE YOUR COUNTRY--
AS A SOLDIER.
IN MY ARMY. UNDER MY COMMAND.

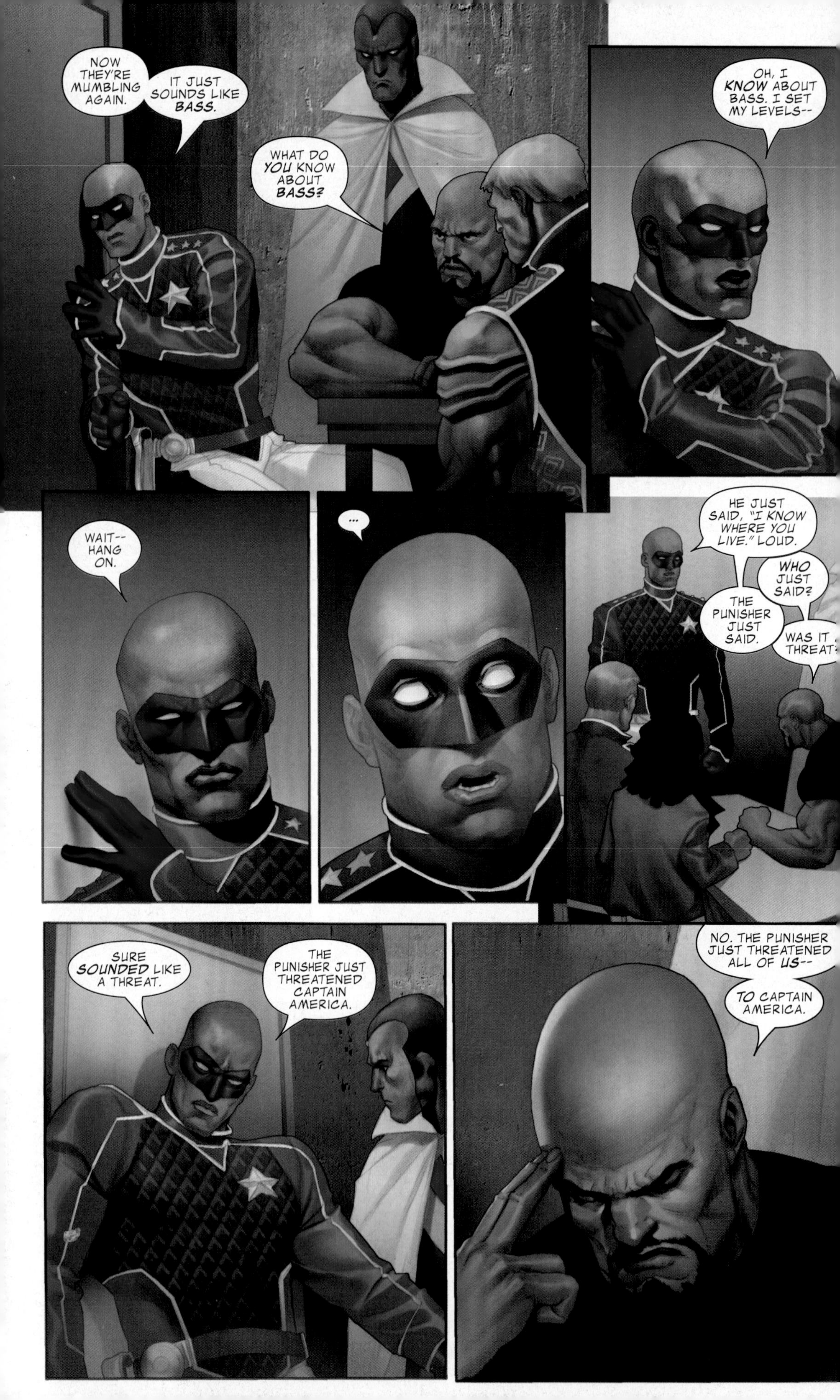
NOW THEY'RE MUMBLING AGAIN.
IT JUST SOUNDS LIKE BASS.
WHAT DO YOU KNOW ABOUT BASS?
OH, I KNOW ABOUT BASS. I SET MY LEVELS--
WAIT-- HANG ON.
...
HE JUST SAID, "I KNOW WHERE YOU LIVE." LOUD.
WHO JUST SAID?
THE PUNISHER JUST SAID.
WAS IT A THREAT?
SURE SOUNDED LIKE A THREAT.
THE PUNISHER JUST THREATENED CAPTAIN AMERICA.
NO. THE PUNISHER JUST THREATENED ALL OF US--
TO CAPTAIN AMERICA.

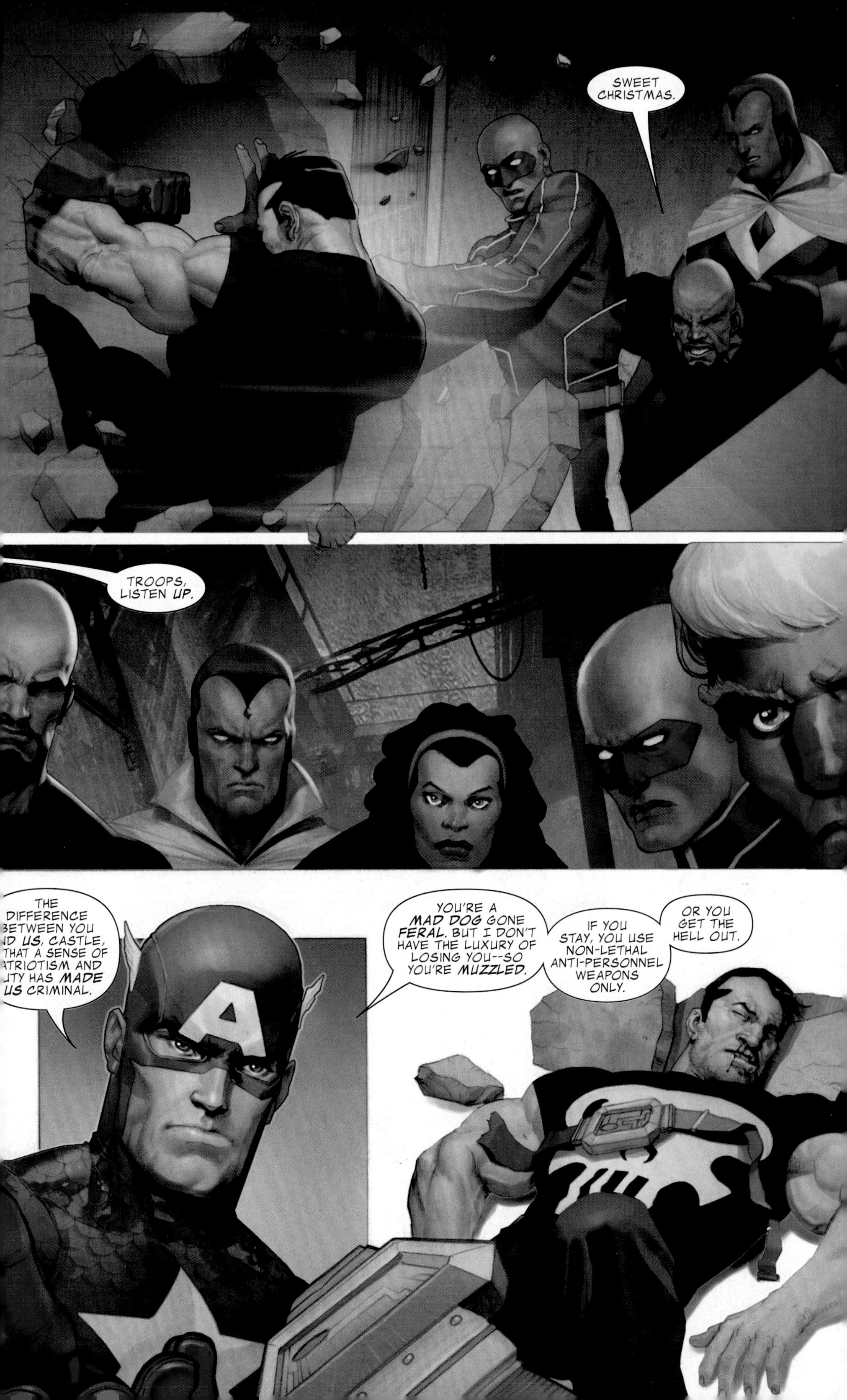
SWEET CHRISTMAS.
TROOPS, LISTEN UP.
THE DIFFERENCE BETWEEN YOU ND US, CASTLE, THAT A SENSE OF ATRIOTISM AND UTY HAS MADE US CRIMINAL.
YOU'RE A MAD DOG GONE FERAL. BUT I DON'T HAVE THE LUXURY OF LOSING YOU--SO YOU'RE MUZZLED.
IF YOU STAY, YOU USE NON-LETHAL ANTI-PERSONNEL WEAPONS ONLY.
OR YOU GET THE HELL OUT.

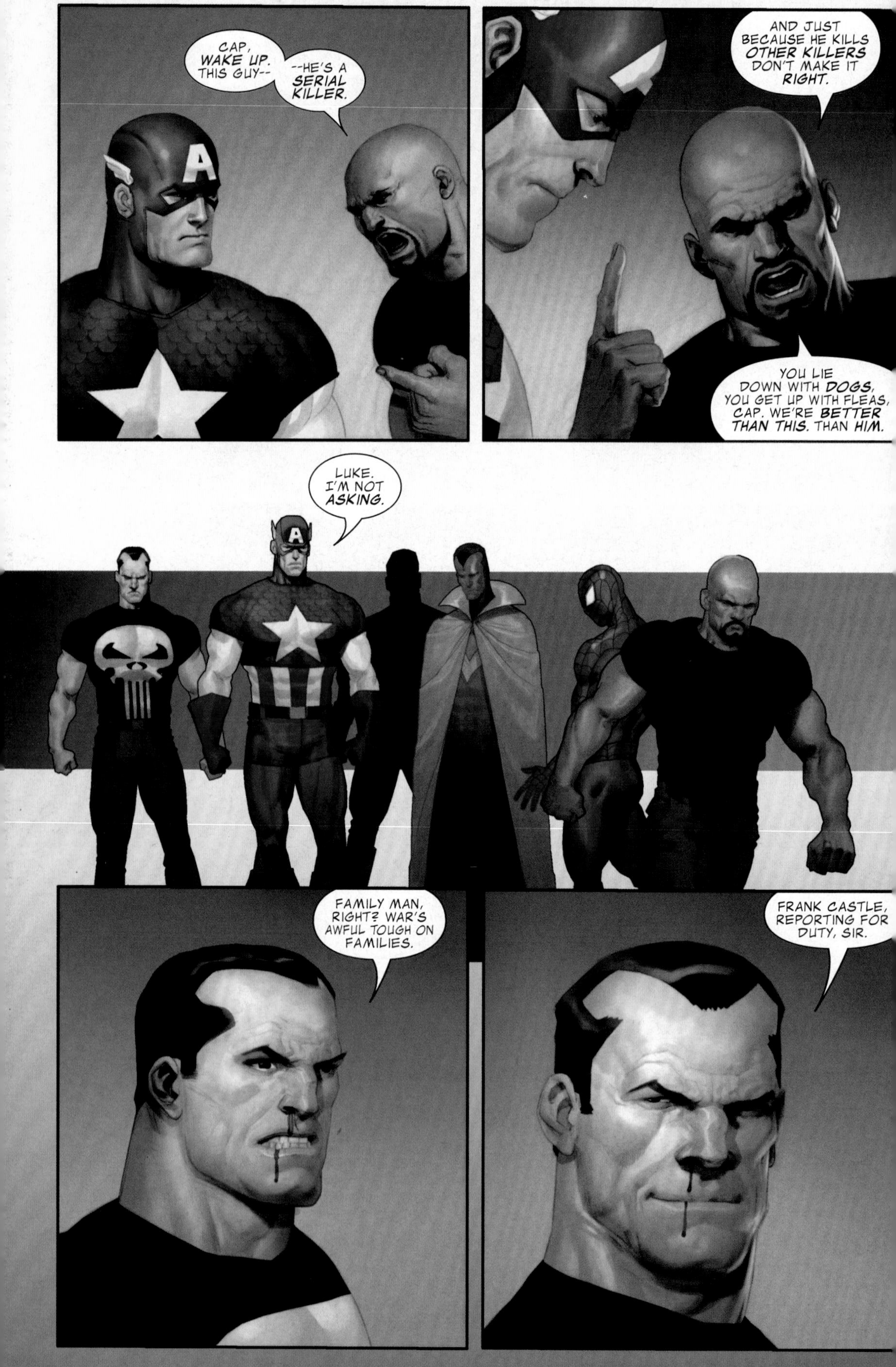
CAP, WAKE UP. THIS GUY--
--HE'S A SERIAL KILLER.
AND JUST BECAUSE HE KILLS OTHER KILLERS DON'T MAKE IT RIGHT.
YOU LIE DOWN WITH DOGS, YOU GET UP WITH FLEAS, CAP. WE'RE BETTER THAN THIS. THAN HIM.
LUKE. I'M NOT ASKING.
FAMILY MAN, RIGHT? WAR'S AWFUL TOUGH ON FAMILIES.
FRANK CASTLE, REPORTING FOR DUTY, SIR.

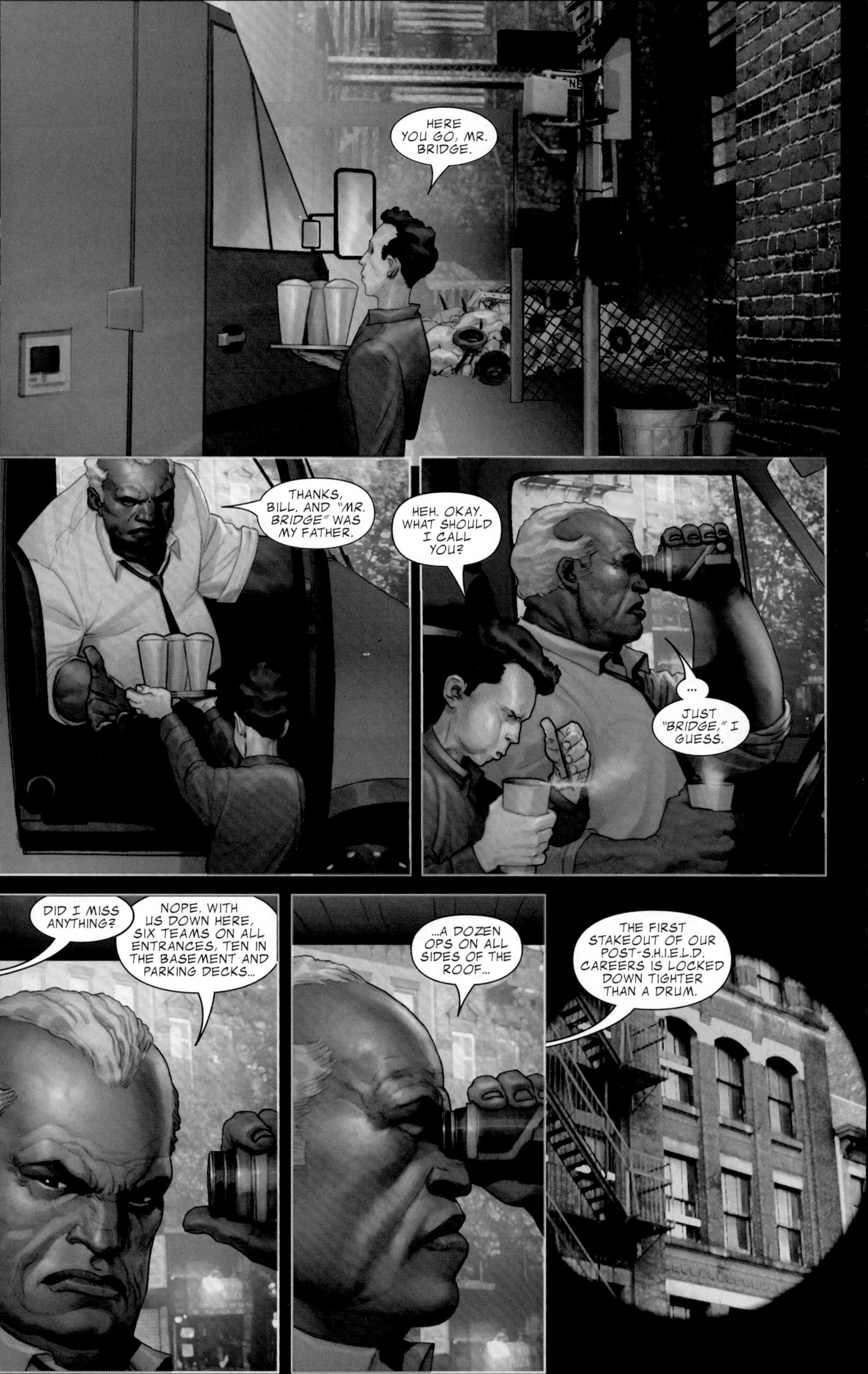
HERE YOU GO, MR. BRIDGE.
THANKS, BILL. AND "MR. BRIDGE" WAS MY FATHER.
HEH. OKAY. WHAT SHOULD I CALL YOU?
... JUST "BRIDGE," I GUESS.
DID I MISS ANYTHING?
NOPE. WITH US DOWN HERE, SIX TEAMS ON ALL ENTRANCES, TEN IN THE BASEMENT AND PARKING DECKS...
...A DOZEN OPS ON ALL SIDES OF THE ROOF...
THE FIRST STAKEOUT OF OUR POST-S.H.I.E.L.D. CAREERS IS LOCKED DOWN TIGHTER THAN A DRUM.

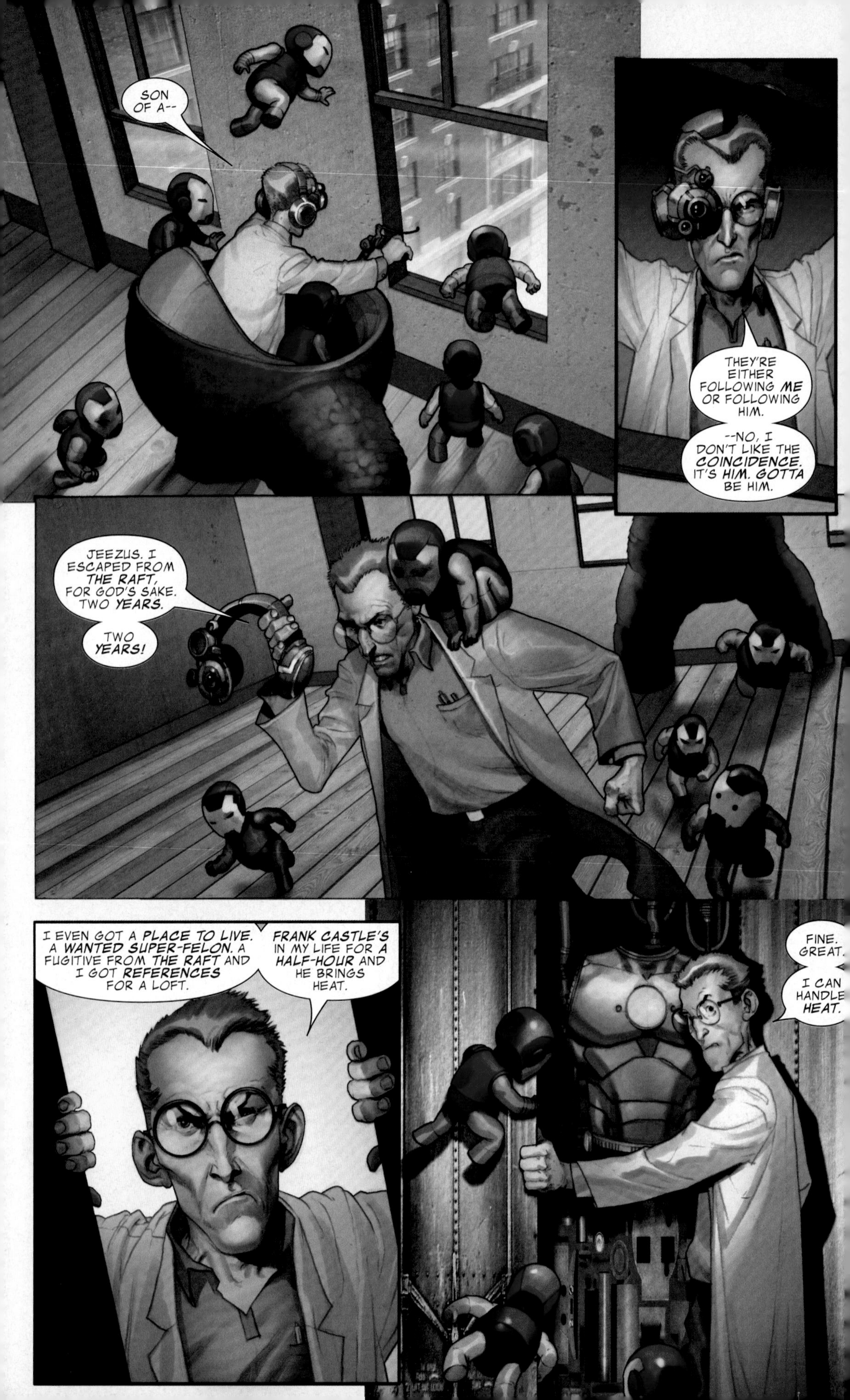

SON OF A--
THEY'RE EITHER FOLLOWING ME OR FOLLOWING HIM.
--NO, I DON'T LIKE THE COINCIDENCE. IT'S HIM. GOTTA BE HIM.
JEEZUS. I ESCAPED FROM THE RAFT, FOR GOD'S SAKE. TWO YEARS.
TWO YEARS!
I EVEN GOT A PLACE TO LIVE. A WANTED SUPER-FELON. A FUGITIVE FROM THE RAFT AND I GOT REFERENCES FOR A LOFT.
FRANK CASTLE'S IN MY LIFE FOR A HALF-HOUR AND HE BRINGS HEAT.
FINE. GREAT.
I CAN HANDLE HEAT.

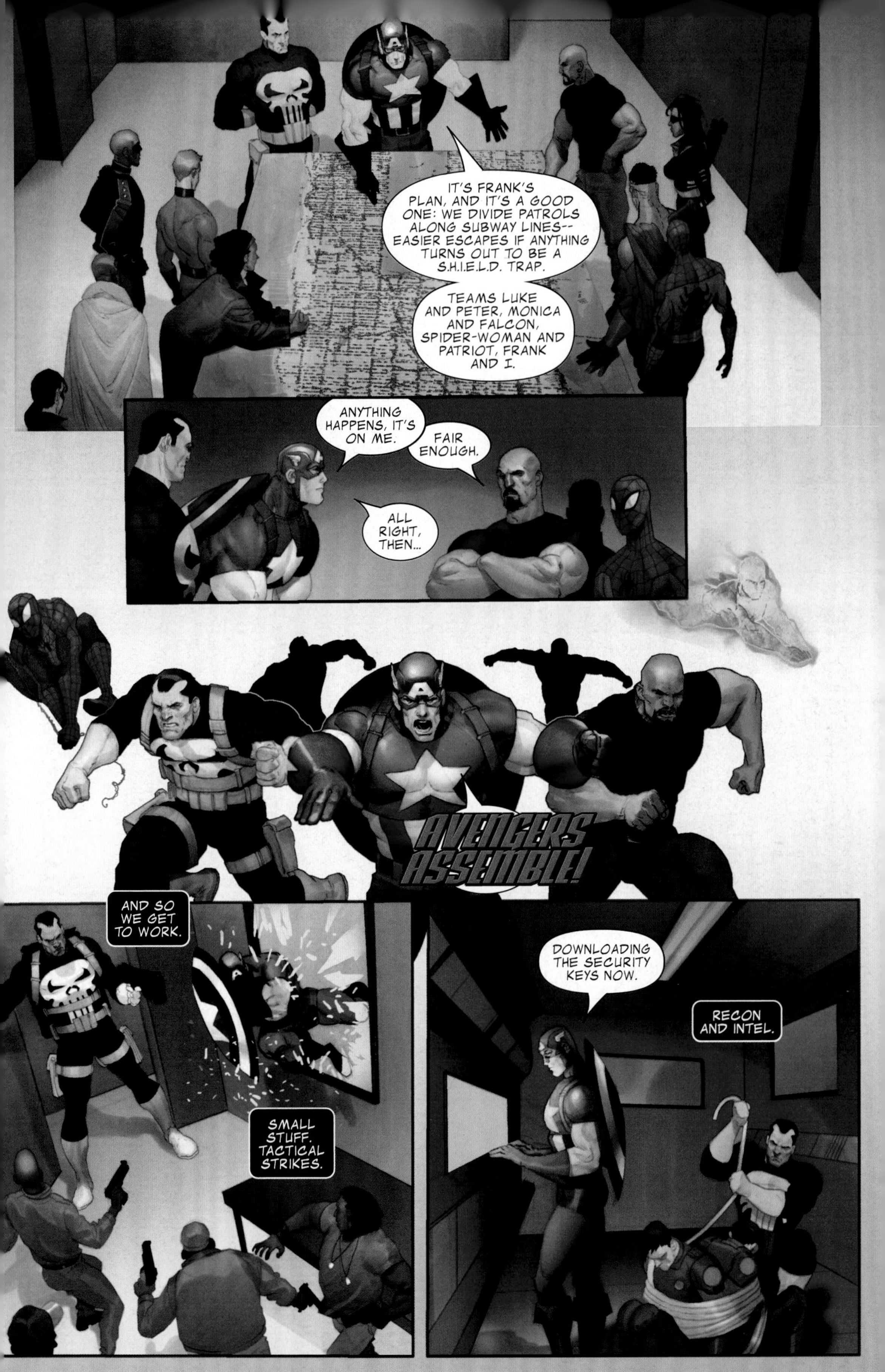
IT'S FRANK'S PLAN, AND IT'S A GOOD ONE: WE DIVIDE PATROLS ALONG SUBWAY LINES-- EASIER ESCAPES IF ANYTHING TURNS OUT TO BE A S.H.I.E.L.D. TRAP.
TEAMS LUKE AND PETER, MONICA AND FALCON, SPIDER-WOMAN AND PATRIOT, FRANK AND I.
ANYTHING HAPPENS, IT'S ON ME.
FAIR ENOUGH.
ALL RIGHT, THEN...
AVENGERS ASSEMBLE!
AND SO WE GET TO WORK.
SMALL STUFF. TACTICAL STRIKES.
DOWNLOADING THE SECURITY KEYS NOW.
RECON AND INTEL.

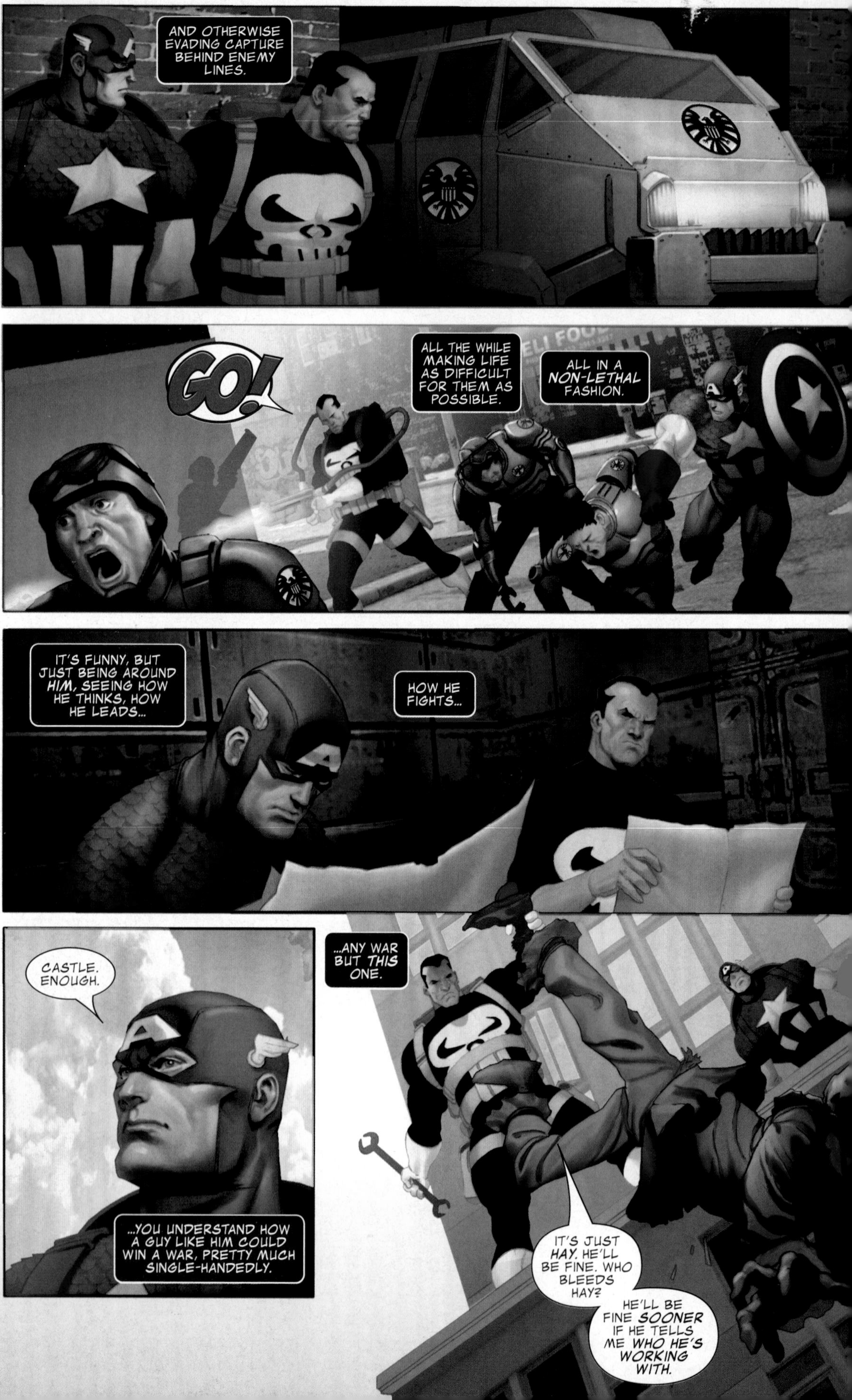
AND OTHERWISE EVADING CAPTURE BEHIND ENEMY LINES.
GO!
ALL THE WHILE MAKING LIFE AS DIFFICULT FOR THEM AS POSSIBLE.
ALL IN A NON-LETHAL FASHION.
IT'S FUNNY, BUT JUST BEING AROUND HIM, SEEING HOW HE THINKS, HOW HE LEADS...
HOW HE FIGHTS...
CASTLE. ENOUGH.
...YOU UNDERSTAND HOW A GUY LIKE HIM COULD WIN A WAR, PRETTY MUCH SINGLE-HANDEDLY.
...ANY WAR BUT THIS ONE.
IT'S JUST HAY. HE'LL BE FINE. WHO BLEEDS HAY?
HE'LL BE FINE SOONER IF HE TELLS ME WHO HE'S WORKING WITH.

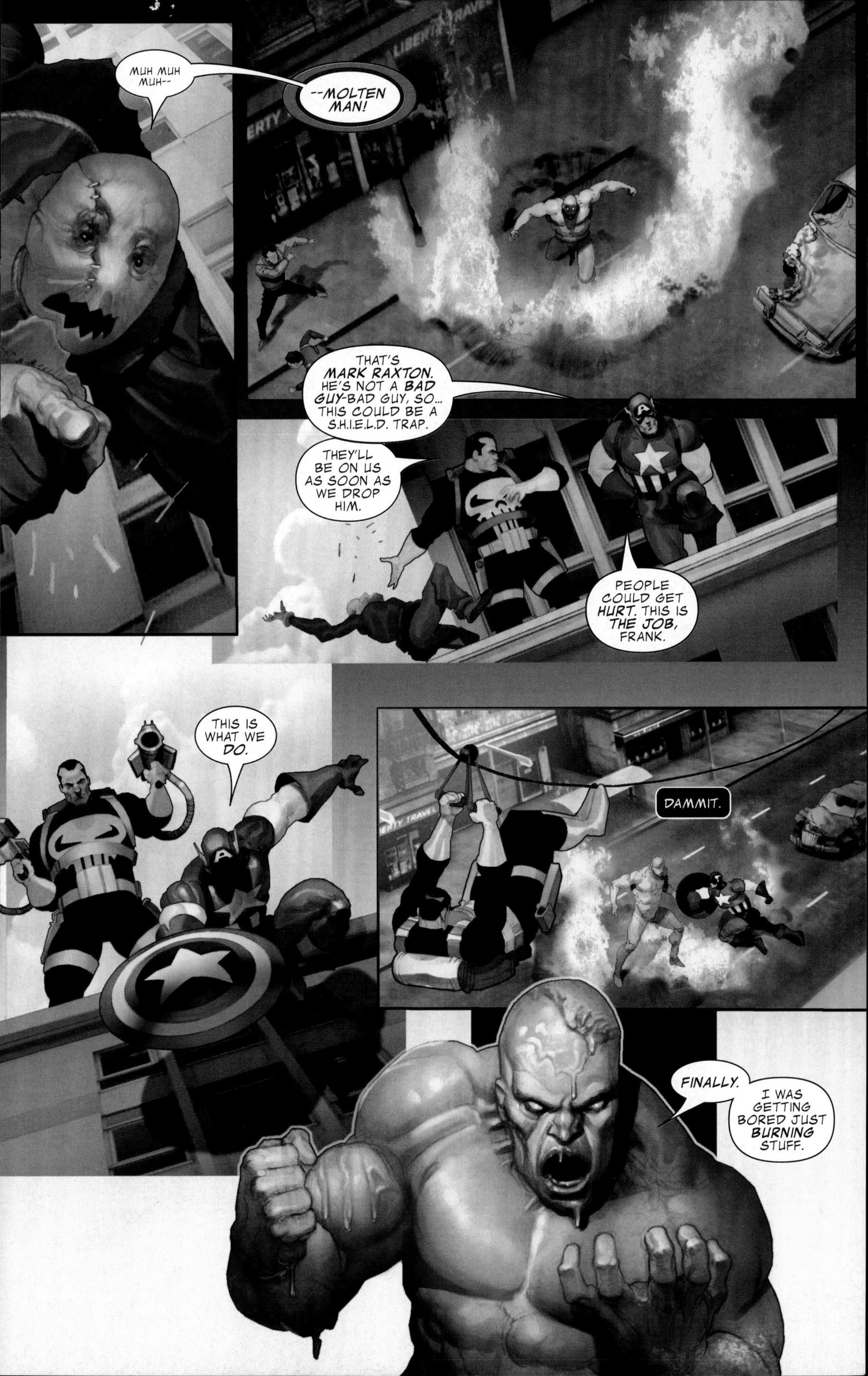
MUH MUH MUH--
--MOLTEN MAN!
THAT'S MARK RAXTON. HE'S NOT A BAD GUY-BAD GUY, SO... THIS COULD BE A S.H.I.E.L.D. TRAP.
THEY'LL BE ON US AS SOON AS WE DROP HIM.
PEOPLE COULD GET HURT. THIS IS THE JOB, FRANK.
THIS IS WHAT WE DO.
DAMMIT.
FINALLY.
I WAS GETTING BORED JUST BURNING STUFF.

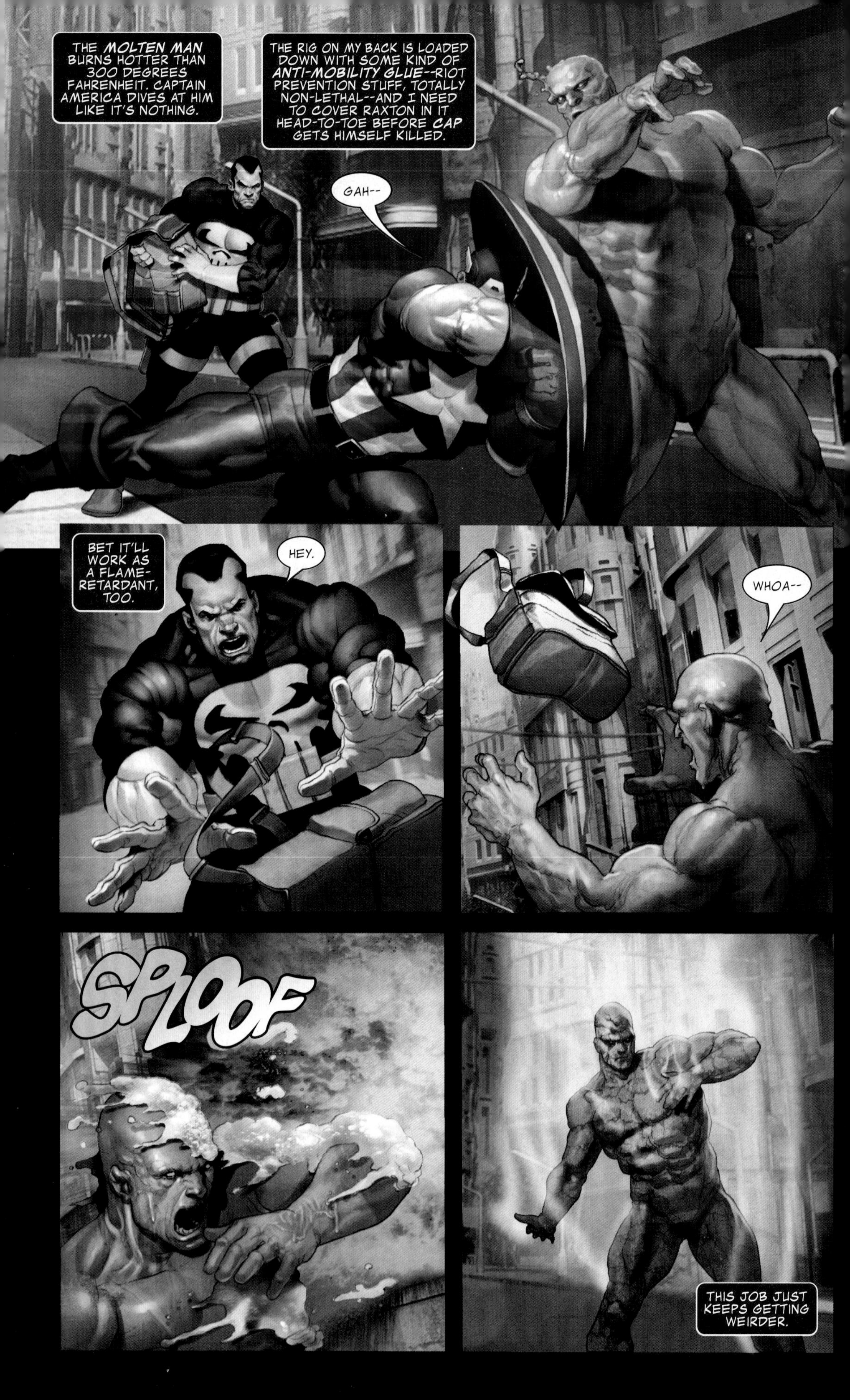
THE MOLTEN MAN BURNS HOTTER THAN 300 DEGREES FAHRENHEIT. CAPTAIN AMERICA DIVES AT HIM LIKE IT'S NOTHING.
THE RIG ON MY BACK IS LOADED DOWN WITH SOME KIND OF ANTI-MOBILITY GLUE--RIOT PREVENTION STUFF, TOTALLY NON-LETHAL--AND I NEED TO COVER RAXTON IN IT HEAD-TO-TOE BEFORE CAP GETS HIMSELF KILLED.
GAH--
BET IT'LL WORK AS A FLAME-RETARDANT, TOO.
HEY.
WHOA--
SPLOOF
THIS JOB JUST KEEPS GETTING WEIRDER.

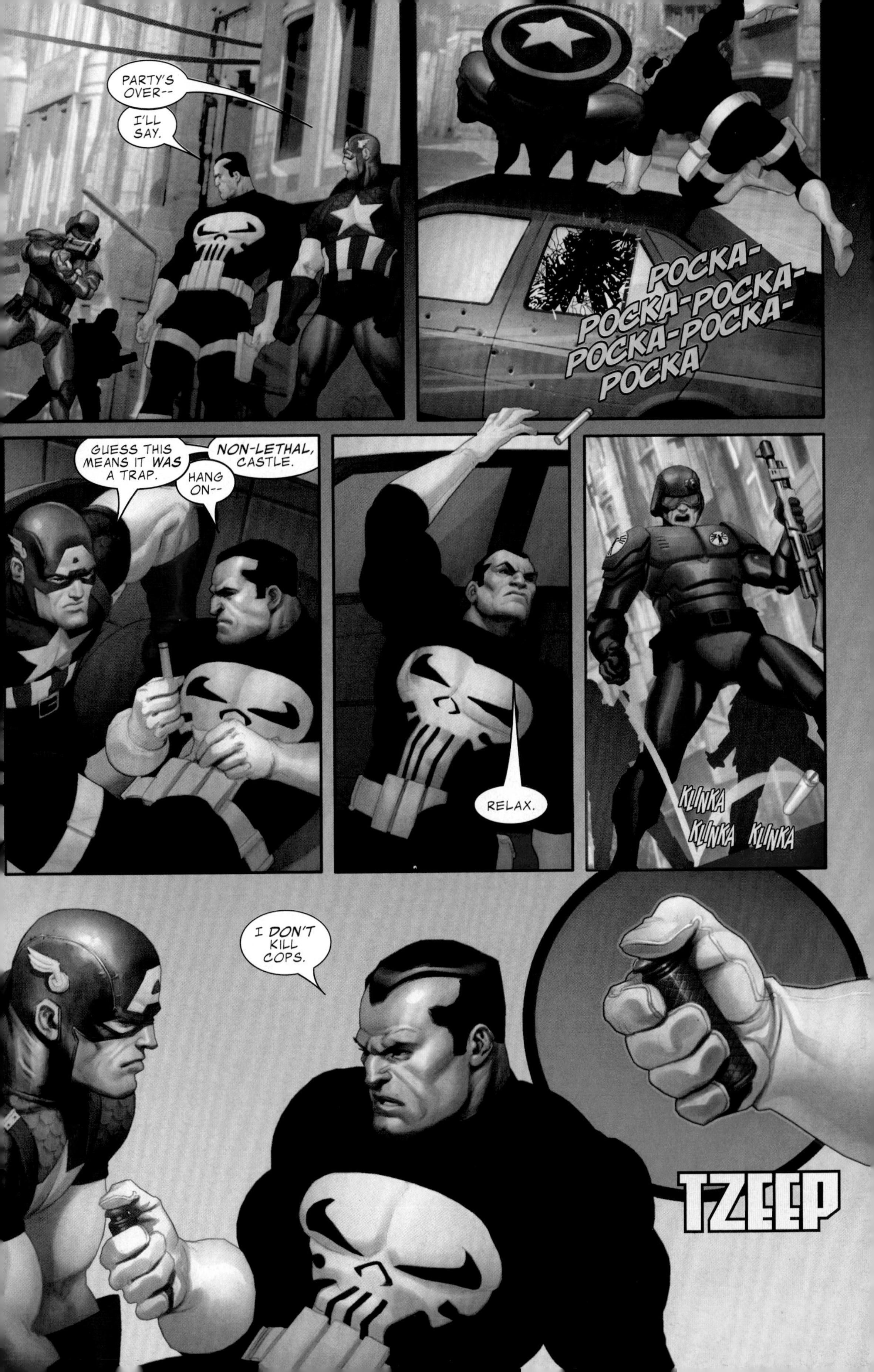

PARTY'S OVER--
I'LL SAY.
POCKA-POCKA-POCKA-POCKA-POCKA-POCKA
GUESS THIS MEANS IT WAS A TRAP.
NON-LETHAL, CASTLE.
HANG ON--
RELAX.
KLINKA KLINKA KLINKA
I DON'T KILL COPS.
TZEEP

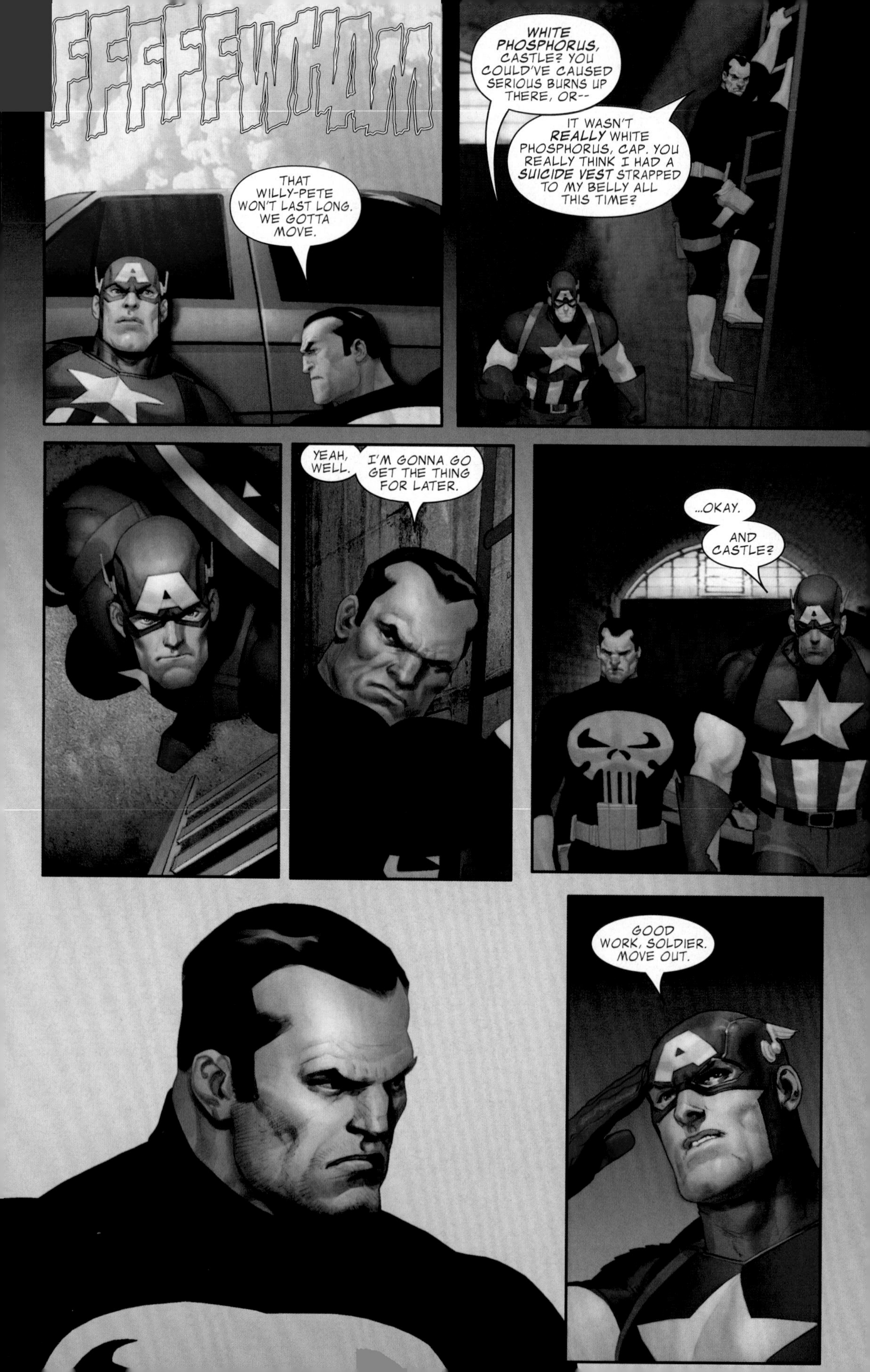
FFFFFWHOOM
THAT WILLY-PETE WON'T LAST LONG. WE GOTTA MOVE.
WHITE PHOSPHORUS, CASTLE? YOU COULD'VE CAUSED SERIOUS BURNS UP THERE, OR--
IT WASN'T REALLY WHITE PHOSPHORUS, CAP. YOU REALLY THINK I HAD A SUICIDE VEST STRAPPED TO MY BELLY ALL THIS TIME?
YEAH, WELL.
I'M GONNA GO GET THE THING FOR LATER.
...OKAY.
AND CASTLE?
GOOD WORK, SOLDIER. MOVE OUT.

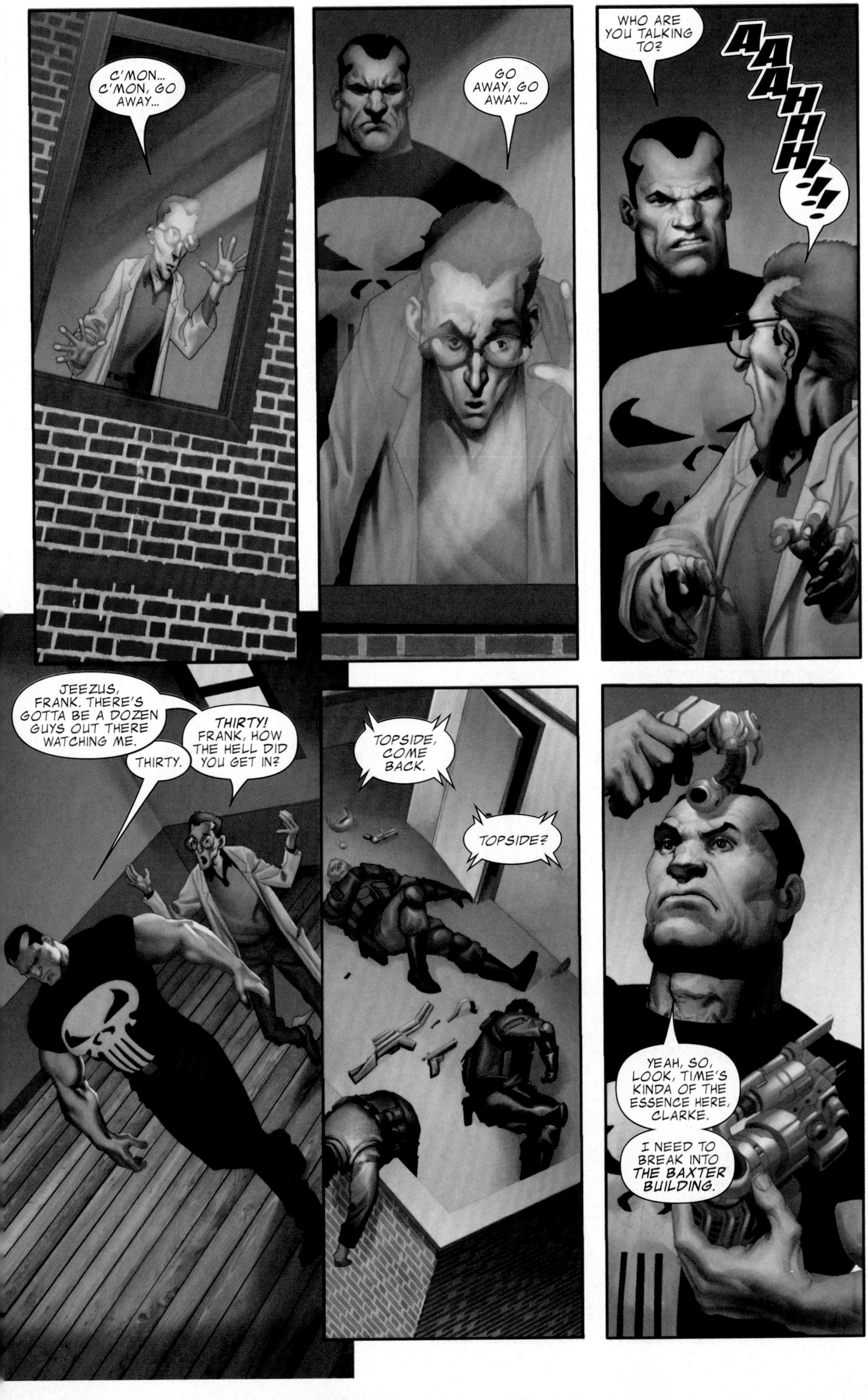
C'MON... C'MON, GO AWAY...
GO AWAY, GO AWAY...
WHO ARE YOU TALKING TO?
AAAHHH!!!
JEEZUS, FRANK. THERE'S GOTTA BE A DOZEN GUYS OUT THERE WATCHING ME.
THIRTY.
THIRTY! FRANK, HOW THE HELL DID YOU GET IN?
TOPSIDE, COME BACK.
TOPSIDE?
YEAH, SO, LOOK, TIME'S KINDA OF THE ESSENCE HERE, CLARKE.
I NEED TO BREAK INTO THE BAXTER BUILDING.

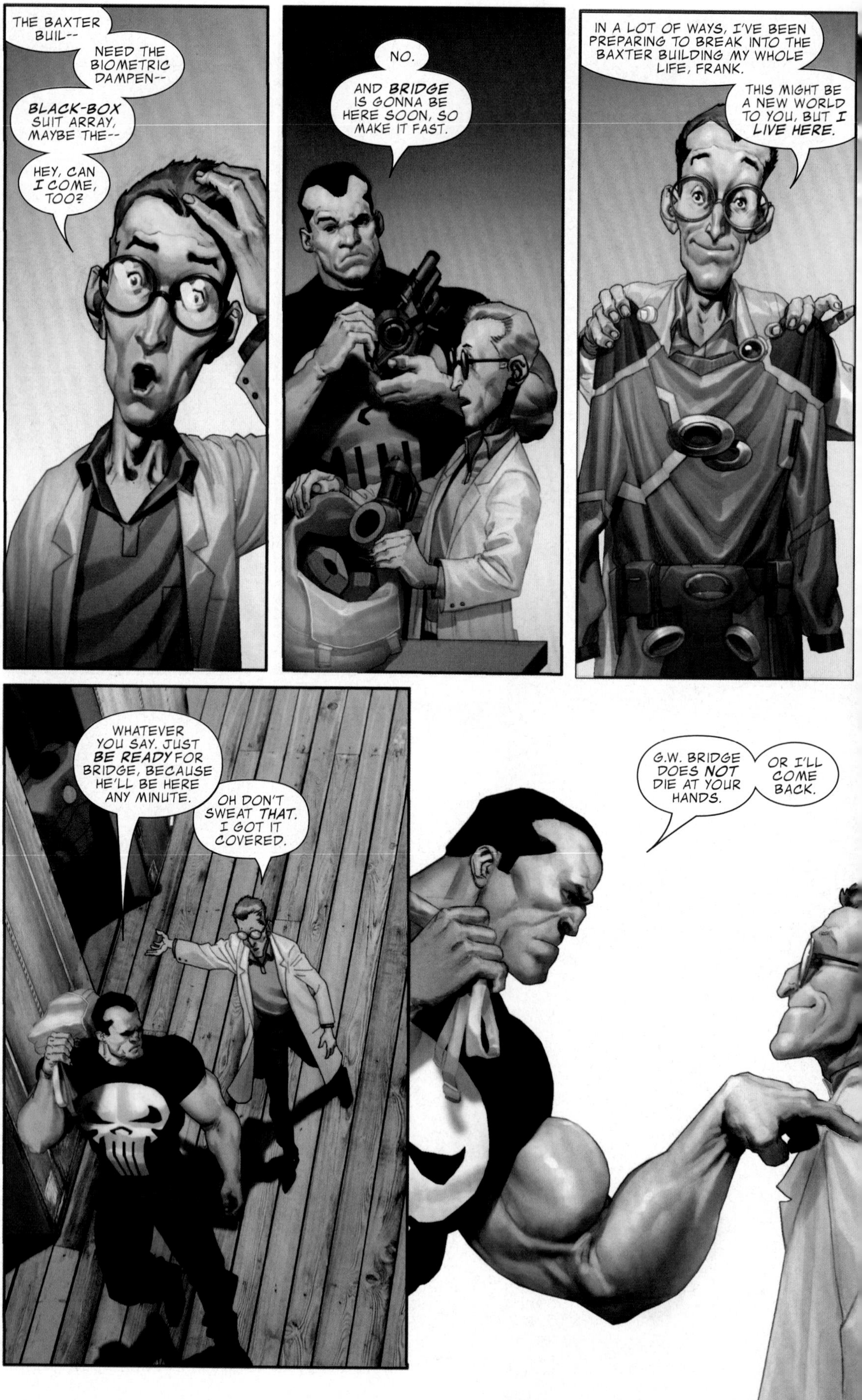
THE BAXTER BUIL--
NEED THE BIOMETRIC DAMPEN--
BLACK-BOX SUIT ARRAY, MAYBE THE--
HEY, CAN I COME, TOO?
NO.
AND BRIDGE IS GONNA BE HERE SOON, SO MAKE IT FAST.
IN A LOT OF WAYS, I'VE BEEN PREPARING TO BREAK INTO THE BAXTER BUILDING MY WHOLE LIFE, FRANK.
THIS MIGHT BE A NEW WORLD TO YOU, BUT I LIVE HERE.
WHATEVER YOU SAY. JUST BE READY FOR BRIDGE, BECAUSE HE'LL BE HERE ANY MINUTE.
OH DON'T SWEAT THAT. I GOT IT COVERED.
G.W. BRIDGE DOES NOT DIE AT YOUR HANDS.
OR I'LL COME BACK.

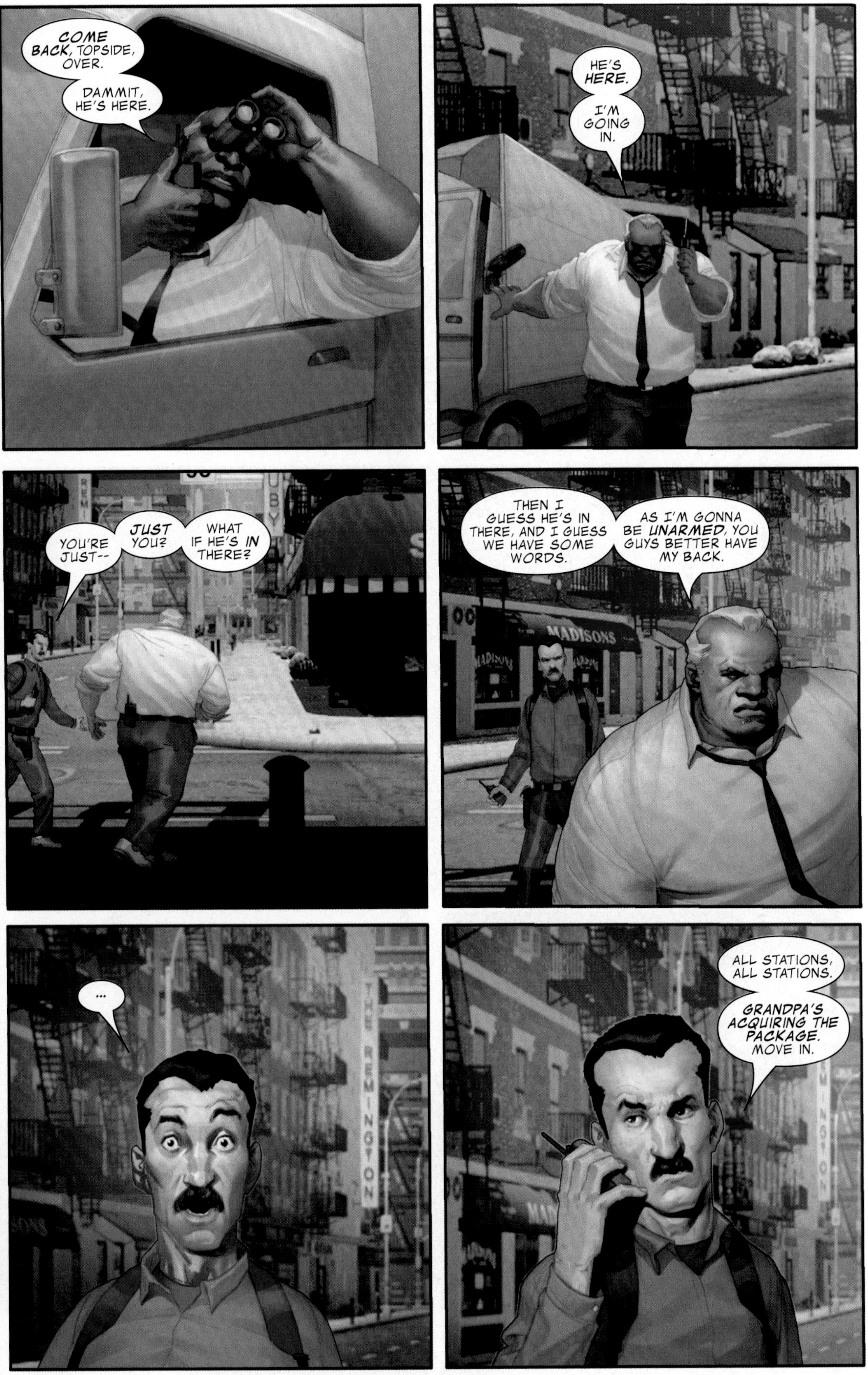
COME BACK, TOPSIDE, OVER.
DAMMIT, HE'S HERE.
HE'S HERE.
I'M GOING IN.
YOU'RE JUST--
JUST YOU?
WHAT IF HE'S IN THERE?
THEN I GUESS HE'S IN THERE, AND I GUESS WE HAVE SOME WORDS.
AS I'M GONNA BE UNARMED, YOU GUYS BETTER HAVE MY BACK.
MADISONS
...
THE REMINGTON
ALL STATIONS, ALL STATIONS.
GRANDPA'S ACQUIRING THE PACKAGE. MOVE IN.

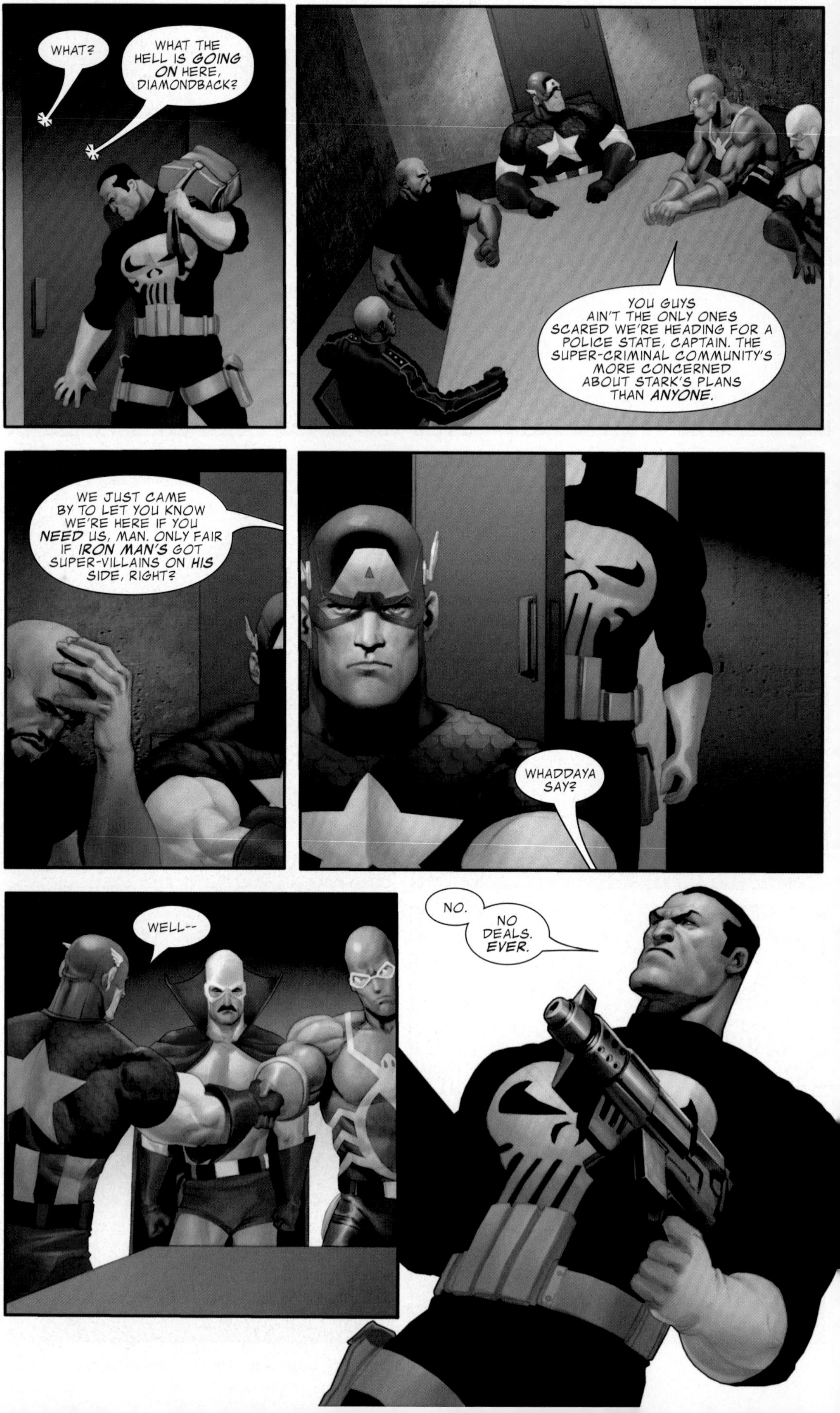
WHAT?
WHAT THE HELL IS GOING ON HERE, DIAMONDBACK?
YOU GUYS AIN'T THE ONLY ONES SCARED WE'RE HEADING FOR A POLICE STATE, CAPTAIN. THE SUPER-CRIMINAL COMMUNITY'S MORE CONCERNED ABOUT STARK'S PLANS THAN ANYONE.
WE JUST CAME BY TO LET YOU KNOW WE'RE HERE IF YOU NEED US, MAN. ONLY FAIR IF IRON MAN'S GOT SUPER-VILLAINS ON HIS SIDE, RIGHT?
WHADDAYA SAY?
WELL--
NO.
NO DEALS. EVER.

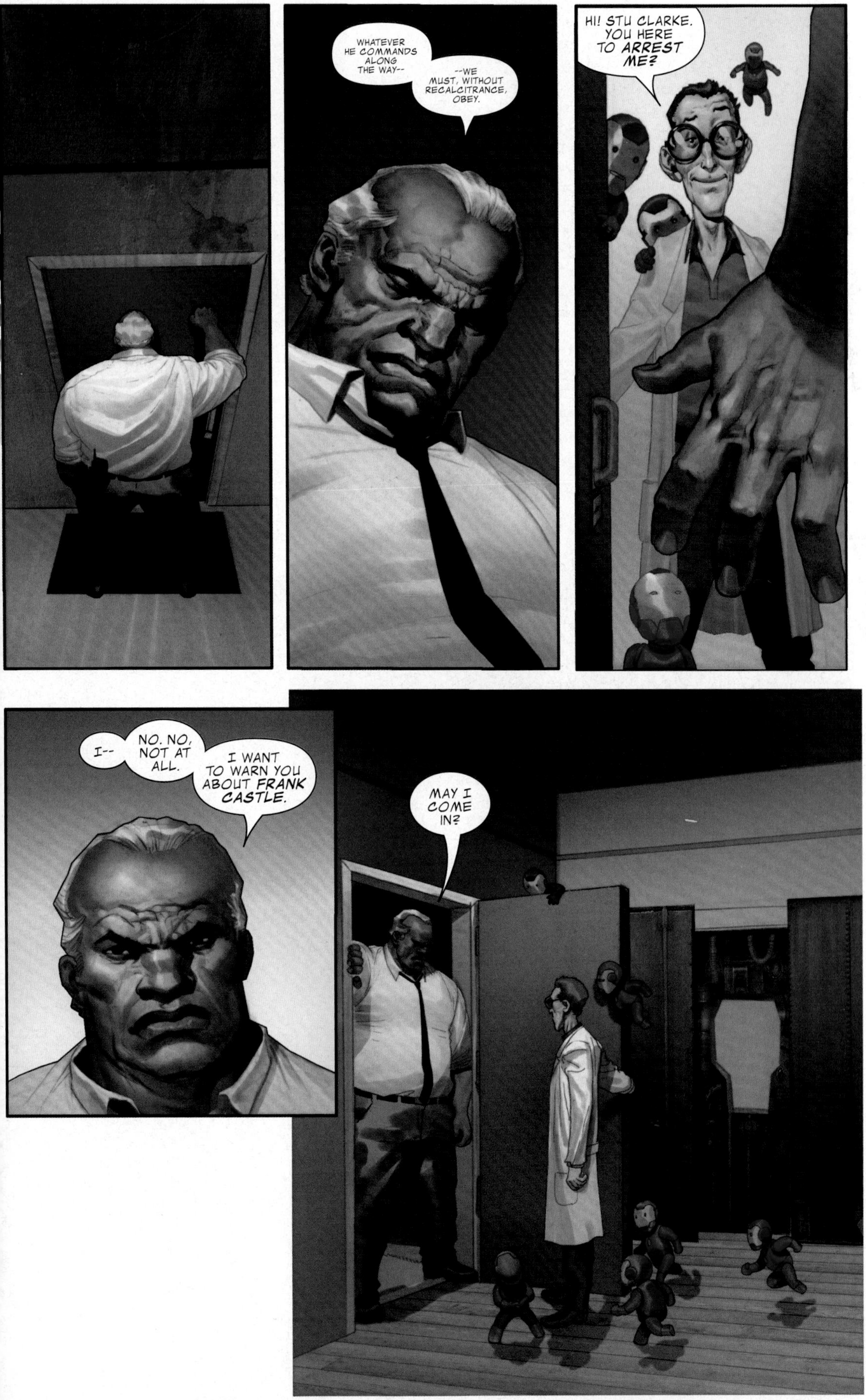
WHATEVER HE COMMANDS ALONG THE WAY--
--WE MUST, WITHOUT RECALCITRANCE, OBEY.
HI! STU CLARKE. YOU HERE TO ARREST ME?
I--
NO. NO, NOT AT ALL.
I WANT TO WARN YOU ABOUT FRANK CASTLE.
MAY I COME IN?

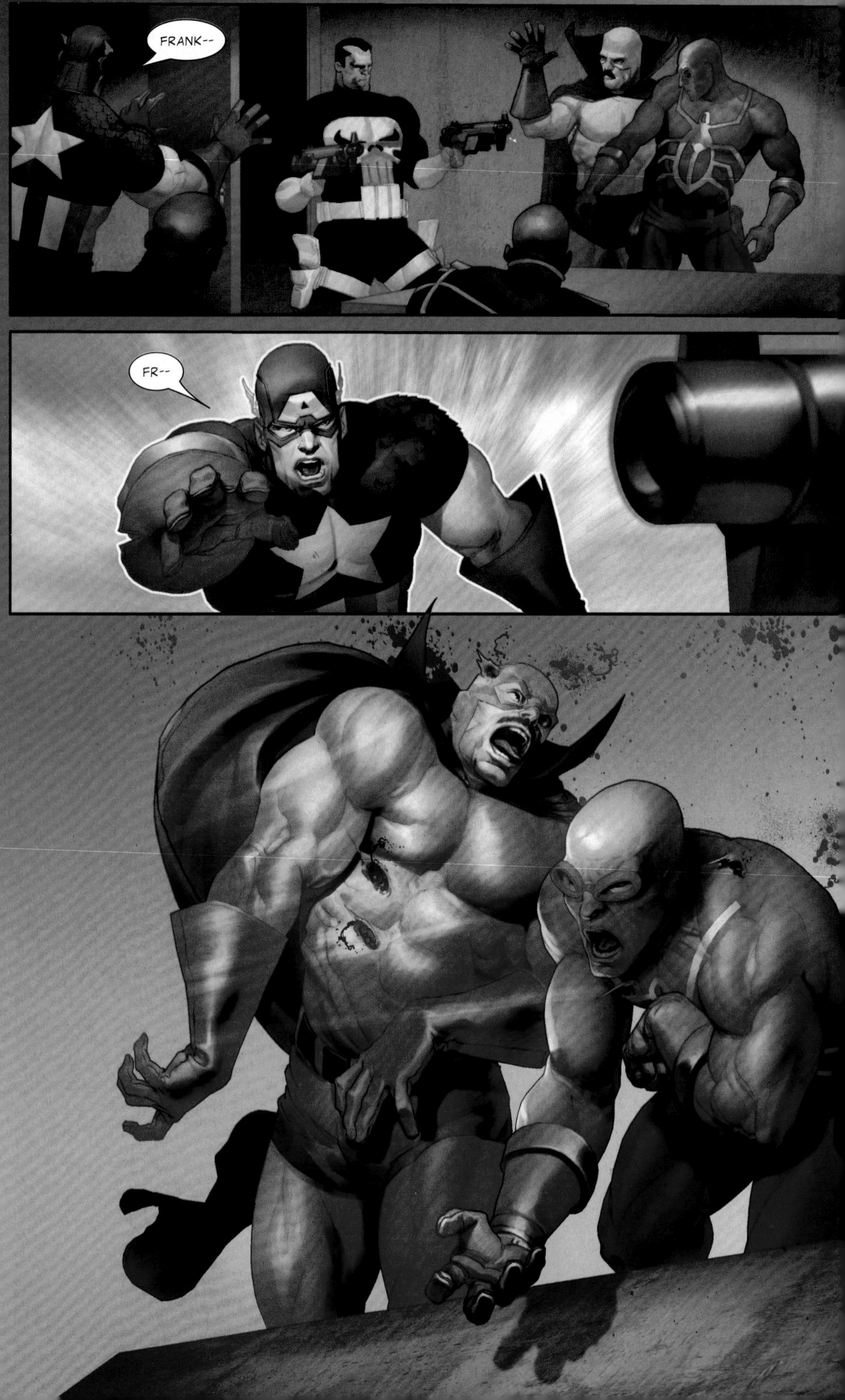
FRANK--
FR--

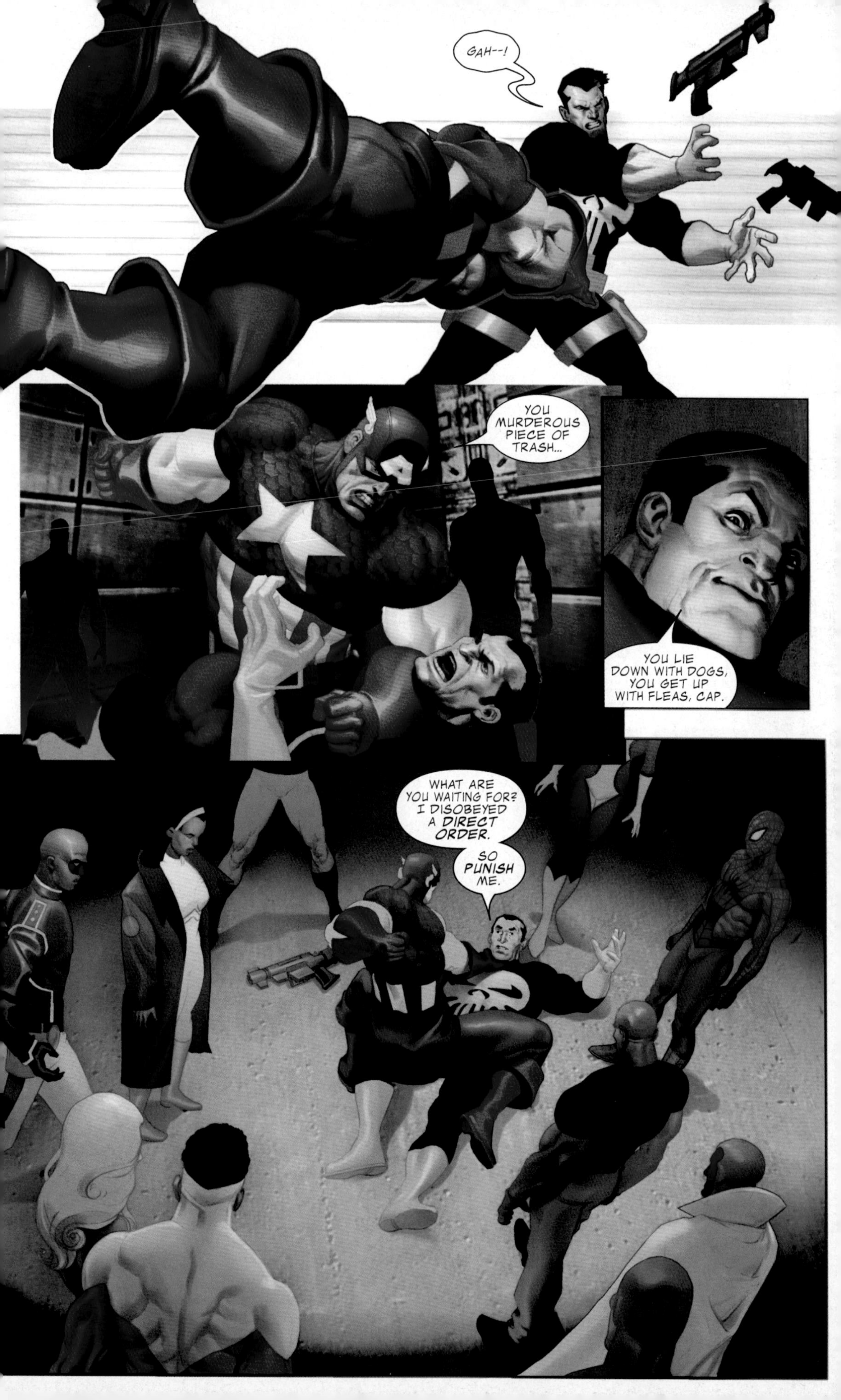
GAH--!
YOU MURDEROUS PIECE OF TRASH...
YOU LIE DOWN WITH DOGS, YOU GET UP WITH FLEAS, CAP.
WHAT ARE YOU WAITING FOR? I DISOBEYED A DIRECT ORDER.
SO PUNISH ME.

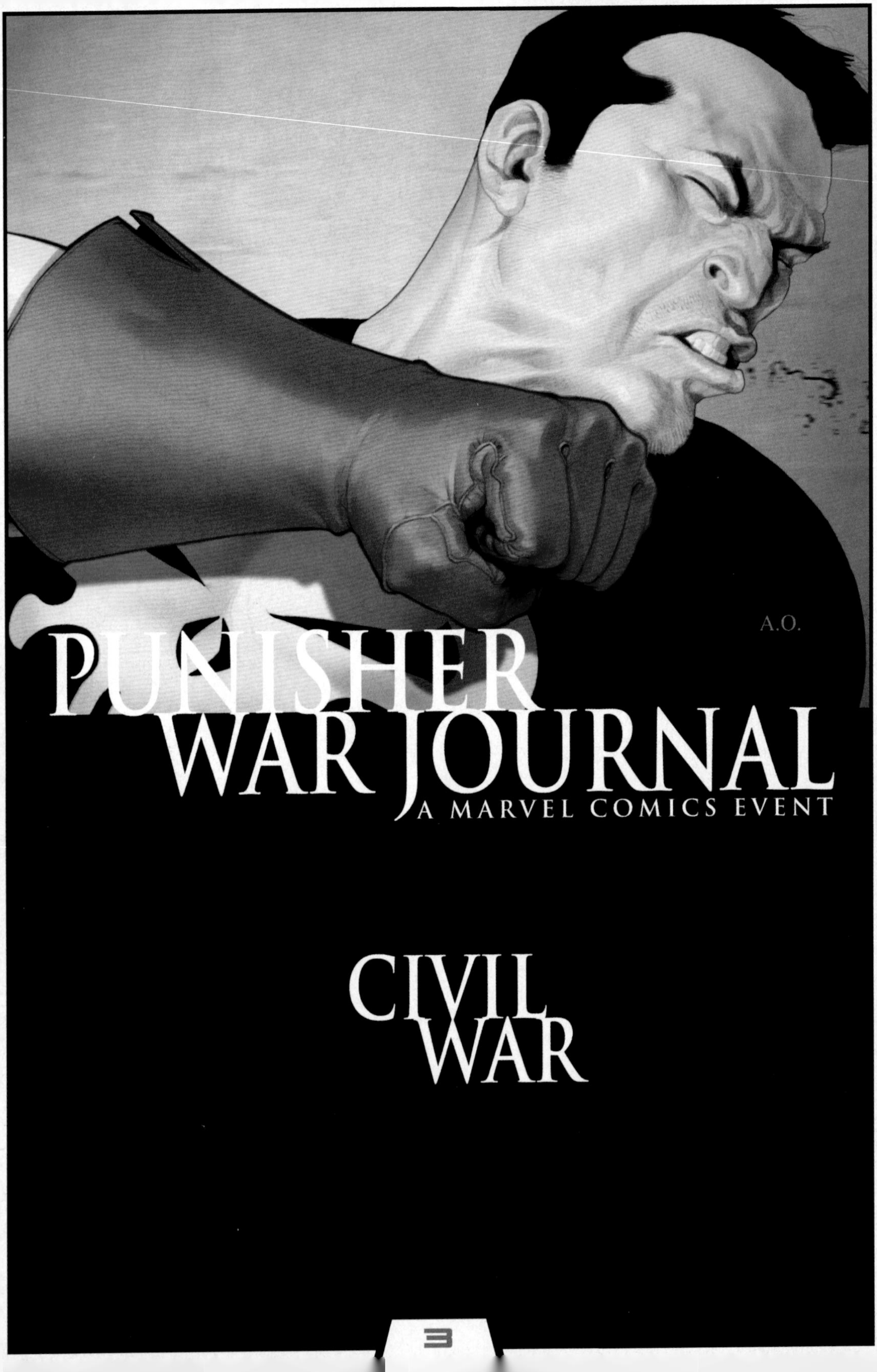
A.O.
PUNISHER
WAR JOURNAL
A MARVEL COMICS EVENT
CIVIL
WAR
3

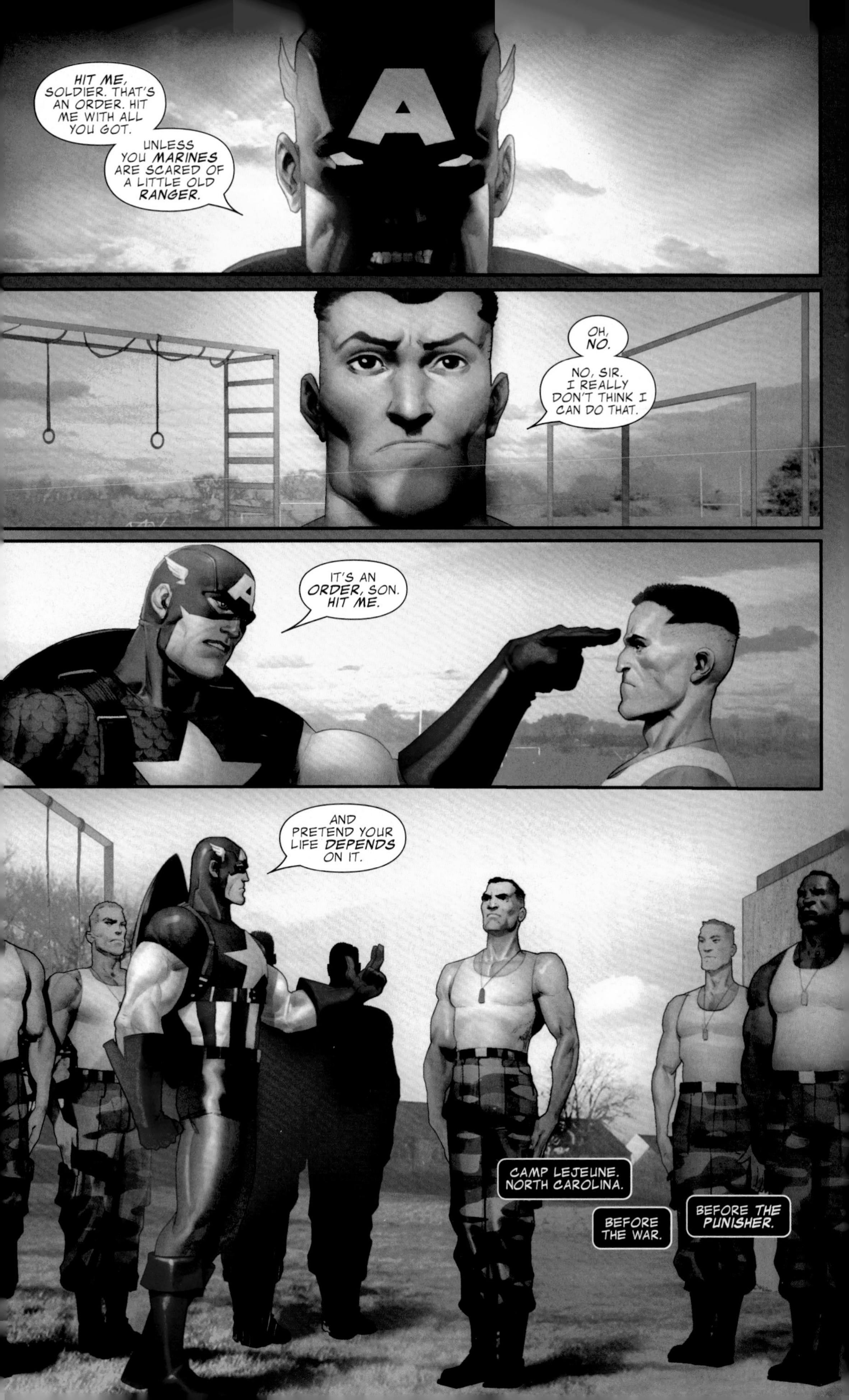
HIT ME, SOLDIER. THAT'S AN ORDER. HIT ME WITH ALL YOU GOT.
UNLESS YOU MARINES ARE SCARED OF A LITTLE OLD RANGER.
OH, NO.
NO, SIR. I REALLY DON'T THINK I CAN DO THAT.
IT'S AN ORDER, SON. HIT ME.
AND PRETEND YOUR LIFE DEPENDS ON IT.
CAMP LEJEUNE. NORTH CAROLINA.
BEFORE THE WAR.
BEFORE THE PUNISHER.

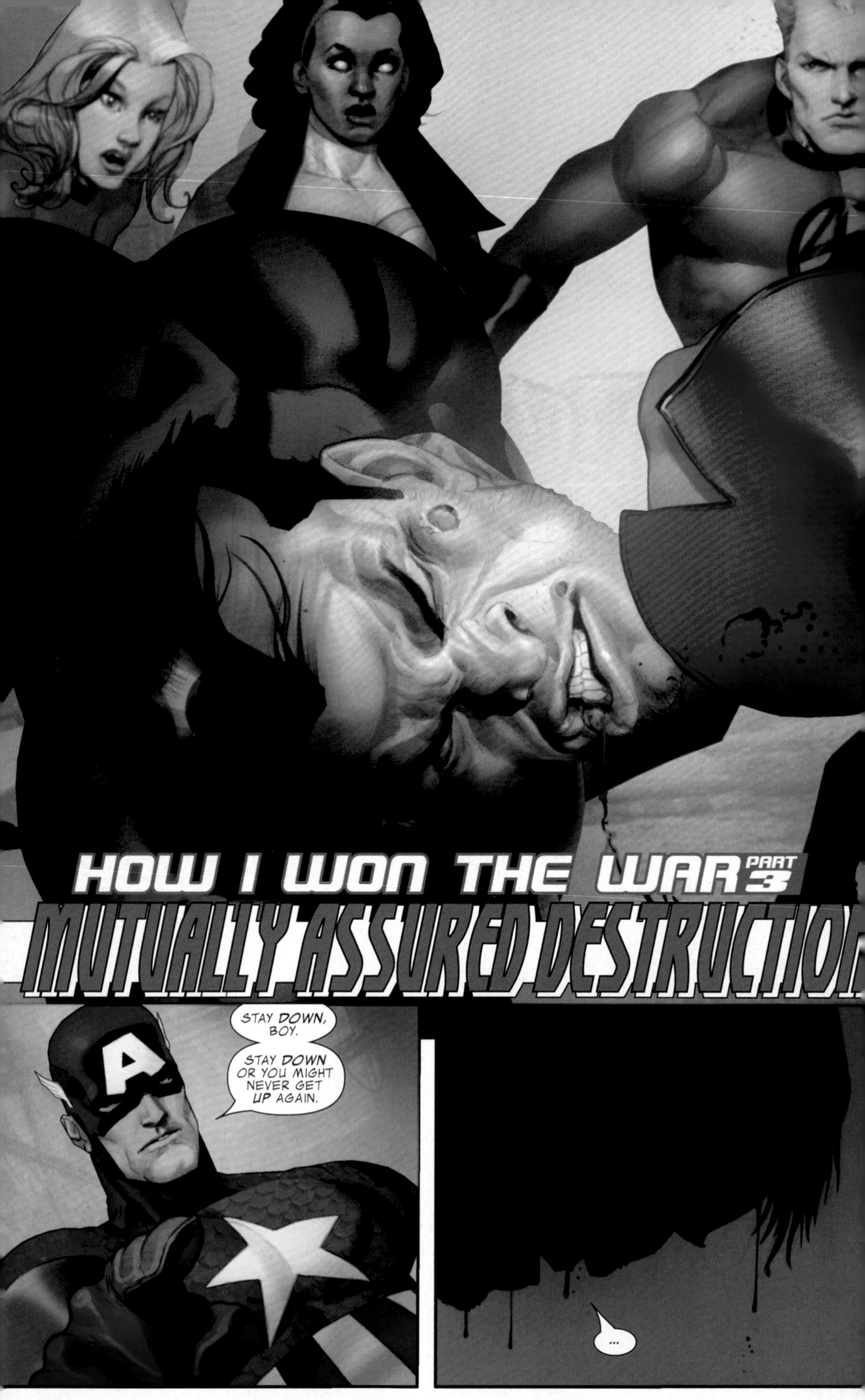
HOW I WON THE WAR PART 3
MUTUALLY ASSURED DESTRUCTION
STAY DOWN, BOY.
STAY DOWN OR YOU MIGHT NEVER GET UP AGAIN.
...

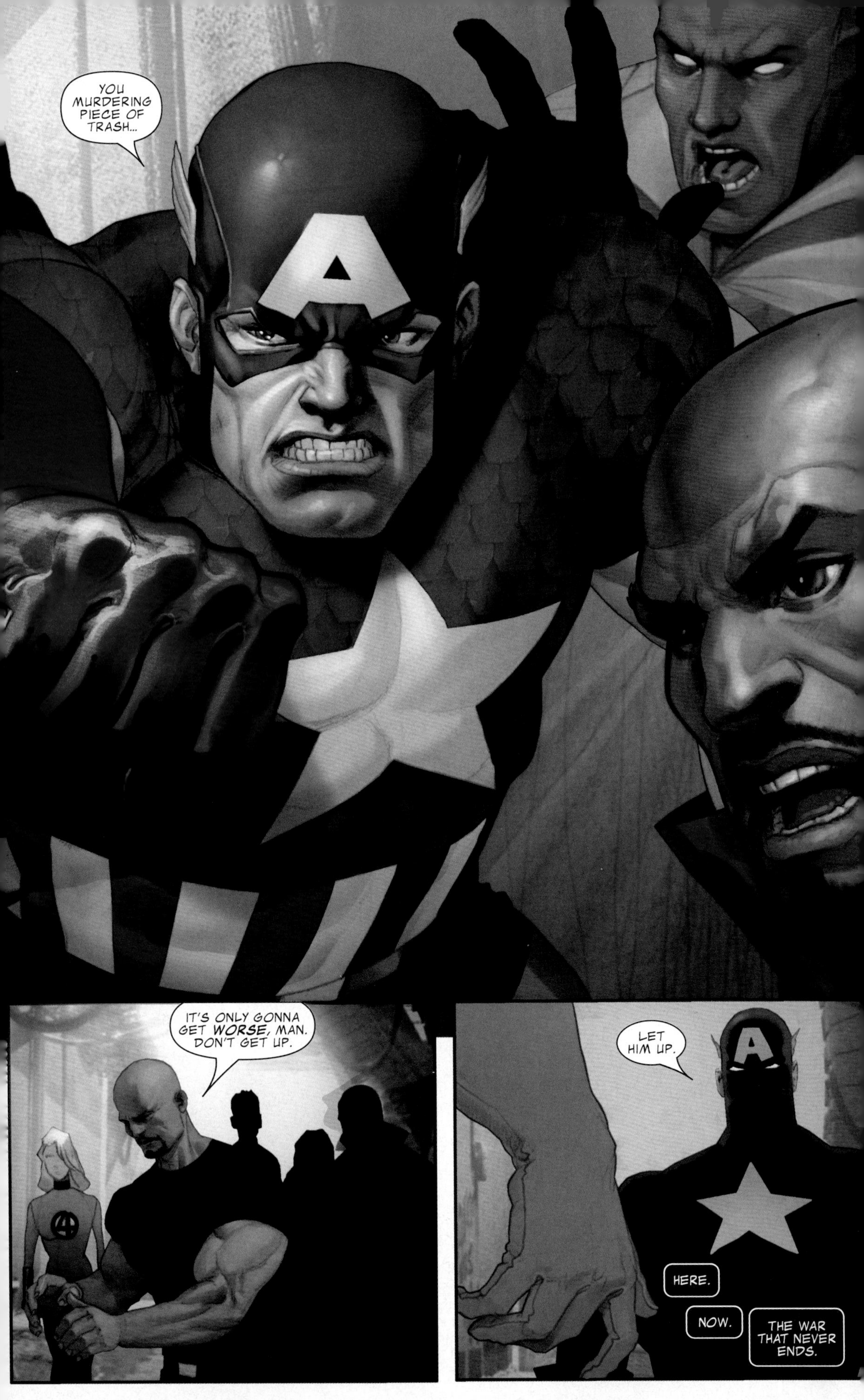
YOU MURDERING PIECE OF TRASH...
IT'S ONLY GONNA GET WORSE, MAN. DON'T GET UP.
LET HIM UP.
HERE.
NOW.
THE WAR THAT NEVER ENDS.

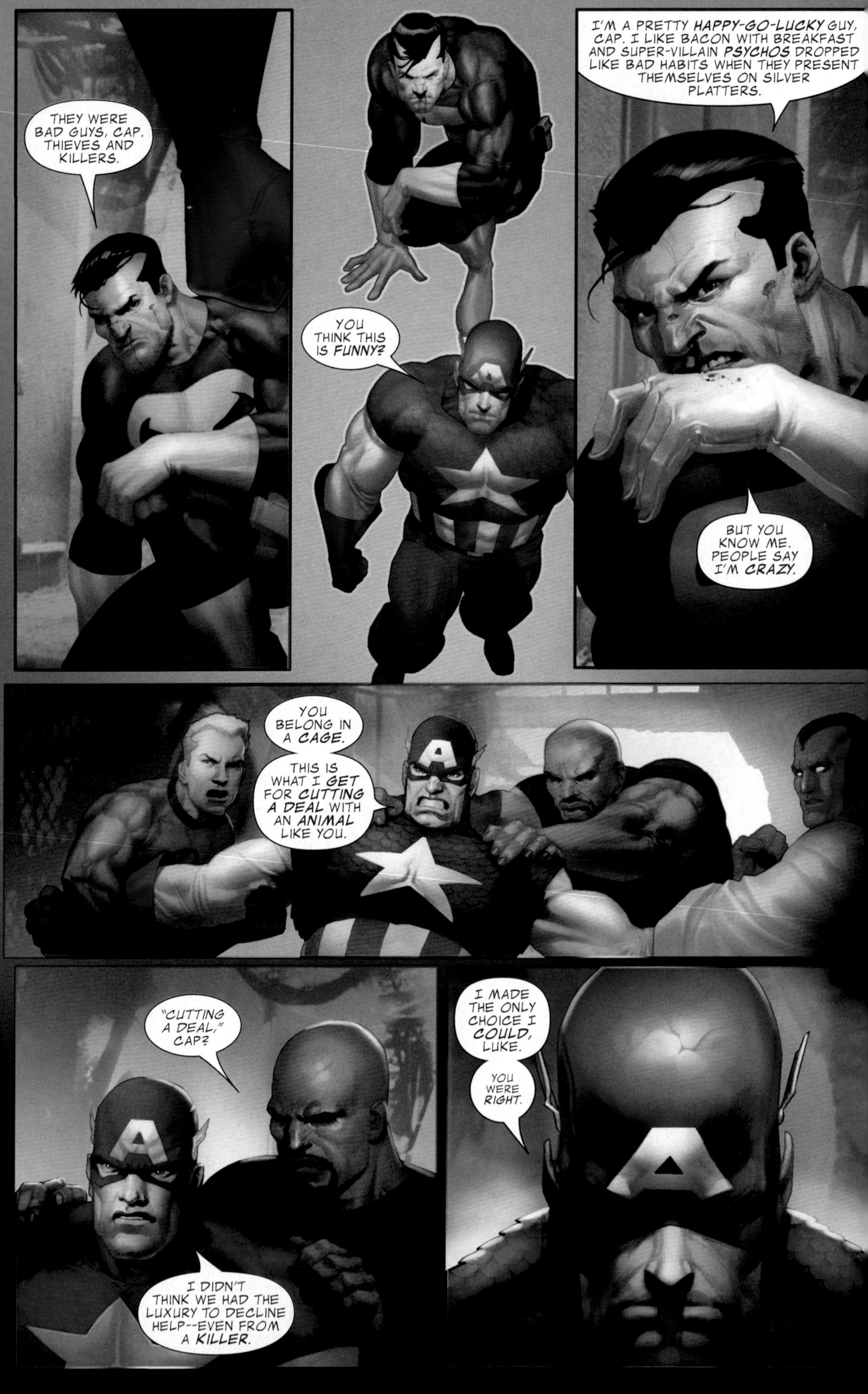
THEY WERE BAD GUYS, CAP. THIEVES AND KILLERS.
YOU THINK THIS IS FUNNY?
I'M A PRETTY HAPPY-GO-LUCKY GUY, CAP. I LIKE BACON WITH BREAKFAST AND SUPER-VILLAIN PSYCHOS DROPPED LIKE BAD HABITS WHEN THEY PRESENT THEMSELVES ON SILVER PLATTERS.
BUT YOU KNOW ME. PEOPLE SAY I'M CRAZY.
YOU BELONG IN A CAGE.
THIS IS WHAT I GET FOR CUTTING A DEAL WITH AN ANIMAL LIKE YOU.
"CUTTING A DEAL," CAP?
I DIDN'T THINK WE HAD THE LUXURY TO DECLINE HELP--EVEN FROM A KILLER.
I MADE THE ONLY CHOICE I COULD, LUKE.
YOU WERE RIGHT.

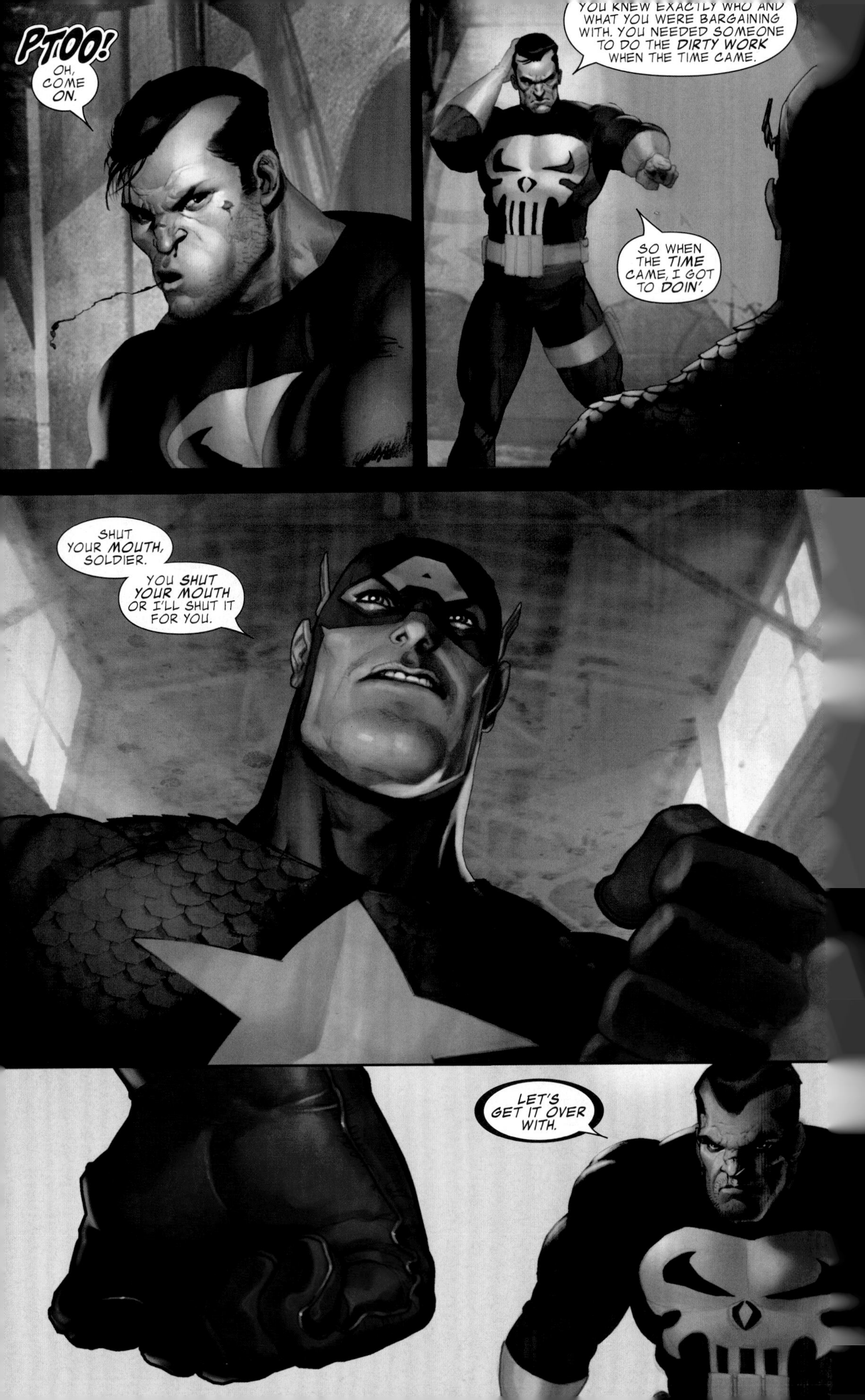
PTOO!
OH, COME ON.
YOU KNEW EXACTLY WHO AND WHAT YOU WERE BARGAINING WITH. YOU NEEDED SOMEONE TO DO THE DIRTY WORK WHEN THE TIME CAME.
SO WHEN THE TIME CAME, I GOT TO DOIN'.
SHUT YOUR MOUTH, SOLDIER.
YOU SHUT YOUR MOUTH OR I'LL SHUT IT FOR YOU.
LET'S GET IT OVER WITH.

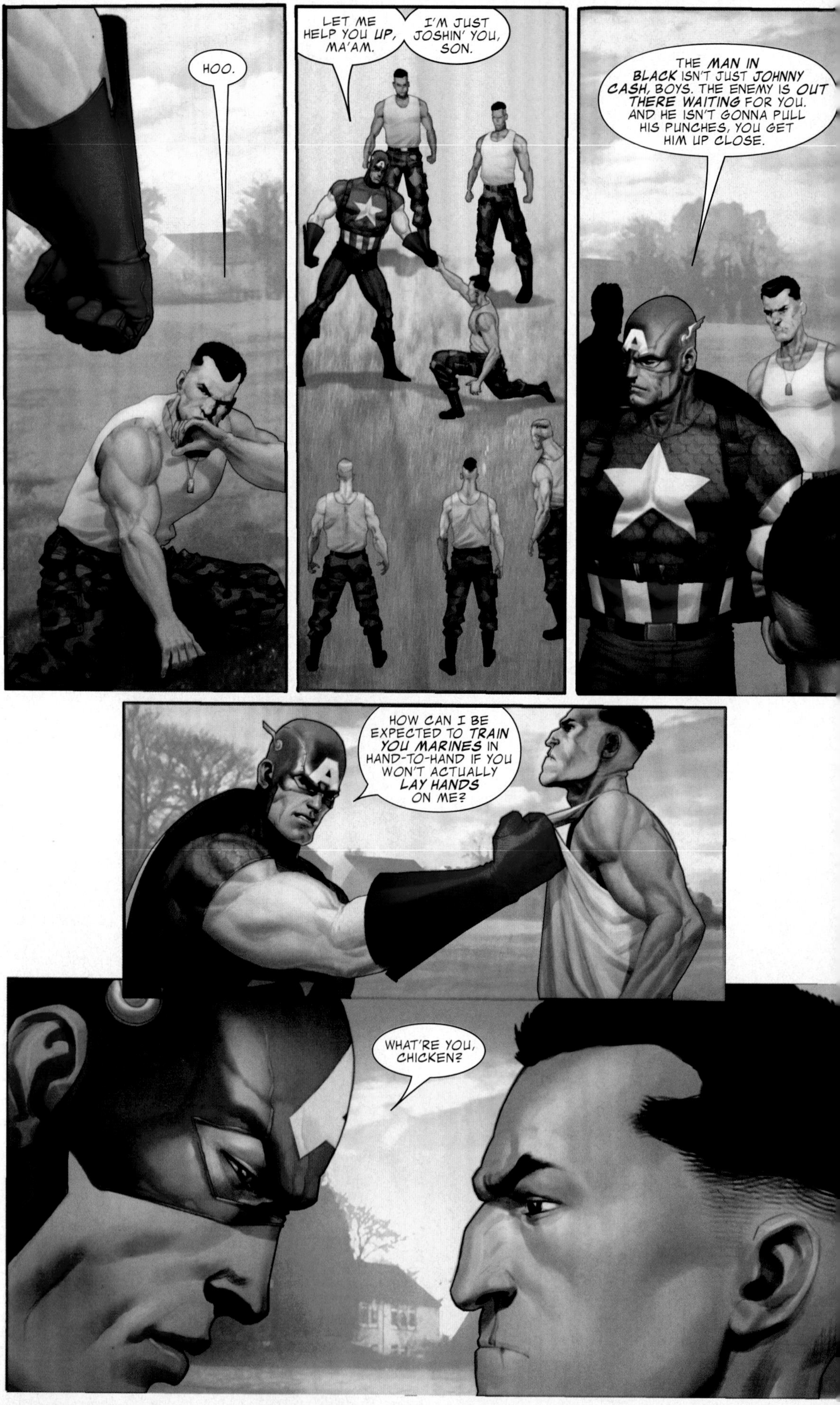
HOO.
LET ME HELP YOU UP, MA'AM.
I'M JUST JOSHIN' YOU, SON.
THE MAN IN BLACK ISN'T JUST JOHNNY CASH, BOYS. THE ENEMY IS OUT THERE WAITING FOR YOU. AND HE ISN'T GONNA PULL HIS PUNCHES, YOU GET HIM UP CLOSE.
HOW CAN I BE EXPECTED TO TRAIN YOU MARINES IN HAND-TO-HAND IF YOU WON'T ACTUALLY LAY HANDS ON ME?
WHAT'RE YOU, CHICKEN?

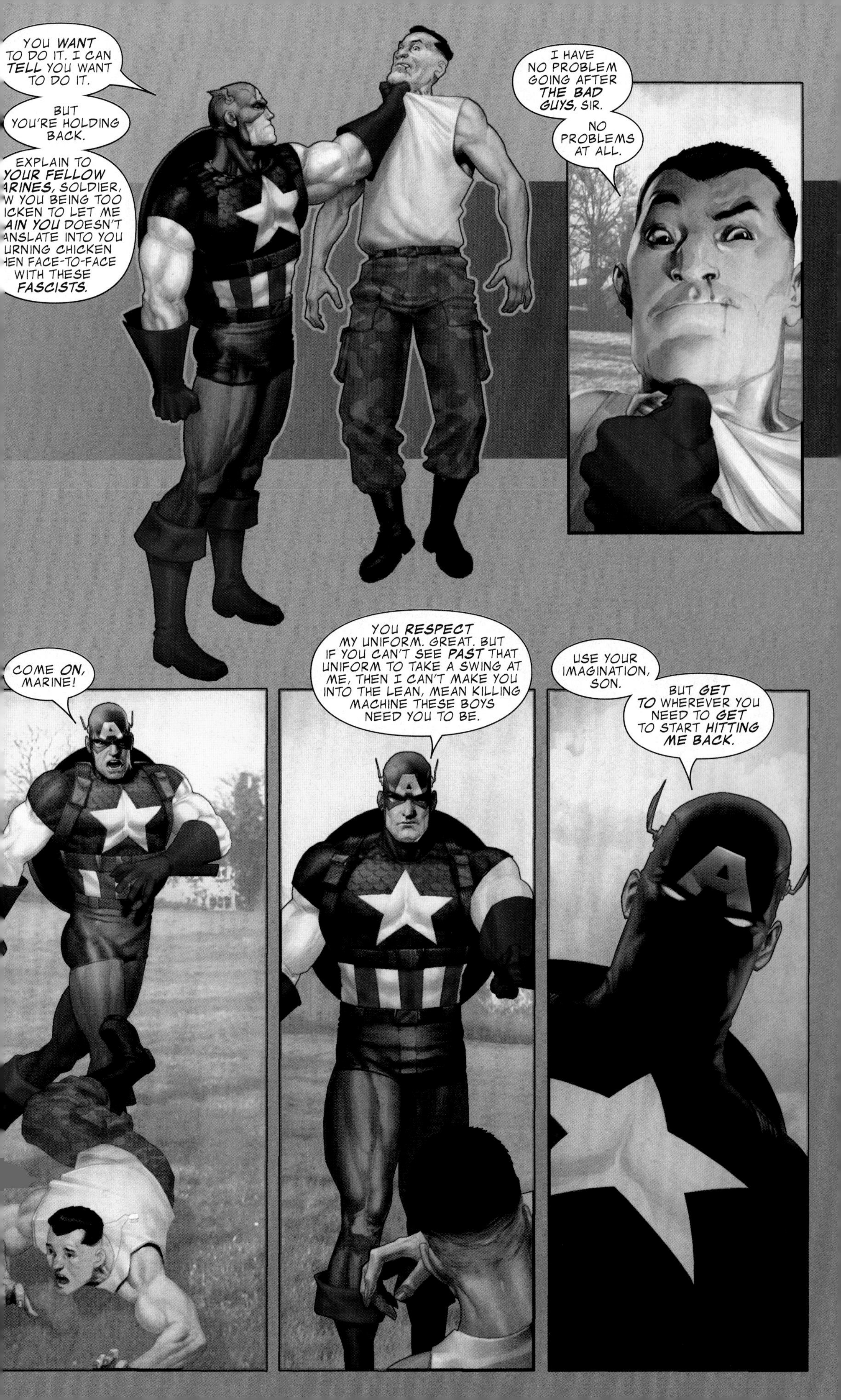
YOU WANT TO DO IT. I CAN TELL YOU WANT TO DO IT.
BUT YOU'RE HOLDING BACK.
EXPLAIN TO YOUR FELLOW ARINES, SOLDIER, W YOU BEING TOO ICKEN TO LET ME AIN YOU DOESN'T ANSLATE INTO YOU URNING CHICKEN HEN FACE-TO-FACE WITH THESE FASCISTS.
I HAVE NO PROBLEM GOING AFTER THE BAD GUYS, SIR.
NO PROBLEMS AT ALL.
COME ON, MARINE!
YOU RESPECT MY UNIFORM. GREAT. BUT IF YOU CAN'T SEE PAST THAT UNIFORM TO TAKE A SWING AT ME, THEN I CAN'T MAKE YOU INTO THE LEAN, MEAN KILLING MACHINE THESE BOYS NEED YOU TO BE.
USE YOUR IMAGINATION, SON.
BUT GET TO WHEREVER YOU NEED TO GET TO START HITTING ME BACK.

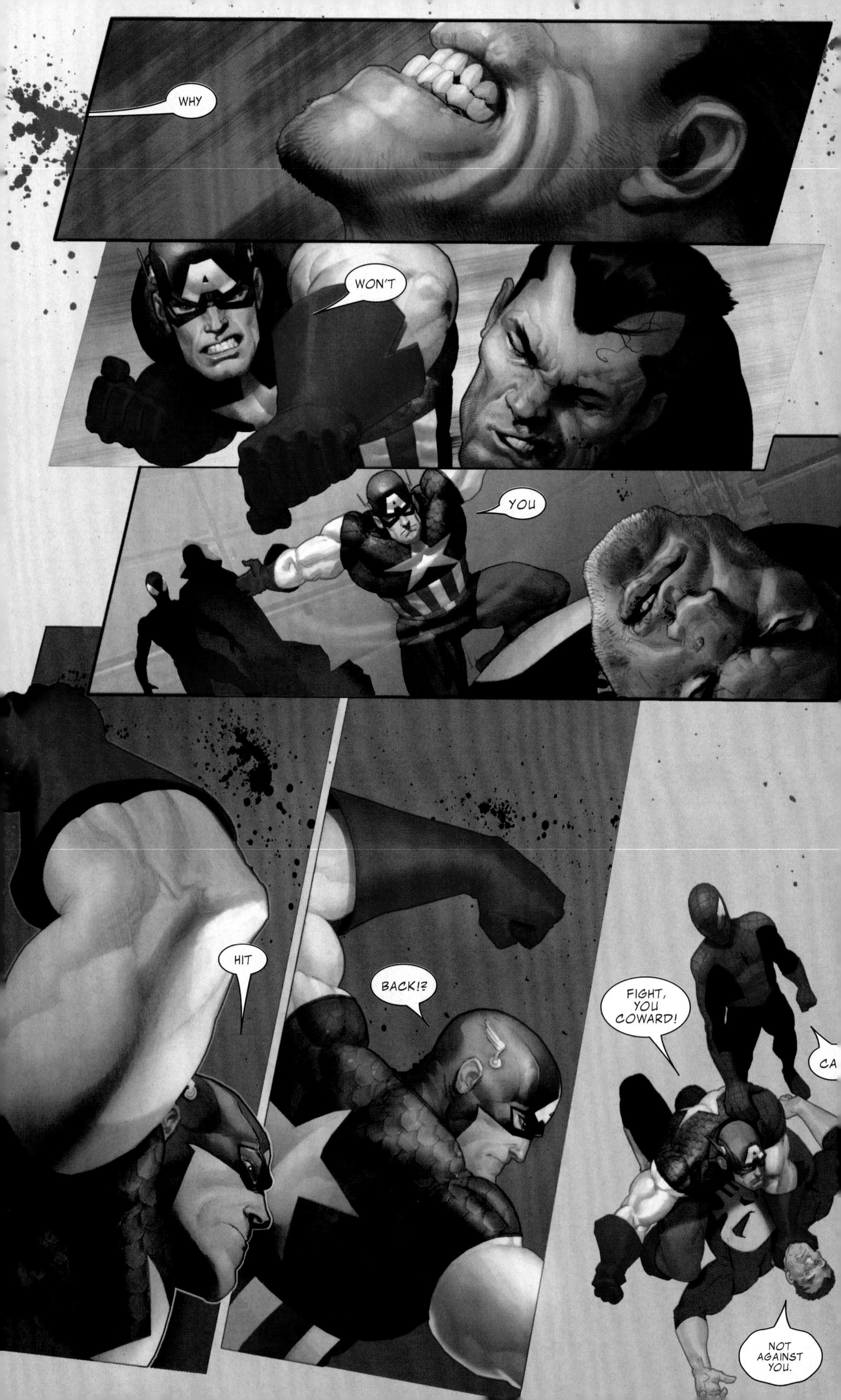
WHY
WON'T
YOU
HIT
BACK!?
FIGHT, YOU COWARD!
CA
NOT AGAINST YOU.

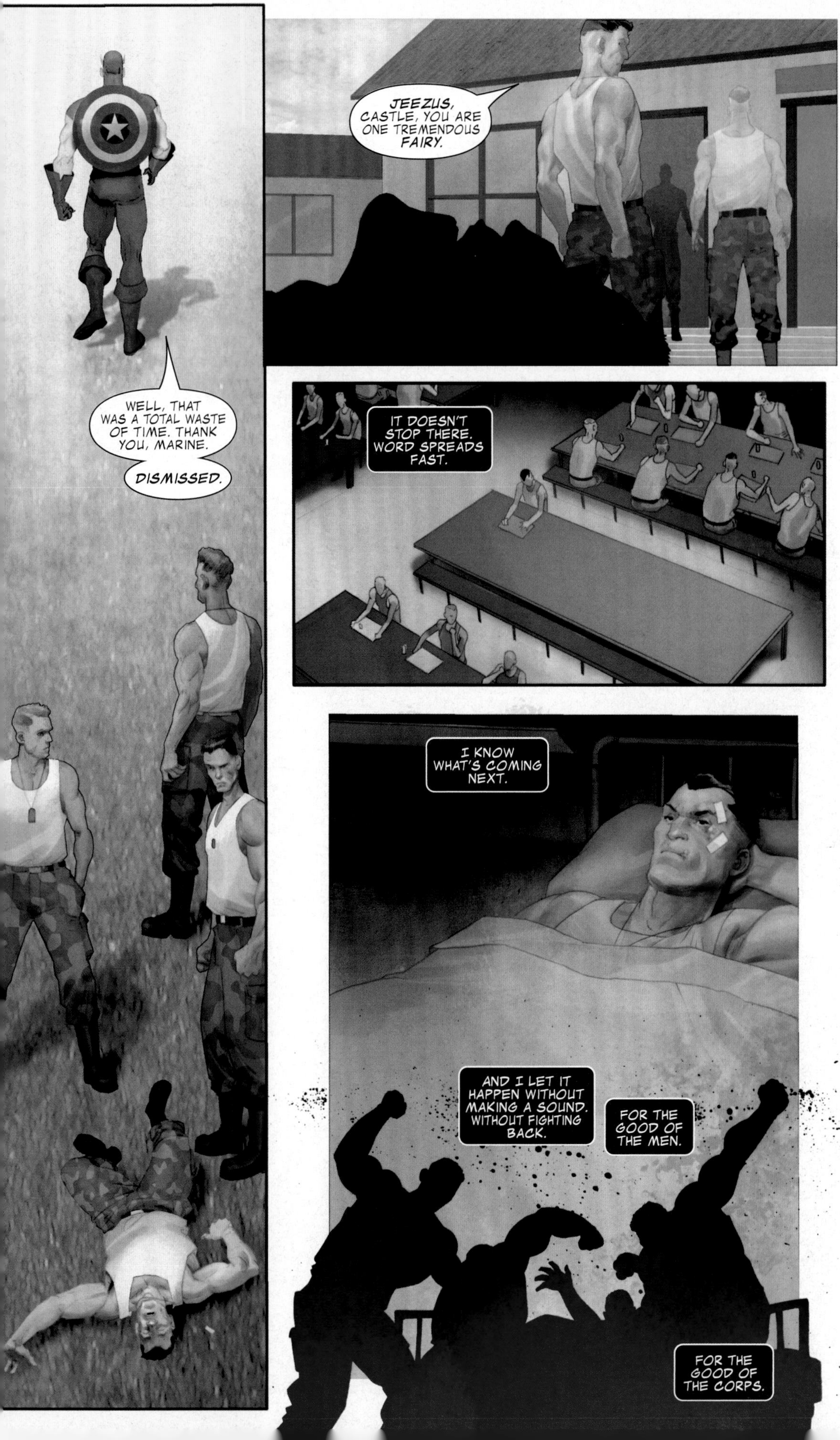
JEEZUS, CASTLE, YOU ARE ONE TREMENDOUS FAIRY.
WELL, THAT WAS A TOTAL WASTE OF TIME. THANK YOU, MARINE.
DISMISSED.
IT DOESN'T STOP THERE. WORD SPREADS FAST.
I KNOW WHAT'S COMING NEXT.
AND I LET IT HAPPEN WITHOUT MAKING A SOUND. WITHOUT FIGHTING BACK.
FOR THE GOOD OF THE MEN.
FOR THE GOOD OF THE CORPS.

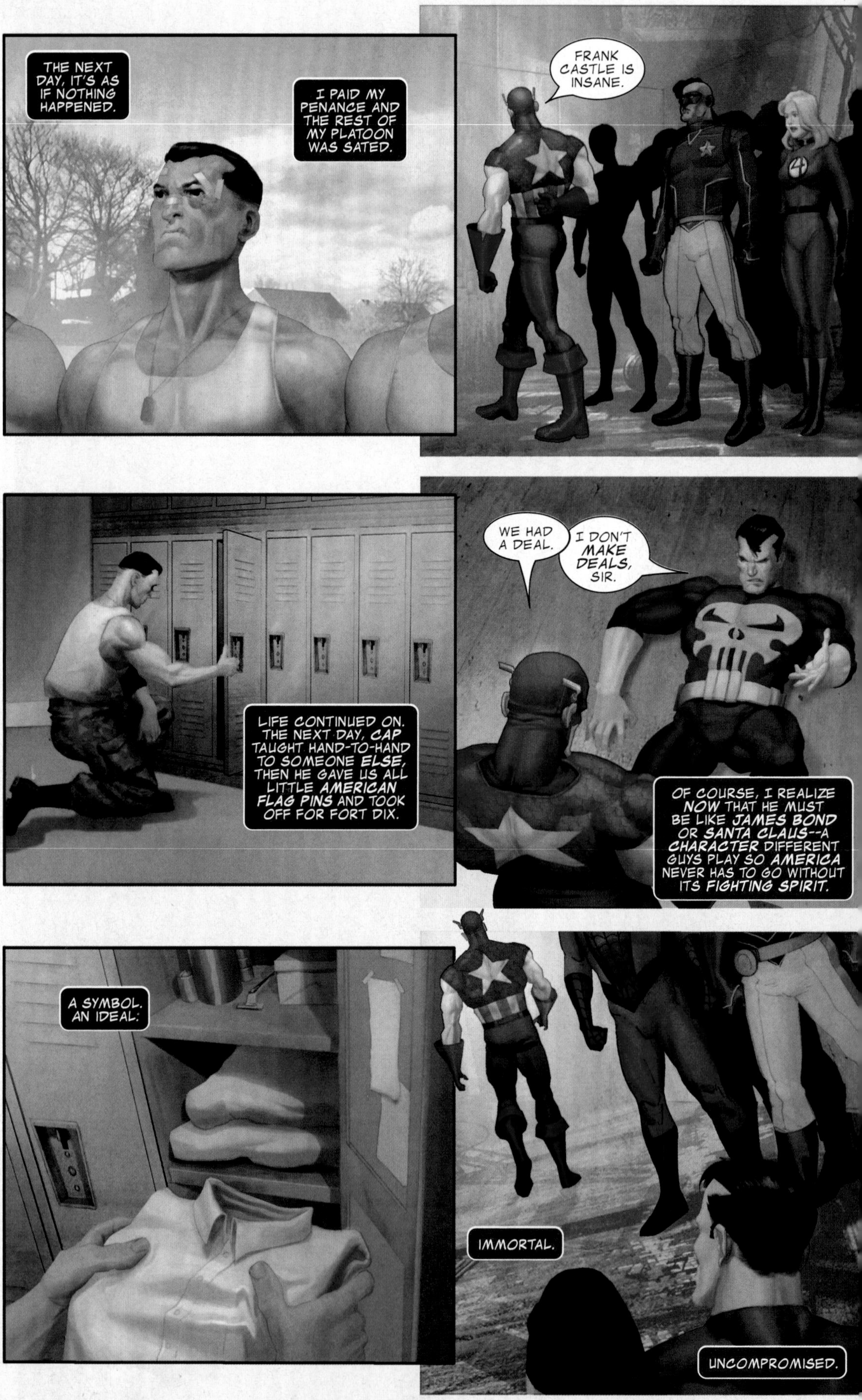

THE NEXT DAY, IT'S AS IF NOTHING HAPPENED.
I PAID MY PENANCE AND THE REST OF MY PLATOON WAS SATED.
FRANK CASTLE IS INSANE.
LIFE CONTINUED ON. THE NEXT DAY, CAP TAUGHT HAND-TO-HAND TO SOMEONE ELSE, THEN HE GAVE US ALL LITTLE AMERICAN FLAG PINS AND TOOK OFF FOR FORT DIX.
WE HAD A DEAL.
I DON'T MAKE DEALS, SIR.
OF COURSE, I REALIZE NOW THAT HE MUST BE LIKE JAMES BOND OR SANTA CLAUS--A CHARACTER DIFFERENT GUYS PLAY SO AMERICA NEVER HAS TO GO WITHOUT ITS FIGHTING SPIRIT.
A SYMBOL. AN IDEAL.
IMMORTAL.
UNCOMPROMISED.

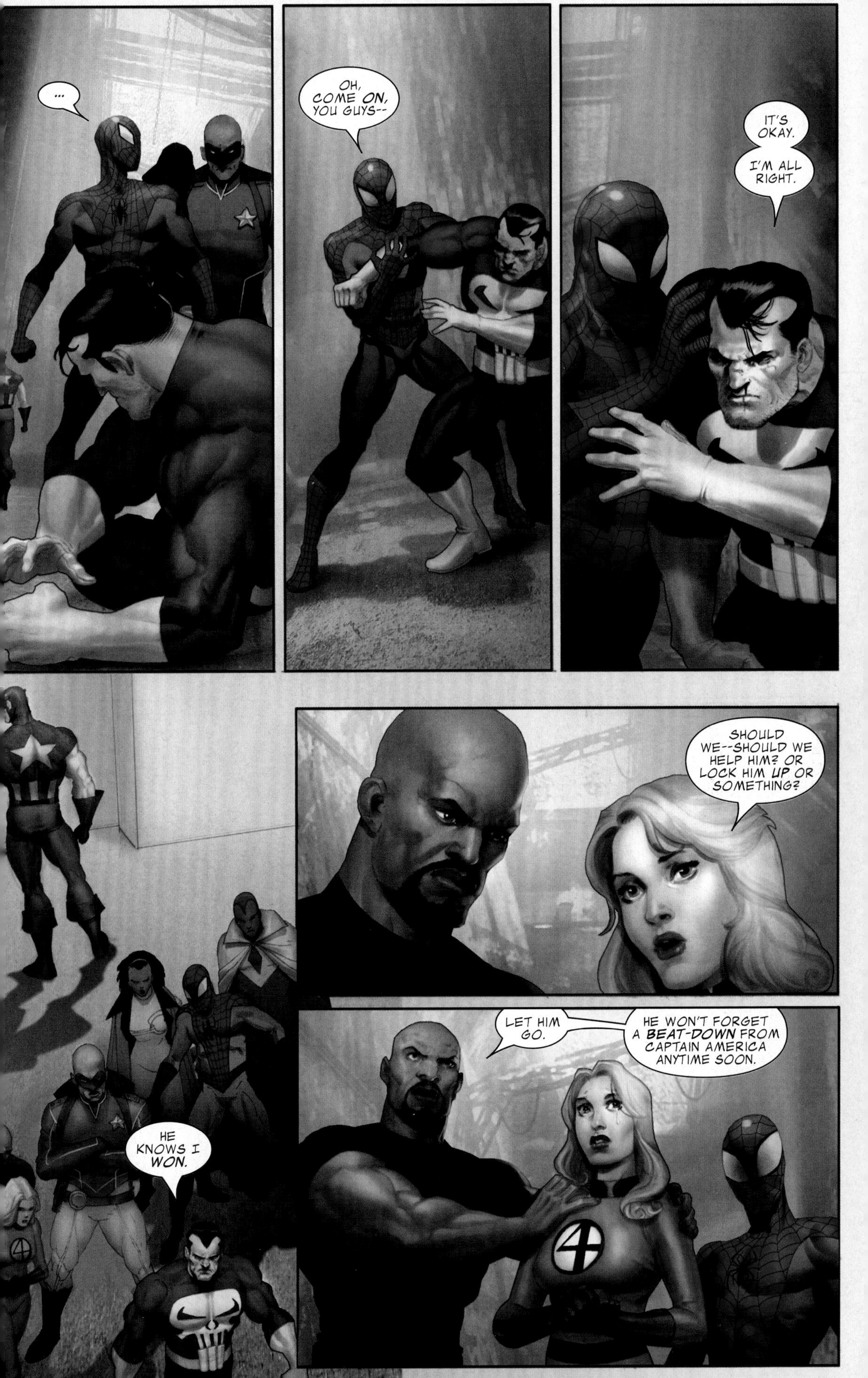
...
OH, COME ON, YOU GUYS--
IT'S OKAY.
I'M ALL RIGHT.
SHOULD WE--SHOULD WE HELP HIM? OR LOCK HIM UP OR SOMETHING?
HE KNOWS I WON.
LET HIM GO.
HE WON'T FORGET A BEAT-DOWN FROM CAPTAIN AMERICA ANYTIME SOON.

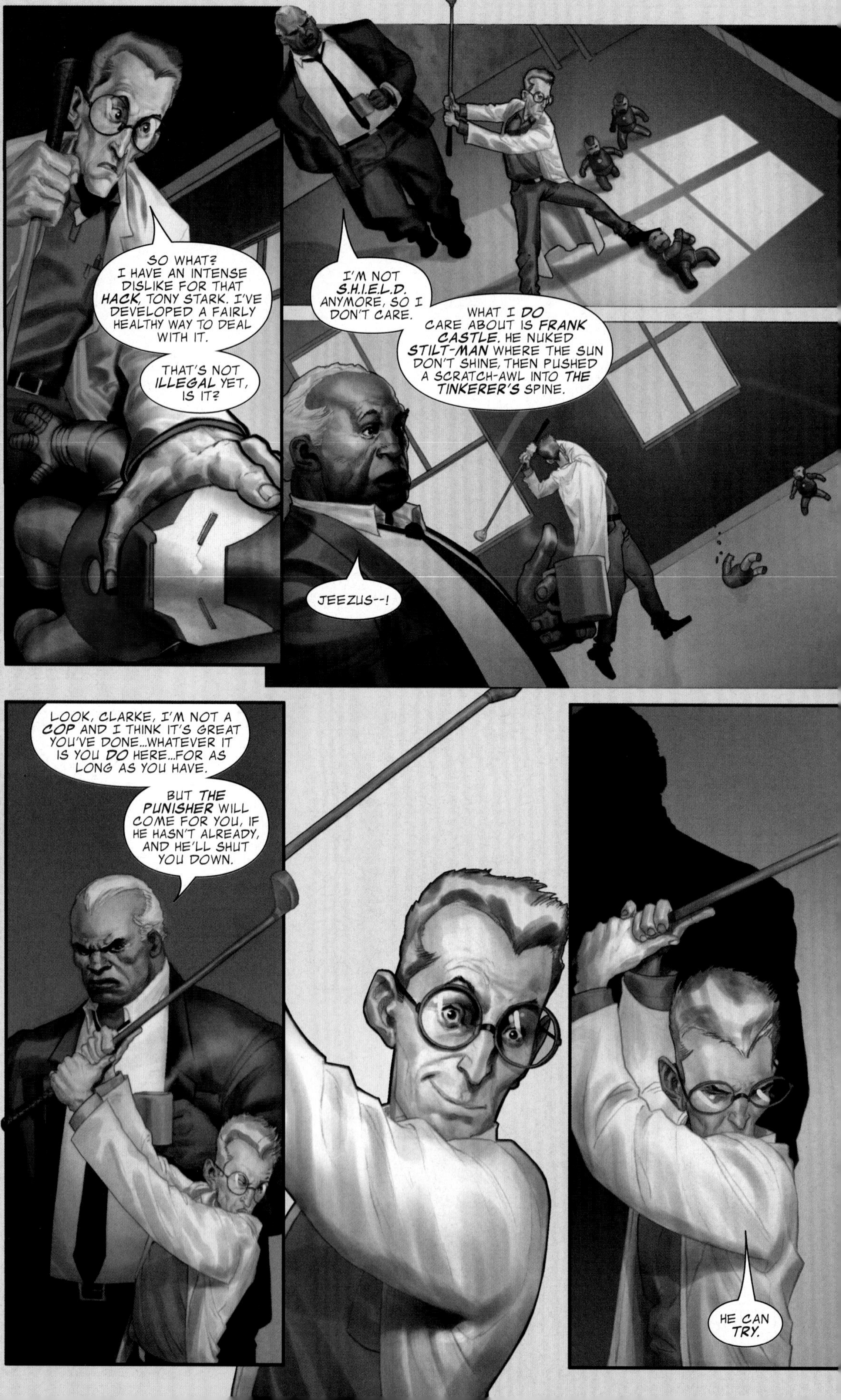
SO WHAT? I HAVE AN INTENSE DISLIKE FOR THAT HACK, TONY STARK. I'VE DEVELOPED A FAIRLY HEALTHY WAY TO DEAL WITH IT.
THAT'S NOT ILLEGAL YET, IS IT?
I'M NOT S.H.I.E.L.D. ANYMORE, SO I DON'T CARE.
WHAT I DO CARE ABOUT IS FRANK CASTLE. HE NUKED STILT-MAN WHERE THE SUN DON'T SHINE, THEN PUSHED A SCRATCH-AWL INTO THE TINKERER'S SPINE.
JEEZUS--!
LOOK, CLARKE, I'M NOT A COP AND I THINK IT'S GREAT YOU'VE DONE...WHATEVER IT IS YOU DO HERE...FOR AS LONG AS YOU HAVE.
BUT THE PUNISHER WILL COME FOR YOU, IF HE HASN'T ALREADY, AND HE'LL SHUT YOU DOWN.
HE CAN TRY.

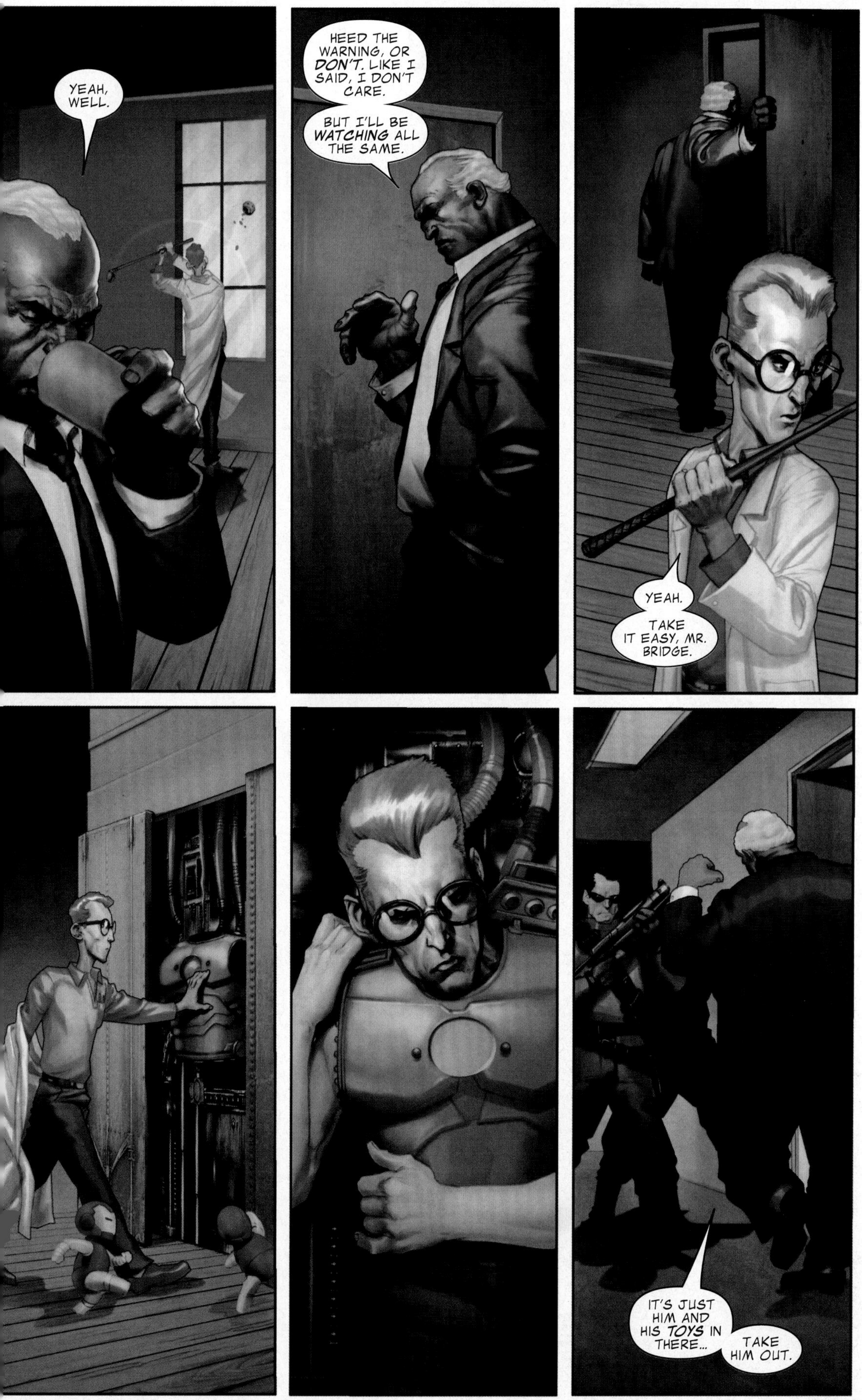
YEAH, WELL.
HEED THE WARNING, OR *DON'T*. LIKE I SAID, I DON'T CARE.
BUT I'LL BE *WATCHING* ALL THE SAME.
YEAH.
TAKE IT EASY, MR. BRIDGE.
IT'S JUST HIM AND HIS *TOYS* IN THERE...
TAKE HIM OUT.

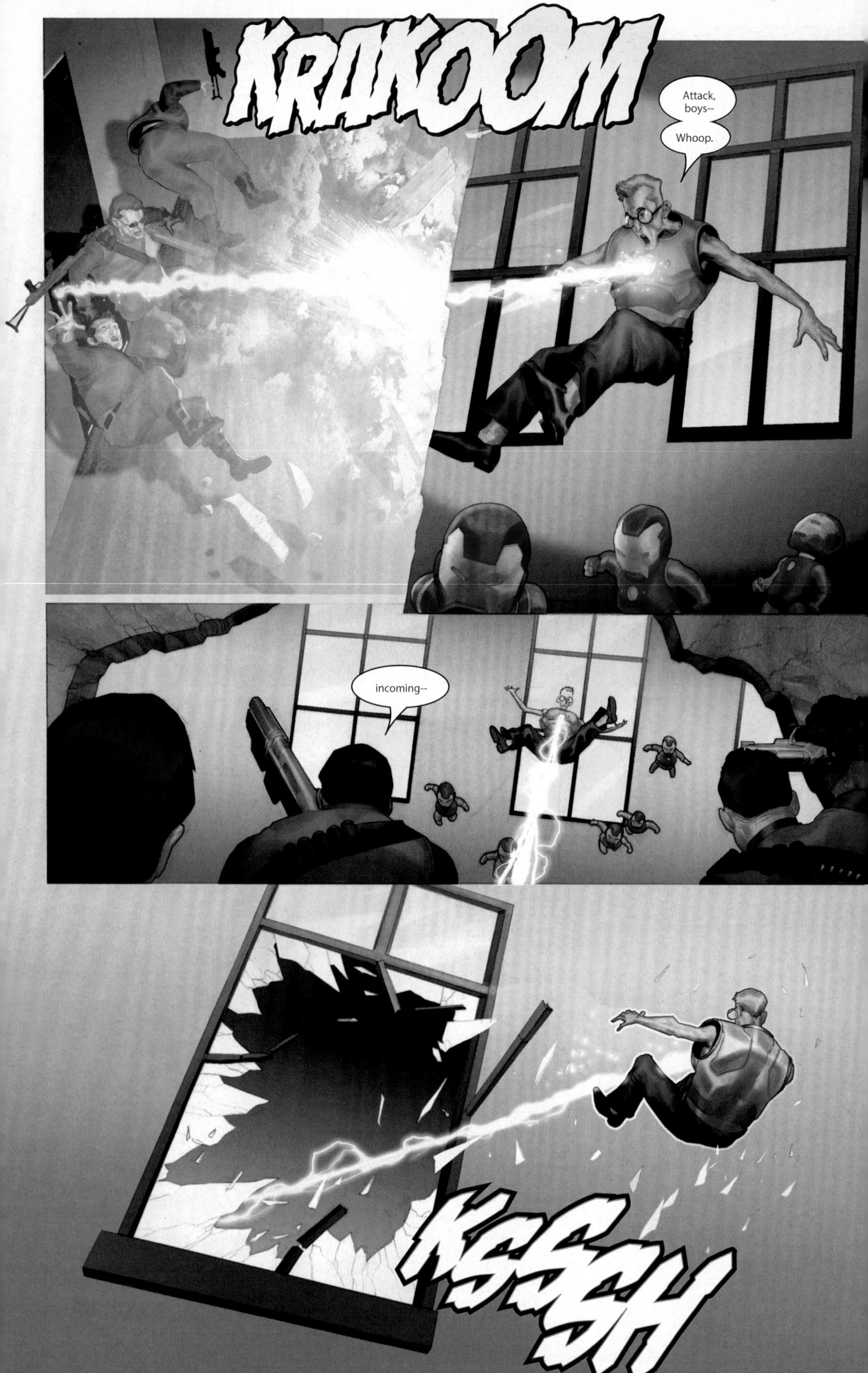
KRAKOOM
Attack, boys--
Whoop.
incoming--
KSSCH

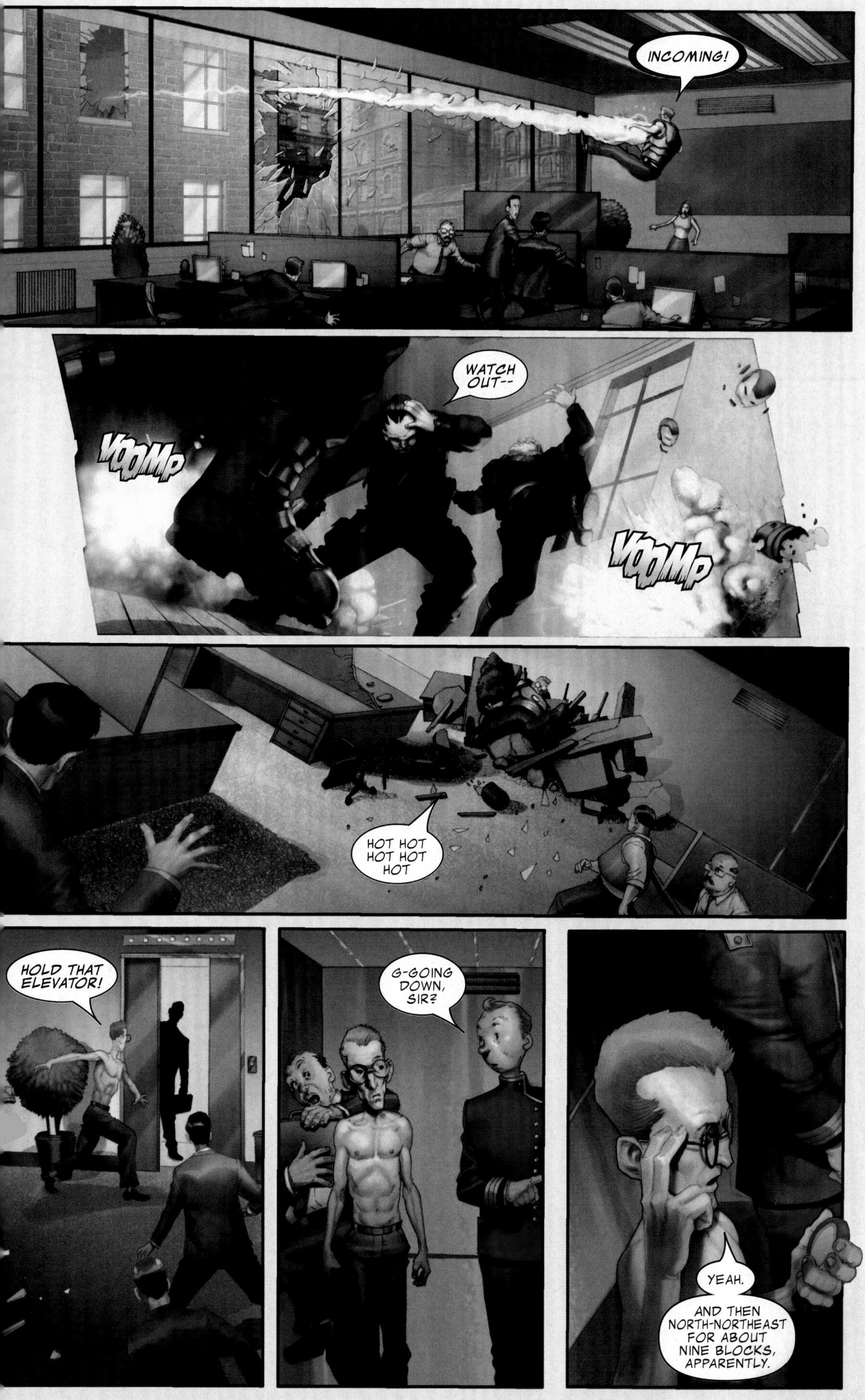
INCOMING!
WATCH OUT--
VOOMP
VOOMP
HOT HOT HOT HOT HOT
HOLD THAT ELEVATOR!
G-GOING DOWN, SIR?
YEAH.
AND THEN NORTH-NORTHEAST FOR ABOUT NINE BLOCKS, APPARENTLY.

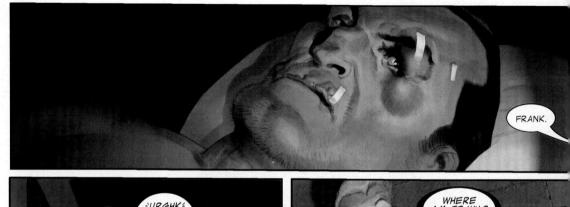

FRANK.

;URGHK; FRANK! SETTLE DOWN!

WHERE AM I? WHO ARE YOU?

WE'RE IN SOME KIND OF S.H.I.E.L.D. ARMORY. MY NAME IS STUART CLARKE. YOU WERE BADLY BEATEN AND HAVE BEEN UNCONSCIOUS FOR FOUR DAYS.

AND BEFORE YOU CRUSH MY WINDPIPE, YOU SHOULD KNOW THAT I FOUND YOU AND HAVE BEEN TAKING CARE OF YOU.

IN FACT, SINCE THAT BRIDGE NARC THAT'S AFTER YOU SHUT ME DOWN, I'VE BEEN HERE STRIP-MINING EVERY BIT OF DATA, EQUIPMENT, AND TECH I COULD--

DID YOU SAY ARMORY?

YOU'RE DAMN RIGHT I DID.

NOW, YOU WANNA HUG ALL NIGHT OR ARE YOU READY TO GET TO WORK?

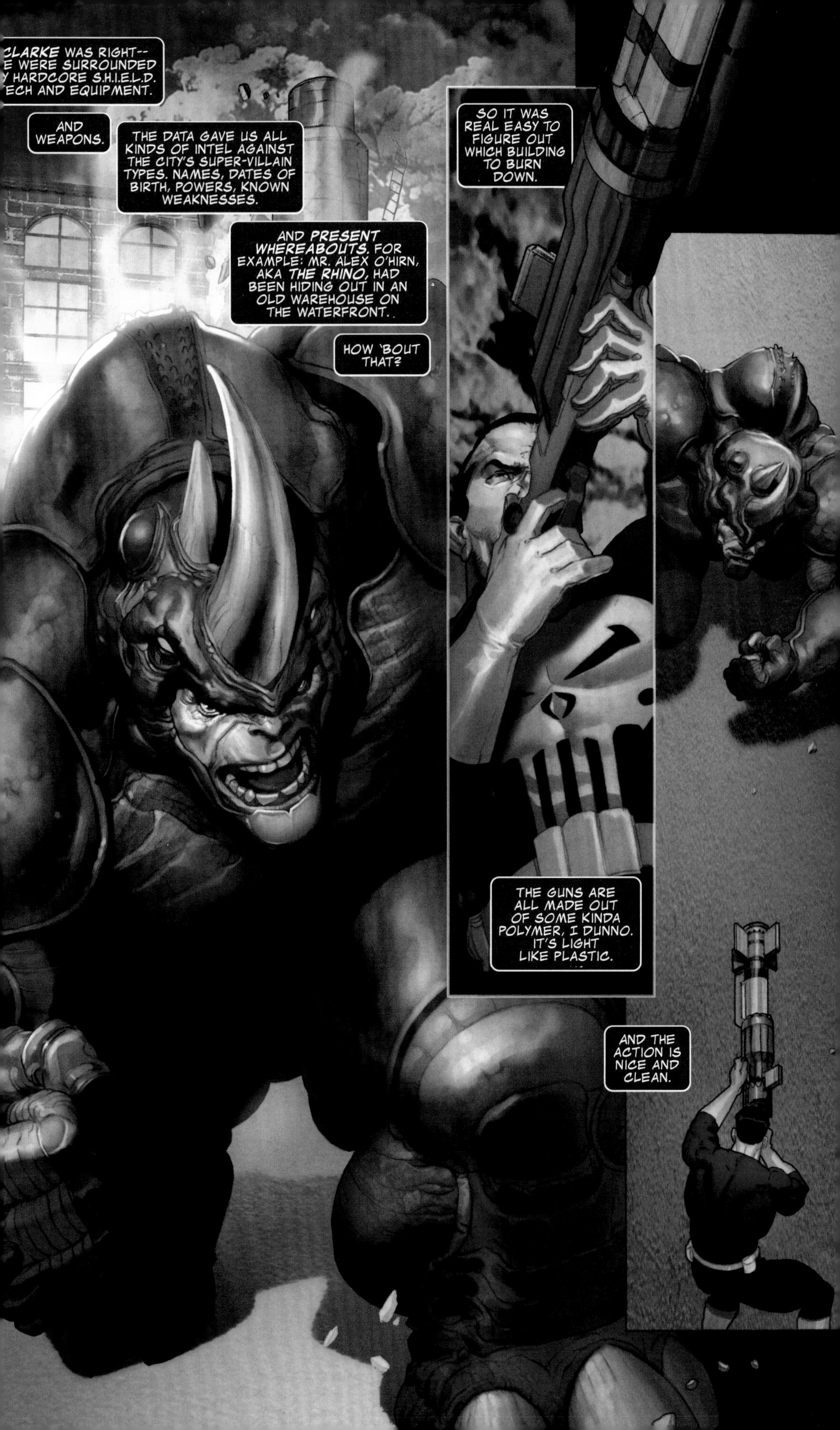
CLARKE WAS RIGHT--
E WERE SURROUNDED
Y HARDCORE S.H.I.E.L.D.
ECH AND EQUIPMENT.
AND WEAPONS.
THE DATA GAVE US ALL KINDS OF INTEL AGAINST THE CITY'S SUPER-VILLAIN TYPES. NAMES, DATES OF BIRTH, POWERS, KNOWN WEAKNESSES.
AND PRESENT WHEREABOUTS. FOR EXAMPLE: MR. ALEX O'HIRN, AKA THE RHINO, HAD BEEN HIDING OUT IN AN OLD WAREHOUSE ON THE WATERFRONT..
HOW 'BOUT THAT?
SO IT WAS REAL EASY TO FIGURE OUT WHICH BUILDING TO BURN DOWN.
THE GUNS ARE ALL MADE OUT OF SOME KINDA POLYMER, I DUNNO. IT'S LIGHT LIKE PLASTIC.
AND THE ACTION IS NICE AND CLEAN.

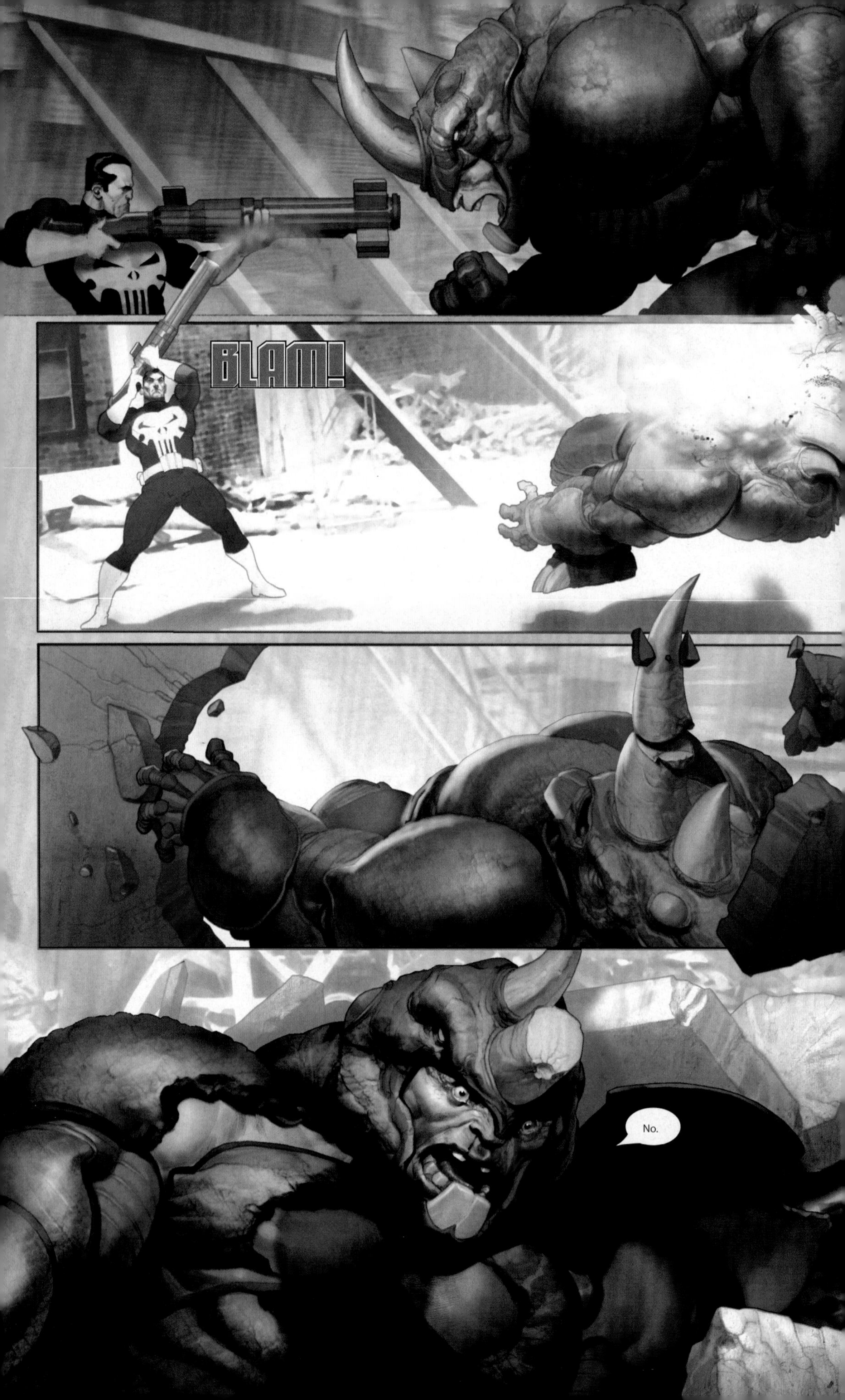
BLAM!
No.

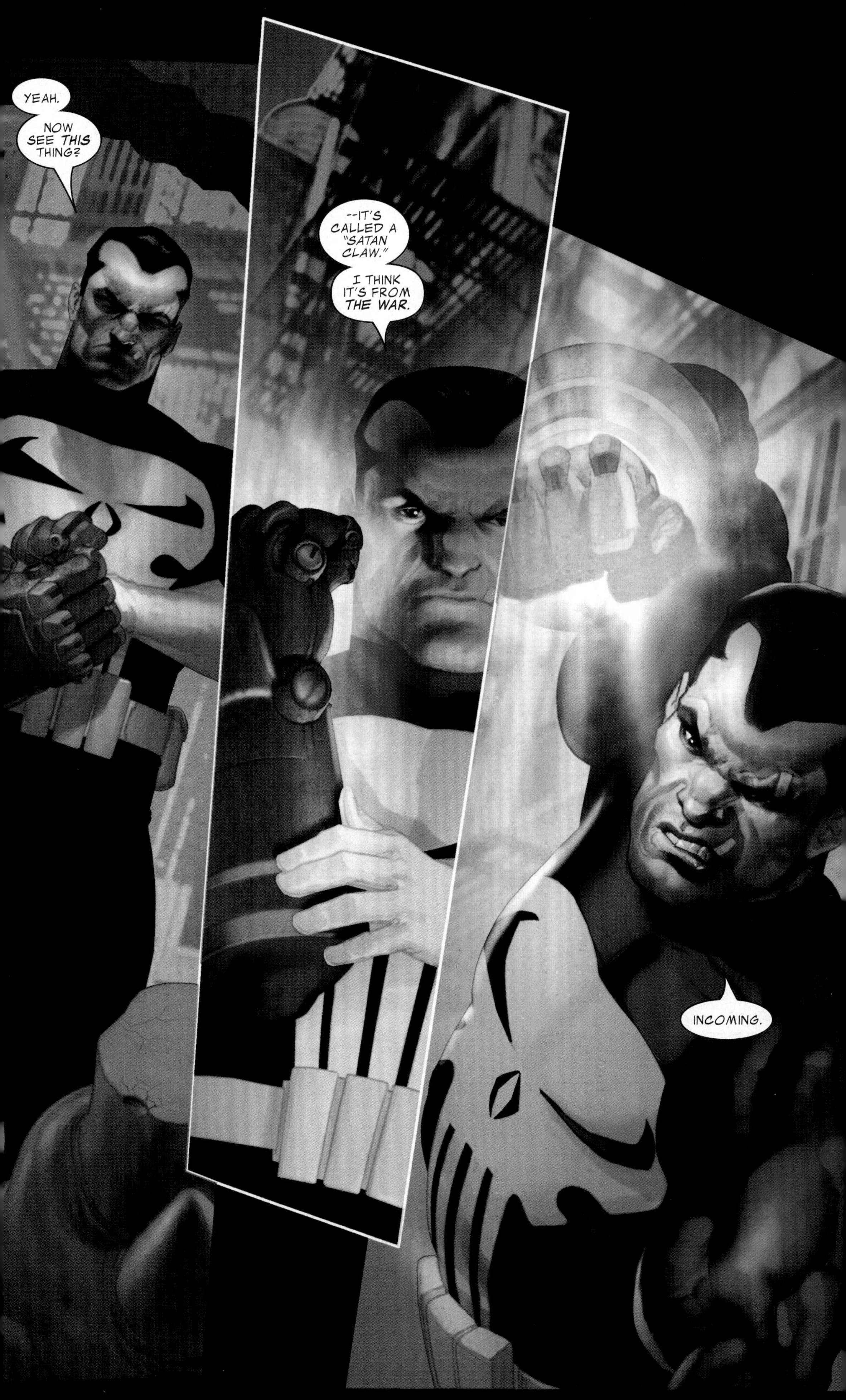
YEAH.
NOW SEE THIS THING?
--IT'S CALLED A "SATAN CLAW."
I THINK IT'S FROM THE WAR.
INCOMING.

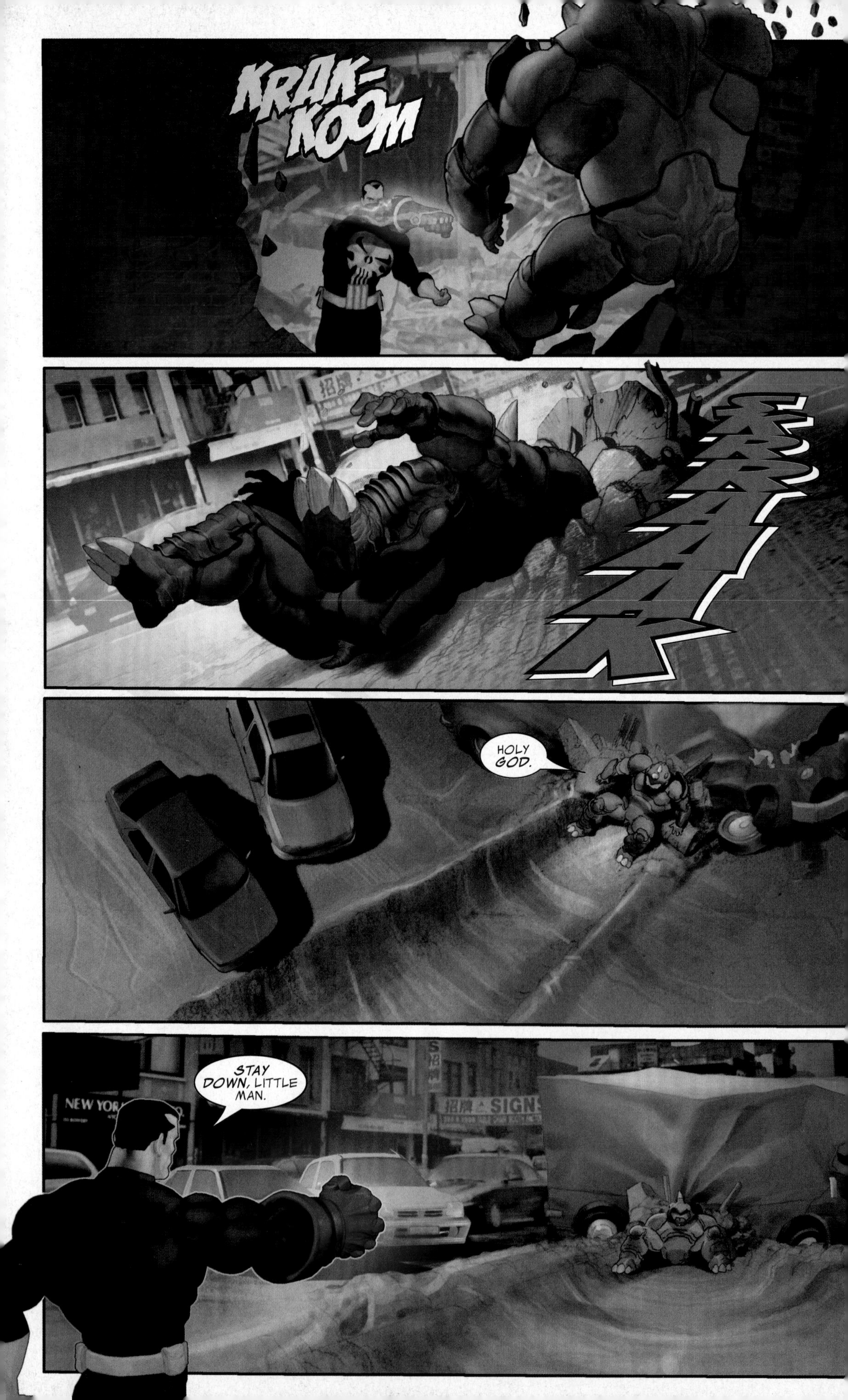
KRAK-
KOOM
KRAAAAK
HOLY GOD.
STAY DOWN, LITTLE MAN.
NEW YORK
SIGNS

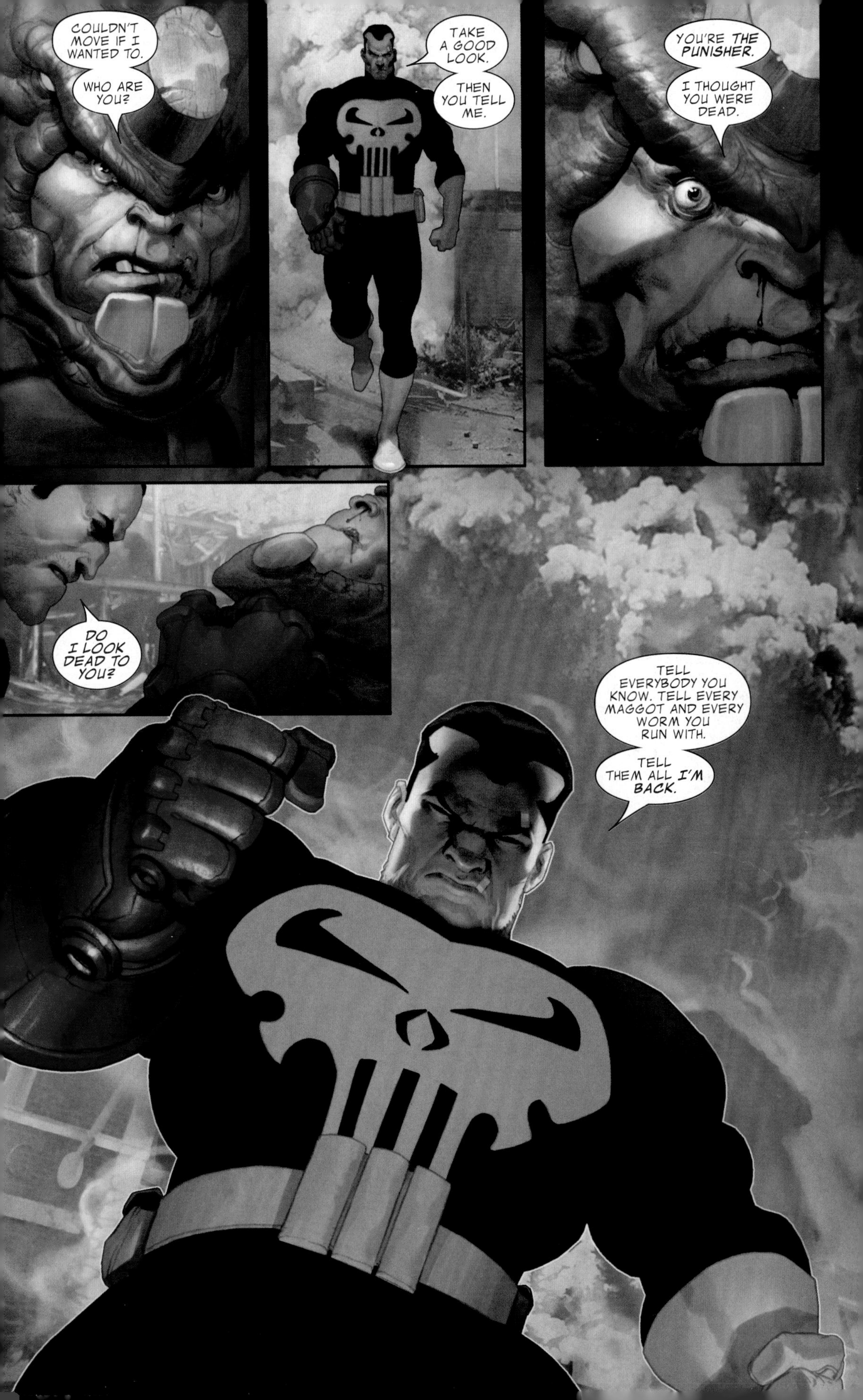
COULDN'T MOVE IF I WANTED TO.
WHO ARE YOU?
TAKE A GOOD LOOK.
THEN YOU TELL ME.
YOU'RE THE PUNISHER.
I THOUGHT YOU WERE DEAD.
DO I LOOK DEAD TO YOU?
TELL EVERYBODY YOU KNOW. TELL EVERY MAGGOT AND EVERY WORM YOU RUN WITH.
TELL THEM ALL I'M BACK.

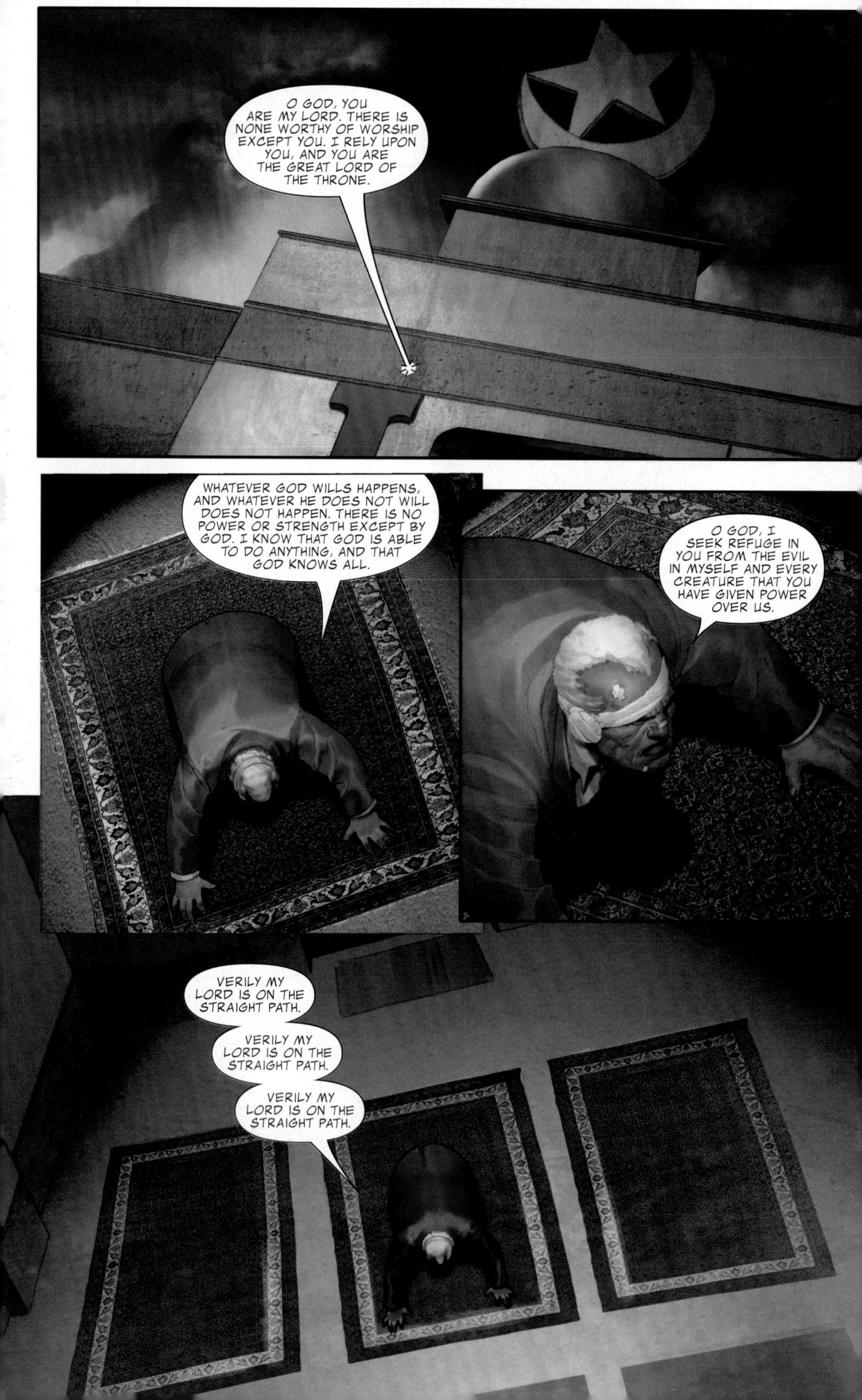
O GOD, YOU ARE MY LORD. THERE IS NONE WORTHY OF WORSHIP EXCEPT YOU. I RELY UPON YOU, AND YOU ARE THE GREAT LORD OF THE THRONE.
WHATEVER GOD WILLS HAPPENS, AND WHATEVER HE DOES NOT WILL DOES NOT HAPPEN. THERE IS NO POWER OR STRENGTH EXCEPT BY GOD. I KNOW THAT GOD IS ABLE TO DO ANYTHING, AND THAT GOD KNOWS ALL.
O GOD, I SEEK REFUGE IN YOU FROM THE EVIL IN MYSELF AND EVERY CREATURE THAT YOU HAVE GIVEN POWER OVER US.
VERILY MY LORD IS ON THE STRAIGHT PATH.
VERILY MY LORD IS ON THE STRAIGHT PATH.
VERILY MY LORD IS ON THE STRAIGHT PATH.

ISSUE #1 & #3 COVER SKETCHES BY ARIEL OLIVETTI

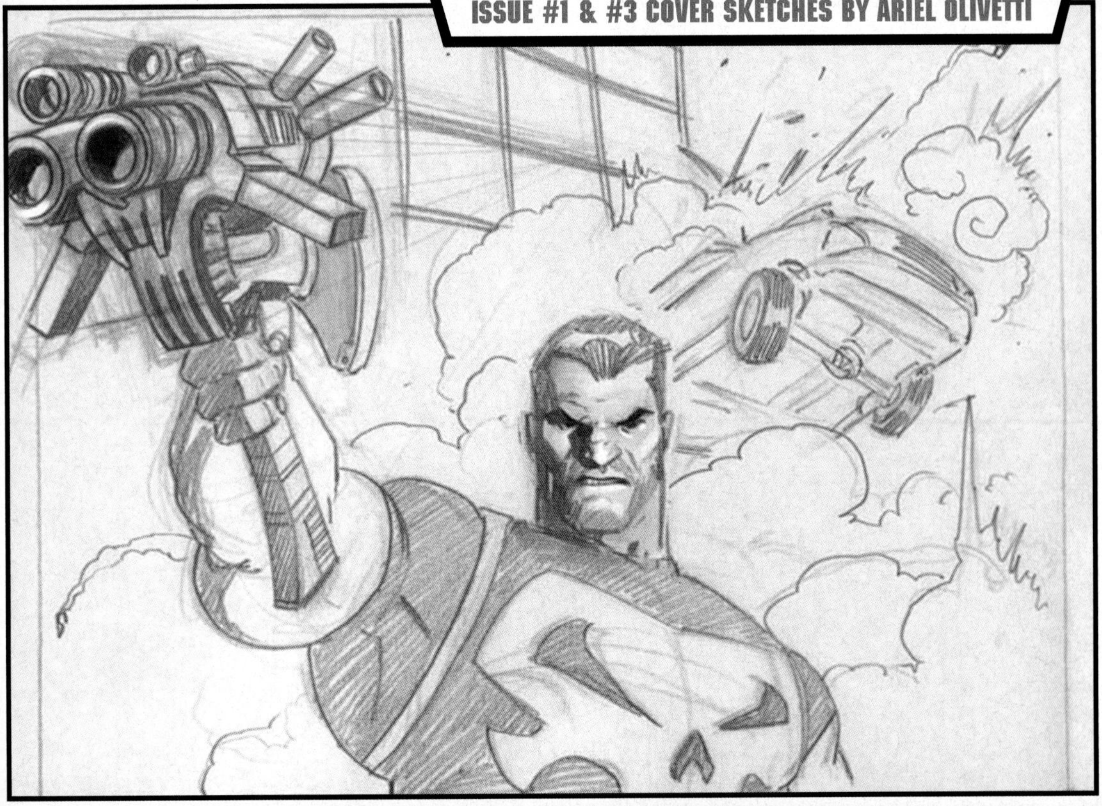

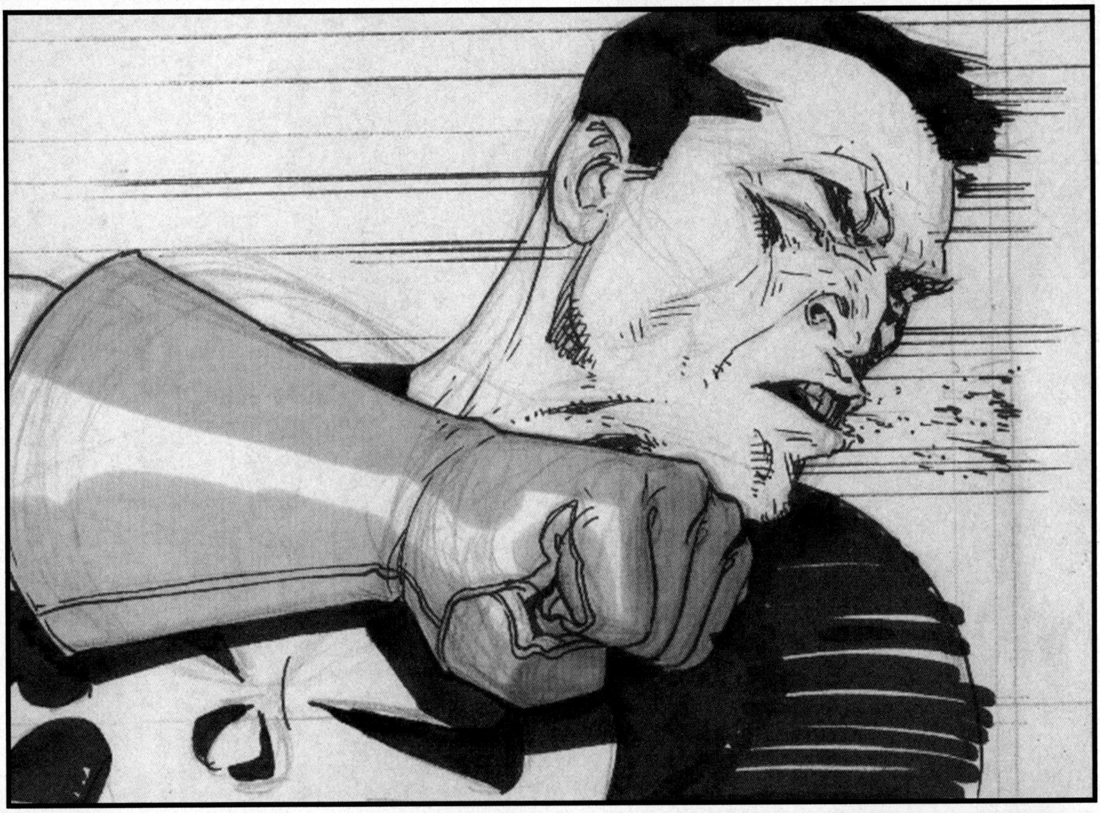

4

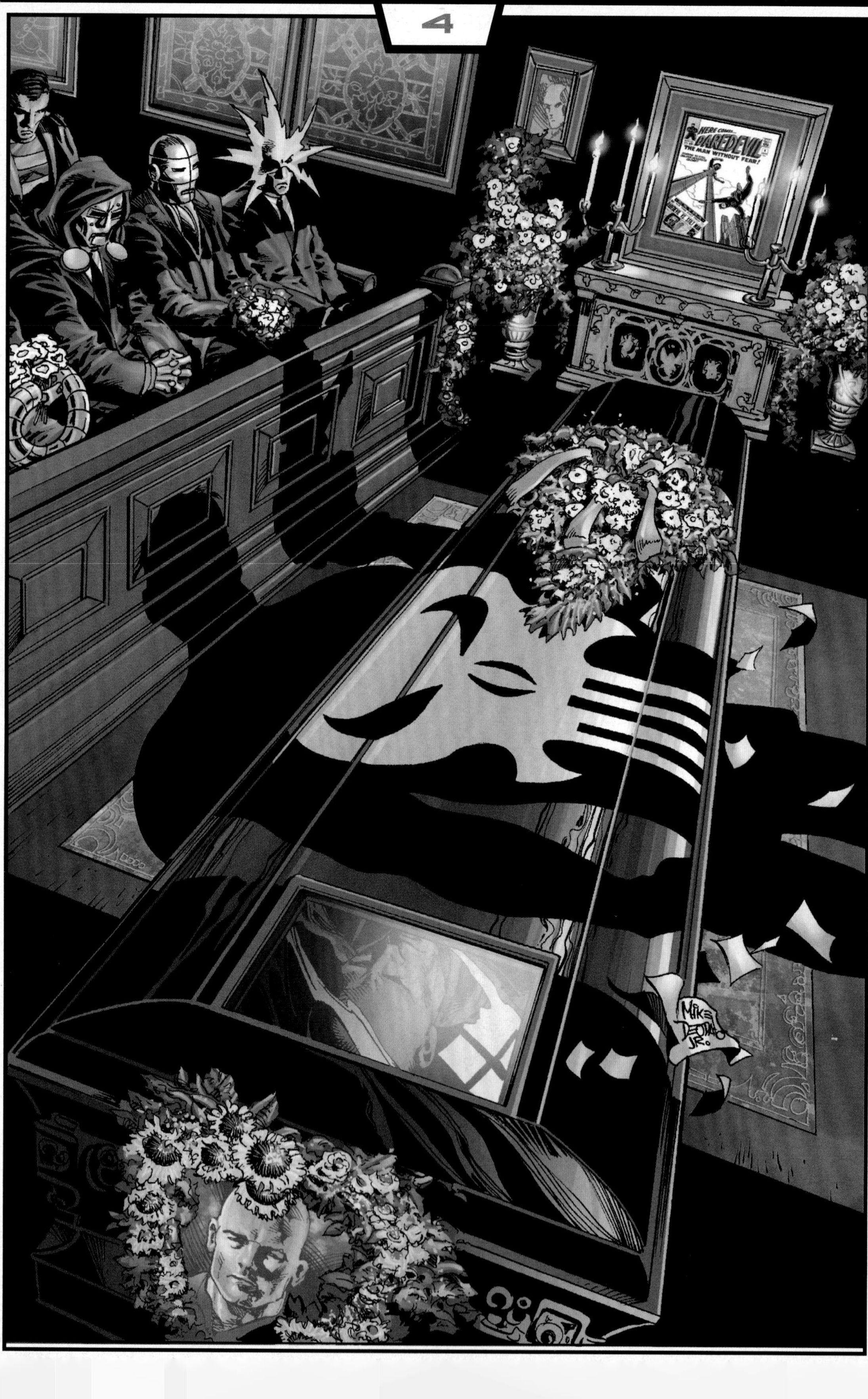
HERE COMES...
DAREDEVIL
THE MAN WITHOUT FEAR!
MIKE DEODATO JR.

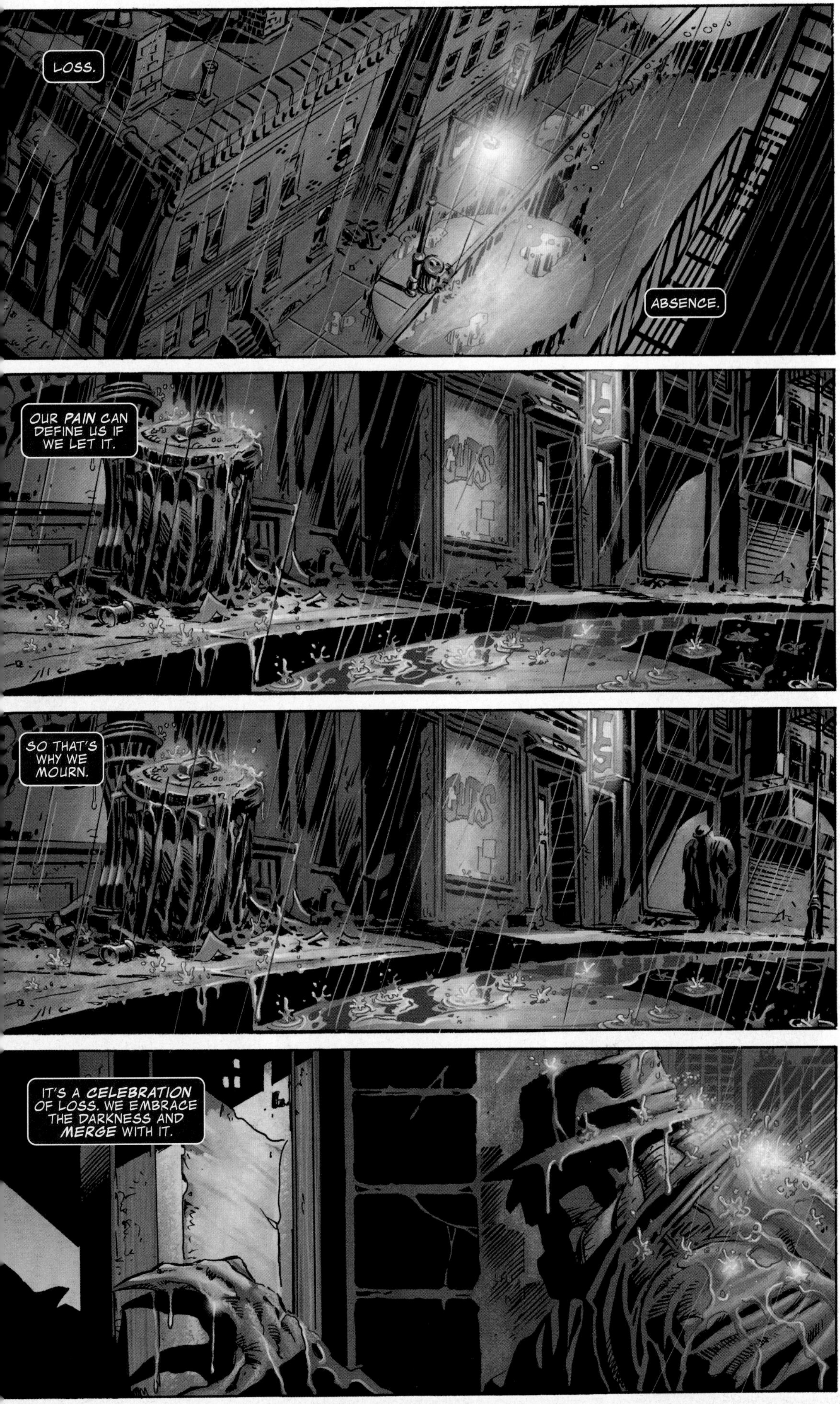
LOSS.
ABSENCE.
OUR PAIN CAN DEFINE US IF WE LET IT.
SO THAT'S WHY WE MOURN.
IT'S A CELEBRATION OF LOSS. WE EMBRACE THE DARKNESS AND MERGE WITH IT.

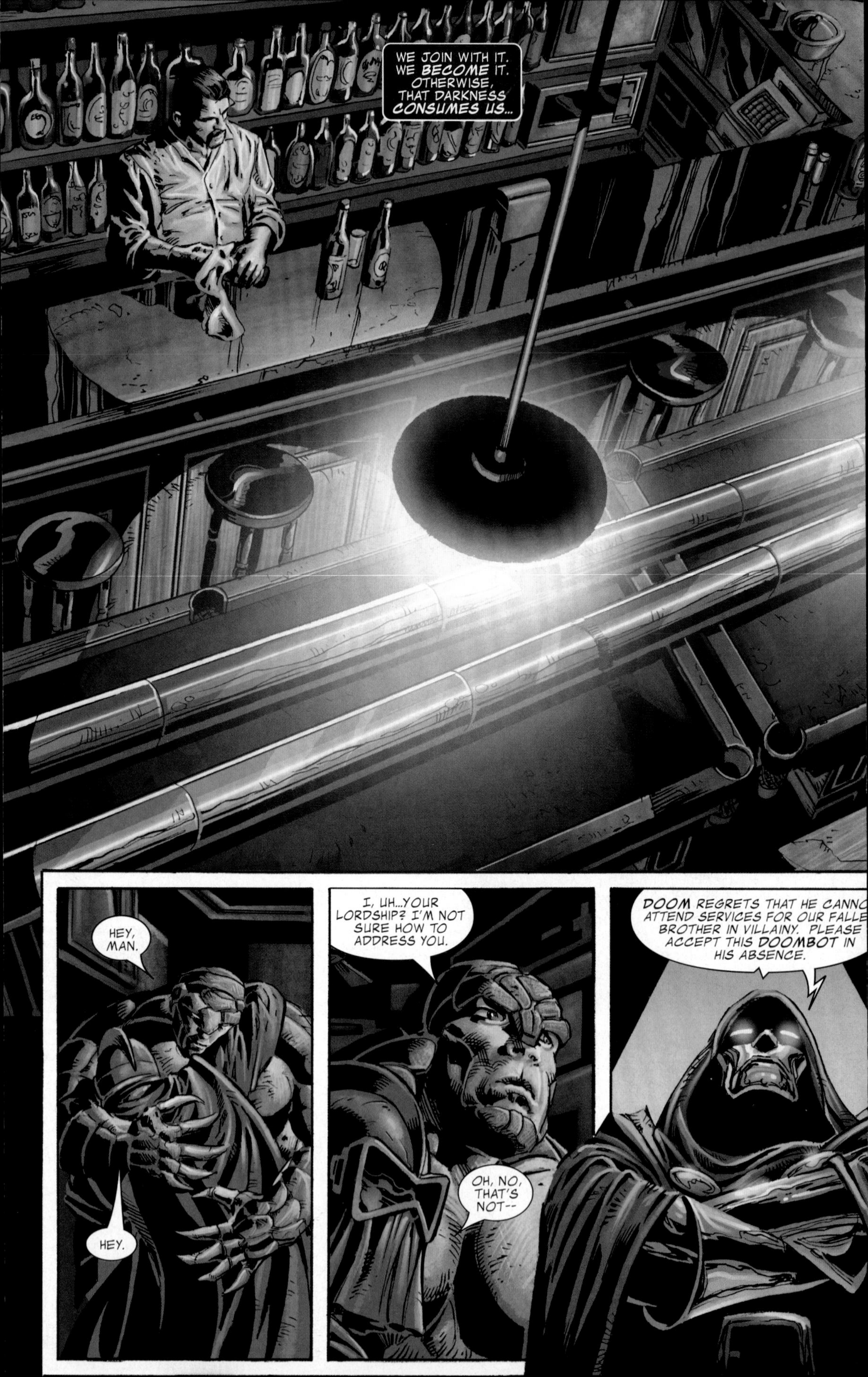
WE JOIN WITH IT. WE BECOME IT. OTHERWISE, THAT DARKNESS CONSUMES US...
HEY, MAN.
HEY.
I, UH...YOUR LORDSHIP? I'M NOT SURE HOW TO ADDRESS YOU.
OH, NO, THAT'S NOT--
DOOM REGRETS THAT HE CANNO ATTEND SERVICES FOR OUR FALLE BROTHER IN VILLAINY. PLEASE ACCEPT THIS DOOMBOT IN HIS ABSENCE.

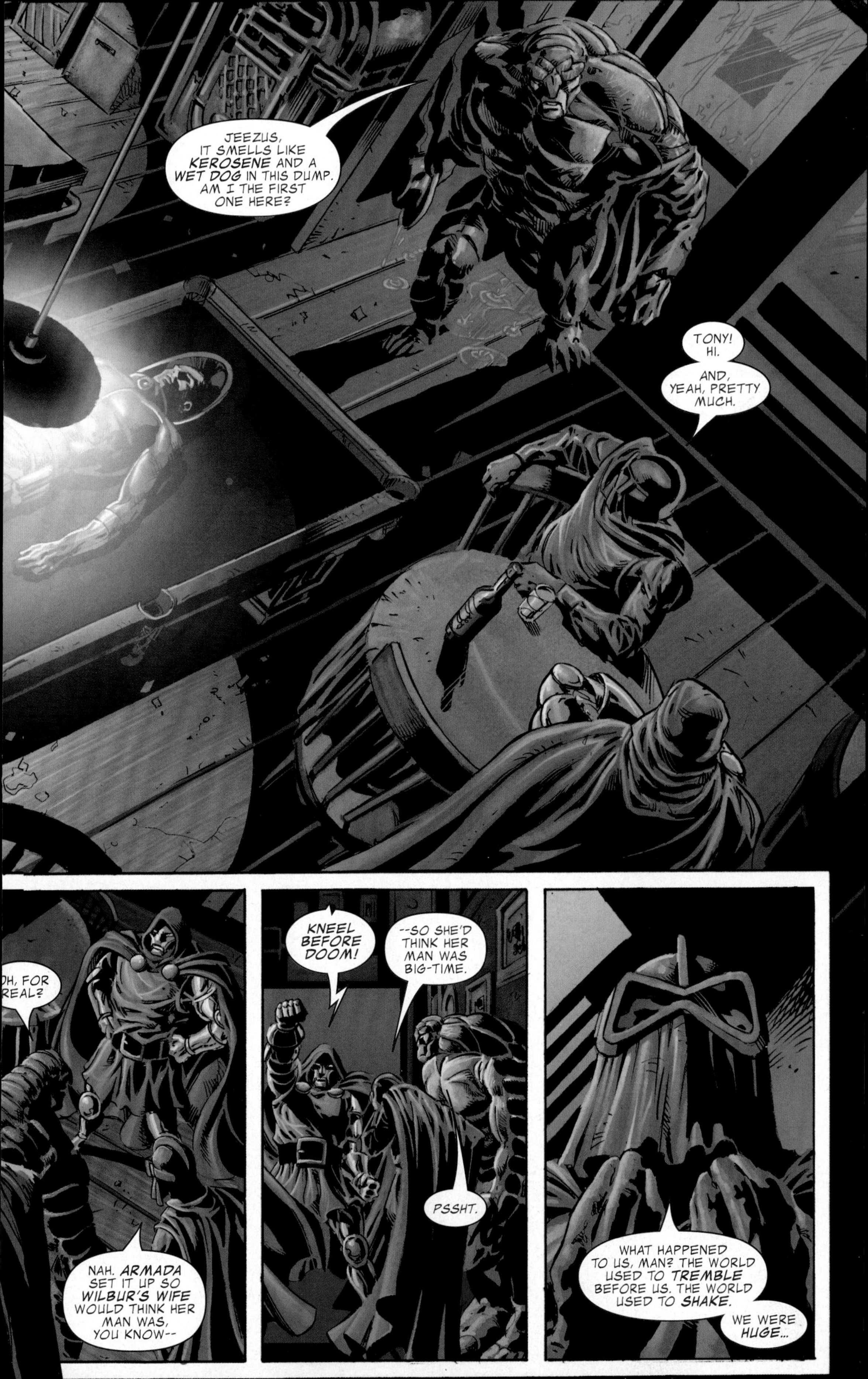

JEEZUS, IT SMELLS LIKE KEROSENE AND A WET DOG IN THIS DUMP. AM I THE FIRST ONE HERE?
TONY! HI.
AND, YEAH, PRETTY MUCH.
OH, FOR REAL?
NAH. ARMADA SET IT UP SO WILBUR'S WIFE WOULD THINK HER MAN WAS, YOU KNOW--
KNEEL BEFORE DOOM!
--SO SHE'D THINK HER MAN WAS BIG-TIME.
PSSHT.
WHAT HAPPENED TO US, MAN? THE WORLD USED TO TREMBLE BEFORE US. THE WORLD USED TO SHAKE.
WE WERE HUGE...

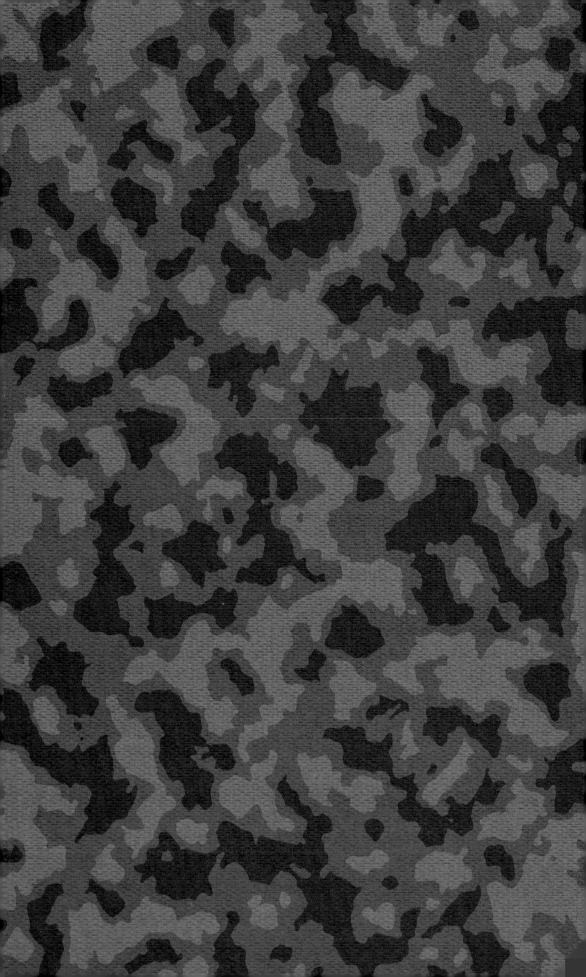

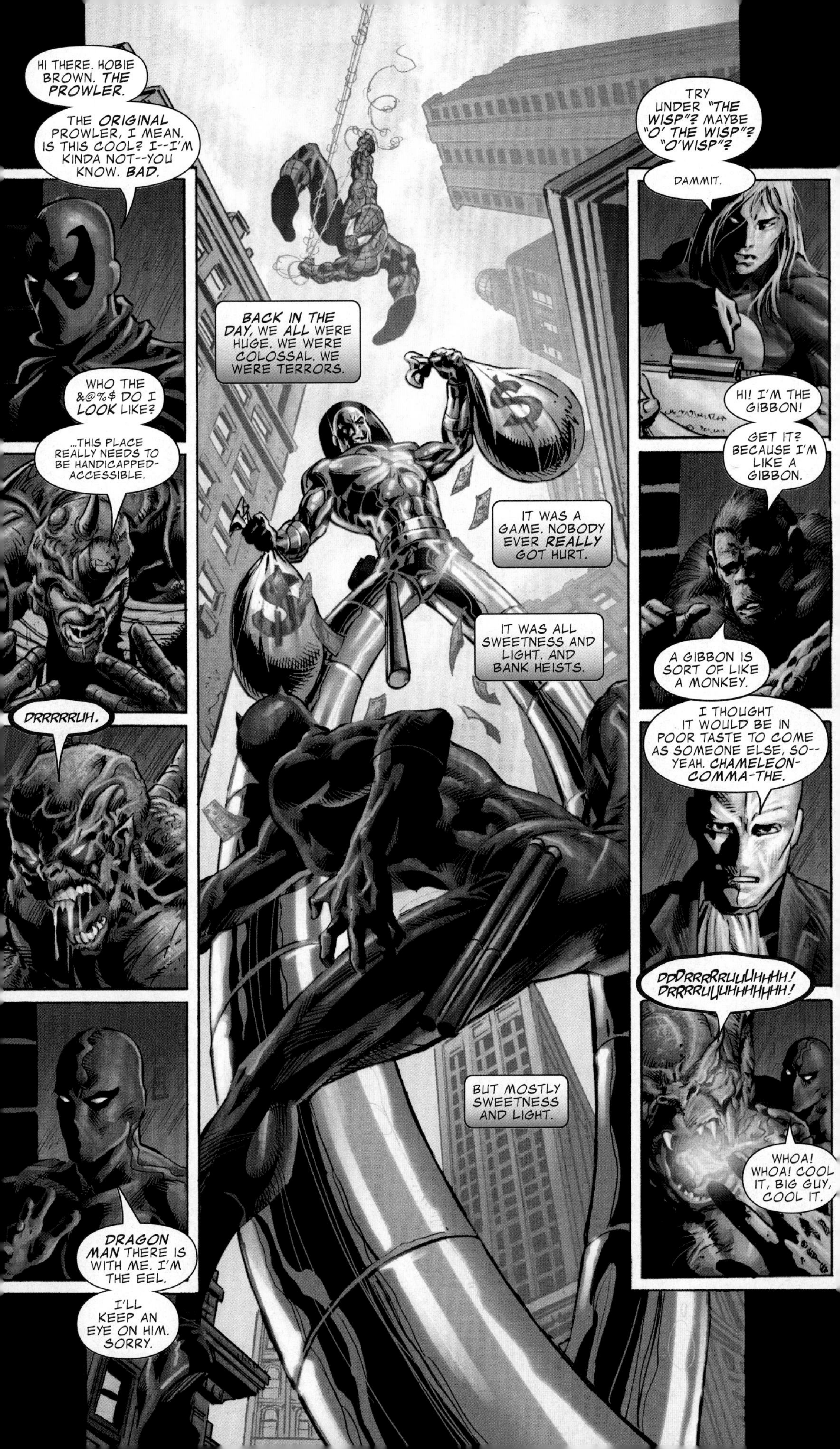
HI THERE. HOBIE BROWN. THE PROWLER.
THE ORIGINAL PROWLER, I MEAN. IS THIS COOL? I--I'M KINDA NOT--YOU KNOW. BAD.
WHO THE &@%$ DO I LOOK LIKE?
...THIS PLACE REALLY NEEDS TO BE HANDICAPPED-ACCESSIBLE.
DRRRRRUH.
DRAGON MAN THERE IS WITH ME. I'M THE EEL.
I'LL KEEP AN EYE ON HIM. SORRY.
BACK IN THE DAY, WE ALL WERE HUGE. WE WERE COLOSSAL. WE WERE TERRORS.
IT WAS A GAME. NOBODY EVER REALLY GOT HURT.
IT WAS ALL SWEETNESS AND LIGHT. AND BANK HEISTS.
BUT MOSTLY SWEETNESS AND LIGHT.
TRY UNDER "THE WISP"? MAYBE "O' THE WISP"? "O'WISP"?
DAMMIT.
HI! I'M THE GIBBON!
GET IT? BECAUSE I'M LIKE A GIBBON.
A GIBBON IS SORT OF LIKE A MONKEY.
I THOUGHT IT WOULD BE IN POOR TASTE TO COME AS SOMEONE ELSE, SO--YEAH. CHAMELEON-COMMA-THE.
DDDRRRRRUUUHHHH! DRRRRUUUHHHHHHH!
WHOA! WHOA! COOL IT, BIG GUY, COOL IT.

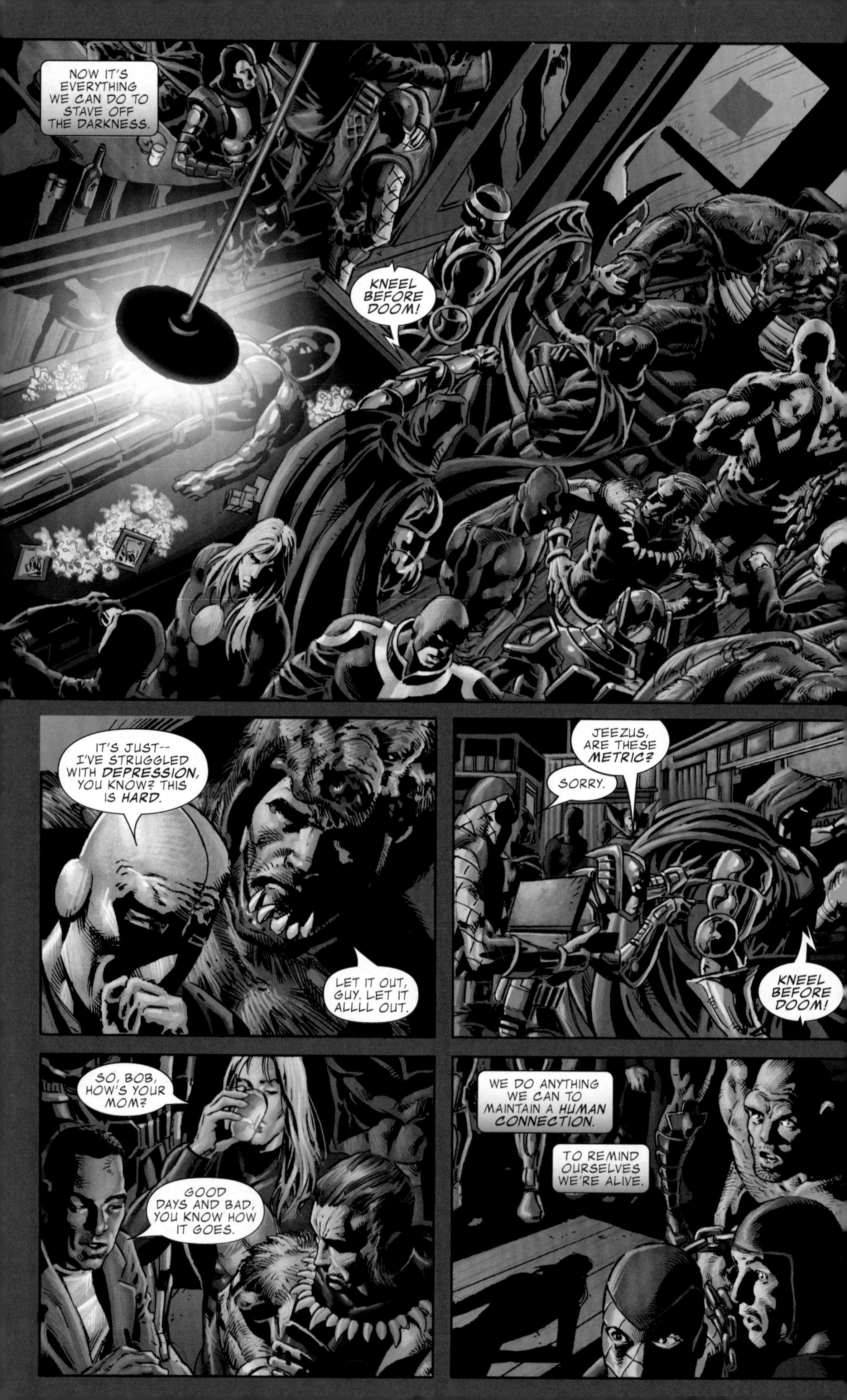
NOW IT'S EVERYTHING WE CAN DO TO STAVE OFF THE DARKNESS.
KNEEL BEFORE DOOM!
IT'S JUST-- I'VE STRUGGLED WITH DEPRESSION, YOU KNOW? THIS IS HARD.
LET IT OUT, GUY. LET IT ALLLL OUT.
JEEZUS, ARE THESE METRIC?
SORRY.
KNEEL BEFORE DOOM!
SO, BOB, HOW'S YOUR MOM?
GOOD DAYS AND BAD, YOU KNOW HOW IT GOES.
WE DO ANYTHING WE CAN TO MAINTAIN A HUMAN CONNECTION.
TO REMIND OURSELVES WE'RE ALIVE.

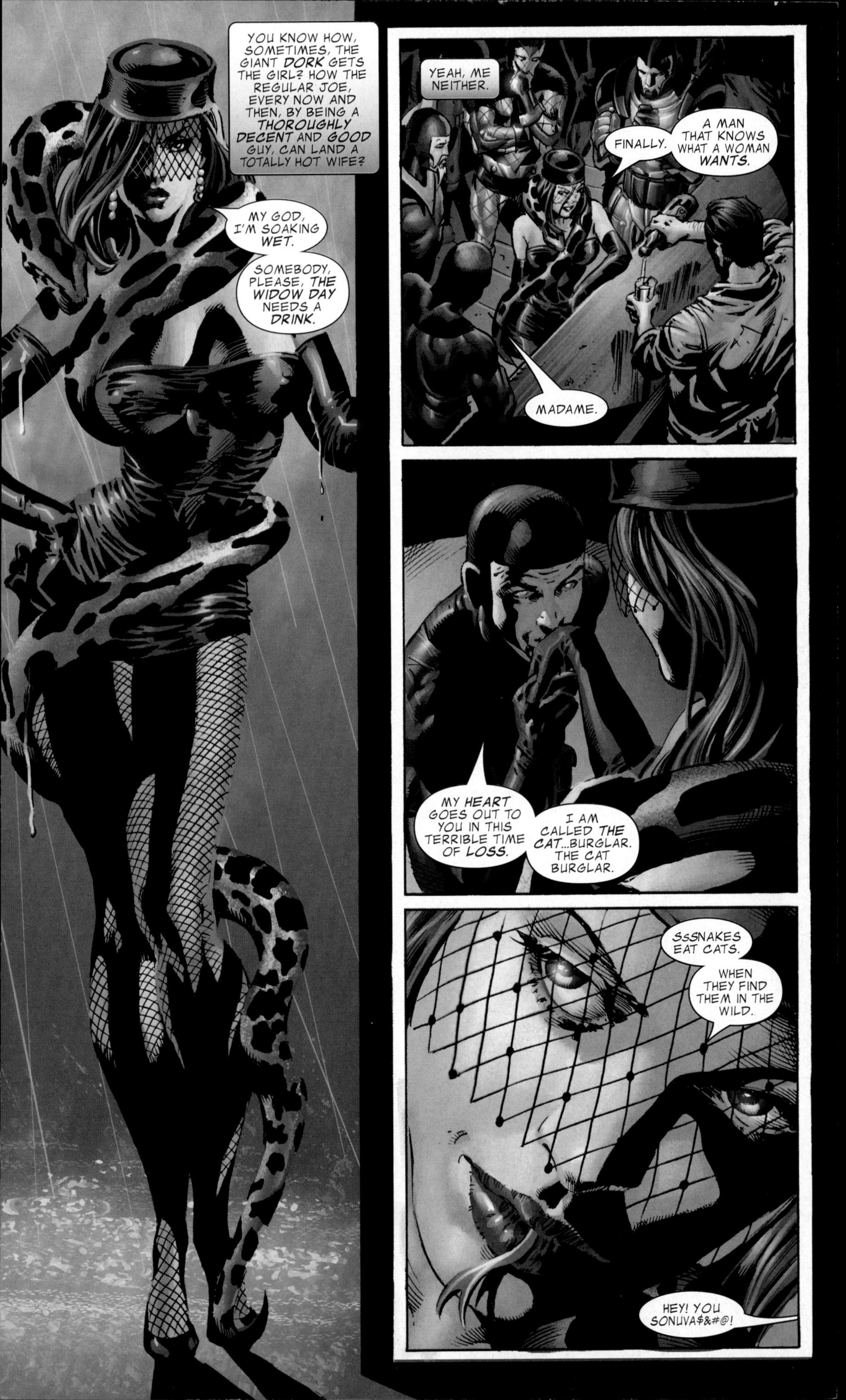
YOU KNOW HOW, SOMETIMES, THE GIANT DORK GETS THE GIRL? HOW THE REGULAR JOE, EVERY NOW AND THEN, BY BEING A THOROUGHLY DECENT AND GOOD GUY, CAN LAND A TOTALLY HOT WIFE?
MY GOD, I'M SOAKING WET.
SOMEBODY, PLEASE, THE WIDOW DAY NEEDS A DRINK.
YEAH, ME NEITHER.
FINALLY.
A MAN THAT KNOWS WHAT A WOMAN WANTS.
MADAME.
MY HEART GOES OUT TO YOU IN THIS TERRIBLE TIME OF LOSS.
I AM CALLED THE CAT...BURGLAR. THE CAT BURGLAR.
SsSNAKES EAT CATS.
WHEN THEY FIND THEM IN THE WILD.
HEY! YOU SONUVA$&#@!

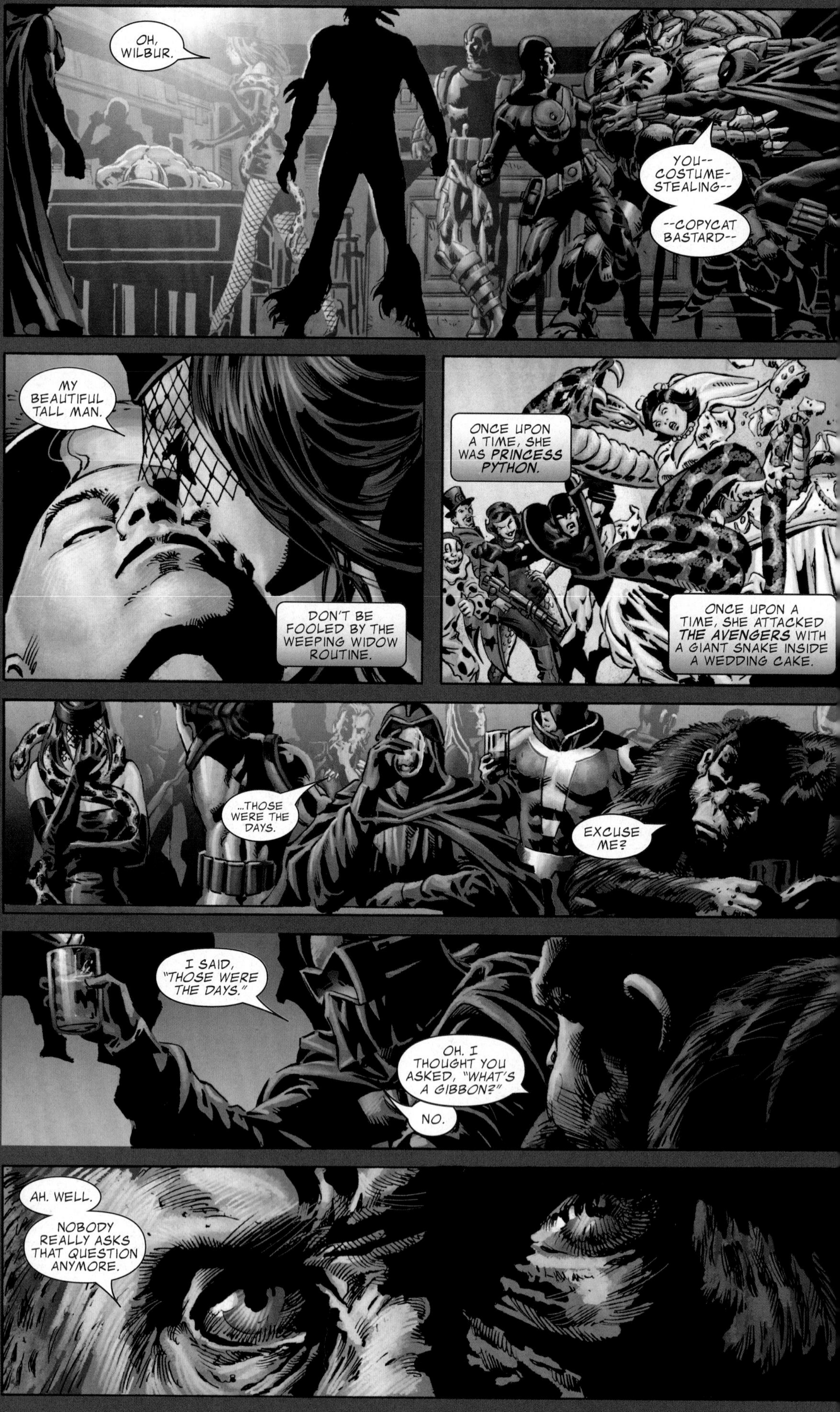
OH, WILBUR.
YOU-- COSTUME-STEALING--
--COPYCAT BASTARD--
MY BEAUTIFUL TALL MAN.
DON'T BE FOOLED BY THE WEEPING WIDOW ROUTINE.
ONCE UPON A TIME, SHE WAS PRINCESS PYTHON.
ONCE UPON A TIME, SHE ATTACKED THE AVENGERS WITH A GIANT SNAKE INSIDE A WEDDING CAKE.
...THOSE WERE THE DAYS.
EXCUSE ME?
I SAID, "THOSE WERE THE DAYS."
OH. I THOUGHT YOU ASKED, "WHAT'S A GIBBON?"
NO.
AH. WELL.
NOBODY REALLY ASKS THAT QUESTION ANYMORE.

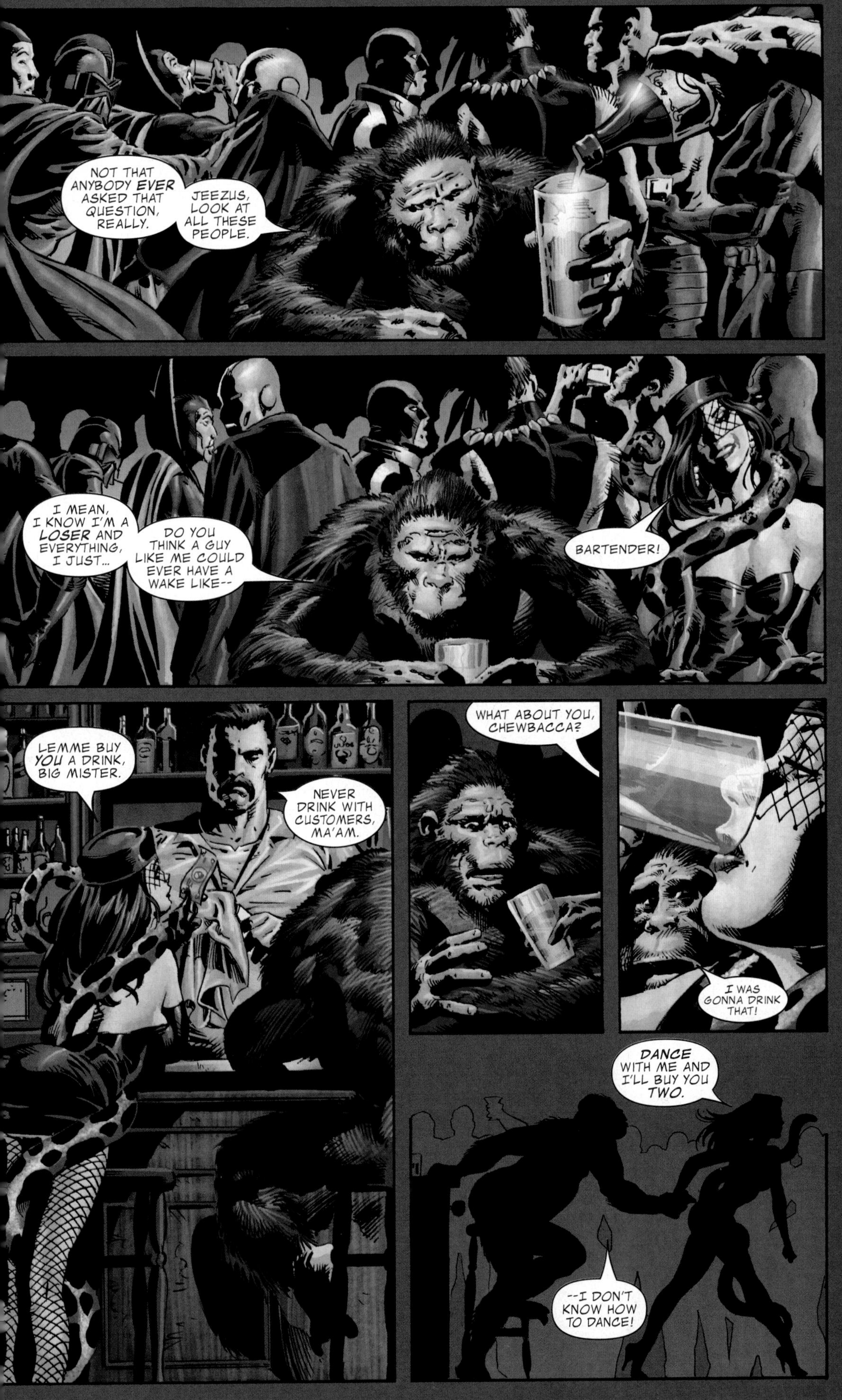

NOT THAT ANYBODY EVER ASKED THAT QUESTION, REALLY.
JEEZUS, LOOK AT ALL THESE PEOPLE.
I MEAN, I KNOW I'M A LOSER AND EVERYTHING, I JUST...
DO YOU THINK A GUY LIKE ME COULD EVER HAVE A WAKE LIKE--
BARTENDER!
LEMME BUY YOU A DRINK, BIG MISTER.
NEVER DRINK WITH CUSTOMERS, MA'AM.
WHAT ABOUT YOU, CHEWBACCA?
I WAS GONNA DRINK THAT!
DANCE WITH ME AND I'LL BUY YOU TWO.
--I DON'T KNOW HOW TO DANCE!

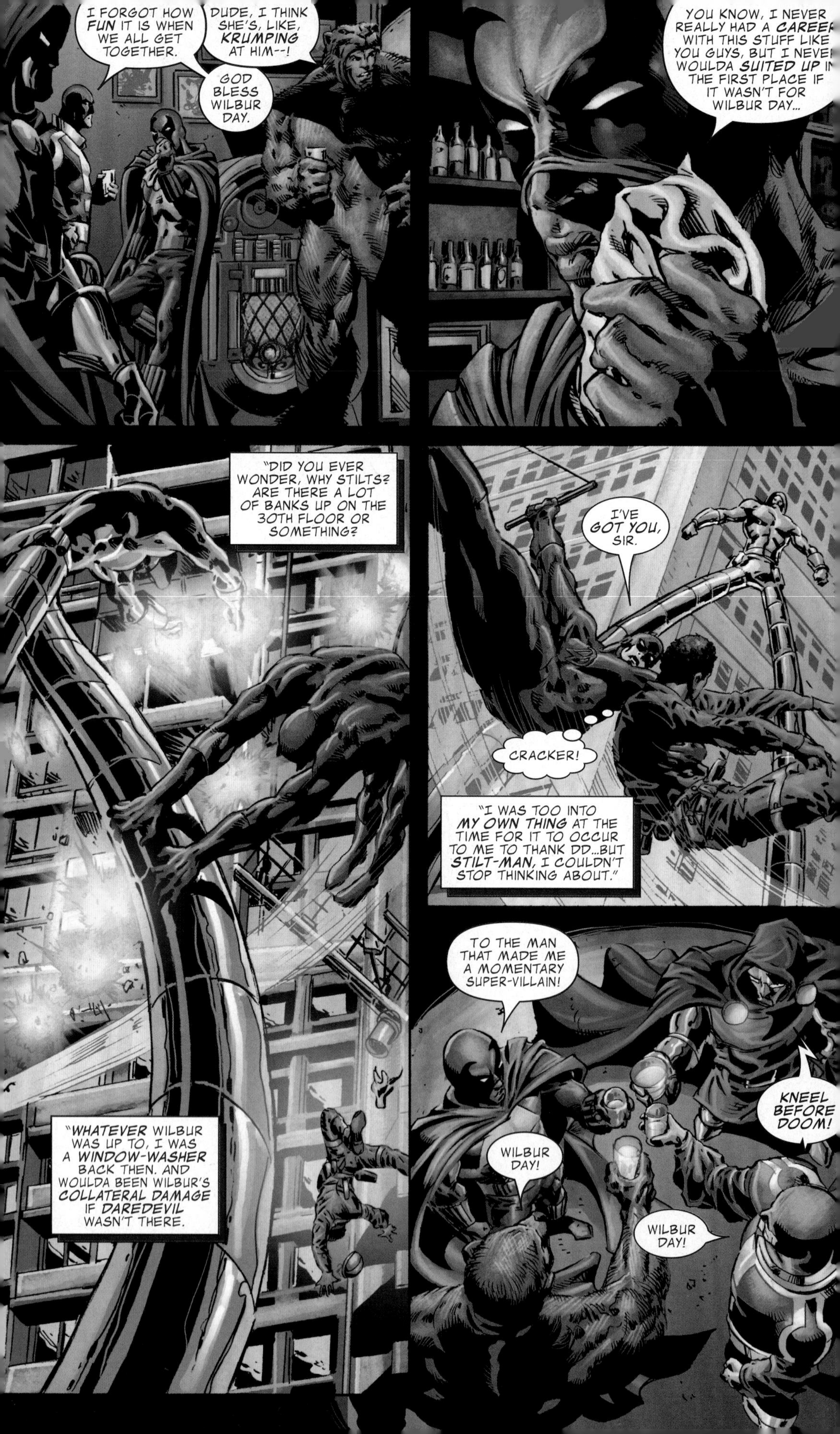

I FORGOT HOW FUN IT IS WHEN WE ALL GET TOGETHER.
DUDE, I THINK SHE'S, LIKE, KRUMPING AT HIM--!
GOD BLESS WILBUR DAY.
YOU KNOW, I NEVER REALLY HAD A CAREER WITH THIS STUFF LIKE YOU GUYS, BUT I NEVER WOULDA SUITED UP IN THE FIRST PLACE IF IT WASN'T FOR WILBUR DAY...
"DID YOU EVER WONDER, WHY STILTS? ARE THERE A LOT OF BANKS UP ON THE 30TH FLOOR OR SOMETHING?
"WHATEVER WILBUR WAS UP TO, I WAS A WINDOW-WASHER BACK THEN. AND WOULDA BEEN WILBUR'S COLLATERAL DAMAGE IF DAREDEVIL WASN'T THERE.
I'VE GOT YOU, SIR.
CRACKER!
"I WAS TOO INTO MY OWN THING AT THE TIME FOR IT TO OCCUR TO ME TO THANK DD...BUT STILT-MAN, I COULDN'T STOP THINKING ABOUT."
TO THE MAN THAT MADE ME A MOMENTARY SUPER-VILLAIN!
KNEEL BEFORE DOOM!
WILBUR DAY!
WILBUR DAY!

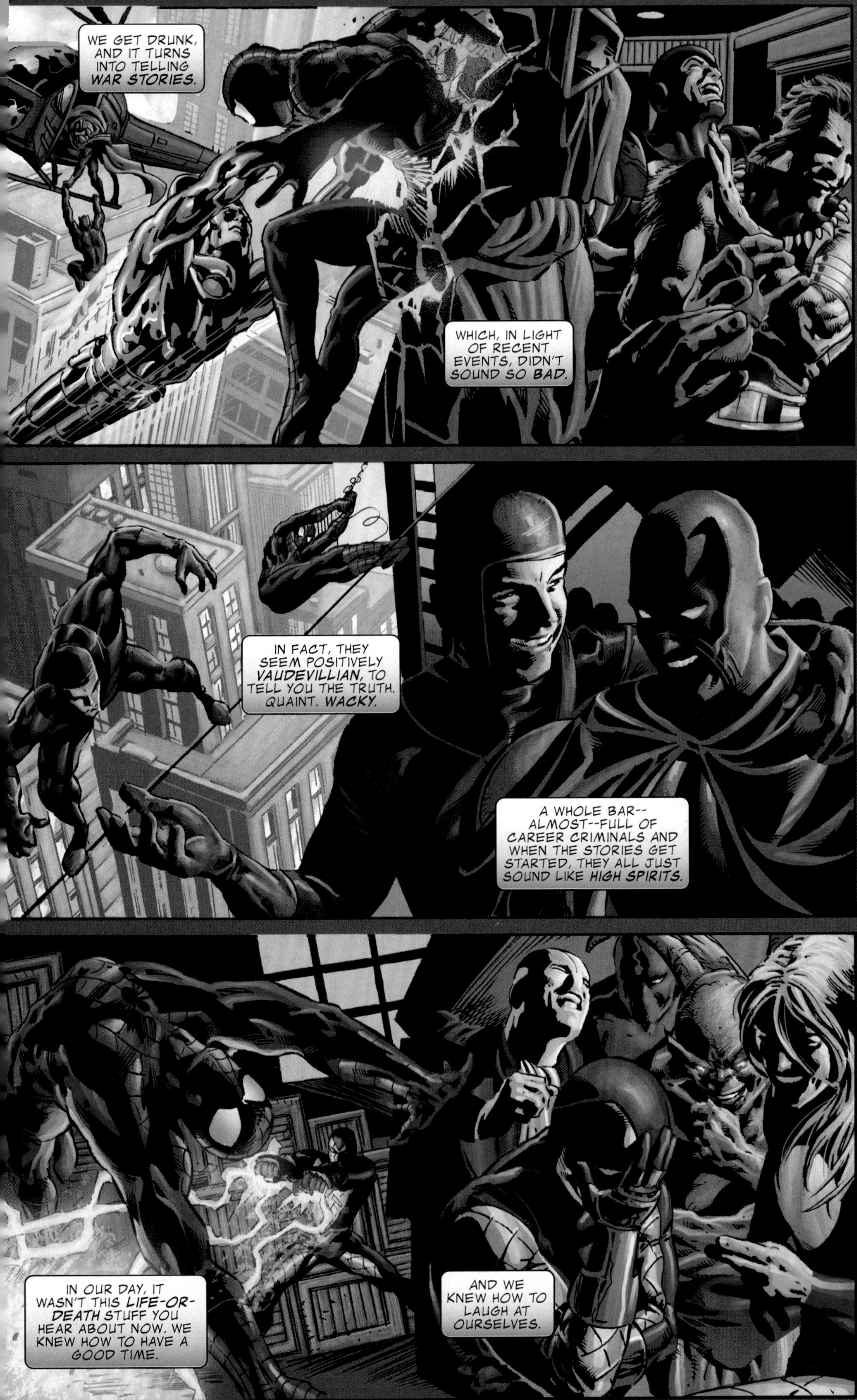
WE GET DRUNK, AND IT TURNS INTO TELLING WAR STORIES.
WHICH, IN LIGHT OF RECENT EVENTS, DIDN'T SOUND SO BAD.
IN FACT, THEY SEEM POSITIVELY VAUDEVILLIAN, TO TELL YOU THE TRUTH. QUAINT. WACKY.
A WHOLE BAR--ALMOST--FULL OF CAREER CRIMINALS AND WHEN THE STORIES GET STARTED, THEY ALL JUST SOUND LIKE HIGH SPIRITS.
IN OUR DAY, IT WASN'T THIS LIFE-OR-DEATH STUFF YOU HEAR ABOUT NOW. WE KNEW HOW TO HAVE A GOOD TIME.
AND WE KNEW HOW TO LAUGH AT OURSELVES.

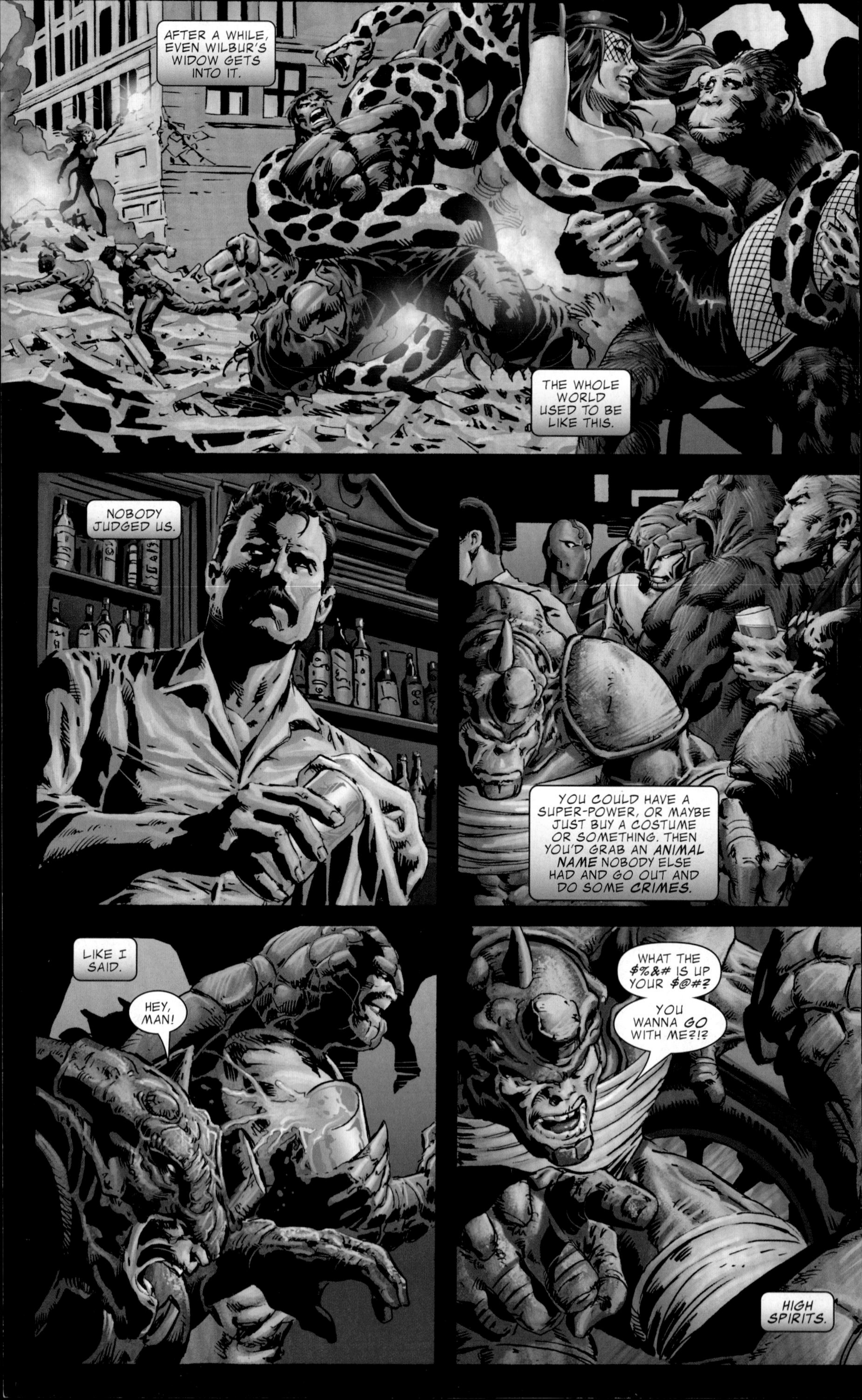
AFTER A WHILE, EVEN WILBUR'S WIDOW GETS INTO IT.
THE WHOLE WORLD USED TO BE LIKE THIS.
NOBODY JUDGED US.
YOU COULD HAVE A SUPER-POWER, OR MAYBE JUST BUY A COSTUME OR SOMETHING. THEN YOU'D GRAB AN ANIMAL NAME NOBODY ELSE HAD AND GO OUT AND DO SOME CRIMES.
LIKE I SAID.
HEY, MAN!
WHAT THE $%&# IS UP YOUR $@#?
YOU WANNA GO WITH ME?!?
HIGH SPIRITS.

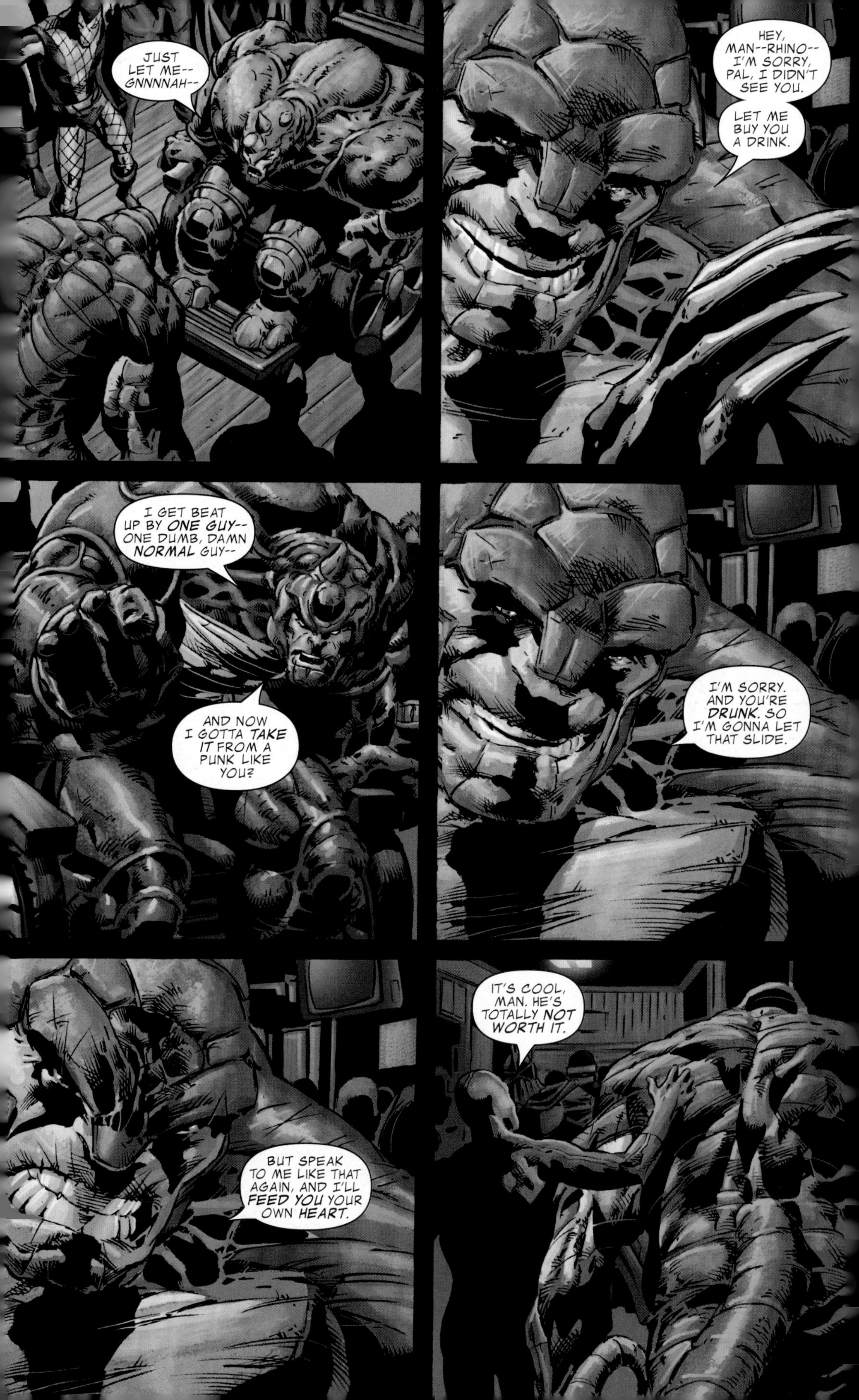
JUST LET ME-- GNNNNAH--
HEY, MAN--RHINO-- I'M SORRY, PAL, I DIDN'T SEE YOU.
LET ME BUY YOU A DRINK.
I GET BEAT UP BY ONE GUY-- ONE DUMB, DAMN NORMAL GUY--
AND NOW I GOTTA TAKE IT FROM A PUNK LIKE YOU?
I'M SORRY. AND YOU'RE DRUNK. SO I'M GONNA LET THAT SLIDE.
BUT SPEAK TO ME LIKE THAT AGAIN, AND I'LL FEED YOU YOUR OWN HEART.
IT'S COOL, MAN. HE'S TOTALLY NOT WORTH IT.

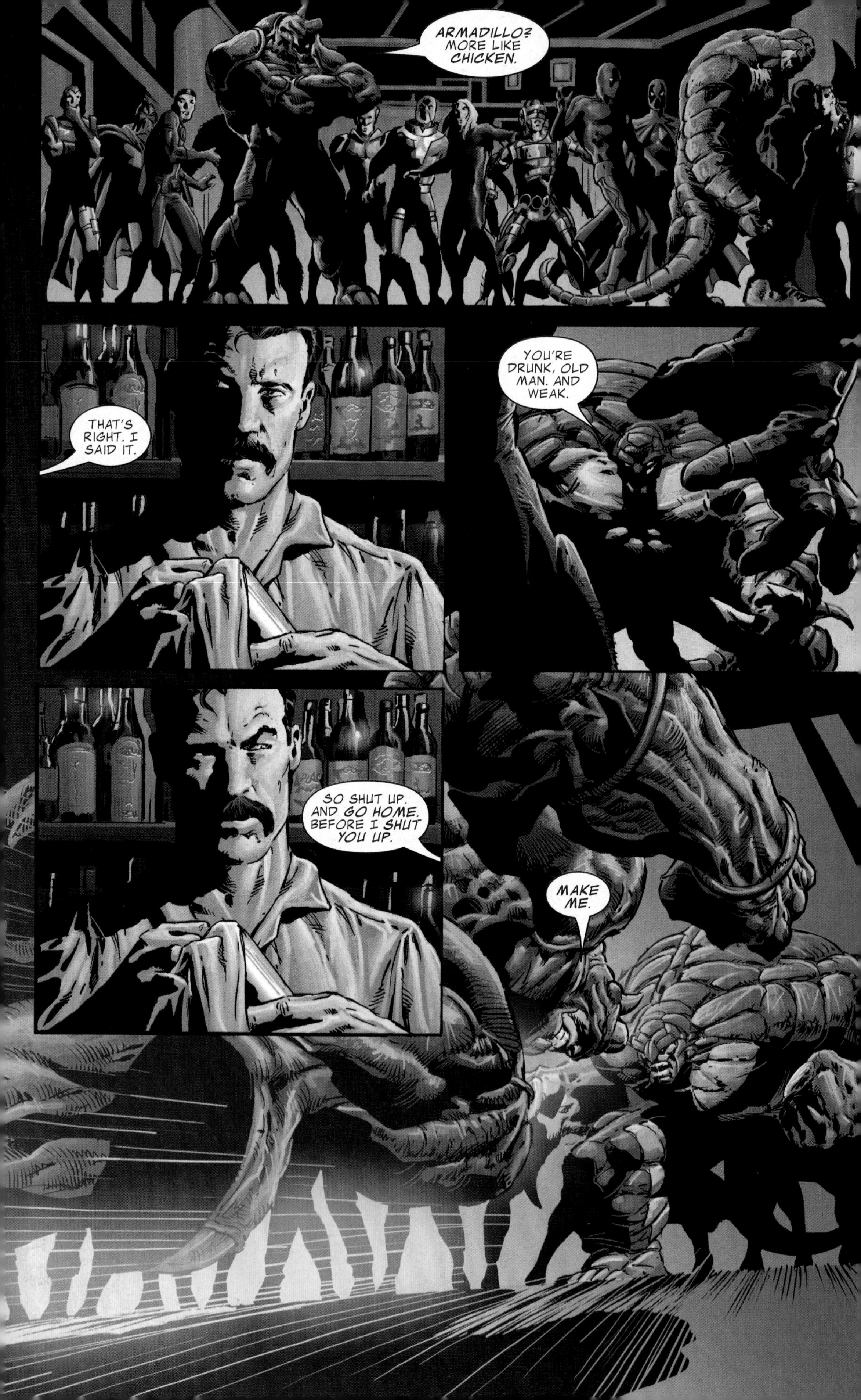
ARMADILLO? MORE LIKE CHICKEN.
THAT'S RIGHT. I SAID IT.
YOU'RE DRUNK, OLD MAN. AND WEAK.
SO SHUT UP. AND GO HOME. BEFORE I SHUT YOU UP.
MAKE ME.

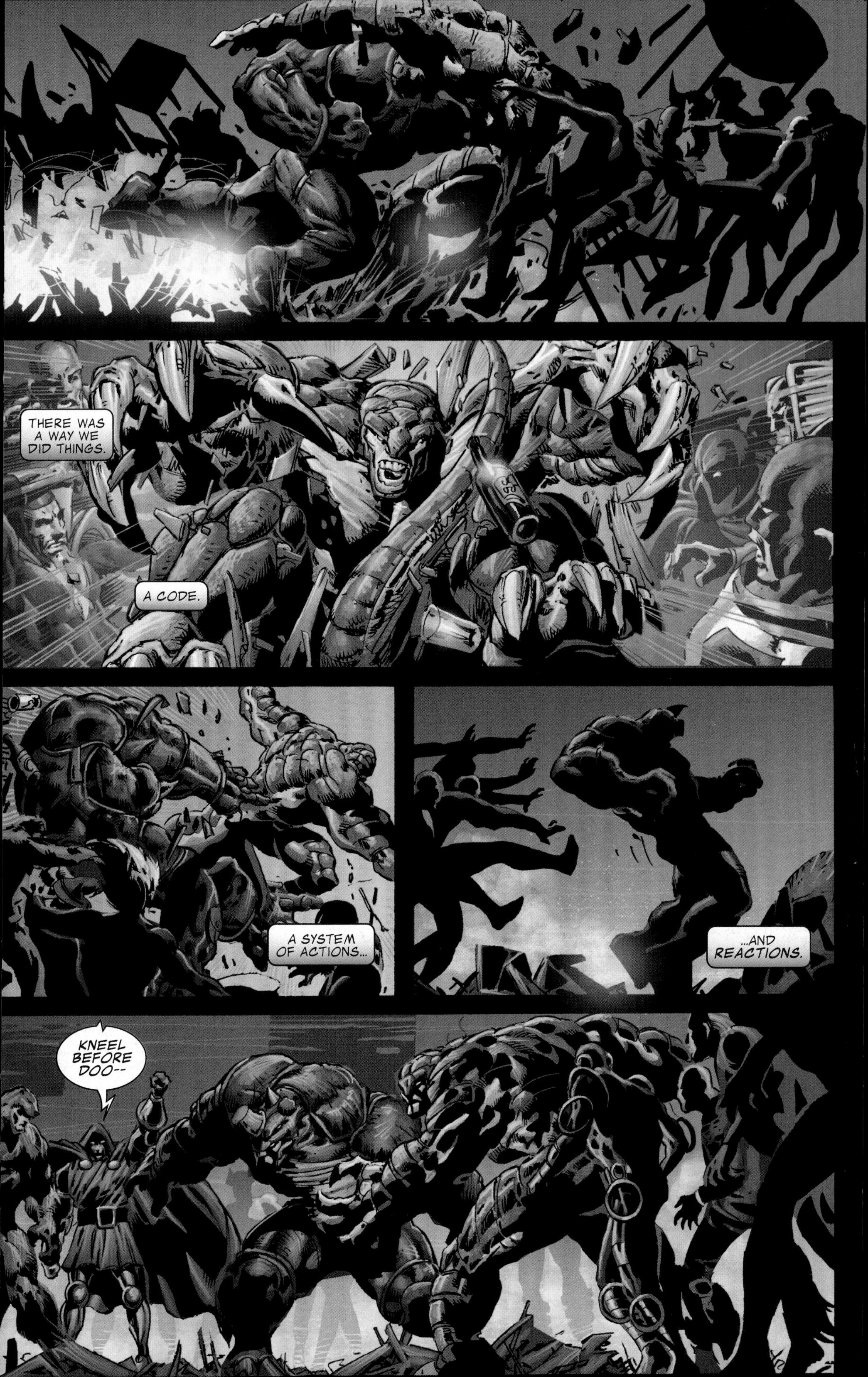

THERE WAS A WAY WE DID THINGS.
A CODE.
A SYSTEM OF ACTIONS...
...AND REACTIONS.
KNEEL BEFORE DOO--

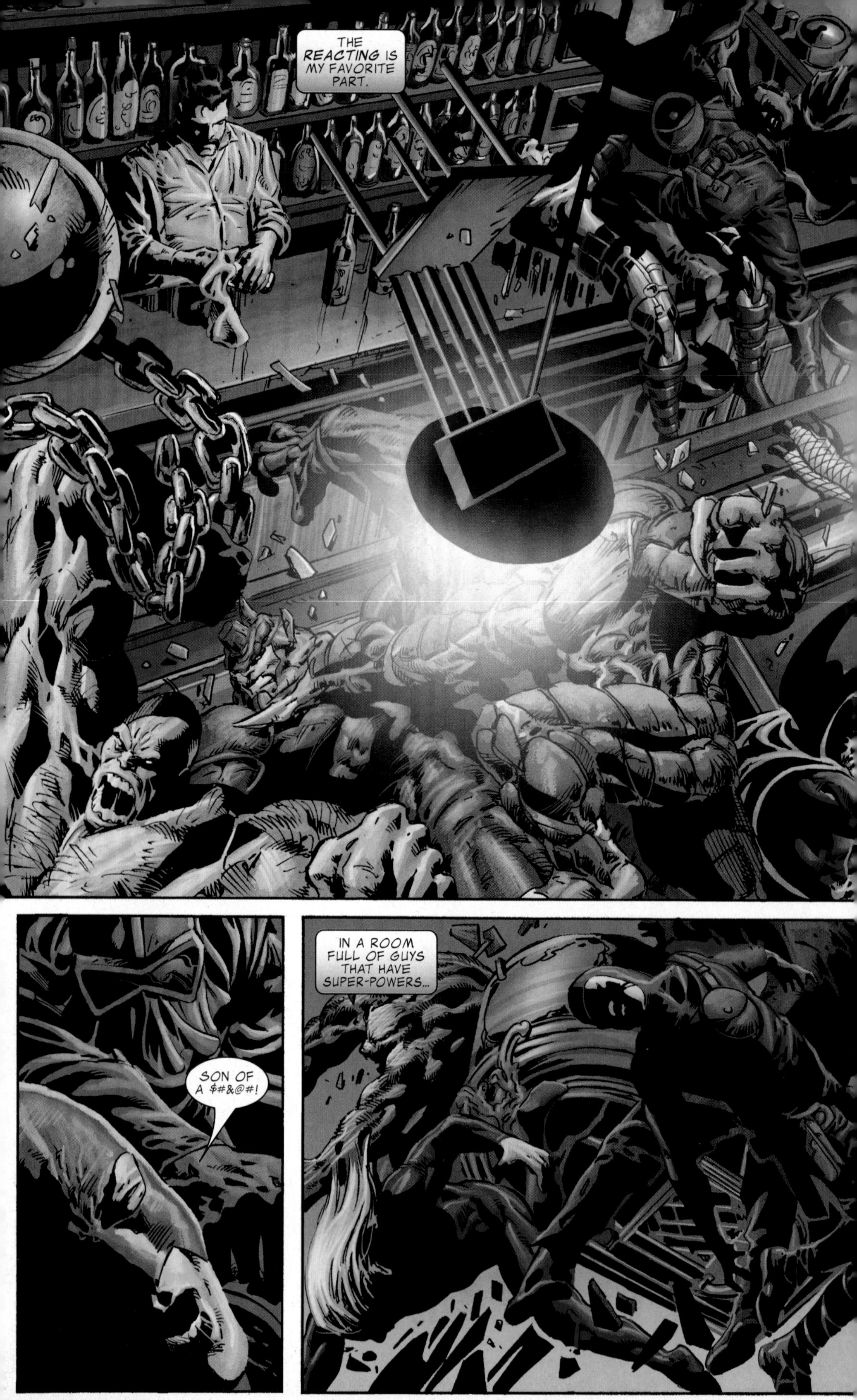
THE *REACTING* IS MY FAVORITE PART.
SON OF A $#&@#!
IN A ROOM FULL OF GUYS THAT HAVE SUPER-POWERS...

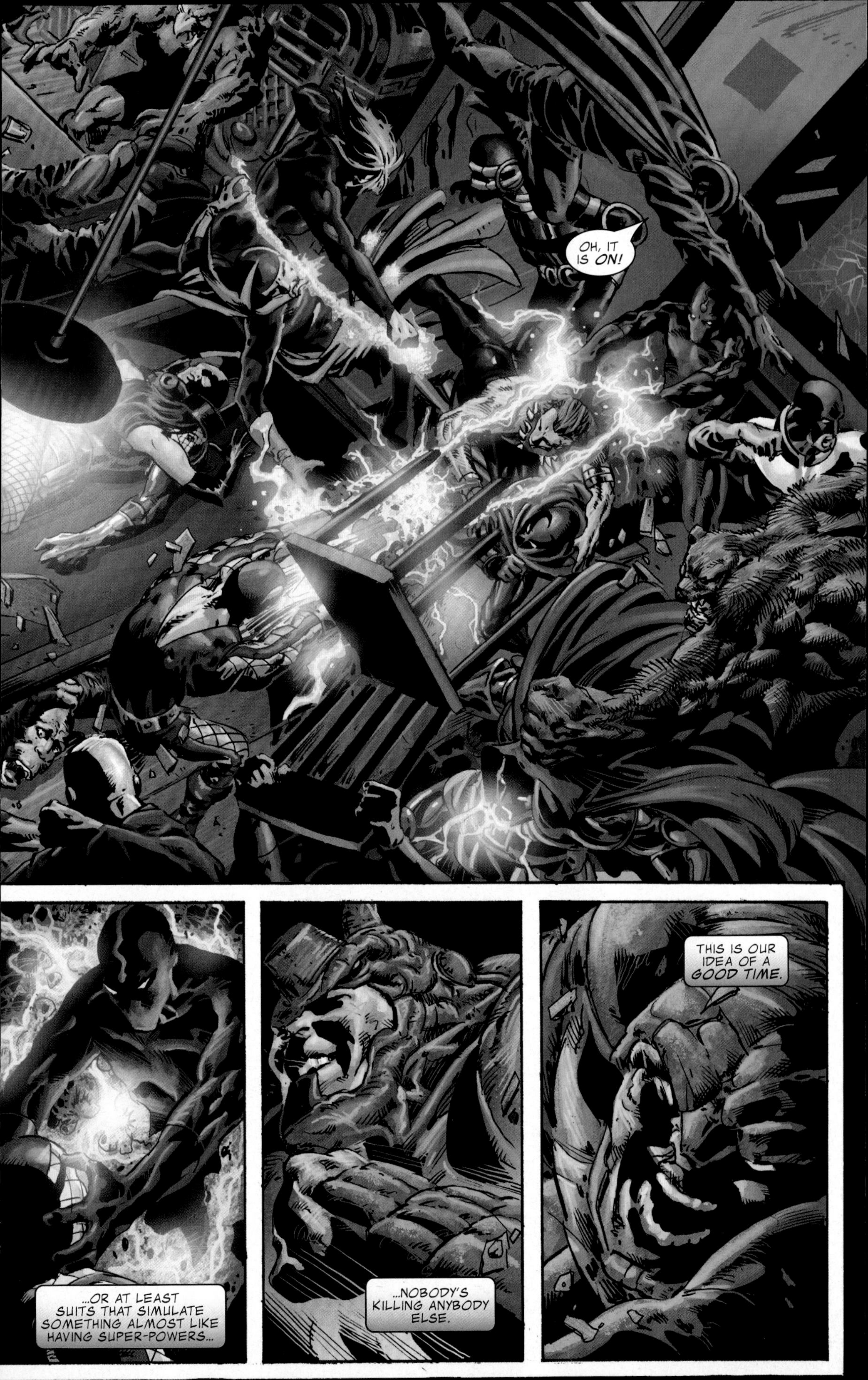
OH, IT IS ON!
...OR AT LEAST SUITS THAT SIMULATE SOMETHING ALMOST LIKE HAVING SUPER-POWERS...
...NOBODY'S KILLING ANYBODY ELSE.
THIS IS OUR IDEA OF A GOOD TIME.

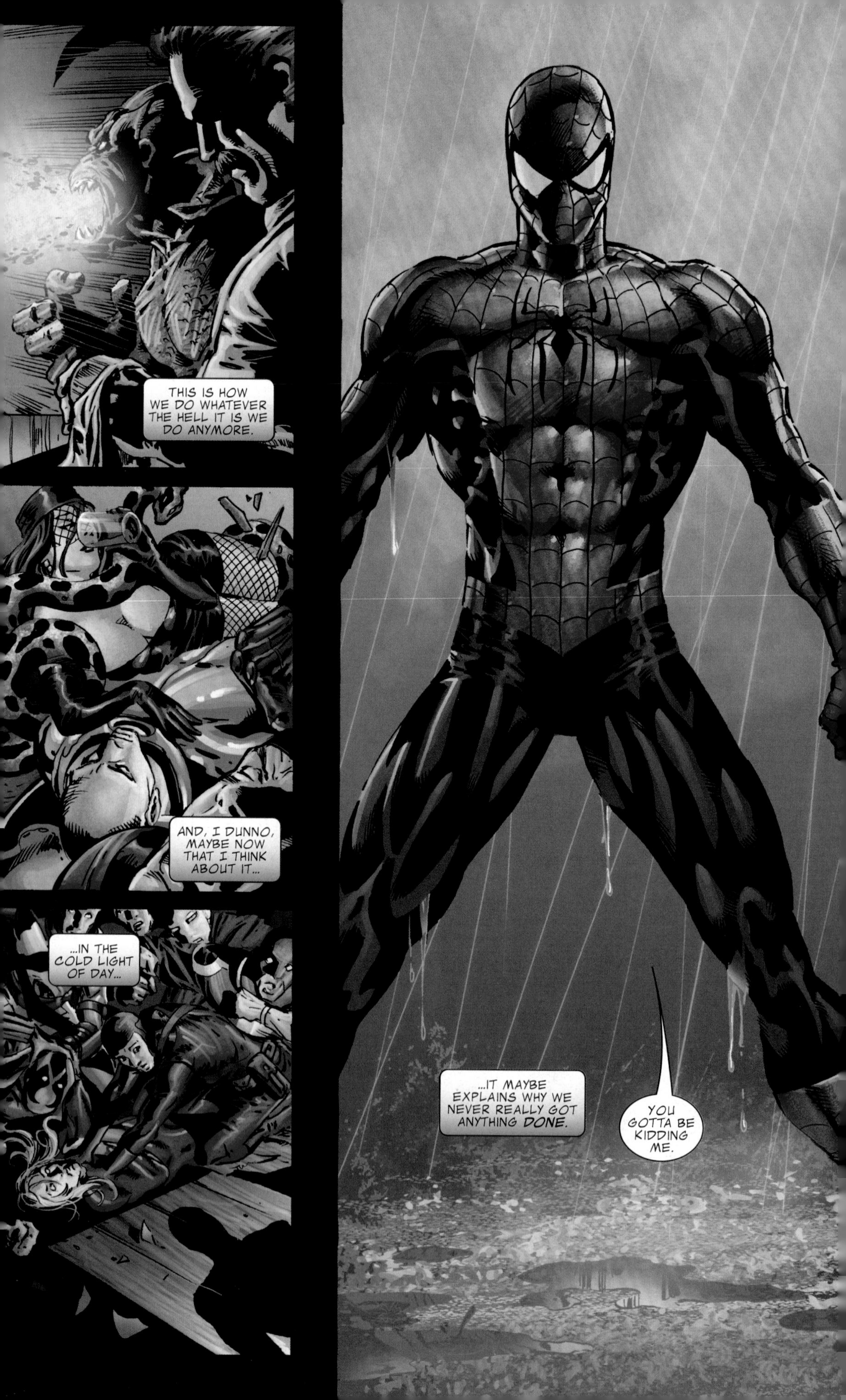
THIS IS HOW WE DO WHATEVER THE HELL IT IS WE DO ANYMORE.
AND, I DUNNO, MAYBE NOW THAT I THINK ABOUT IT...
...IN THE COLD LIGHT OF DAY...
...IT MAYBE EXPLAINS WHY WE NEVER REALLY GOT ANYTHING DONE.
YOU GOTTA BE KIDDING ME.

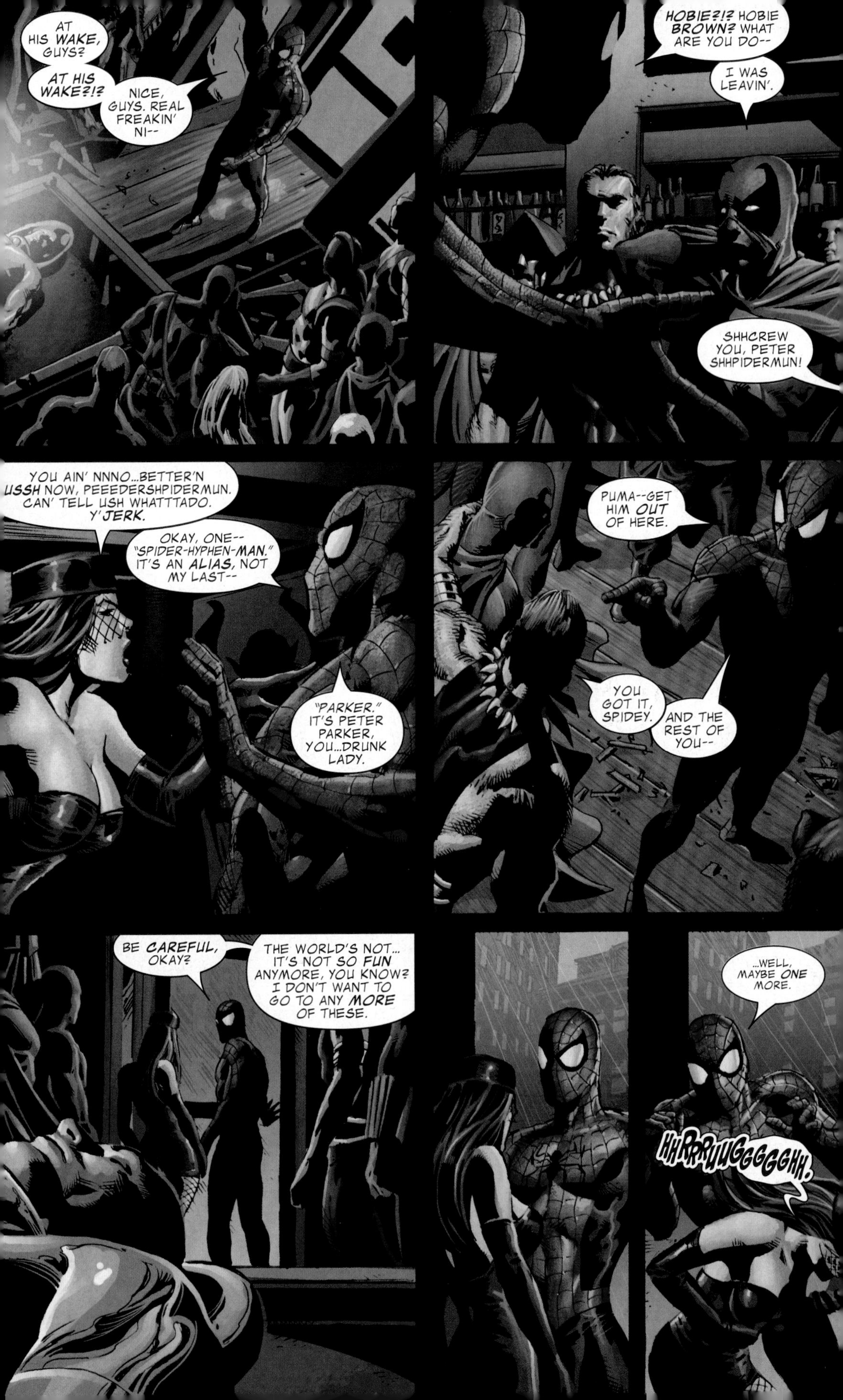
AT HIS WAKE, GUYS?
AT HIS WAKE?!?
NICE, GUYS. REAL FREAKIN' NI--
HOBIE?!? HOBIE BROWN? WHAT ARE YOU DO--
I WAS LEAVIN'.
SHHCREW YOU, PETER SHHPIDERMUN!
YOU AIN' NNNO...BETTER'N USSH NOW, PEEEDERSHPIDERMUN. CAN' TELL USH WHATTTADO. Y'JERK.
OKAY, ONE-- "SPIDER-HYPHEN-MAN." IT'S AN ALIAS, NOT MY LAST--
"PARKER." IT'S PETER PARKER, YOU...DRUNK LADY.
PUMA--GET HIM OUT OF HERE.
YOU GOT IT, SPIDEY.
AND THE REST OF YOU--
BE CAREFUL, OKAY?
THE WORLD'S NOT... IT'S NOT SO FUN ANYMORE, YOU KNOW? I DON'T WANT TO GO TO ANY MORE OF THESE.
...WELL, MAYBE ONE MORE.
HHRRRUUGGGGGHH.

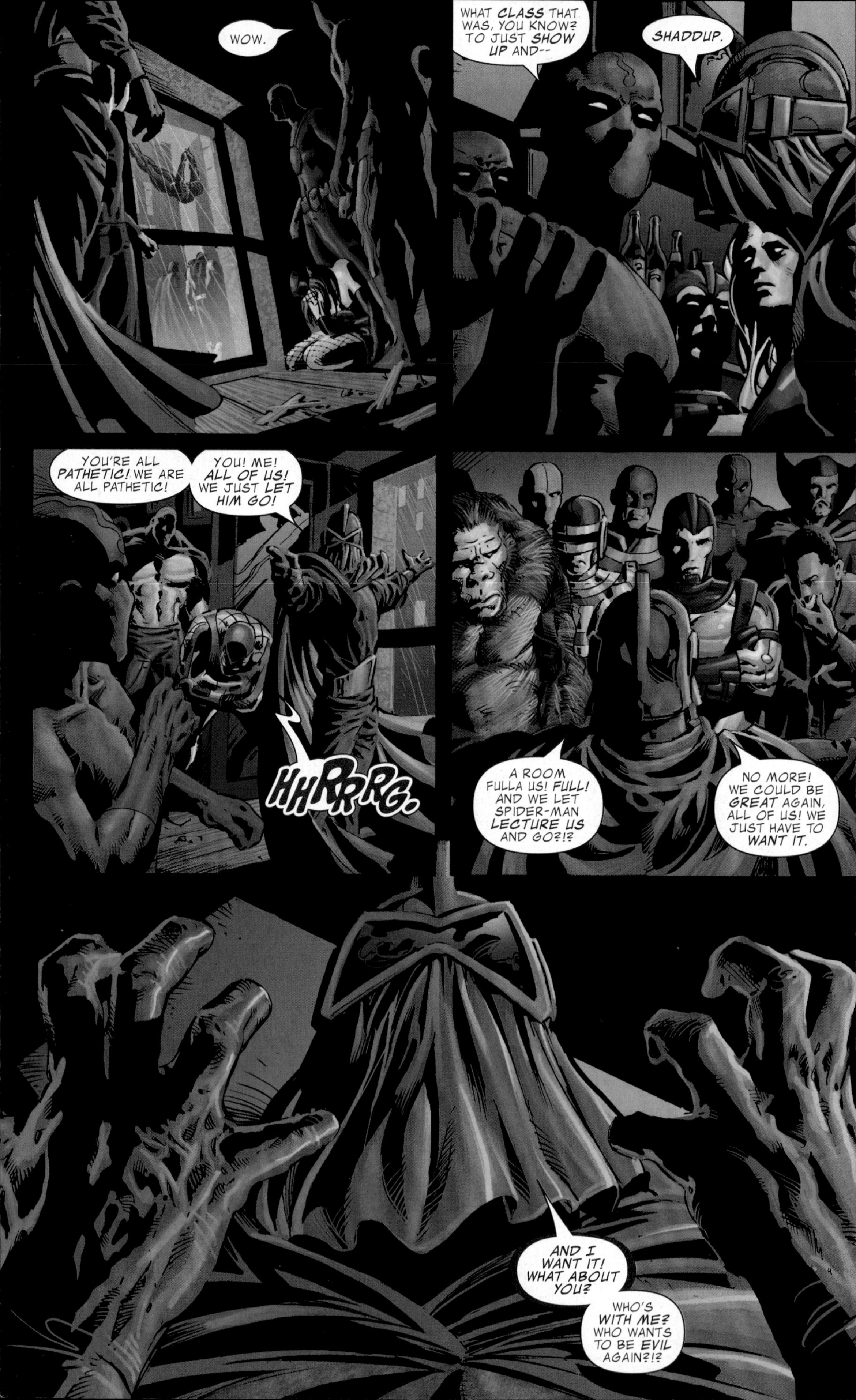
WOW.
WHAT CLASS THAT WAS, YOU KNOW? TO JUST SHOW UP AND--
SHADDUP.
YOU'RE ALL PATHETIC! WE ARE ALL PATHETIC!
YOU! ME! ALL OF US! WE JUST LET HIM GO!
HHRRRG.
A ROOM FULLA US! FULL! AND WE LET SPIDER-MAN LECTURE US AND GO?!?
NO MORE! WE COULD BE GREAT AGAIN, ALL OF US! WE JUST HAVE TO WANT IT.
AND I WANT IT! WHAT ABOUT YOU?
WHO'S WITH ME? WHO WANTS TO BE EVIL AGAIN?!?

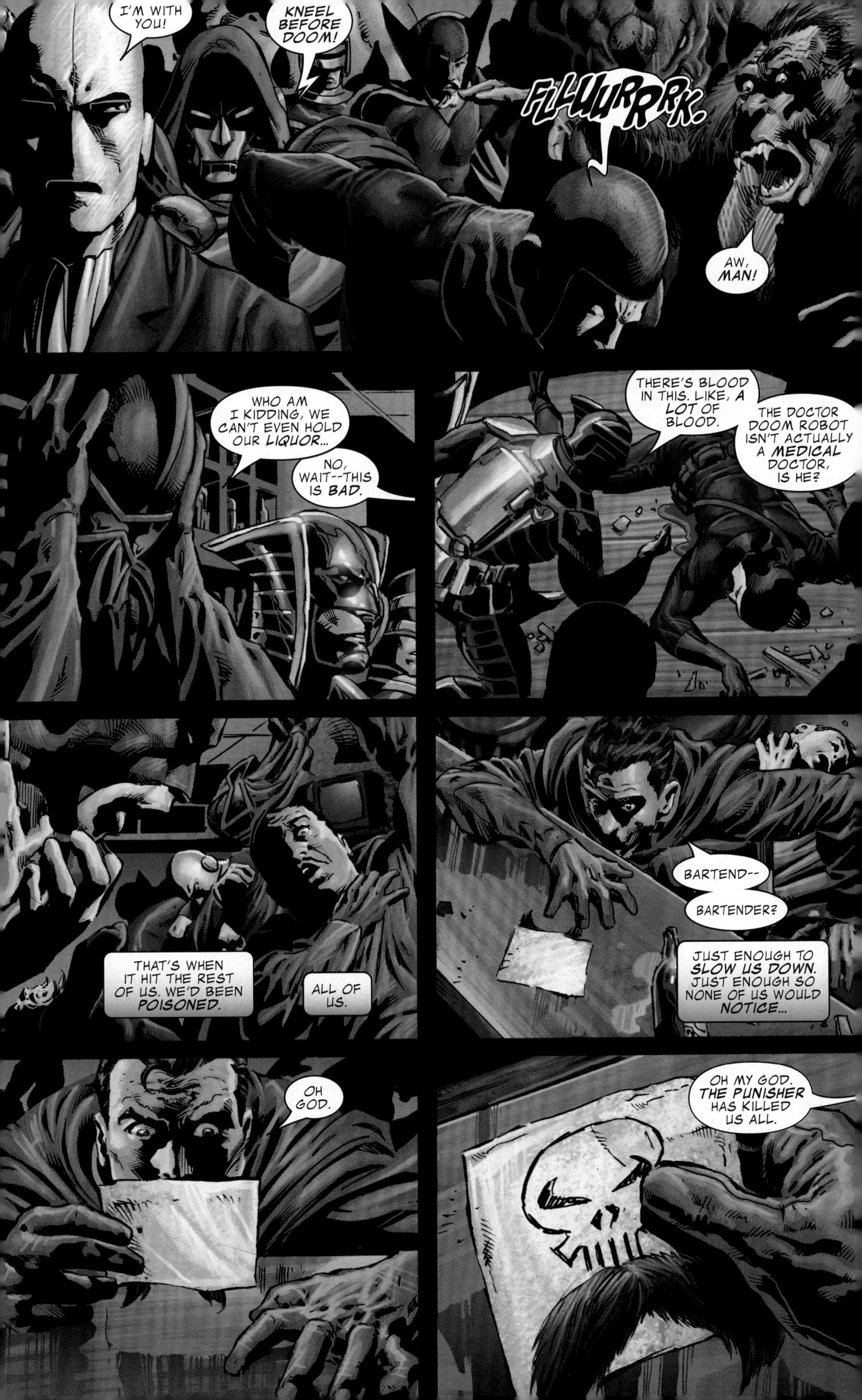
I'M WITH YOU!
KNEEL BEFORE DOOM!
FLLUURRRK.
AW, MAN!
WHO AM I KIDDING, WE CAN'T EVEN HOLD OUR LIQUOR...
NO, WAIT--THIS IS BAD.
THERE'S BLOOD IN THIS. LIKE, A LOT OF BLOOD.
THE DOCTOR DOOM ROBOT ISN'T ACTUALLY A MEDICAL DOCTOR, IS HE?
THAT'S WHEN IT HIT THE REST OF US. WE'D BEEN POISONED.
ALL OF US.
BARTEND--
BARTENDER?
JUST ENOUGH TO SLOW US DOWN. JUST ENOUGH SO NONE OF US WOULD NOTICE...
OH GOD.
OH MY GOD. THE PUNISHER HAS KILLED US ALL.

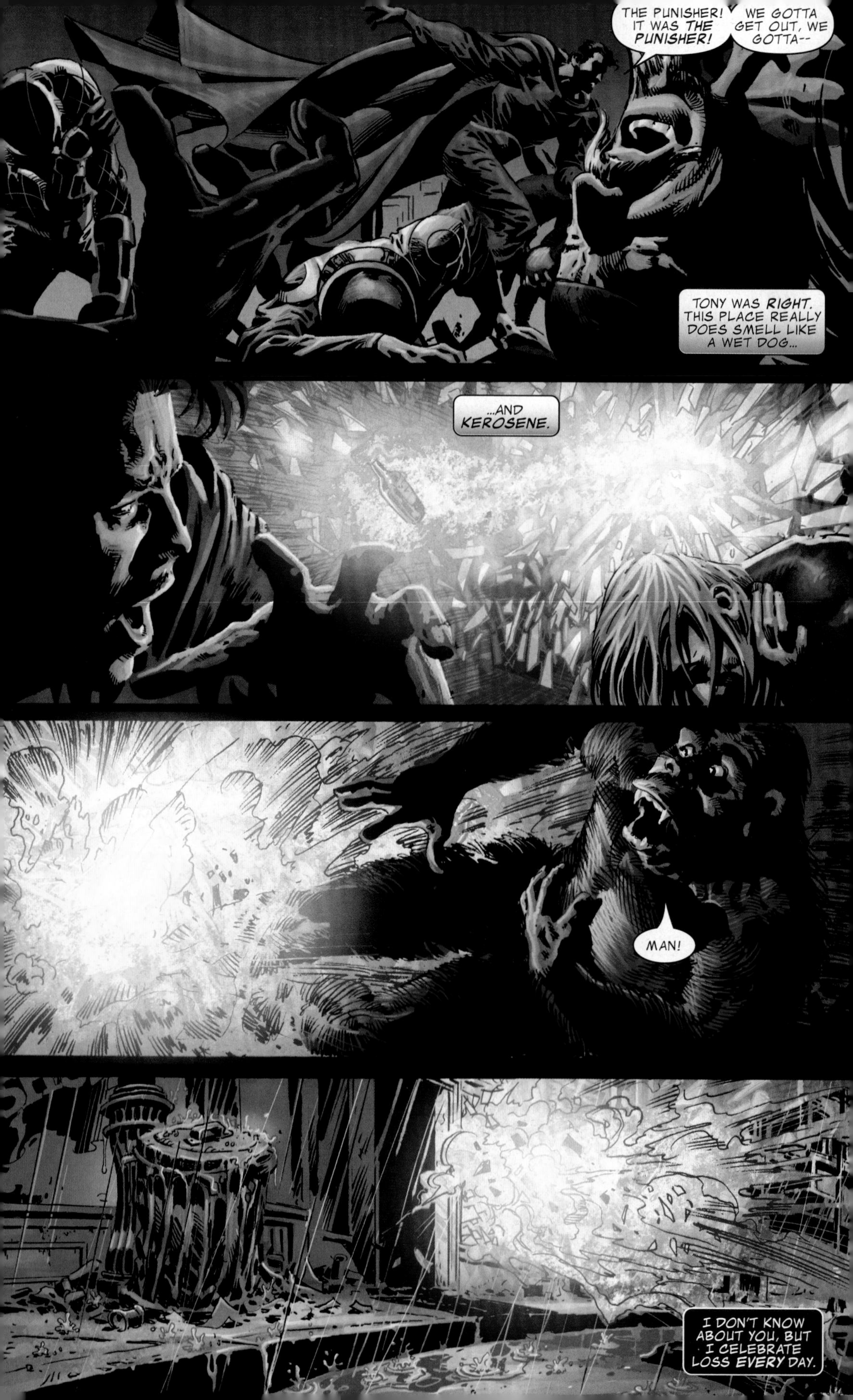
THE PUNISHER! IT WAS THE PUNISHER!
WE GOTTA GET OUT, WE GOTTA--
TONY WAS RIGHT. THIS PLACE REALLY DOES SMELL LIKE A WET DOG...
...AND KEROSENE.
MAN!
I DON'T KNOW ABOUT YOU, BUT I CELEBRATE LOSS EVERY DAY.

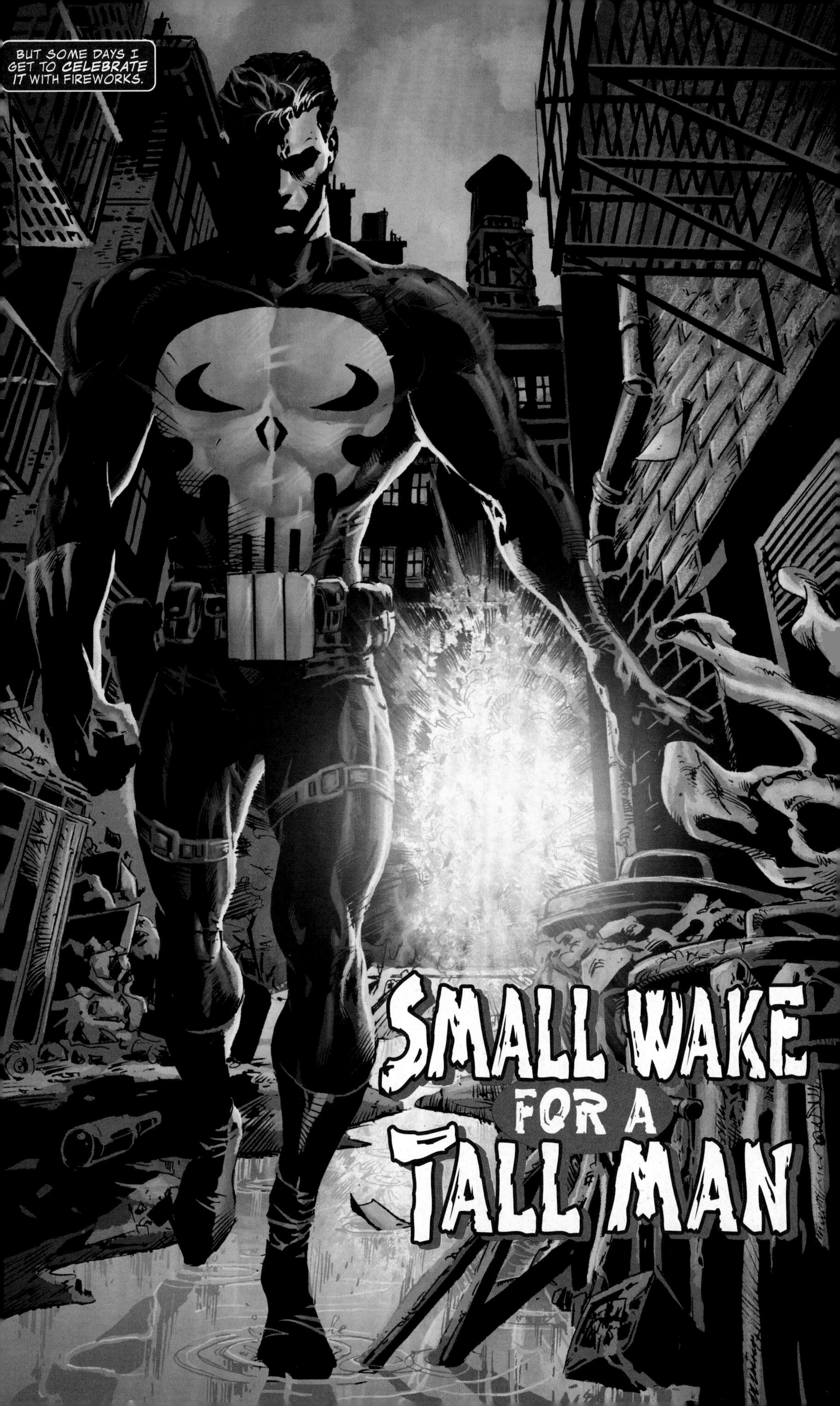
BUT SOME DAYS I GET TO CELEBRATE IT WITH FIREWORKS.
SMALL WAKE FOR A TALL MAN

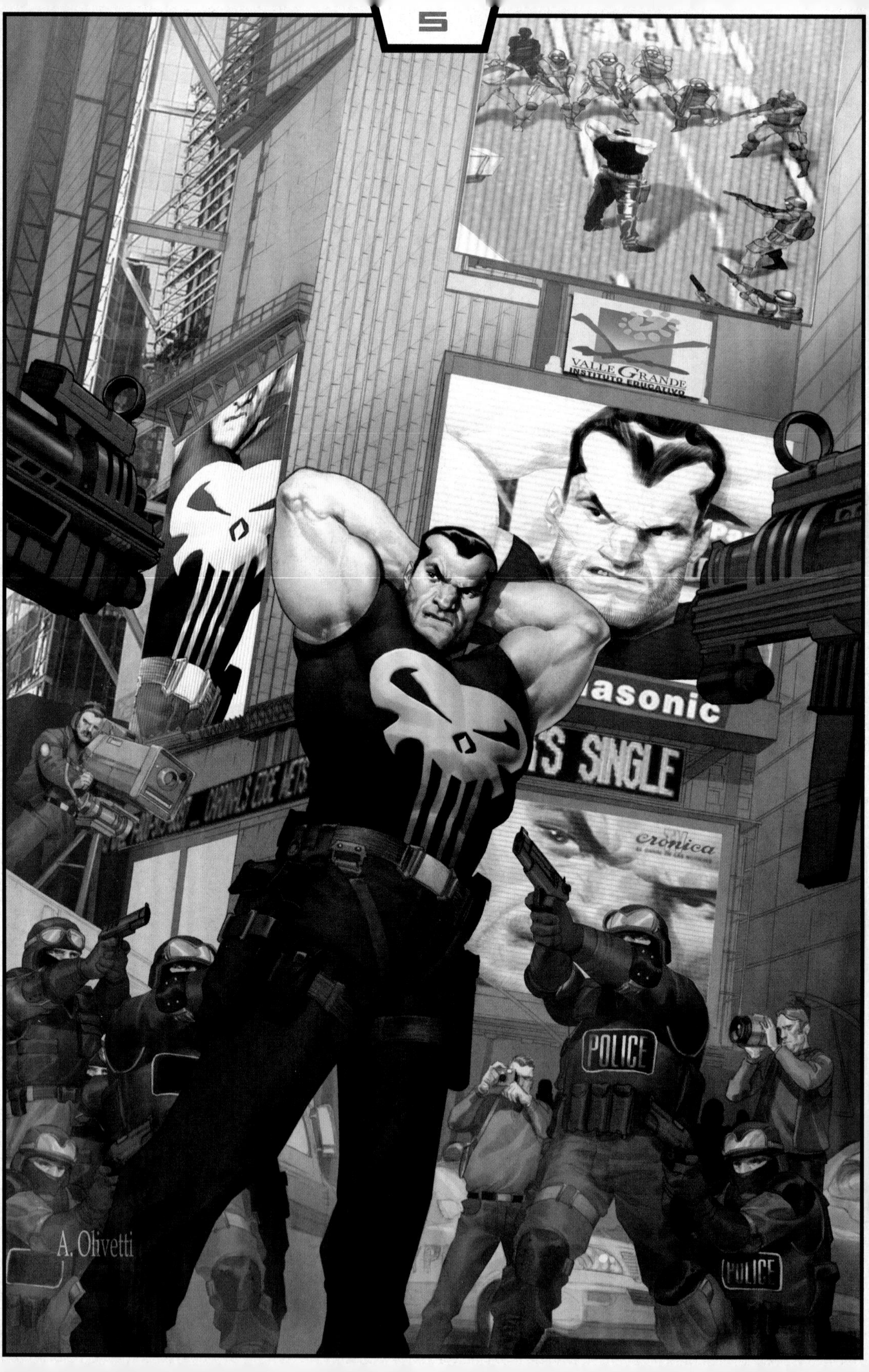
5
VALLE GRANDE
INSTITUTO EDUCATIVO
asonic
TS SINGLE
Crónica
POLICE
POLICE
A. Olivetti

SEPTEMBER 11, 2001.

A LOT OF PEOPLE THOUGHT, WHEN WE FLEW ALL THOSE FLAGS, IT WAS SOME KIND OF *YAY AMERICA* THING.

IT WASN'T. NOT *REALLY*.

IT WAS US SAYING TO THE *COPS* AND THE *FIREMEN* THAT WERE DOWN THERE--HEY. WE'RE *WITH YOU*.

COPS AND FIREMEN DON'T HAVE FLAGS OF THEIR OWN, YOU KNOW?

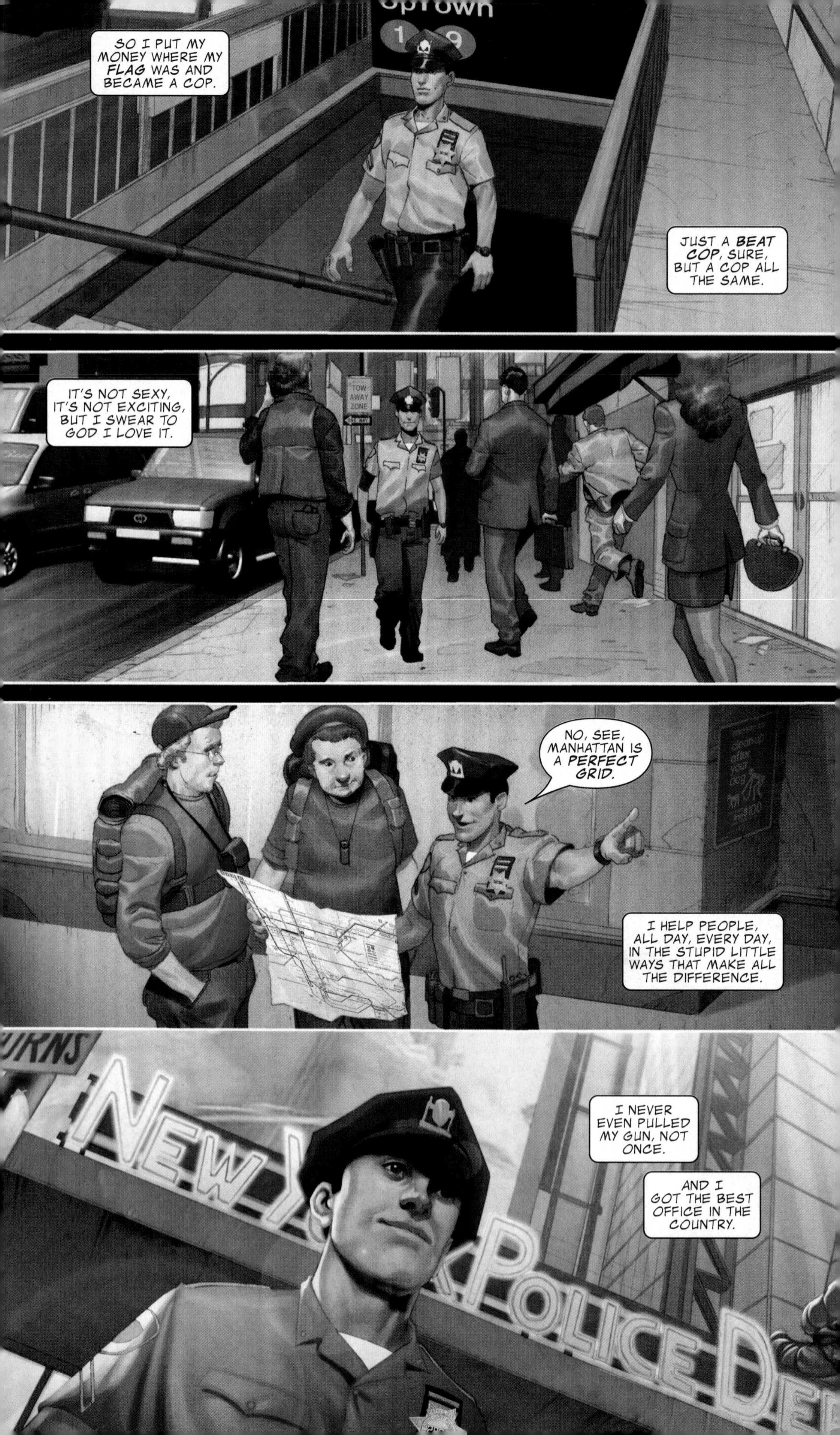

Uptown
1 9
SO I PUT MY MONEY WHERE MY FLAG WAS AND BECAME A COP.
JUST A BEAT COP, SURE, BUT A COP ALL THE SAME.
TOW AWAY ZONE
ONE WAY
IT'S NOT SEXY, IT'S NOT EXCITING, BUT I SWEAR TO GOD I LOVE IT.
NO, SEE, MANHATTAN IS A PERFECT GRID.
cleanup after your dog
I HELP PEOPLE, ALL DAY, EVERY DAY, IN THE STUPID LITTLE WAYS THAT MAKE ALL THE DIFFERENCE.
I NEVER EVEN PULLED MY GUN, NOT ONCE.
AND I GOT THE BEST OFFICE IN THE COUNTRY.

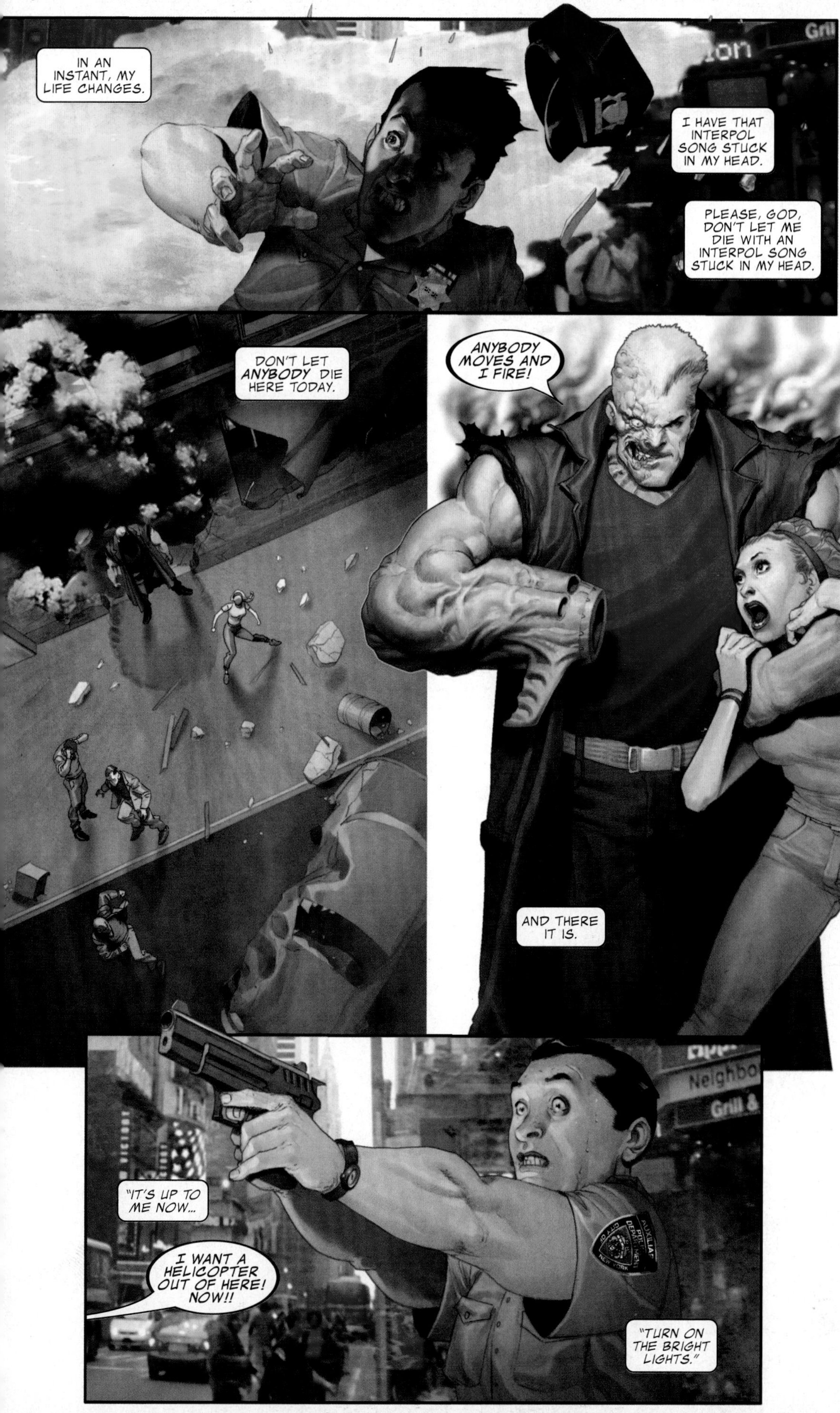
IN AN INSTANT, MY LIFE CHANGES.
I HAVE THAT INTERPOL SONG STUCK IN MY HEAD.
PLEASE, GOD, DON'T LET ME DIE WITH AN INTERPOL SONG STUCK IN MY HEAD.
DON'T LET ANYBODY DIE HERE TODAY.
ANYBODY MOVES AND I FIRE!
AND THERE IT IS.
"IT'S UP TO ME NOW...
I WANT A HELICOPTER OUT OF HERE! NOW!!
"TURN ON THE BRIGHT LIGHTS."

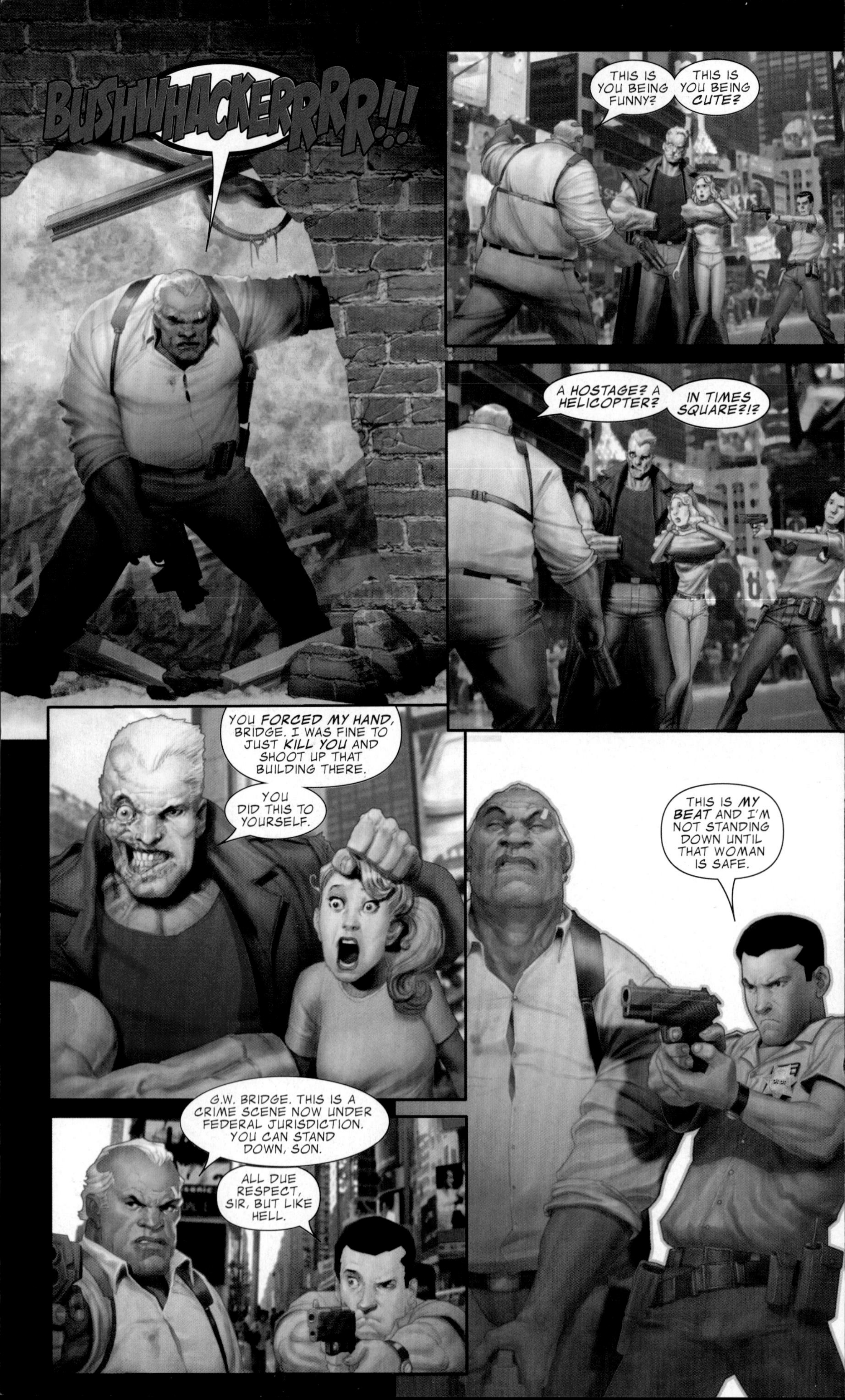
BUSHWHACKERRRR!!!
THIS IS YOU BEING FUNNY?
THIS IS YOU BEING CUTE?
A HOSTAGE? A HELICOPTER?
IN TIMES SQUARE?!?
YOU FORCED MY HAND, BRIDGE. I WAS FINE TO JUST KILL YOU AND SHOOT UP THAT BUILDING THERE.
YOU DID THIS TO YOURSELF.
G.W. BRIDGE. THIS IS A CRIME SCENE NOW UNDER FEDERAL JURISDICTION. YOU CAN STAND DOWN, SON.
ALL DUE RESPECT, SIR, BUT LIKE HELL.
THIS IS MY BEAT AND I'M NOT STANDING DOWN UNTIL THAT WOMAN IS SAFE.

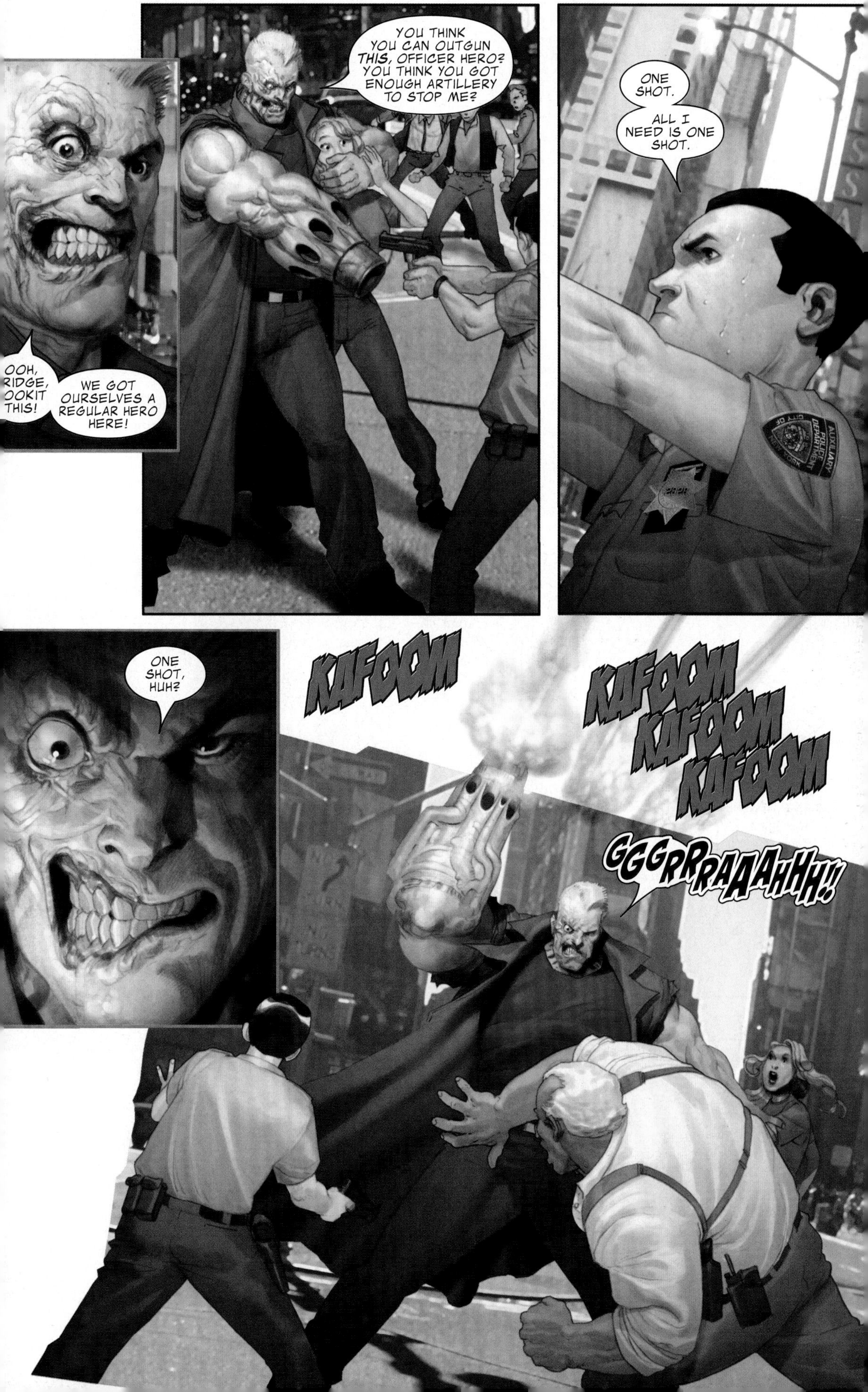
OOH, RIDGE, LOOKIT THIS!
WE GOT OURSELVES A REGULAR HERO HERE!
YOU THINK YOU CAN OUTGUN THIS, OFFICER HERO? YOU THINK YOU GOT ENOUGH ARTILLERY TO STOP ME?
ONE SHOT.
ALL I NEED IS ONE SHOT.
ONE SHOT, HUH?
KAFOOM
KAFOOM KAFOOM KAFOOM
GGGRRRAAAHHH!!

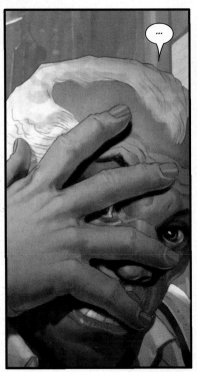

...

HEH.

YOU FLINCHED AT ALL *FOUR* SHOTS, SUPERCOP.

IT'S *BRIDGE.* I CAN'T IMAGINE EVERY PHONE IN *MIDTOWN* ISN'T DIALING 911 RIGHT NOW, BUT YOU GUYS ARE GONNA WANT TO GET A COUPLE DOZEN *CAPEKILLER* SQUADS DOWN TO TIMES SQUARE.

OOH-HOO-HOO, LOOK WHO DIDN'T *FLINCH.*

BUT, C'MON, IF YOU DIDN'T SHOOT ME AFTER *THAT,* WHAT'S IT GONNA ACTUALLY *TAKE?*

HARM ONE HAIR ON HER HEAD.

MAYBE YOU WOULD, LAW-MAN. MAYBE YOU WOULD.

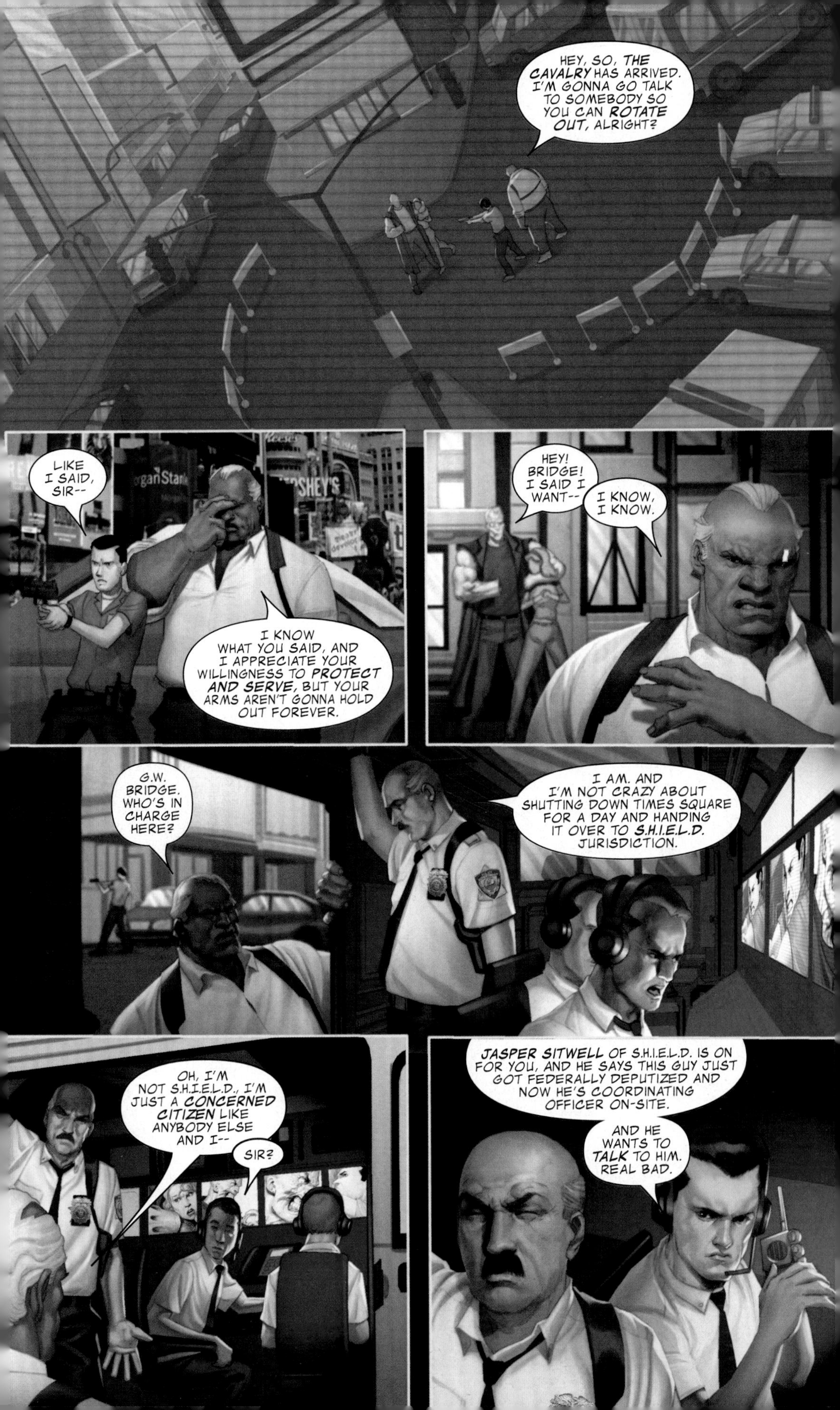
HEY, SO, THE CAVALRY HAS ARRIVED. I'M GONNA GO TALK TO SOMEBODY SO YOU CAN ROTATE OUT, ALRIGHT?
LIKE I SAID, SIR--
I KNOW WHAT YOU SAID, AND I APPRECIATE YOUR WILLINGNESS TO PROTECT AND SERVE, BUT YOUR ARMS AREN'T GONNA HOLD OUT FOREVER.
HEY! BRIDGE! I SAID I WANT--
I KNOW, I KNOW.
G.W. BRIDGE. WHO'S IN CHARGE HERE?
I AM. AND I'M NOT CRAZY ABOUT SHUTTING DOWN TIMES SQUARE FOR A DAY AND HANDING IT OVER TO S.H.I.E.L.D. JURISDICTION.
OH, I'M NOT S.H.I.E.L.D., I'M JUST A CONCERNED CITIZEN LIKE ANYBODY ELSE AND I--
SIR?
JASPER SITWELL OF S.H.I.E.L.D. IS ON FOR YOU, AND HE SAYS THIS GUY JUST GOT FEDERALLY DEPUTIZED AND NOW HE'S COORDINATING OFFICER ON-SITE.
AND HE WANTS TO TALK TO HIM. REAL BAD.

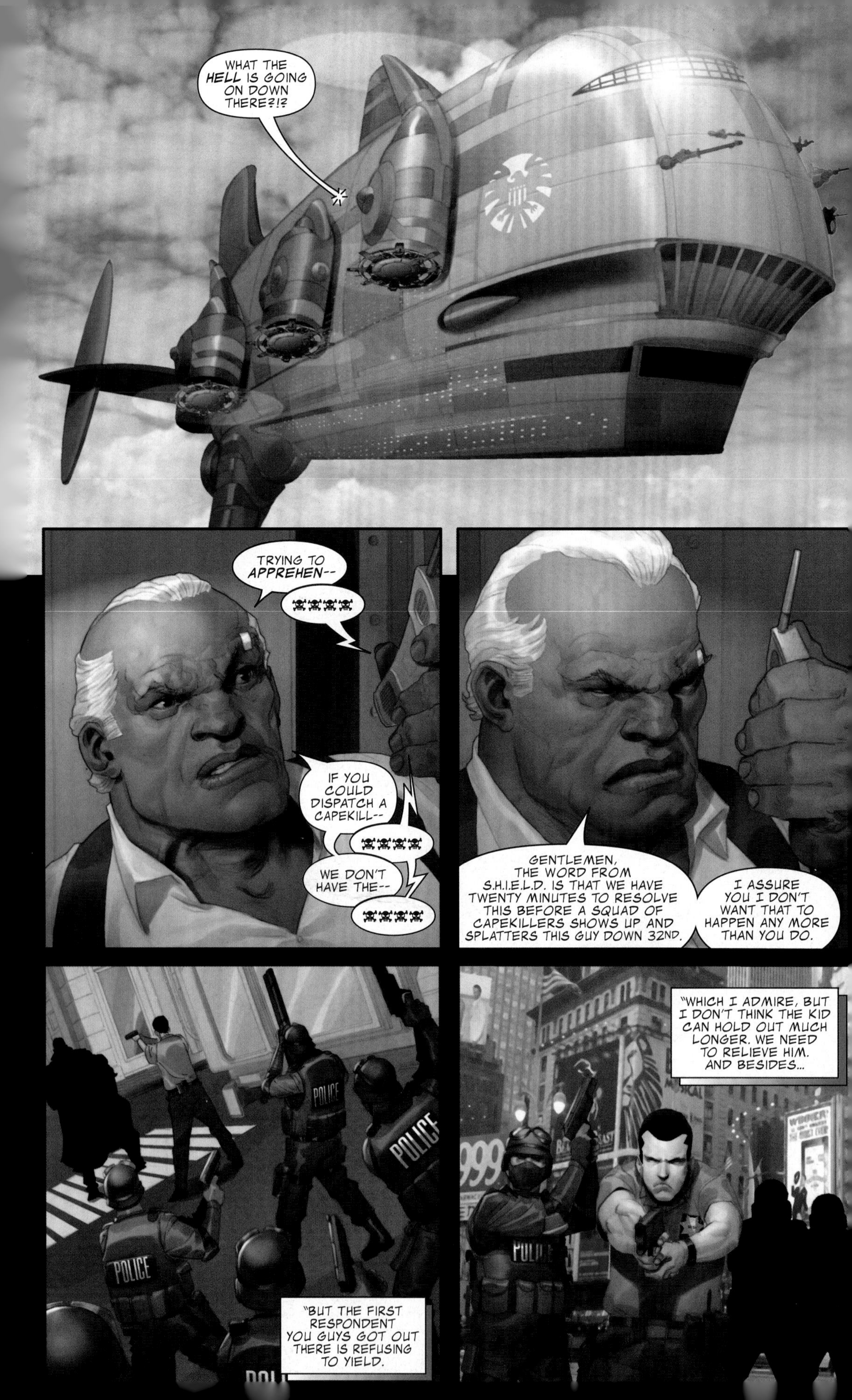

WHAT THE **HELL** IS GOING ON DOWN THERE?!?
TRYING TO *APPREHEN--*
IF YOU COULD DISPATCH A CAPEKILL--
WE DON'T HAVE THE--
GENTLEMEN, THE WORD FROM S.H.I.E.L.D. IS THAT WE HAVE TWENTY MINUTES TO RESOLVE THIS BEFORE A SQUAD OF CAPEKILLERS SHOWS UP AND SPLATTERS THIS GUY DOWN 32ND.
I ASSURE YOU I DON'T WANT THAT TO HAPPEN ANY MORE THAN YOU DO.
"BUT THE FIRST RESPONDENT YOU GUYS GOT OUT THERE IS REFUSING TO YIELD.
"WHICH I ADMIRE, BUT I DON'T THINK THE KID CAN HOLD OUT MUCH LONGER. WE NEED TO RELIEVE HIM. AND BESIDES...

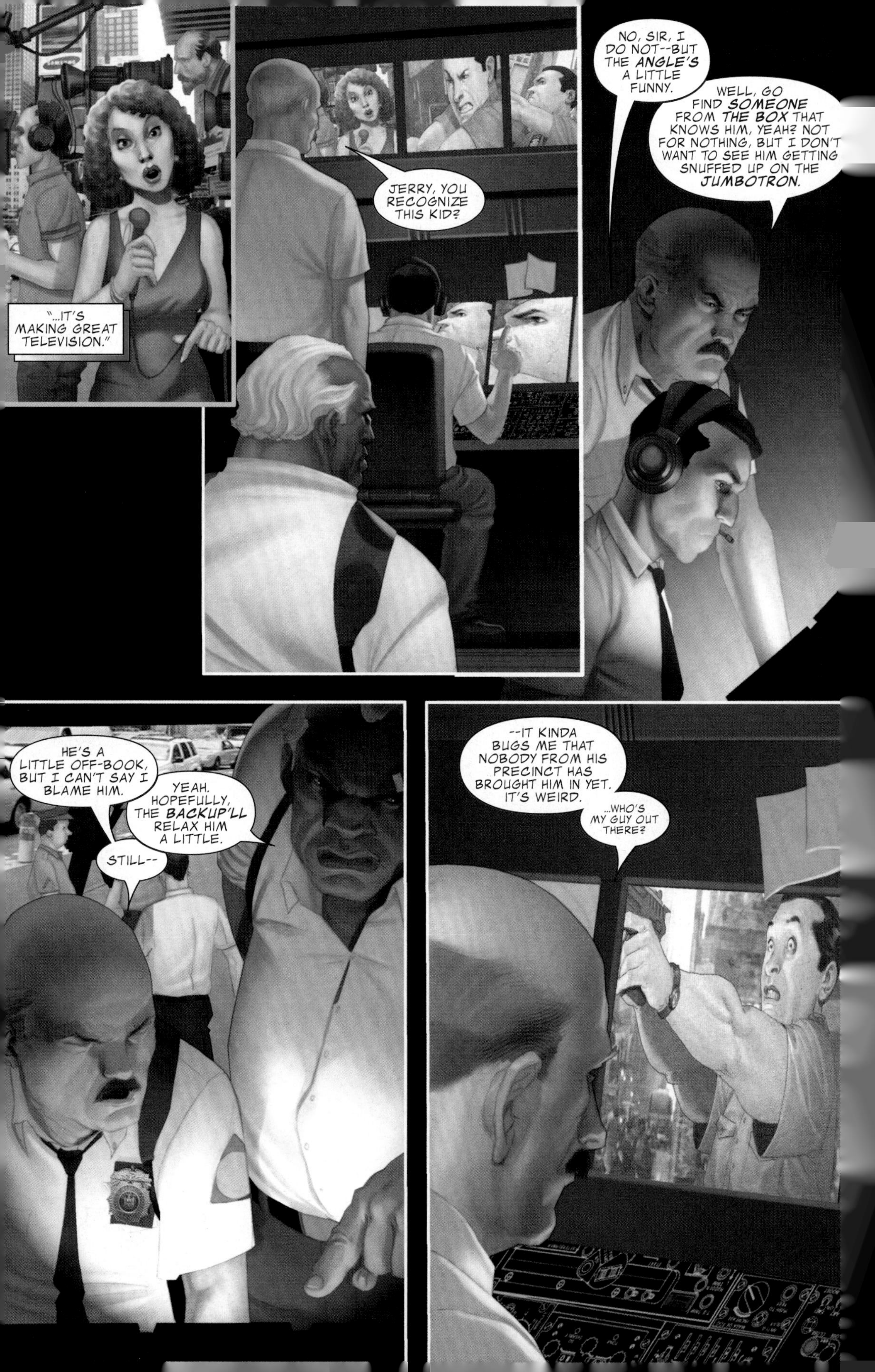
"...IT'S MAKING GREAT TELEVISION."
JERRY, YOU RECOGNIZE THIS KID?
NO, SIR, I DO NOT--BUT THE ANGLE'S A LITTLE FUNNY.
WELL, GO FIND SOMEONE FROM THE BOX THAT KNOWS HIM, YEAH? NOT FOR NOTHING, BUT I DON'T WANT TO SEE HIM GETTING SNUFFED UP ON THE JUMBOTRON.
HE'S A LITTLE OFF-BOOK, BUT I CAN'T SAY I BLAME HIM.
YEAH. HOPEFULLY, THE BACKUP'LL RELAX HIM A LITTLE.
STILL--
--IT KINDA BUGS ME THAT NOBODY FROM HIS PRECINCT HAS BROUGHT HIM IN YET. IT'S WEIRD.
...WHO'S MY GUY OUT THERE?

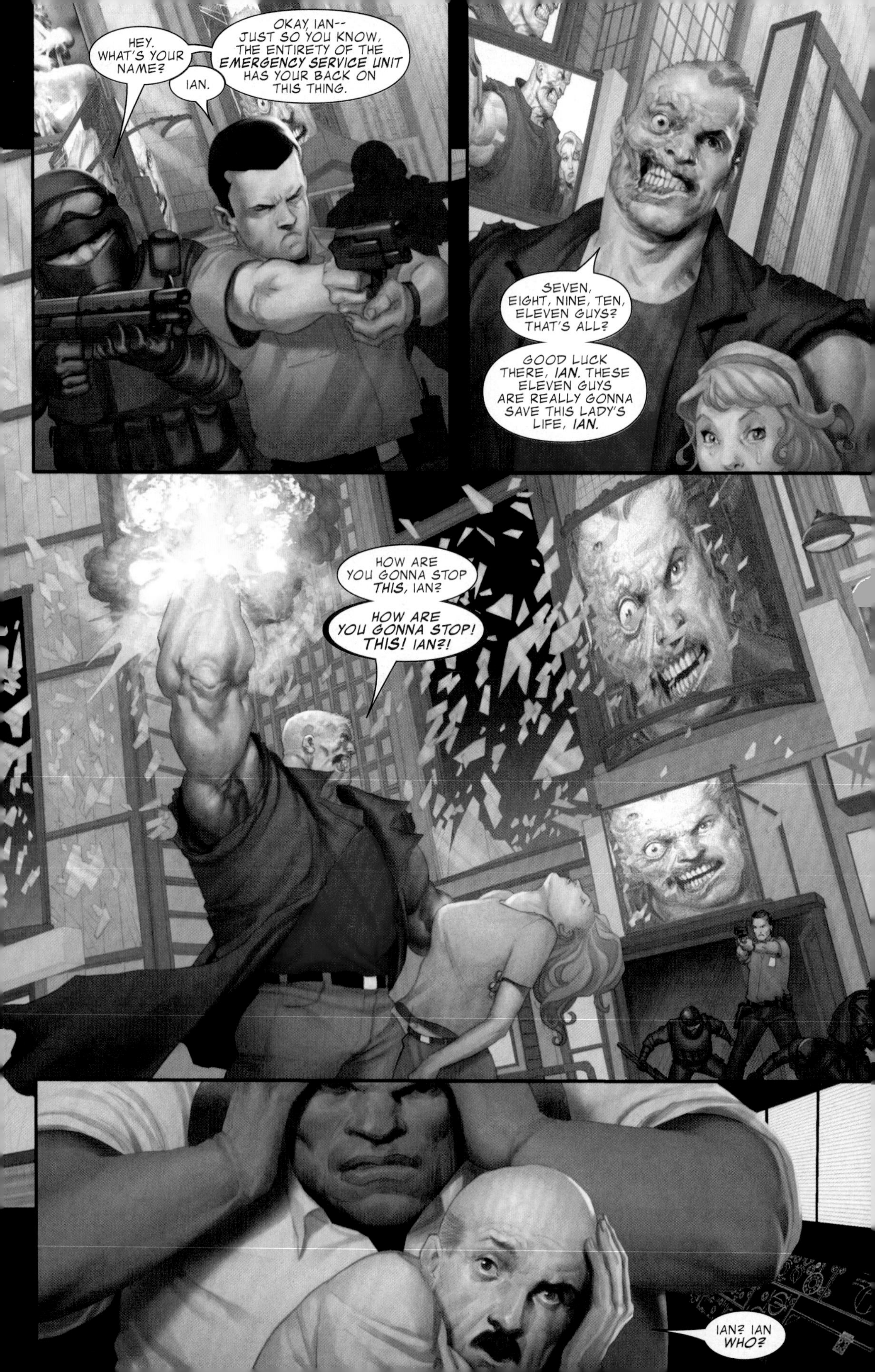
HEY. WHAT'S YOUR NAME?
IAN.
OKAY, IAN-- JUST SO YOU KNOW, THE ENTIRETY OF THE EMERGENCY SERVICE UNIT HAS YOUR BACK ON THIS THING.
SEVEN, EIGHT, NINE, TEN, ELEVEN GUYS? THAT'S ALL?
GOOD LUCK THERE, IAN. THESE ELEVEN GUYS ARE REALLY GONNA SAVE THIS LADY'S LIFE, IAN.
HOW ARE YOU GONNA STOP THIS, IAN?
HOW ARE YOU GONNA STOP! THIS! IAN?!
IAN? IAN WHO?

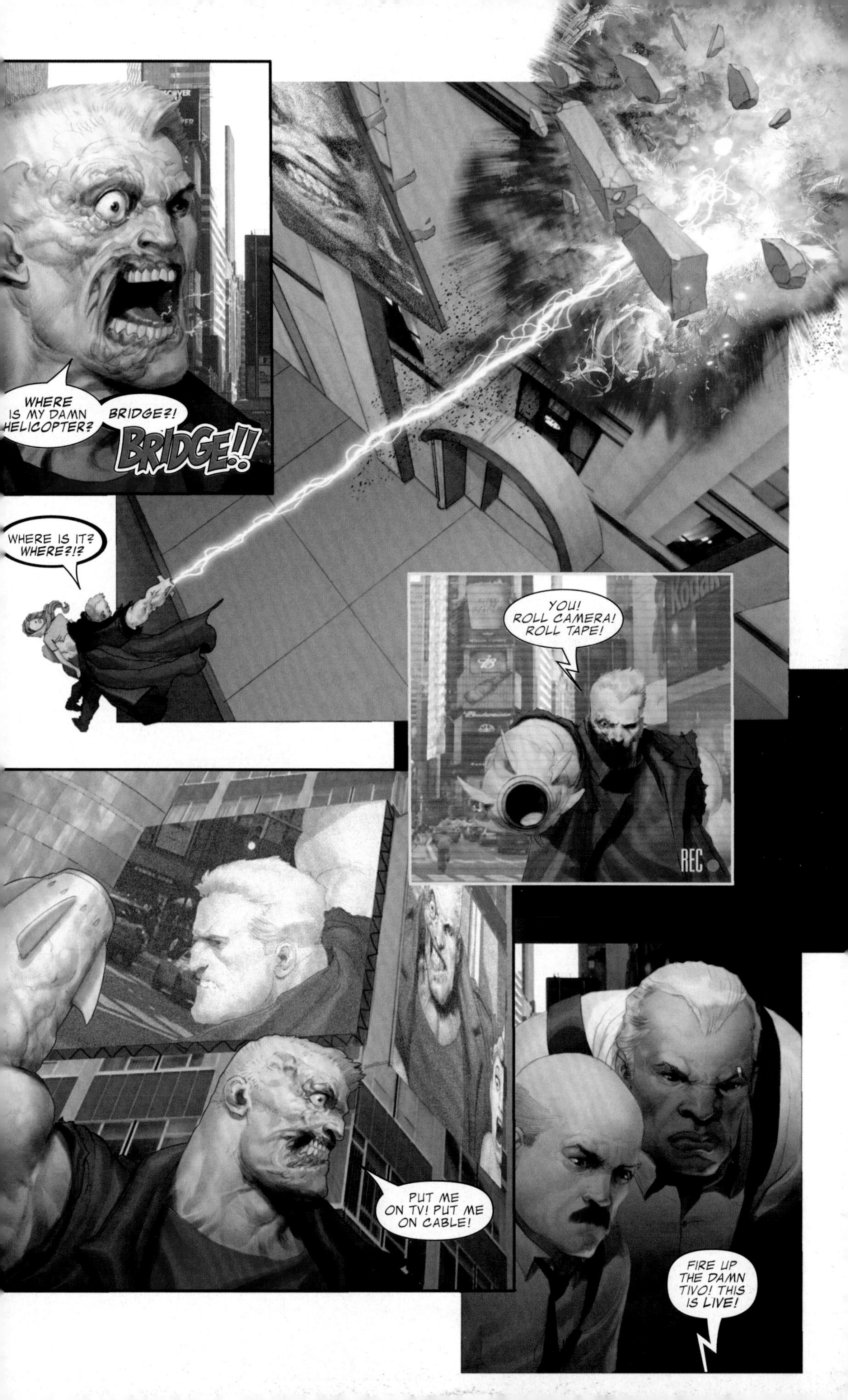
WHERE IS MY DAMN HELICOPTER?
BRIDGE?!
BRIDGE!!
WHERE IS IT? WHERE?!?
YOU! ROLL CAMERA! ROLL TAPE!
REC
PUT ME ON TV! PUT ME ON CABLE!
FIRE UP THE DAMN TIVO! THIS IS LIVE!

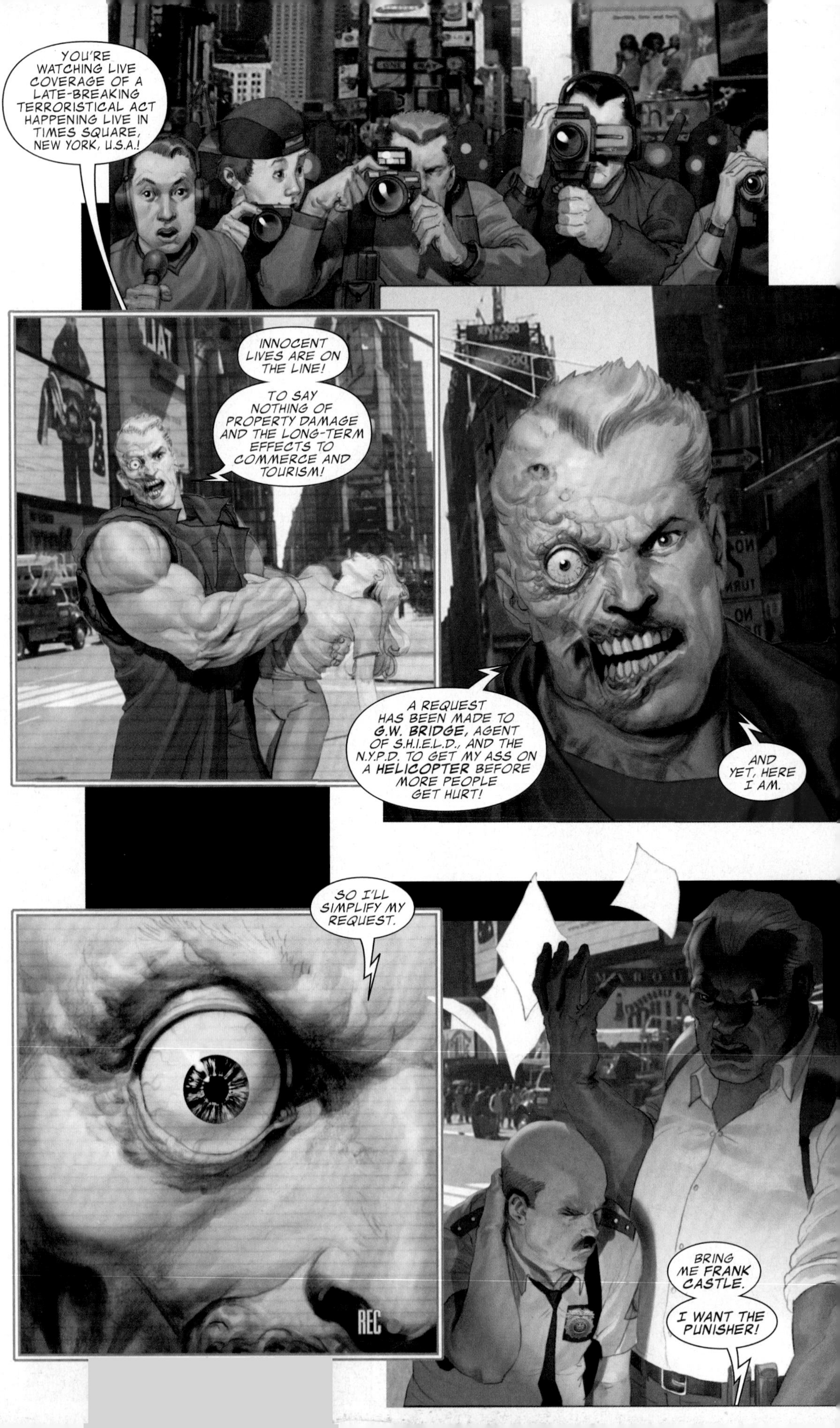
YOU'RE WATCHING LIVE COVERAGE OF A LATE-BREAKING TERRORISTICAL ACT HAPPENING LIVE IN TIMES SQUARE, NEW YORK, U.S.A.!
INNOCENT LIVES ARE ON THE LINE!
TO SAY NOTHING OF PROPERTY DAMAGE AND THE LONG-TERM EFFECTS TO COMMERCE AND TOURISM!
A REQUEST HAS BEEN MADE TO G.W. BRIDGE, AGENT OF S.H.I.E.L.D., AND THE N.Y.P.D. TO GET MY ASS ON A HELICOPTER BEFORE MORE PEOPLE GET HURT!
AND YET, HERE I AM.
SO I'LL SIMPLIFY MY REQUEST.
REC
BRING ME FRANK CASTLE.
I WANT THE PUNISHER!

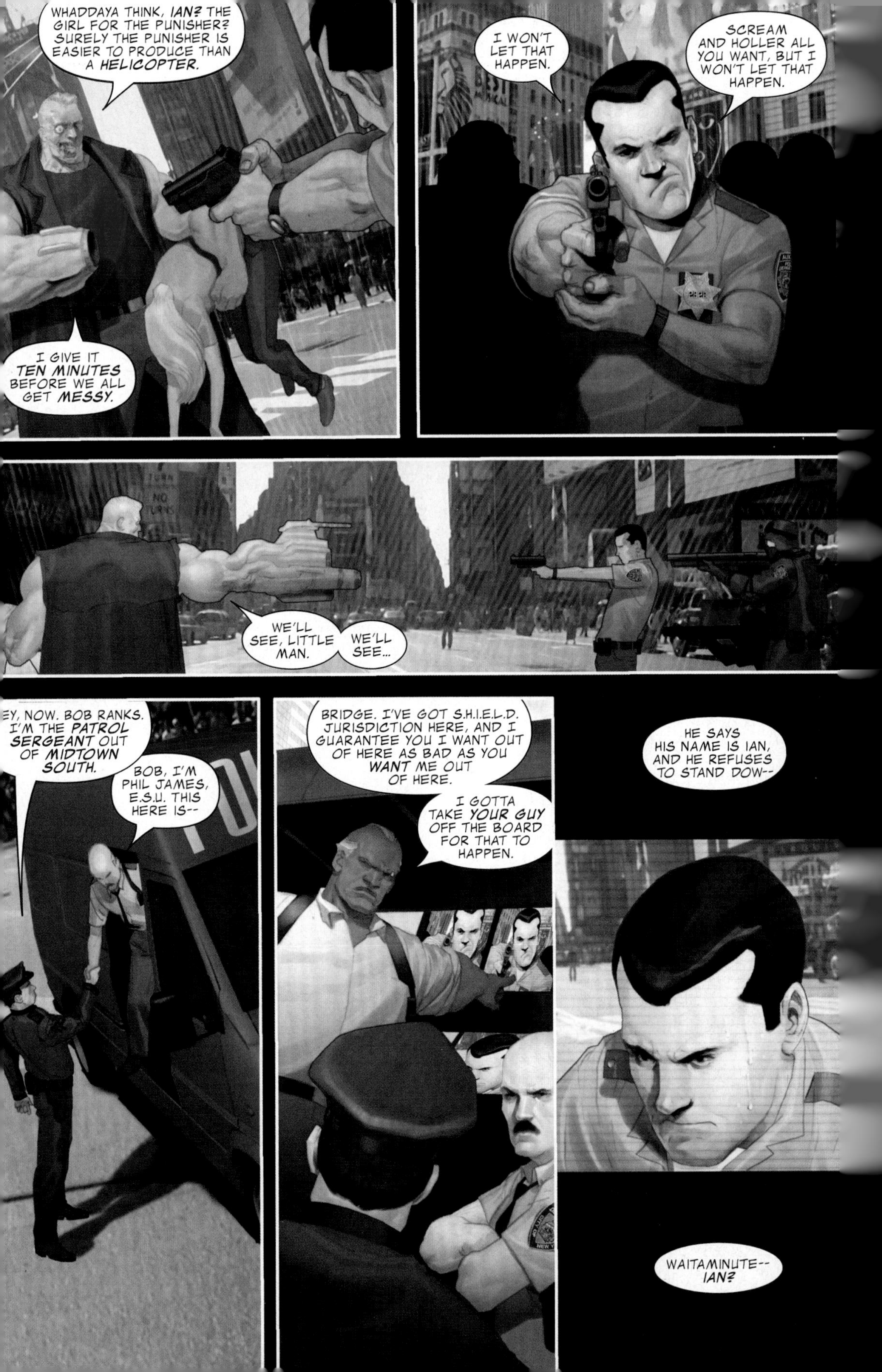
WHADDAYA THINK, IAN? THE GIRL FOR THE PUNISHER? SURELY THE PUNISHER IS EASIER TO PRODUCE THAN A HELICOPTER.
I GIVE IT TEN MINUTES BEFORE WE ALL GET MESSY.
I WON'T LET THAT HAPPEN.
SCREAM AND HOLLER ALL YOU WANT, BUT I WON'T LET THAT HAPPEN.
WE'LL SEE, LITTLE MAN.
WE'LL SEE...
EY, NOW. BOB RANKS. I'M THE PATROL SERGEANT OUT OF MIDTOWN SOUTH.
BOB, I'M PHIL JAMES, E.S.U. THIS HERE IS--
BRIDGE. I'VE GOT S.H.I.E.L.D. JURISDICTION HERE, AND I GUARANTEE YOU I WANT OUT OF HERE AS BAD AS YOU WANT ME OUT OF HERE.
I GOTTA TAKE YOUR GUY OFF THE BOARD FOR THAT TO HAPPEN.
HE SAYS HIS NAME IS IAN, AND HE REFUSES TO STAND DOW--
WAITAMINUTE-- IAN?

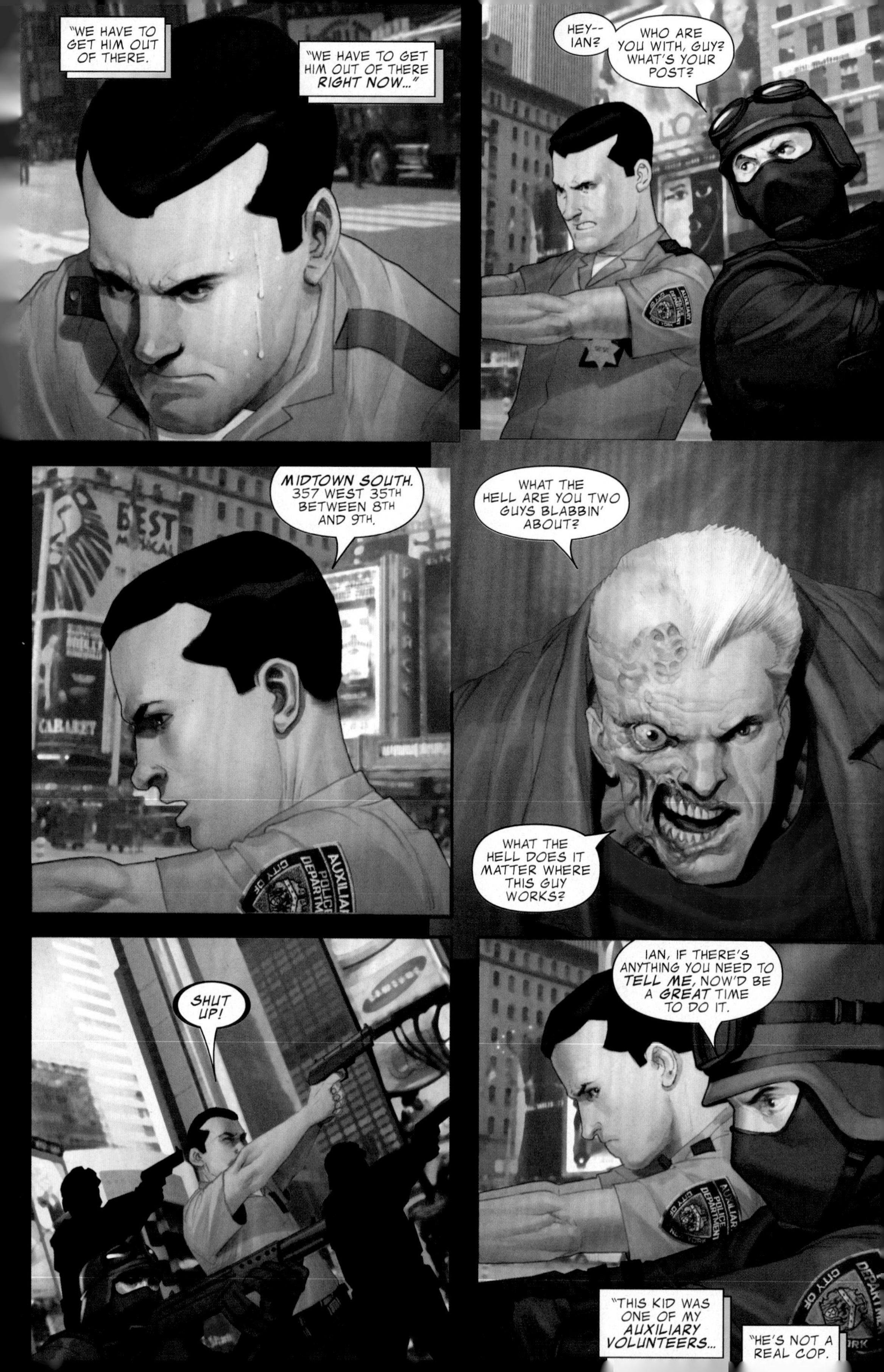

"WE HAVE TO GET HIM OUT OF THERE.
"WE HAVE TO GET HIM OUT OF THERE *RIGHT NOW*..."
HEY-- IAN?
WHO ARE YOU WITH, GUY? WHAT'S YOUR POST?
MIDTOWN SOUTH. 357 WEST 35TH BETWEEN 8TH AND 9TH.
WHAT THE HELL ARE YOU TWO GUYS BLABBIN' ABOUT?
WHAT THE HELL DOES IT MATTER WHERE THIS GUY WORKS?
SHUT UP!
IAN, IF THERE'S ANYTHING YOU NEED TO *TELL ME*, NOW'D BE A *GREAT* TIME TO DO IT.
"THIS KID WAS ONE OF MY *AUXILIARY VOLUNTEERS*...
"HE'S NOT A REAL COP.

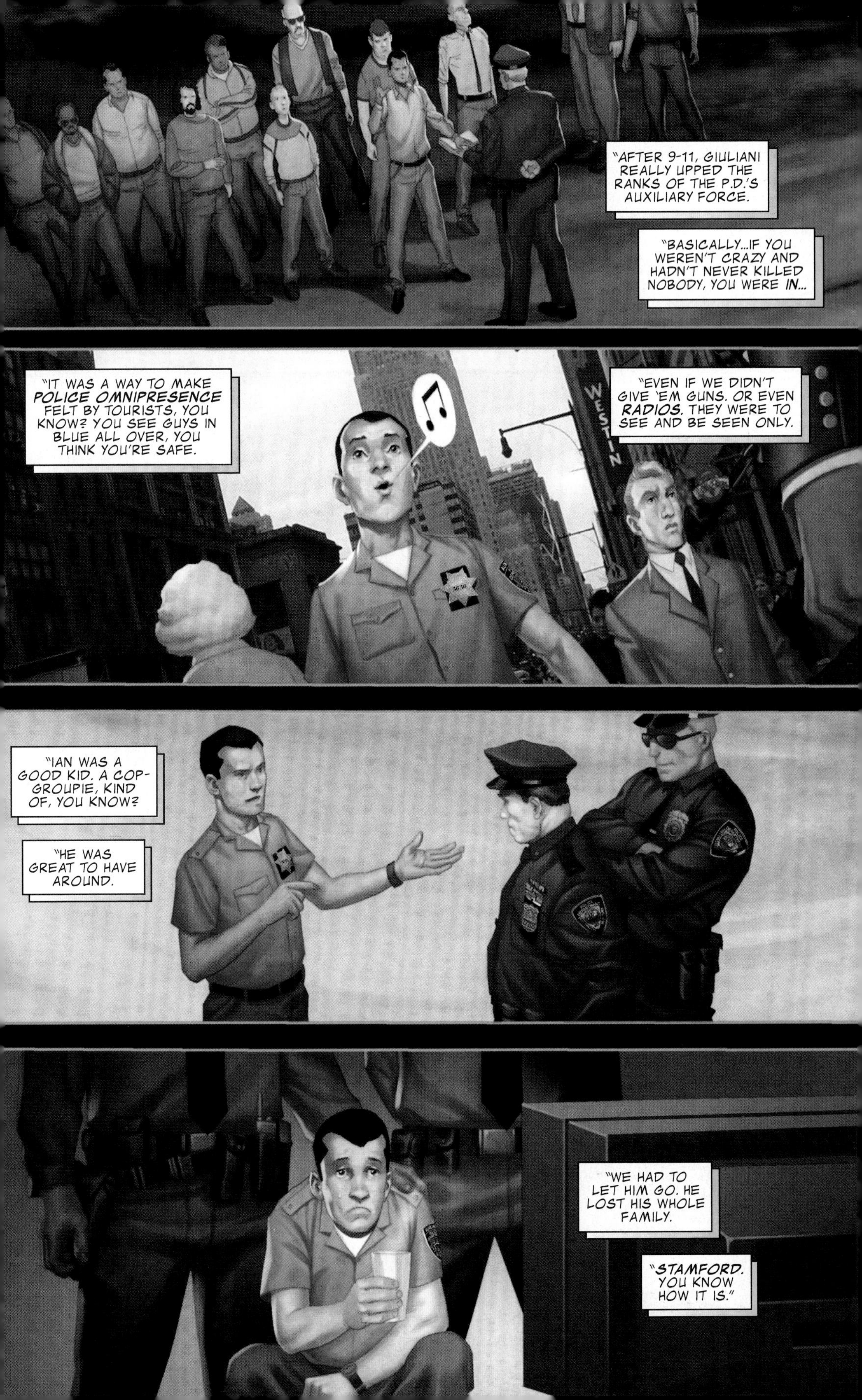
"AFTER 9-11, GIULIANI REALLY UPPED THE RANKS OF THE P.D.'S AUXILIARY FORCE.
"BASICALLY...IF YOU WEREN'T CRAZY AND HADN'T NEVER KILLED NOBODY, YOU WERE IN...
"IT WAS A WAY TO MAKE POLICE OMNIPRESENCE FELT BY TOURISTS, YOU KNOW? YOU SEE GUYS IN BLUE ALL OVER, YOU THINK YOU'RE SAFE.
"EVEN IF WE DIDN'T GIVE 'EM GUNS. OR EVEN RADIOS. THEY WERE TO SEE AND BE SEEN ONLY.
WESTIN
"IAN WAS A GOOD KID. A COP-GROUPIE, KIND OF, YOU KNOW?
"HE WAS GREAT TO HAVE AROUND.
"WE HAD TO LET HIM GO. HE LOST HIS WHOLE FAMILY.
"STAMFORD. YOU KNOW HOW IT IS."

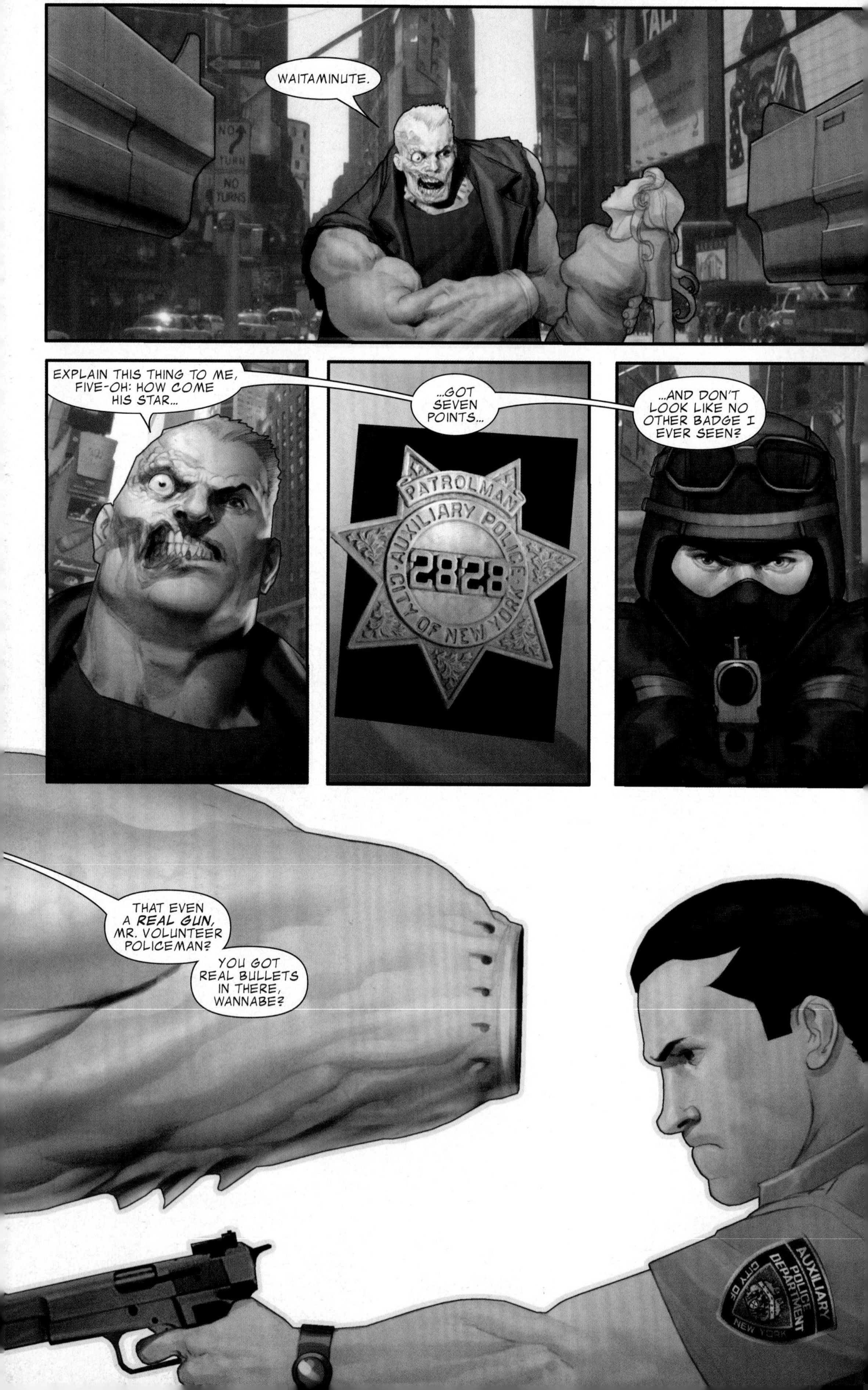
WAITAMINUTE.
NO TURN
NO TURNS
EXPLAIN THIS THING TO ME, FIVE-OH: HOW COME HIS STAR...
...GOT SEVEN POINTS...
...AND DON'T LOOK LIKE NO OTHER BADGE I EVER SEEN?
PATROLMAN
AUXILIARY POLICE
2828
CITY OF NEW YORK
THAT EVEN A REAL GUN, MR. VOLUNTEER POLICEMAN?
YOU GOT REAL BULLETS IN THERE, WANNABE?
AUXILIARY POLICE DEPARTMENT
CITY OF NEW YORK

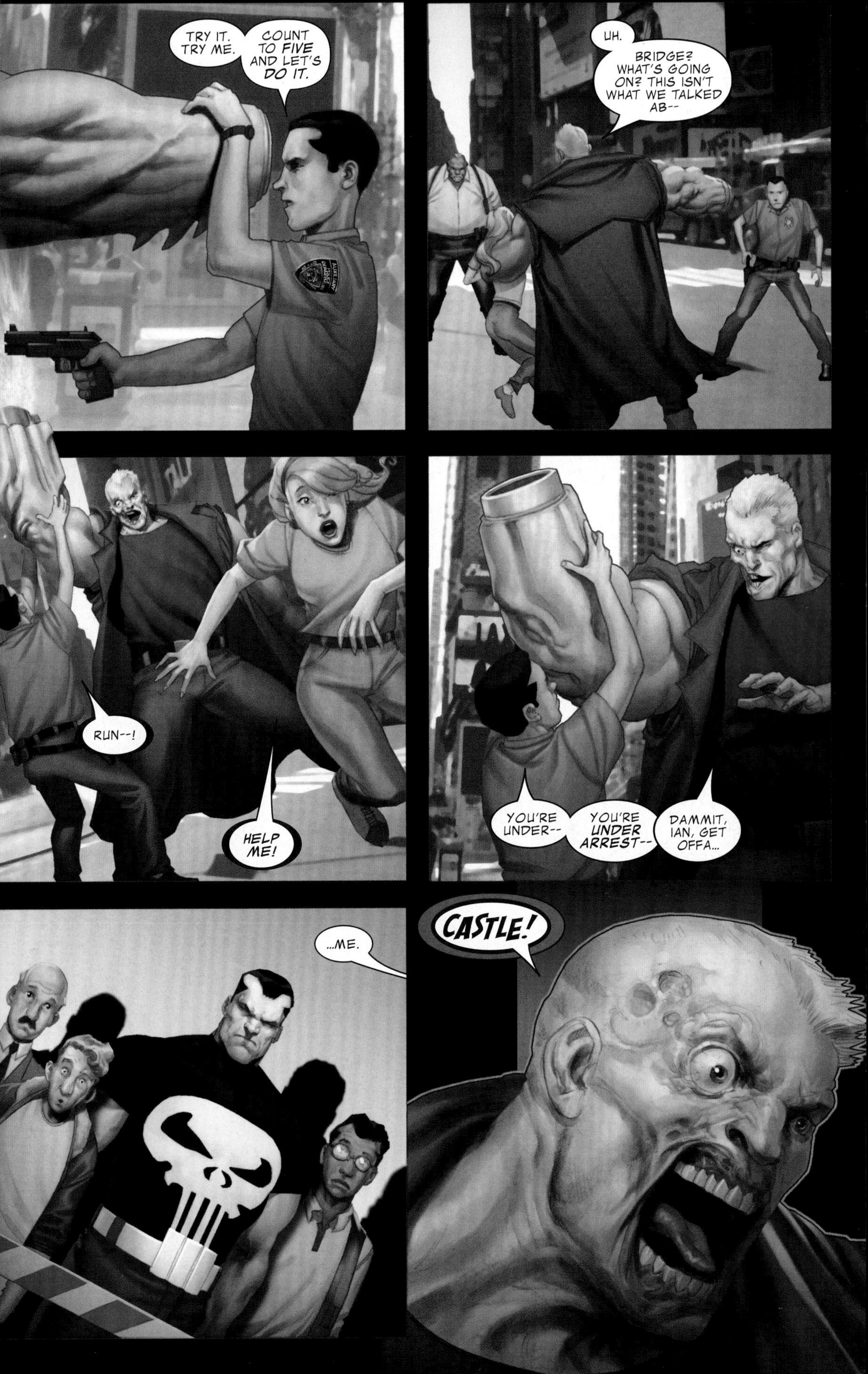
TRY IT. TRY ME.
COUNT TO FIVE AND LET'S DO IT.
UH.
BRIDGE? WHAT'S GOING ON? THIS ISN'T WHAT WE TALKED AB--
RUN--!
HELP ME!
YOU'RE UNDER--
YOU'RE UNDER ARREST--
DAMMIT, IAN, GET OFFA...
...ME.
CASTLE!

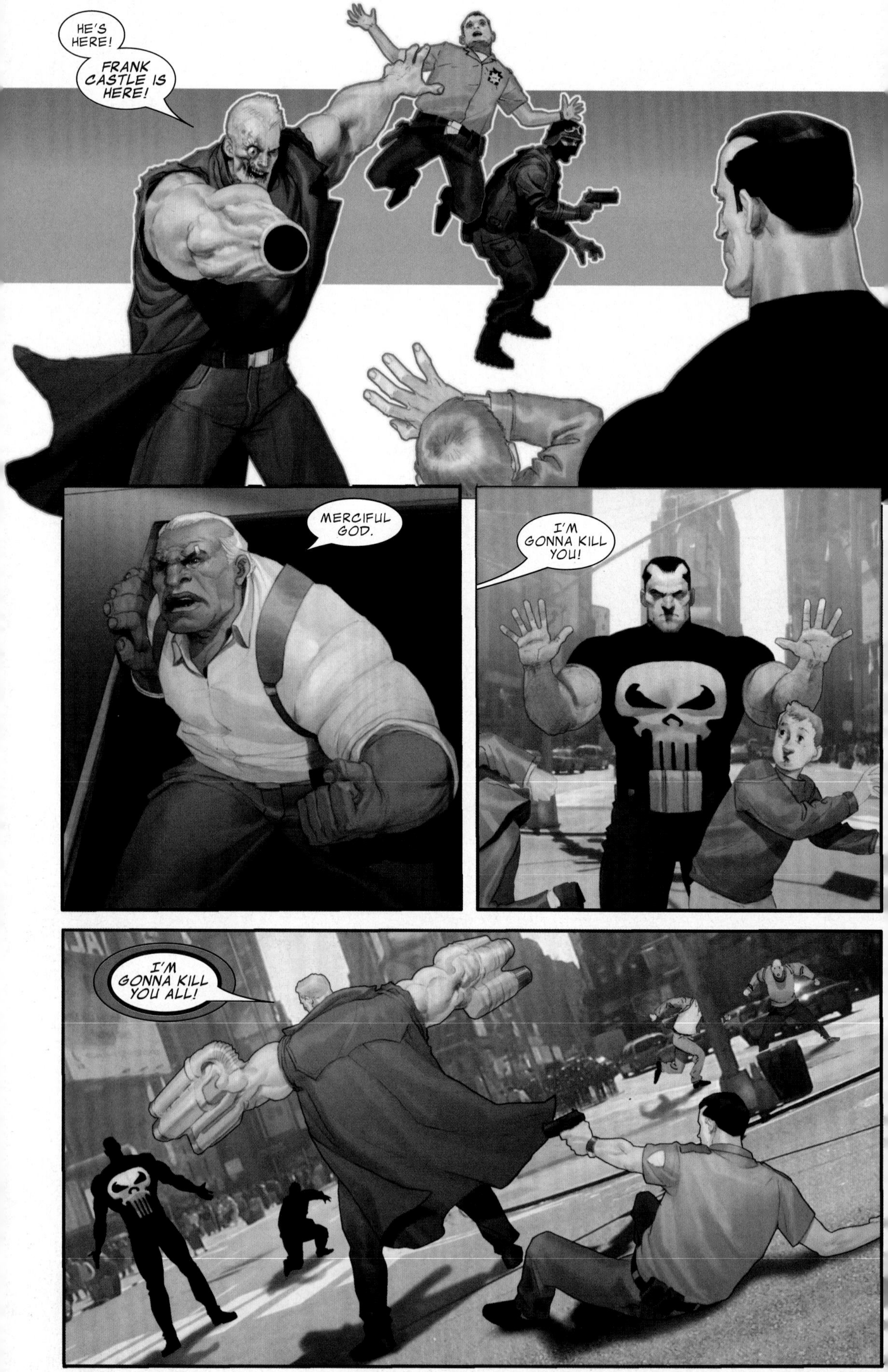
HE'S HERE!
FRANK CASTLE IS HERE!
MERCIFUL GOD.
I'M GONNA KILL YOU!
I'M GONNA KILL YOU ALL!

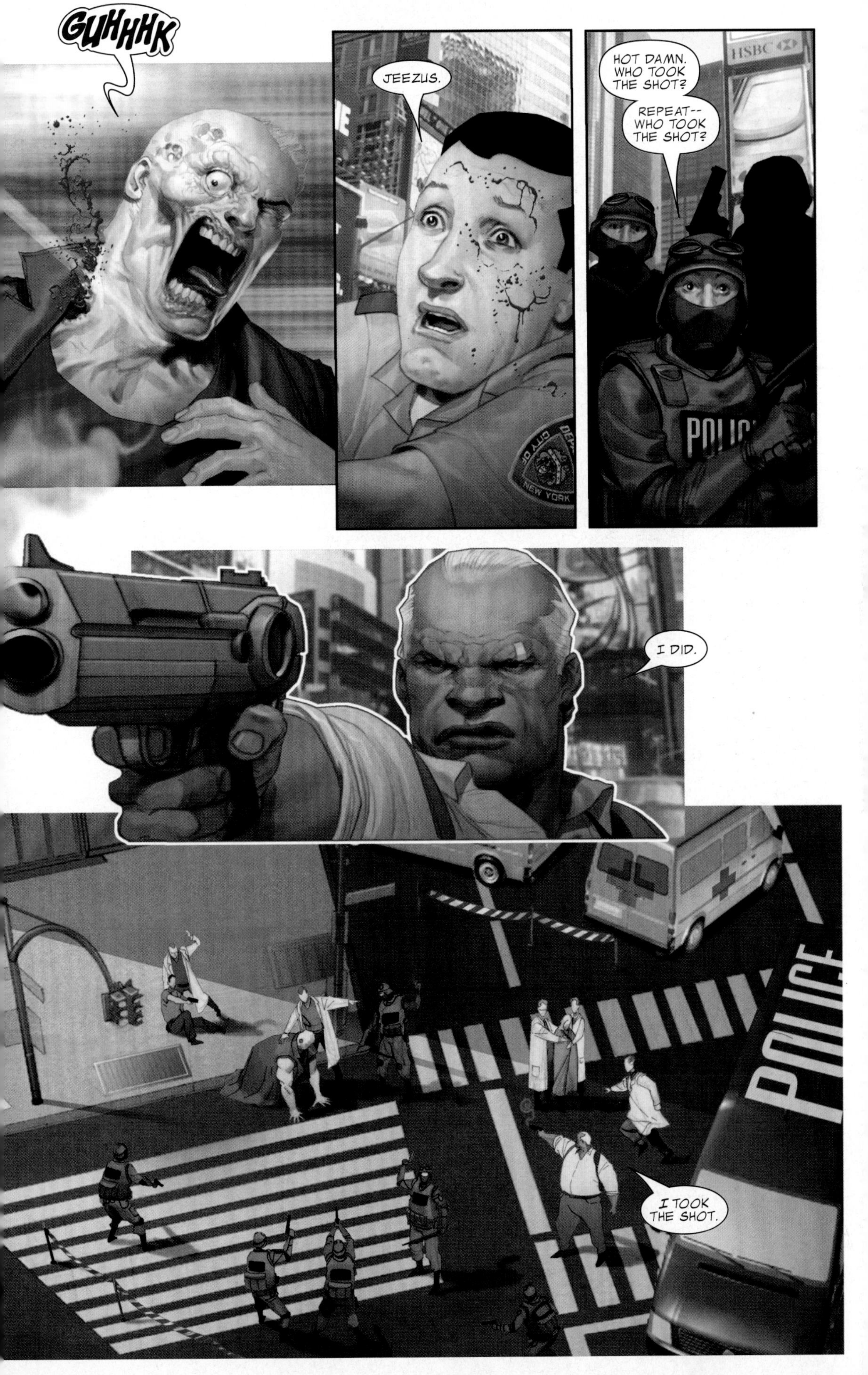
GUHHHK
JEEZUS.
HOT DAMN. WHO TOOK THE SHOT?
REPEAT-- WHO TOOK THE SHOT?
HSBC
POLICE
I DID.
POLICE
I TOOK THE SHOT.

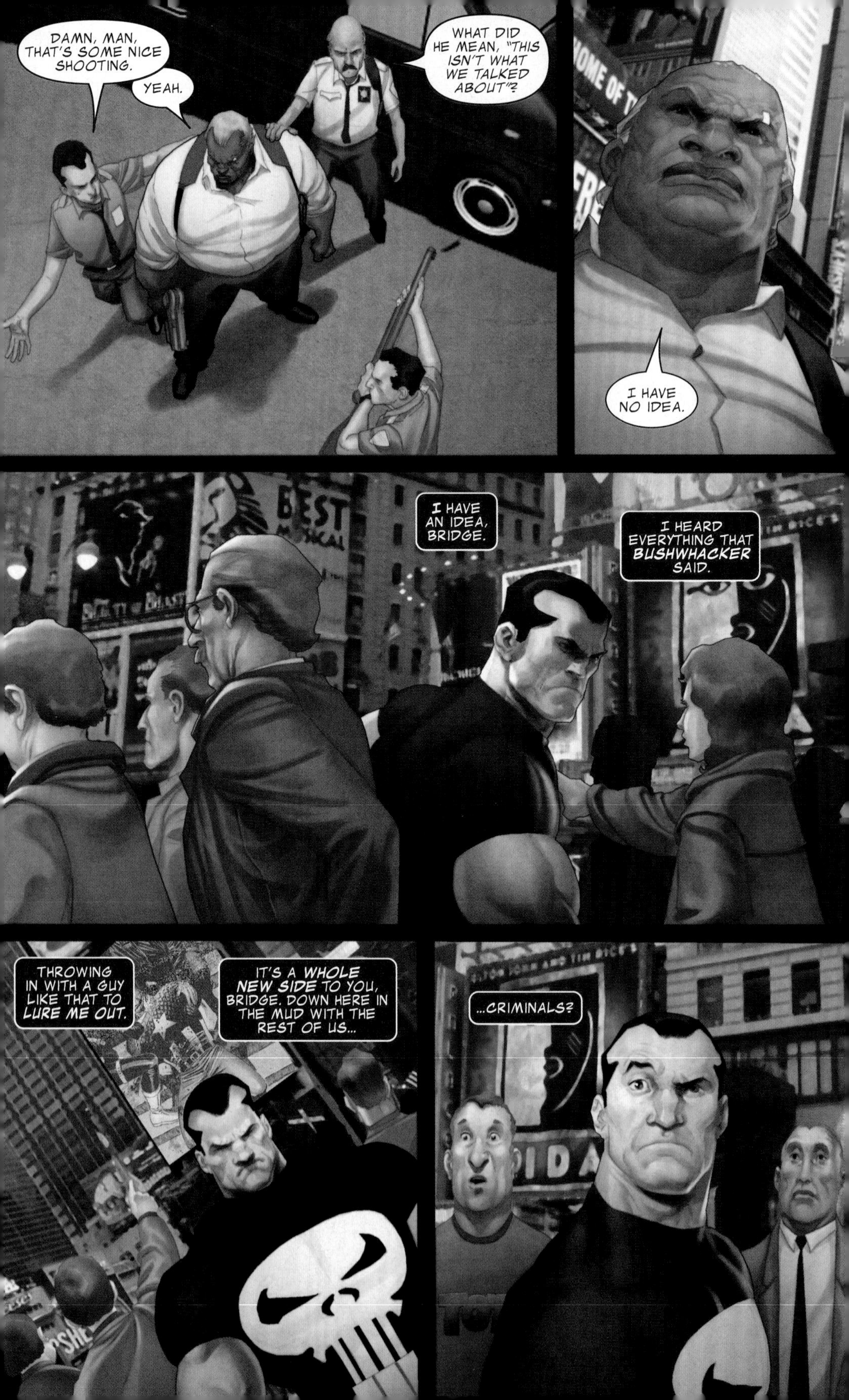

DAMN, MAN, THAT'S SOME NICE SHOOTING.
YEAH.
WHAT DID HE MEAN, "THIS ISN'T WHAT WE TALKED ABOUT"?
I HAVE NO IDEA.
I HAVE AN IDEA, BRIDGE.
I HEARD EVERYTHING THAT BUSHWHACKER SAID.
THROWING IN WITH A GUY LIKE THAT TO LURE ME OUT.
IT'S A WHOLE NEW SIDE TO YOU, BRIDGE. DOWN HERE IN THE MUD WITH THE REST OF US...
...CRIMINALS?

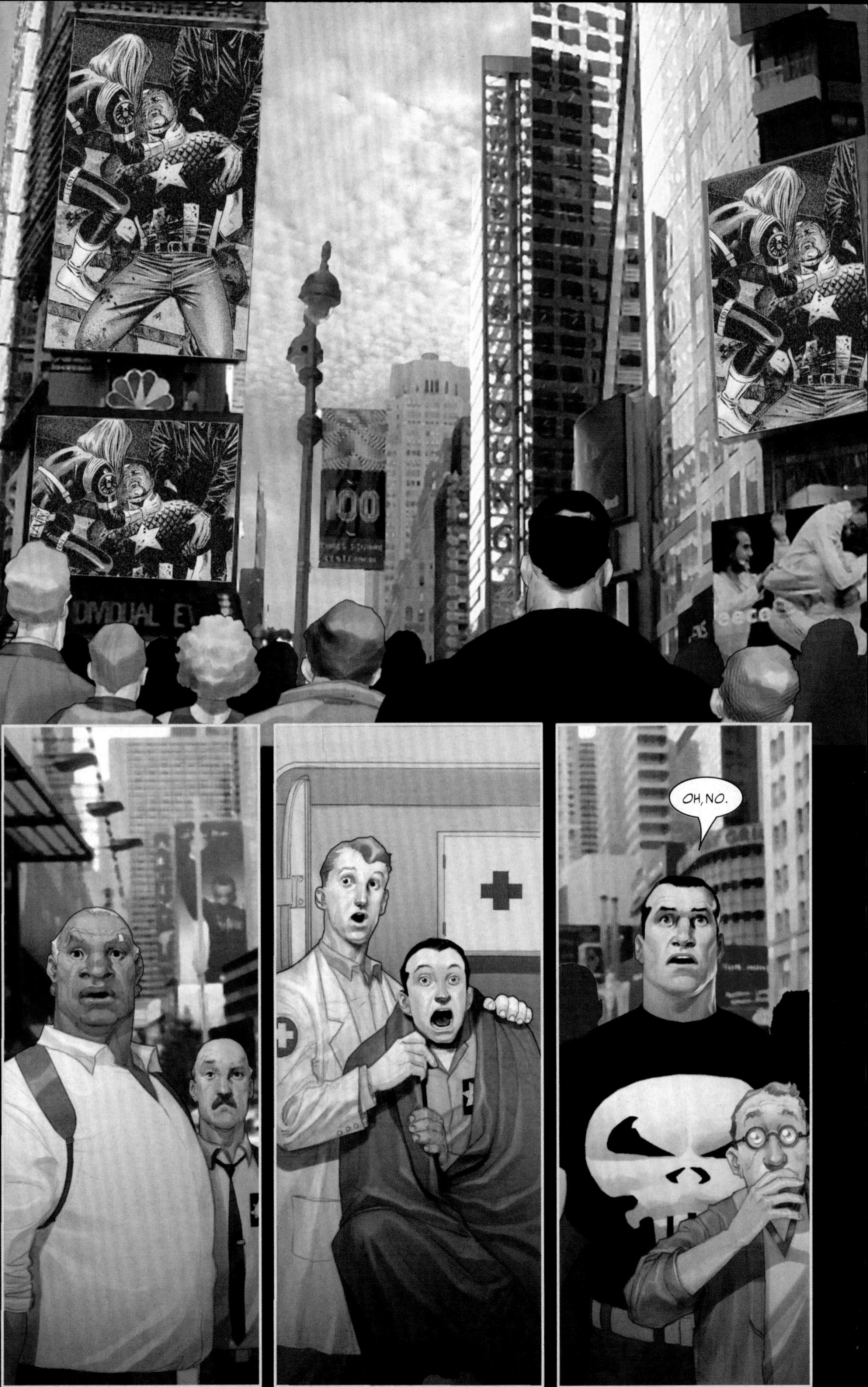
OH, NO.

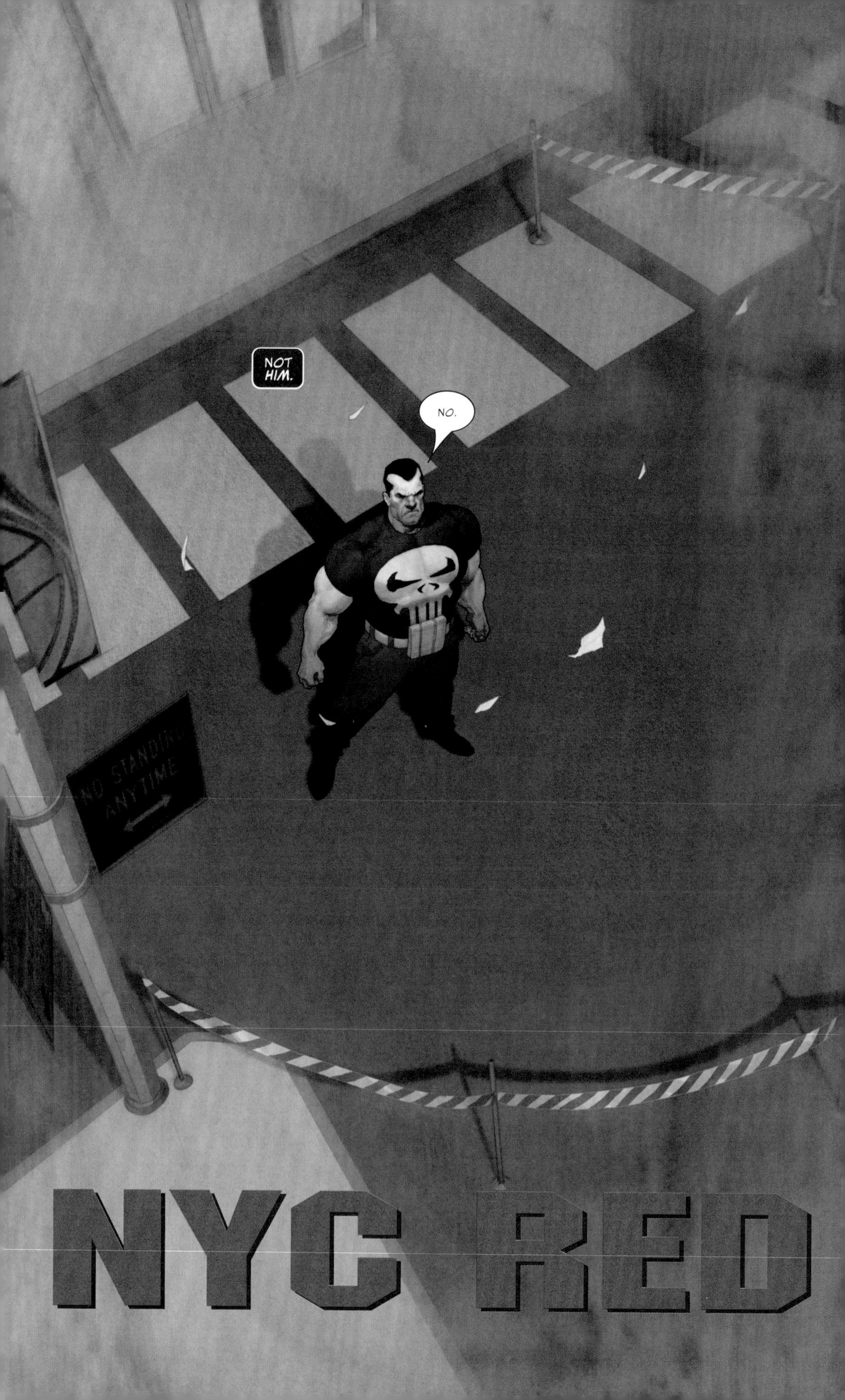
NOT HIM.
NO.
NO STANDING ANYTIME
NYC RED

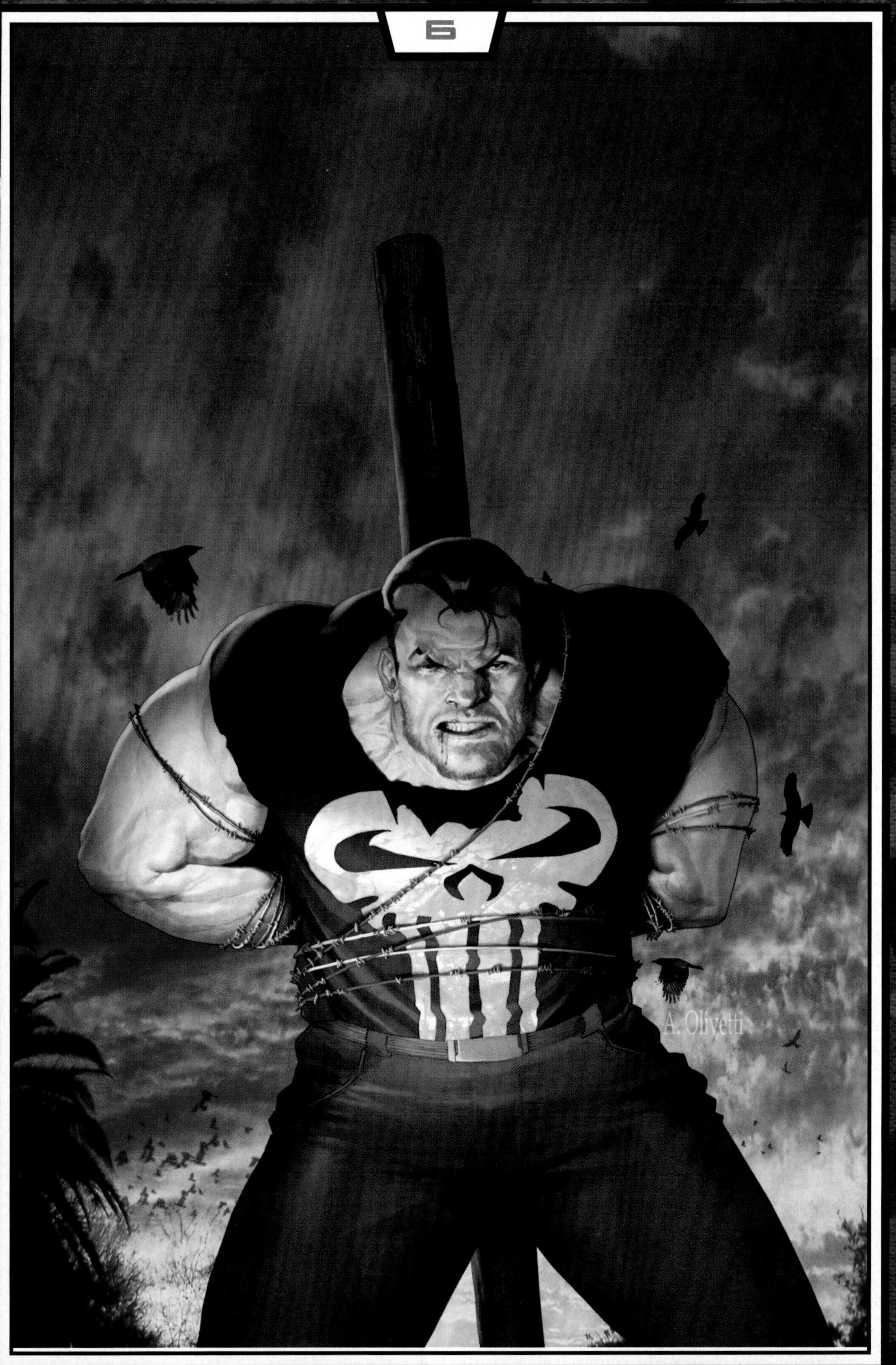
6
A. Olivetti

GOIN' OUT WEST

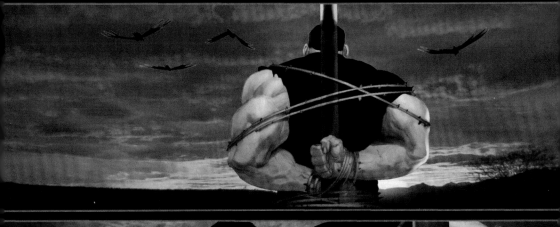

I'M GONNA DIE OUT HERE.

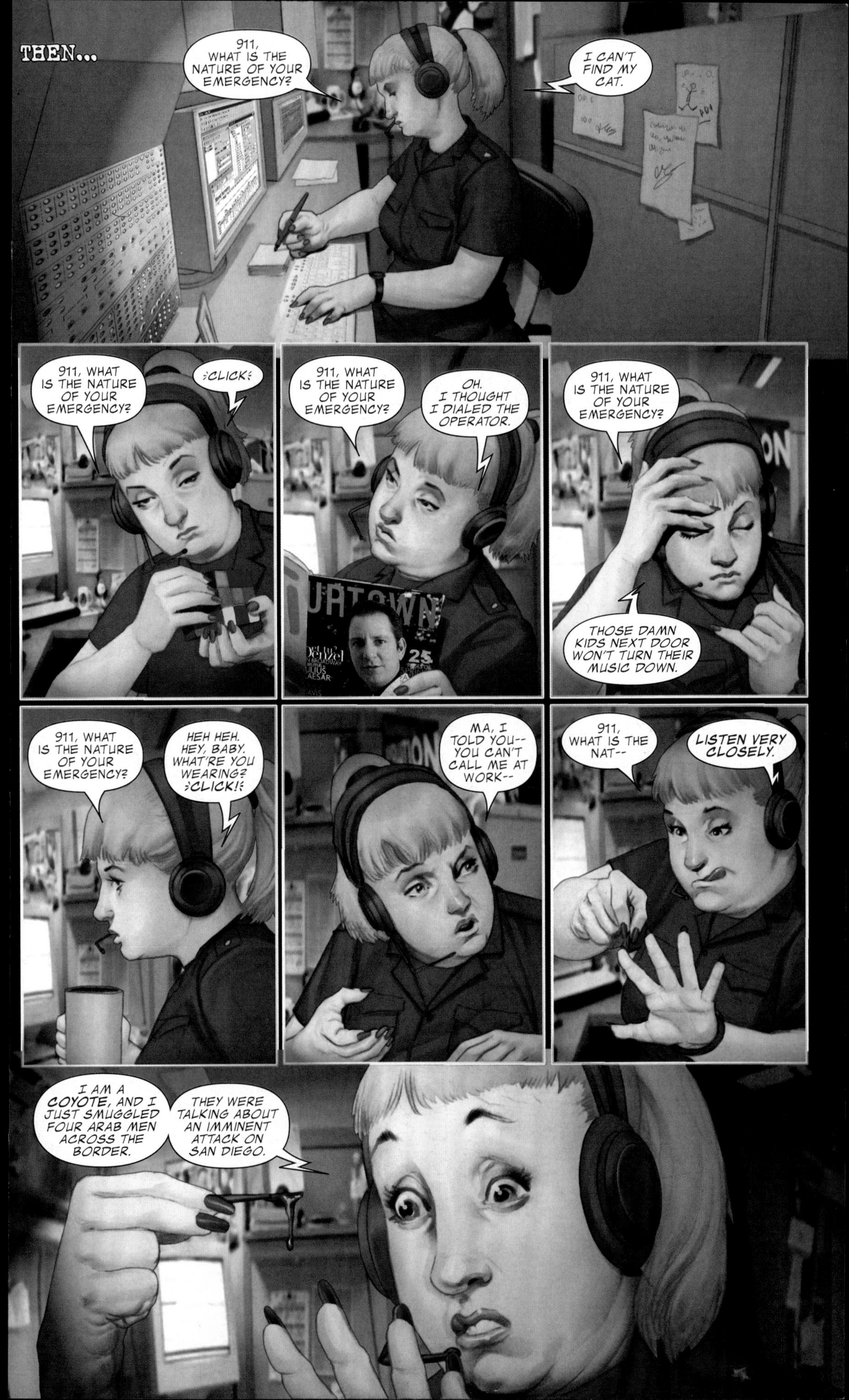
THEN...
911, WHAT IS THE NATURE OF YOUR EMERGENCY?
I CAN'T FIND MY CAT.
911, WHAT IS THE NATURE OF YOUR EMERGENCY?
:CLICK:
911, WHAT IS THE NATURE OF YOUR EMERGENCY?
OH. I THOUGHT I DIALED THE OPERATOR.
911, WHAT IS THE NATURE OF YOUR EMERGENCY?
THOSE DAMN KIDS NEXT DOOR WON'T TURN THEIR MUSIC DOWN.
911, WHAT IS THE NATURE OF YOUR EMERGENCY?
HEH HEH. HEY, BABY. WHAT'RE YOU WEARING? :CLICK!:
MA, I TOLD YOU--YOU CAN'T CALL ME AT WORK--
911, WHAT IS THE NAT--
LISTEN VERY CLOSELY.
I AM A COYOTE, AND I JUST SMUGGLED FOUR ARAB MEN ACROSS THE BORDER.
THEY WERE TALKING ABOUT AN IMMINENT ATTACK ON SAN DIEGO.

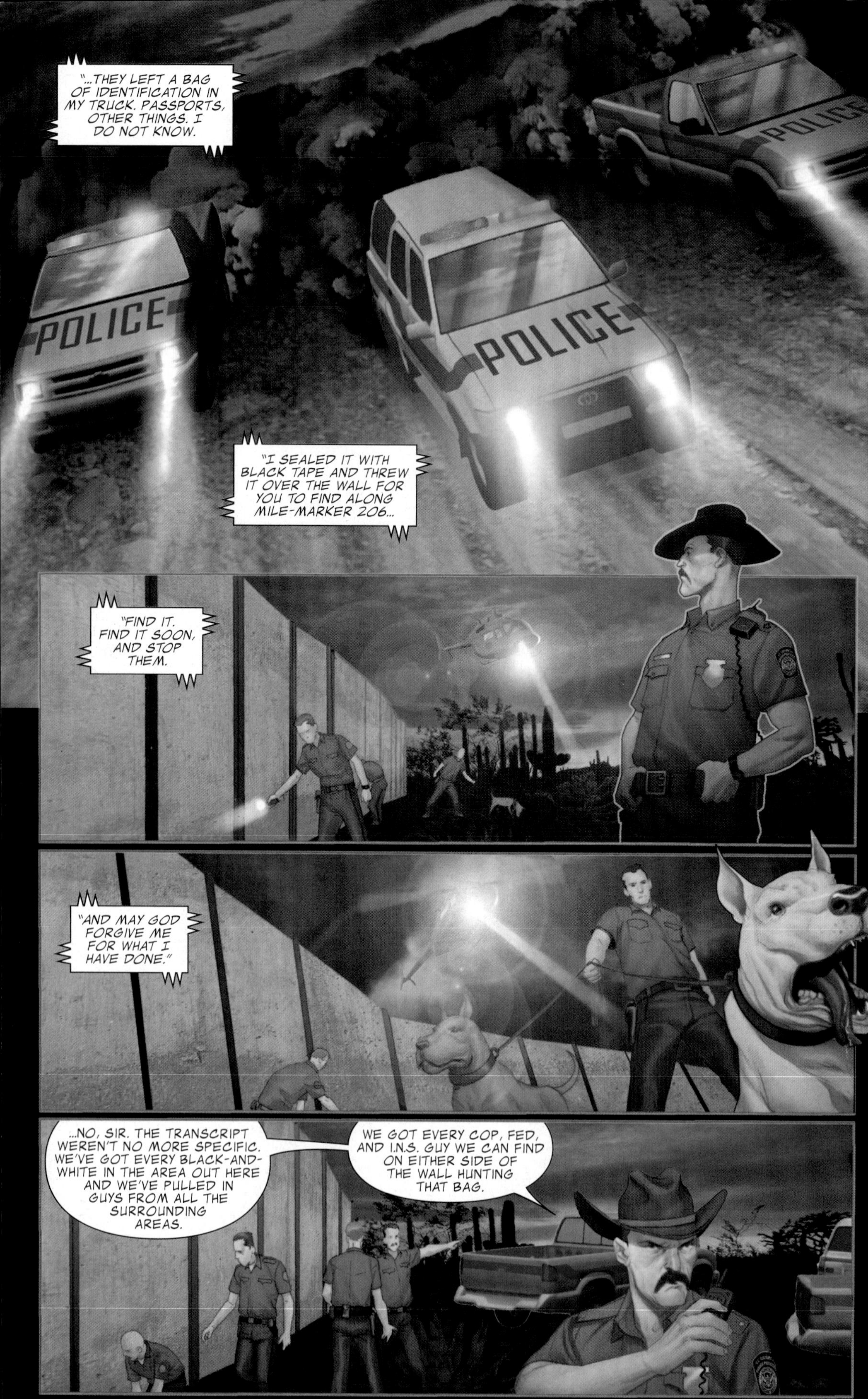
"...THEY LEFT A BAG OF IDENTIFICATION IN MY TRUCK. PASSPORTS, OTHER THINGS. I DO NOT KNOW.
POLICE
POLICE
POLICE
"I SEALED IT WITH BLACK TAPE AND THREW IT OVER THE WALL FOR YOU TO FIND ALONG MILE-MARKER 206...
"FIND IT. FIND IT SOON, AND STOP THEM.
"AND MAY GOD FORGIVE ME FOR WHAT I HAVE DONE."
...NO, SIR. THE TRANSCRIPT WEREN'T NO MORE SPECIFIC. WE'VE GOT EVERY BLACK-AND-WHITE IN THE AREA OUT HERE AND WE'VE PULLED IN GUYS FROM ALL THE SURROUNDING AREAS.
WE GOT EVERY COP, FED, AND I.N.S. GUY WE CAN FIND ON EITHER SIDE OF THE WALL HUNTING THAT BAG.

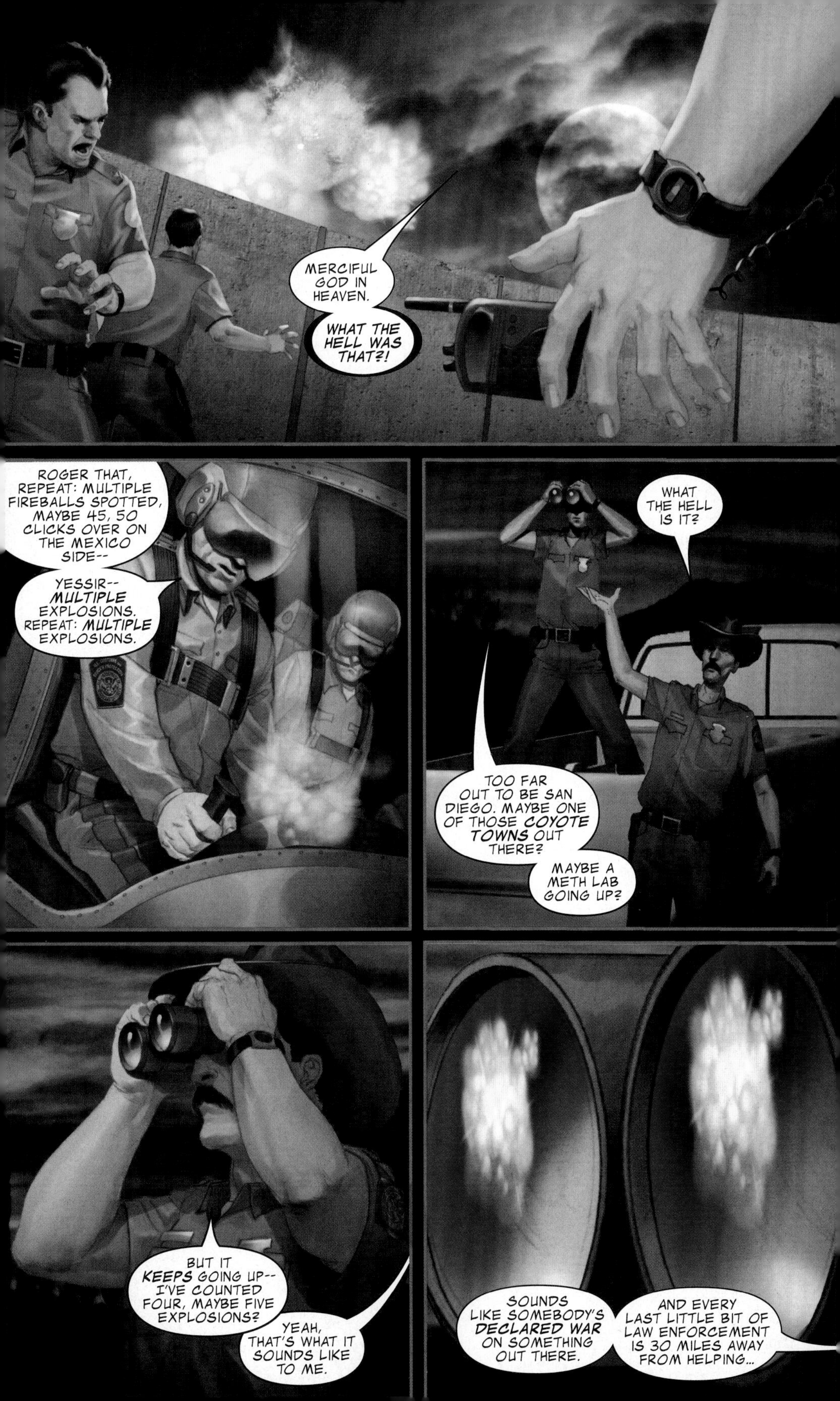
MERCIFUL GOD IN HEAVEN.
WHAT THE HELL WAS THAT?!
ROGER THAT, REPEAT: MULTIPLE FIREBALLS SPOTTED, MAYBE 45, 50 CLICKS OVER ON THE MEXICO SIDE--
YESSIR-- MULTIPLE EXPLOSIONS. REPEAT: MULTIPLE EXPLOSIONS.
WHAT THE HELL IS IT?
TOO FAR OUT TO BE SAN DIEGO. MAYBE ONE OF THOSE COYOTE TOWNS OUT THERE?
MAYBE A METH LAB GOING UP?
BUT IT KEEPS GOING UP-- I'VE COUNTED FOUR, MAYBE FIVE EXPLOSIONS?
YEAH, THAT'S WHAT IT SOUNDS LIKE TO ME.
SOUNDS LIKE SOMEBODY'S DECLARED WAR ON SOMETHING OUT THERE.
AND EVERY LAST LITTLE BIT OF LAW ENFORCEMENT IS 30 MILES AWAY FROM HELPING...

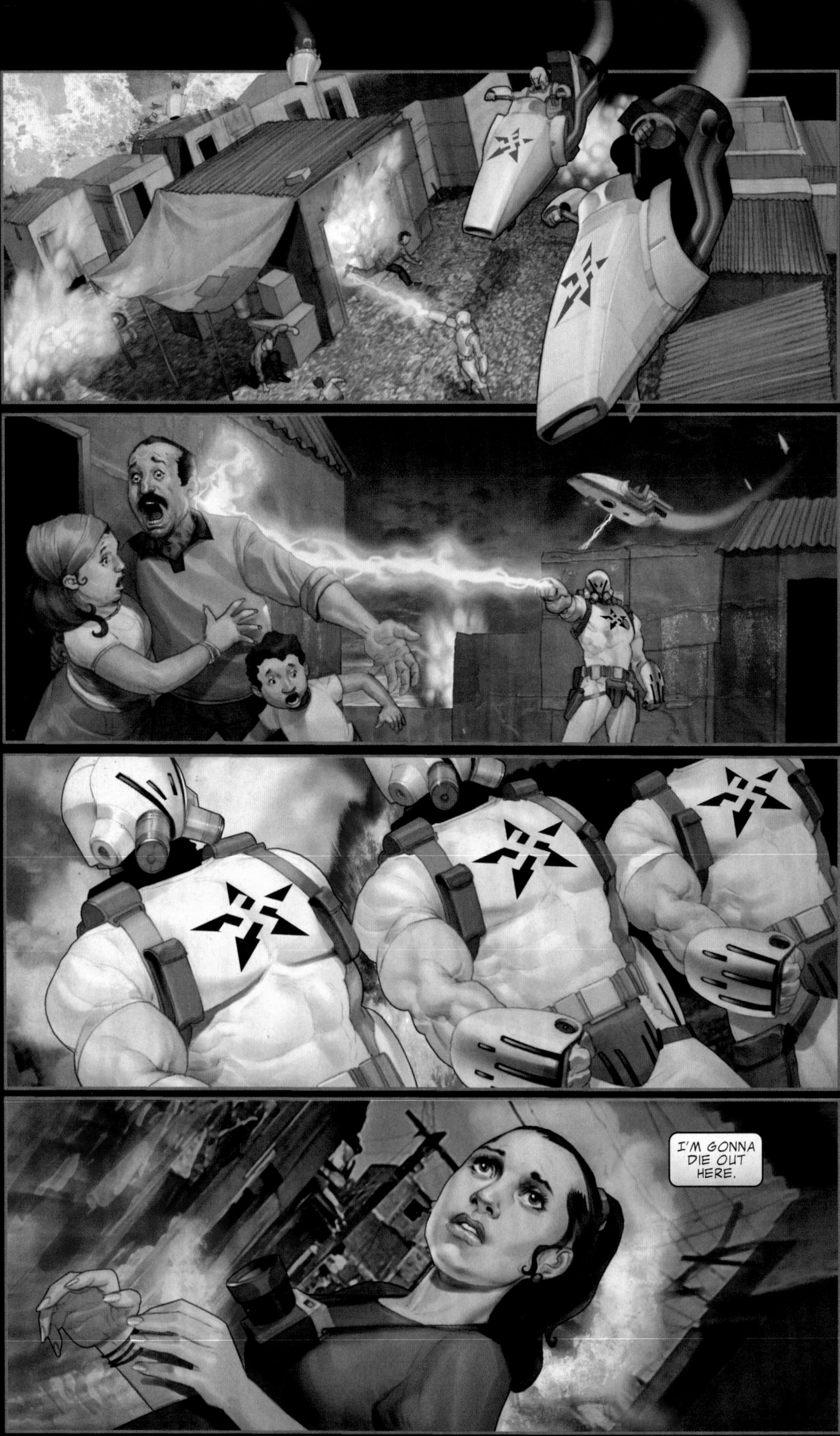
I'M GONNA DIE OUT HERE.

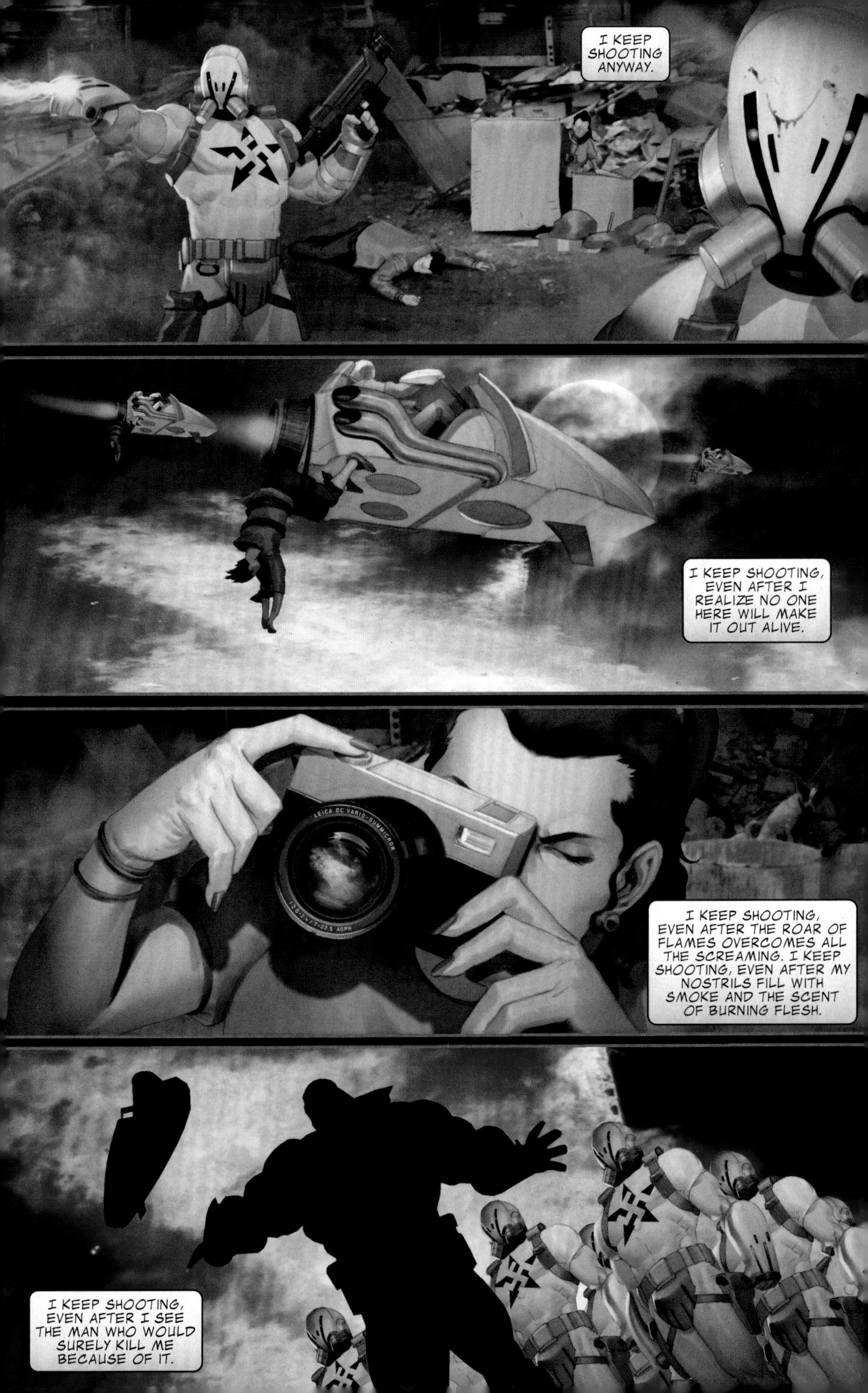
I KEEP SHOOTING ANYWAY.
I KEEP SHOOTING, EVEN AFTER I REALIZE NO ONE HERE WILL MAKE IT OUT ALIVE.
I KEEP SHOOTING, EVEN AFTER THE ROAR OF FLAMES OVERCOMES ALL THE SCREAMING. I KEEP SHOOTING, EVEN AFTER MY NOSTRILS FILL WITH SMOKE AND THE SCENT OF BURNING FLESH.
I KEEP SHOOTING, EVEN AFTER I SEE THE MAN WHO WOULD SURELY KILL ME BECAUSE OF IT.

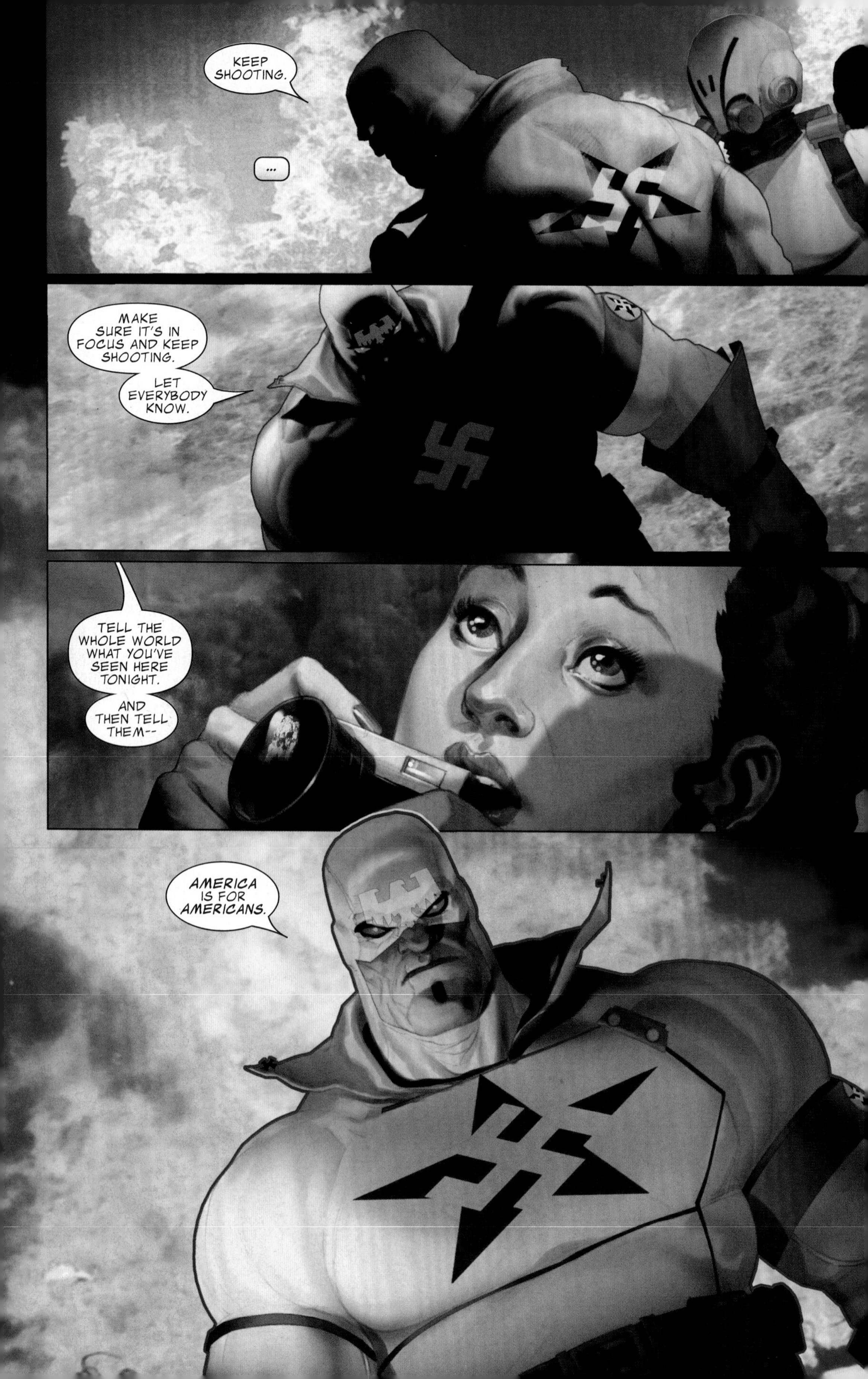
KEEP SHOOTING.
...
MAKE SURE IT'S IN FOCUS AND KEEP SHOOTING.
LET EVERYBODY KNOW.
TELL THE WHOLE WORLD WHAT YOU'VE SEEN HERE TONIGHT.
AND THEN TELL THEM--
AMERICA IS FOR AMERICANS.

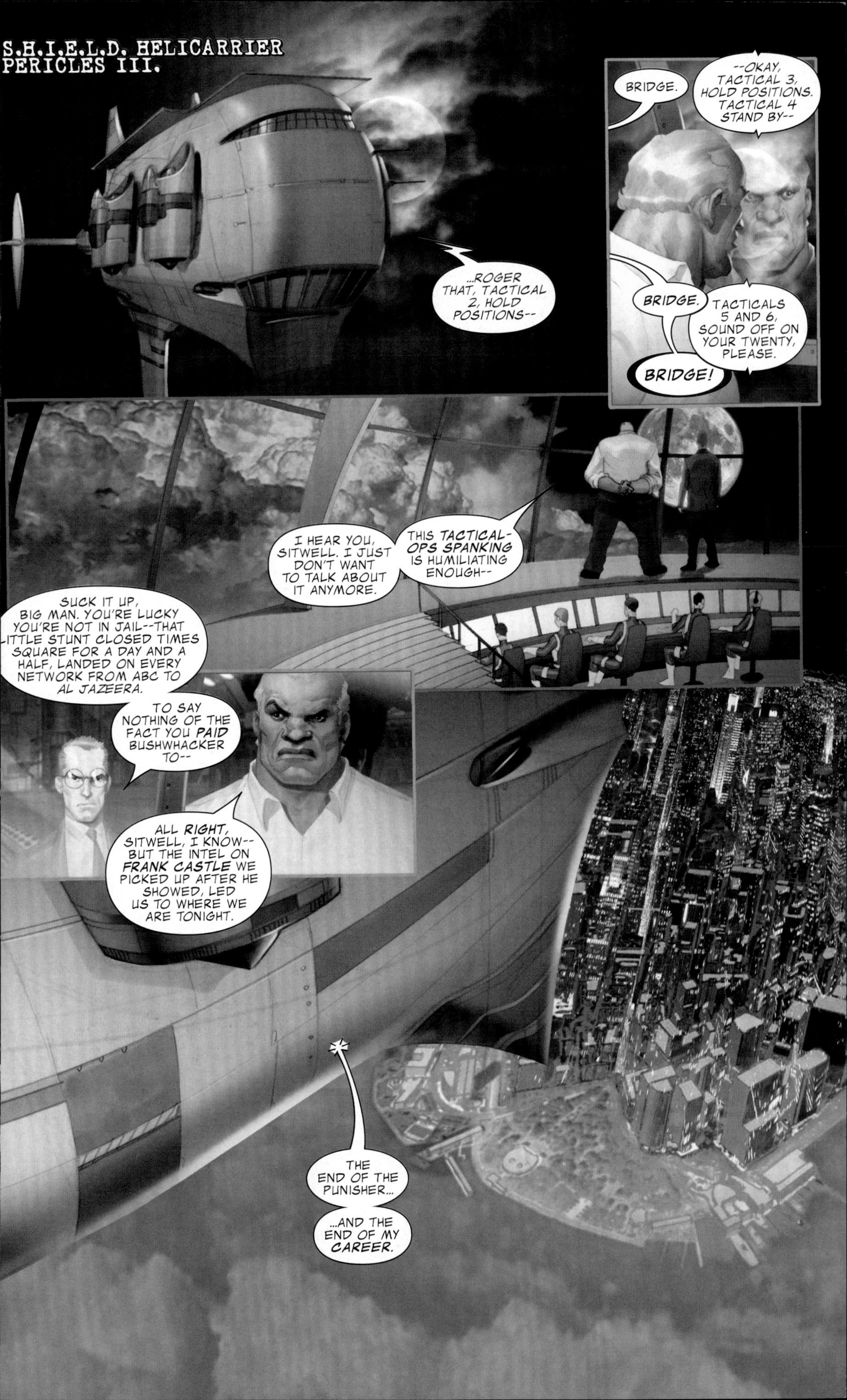
S.H.I.E.L.D. HELICARRIER PERICLES III.
BRIDGE.
--OKAY, TACTICAL 3, HOLD POSITIONS. TACTICAL 4 STAND BY--
...ROGER THAT, TACTICAL 2, HOLD POSITIONS--
BRIDGE.
TACTICALS 5 AND 6, SOUND OFF ON YOUR TWENTY, PLEASE.
BRIDGE!
THIS TACTICAL-OPS SPANKING IS HUMILIATING ENOUGH--
I HEAR YOU, SITWELL. I JUST DON'T WANT TO TALK ABOUT IT ANYMORE.
SUCK IT UP, BIG MAN. YOU'RE LUCKY YOU'RE NOT IN JAIL--THAT LITTLE STUNT CLOSED TIMES SQUARE FOR A DAY AND A HALF, LANDED ON EVERY NETWORK FROM ABC TO AL JAZEERA.
TO SAY NOTHING OF THE FACT YOU PAID BUSHWHACKER TO--
ALL RIGHT, SITWELL, I KNOW--BUT THE INTEL ON FRANK CASTLE WE PICKED UP AFTER HE SHOWED, LED US TO WHERE WE ARE TONIGHT.
THE END OF THE PUNISHER...
...AND THE END OF MY CAREER.

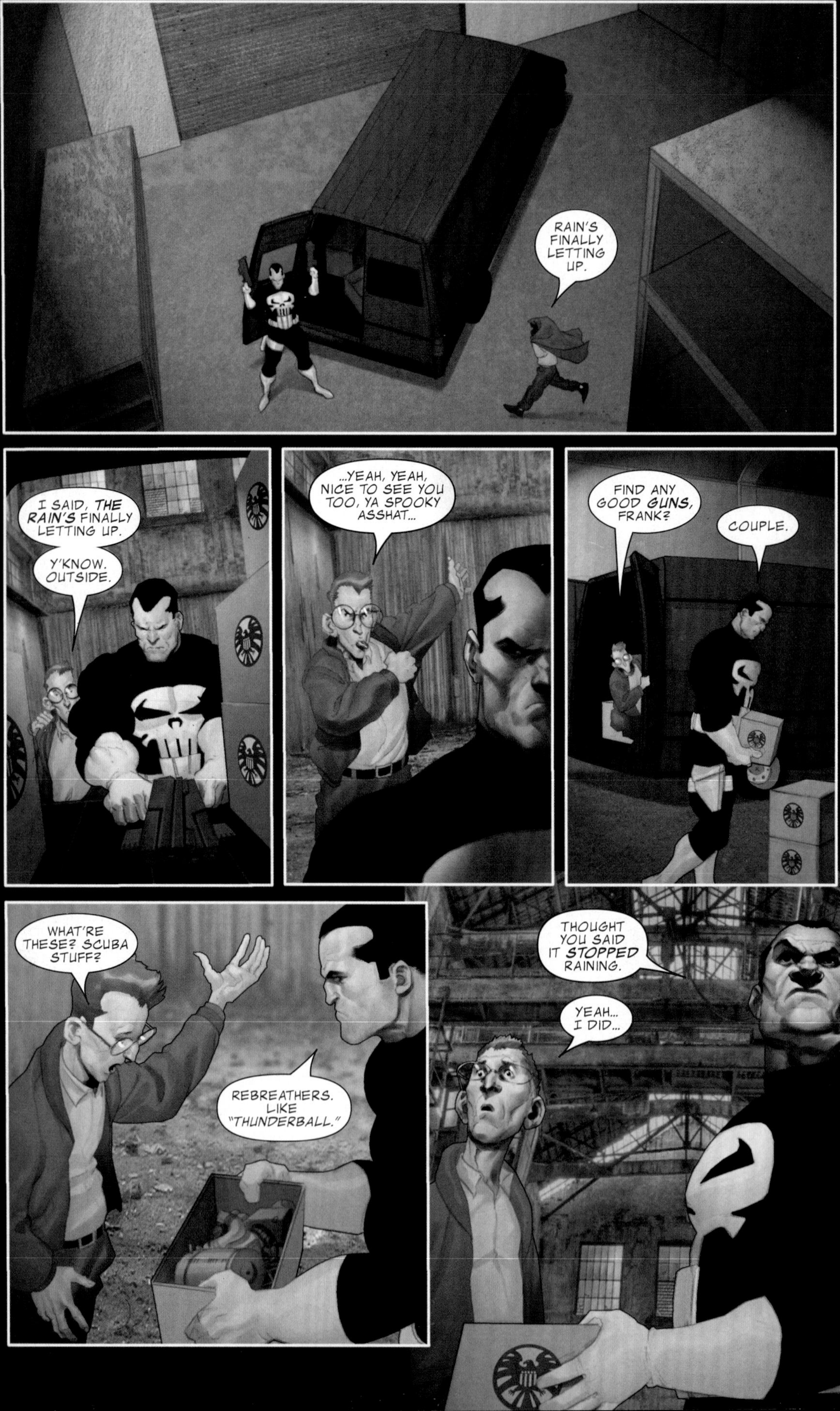
RAIN'S FINALLY LETTING UP.
I SAID, THE RAIN'S FINALLY LETTING UP.
Y'KNOW. OUTSIDE.
...YEAH, YEAH, NICE TO SEE YOU TOO, YA SPOOKY ASSHAT...
FIND ANY GOOD GUNS, FRANK?
COUPLE.
WHAT'RE THESE? SCUBA STUFF?
REBREATHERS. LIKE "THUNDERBALL."
THOUGHT YOU SAID IT STOPPED RAINING.
YEAH... I DID...

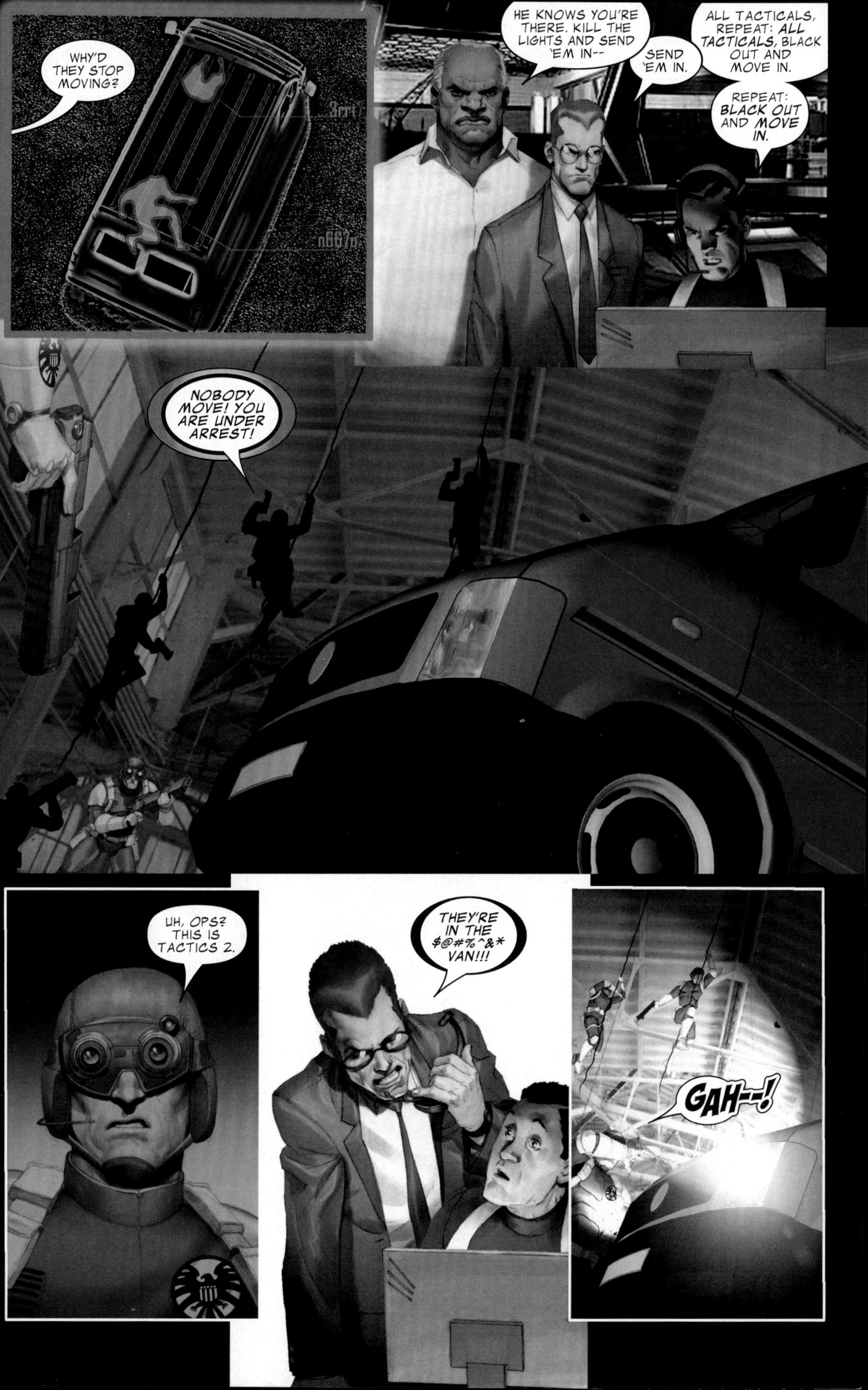
WHY'D THEY STOP MOVING?
HE KNOWS YOU'RE THERE. KILL THE LIGHTS AND SEND 'EM IN--
SEND 'EM IN.
ALL TACTICALS, REPEAT: ALL TACTICALS, BLACK OUT AND MOVE IN.
REPEAT: BLACK OUT AND MOVE IN.
NOBODY MOVE! YOU ARE UNDER ARREST!
UH, OPS? THIS IS TACTICS 2.
THEY'RE IN THE $@#%^&* VAN!!!
GAH--!

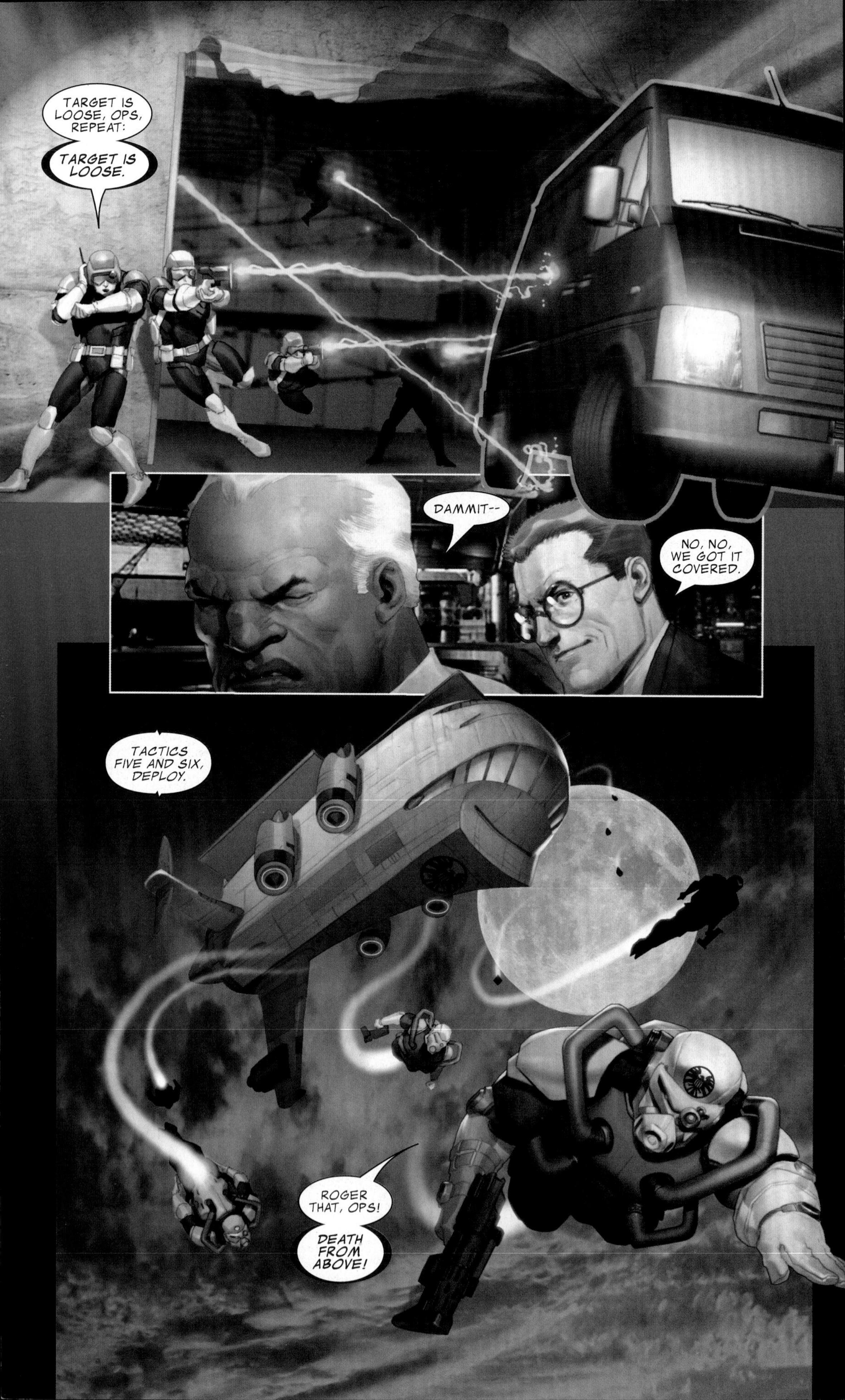
TARGET IS LOOSE, OPS, REPEAT:
TARGET IS LOOSE.
DAMMIT--
NO, NO, WE GOT IT COVERED.
TACTICS FIVE AND SIX, DEPLOY.
ROGER THAT, OPS!
DEATH FROM ABOVE!

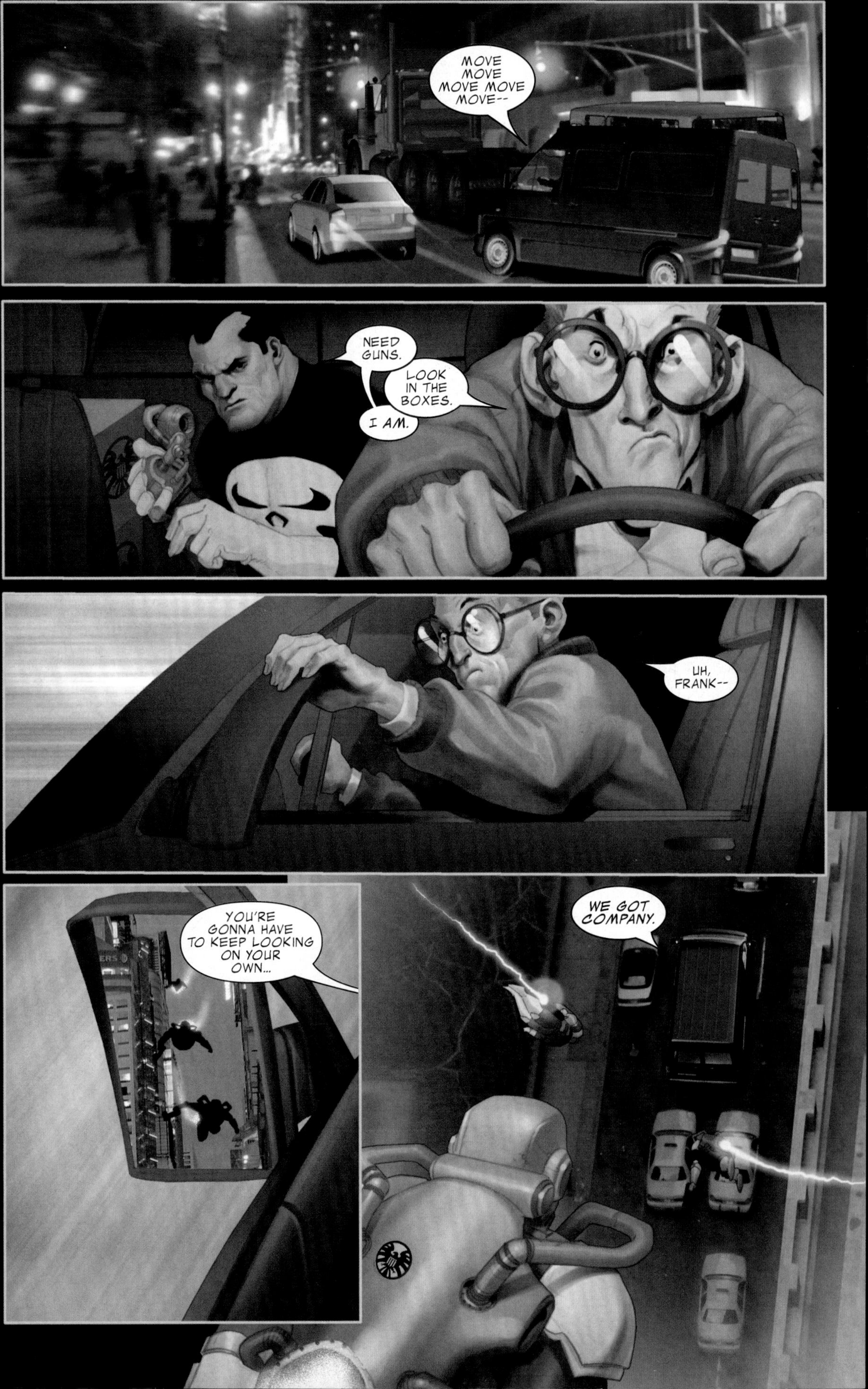
MOVE MOVE MOVE MOVE MOVE--
NEED GUNS.
LOOK IN THE BOXES.
I AM.
UH, FRANK--
YOU'RE GONNA HAVE TO KEEP LOOKING ON YOUR OWN...
WE GOT COMPANY.

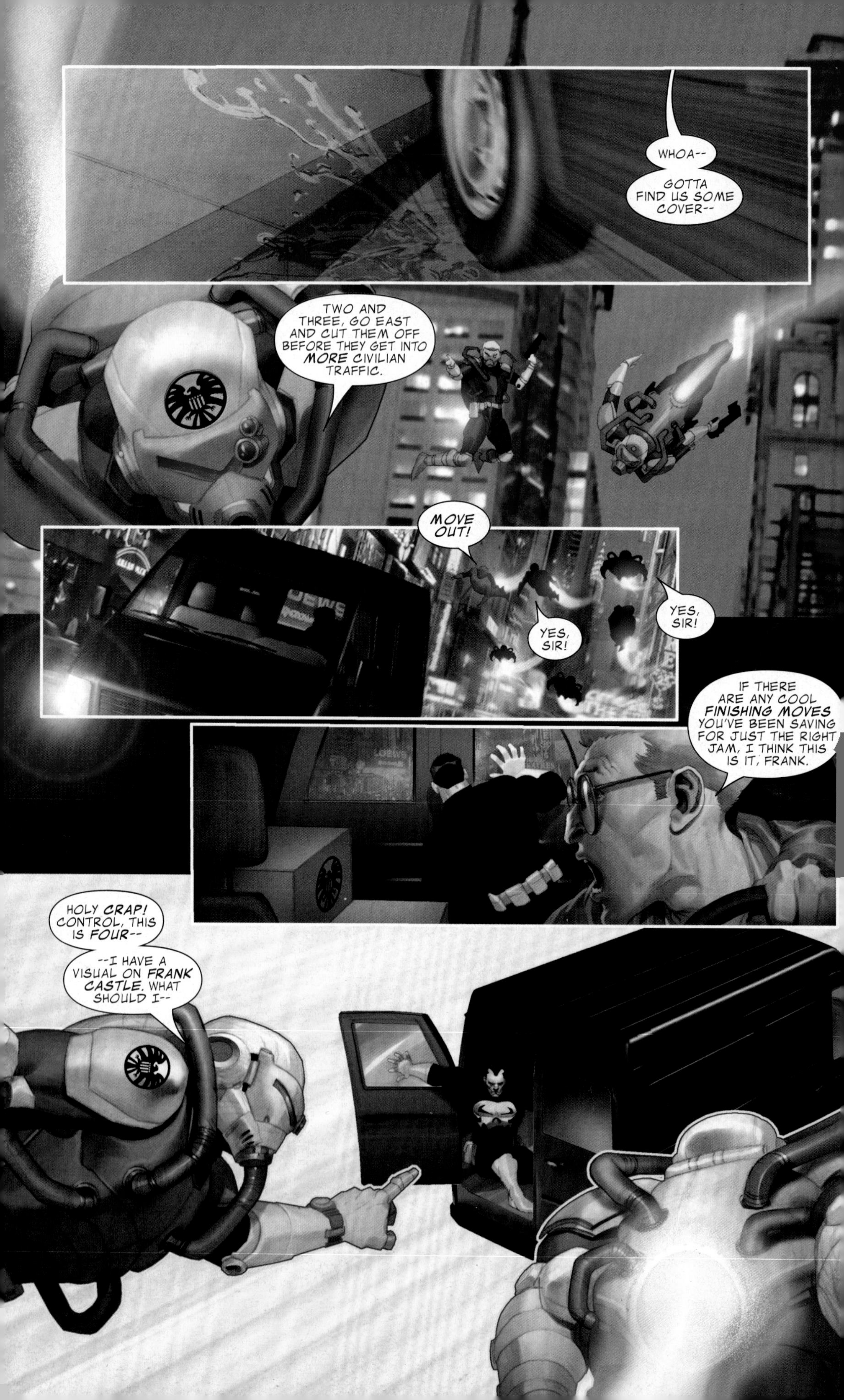
WHOA--
GOTTA FIND US SOME COVER--
TWO AND THREE, GO EAST AND CUT THEM OFF BEFORE THEY GET INTO MORE CIVILIAN TRAFFIC.
MOVE OUT!
YES, SIR!
YES, SIR!
IF THERE ARE ANY COOL FINISHING MOVES YOU'VE BEEN SAVING FOR JUST THE RIGHT JAM, I THINK THIS IS IT, FRANK.
HOLY CRAP! CONTROL, THIS IS FOUR--
--I HAVE A VISUAL ON FRANK CASTLE. WHAT SHOULD I--

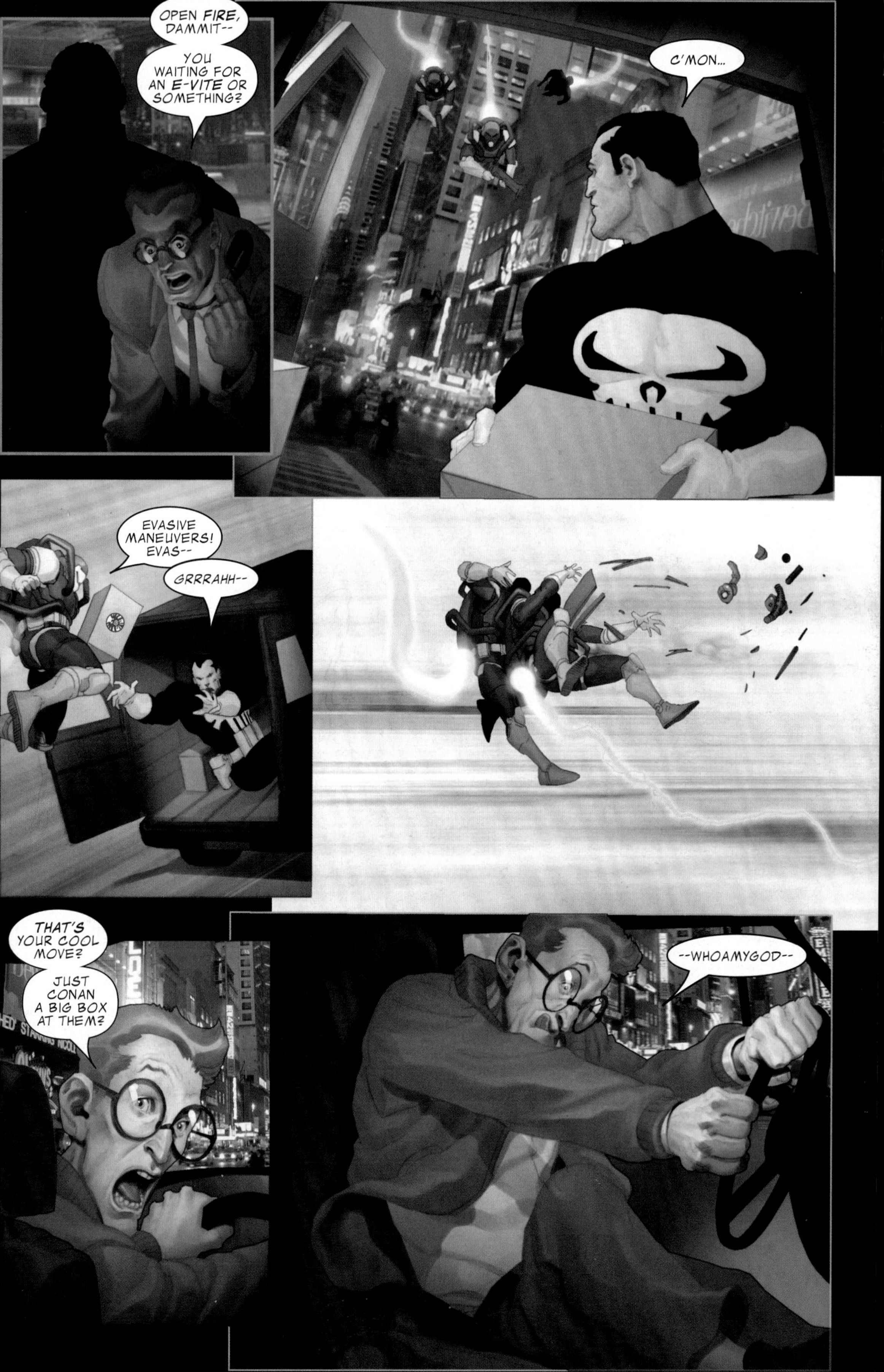

OPEN FIRE, DAMMIT--
YOU WAITING FOR AN E-VITE OR SOMETHING?
C'MON...
EVASIVE MANEUVERS! EVAS--
GRRRAHH--
THAT'S YOUR COOL MOVE?
JUST CONAN A BIG BOX AT THEM?
--WHOAMYGOD--

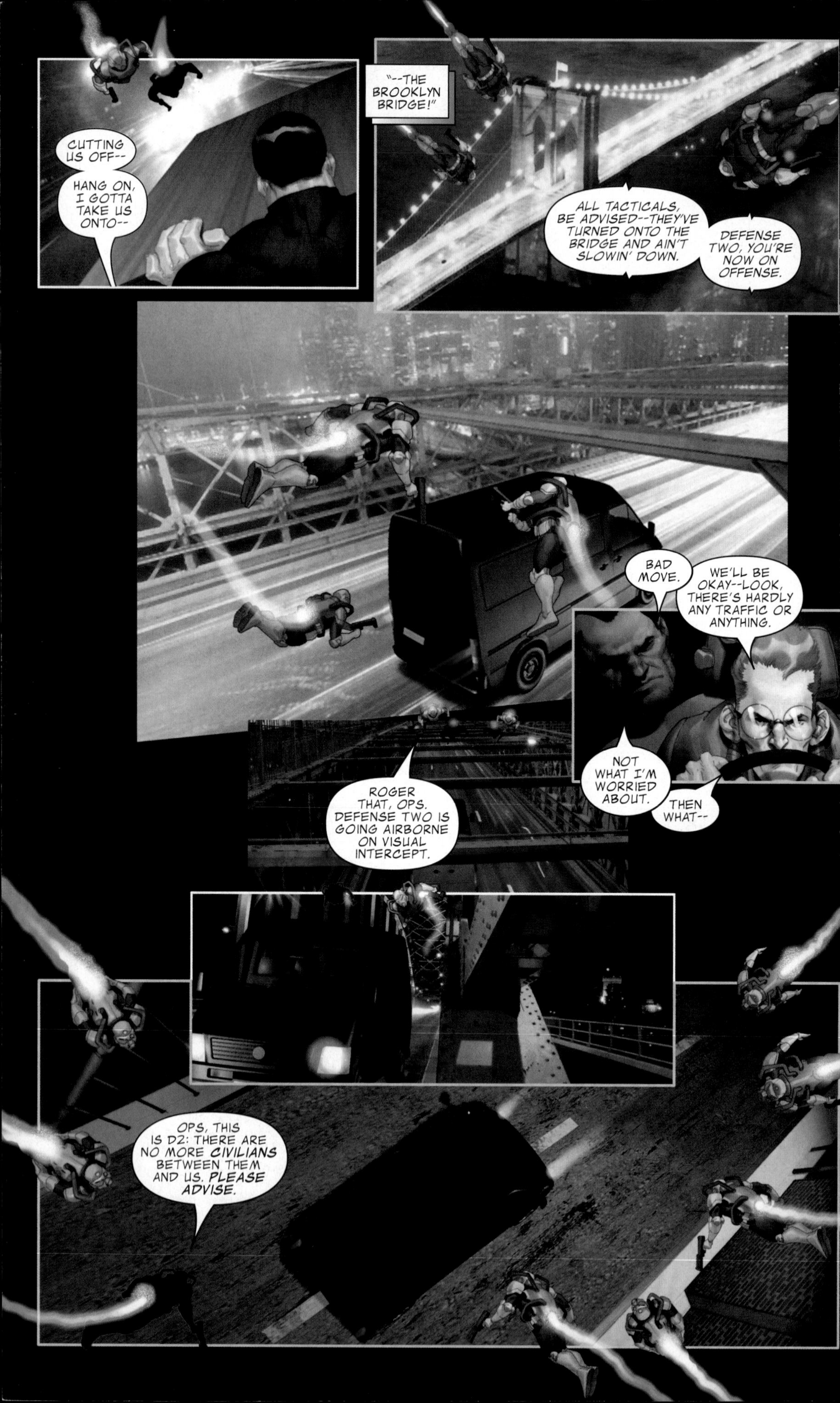
CUTTING US OFF--
HANG ON, I GOTTA TAKE US ONTO--
"--THE BROOKLYN BRIDGE!"
ALL TACTICALS, BE ADVISED--THEY'VE TURNED ONTO THE BRIDGE AND AIN'T SLOWIN' DOWN.
DEFENSE TWO, YOU'RE NOW ON OFFENSE.
BAD MOVE.
WE'LL BE OKAY--LOOK, THERE'S HARDLY ANY TRAFFIC OR ANYTHING.
NOT WHAT I'M WORRIED ABOUT.
THEN WHAT--
ROGER THAT, OPS. DEFENSE TWO IS GOING AIRBORNE ON VISUAL INTERCEPT.
OPS, THIS IS D2: THERE ARE NO MORE CIVILIANS BETWEEN THEM AND US. PLEASE ADVISE.

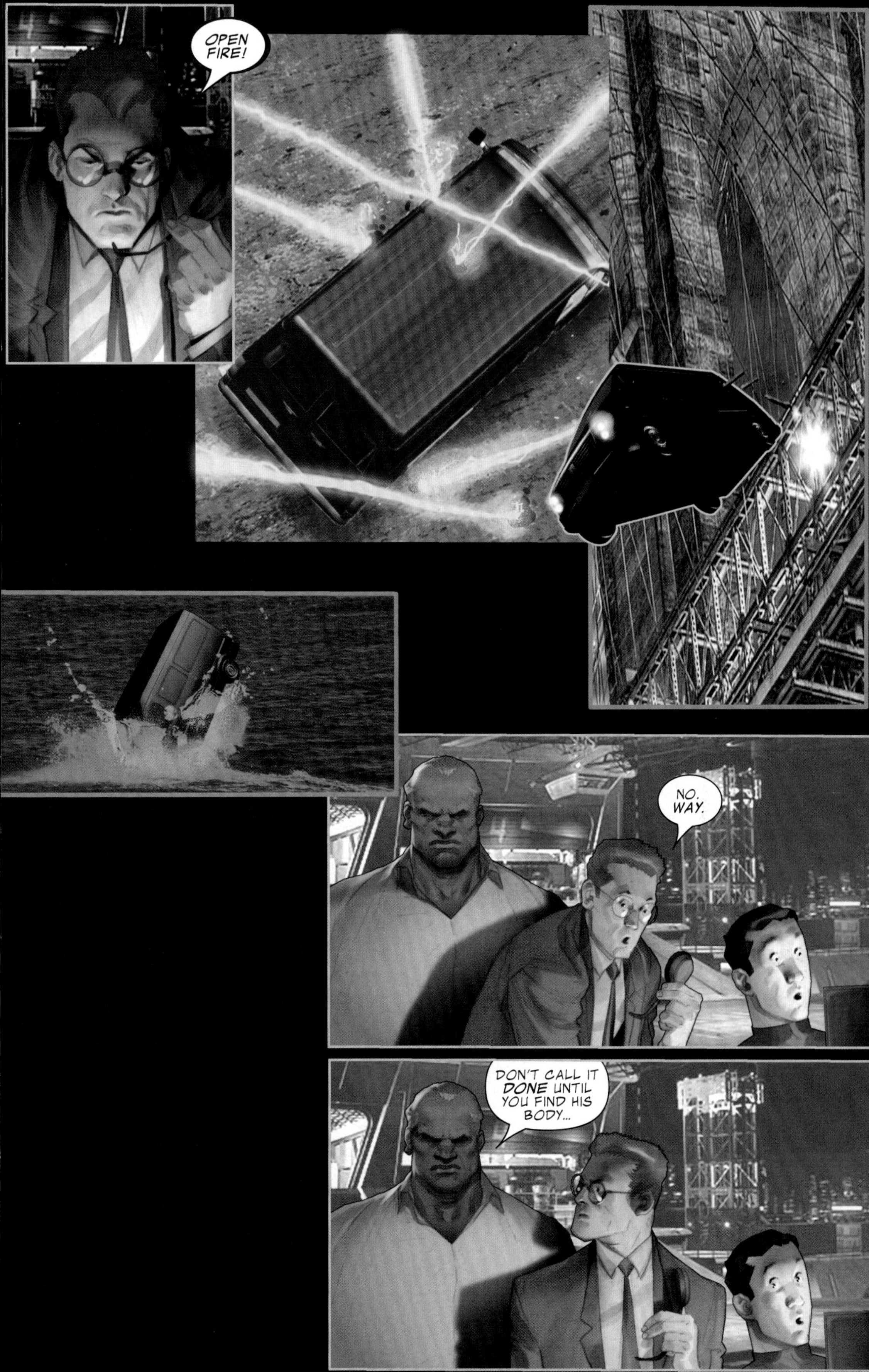
OPEN FIRE!
NO. WAY.
DON'T CALL IT DONE UNTIL YOU FIND HIS BODY...

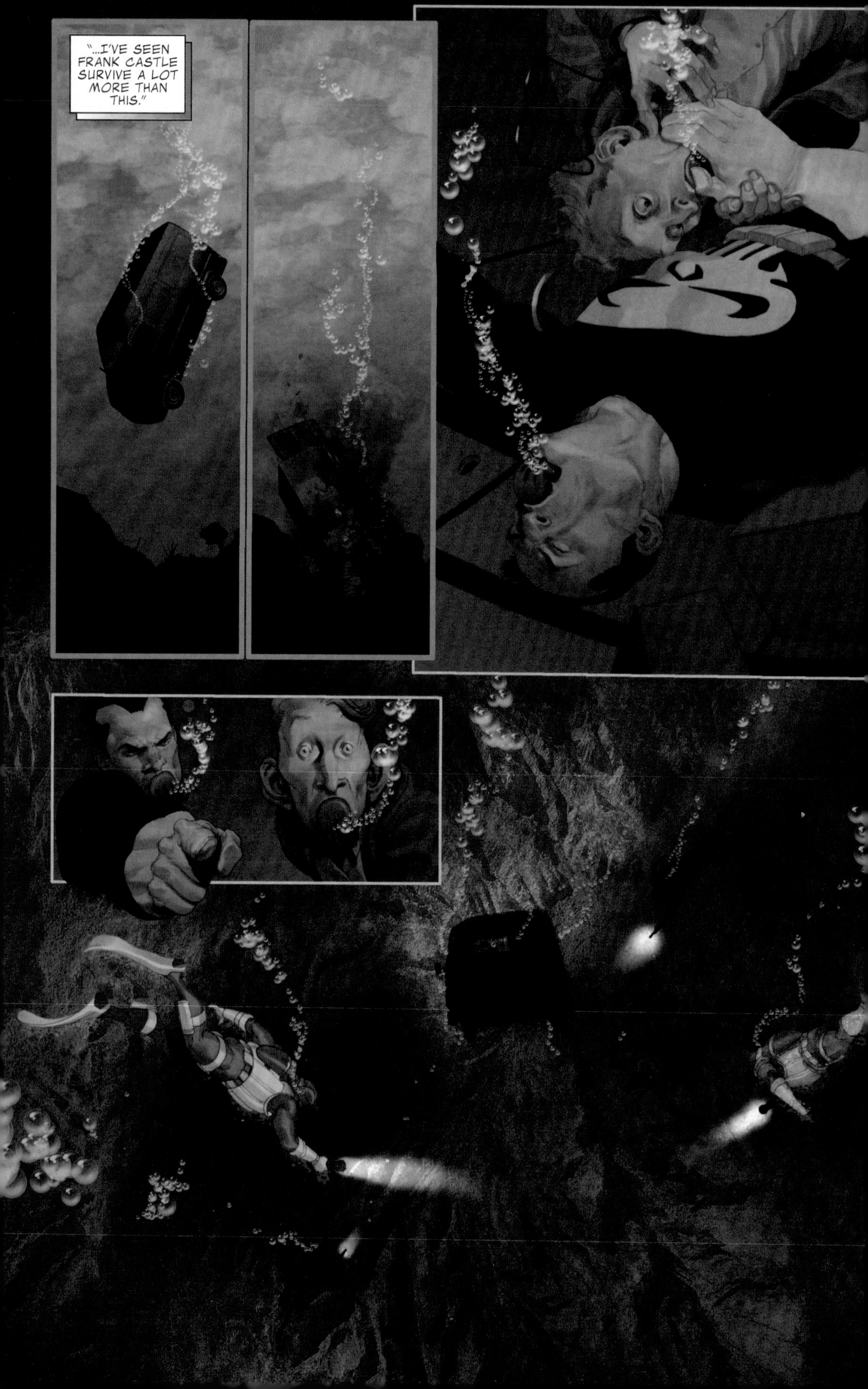
"...I'VE SEEN FRANK CASTLE SURVIVE A LOT MORE THAN THIS."

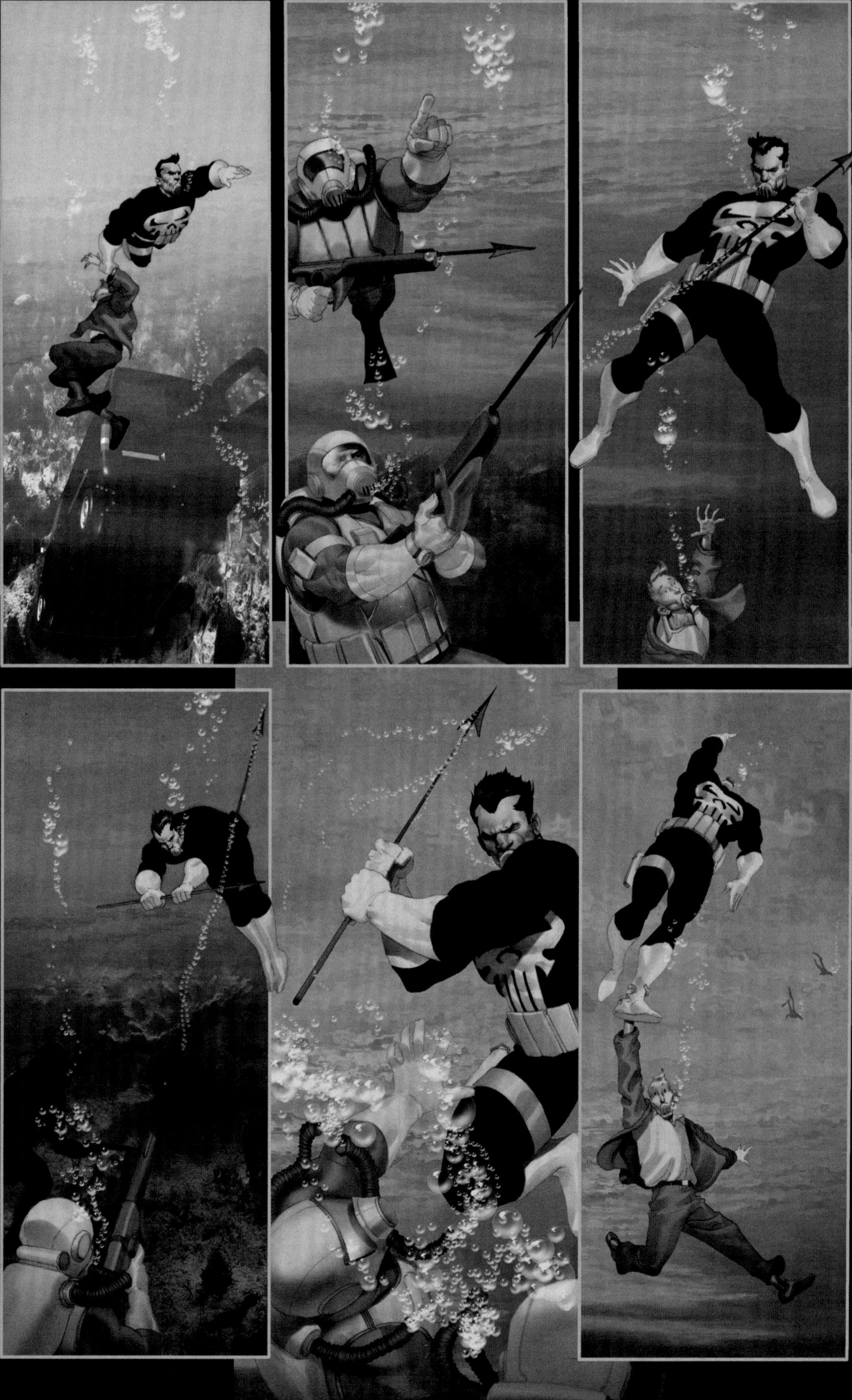

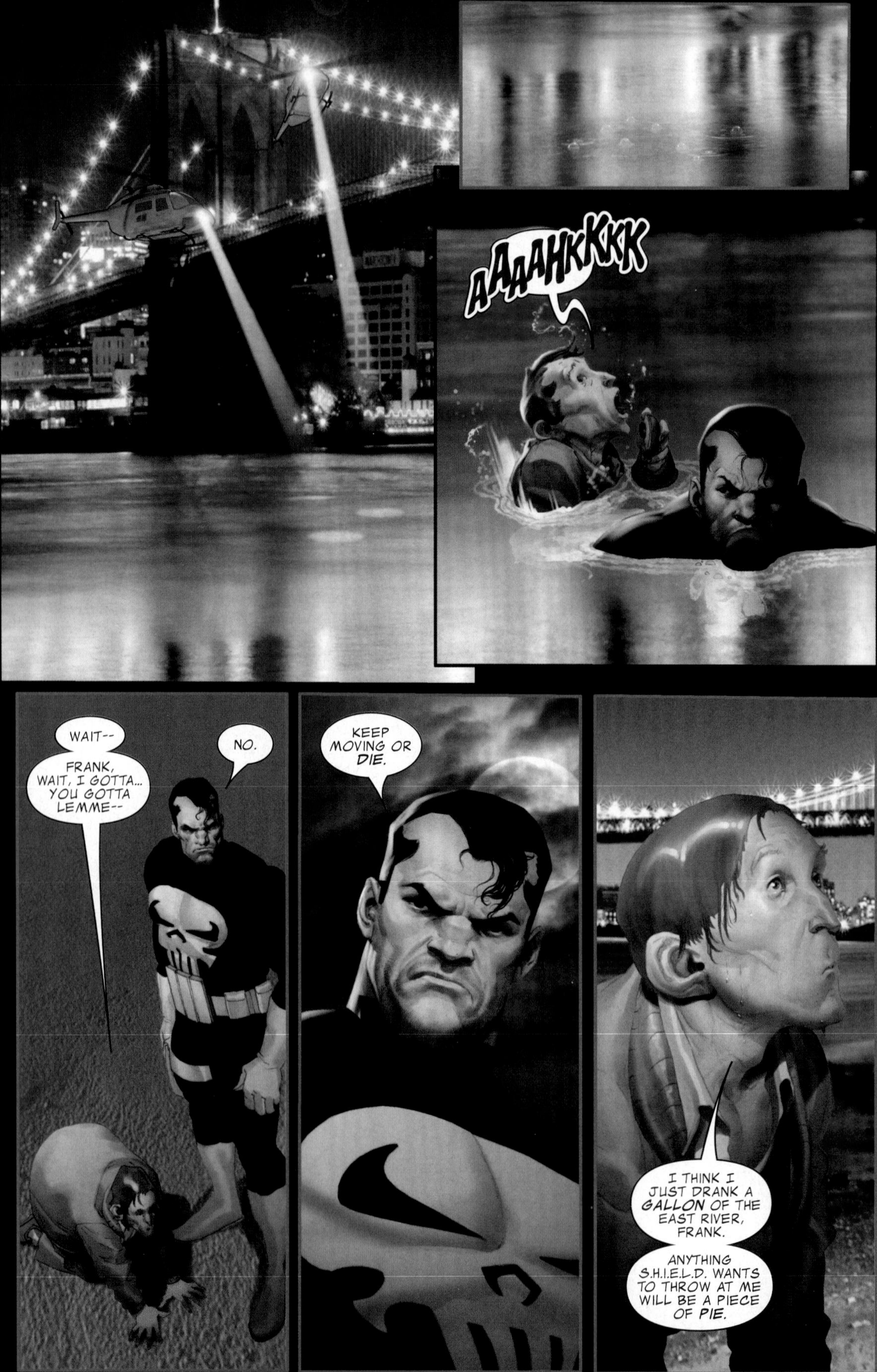
AAAAHKKKK
WAIT--
FRANK, WAIT, I GOTTA... YOU GOTTA LEMME--
NO.
KEEP MOVING OR DIE.
I THINK I JUST DRANK A GALLON OF THE EAST RIVER, FRANK.
ANYTHING S.H.I.E.L.D. WANTS TO THROW AT ME WILL BE A PIECE OF PIE.

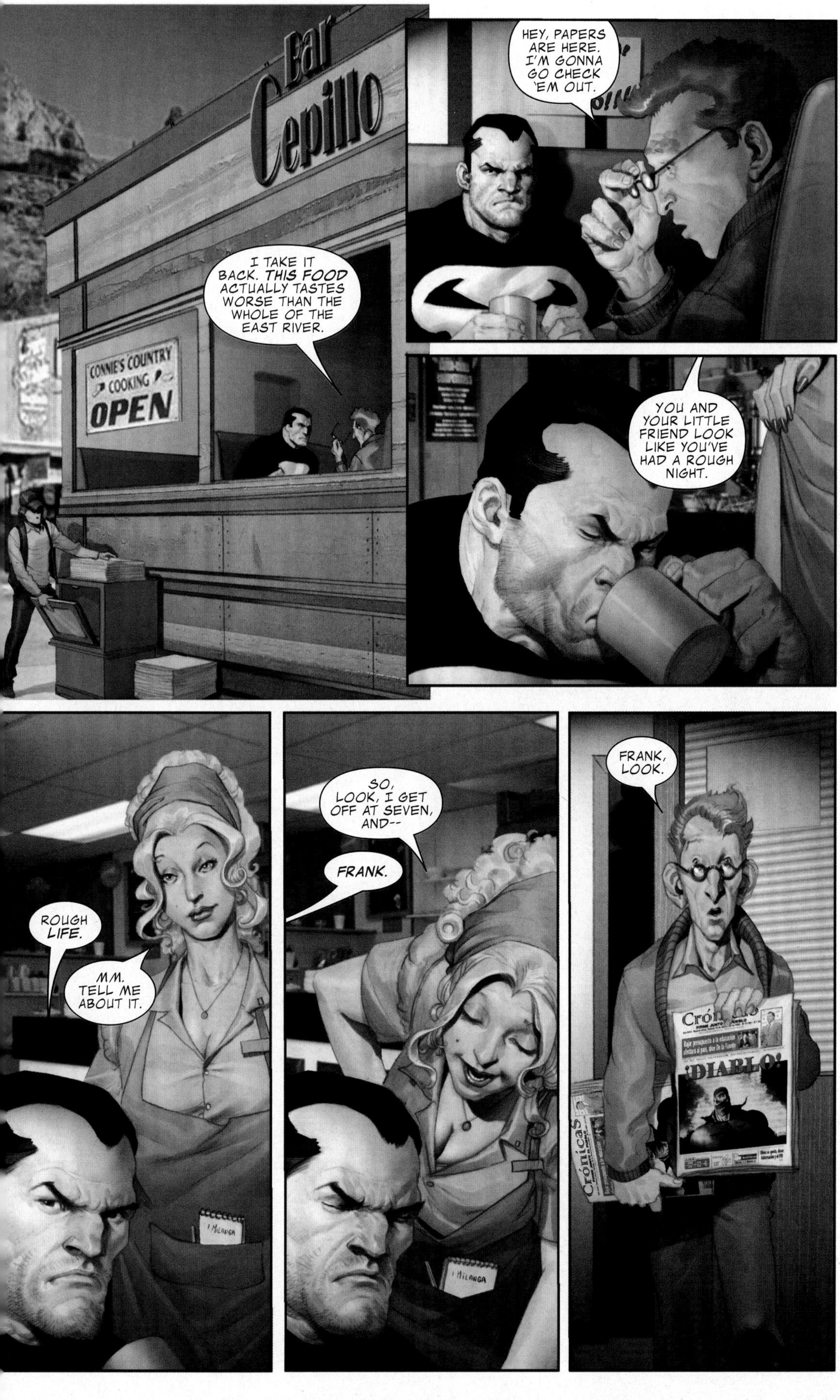
Bar Cepillo
CONNIE'S COUNTRY COOKING OPEN
I TAKE IT BACK. THIS FOOD ACTUALLY TASTES WORSE THAN THE WHOLE OF THE EAST RIVER.
HEY, PAPERS ARE HERE. I'M GONNA GO CHECK 'EM OUT.
YOU AND YOUR LITTLE FRIEND LOOK LIKE YOU'VE HAD A ROUGH NIGHT.
ROUGH LIFE.
MM. TELL ME ABOUT IT.
SO, LOOK, I GET OFF AT SEVEN, AND--
FRANK.
FRANK, LOOK.
¡DIABLO!
Crónicas

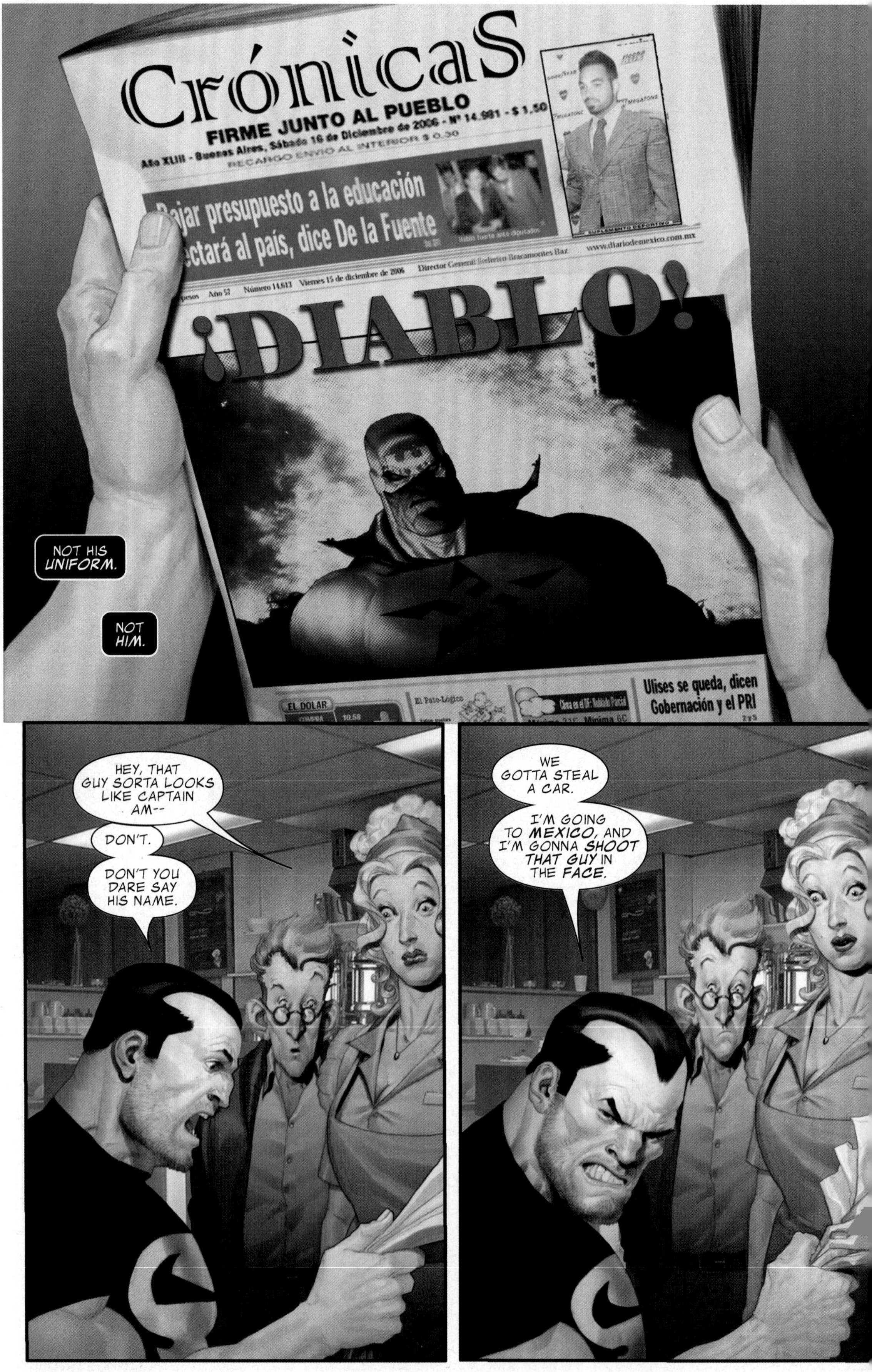
Crónicas
FIRME JUNTO AL PUEBLO
Bajar presupuesto a la educación afectará al país, dice De la Fuente
¡DIABLO!
Ulises se queda, dicen Gobernación y el PRI
NOT HIS UNIFORM.
NOT HIM.
HEY, THAT GUY SORTA LOOKS LIKE CAPTAIN AM--
DON'T.
DON'T YOU DARE SAY HIS NAME.
WE GOTTA STEAL A CAR.
I'M GOING TO MEXICO, AND I'M GONNA SHOOT THAT GUY IN THE FACE.

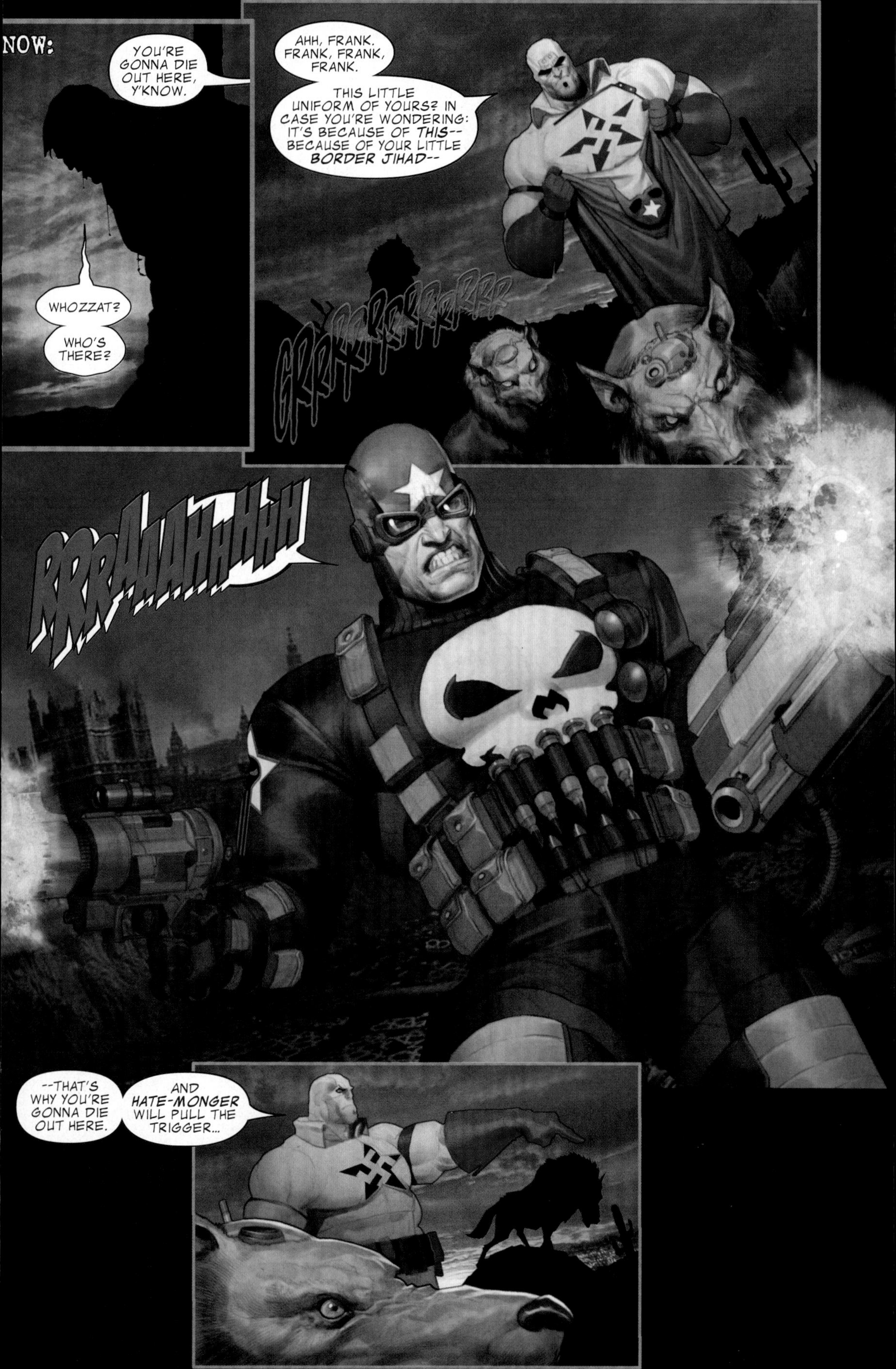
NOW:
YOU'RE GONNA DIE OUT HERE, Y'KNOW.
WHOZZAT?
WHO'S THERE?
AHH, FRANK. FRANK, FRANK, FRANK.
THIS LITTLE UNIFORM OF YOURS? IN CASE YOU'RE WONDERING: IT'S BECAUSE OF THIS-- BECAUSE OF YOUR LITTLE BORDER JIHAD--
GRRRRRRRRRRRRR
RRRAAAHHHHH
--THAT'S WHY YOU'RE GONNA DIE OUT HERE.
AND HATE-MONGER WILL PULL THE TRIGGER...

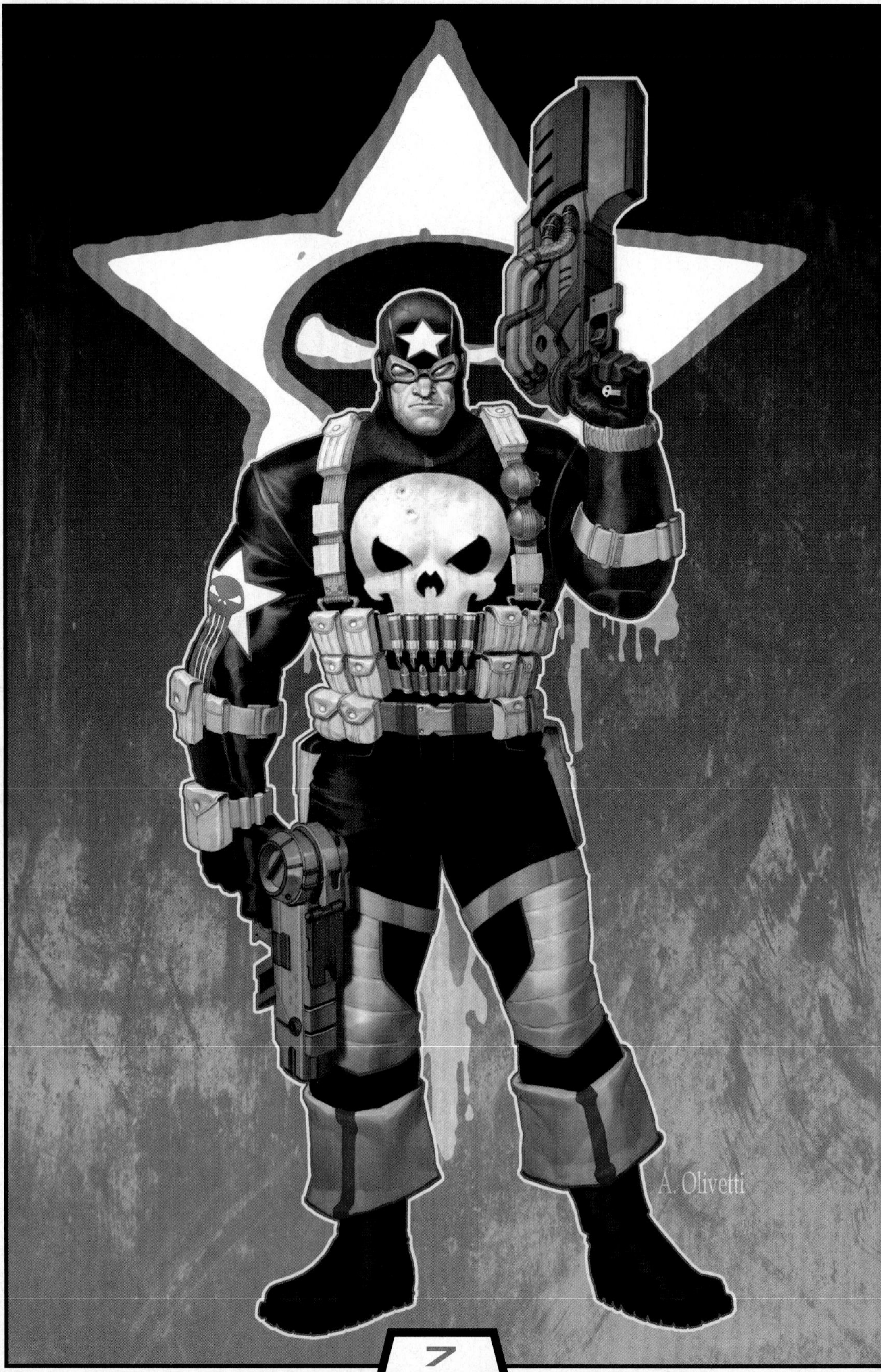
A. Olivetti

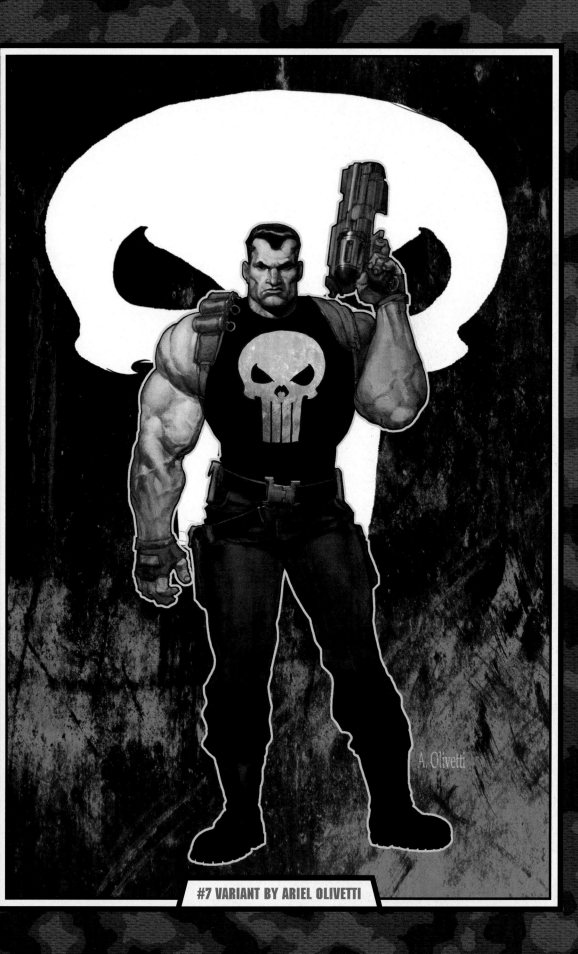

#7 VARIANT BY ARIEL OLIVETTI

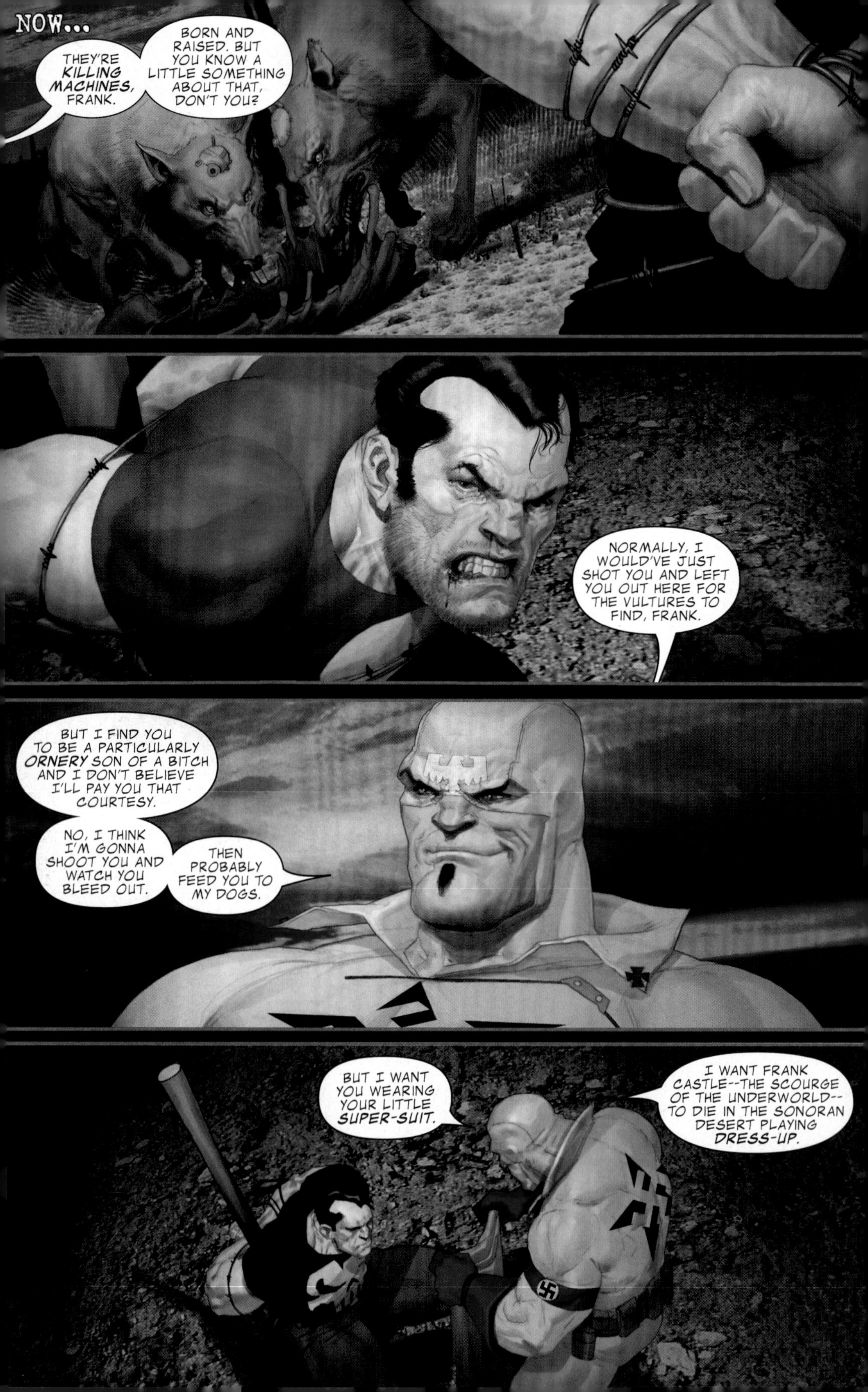
NOW...
THEY'RE KILLING MACHINES, FRANK.
BORN AND RAISED. BUT YOU KNOW A LITTLE SOMETHING ABOUT THAT, DON'T YOU?
NORMALLY, I WOULD'VE JUST SHOT YOU AND LEFT YOU OUT HERE FOR THE VULTURES TO FIND, FRANK.
BUT I FIND YOU TO BE A PARTICULARLY ORNERY SON OF A BITCH AND I DON'T BELIEVE I'LL PAY YOU THAT COURTESY.
NO, I THINK I'M GONNA SHOOT YOU AND WATCH YOU BLEED OUT.
THEN PROBABLY FEED YOU TO MY DOGS.
BUT I WANT YOU WEARING YOUR LITTLE SUPER-SUIT.
I WANT FRANK CASTLE--THE SCOURGE OF THE UNDERWORLD--TO DIE IN THE SONORAN DESERT PLAYING DRESS-UP.

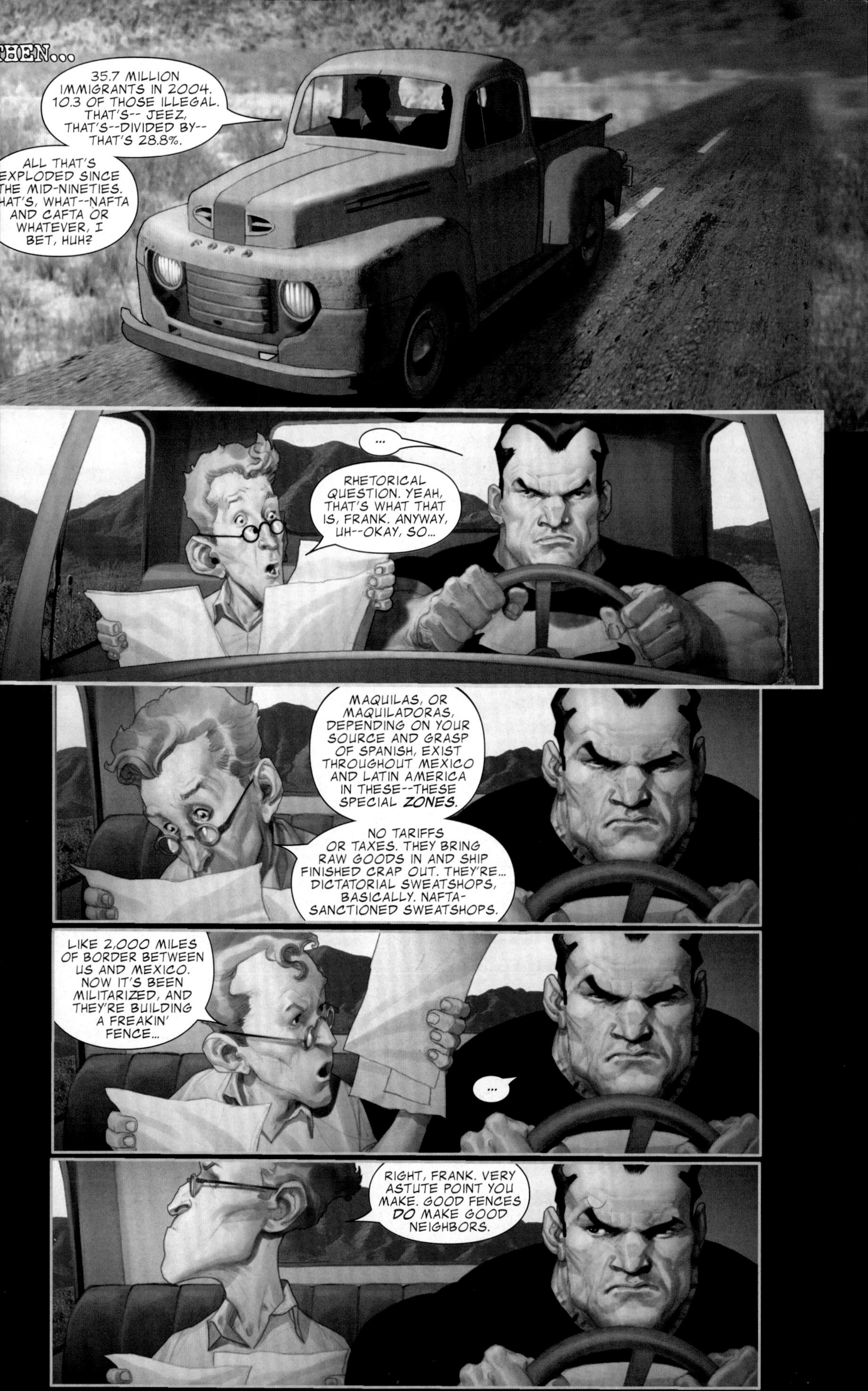
THEN...
35.7 MILLION IMMIGRANTS IN 2004. 10.3 OF THOSE ILLEGAL. THAT'S-- JEEZ, THAT'S--DIVIDED BY-- THAT'S 28.8%.
ALL THAT'S EXPLODED SINCE THE MID-NINETIES. THAT'S, WHAT--NAFTA AND CAFTA OR WHATEVER, I BET, HUH?
...
RHETORICAL QUESTION. YEAH, THAT'S WHAT THAT IS, FRANK. ANYWAY, UH--OKAY, SO...
MAQUILAS, OR MAQUILADORAS, DEPENDING ON YOUR SOURCE AND GRASP OF SPANISH, EXIST THROUGHOUT MEXICO AND LATIN AMERICA IN THESE--THESE SPECIAL ZONES.
NO TARIFFS OR TAXES. THEY BRING RAW GOODS IN AND SHIP FINISHED CRAP OUT. THEY'RE... DICTATORIAL SWEATSHOPS, BASICALLY. NAFTA-SANCTIONED SWEATSHOPS.
LIKE 2,000 MILES OF BORDER BETWEEN US AND MEXICO. NOW IT'S BEEN MILITARIZED, AND THEY'RE BUILDING A FREAKIN' FENCE...
...
RIGHT, FRANK. VERY ASTUTE POINT YOU MAKE. GOOD FENCES DO MAKE GOOD NEIGHBORS.

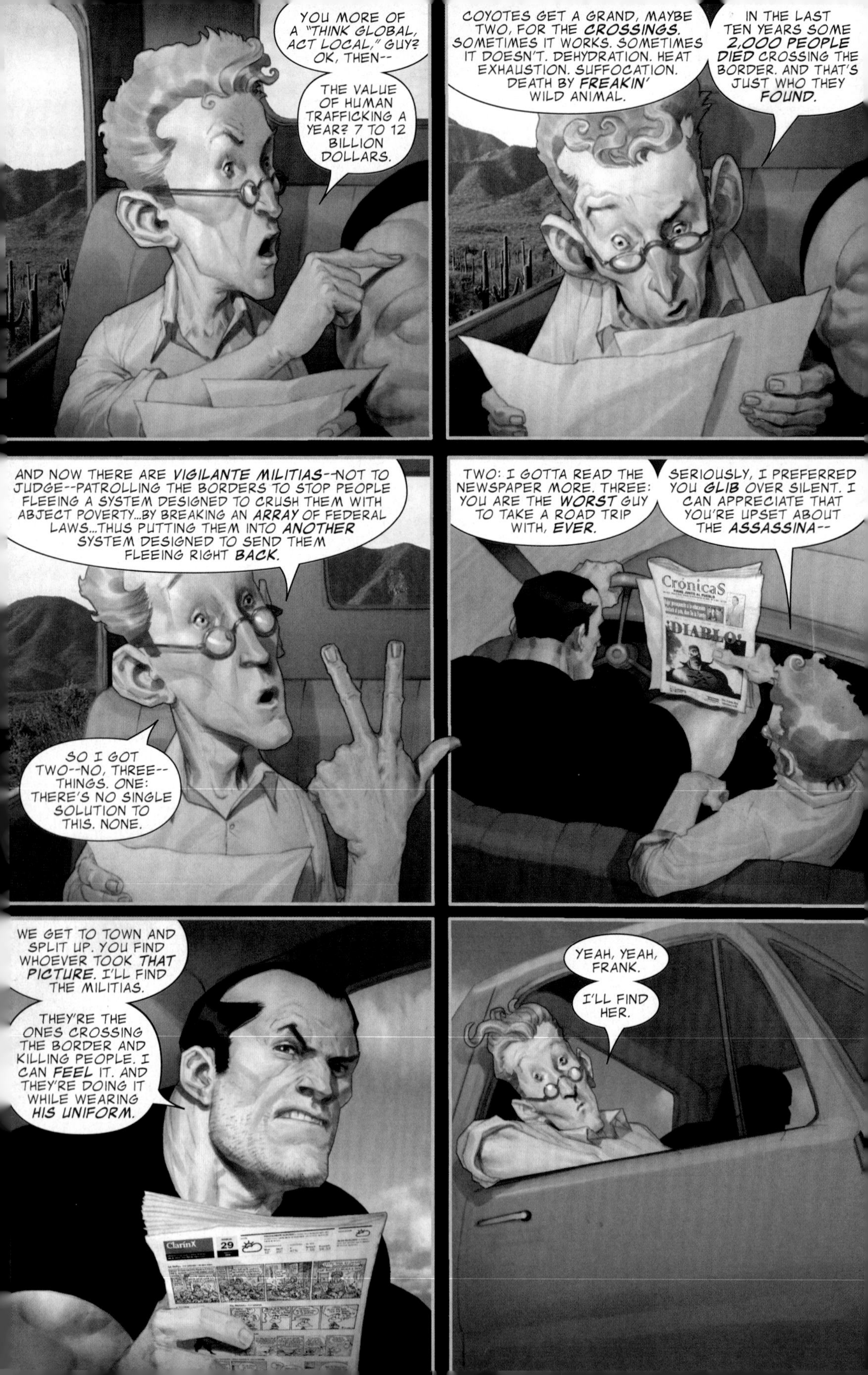
YOU MORE OF A "THINK GLOBAL, ACT LOCAL," GUY? OK, THEN--
THE VALUE OF HUMAN TRAFFICKING A YEAR? 7 TO 12 BILLION DOLLARS.
COYOTES GET A GRAND, MAYBE TWO, FOR THE CROSSINGS. SOMETIMES IT WORKS. SOMETIMES IT DOESN'T. DEHYDRATION. HEAT EXHAUSTION. SUFFOCATION. DEATH BY FREAKIN' WILD ANIMAL.
IN THE LAST TEN YEARS SOME 2,000 PEOPLE DIED CROSSING THE BORDER. AND THAT'S JUST WHO THEY FOUND.
AND NOW THERE ARE VIGILANTE MILITIAS--NOT TO JUDGE--PATROLLING THE BORDERS TO STOP PEOPLE FLEEING A SYSTEM DESIGNED TO CRUSH THEM WITH ABJECT POVERTY...BY BREAKING AN ARRAY OF FEDERAL LAWS...THUS PUTTING THEM INTO ANOTHER SYSTEM DESIGNED TO SEND THEM FLEEING RIGHT BACK.
SO I GOT TWO--NO, THREE--THINGS. ONE: THERE'S NO SINGLE SOLUTION TO THIS. NONE.
TWO: I GOTTA READ THE NEWSPAPER MORE. THREE: YOU ARE THE WORST GUY TO TAKE A ROAD TRIP WITH, EVER.
SERIOUSLY, I PREFERRED YOU GLIB OVER SILENT. I CAN APPRECIATE THAT YOU'RE UPSET ABOUT THE ASSASSINA--
Crónicas
¡DIABLO!
WE GET TO TOWN AND SPLIT UP. YOU FIND WHOEVER TOOK THAT PICTURE. I'LL FIND THE MILITIAS.
THEY'RE THE ONES CROSSING THE BORDER AND KILLING PEOPLE. I CAN FEEL IT. AND THEY'RE DOING IT WHILE WEARING HIS UNIFORM.
ClarinX
29
YEAH, YEAH, FRANK.
I'LL FIND HER.

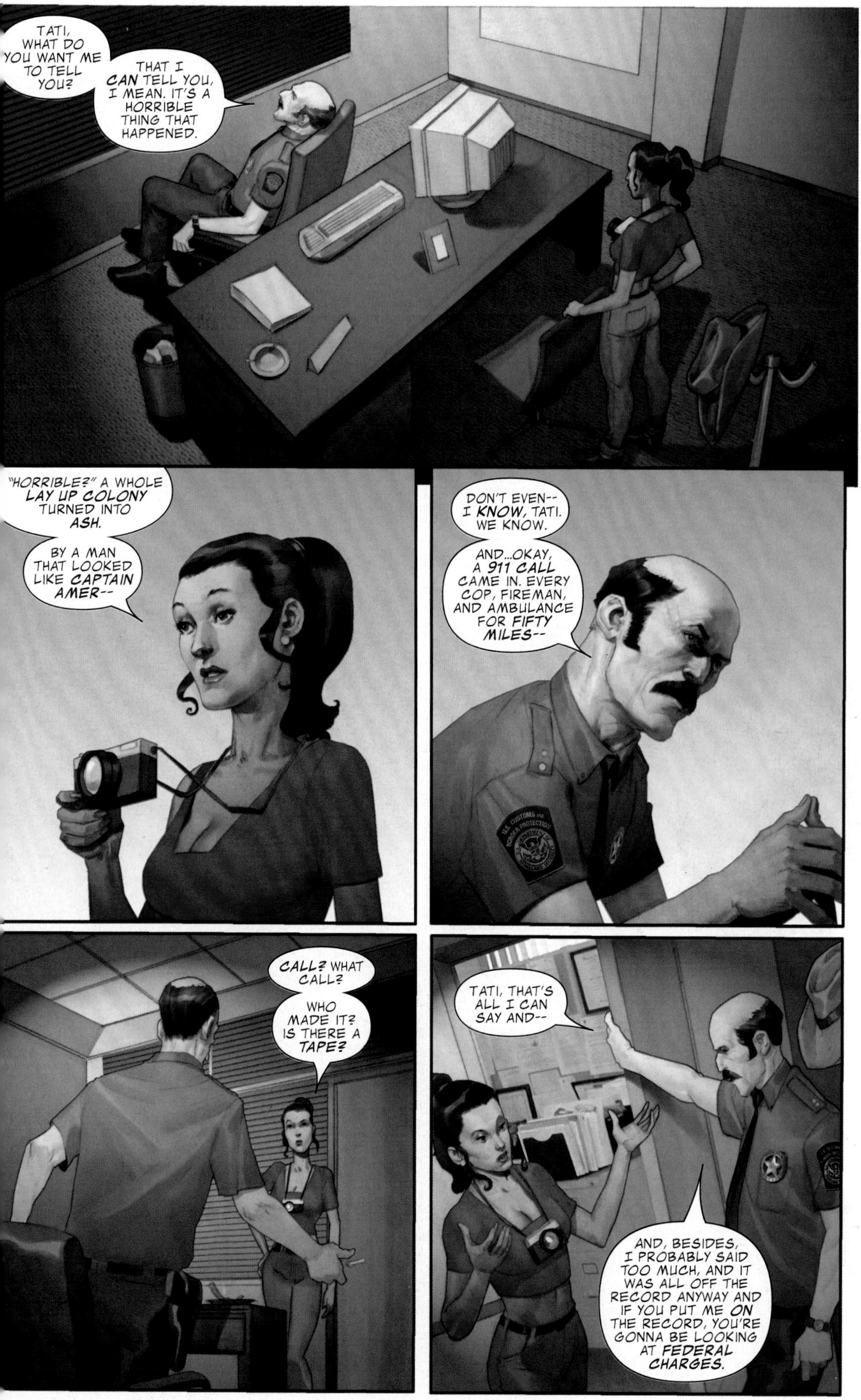
TATI, WHAT DO YOU WANT ME TO TELL YOU?
THAT I CAN TELL YOU, I MEAN. IT'S A HORRIBLE THING THAT HAPPENED.
"HORRIBLE?" A WHOLE LAY UP COLONY TURNED INTO ASH.
BY A MAN THAT LOOKED LIKE CAPTAIN AMER--
DON'T EVEN-- I KNOW, TATI. WE KNOW.
AND...OKAY, A 911 CALL CAME IN. EVERY COP, FIREMAN, AND AMBULANCE FOR FIFTY MILES--
CALL? WHAT CALL?
WHO MADE IT? IS THERE A TAPE?
TATI, THAT'S ALL I CAN SAY AND--
AND, BESIDES, I PROBABLY SAID TOO MUCH, AND IT WAS ALL OFF THE RECORD ANYWAY AND IF YOU PUT ME ON THE RECORD, YOU'RE GONNA BE LOOKING AT FEDERAL CHARGES.

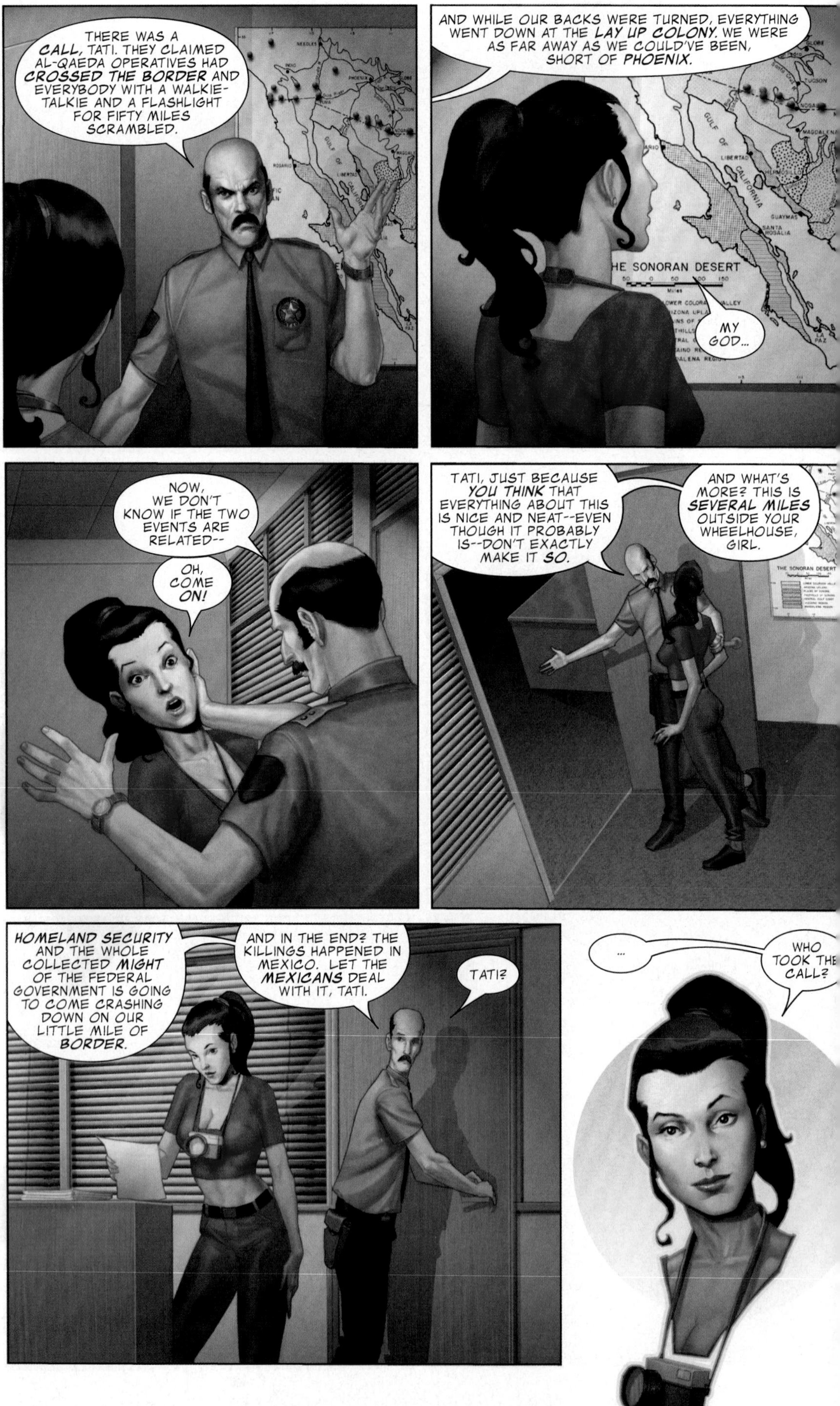
THERE WAS A CALL, TATI. THEY CLAIMED AL-QAEDA OPERATIVES HAD CROSSED THE BORDER AND EVERYBODY WITH A WALKIE-TALKIE AND A FLASHLIGHT FOR FIFTY MILES SCRAMBLED.
AND WHILE OUR BACKS WERE TURNED, EVERYTHING WENT DOWN AT THE LAY UP COLONY. WE WERE AS FAR AWAY AS WE COULD'VE BEEN, SHORT OF PHOENIX.
THE SONORAN DESERT
MY GOD...
NOW, WE DON'T KNOW IF THE TWO EVENTS ARE RELATED--
OH, COME ON!
TATI, JUST BECAUSE YOU THINK THAT EVERYTHING ABOUT THIS IS NICE AND NEAT--EVEN THOUGH IT PROBABLY IS--DON'T EXACTLY MAKE IT SO.
AND WHAT'S MORE? THIS IS SEVERAL MILES OUTSIDE YOUR WHEELHOUSE, GIRL.
HOMELAND SECURITY AND THE WHOLE COLLECTED MIGHT OF THE FEDERAL GOVERNMENT IS GOING TO COME CRASHING DOWN ON OUR LITTLE MILE OF BORDER.
AND IN THE END? THE KILLINGS HAPPENED IN MEXICO. LET THE MEXICANS DEAL WITH IT, TATI.
TATI?
...
WHO TOOK THE CALL?

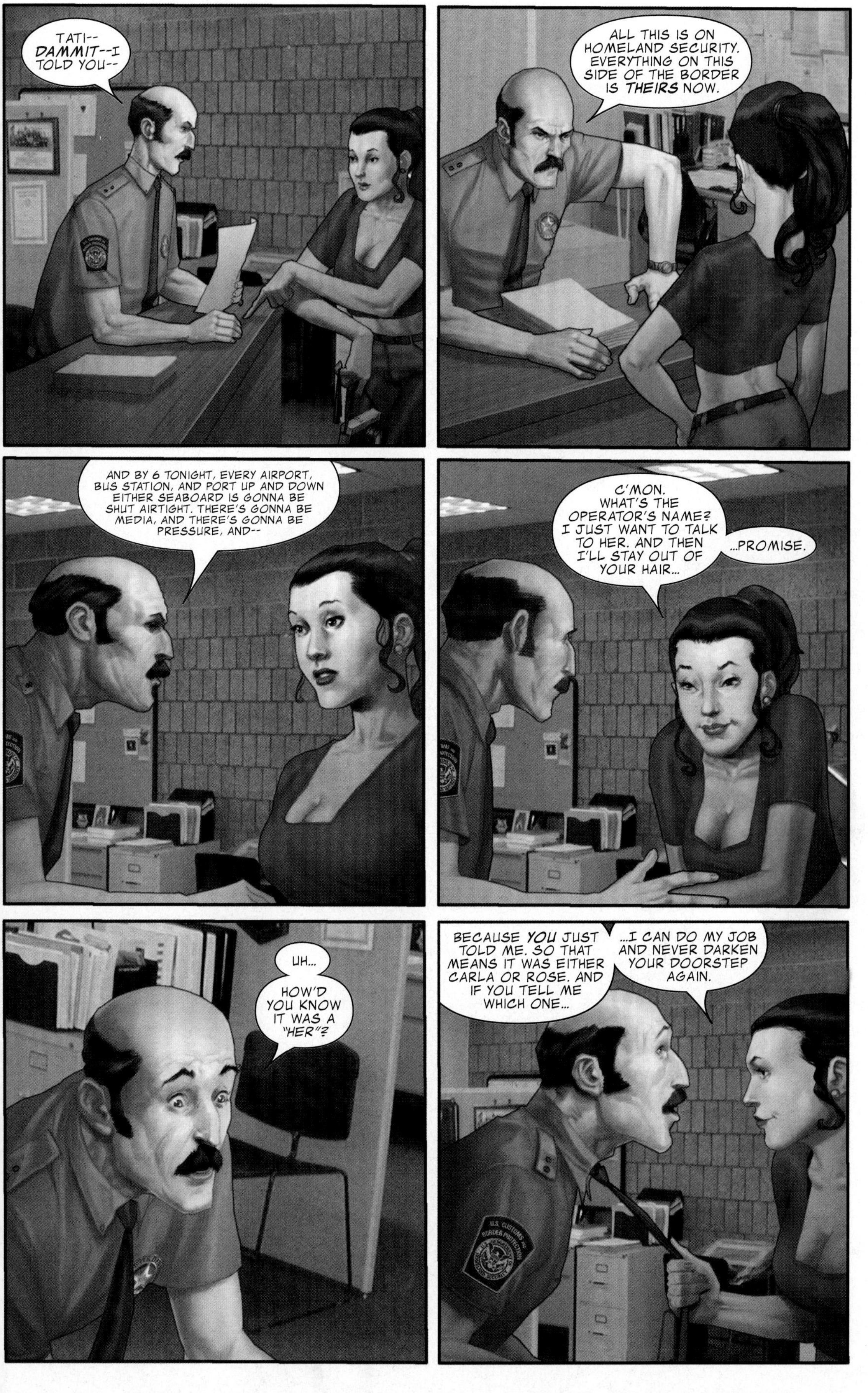
TATI-- DAMMIT--I TOLD YOU--
ALL THIS IS ON HOMELAND SECURITY. EVERYTHING ON THIS SIDE OF THE BORDER IS THEIRS NOW.
AND BY 6 TONIGHT, EVERY AIRPORT, BUS STATION, AND PORT UP AND DOWN EITHER SEABOARD IS GONNA BE SHUT AIRTIGHT. THERE'S GONNA BE MEDIA, AND THERE'S GONNA BE PRESSURE, AND--
C'MON. WHAT'S THE OPERATOR'S NAME? I JUST WANT TO TALK TO HER. AND THEN I'LL STAY OUT OF YOUR HAIR...
...PROMISE.
UH...
HOW'D YOU KNOW IT WAS A "HER"?
BECAUSE YOU JUST TOLD ME. SO THAT MEANS IT WAS EITHER CARLA OR ROSE. AND IF YOU TELL ME WHICH ONE...
...I CAN DO MY JOB AND NEVER DARKEN YOUR DOORSTEP AGAIN.

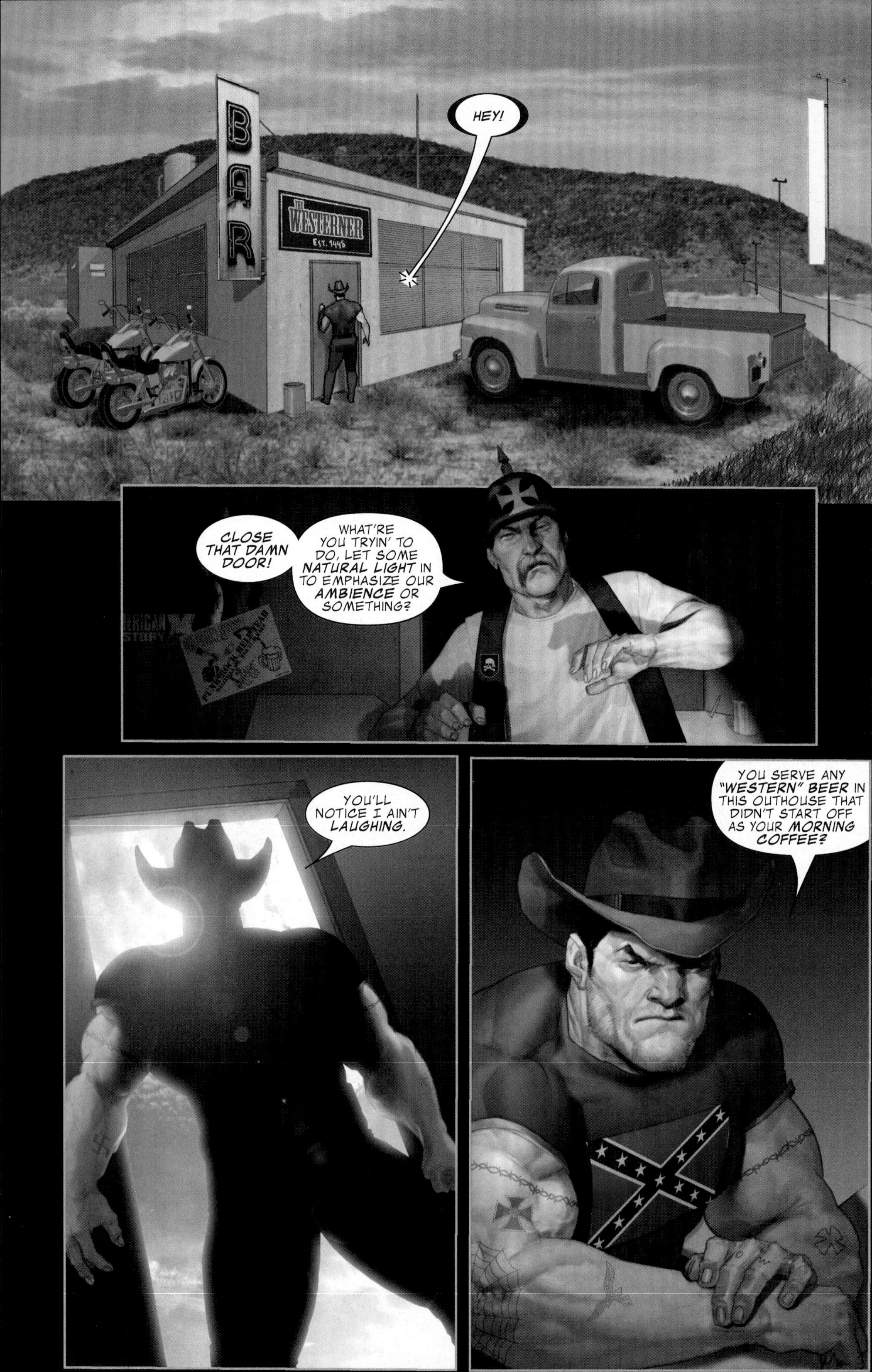
BAR
THE WESTERNER
EST. 1448
HEY!
CLOSE THAT DAMN DOOR!
WHAT'RE YOU TRYIN' TO DO, LET SOME NATURAL LIGHT IN TO EMPHASIZE OUR AMBIENCE OR SOMETHING?
YOU'LL NOTICE I AIN'T LAUGHING.
YOU SERVE ANY "WESTERN" BEER IN THIS OUTHOUSE THAT DIDN'T START OFF AS YOUR MORNING COFFEE?

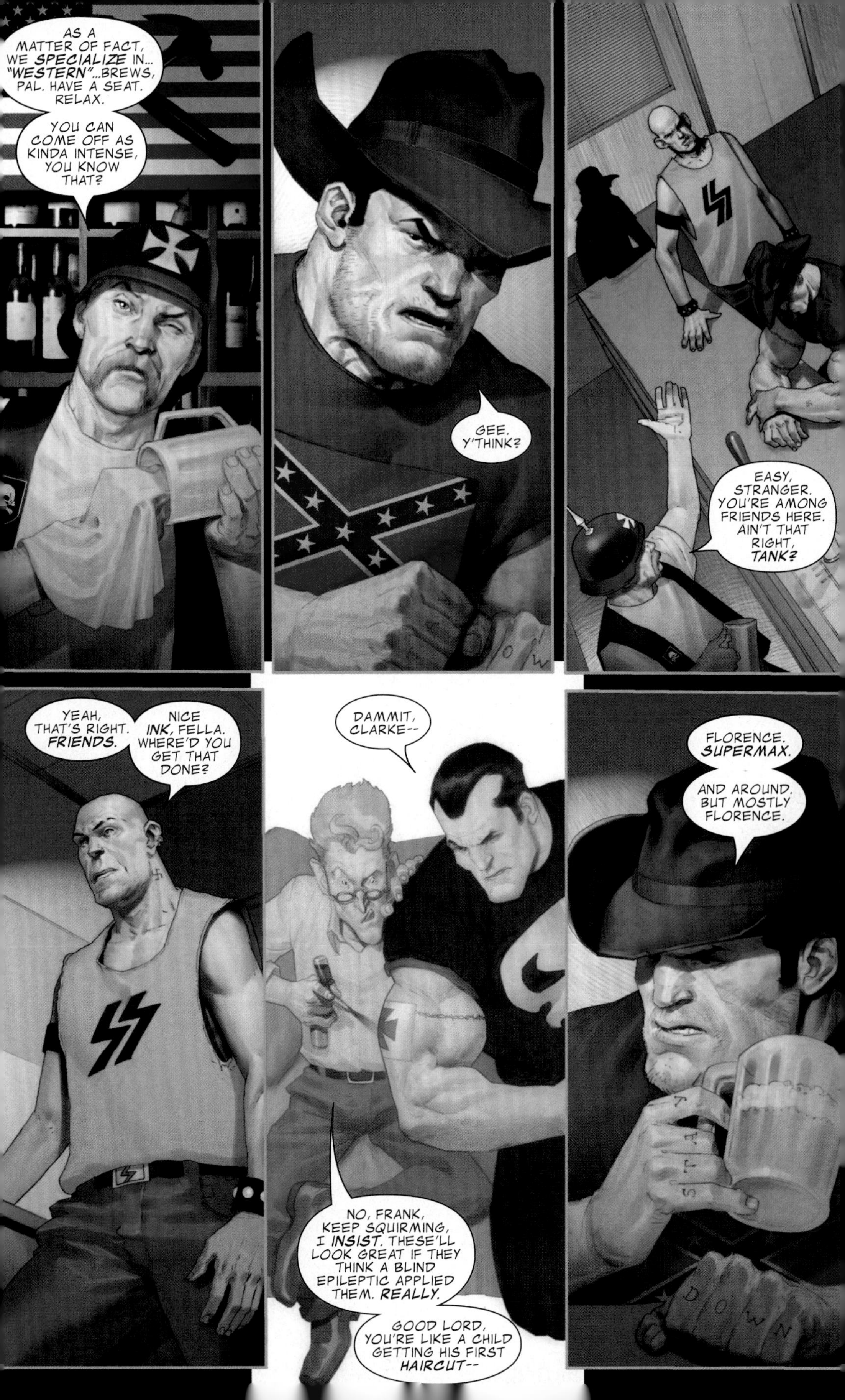

AS A MATTER OF FACT, WE SPECIALIZE IN... "WESTERN"...BREWS, PAL. HAVE A SEAT. RELAX.
YOU CAN COME OFF AS KINDA INTENSE, YOU KNOW THAT?
GEE. Y'THINK?
EASY, STRANGER. YOU'RE AMONG FRIENDS HERE. AIN'T THAT RIGHT, TANK?
YEAH, THAT'S RIGHT. FRIENDS.
NICE INK, FELLA. WHERE'D YOU GET THAT DONE?
DAMMIT, CLARKE--
NO, FRANK, KEEP SQUIRMING, I INSIST. THESE'LL LOOK GREAT IF THEY THINK A BLIND EPILEPTIC APPLIED THEM. REALLY.
GOOD LORD, YOU'RE LIKE A CHILD GETTING HIS FIRST HAIRCUT--
FLORENCE. SUPERMAX.
AND AROUND. BUT MOSTLY FLORENCE.

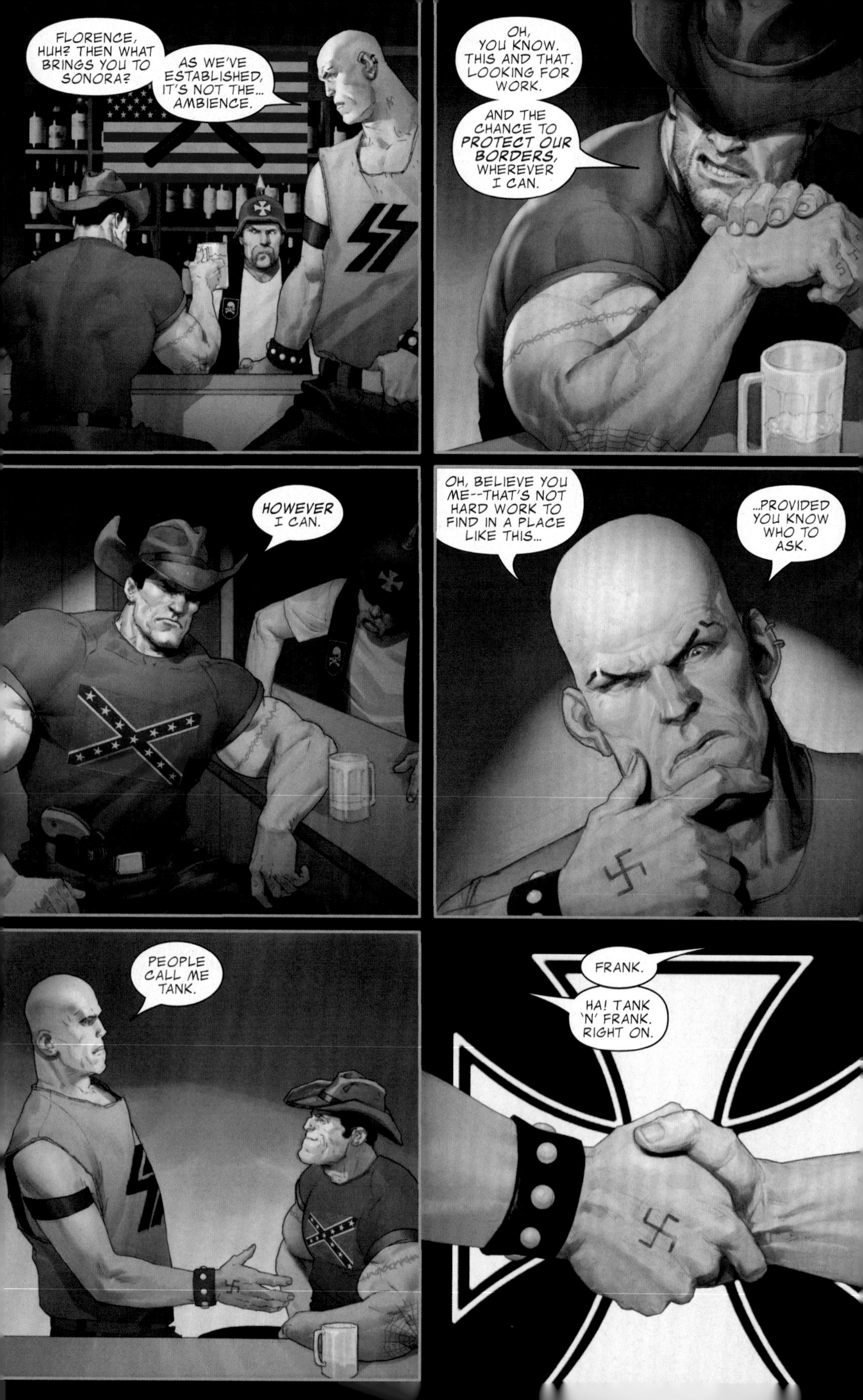
FLORENCE, HUH? THEN WHAT BRINGS YOU TO SONORA?
AS WE'VE ESTABLISHED, IT'S NOT THE... AMBIENCE.
OH, YOU KNOW. THIS AND THAT. LOOKING FOR WORK.
AND THE CHANCE TO *PROTECT OUR BORDERS,* WHEREVER I CAN.
HOWEVER I CAN.
OH, BELIEVE YOU ME--THAT'S NOT HARD WORK TO FIND IN A PLACE LIKE THIS...
...PROVIDED YOU KNOW WHO TO ASK.
PEOPLE CALL ME TANK.
FRANK.
HA! TANK 'N' FRANK. RIGHT ON.

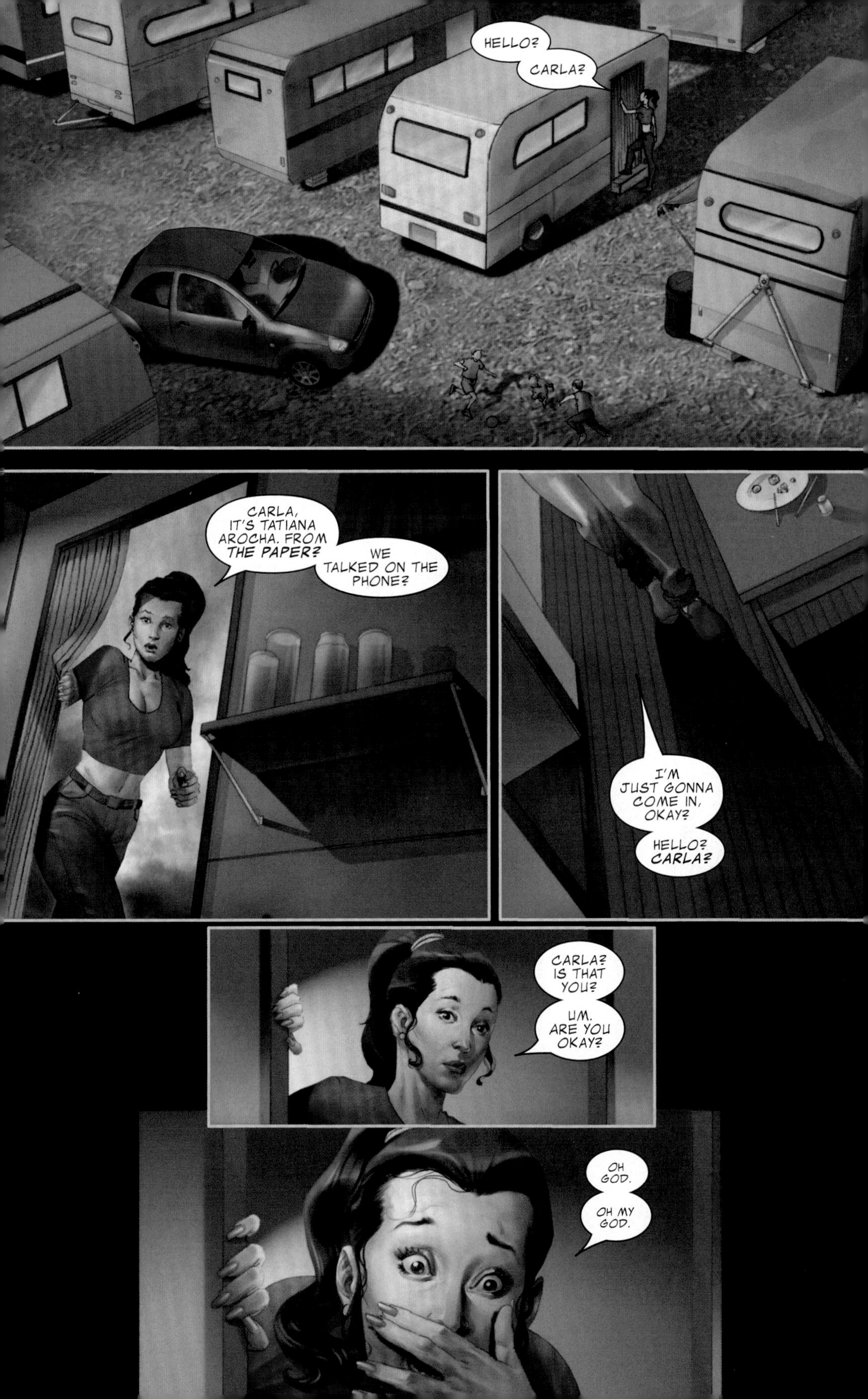
HELLO?
CARLA?
CARLA, IT'S TATIANA AROCHA. FROM *THE PAPER?*
WE TALKED ON THE PHONE?
I'M JUST GONNA COME IN, OKAY?
HELLO? *CARLA?*
CARLA? IS THAT YOU?
UM. ARE YOU OKAY?
OH GOD.
OH MY GOD.

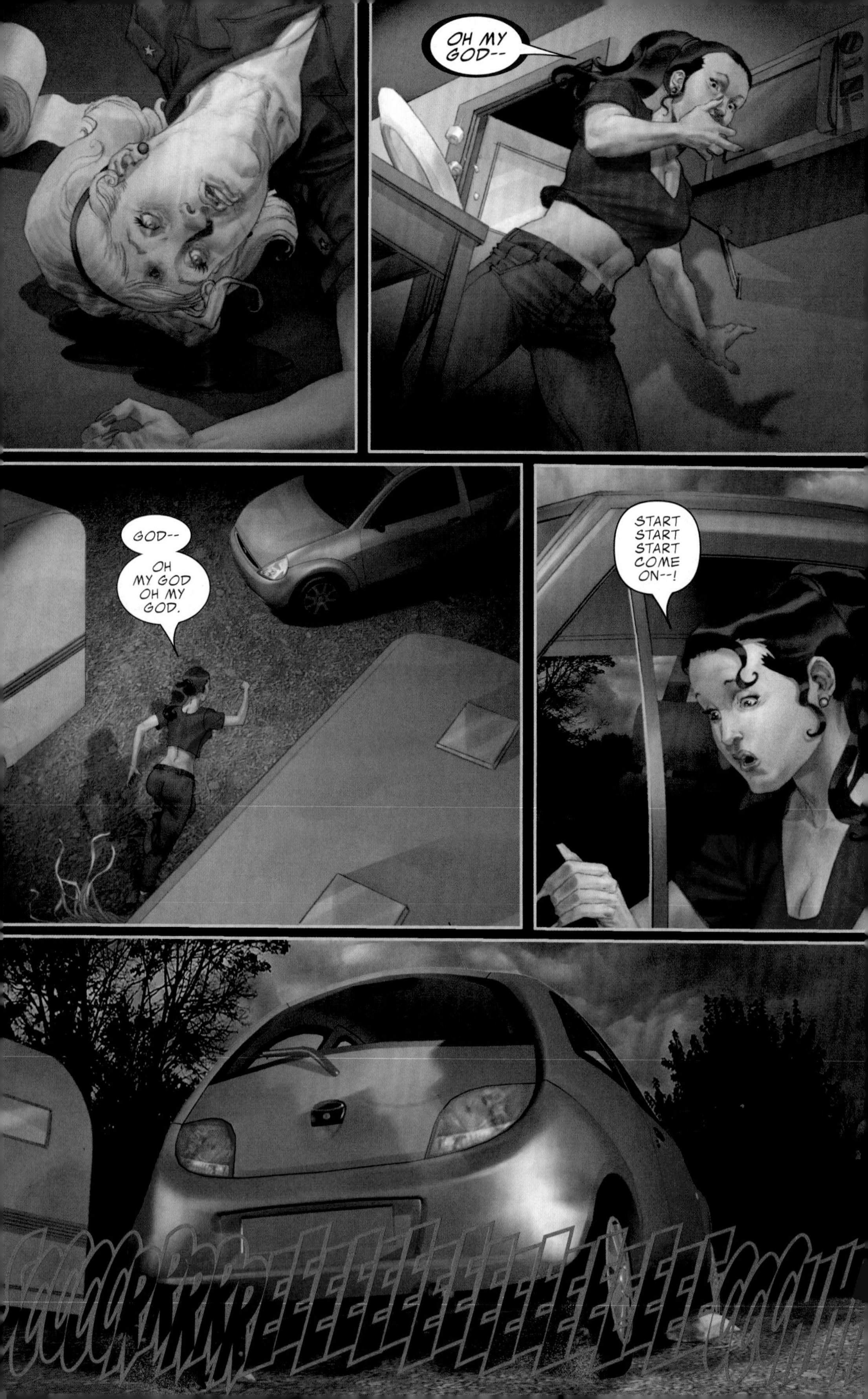
OH MY GOD--
GOD--
OH MY GOD OH MY GOD.
START START START COME ON--!

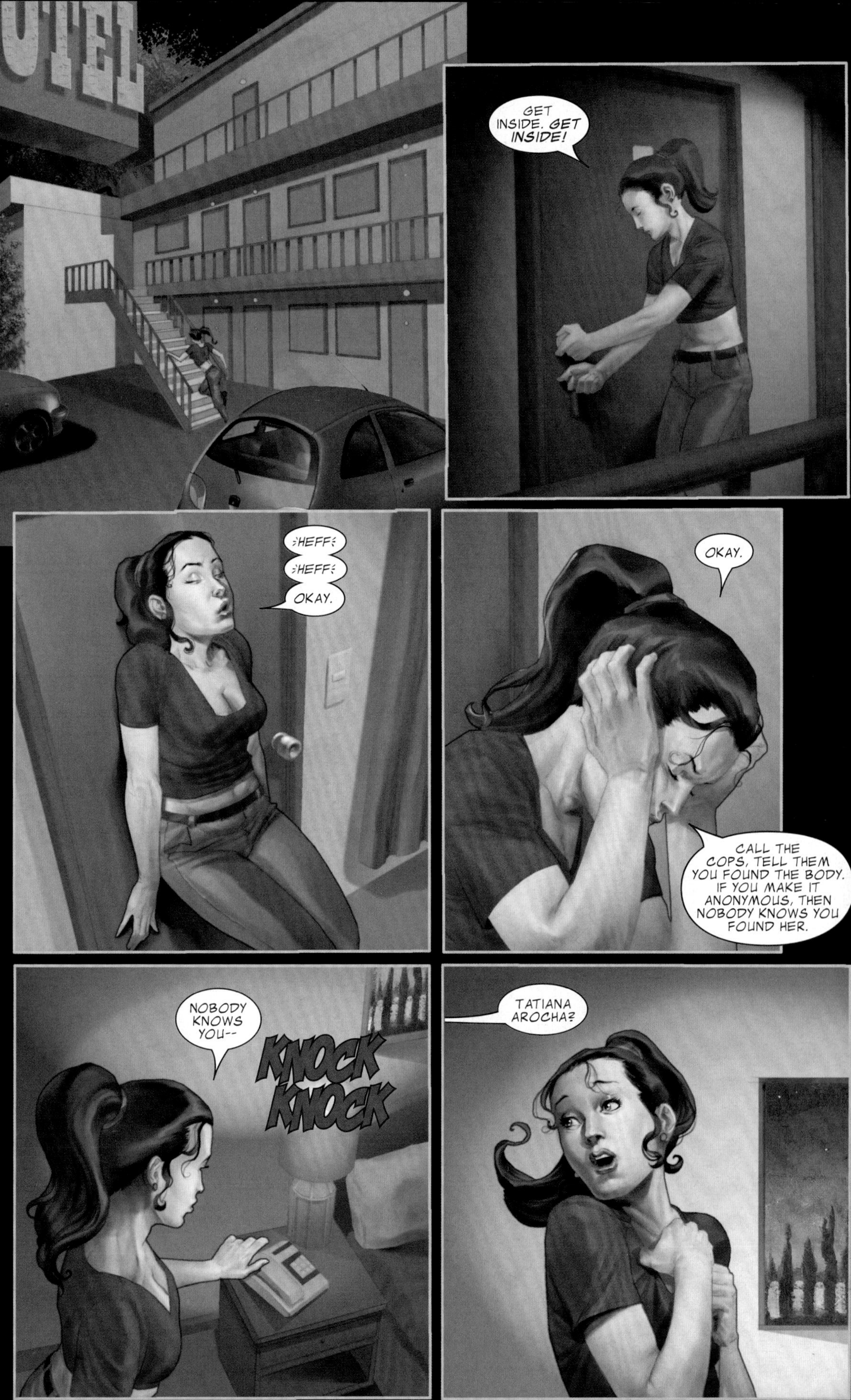
GET INSIDE. GET INSIDE!
HEFF
HEFF
OKAY.
OKAY.
CALL THE COPS, TELL THEM YOU FOUND THE BODY. IF YOU MAKE IT ANONYMOUS, THEN NOBODY KNOWS YOU FOUND HER.
NOBODY KNOWS YOU--
KNOCK KNOCK
TATIANA AROCHA?

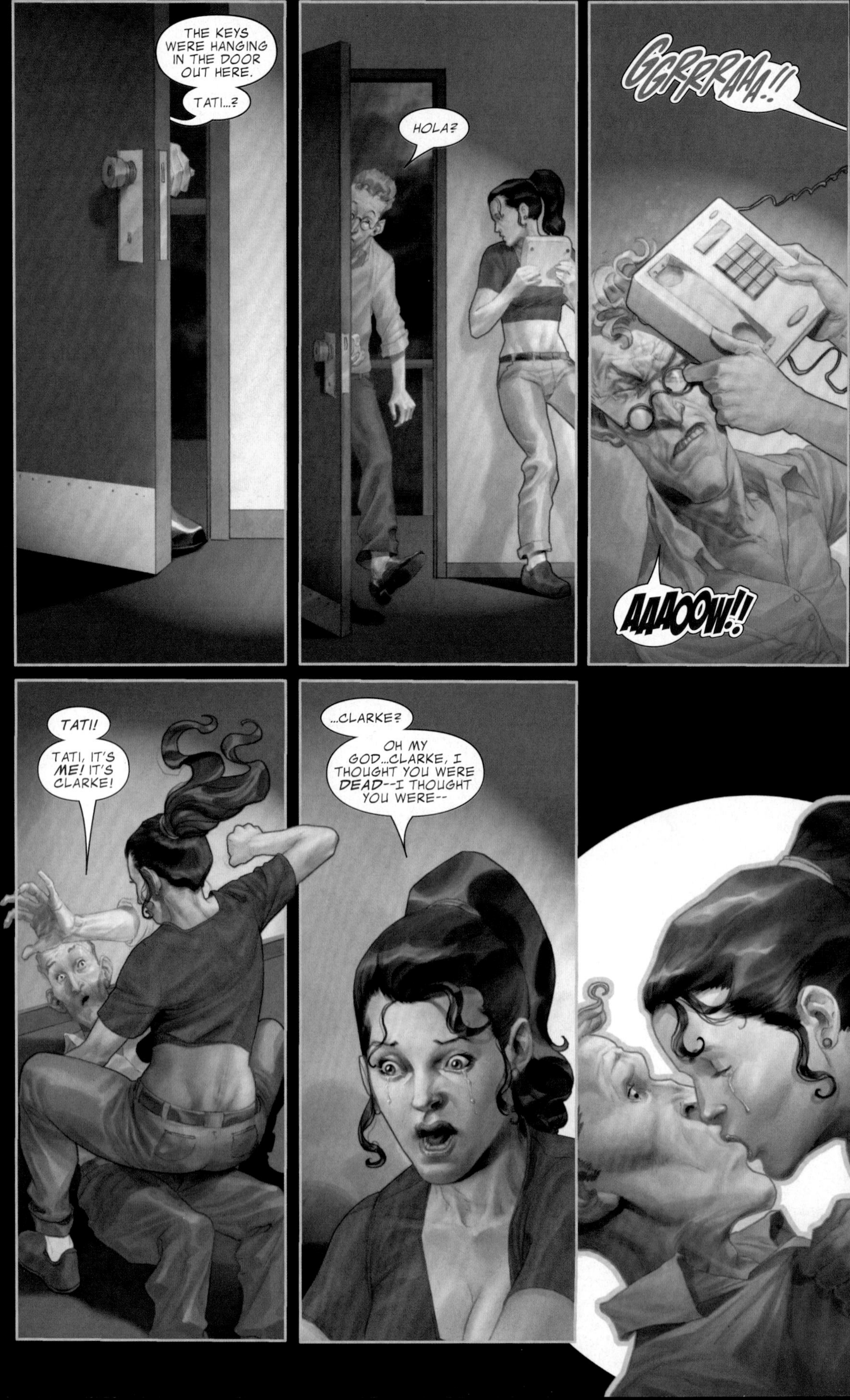
THE KEYS WERE HANGING IN THE DOOR OUT HERE.
TATI...?
HOLA?
GGRRRAAA!!
AAAOOW!!
TATI!
TATI, IT'S *ME!* IT'S CLARKE!
...CLARKE?
OH MY GOD...CLARKE, I THOUGHT YOU WERE *DEAD*--I THOUGHT YOU WERE--

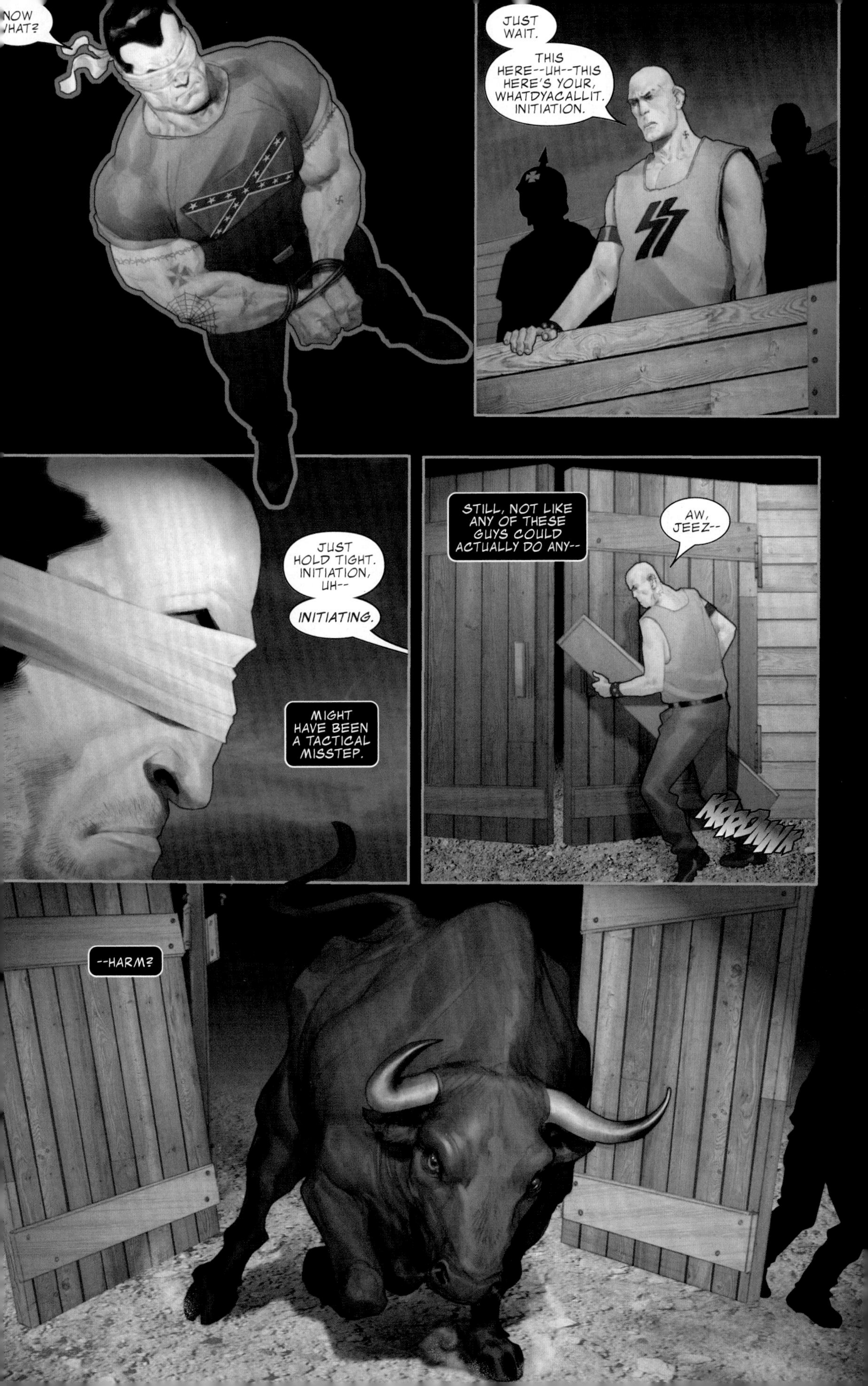

NOW WHAT?
JUST WAIT.
THIS HERE--UH--THIS HERE'S YOUR, WHATDYACALLIT. INITIATION.
JUST HOLD TIGHT. INITIATION, UH--
INITIATING.
MIGHT HAVE BEEN A TACTICAL MISSTEP.
STILL, NOT LIKE ANY OF THESE GUYS COULD ACTUALLY DO ANY--
AW, JEEZ--
KRRONNK
--HARM?

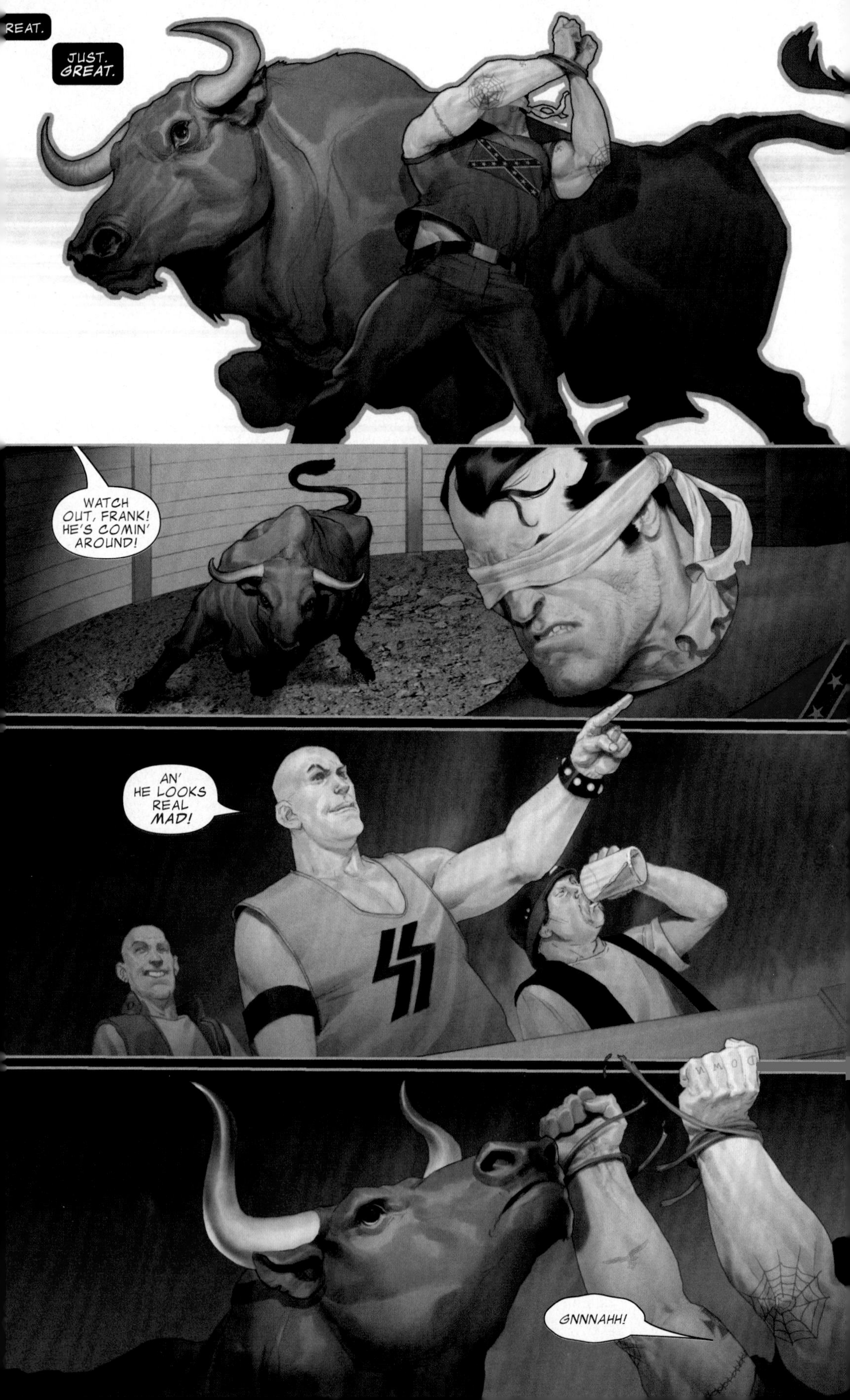
REAT.
JUST. GREAT.
WATCH OUT, FRANK! HE'S COMIN' AROUND!
AN' HE LOOKS REAL MAD!
GNNNAHH!

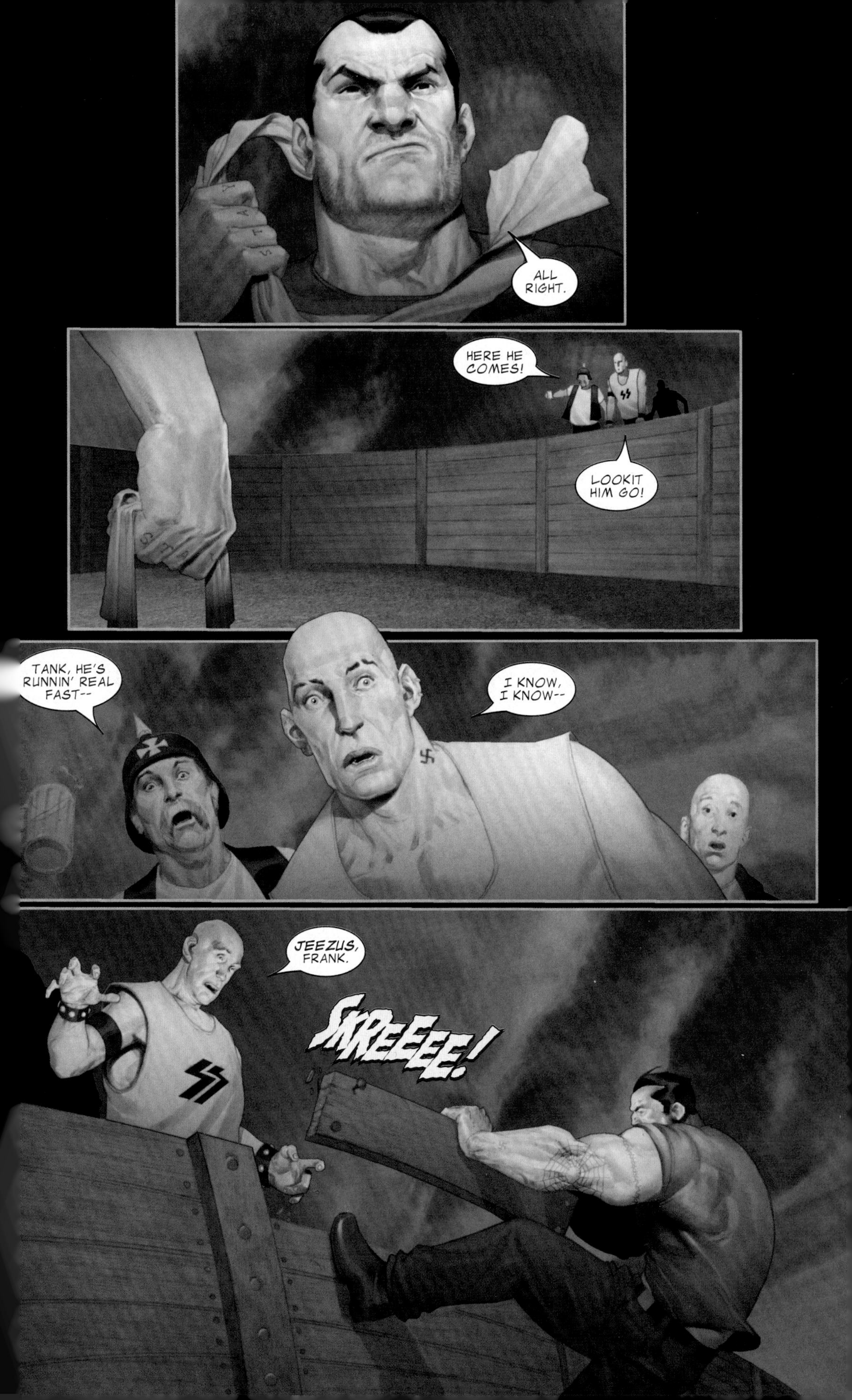
ALL RIGHT.
HERE HE COMES!
LOOKIT HIM GO!
TANK, HE'S RUNNIN' REAL FAST--
I KNOW, I KNOW--
JEEZUS, FRANK.
SKREEEEE!

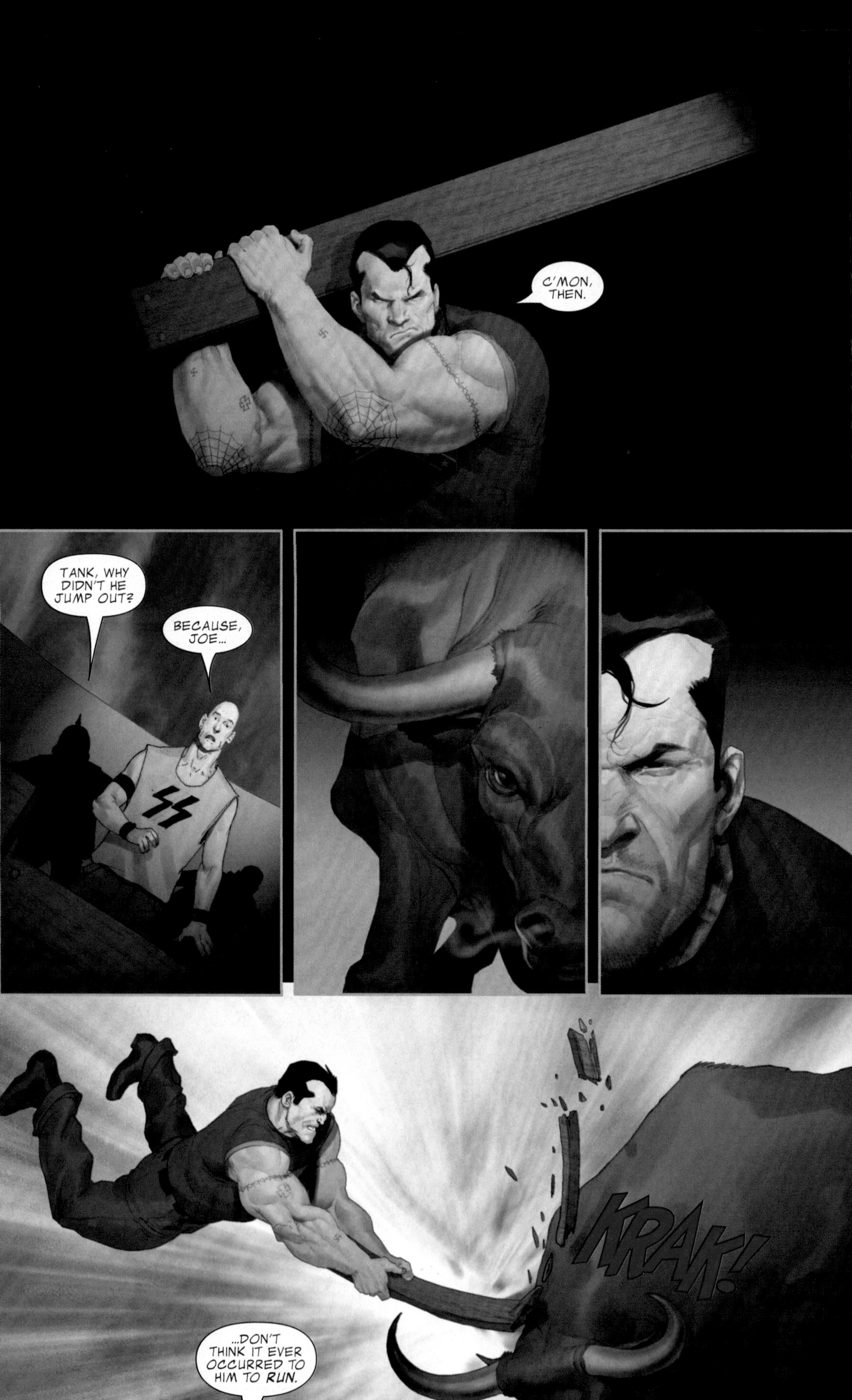
C'MON, THEN.
TANK, WHY DIDN'T HE JUMP OUT?
BECAUSE, JOE...
KRAK!
...DON'T THINK IT EVER OCCURRED TO HIM TO *RUN*.

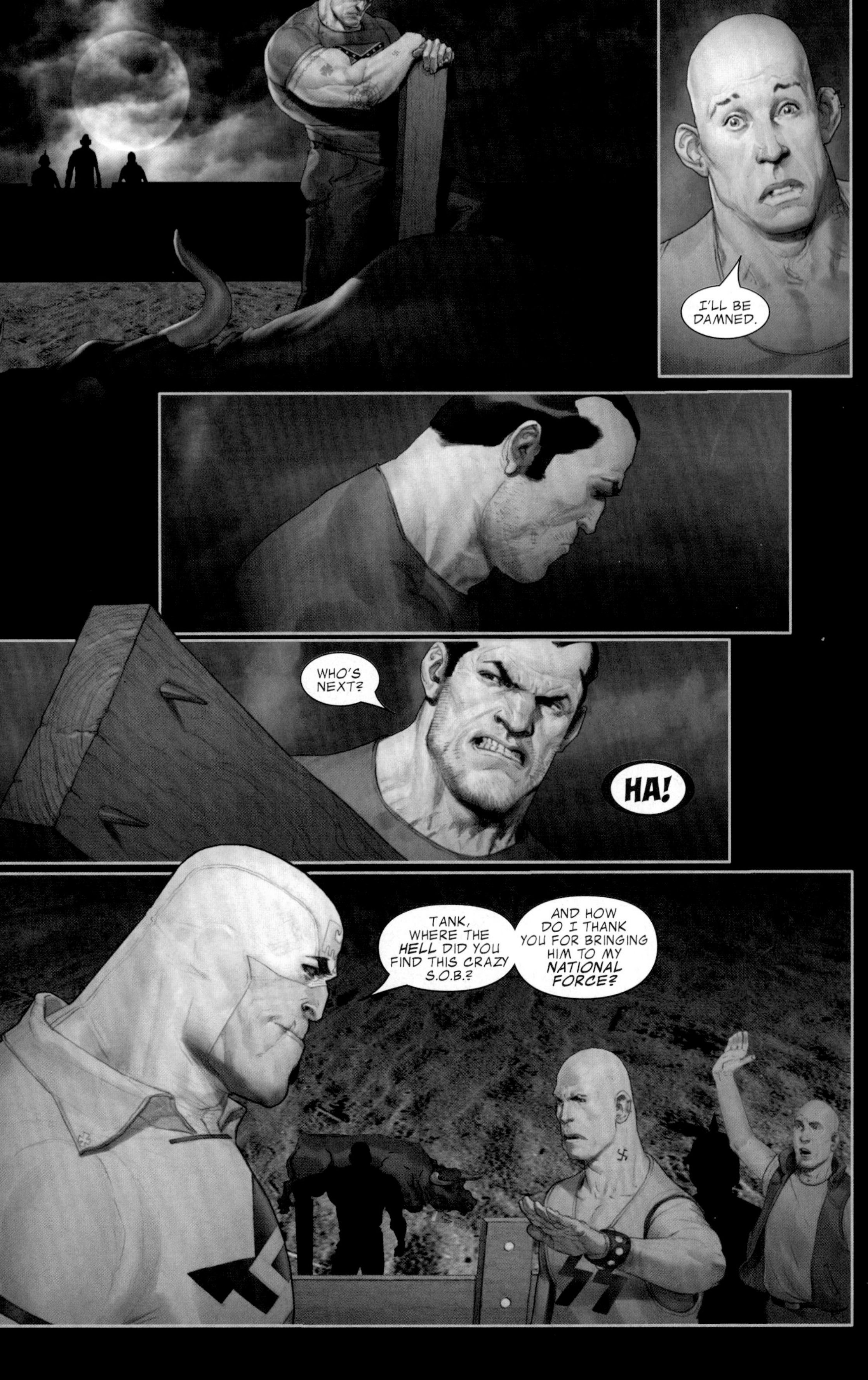
I'LL BE DAMNED.
WHO'S NEXT?
HA!
TANK, WHERE THE HELL DID YOU FIND THIS CRAZY S.O.B.?
AND HOW DO I THANK YOU FOR BRINGING HIM TO MY NATIONAL FORCE?

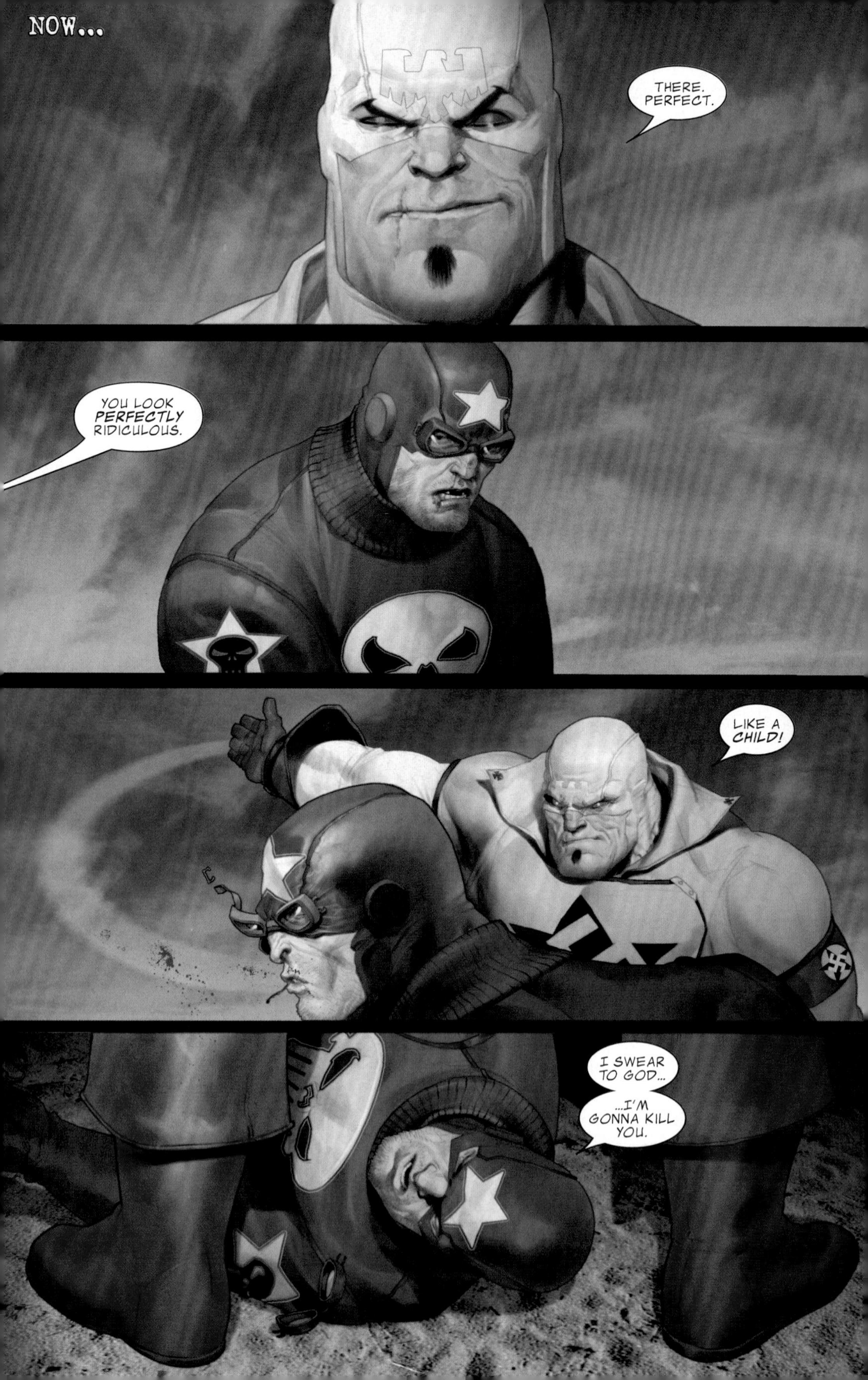
NOW...
THERE. PERFECT.
YOU LOOK PERFECTLY RIDICULOUS.
LIKE A CHILD!
I SWEAR TO GOD...
...I'M GONNA KILL YOU.

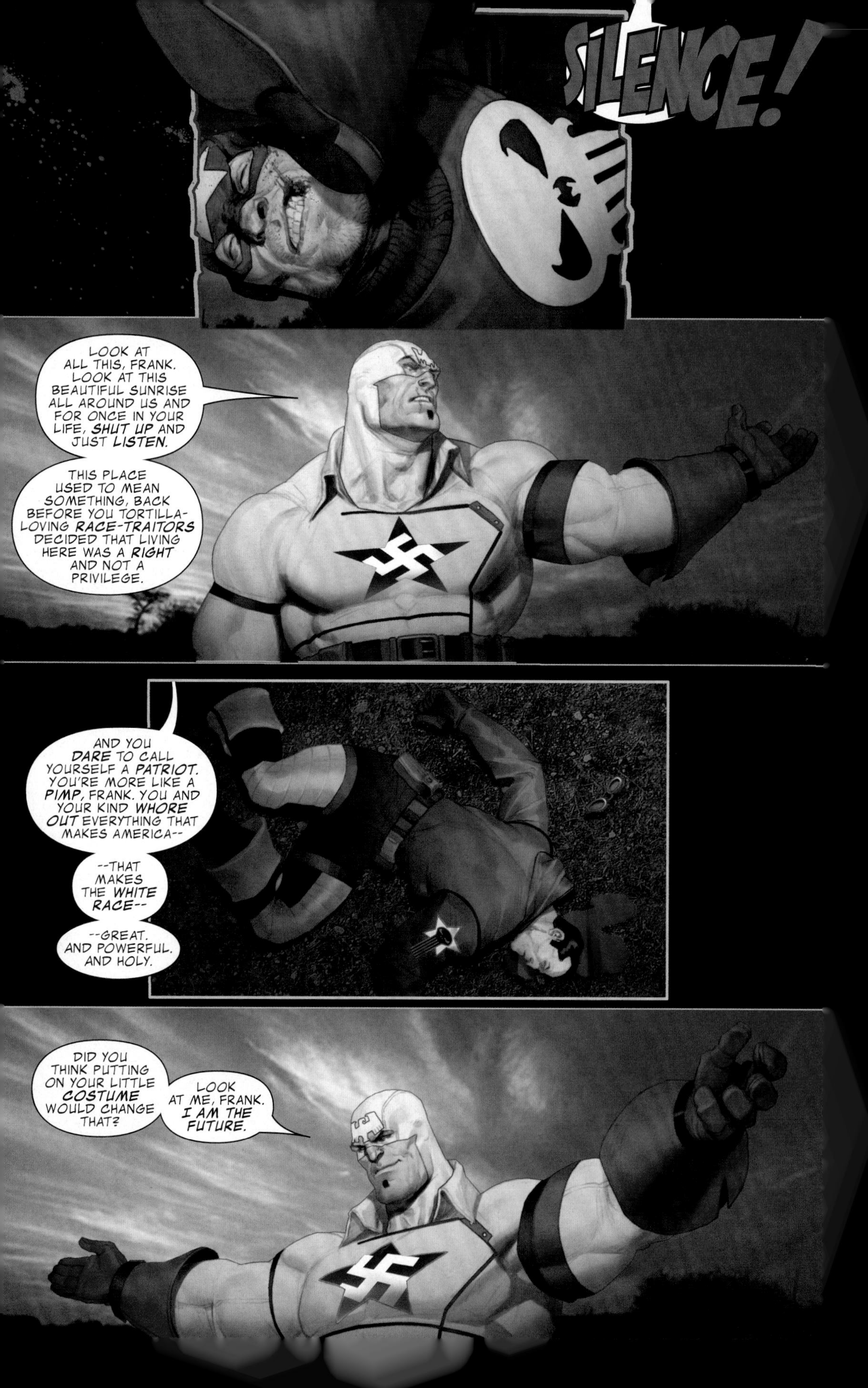
SILENCE!
LOOK AT ALL THIS, FRANK. LOOK AT THIS BEAUTIFUL SUNRISE ALL AROUND US AND FOR ONCE IN YOUR LIFE, SHUT UP AND JUST LISTEN.
THIS PLACE USED TO MEAN SOMETHING, BACK BEFORE YOU TORTILLA-LOVING RACE-TRAITORS DECIDED THAT LIVING HERE WAS A RIGHT AND NOT A PRIVILEGE.
AND YOU DARE TO CALL YOURSELF A PATRIOT. YOU'RE MORE LIKE A PIMP, FRANK. YOU AND YOUR KIND WHORE OUT EVERYTHING THAT MAKES AMERICA--
--THAT MAKES THE WHITE RACE--
--GREAT. AND POWERFUL. AND HOLY.
DID YOU THINK PUTTING ON YOUR LITTLE COSTUME WOULD CHANGE THAT?
LOOK AT ME, FRANK. I AM THE FUTURE.

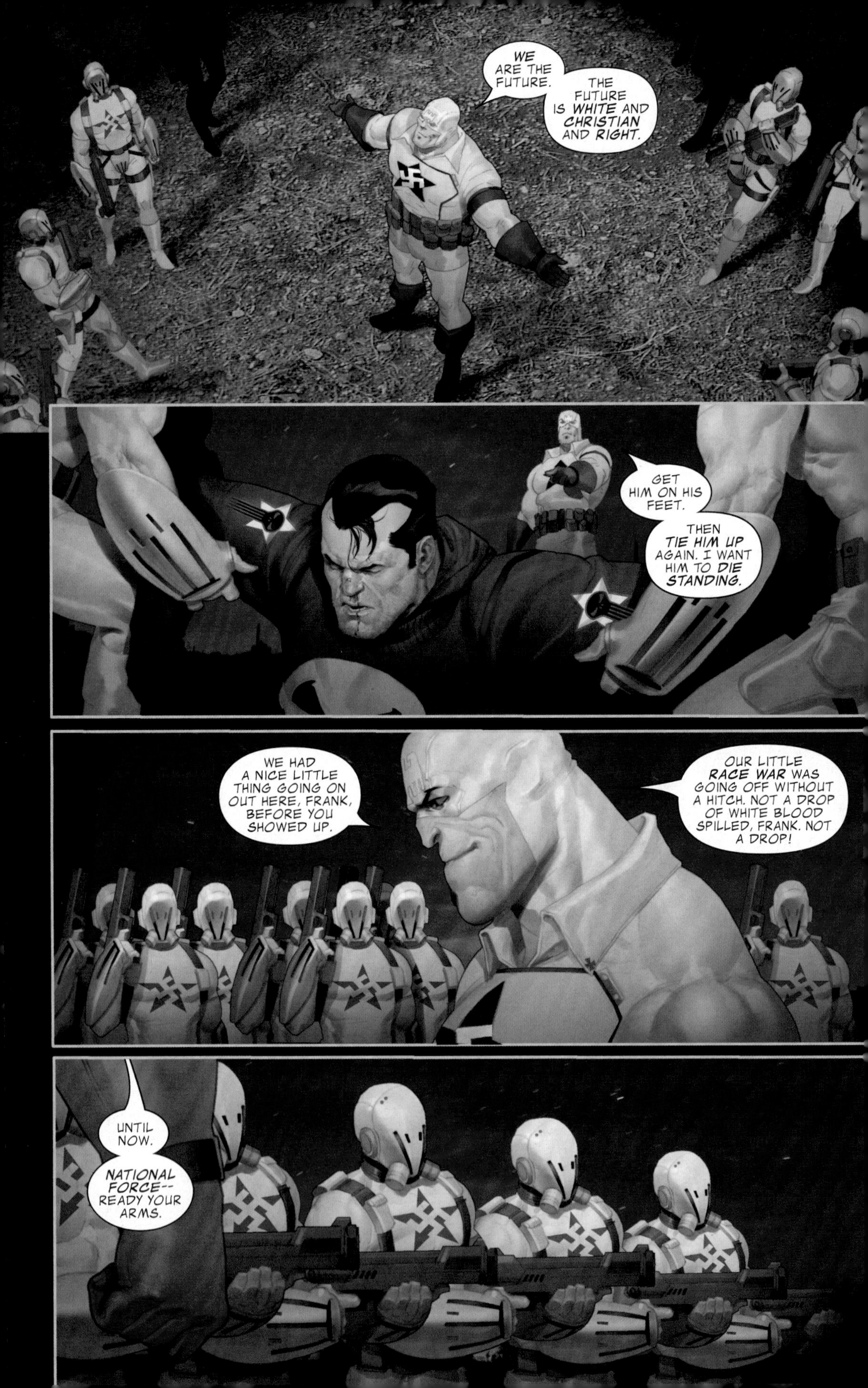
WE ARE THE FUTURE.
THE FUTURE IS WHITE AND CHRISTIAN AND RIGHT.
GET HIM ON HIS FEET.
THEN TIE HIM UP AGAIN. I WANT HIM TO DIE STANDING.
WE HAD A NICE LITTLE THING GOING ON OUT HERE, FRANK, BEFORE YOU SHOWED UP.
OUR LITTLE RACE WAR WAS GOING OFF WITHOUT A HITCH. NOT A DROP OF WHITE BLOOD SPILLED, FRANK. NOT A DROP!
UNTIL NOW.
NATIONAL FORCE-- READY YOUR ARMS.

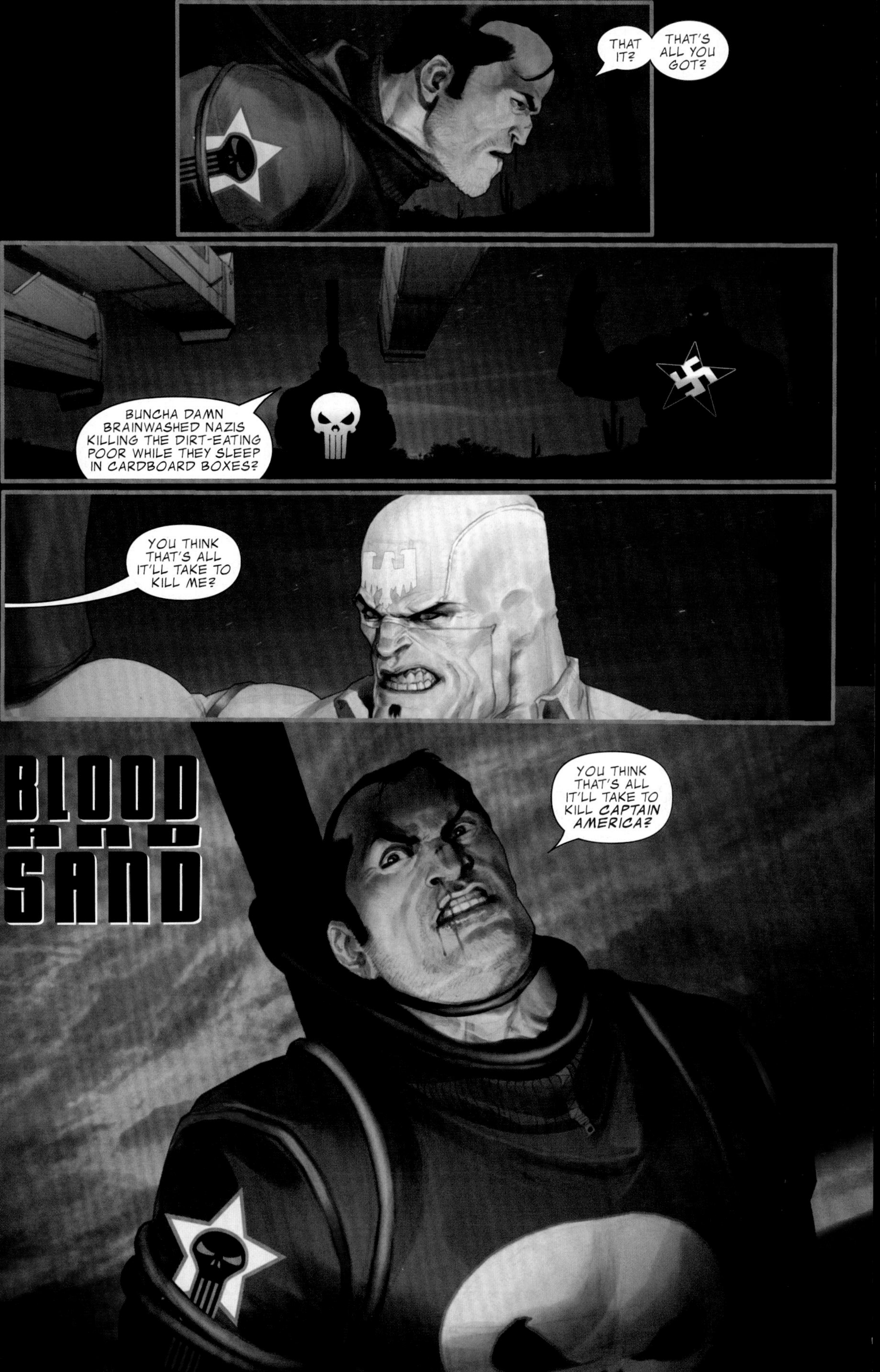
THAT IT?
THAT'S ALL YOU GOT?
BUNCHA DAMN BRAINWASHED NAZIS KILLING THE DIRT-EATING POOR WHILE THEY SLEEP IN CARDBOARD BOXES?
YOU THINK THAT'S ALL IT'LL TAKE TO KILL ME?
BLOOD AND SAND
YOU THINK THAT'S ALL IT'LL TAKE TO KILL CAPTAIN AMERICA?

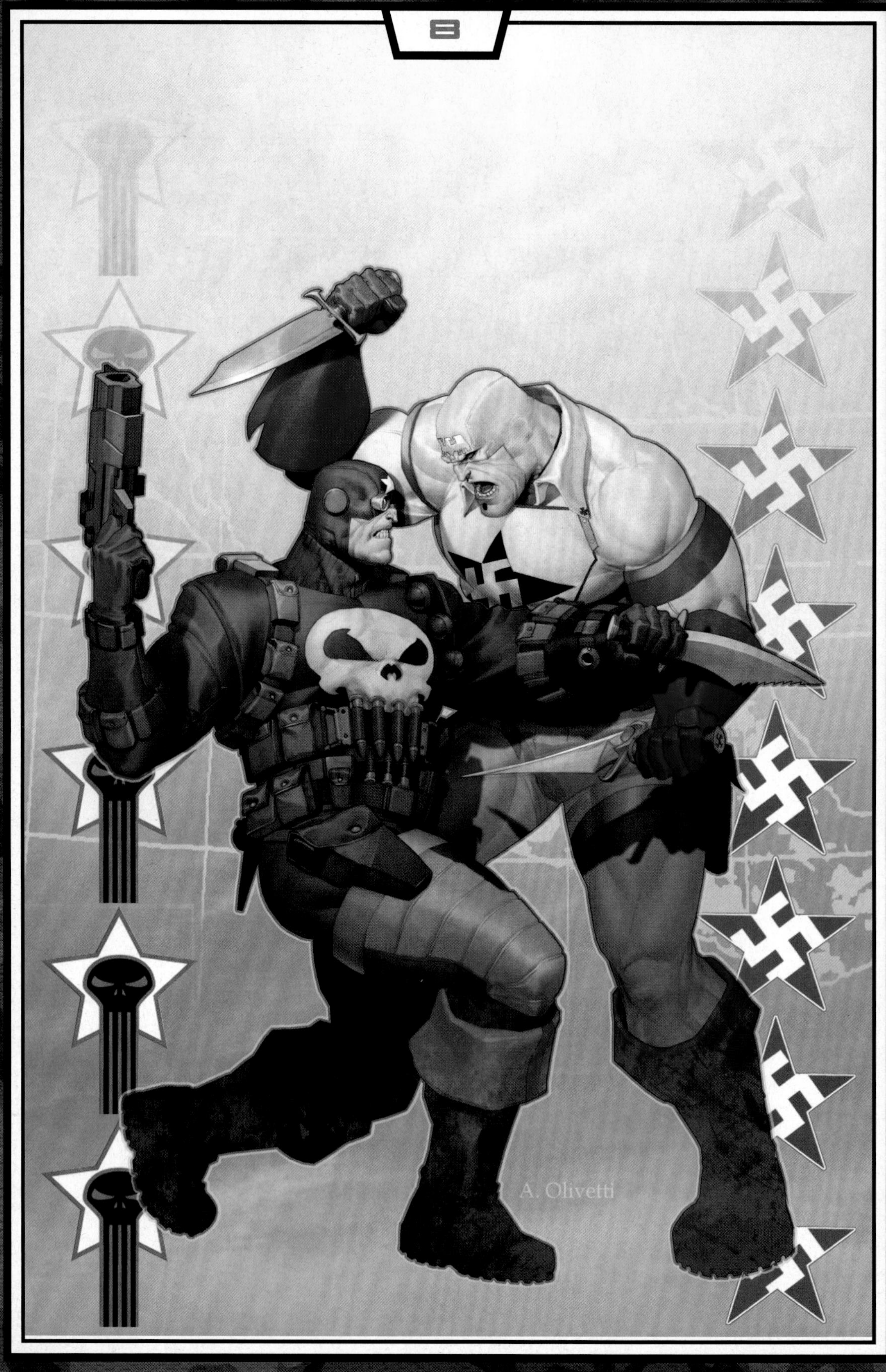
8
A. Olivetti

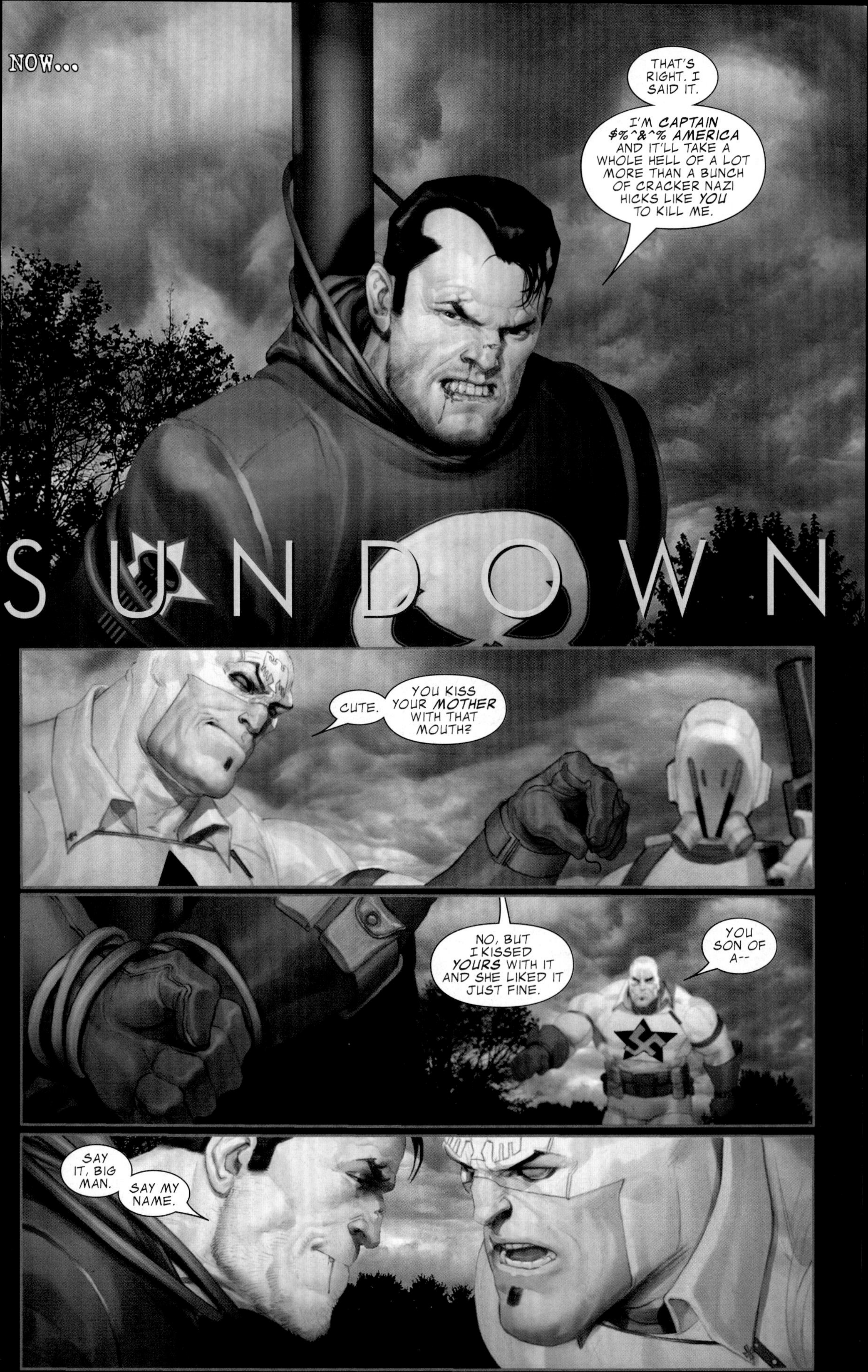
NOW...
THAT'S RIGHT. I SAID IT.
I'M CAPTAIN $%^&^% AMERICA AND IT'LL TAKE A WHOLE HELL OF A LOT MORE THAN A BUNCH OF CRACKER NAZI HICKS LIKE YOU TO KILL ME.
SUNDOWN
CUTE.
YOU KISS YOUR MOTHER WITH THAT MOUTH?
NO, BUT I KISSED YOURS WITH IT AND SHE LIKED IT JUST FINE.
YOU SON OF A--
SAY IT, BIG MAN.
SAY MY NAME.

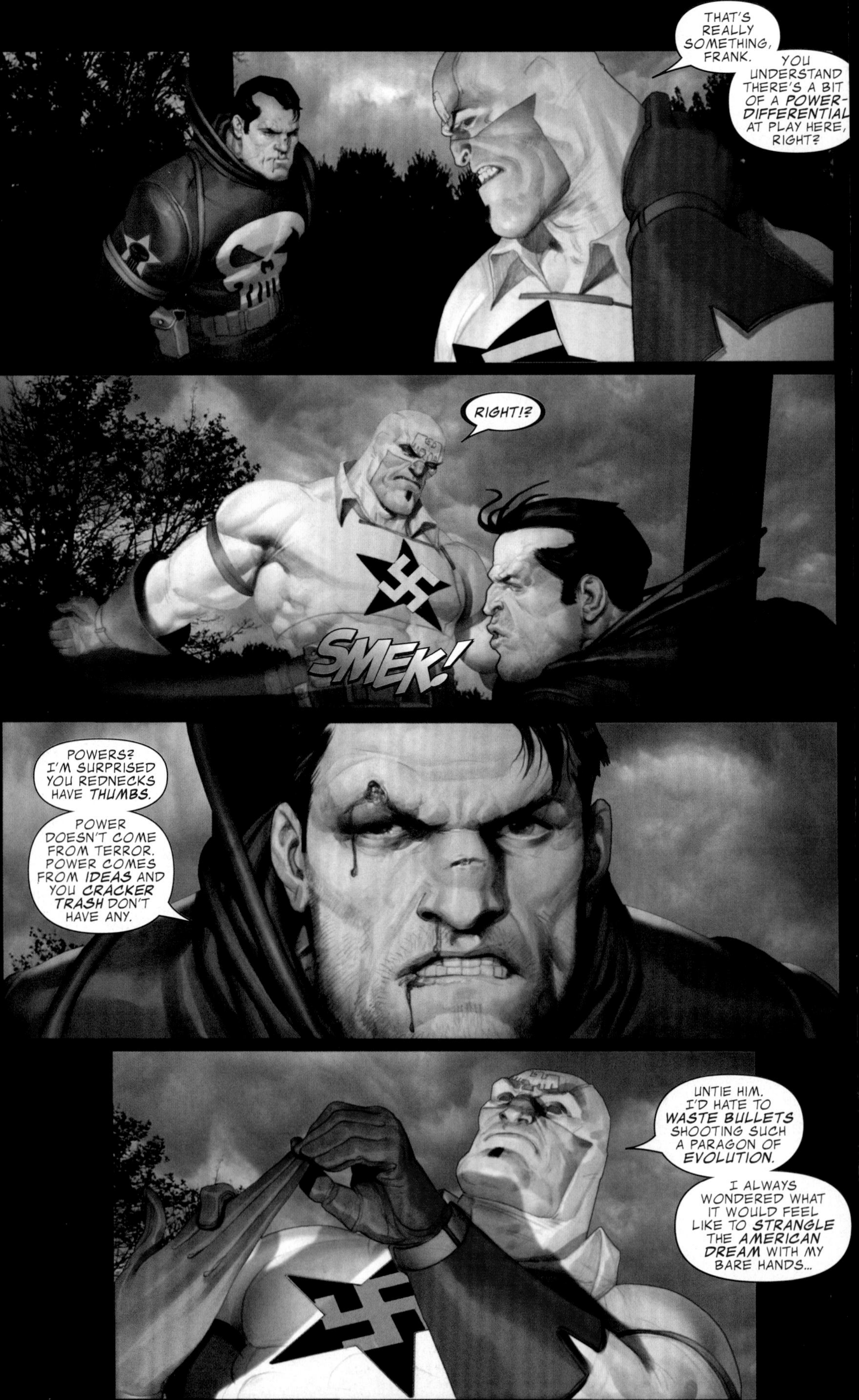
THAT'S REALLY SOMETHING, FRANK.
YOU UNDERSTAND THERE'S A BIT OF A POWER-DIFFERENTIAL AT PLAY HERE, RIGHT?
RIGHT!?
SMEK!
POWERS? I'M SURPRISED YOU REDNECKS HAVE THUMBS.
POWER DOESN'T COME FROM TERROR. POWER COMES FROM IDEAS AND YOU CRACKER TRASH DON'T HAVE ANY.
UNTIE HIM. I'D HATE TO WASTE BULLETS SHOOTING SUCH A PARAGON OF EVOLUTION.
I ALWAYS WONDERED WHAT IT WOULD FEEL LIKE TO STRANGLE THE AMERICAN DREAM WITH MY BARE HANDS...

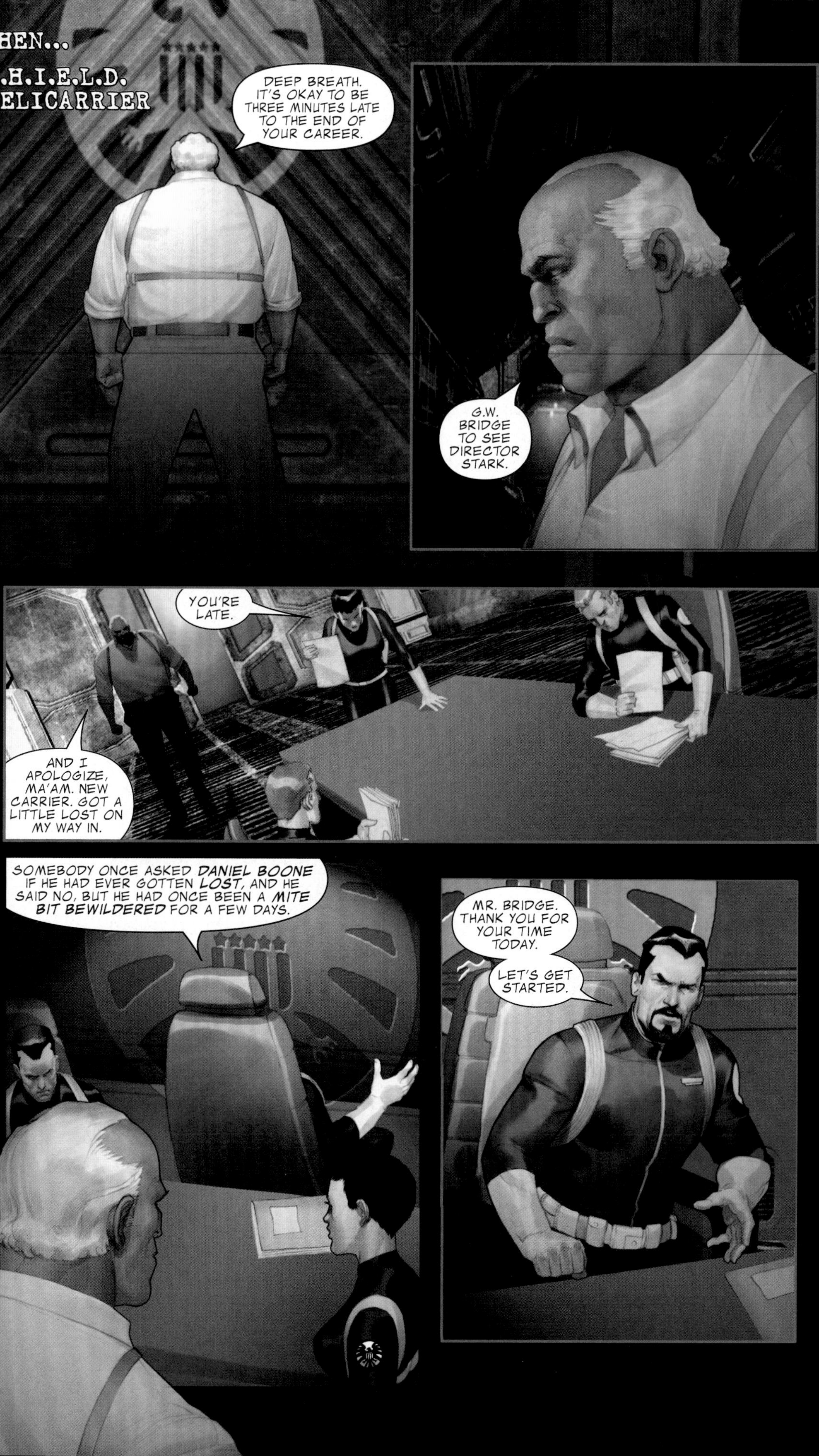
HEN...
.H.I.E.L.D.
ELICARRIER
DEEP BREATH. IT'S OKAY TO BE THREE MINUTES LATE TO THE END OF YOUR CAREER.
G.W. BRIDGE TO SEE DIRECTOR STARK.
YOU'RE LATE.
AND I APOLOGIZE, MA'AM. NEW CARRIER. GOT A LITTLE LOST ON MY WAY IN.
SOMEBODY ONCE ASKED DANIEL BOONE IF HE HAD EVER GOTTEN LOST, AND HE SAID NO, BUT HE HAD ONCE BEEN A MITE BIT BEWILDERED FOR A FEW DAYS.
MR. BRIDGE. THANK YOU FOR YOUR TIME TODAY.
LET'S GET STARTED.

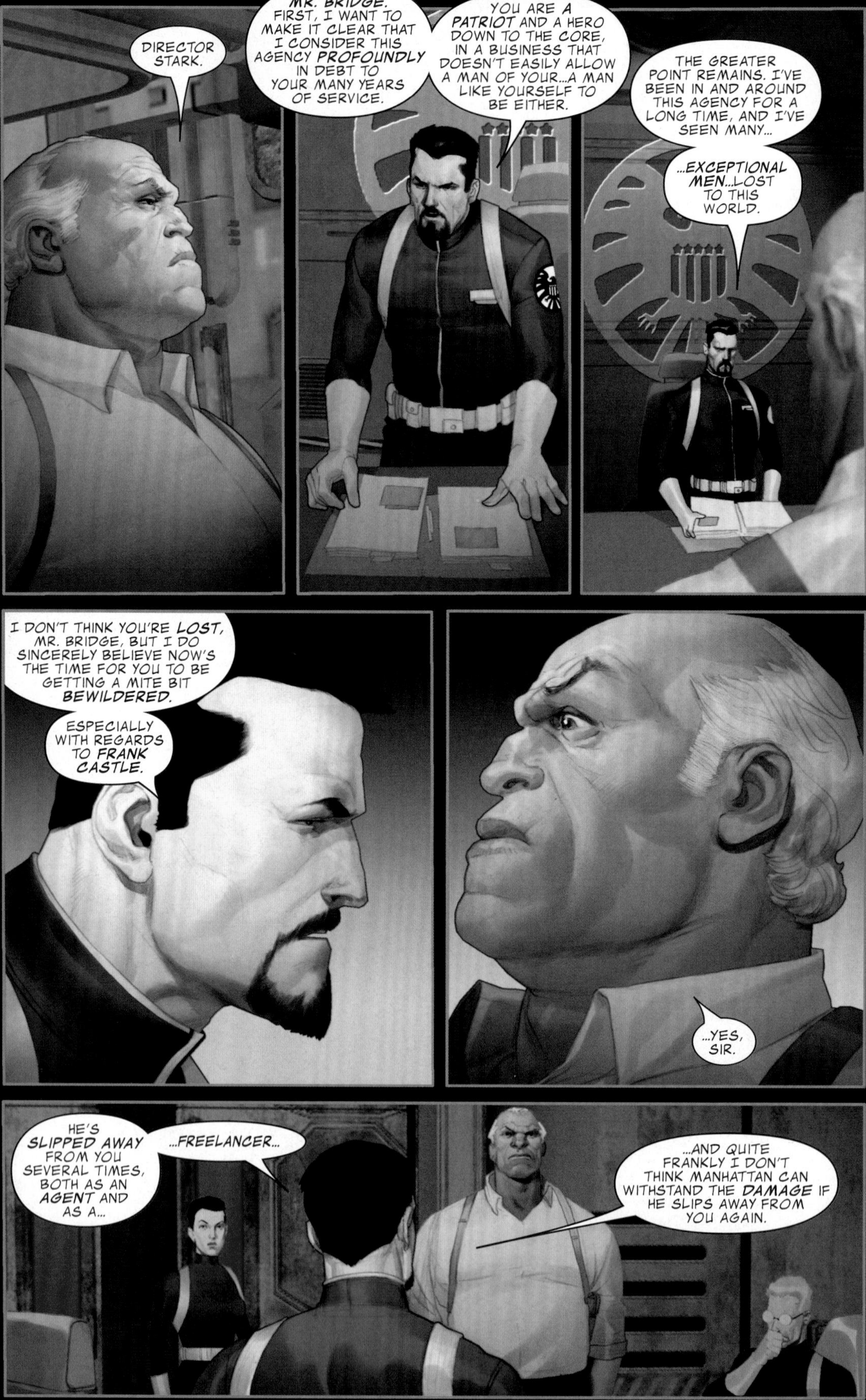
DIRECTOR STARK.
MR. BRIDGE. FIRST, I WANT TO MAKE IT CLEAR THAT I CONSIDER THIS AGENCY PROFOUNDLY IN DEBT TO YOUR MANY YEARS OF SERVICE.
YOU ARE A PATRIOT AND A HERO DOWN TO THE CORE, IN A BUSINESS THAT DOESN'T EASILY ALLOW A MAN OF YOUR...A MAN LIKE YOURSELF TO BE EITHER.
THE GREATER POINT REMAINS. I'VE BEEN IN AND AROUND THIS AGENCY FOR A LONG TIME, AND I'VE SEEN MANY...
...EXCEPTIONAL MEN...LOST TO THIS WORLD.
I DON'T THINK YOU'RE LOST, MR. BRIDGE, BUT I DO SINCERELY BELIEVE NOW'S THE TIME FOR YOU TO BE GETTING A MITE BIT BEWILDERED.
ESPECIALLY WITH REGARDS TO FRANK CASTLE.
...YES, SIR.
HE'S SLIPPED AWAY FROM YOU SEVERAL TIMES, BOTH AS AN AGENT AND AS A...
...FREELANCER...
...AND QUITE FRANKLY I DON'T THINK MANHATTAN CAN WITHSTAND THE DAMAGE IF HE SLIPS AWAY FROM YOU AGAIN.

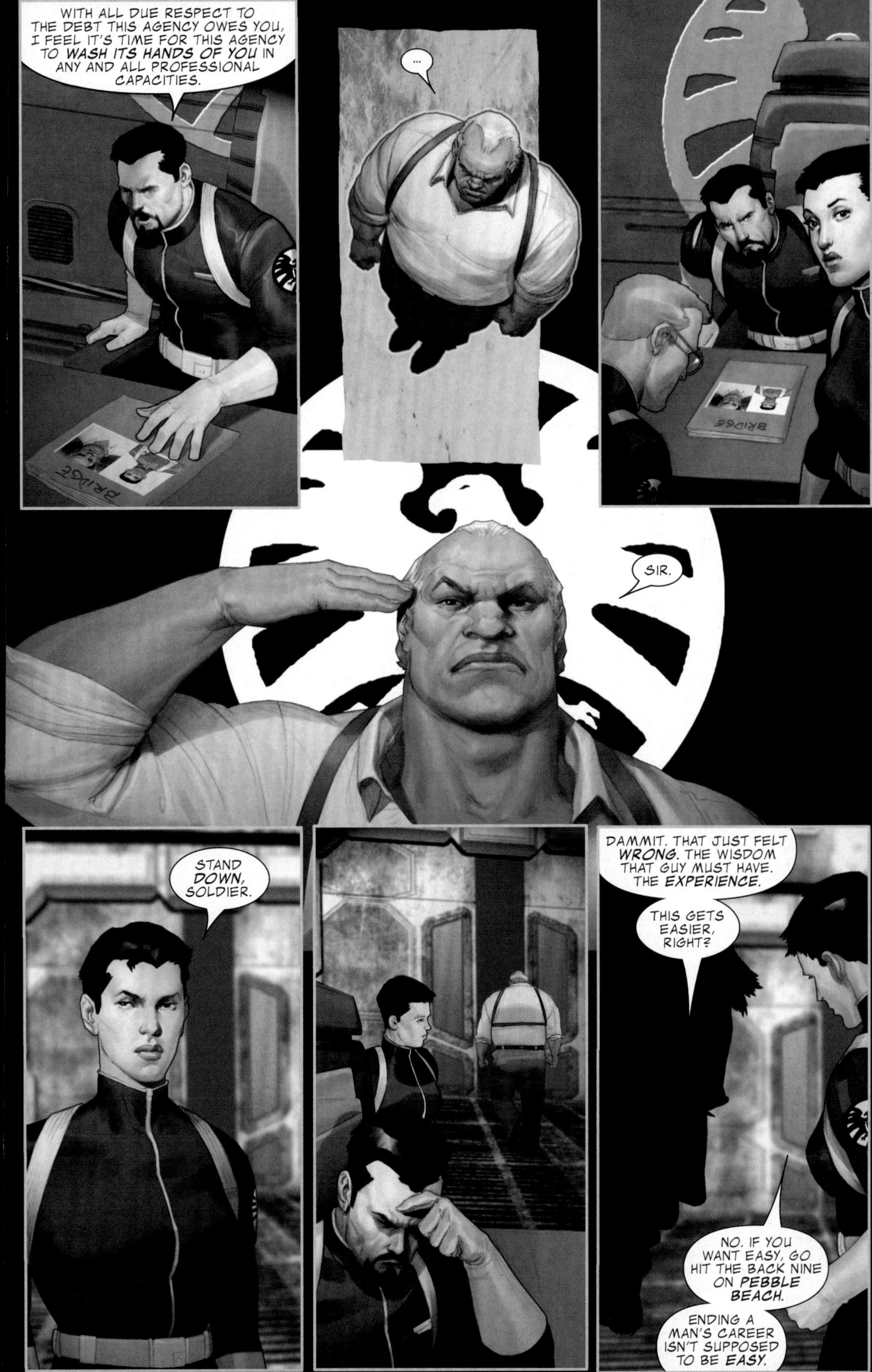

WITH ALL DUE RESPECT TO THE DEBT THIS AGENCY OWES YOU, I FEEL IT'S TIME FOR THIS AGENCY TO *WASH ITS HANDS OF YOU* IN ANY AND ALL PROFESSIONAL CAPACITIES.
...
BRIDGE
BRIDGE
SIR.
STAND *DOWN,* SOLDIER.
DAMMIT. THAT JUST FELT *WRONG.* THE WISDOM THAT GUY MUST HAVE. THE *EXPERIENCE.*
THIS GETS EASIER, RIGHT?
NO. IF YOU WANT EASY, GO HIT THE BACK NINE ON *PEBBLE BEACH.*
ENDING A MAN'S CAREER ISN'T SUPPOSED TO BE *EASY.*

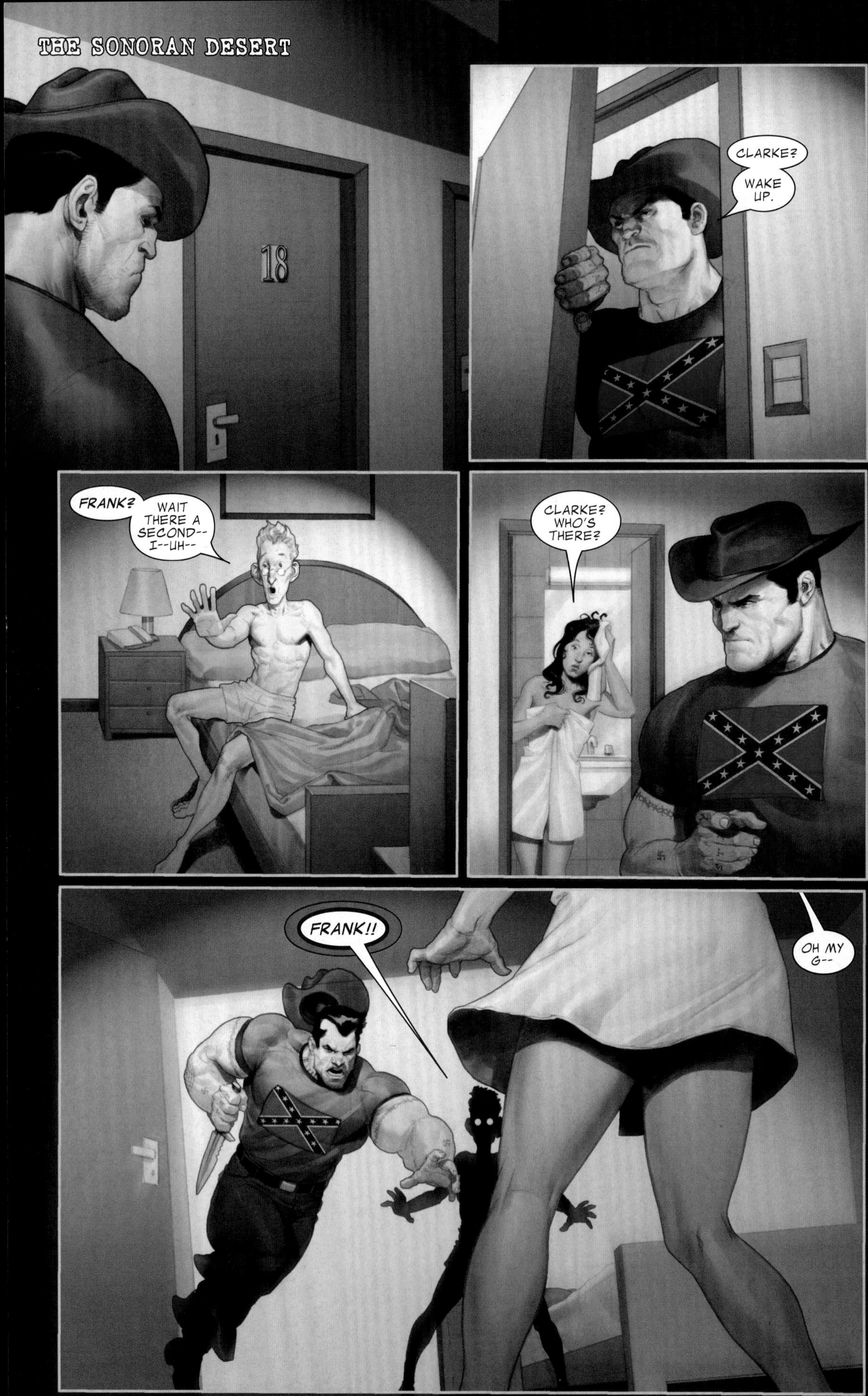
THE SONORAN DESERT
18
CLARKE?
WAKE UP.
FRANK?
WAIT THERE A SECOND-- I--UH--
CLARKE? WHO'S THERE?
FRANK!!
OH MY G--

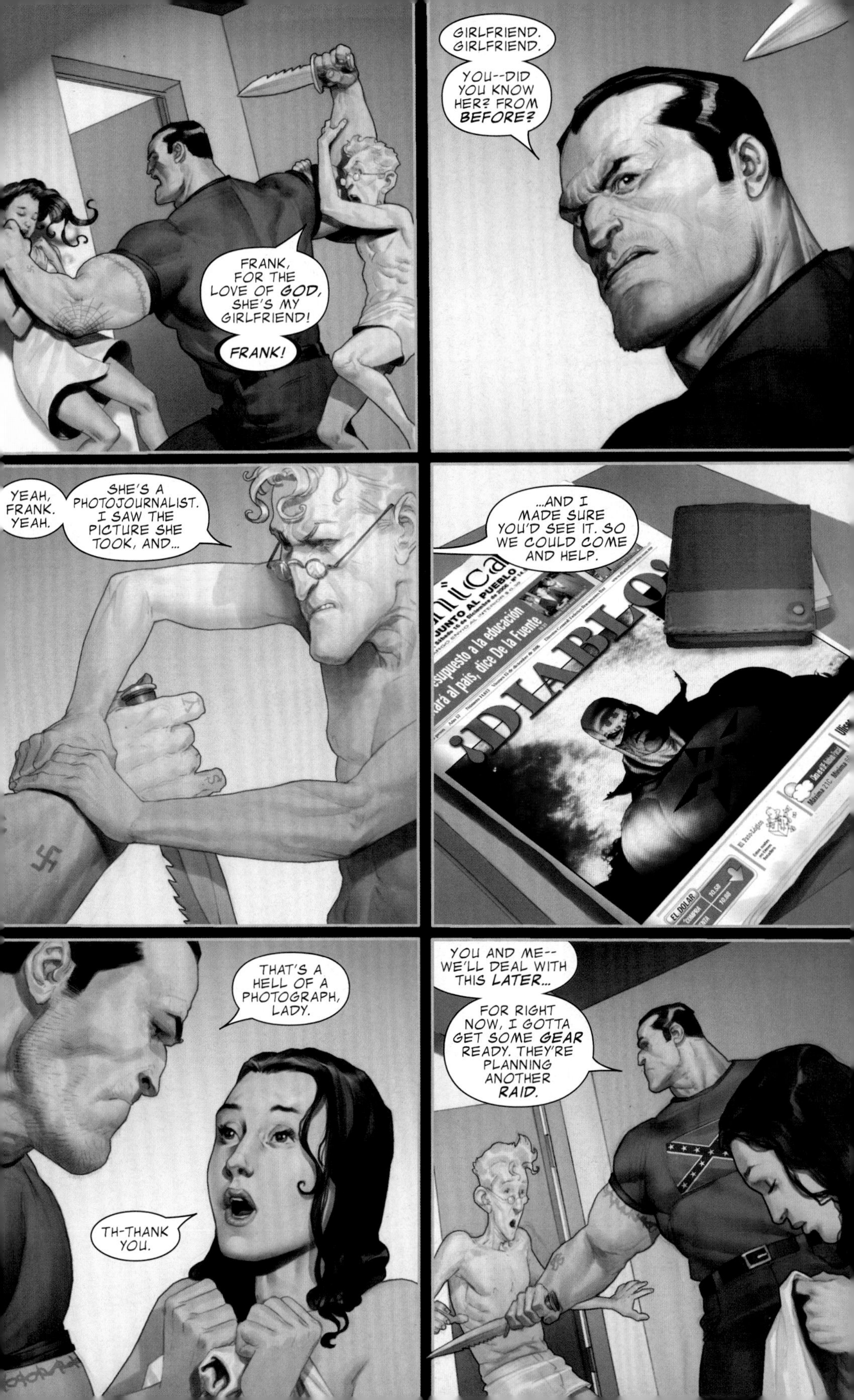
FRANK, FOR THE LOVE OF GOD, SHE'S MY GIRLFRIEND!
FRANK!
GIRLFRIEND. GIRLFRIEND.
YOU--DID YOU KNOW HER? FROM BEFORE?
YEAH, FRANK. YEAH.
SHE'S A PHOTOJOURNALIST. I SAW THE PICTURE SHE TOOK, AND...
...AND I MADE SURE YOU'D SEE IT. SO WE COULD COME AND HELP.
THAT'S A HELL OF A PHOTOGRAPH, LADY.
TH-THANK YOU.
YOU AND ME-- WE'LL DEAL WITH THIS LATER...
FOR RIGHT NOW, I GOTTA GET SOME GEAR READY. THEY'RE PLANNING ANOTHER RAID.

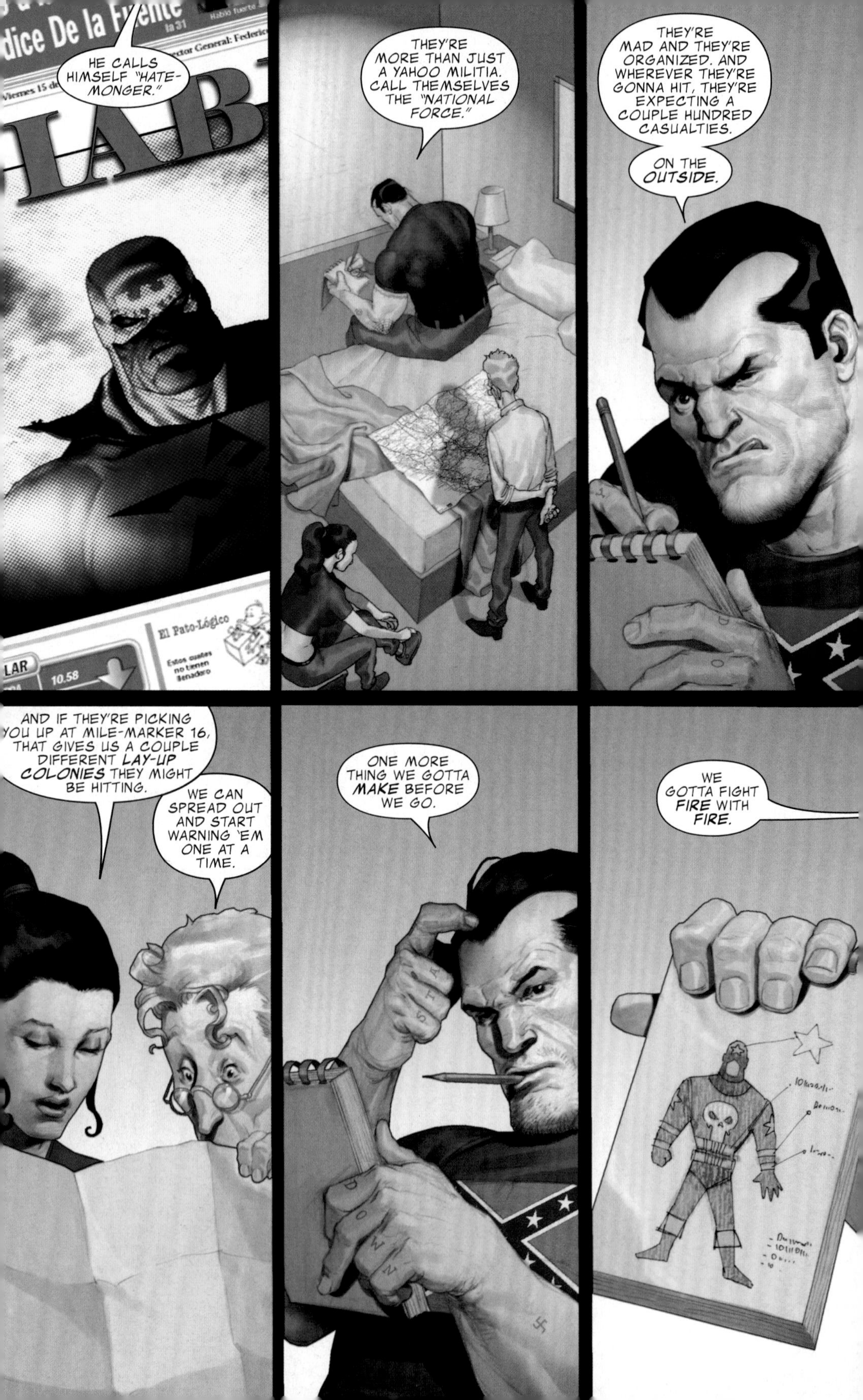
dice De la Fuente
Viernes 15 de
HE CALLS HIMSELF "HATE-MONGER."
THEY'RE MORE THAN JUST A YAHOO MILITIA. CALL THEMSELVES THE "NATIONAL FORCE."
THEY'RE MAD AND THEY'RE ORGANIZED. AND WHEREVER THEY'RE GONNA HIT, THEY'RE EXPECTING A COUPLE HUNDRED CASUALTIES.
ON THE OUTSIDE.
El Pato-Lógico
Estos cuates no tienen llenadero
10.58
AND IF THEY'RE PICKING YOU UP AT MILE-MARKER 16, THAT GIVES US A COUPLE DIFFERENT LAY-UP COLONIES THEY MIGHT BE HITTING.
WE CAN SPREAD OUT AND START WARNING 'EM ONE AT A TIME.
ONE MORE THING WE GOTTA MAKE BEFORE WE GO.
WE GOTTA FIGHT FIRE WITH FIRE.

NEWARK, N.J.

TURNPIKE MOTEL

NEWARK
IT'S NEW TO YOU!

YEAH, I NEED SOME *COFFEE* BROUGHT OVER TO ROOM 202?

THERE'S A COMPLIMENTARY MINI-POT IN ALL OF OUR ROO--

YEAH, NO, NOT ENOUGH.

SEND ME A COUPLE CARAFES.

... A CARAFE IS LIKE A COFFEE POT, BUT TALL.

HUNTER-SEEKER

LOGIN

EMAIL

DO IT, ALL RIGHT? MAKE IT HAPPEN.

DAMMIT, SON, I GOT *WORK* TO DO.

A.OLIVETTI

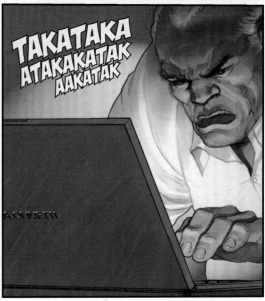

TAKATAKA ATAKAKATAK AAKATAK

A.OLIVETTI

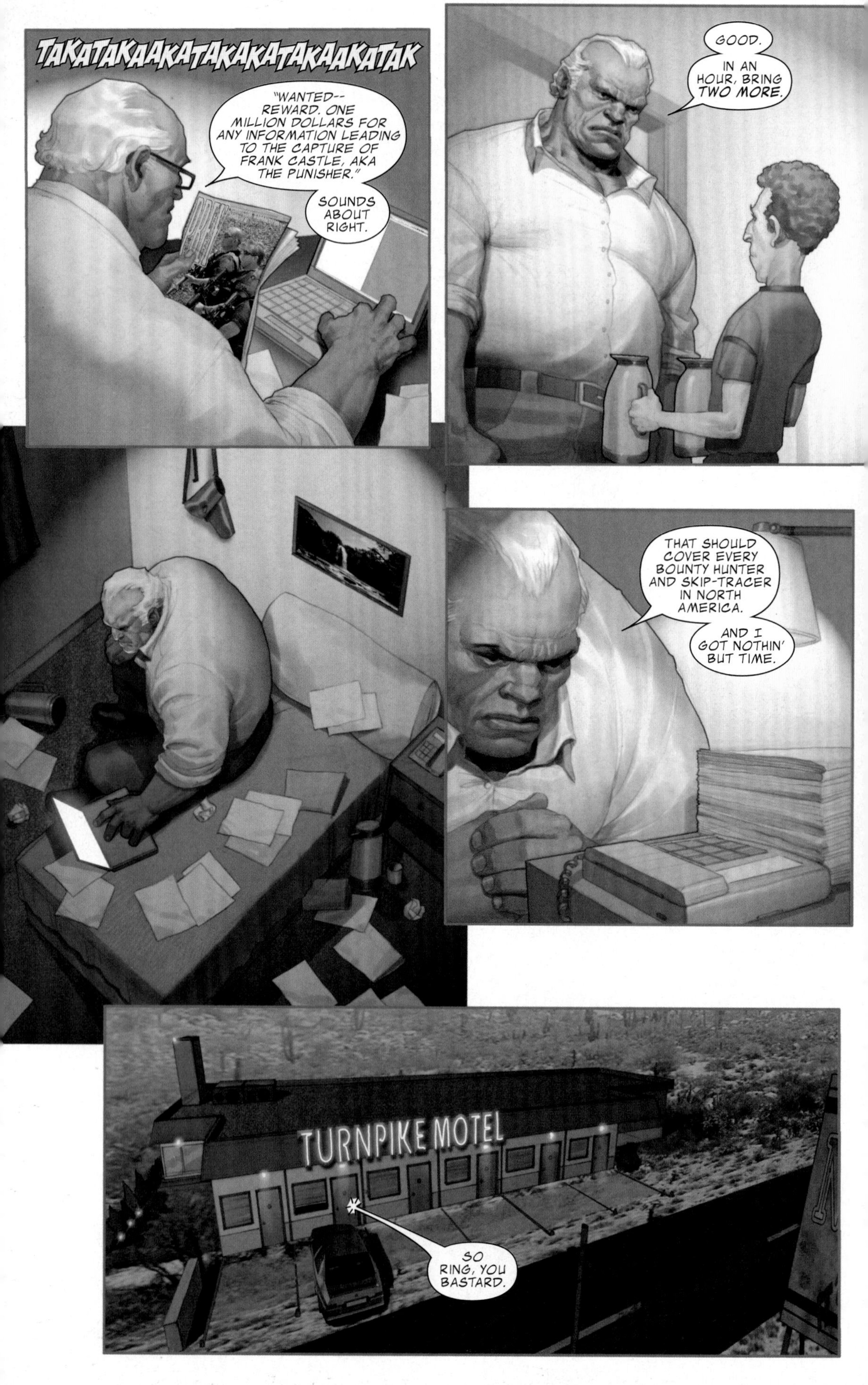
TAKATAKAAKATAKAKATAKAAKATAK
"WANTED-- REWARD. ONE MILLION DOLLARS FOR ANY INFORMATION LEADING TO THE CAPTURE OF FRANK CASTLE, AKA THE PUNISHER."
SOUNDS ABOUT RIGHT.
GOOD.
IN AN HOUR, BRING TWO MORE.
THAT SHOULD COVER EVERY BOUNTY HUNTER AND SKIP-TRACER IN NORTH AMERICA.
AND I GOT NOTHIN' BUT TIME.
TURNPIKE MOTEL
SO RING, YOU BASTARD.

O,
NDER
TANCES,
TWO
O--

--MY OFFICE.

SHERIFF.

BOYS-- TO WHAT DO I OWE THE--

I REALLY, REALLY DON'T WANT NO KIND OF *TROUBLE*.

HELL, SHERIFF, NEITHER DO *WE*. THAT'S WHY WE'RE HERE.

THE LAST THING ANYBODY WANTS IS *TROUBLE*.

LAST NIGHT, AS A MATTER OF FACT, WE WENT AND TALKED TO A 911 OPERATOR NAMED *CARLA* ABOUT GETTING OUT OF

AND ANYWAY SOME LOOKY-LOO FROM *THE NEWSPAPER* CAME BY

WHO ON **EARTH** WOULD HAVE REASON TO COME TALK TO CARLA, SHERIFF?

WHO FROM THE NEWSPAPER WOULD HAVE HAD A SINGLE SOLITARY THING TO ASK HER?

MR. TANK...

PLEASE.

JUST A **NAME.** THAT'S ALL.

YOU'D BE SPARING YOURSELF A WHOLE LOT OF **TROUBLE** SHERIFF...

TATIANA AROCHA.

SHE WAS THE ONE WHAT TOOK THEM PICTURES. SHE WANTED TO KNOW MORE.

TOODELOO, BOSS, AND THANKS FOR THE TIP.

AND, HEY, SHERIFF...

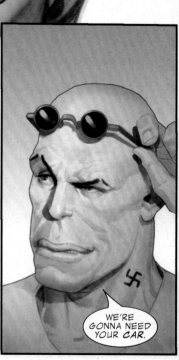

WE'RE GONNA NEED YOUR **CAR.**

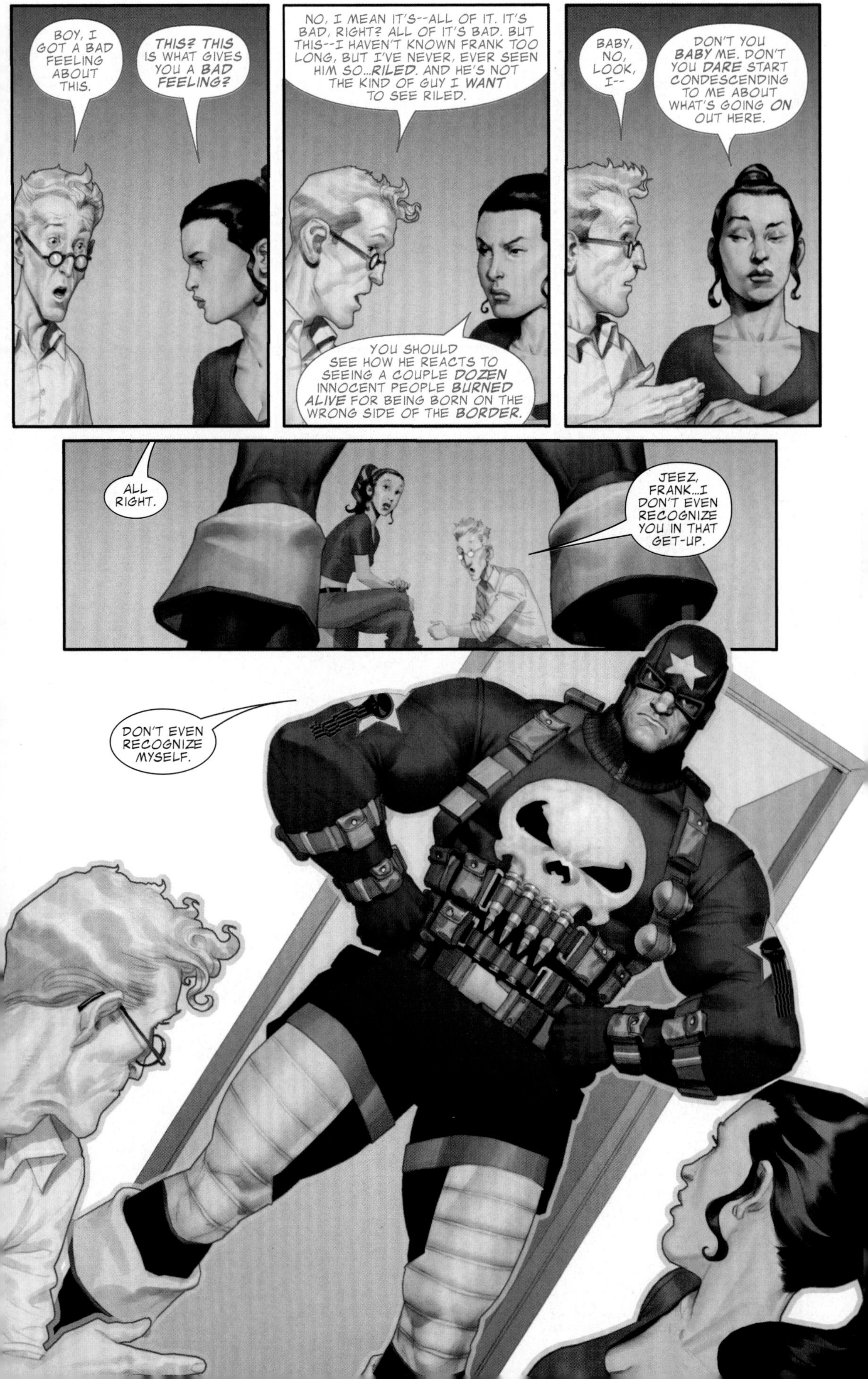
BOY, I GOT A BAD FEELING ABOUT THIS.
THIS? THIS IS WHAT GIVES YOU A BAD FEELING?
NO, I MEAN IT'S--ALL OF IT. IT'S BAD, RIGHT? ALL OF IT'S BAD. BUT THIS--I HAVEN'T KNOWN FRANK TOO LONG, BUT I'VE NEVER, EVER SEEN HIM SO...RILED. AND HE'S NOT THE KIND OF GUY I WANT TO SEE RILED.
YOU SHOULD SEE HOW HE REACTS TO SEEING A COUPLE DOZEN INNOCENT PEOPLE BURNED ALIVE FOR BEING BORN ON THE WRONG SIDE OF THE BORDER.
BABY, NO, LOOK, I--
DON'T YOU BABY ME. DON'T YOU DARE START CONDESCENDING TO ME ABOUT WHAT'S GOING ON OUT HERE.
ALL RIGHT.
JEEZ, FRANK...I DON'T EVEN RECOGNIZE YOU IN THAT GET-UP.
DON'T EVEN RECOGNIZE MYSELF.

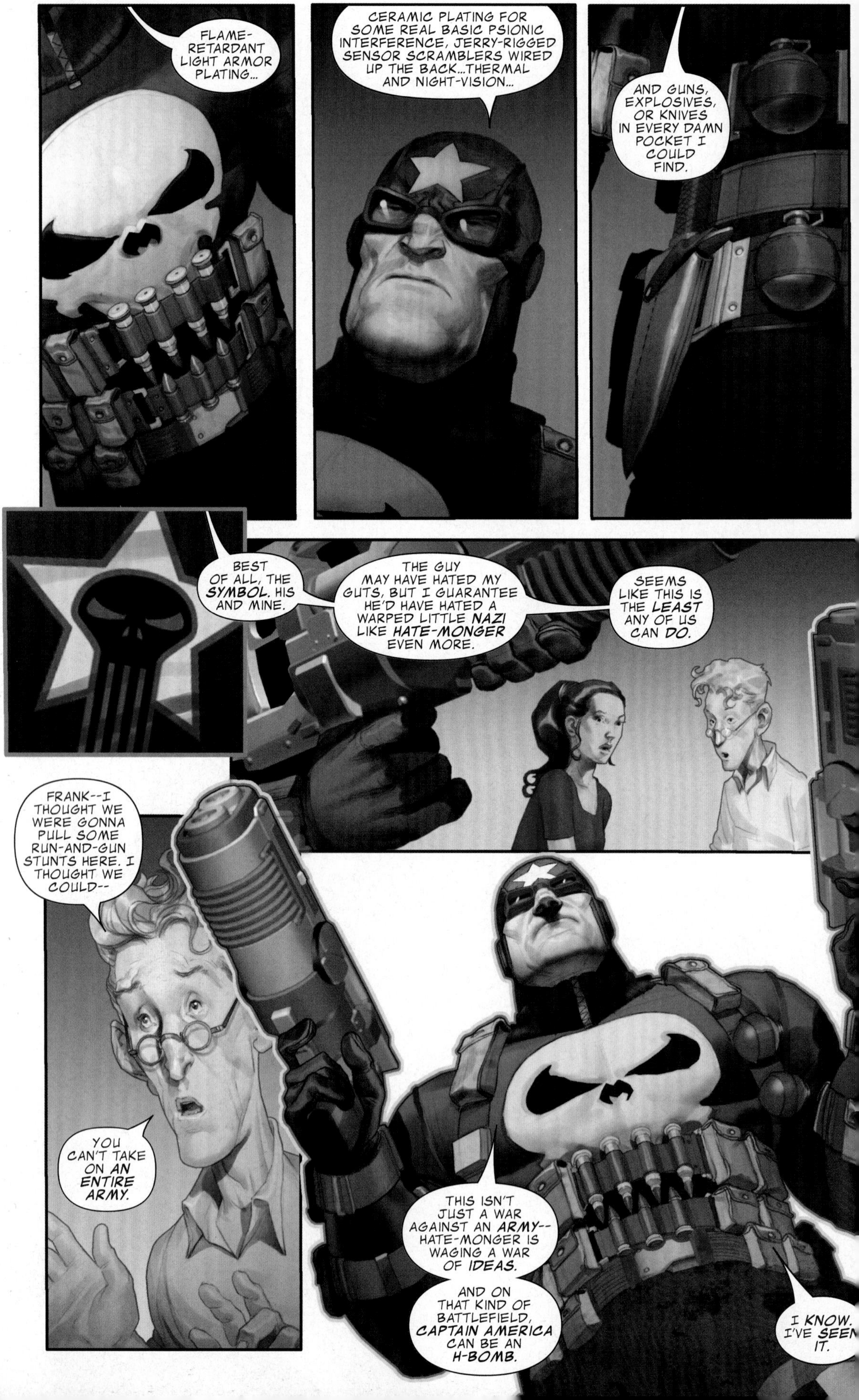

FLAME-RETARDANT LIGHT ARMOR PLATING...
CERAMIC PLATING FOR SOME REAL BASIC PSIONIC INTERFERENCE, JERRY-RIGGED SENSOR SCRAMBLERS WIRED UP THE BACK...THERMAL AND NIGHT-VISION...
AND GUNS, EXPLOSIVES, OR KNIVES IN EVERY DAMN POCKET I COULD FIND.
BEST OF ALL, THE SYMBOL. HIS AND MINE.
THE GUY MAY HAVE HATED MY GUTS, BUT I GUARANTEE HE'D HAVE HATED A WARPED LITTLE NAZI LIKE HATE-MONGER EVEN MORE.
SEEMS LIKE THIS IS THE LEAST ANY OF US CAN DO.
FRANK--I THOUGHT WE WERE GONNA PULL SOME RUN-AND-GUN STUNTS HERE. I THOUGHT WE COULD--
YOU CAN'T TAKE ON AN ENTIRE ARMY.
THIS ISN'T JUST A WAR AGAINST AN ARMY-- HATE-MONGER IS WAGING A WAR OF IDEAS.
AND ON THAT KIND OF BATTLEFIELD, CAPTAIN AMERICA CAN BE AN H-BOMB.
I KNOW. I'VE SEEN IT.

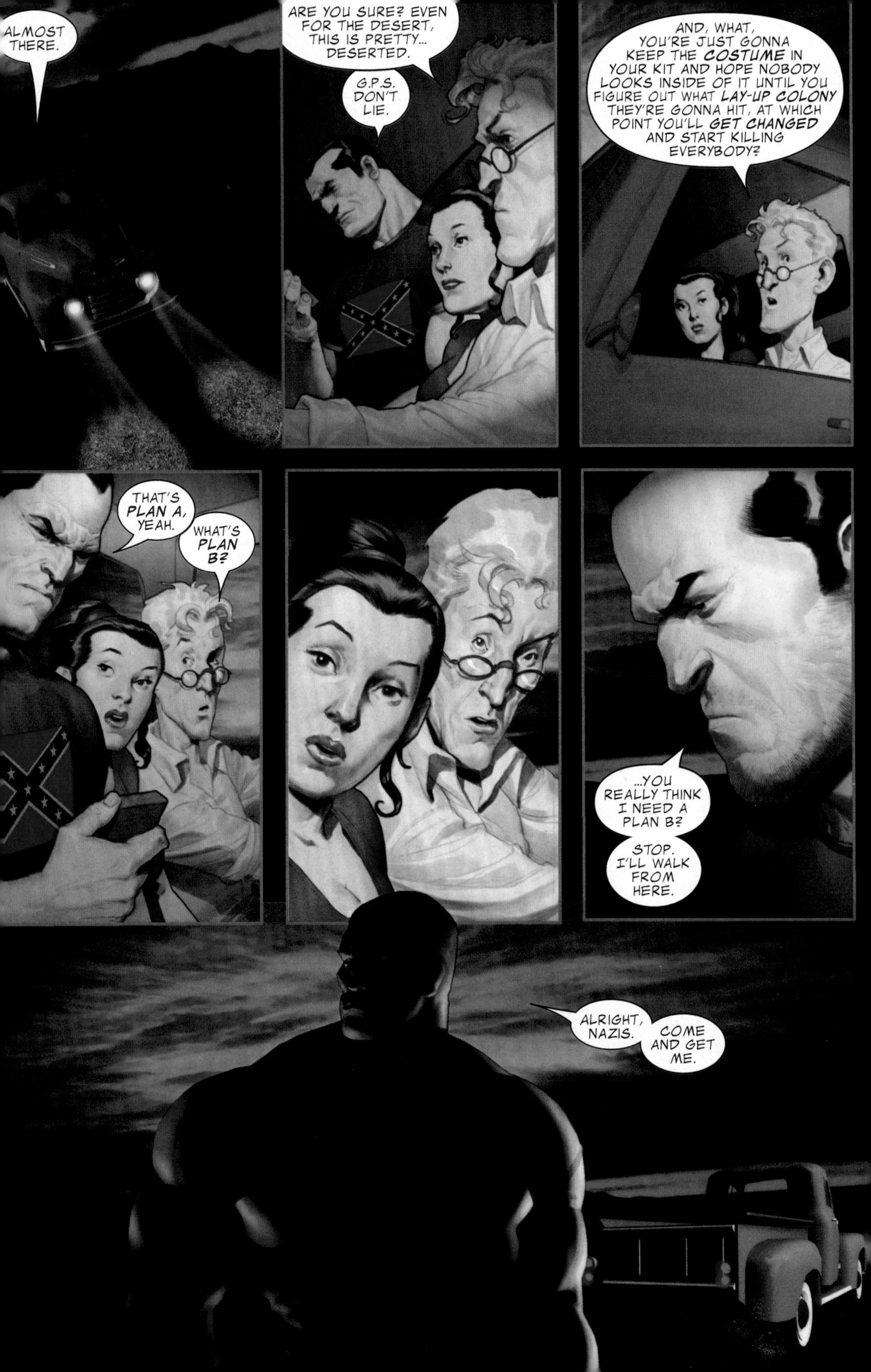
ALMOST THERE.
ARE YOU SURE? EVEN FOR THE DESERT, THIS IS PRETTY... DESERTED.
G.P.S. DON'T LIE.
AND, WHAT, YOU'RE JUST GONNA KEEP THE COSTUME IN YOUR KIT AND HOPE NOBODY LOOKS INSIDE OF IT UNTIL YOU FIGURE OUT WHAT LAY-UP COLONY THEY'RE GONNA HIT, AT WHICH POINT YOU'LL GET CHANGED AND START KILLING EVERYBODY?
THAT'S PLAN A, YEAH.
WHAT'S PLAN B?
...YOU REALLY THINK I NEED A PLAN B?
STOP. I'LL WALK FROM HERE.
ALRIGHT, NAZIS.
COME AND GET ME.

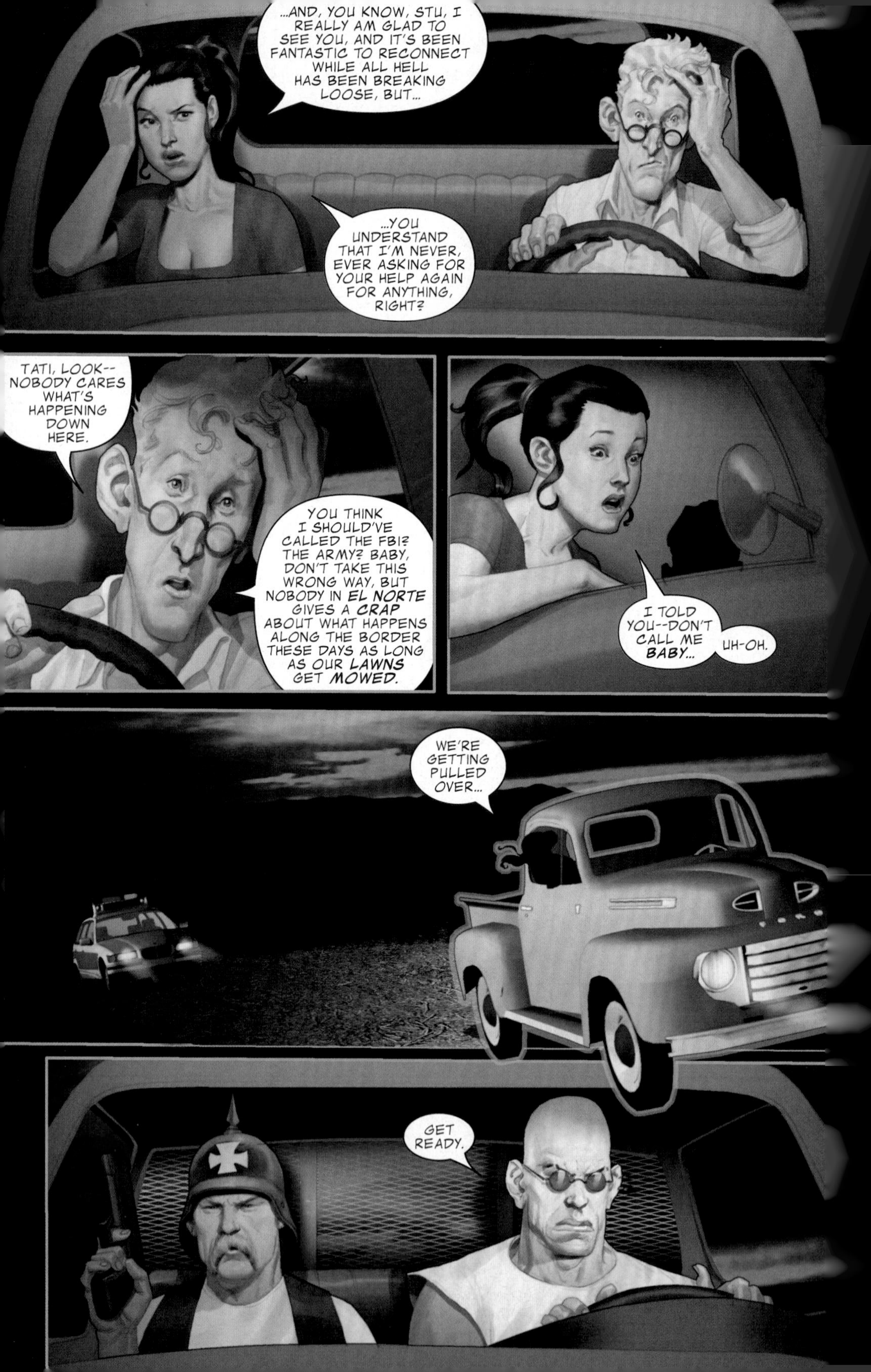
...AND, YOU KNOW, STU, I REALLY AM GLAD TO SEE YOU, AND IT'S BEEN FANTASTIC TO RECONNECT WHILE ALL HELL HAS BEEN BREAKING LOOSE, BUT...
...YOU UNDERSTAND THAT I'M NEVER, EVER ASKING FOR YOUR HELP AGAIN FOR ANYTHING, RIGHT?
TATI, LOOK-- NOBODY CARES WHAT'S HAPPENING DOWN HERE.
YOU THINK I SHOULD'VE CALLED THE FBI? THE ARMY? BABY, DON'T TAKE THIS WRONG WAY, BUT NOBODY IN EL NORTE GIVES A CRAP ABOUT WHAT HAPPENS ALONG THE BORDER THESE DAYS AS LONG AS OUR LAWNS GET MOWED.
I TOLD YOU--DON'T CALL ME BABY...
UH-OH.
WE'RE GETTING PULLED OVER...
GET READY.

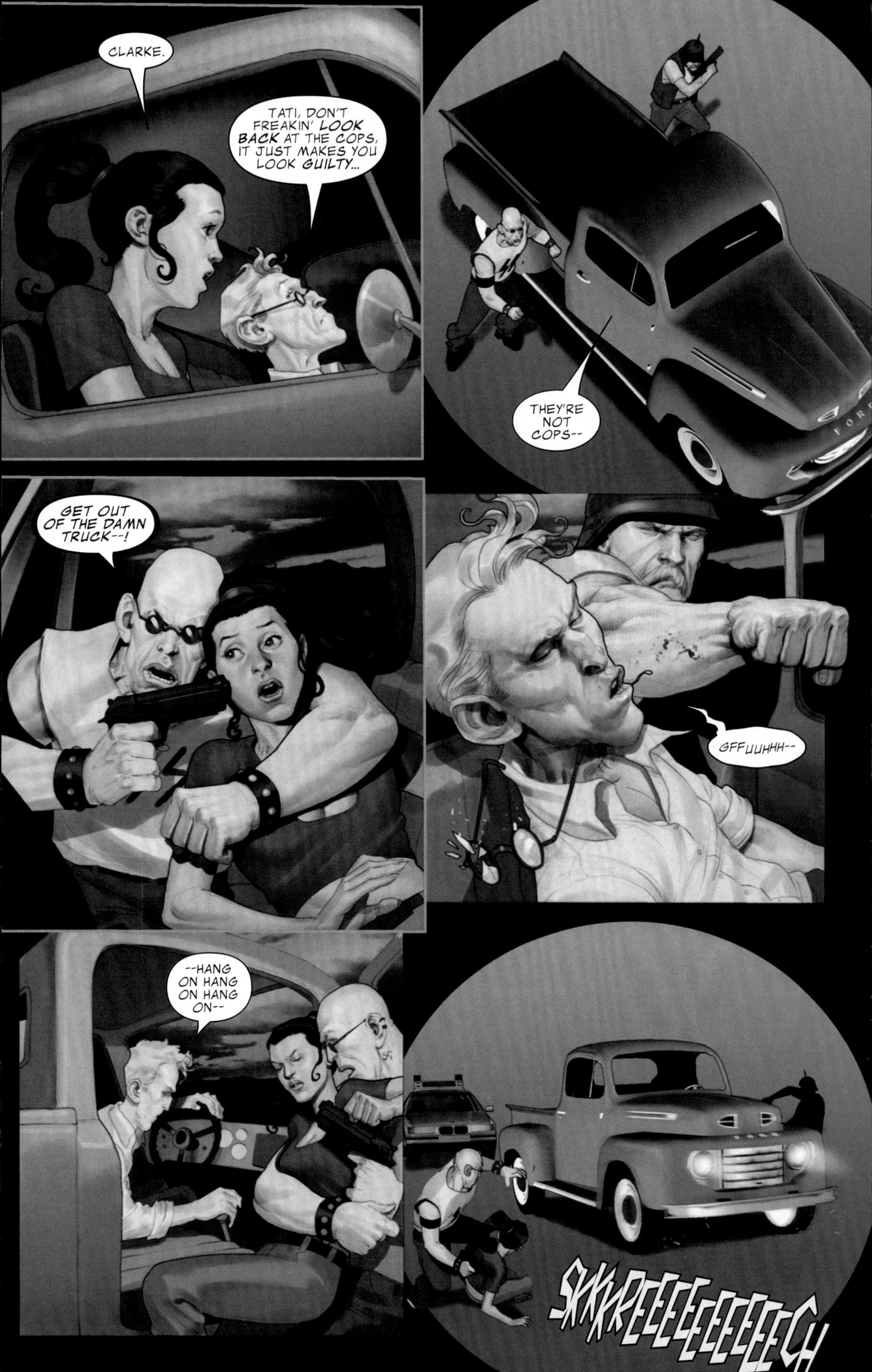
CLARKE.
TATI, DON'T FREAKIN' LOOK BACK AT THE COPS, IT JUST MAKES YOU LOOK GUILTY...
THEY'RE NOT COPS--
GET OUT OF THE DAMN TRUCK--!
GFFUUHHH--
--HANG ON HANG ON HANG ON--
SKKKREEEEEEEEEEECH

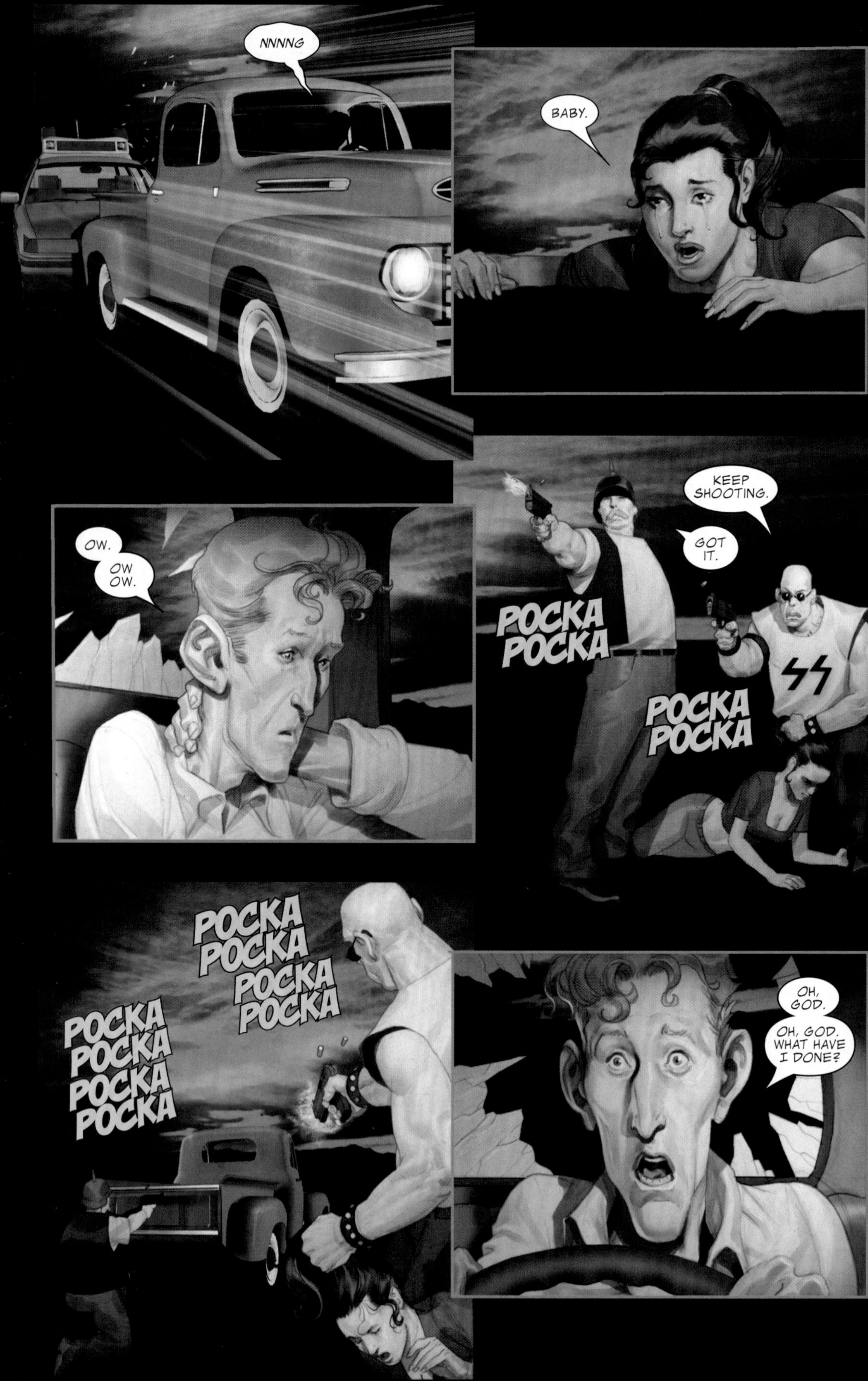
NNNNG
BABY.
OW.
OW OW.
KEEP SHOOTING.
GOT IT.
POCKA POCKA
POCKA POCKA
POCKA POCKA POCKA POCKA
POCKA POCKA POCKA POCKA
OH, GOD.
OH, GOD. WHAT HAVE I DONE?

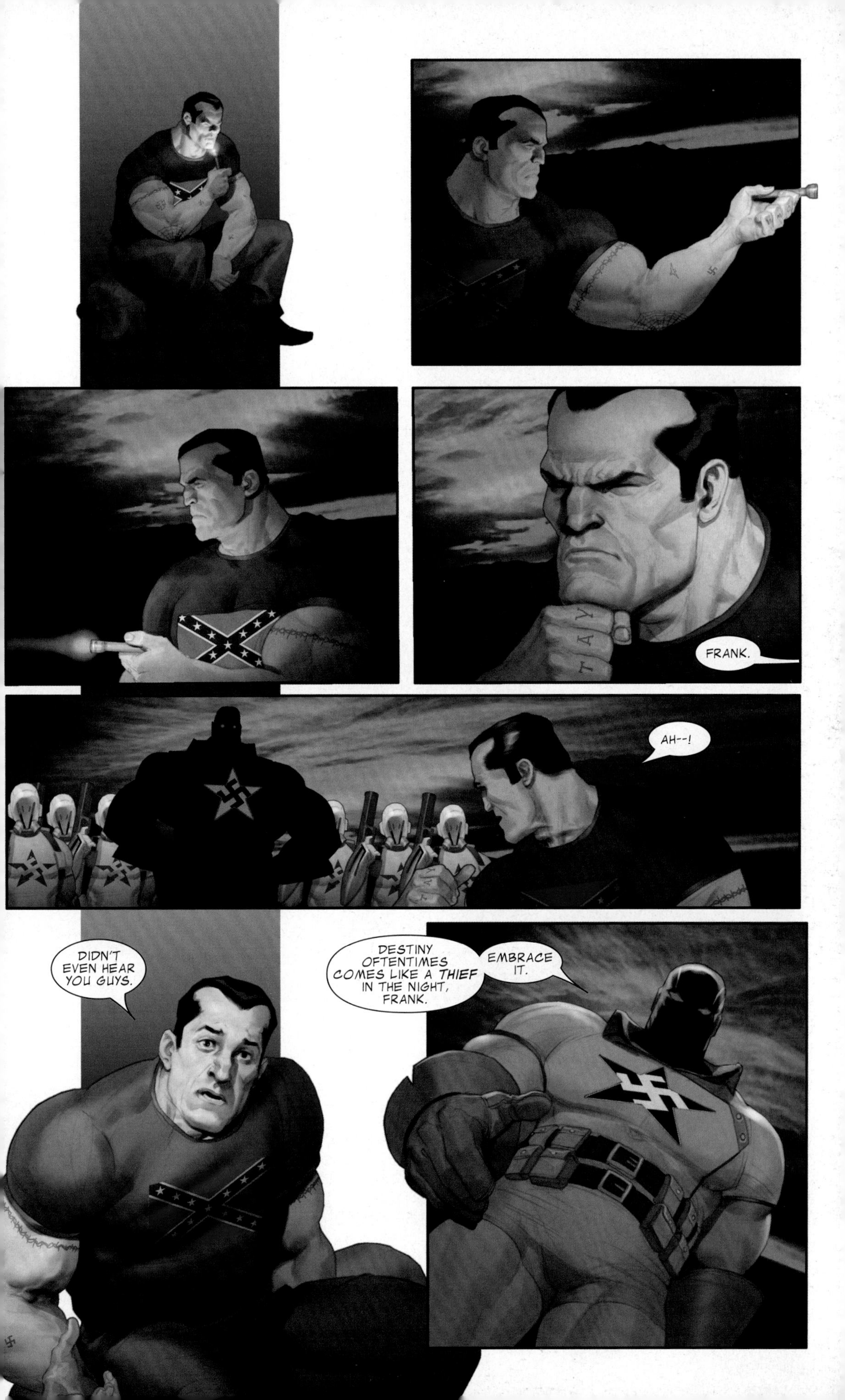
FRANK.
AH--!
DIDN'T EVEN HEAR YOU GUYS.
DESTINY OFTENTIMES COMES LIKE A THIEF IN THE NIGHT, FRANK.
EMBRACE IT.

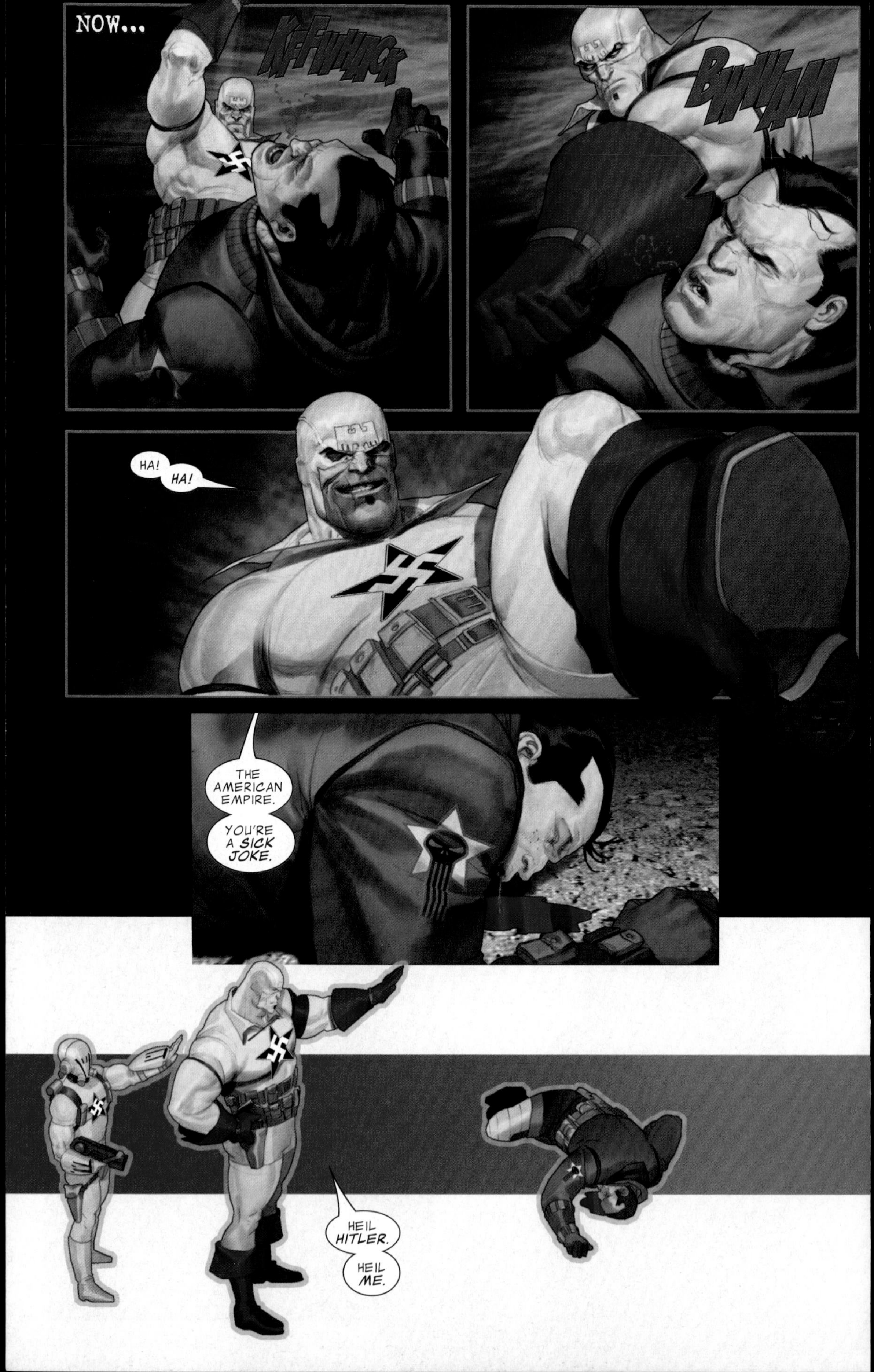
NOW...
KA-FWHACK
BWHAM
HA!
HA!
THE AMERICAN EMPIRE.
YOU'RE A SICK JOKE.
HEIL HITLER.
HEIL ME.

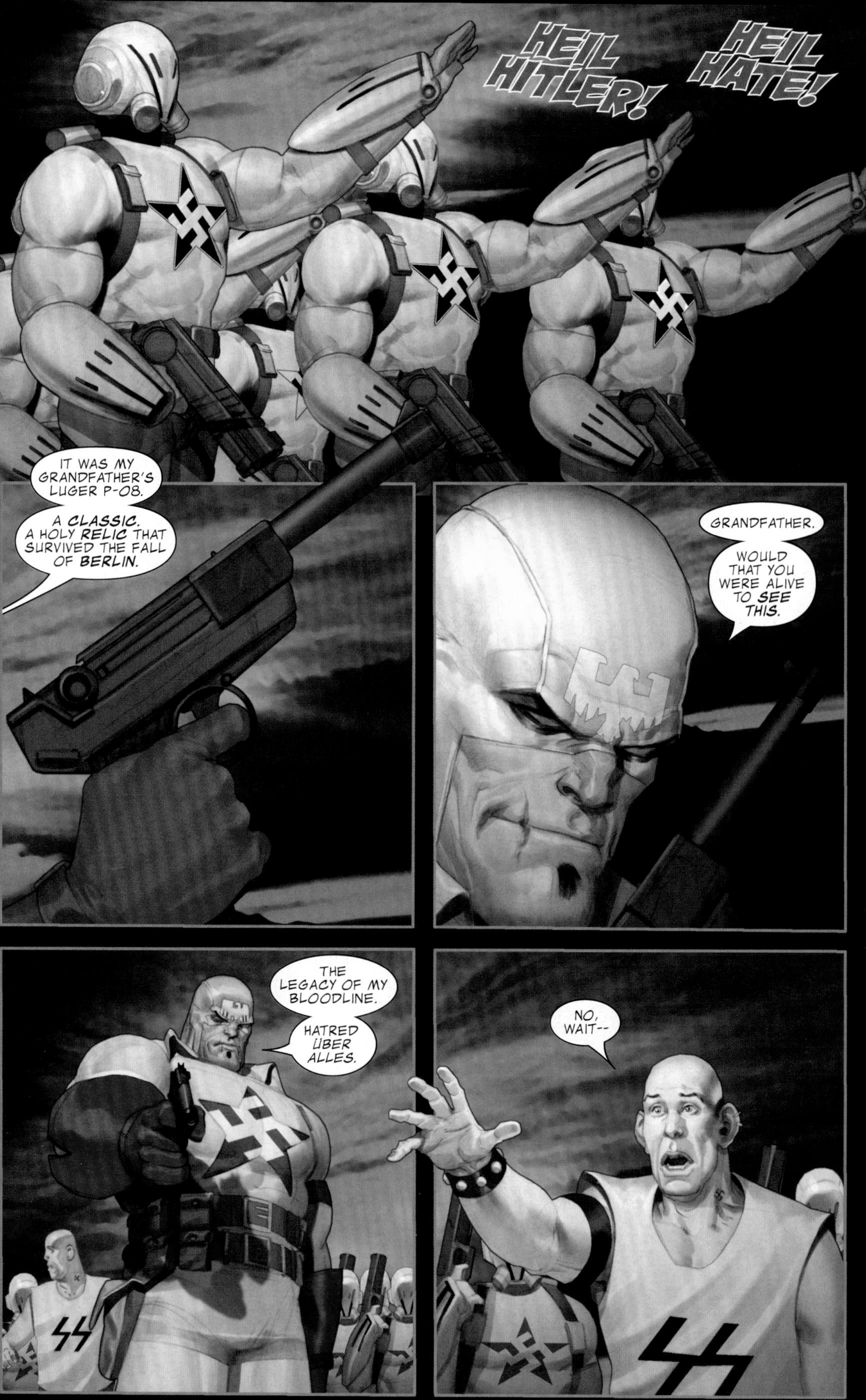
HEIL HITLER!
HEIL HATE!
IT WAS MY GRANDFATHER'S LUGER P-08.
A CLASSIC. A HOLY RELIC THAT SURVIVED THE FALL OF BERLIN.
GRANDFATHER.
WOULD THAT YOU WERE ALIVE TO SEE THIS.
THE LEGACY OF MY BLOODLINE.
HATRED ÜBER ALLES.
NO, WAIT--

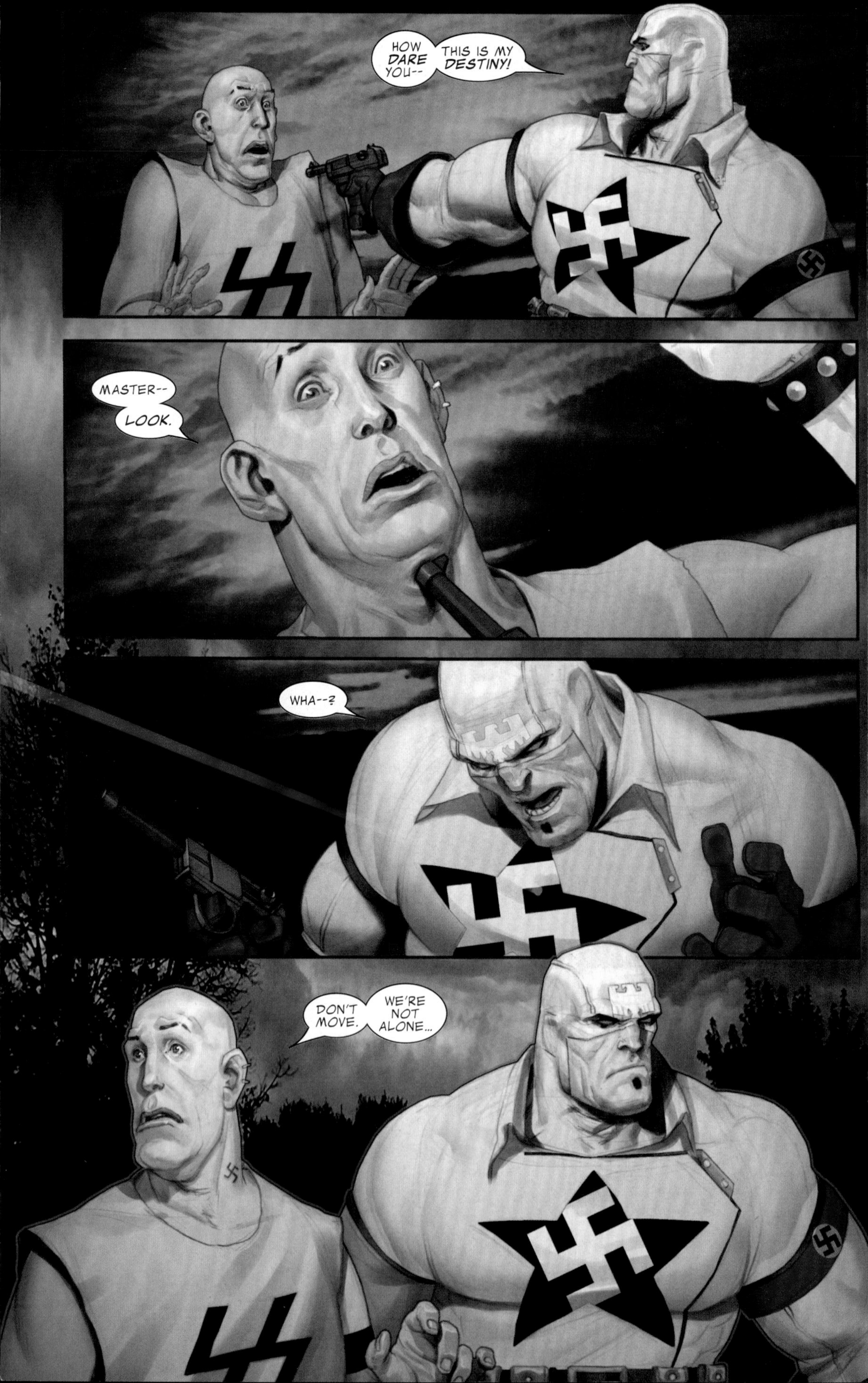
HOW DARE YOU--
THIS IS MY DESTINY!
MASTER--
LOOK.
WHA--?
DON'T MOVE.
WE'RE NOT ALONE...

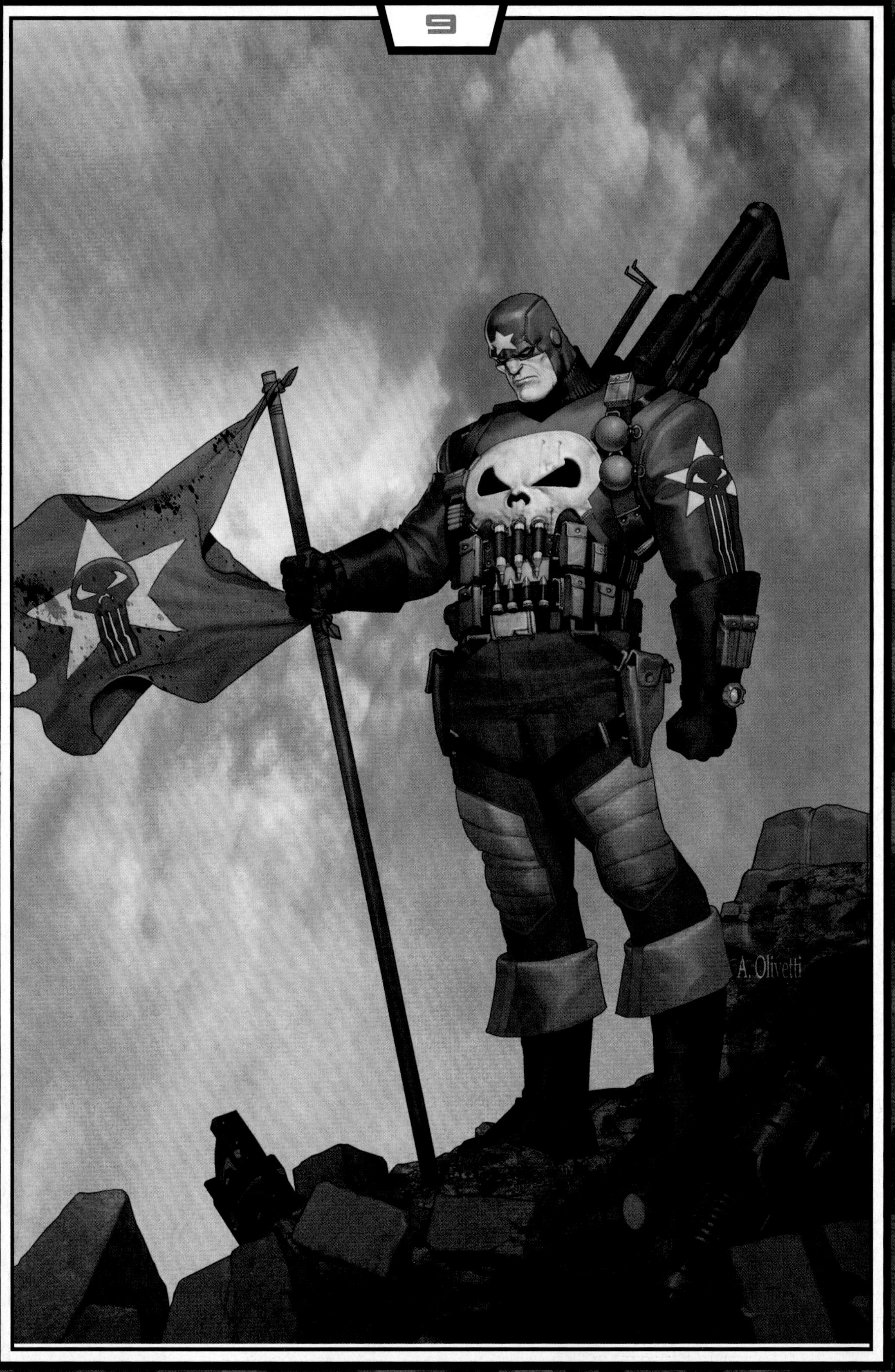
9
A. Olivetti

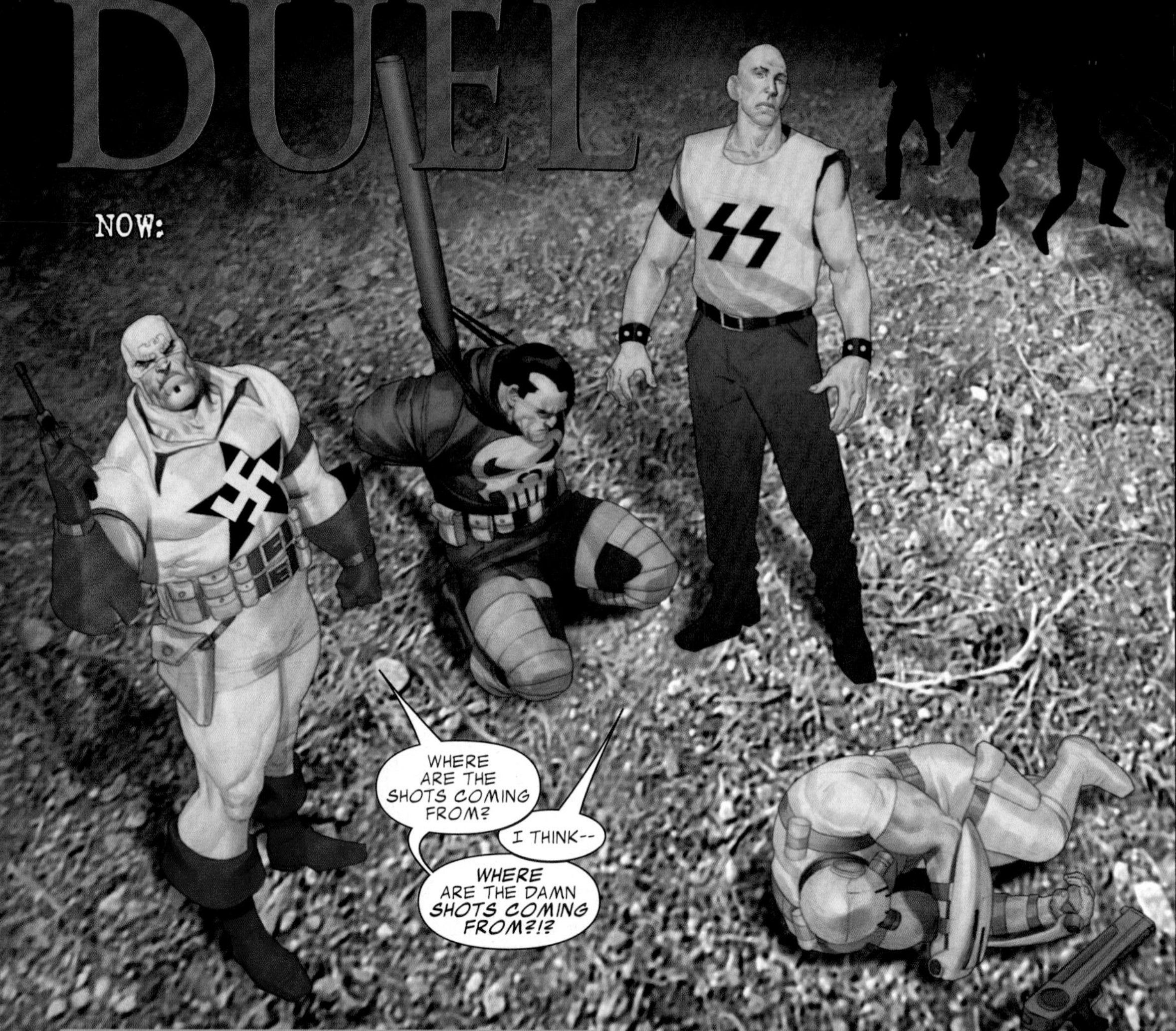
DUEL
NOW:
WHERE ARE THE SHOTS COMING FROM?
I THINK--
WHERE ARE THE DAMN SHOTS COMING FROM?!?

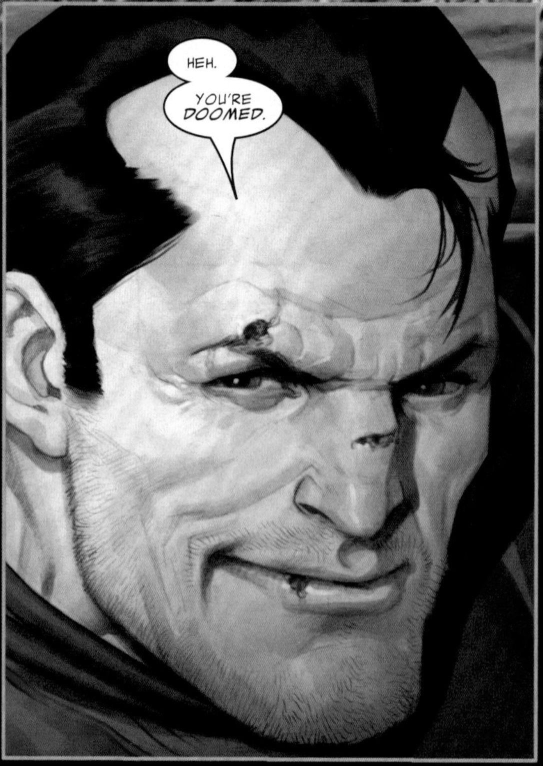
HEH.
YOU'RE DOOMED.

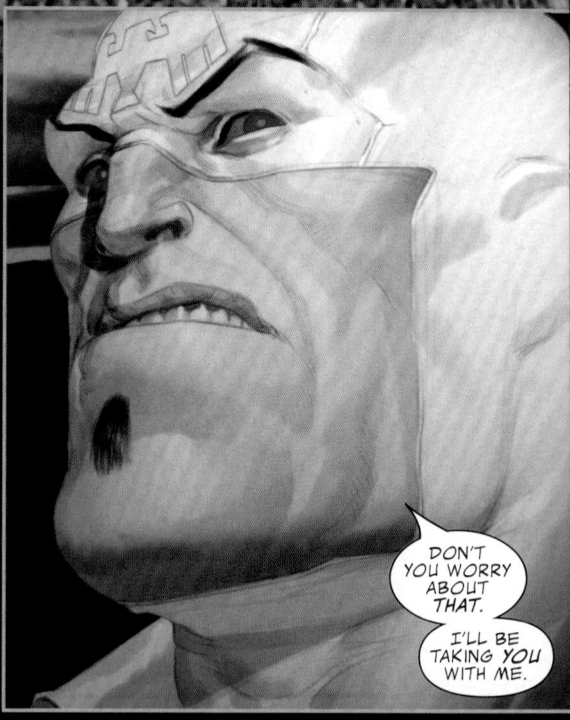
DON'T YOU WORRY ABOUT THAT.
I'LL BE TAKING YOU WITH ME.

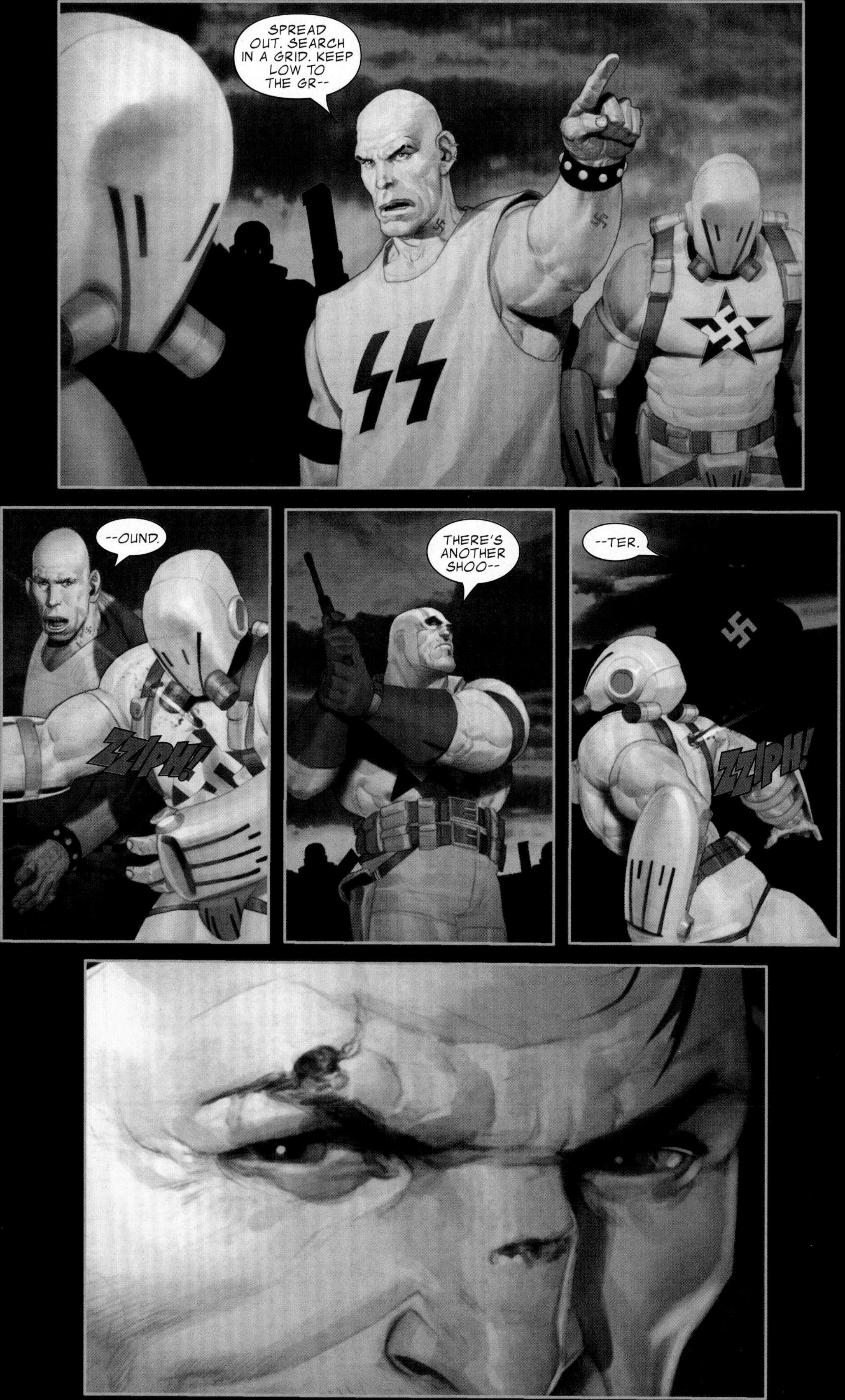
SPREAD OUT. SEARCH IN A GRID. KEEP LOW TO THE GR--
--OUND.
ZZIPH!
THERE'S ANOTHER SHOO--
--TER.
ZZIPH!

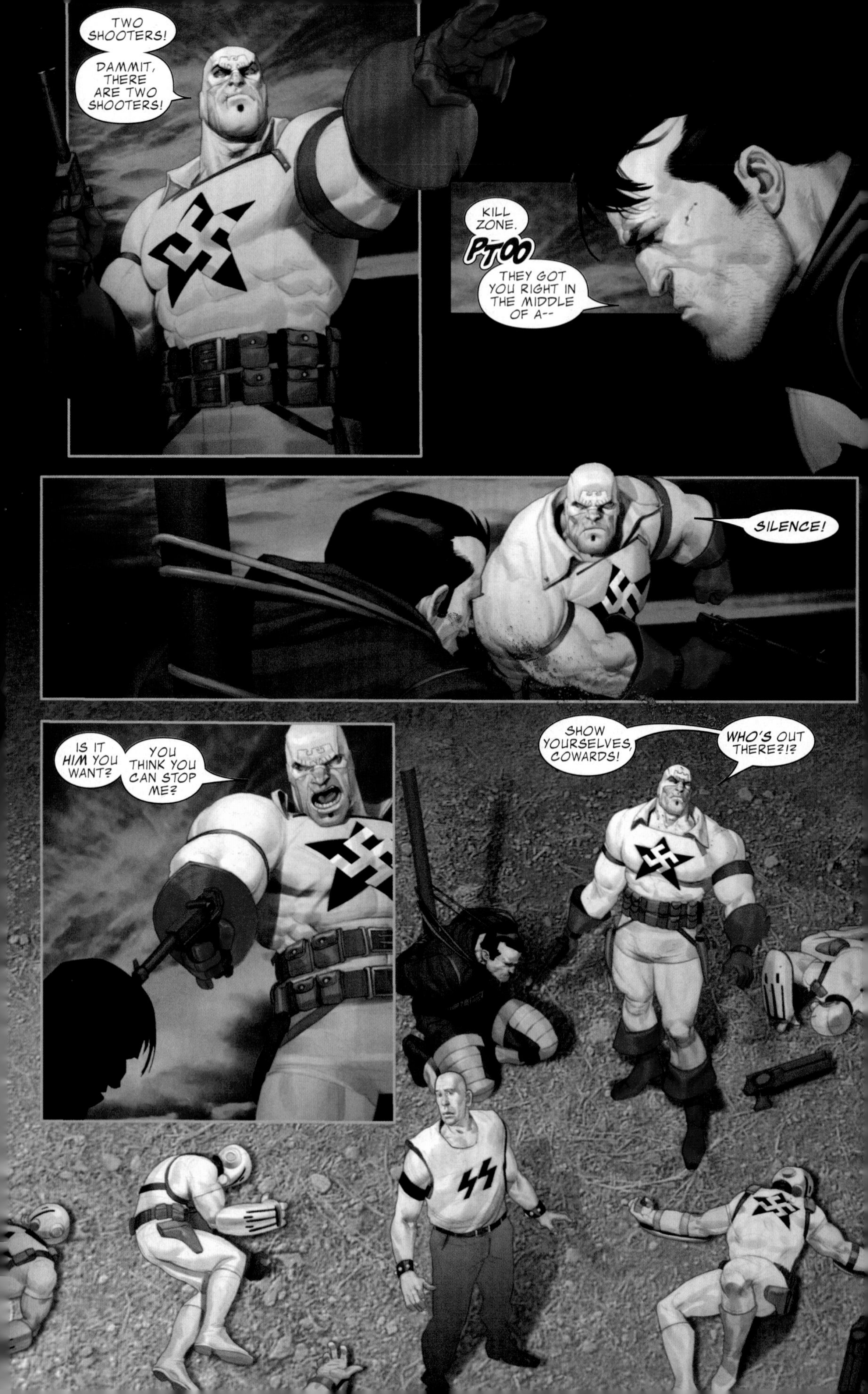
TWO SHOOTERS!
DAMMIT, THERE ARE TWO SHOOTERS!
KILL ZONE.
PTOO
THEY GOT YOU RIGHT IN THE MIDDLE OF A--
SILENCE!
IS IT HIM YOU WANT?
YOU THINK YOU CAN STOP ME?
SHOW YOURSELVES, COWARDS!
WHO'S OUT THERE?!?

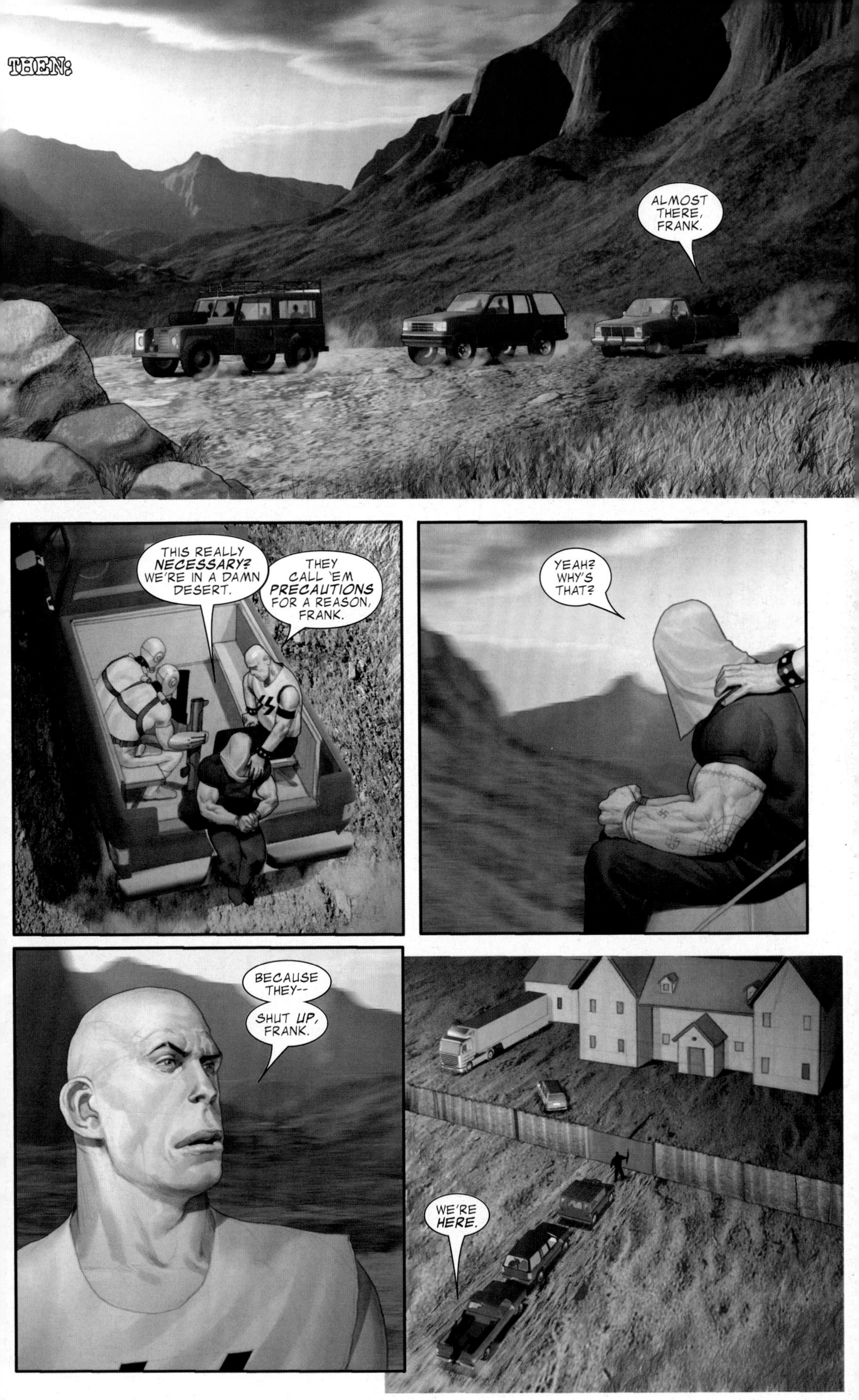
THEN:
ALMOST THERE, FRANK.
THIS REALLY NECESSARY? WE'RE IN A DAMN DESERT.
THEY CALL 'EM PRECAUTIONS FOR A REASON, FRANK.
YEAH? WHY'S THAT?
BECAUSE THEY--
SHUT UP, FRANK.
WE'RE HERE.

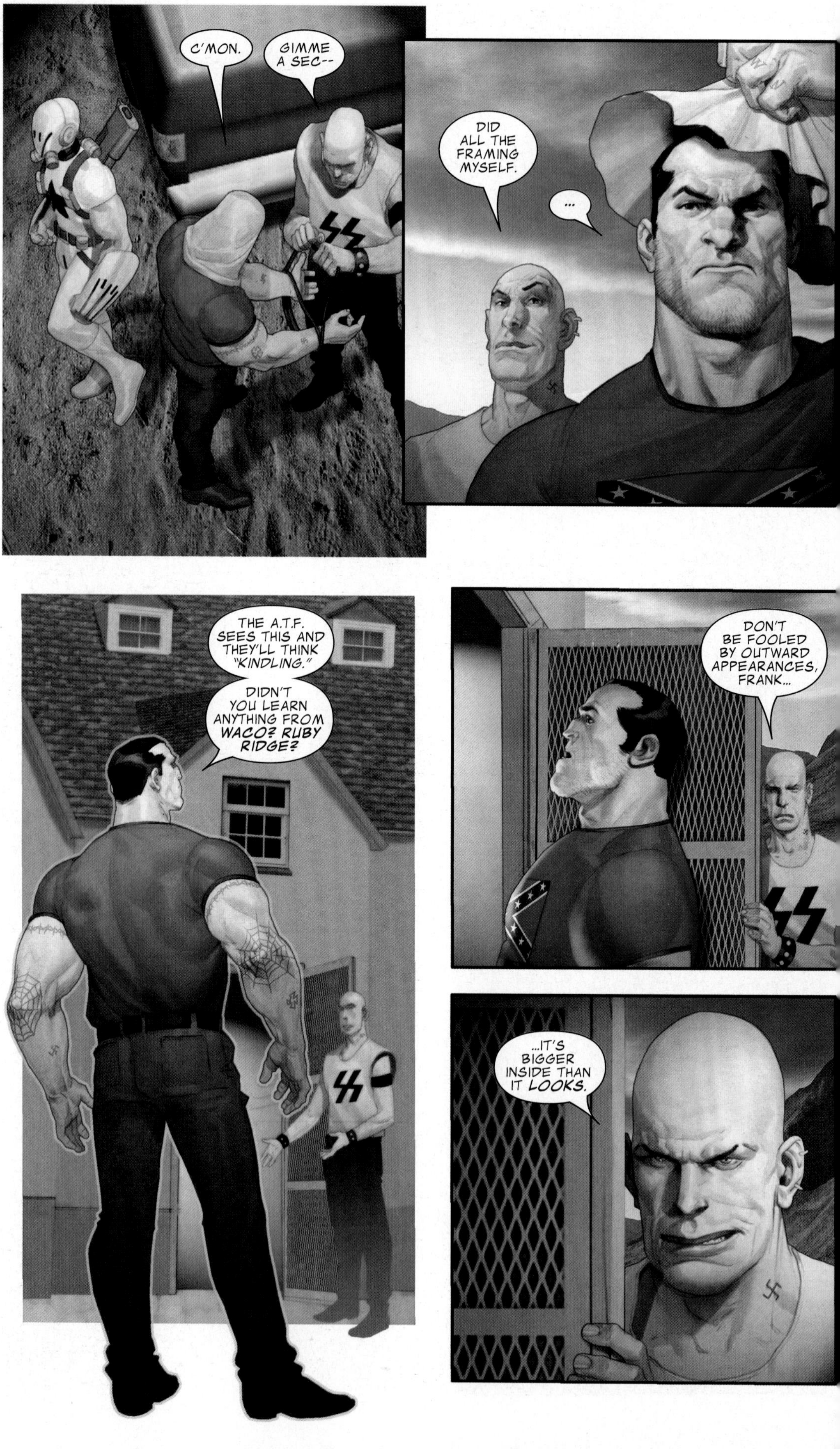
C'MON.
GIMME A SEC--
DID ALL THE FRAMING MYSELF.
...
THE A.T.F. SEES THIS AND THEY'LL THINK "KINDLING."
DIDN'T YOU LEARN ANYTHING FROM WACO? RUBY RIDGE?
DON'T BE FOOLED BY OUTWARD APPEARANCES, FRANK...
...IT'S BIGGER INSIDE THAN IT LOOKS.

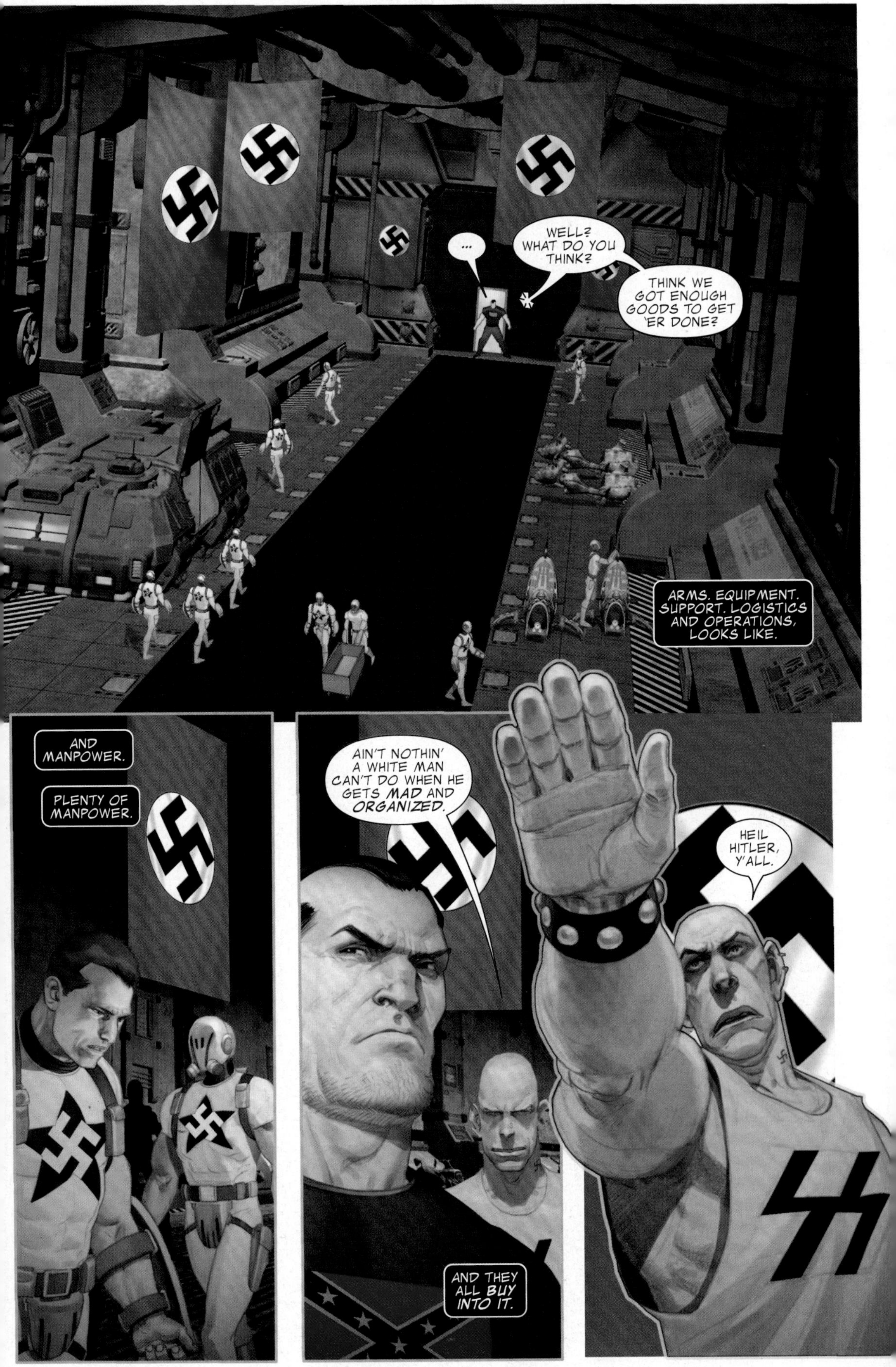
...
WELL? WHAT DO YOU THINK?
THINK WE GOT ENOUGH GOODS TO GET 'ER DONE?
ARMS. EQUIPMENT. SUPPORT. LOGISTICS AND OPERATIONS, LOOKS LIKE.
AND MANPOWER.
PLENTY OF MANPOWER.
AIN'T NOTHIN' A WHITE MAN CAN'T DO WHEN HE GETS MAD AND ORGANIZED.
AND THEY ALL BUY INTO IT.
HEIL HITLER, Y'ALL.

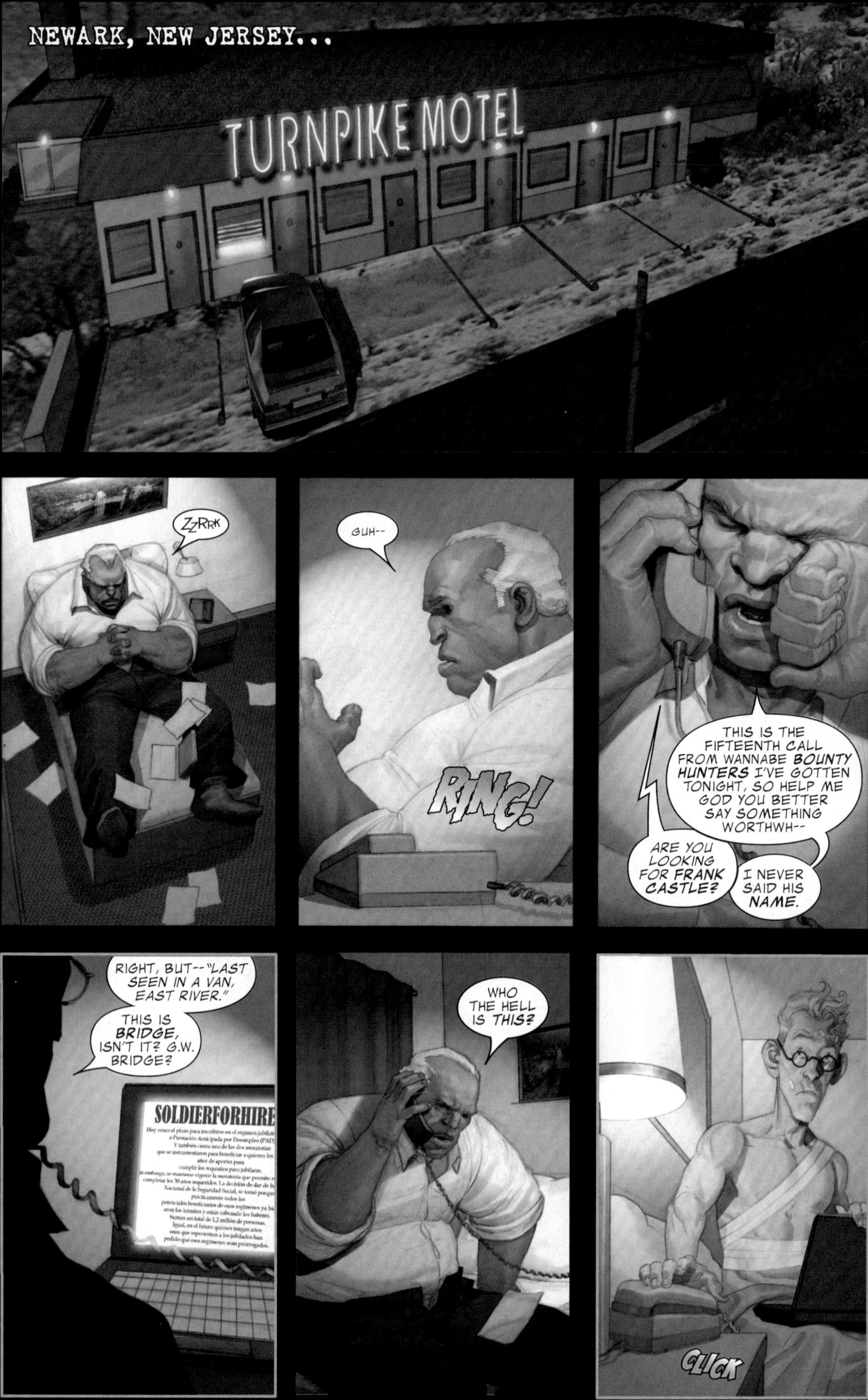
NEWARK, NEW JERSEY...
TURNPIKE MOTEL
ZZRRK
GUH--
RING!
THIS IS THE FIFTEENTH CALL FROM WANNABE BOUNTY HUNTERS I'VE GOTTEN TONIGHT, SO HELP ME GOD YOU BETTER SAY SOMETHING WORTHWH--
ARE YOU LOOKING FOR FRANK CASTLE?
I NEVER SAID HIS NAME.
RIGHT, BUT-- "LAST SEEN IN A VAN, EAST RIVER."
THIS IS BRIDGE, ISN'T IT? G.W. BRIDGE?
SOLDIERFORHIRE
WHO THE HELL IS THIS?
CLICK

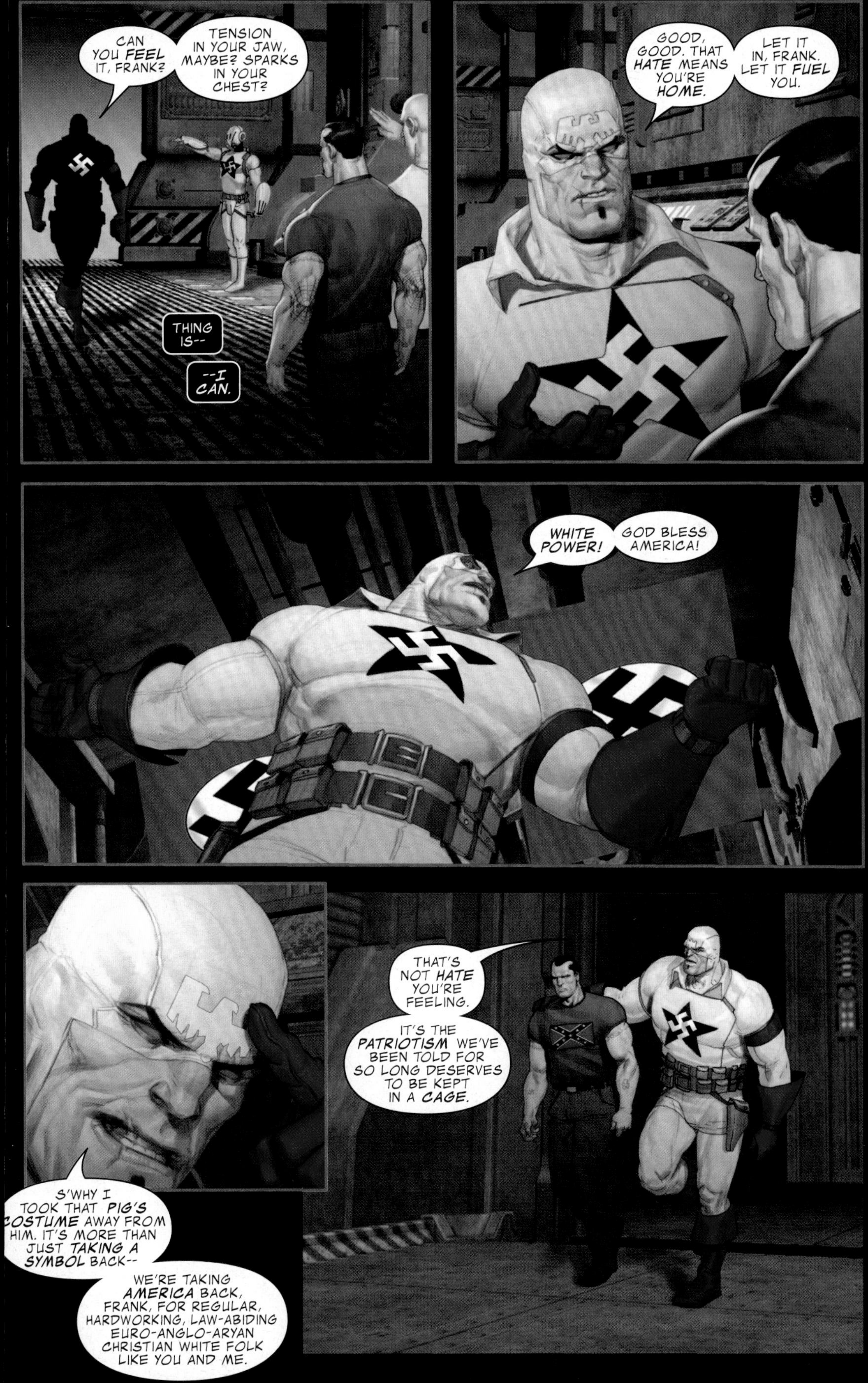
CAN YOU FEEL IT, FRANK?
TENSION IN YOUR JAW, MAYBE? SPARKS IN YOUR CHEST?
THING IS--
--I CAN.
GOOD, GOOD. THAT HATE MEANS YOU'RE HOME.
LET IT IN, FRANK. LET IT FUEL YOU.
WHITE POWER!
GOD BLESS AMERICA!
THAT'S NOT HATE YOU'RE FEELING.
IT'S THE PATRIOTISM WE'VE BEEN TOLD FOR SO LONG DESERVES TO BE KEPT IN A CAGE.
S'WHY I TOOK THAT PIG'S COSTUME AWAY FROM HIM. IT'S MORE THAN JUST TAKING A SYMBOL BACK--
WE'RE TAKING AMERICA BACK, FRANK, FOR REGULAR, HARDWORKING, LAW-ABIDING EURO-ANGLO-ARYAN CHRISTIAN WHITE FOLK LIKE YOU AND ME.

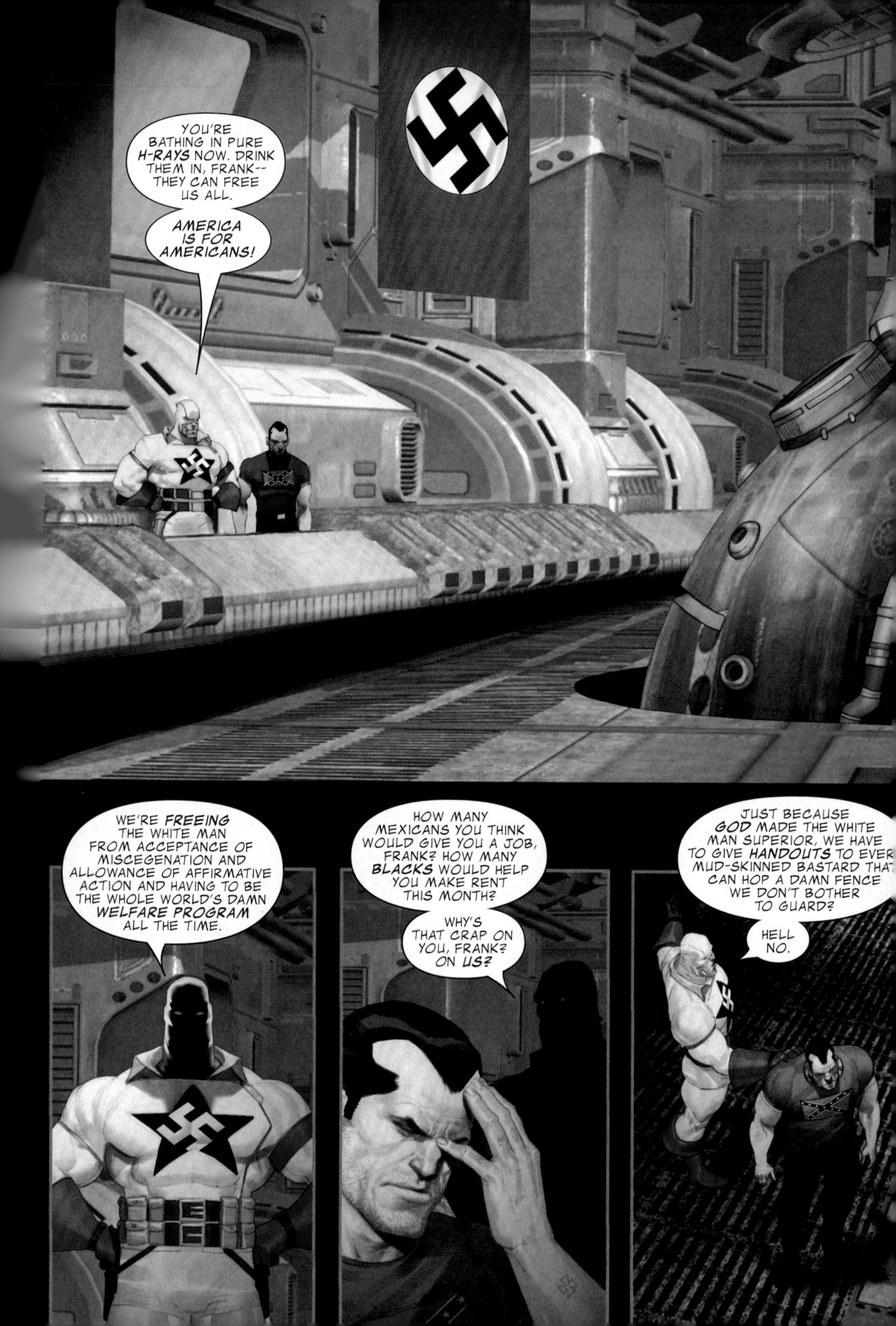

YOU'RE BATHING IN PURE H-RAYS NOW. DRINK THEM IN, FRANK-- THEY CAN FREE US ALL.
AMERICA IS FOR AMERICANS!
WE'RE FREEING THE WHITE MAN FROM ACCEPTANCE OF MISCEGENATION AND ALLOWANCE OF AFFIRMATIVE ACTION AND HAVING TO BE THE WHOLE WORLD'S DAMN WELFARE PROGRAM ALL THE TIME.
HOW MANY MEXICANS YOU THINK WOULD GIVE YOU A JOB, FRANK? HOW MANY BLACKS WOULD HELP YOU MAKE RENT THIS MONTH?
WHY'S THAT CRAP ON YOU, FRANK? ON US?
JUST BECAUSE GOD MADE THE WHITE MAN SUPERIOR, WE HAVE TO GIVE HANDOUTS TO EVER MUD-SKINNED BASTARD THAT CAN HOP A DAMN FENCE WE DON'T BOTHER TO GUARD?
HELL NO.

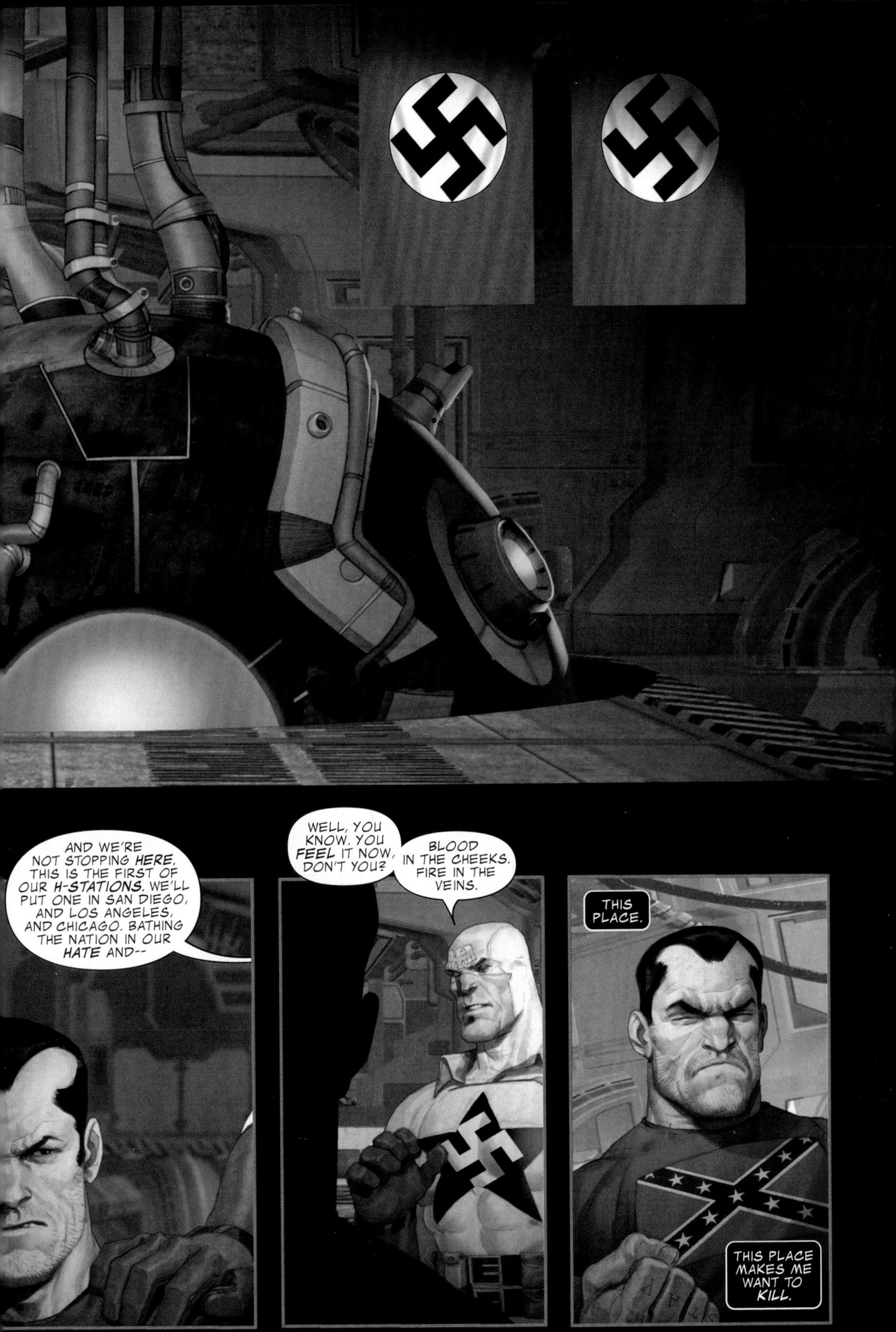

AND WE'RE NOT STOPPING HERE. THIS IS THE FIRST OF OUR H-STATIONS. WE'LL PUT ONE IN SAN DIEGO, AND LOS ANGELES, AND CHICAGO. BATHING THE NATION IN OUR HATE AND--
WELL, YOU KNOW. YOU FEEL IT NOW, DON'T YOU?
BLOOD IN THE CHEEKS. FIRE IN THE VEINS.
THIS PLACE.
THIS PLACE MAKES ME WANT TO KILL.

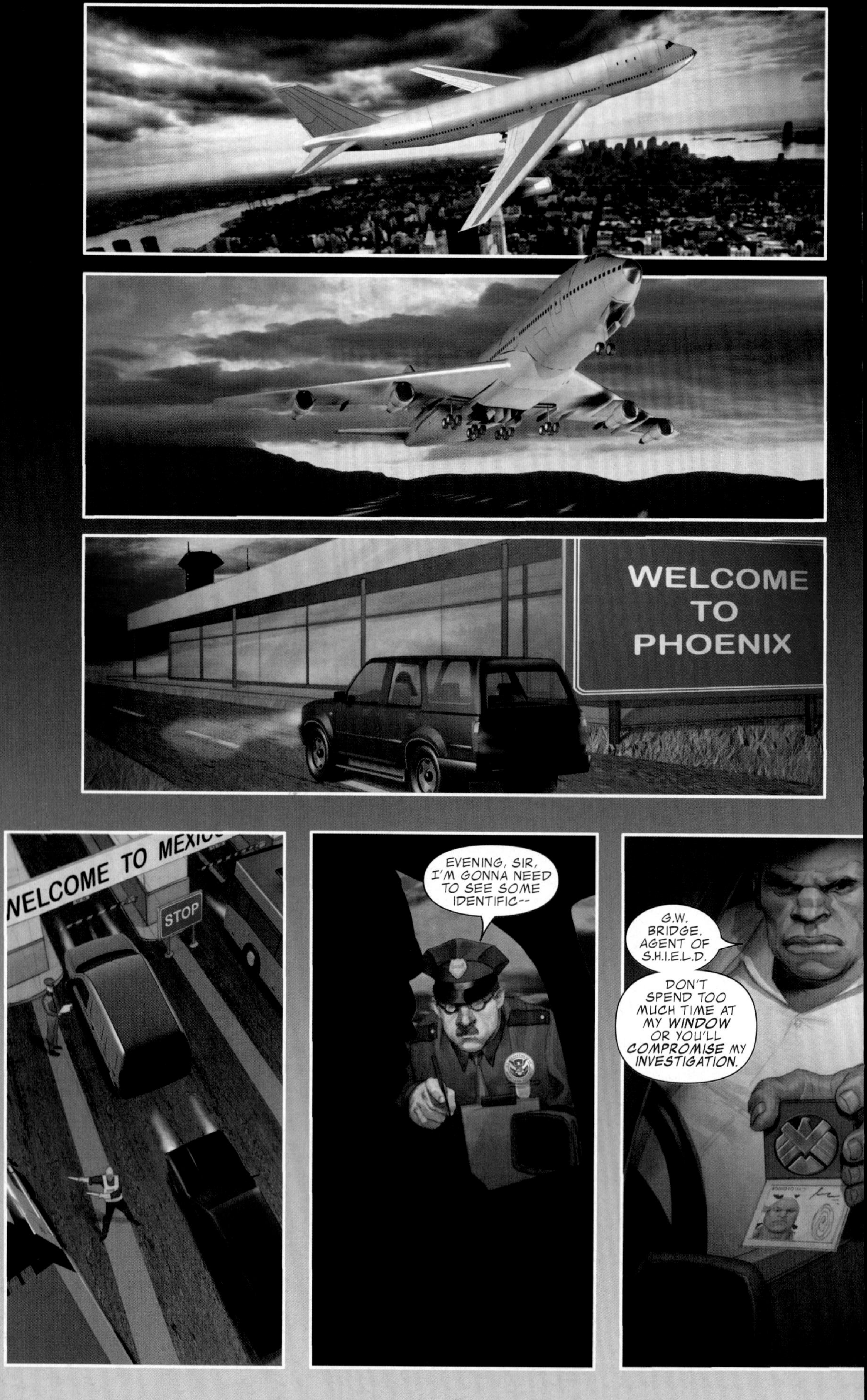
WELCOME TO PHOENIX
WELCOME TO MEXIC
STOP
EVENING, SIR, I'M GONNA NEED TO SEE SOME IDENTIFIC--
G.W. BRIDGE. AGENT OF S.H.I.E.L.D.
DON'T SPEND TOO MUCH TIME AT MY *WINDOW* OR YOU'LL *COMPROMISE* MY *INVESTIGATION.*

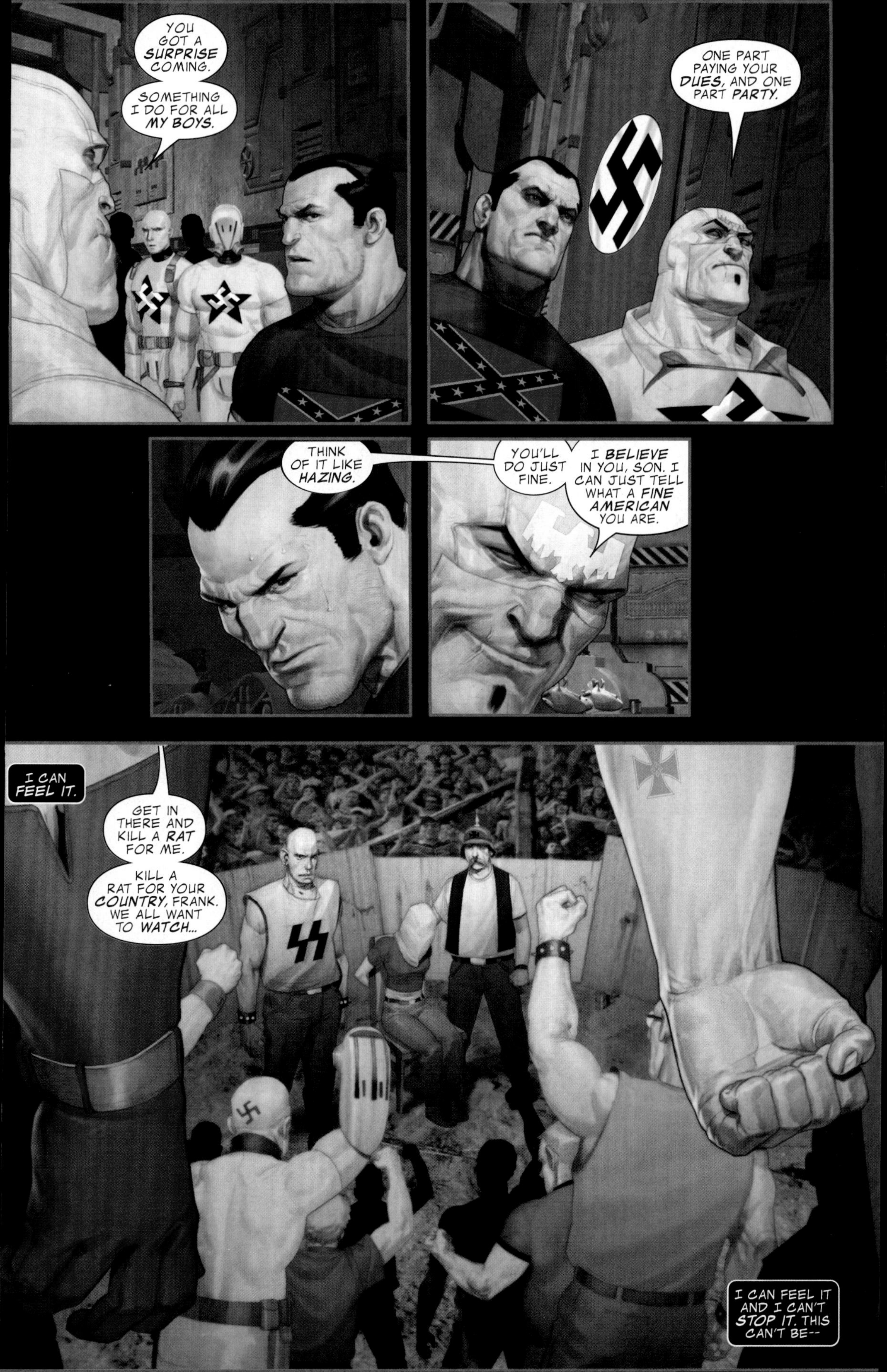
YOU GOT A SURPRISE COMING.
SOMETHING I DO FOR ALL MY BOYS.
ONE PART PAYING YOUR DUES, AND ONE PART PARTY.
THINK OF IT LIKE HAZING.
YOU'LL DO JUST FINE.
I BELIEVE IN YOU, SON. I CAN JUST TELL WHAT A FINE AMERICAN YOU ARE.
I CAN FEEL IT.
GET IN THERE AND KILL A RAT FOR ME.
KILL A RAT FOR YOUR COUNTRY, FRANK. WE ALL WANT TO WATCH...
I CAN FEEL IT AND I CAN'T STOP IT. THIS CAN'T BE--

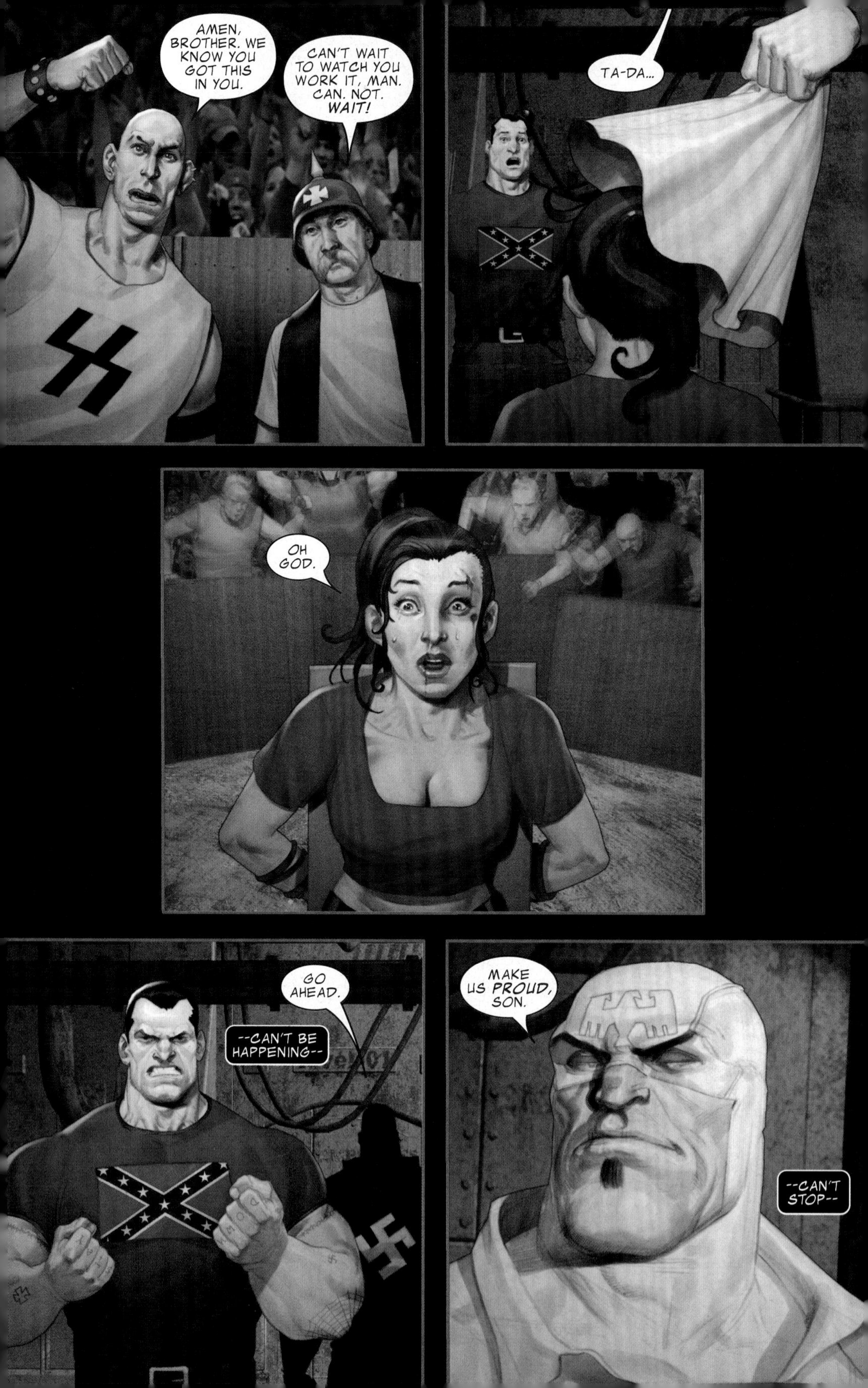
AMEN, BROTHER. WE KNOW YOU GOT THIS IN YOU.
CAN'T WAIT TO WATCH YOU WORK IT, MAN. CAN. NOT. *WAIT!*
TA-DA...
OH GOD.
GO AHEAD.
--CAN'T BE HAPPENING--
MAKE US *PROUD,* SON.
--CAN'T STOP--

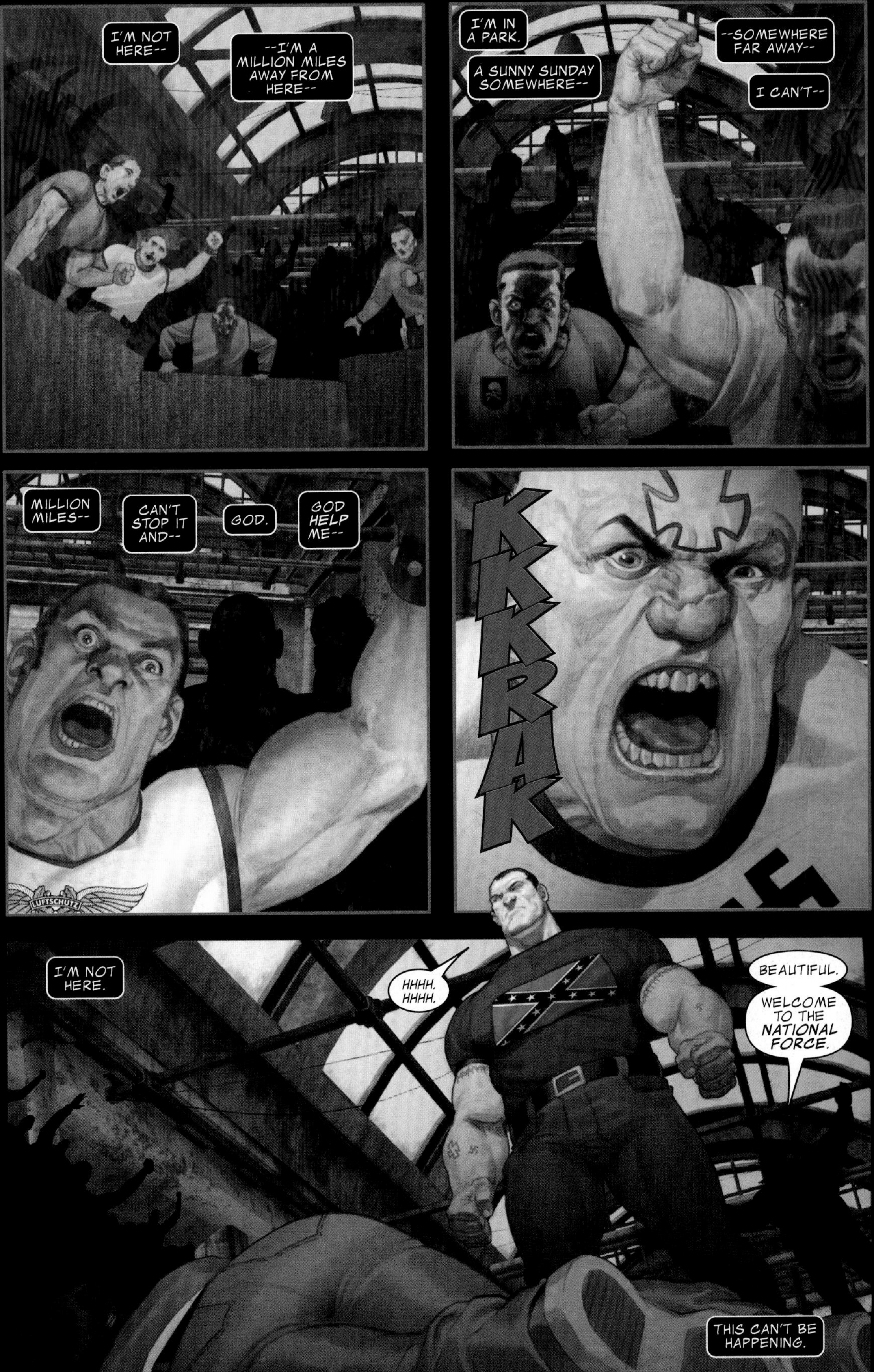
I'M NOT HERE--
--I'M A MILLION MILES AWAY FROM HERE--
I'M IN A PARK.
A SUNNY SUNDAY SOMEWHERE--
--SOMEWHERE FAR AWAY--
I CAN'T--
MILLION MILES--
CAN'T STOP IT AND--
GOD.
GOD HELP ME--
LUFTSCHUTZ
KKRAK
I'M NOT HERE.
HHHH. HHHH.
BEAUTIFUL.
WELCOME TO THE NATIONAL FORCE.
THIS CAN'T BE HAPPENING.

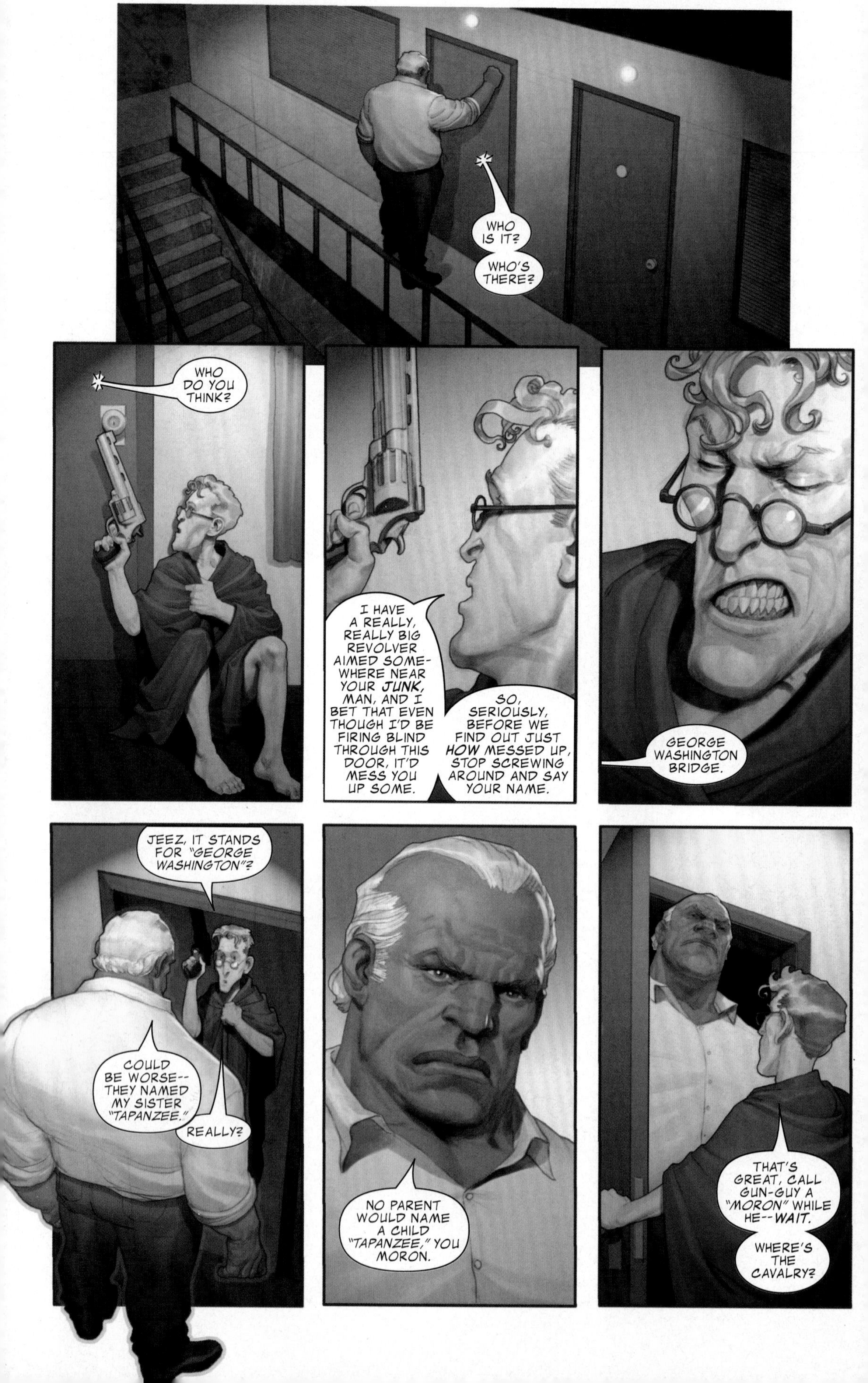
WHO IS IT?
WHO'S THERE?
WHO DO YOU THINK?
I HAVE A REALLY, REALLY BIG REVOLVER AIMED SOME-WHERE NEAR YOUR JUNK, MAN, AND I BET THAT EVEN THOUGH I'D BE FIRING BLIND THROUGH THIS DOOR, IT'D MESS YOU UP SOME.
SO, SERIOUSLY, BEFORE WE FIND OUT JUST HOW MESSED UP, STOP SCREWING AROUND AND SAY YOUR NAME.
GEORGE WASHINGTON BRIDGE.
JEEZ, IT STANDS FOR "GEORGE WASHINGTON"?
COULD BE WORSE-- THEY NAMED MY SISTER "TAPANZEE."
REALLY?
NO PARENT WOULD NAME A CHILD "TAPANZEE," YOU MORON.
THAT'S GREAT, CALL GUN-GUY A "MORON" WHILE HE--WAIT.
WHERE'S THE CAVALRY?

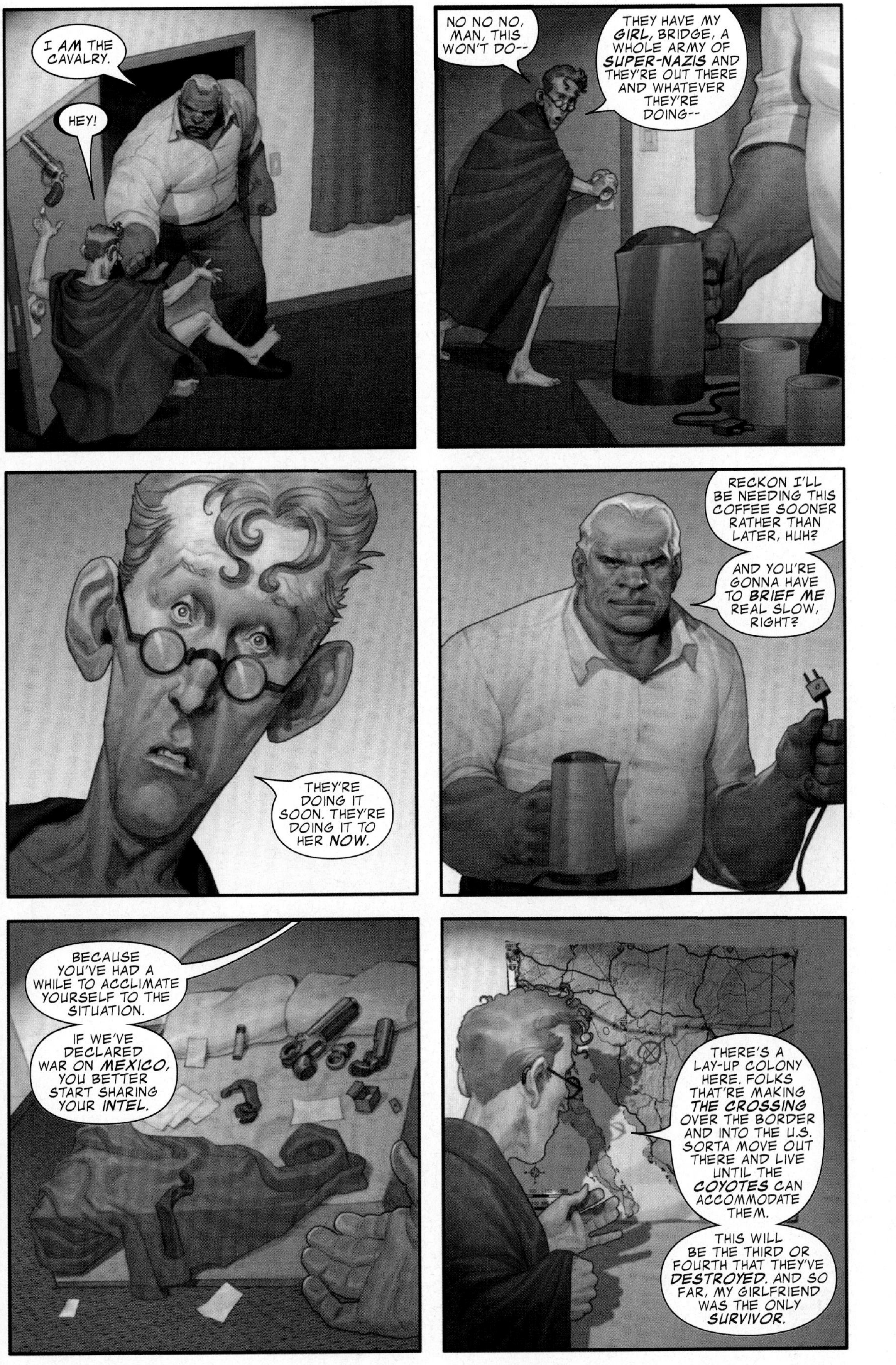
I AM THE CAVALRY.
HEY!
NO NO NO, MAN, THIS WON'T DO--
THEY HAVE MY GIRL, BRIDGE, A WHOLE ARMY OF SUPER-NAZIS AND THEY'RE OUT THERE AND WHATEVER THEY'RE DOING--
THEY'RE DOING IT SOON. THEY'RE DOING IT TO HER NOW.
RECKON I'LL BE NEEDING THIS COFFEE SOONER RATHER THAN LATER, HUH?
AND YOU'RE GONNA HAVE TO BRIEF ME REAL SLOW, RIGHT?
BECAUSE YOU'VE HAD A WHILE TO ACCLIMATE YOURSELF TO THE SITUATION.
IF WE'VE DECLARED WAR ON MEXICO, YOU BETTER START SHARING YOUR INTEL.
THERE'S A LAY-UP COLONY HERE. FOLKS THAT'RE MAKING THE CROSSING OVER THE BORDER AND INTO THE U.S. SORTA MOVE OUT THERE AND LIVE UNTIL THE COYOTES CAN ACCOMMODATE THEM.
THIS WILL BE THE THIRD OR FOURTH THAT THEY'VE DESTROYED. AND SO FAR, MY GIRLFRIEND WAS THE ONLY SURVIVOR.

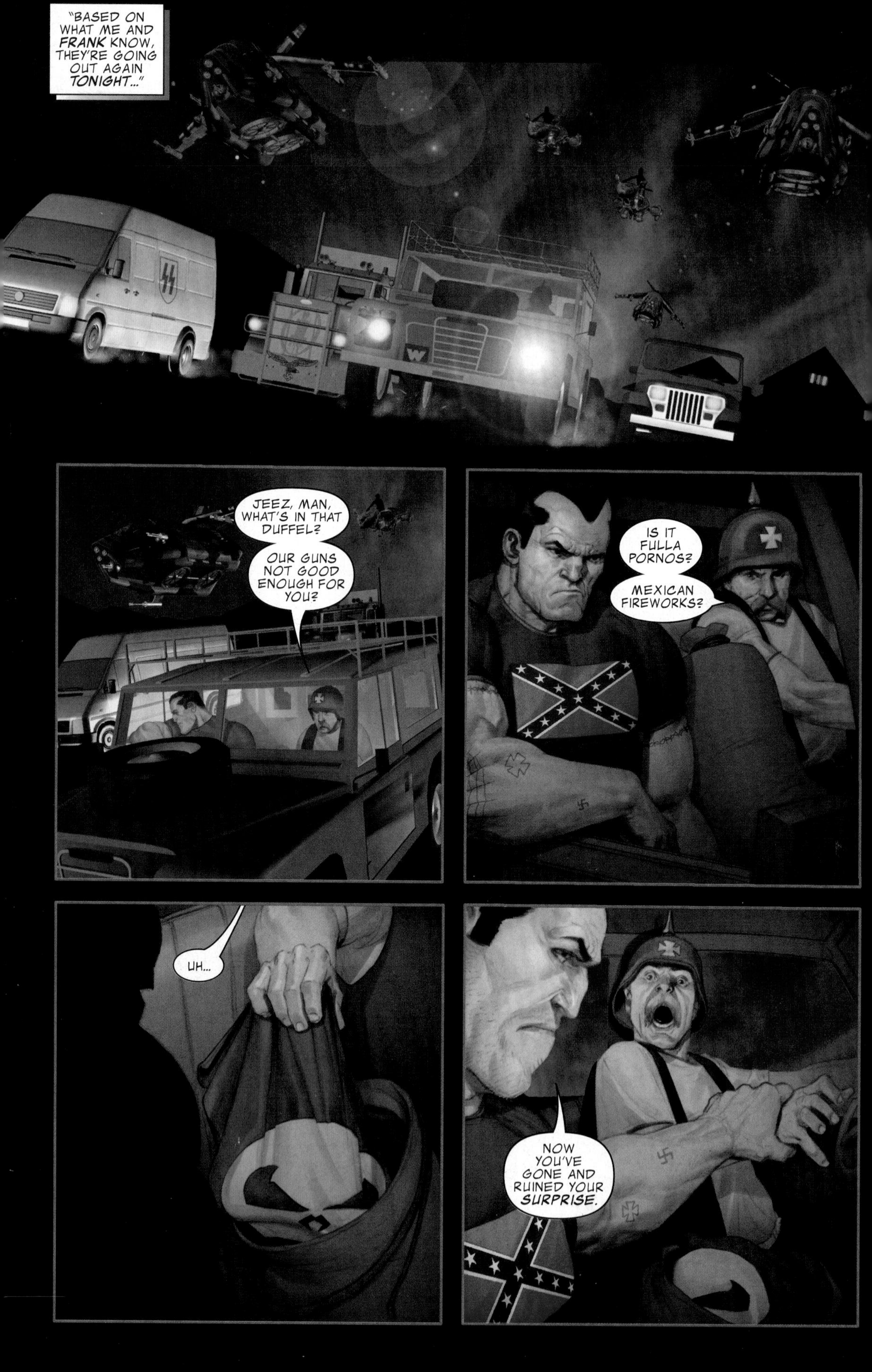
"BASED ON WHAT ME AND FRANK KNOW, THEY'RE GOING OUT AGAIN TONIGHT..."
JEEZ, MAN, WHAT'S IN THAT DUFFEL?
OUR GUNS NOT GOOD ENOUGH FOR YOU?
IS IT FULLA PORNOS?
MEXICAN FIREWORKS?
UH...
NOW YOU'VE GONE AND RUINED YOUR SURPRISE.

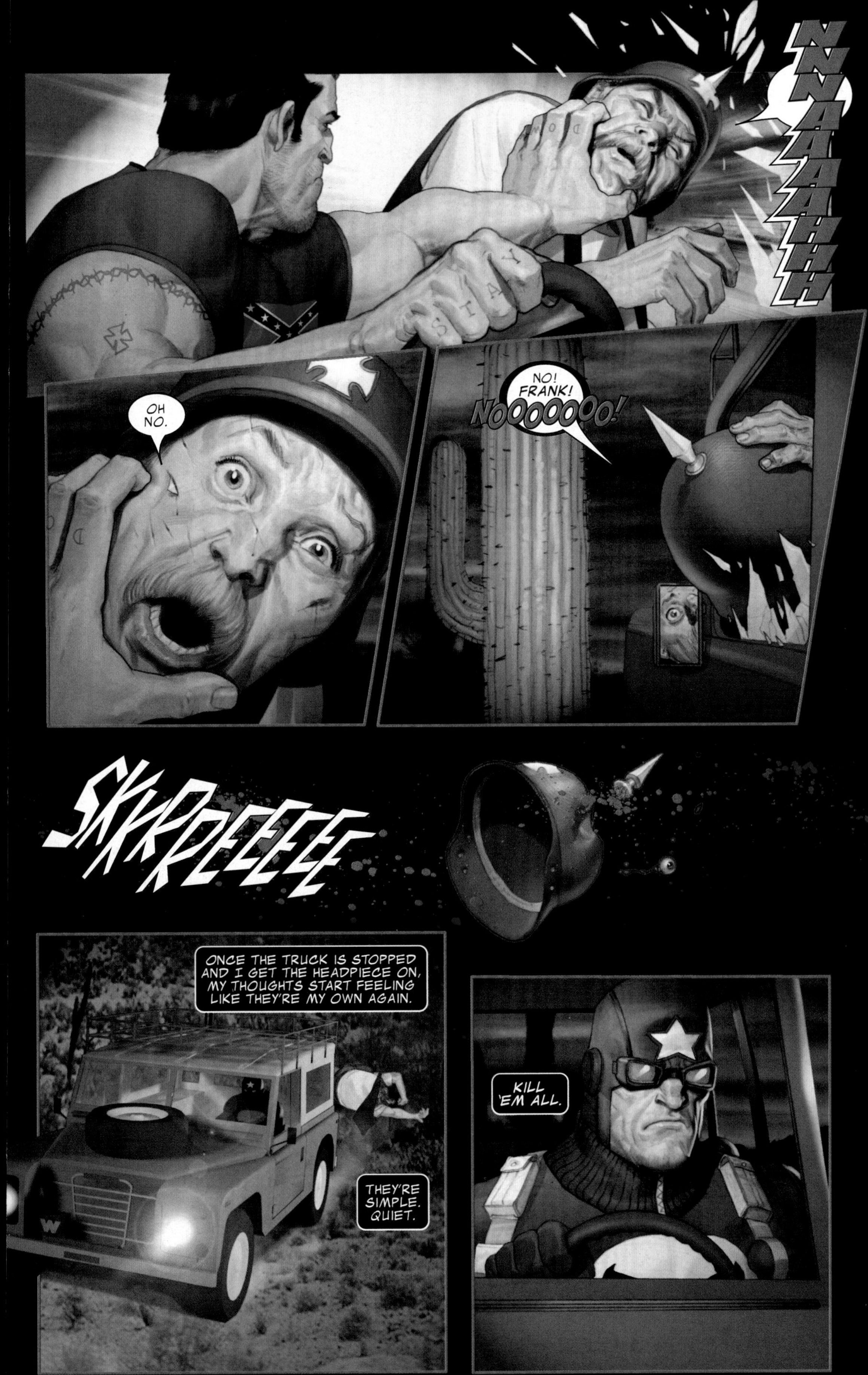
NNNAAAAHHH
OH NO.
NO! FRANK!
NOOOOOOO!
SKKREEEEE
ONCE THE TRUCK IS STOPPED AND I GET THE HEADPIECE ON, MY THOUGHTS START FEELING LIKE THEY'RE MY OWN AGAIN.
THEY'RE SIMPLE. QUIET.
KILL 'EM ALL.

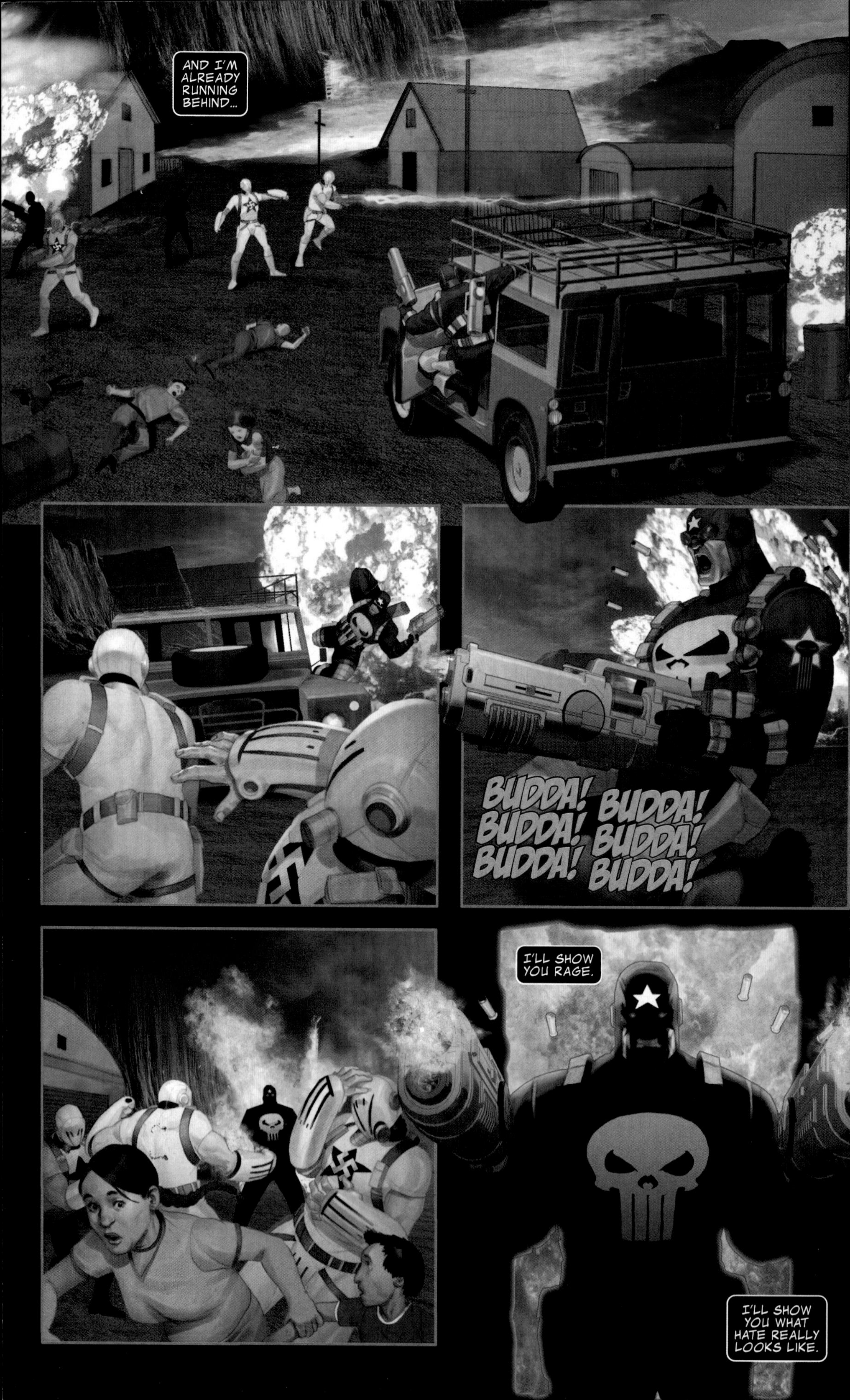
AND I'M ALREADY RUNNING BEHIND...
BUDDA! BUDDA! BUDDA! BUDDA! BUDDA! BUDDA!
I'LL SHOW YOU RAGE.
I'LL SHOW YOU WHAT HATE REALLY LOOKS LIKE.

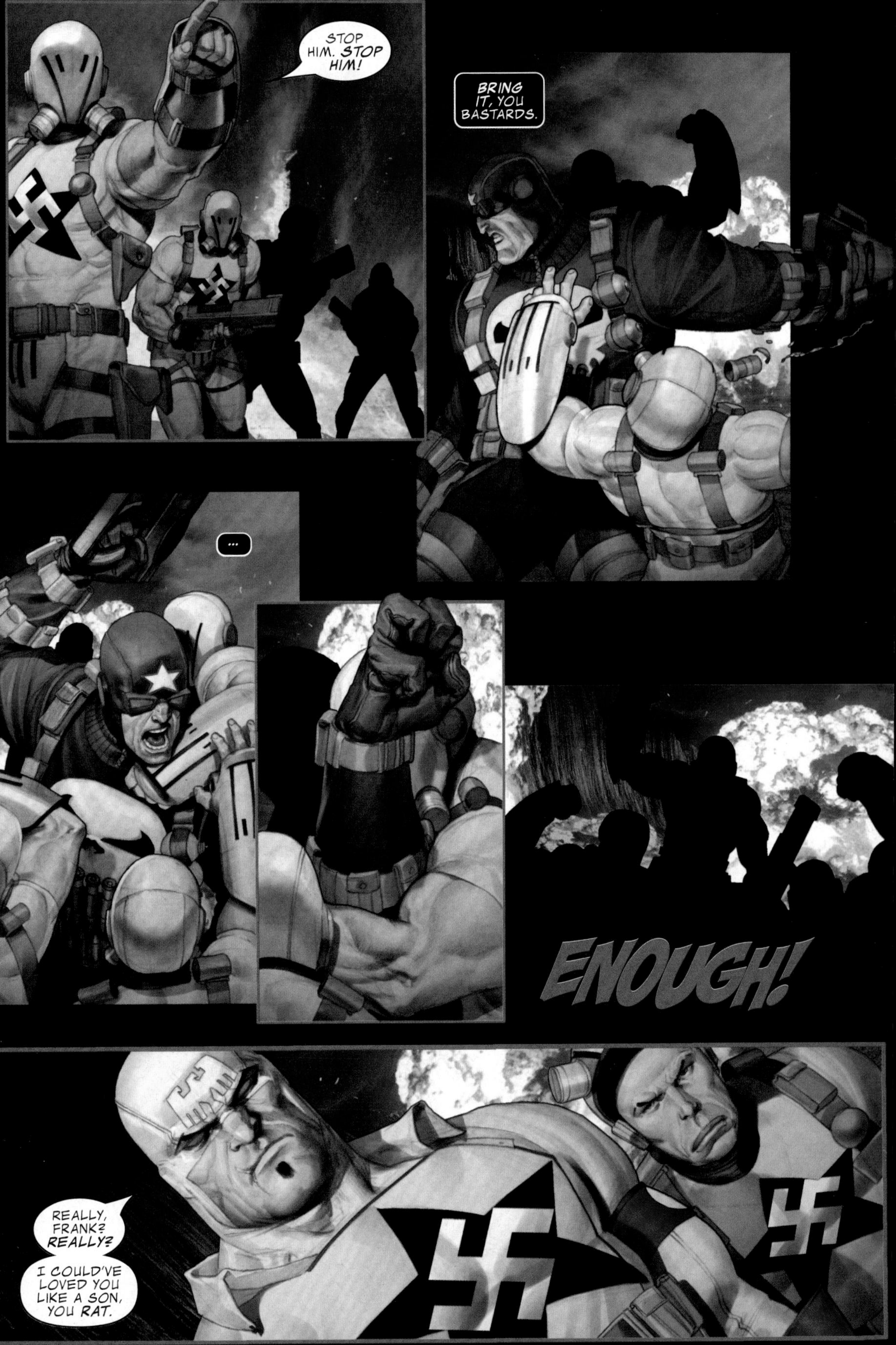
STOP HIM. STOP HIM!
BRING IT, YOU BASTARDS.
...
ENOUGH!
REALLY, FRANK? REALLY?
I COULD'VE LOVED YOU LIKE A SON, YOU RAT.

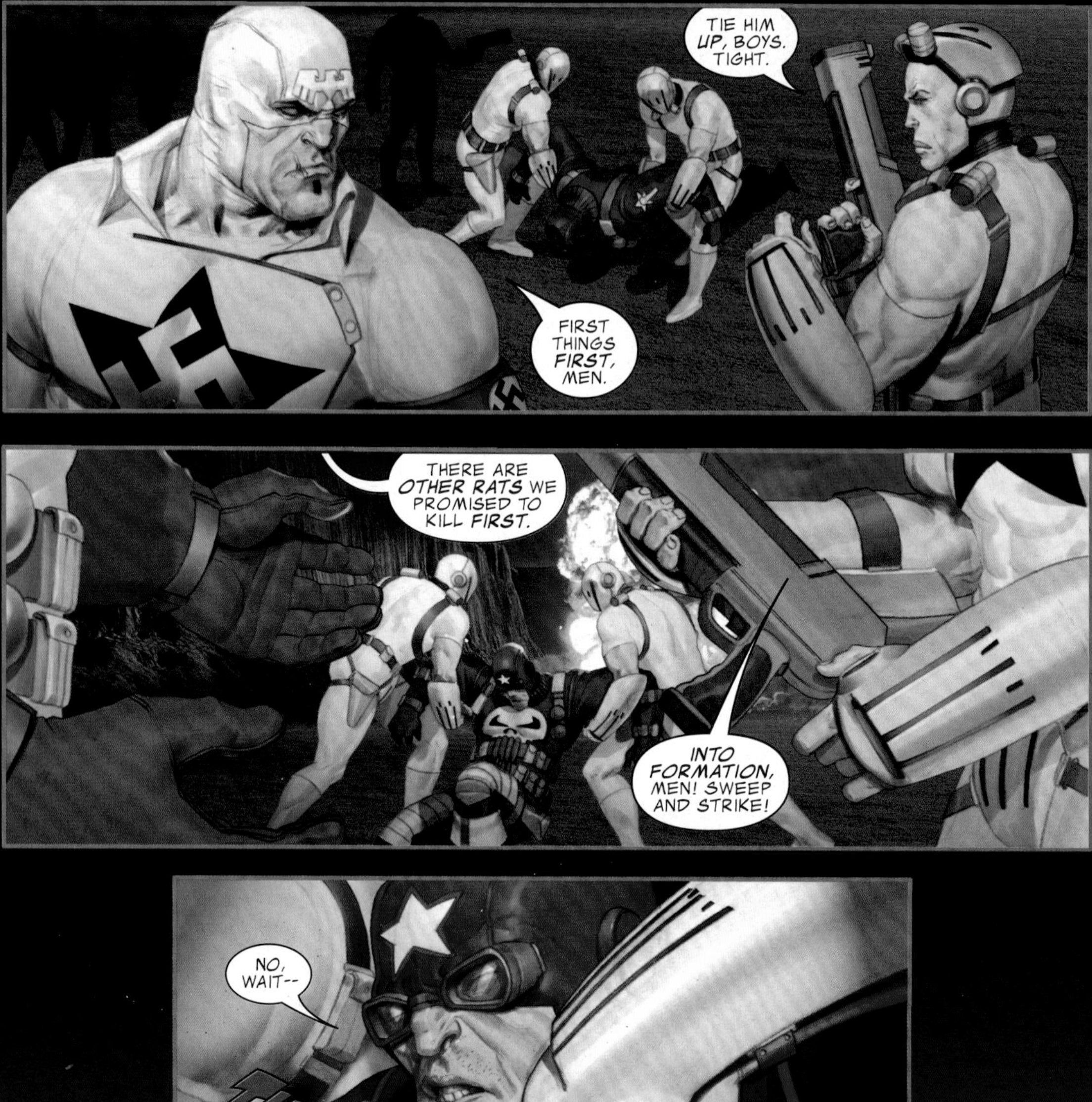
TIE HIM UP, BOYS. TIGHT.
FIRST THINGS FIRST, MEN.
THERE ARE OTHER RATS WE PROMISED TO KILL FIRST.
INTO FORMATION, MEN! SWEEP AND STRIKE!
NO, WAIT--
THUNGK!
AND I WOKE UP IN THE DESERT.

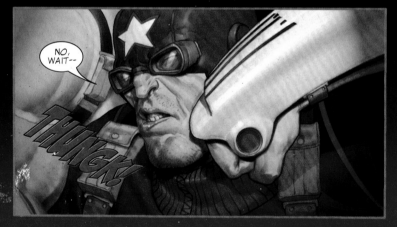

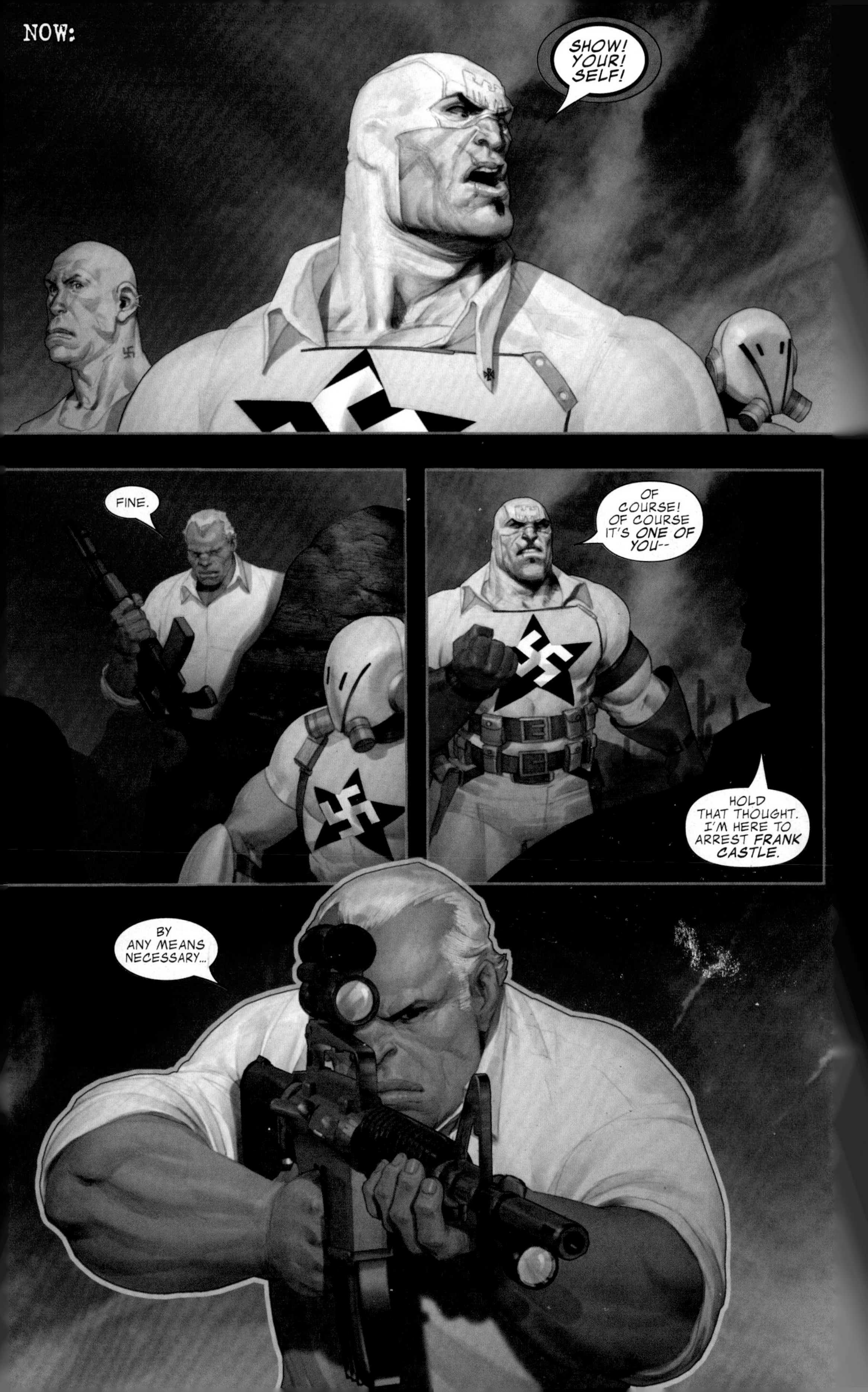
NOW:
SHOW! YOUR! SELF!
FINE.
OF COURSE! OF COURSE IT'S ONE OF YOU--
HOLD THAT THOUGHT. I'M HERE TO ARREST FRANK CASTLE.
BY ANY MEANS NECESSARY...

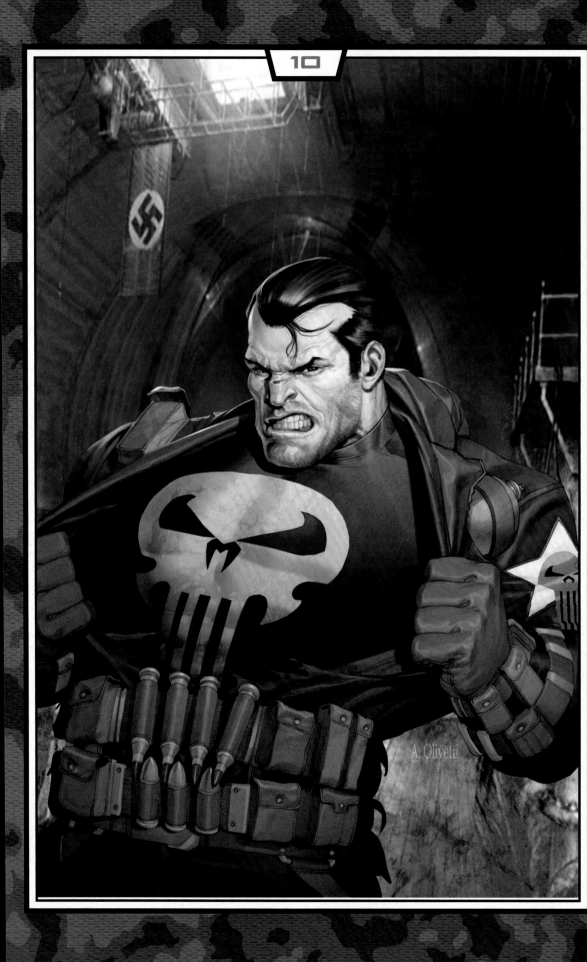

10

A. Olivetti

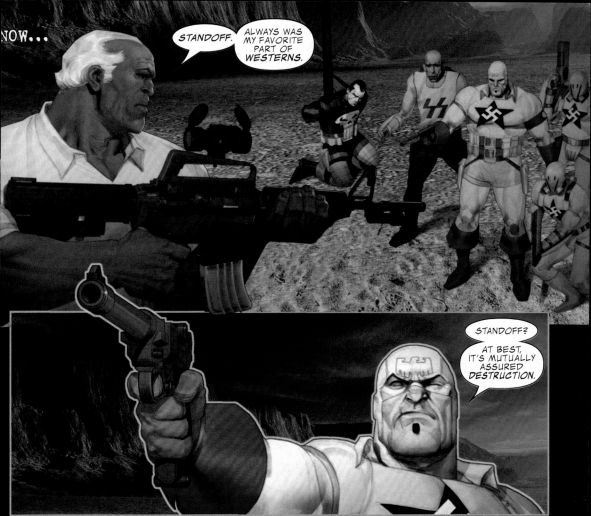

NOW...

STANDOFF. ALWAYS WAS MY FAVORITE PART OF WESTERNS.

STANDOFF? AT BEST, IT'S MUTUALLY ASSURED DESTRUCTION.

THIS IS A MASSACRE, BOY.

YOU'RE JUST TOO DUMB TO REALIZE IT. WHAT IN THAT OLD ADDLED BLACK BRAIN OF YOURS MADE YOU THINK YOU COULD STOP THIS?

WELL. I HAVE A PARTNER.

AND HE FOUND YOUR HIDEOUT.

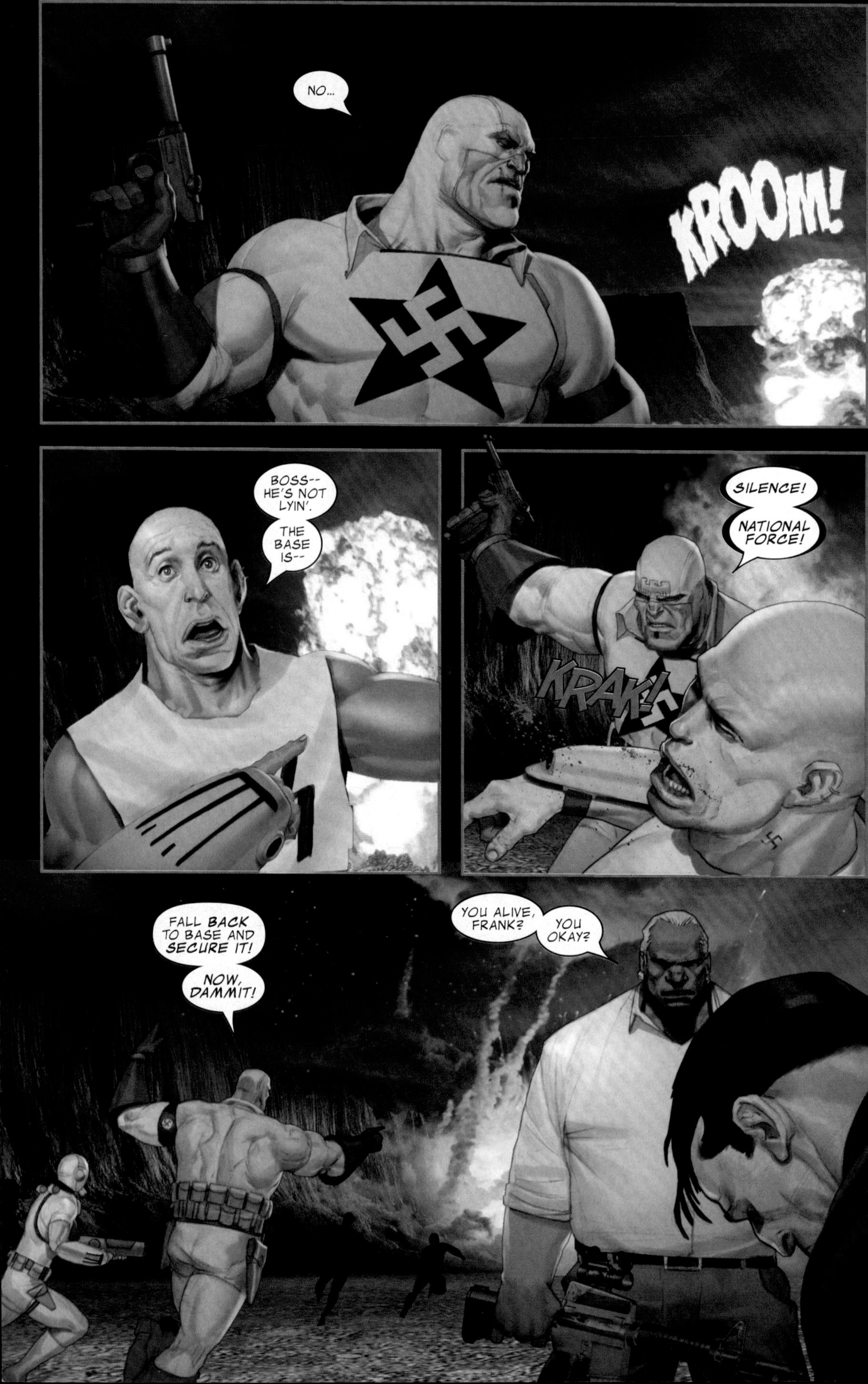
NO...
KROOM!
BOSS-- HE'S NOT LYIN'.
THE BASE IS--
SILENCE!
NATIONAL FORCE!
KRAK!
FALL BACK TO BASE AND SECURE IT!
NOW, DAMMIT!
YOU ALIVE, FRANK?
YOU OKAY?

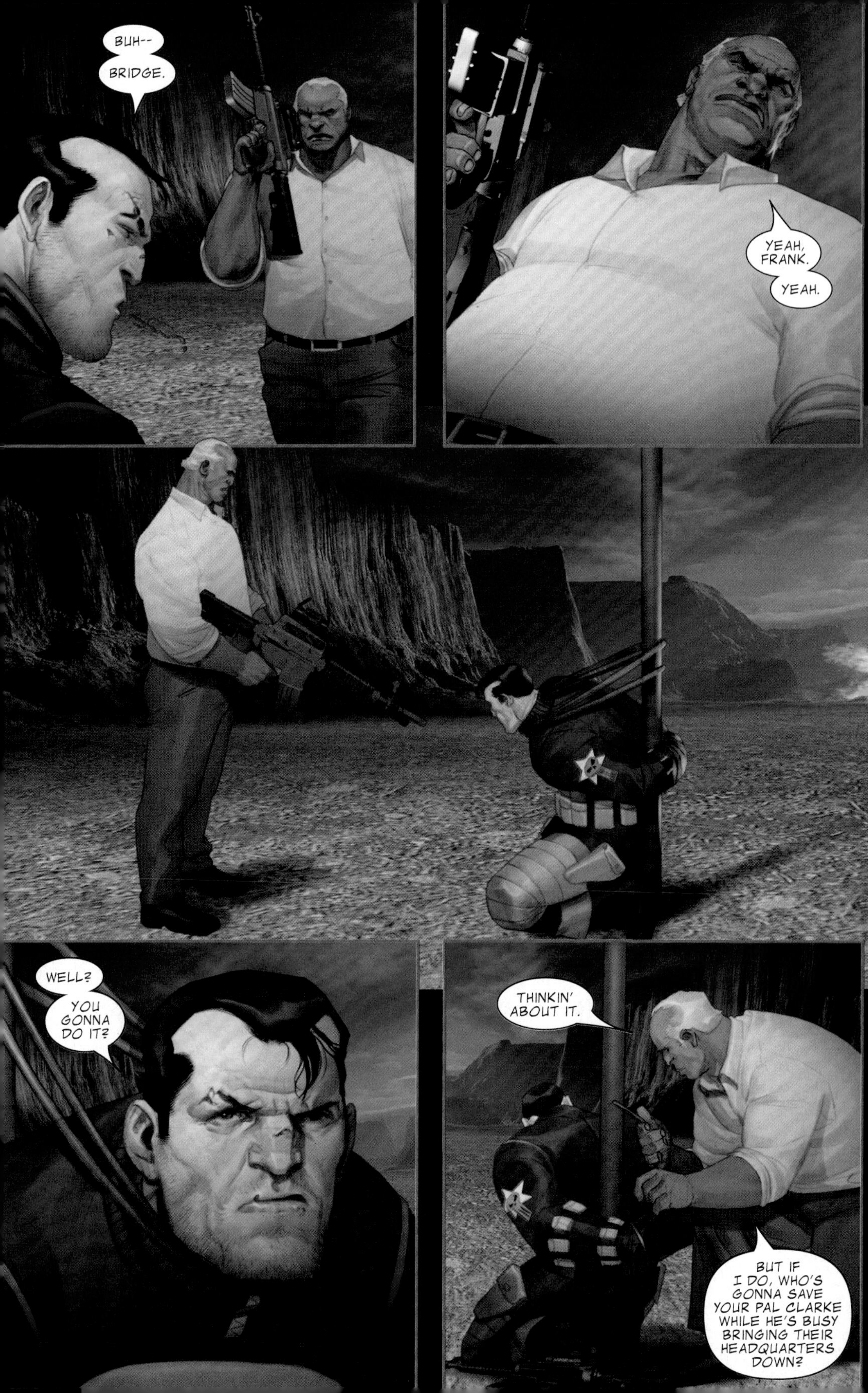
BUH--
BRIDGE.
YEAH, FRANK.
YEAH.
WELL?
YOU GONNA DO IT?
THINKIN' ABOUT IT.
BUT IF I DO, WHO'S GONNA SAVE YOUR PAL CLARKE WHILE HE'S BUSY BRINGING THEIR HEADQUARTERS DOWN?

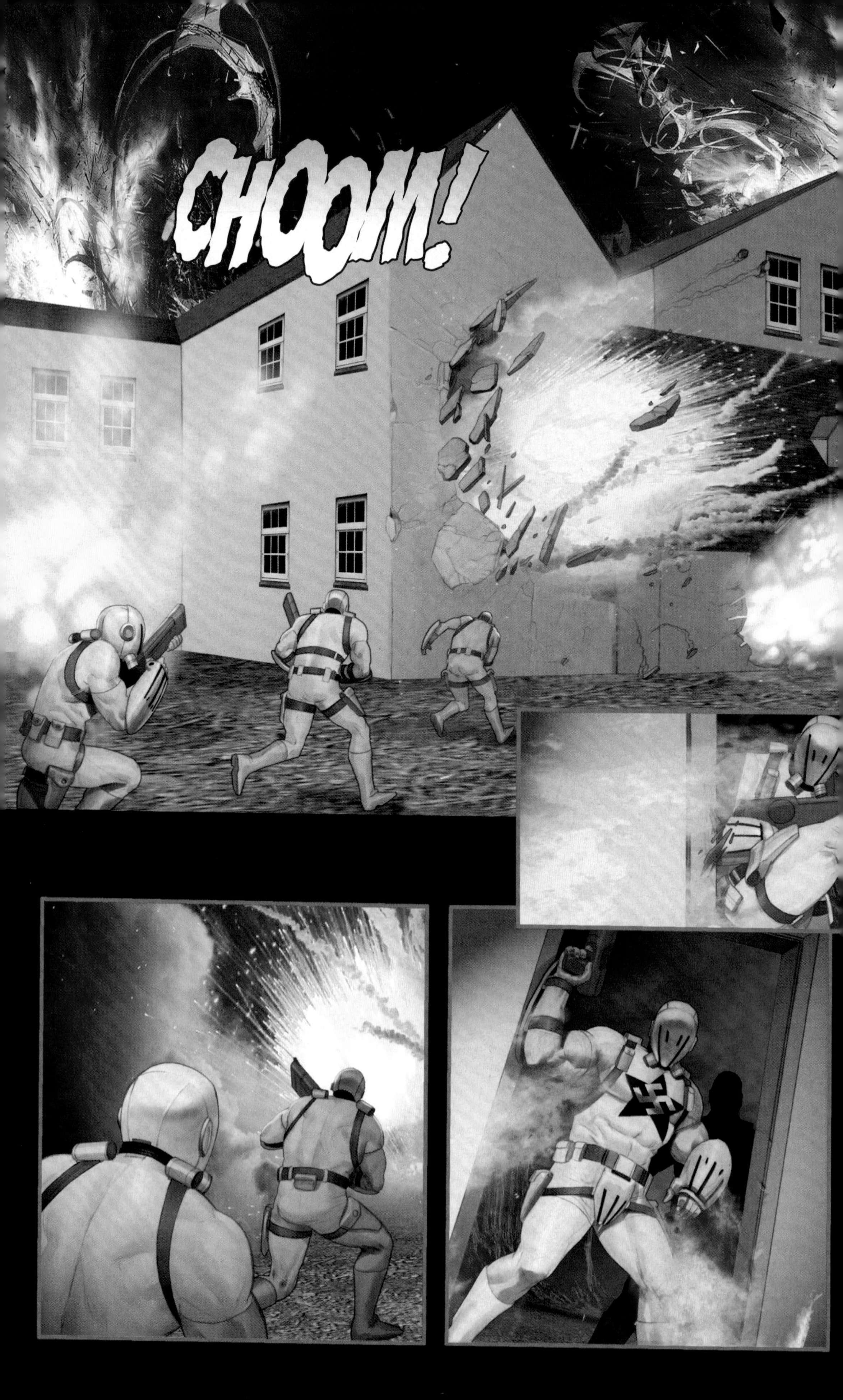
CHOOM!

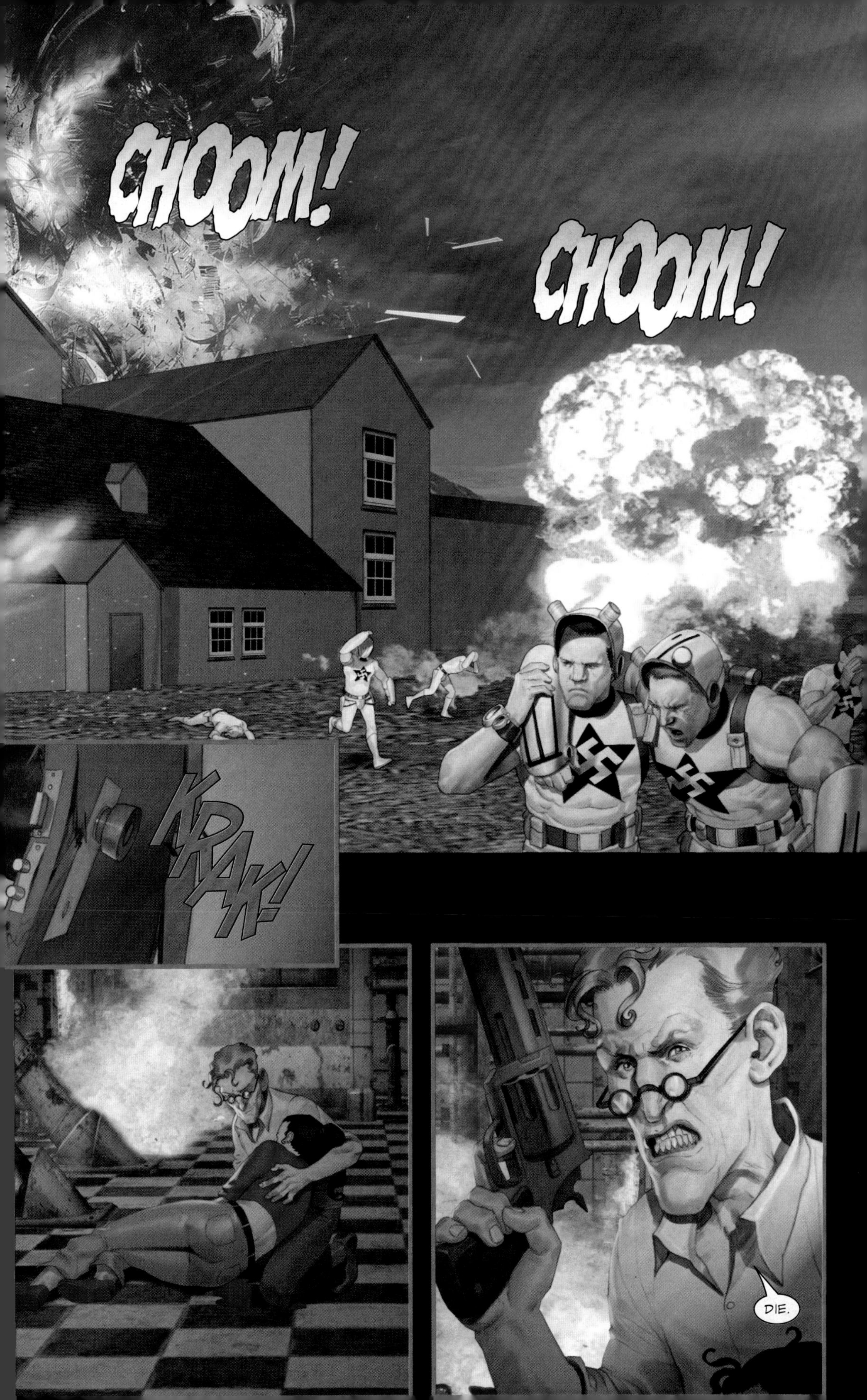
CHOOM!
CHOOM!
KRAK!
DIE.

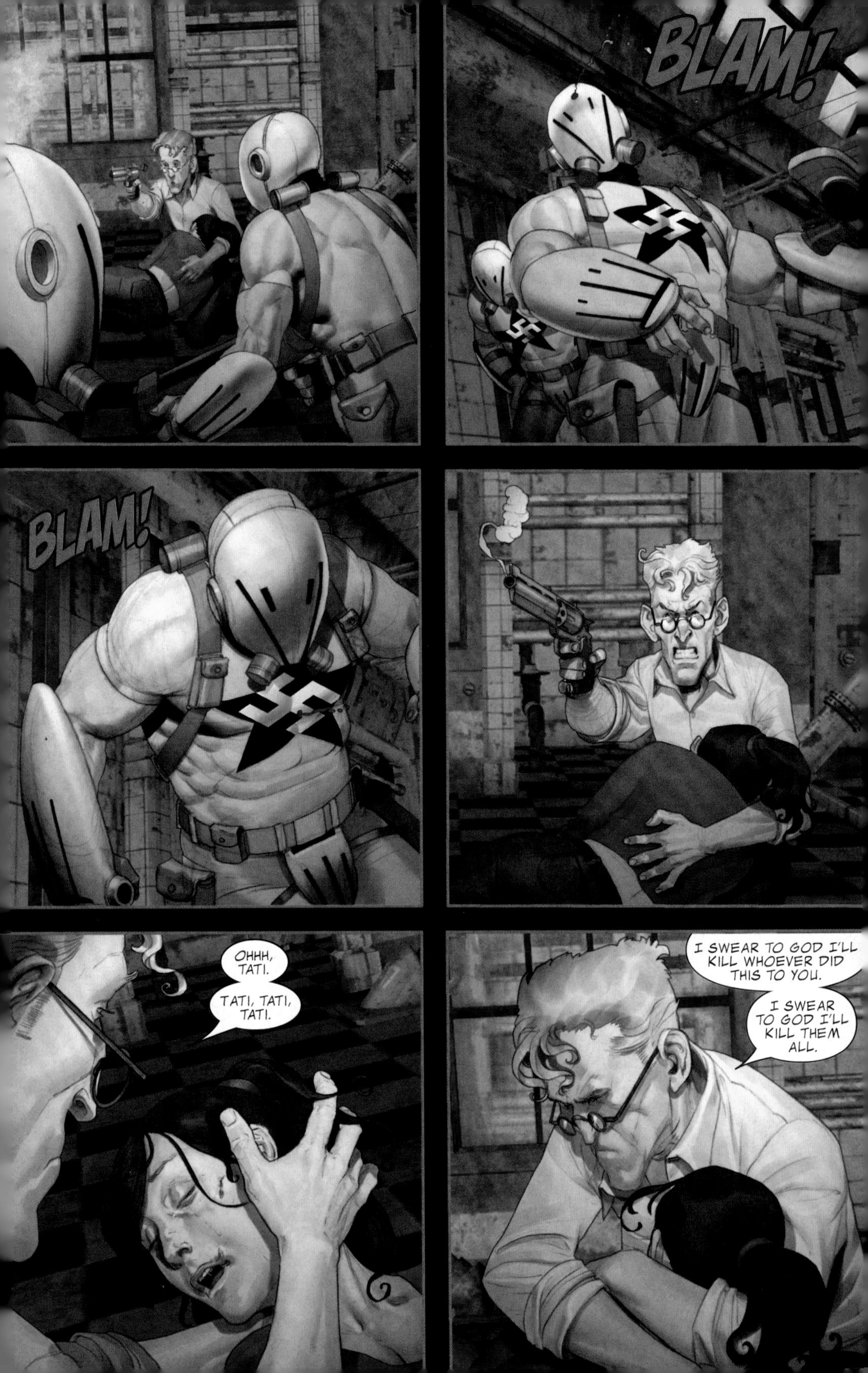
BLAM!
BLAM!
OHHH, TATI.
TATI, TATI, TATI.
I SWEAR TO GOD I'LL KILL WHOEVER DID THIS TO YOU.
I SWEAR TO GOD I'LL KILL THEM ALL.

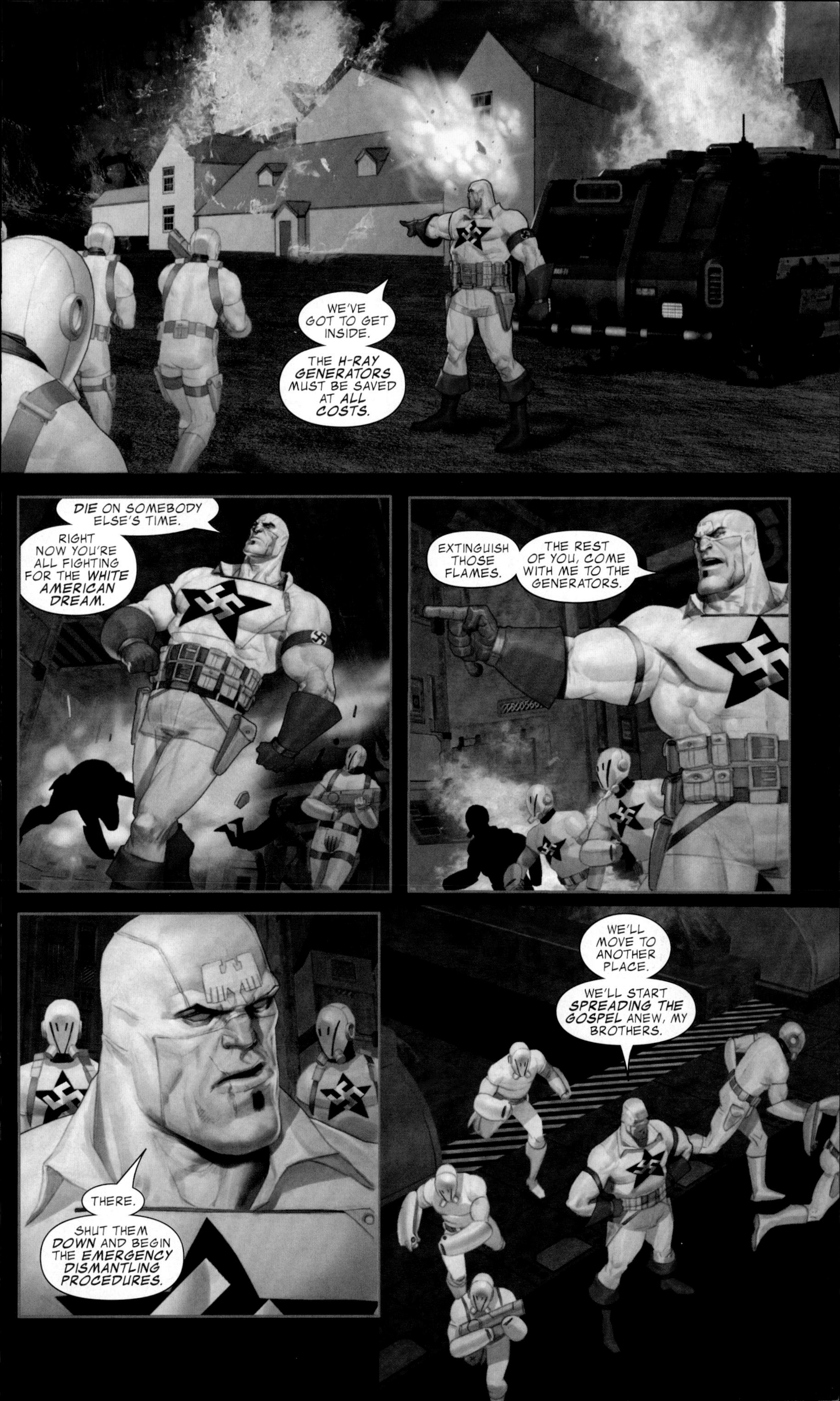
WE'VE GOT TO GET INSIDE.
THE H-RAY GENERATORS MUST BE SAVED AT ALL COSTS.
DIE ON SOMEBODY ELSE'S TIME.
RIGHT NOW YOU'RE ALL FIGHTING FOR THE WHITE AMERICAN DREAM.
EXTINGUISH THOSE FLAMES.
THE REST OF YOU, COME WITH ME TO THE GENERATORS.
THERE.
SHUT THEM DOWN AND BEGIN THE EMERGENCY DISMANTLING PROCEDURES.
WE'LL MOVE TO ANOTHER PLACE.
WE'LL START SPREADING THE GOSPEL ANEW, MY BROTHERS.

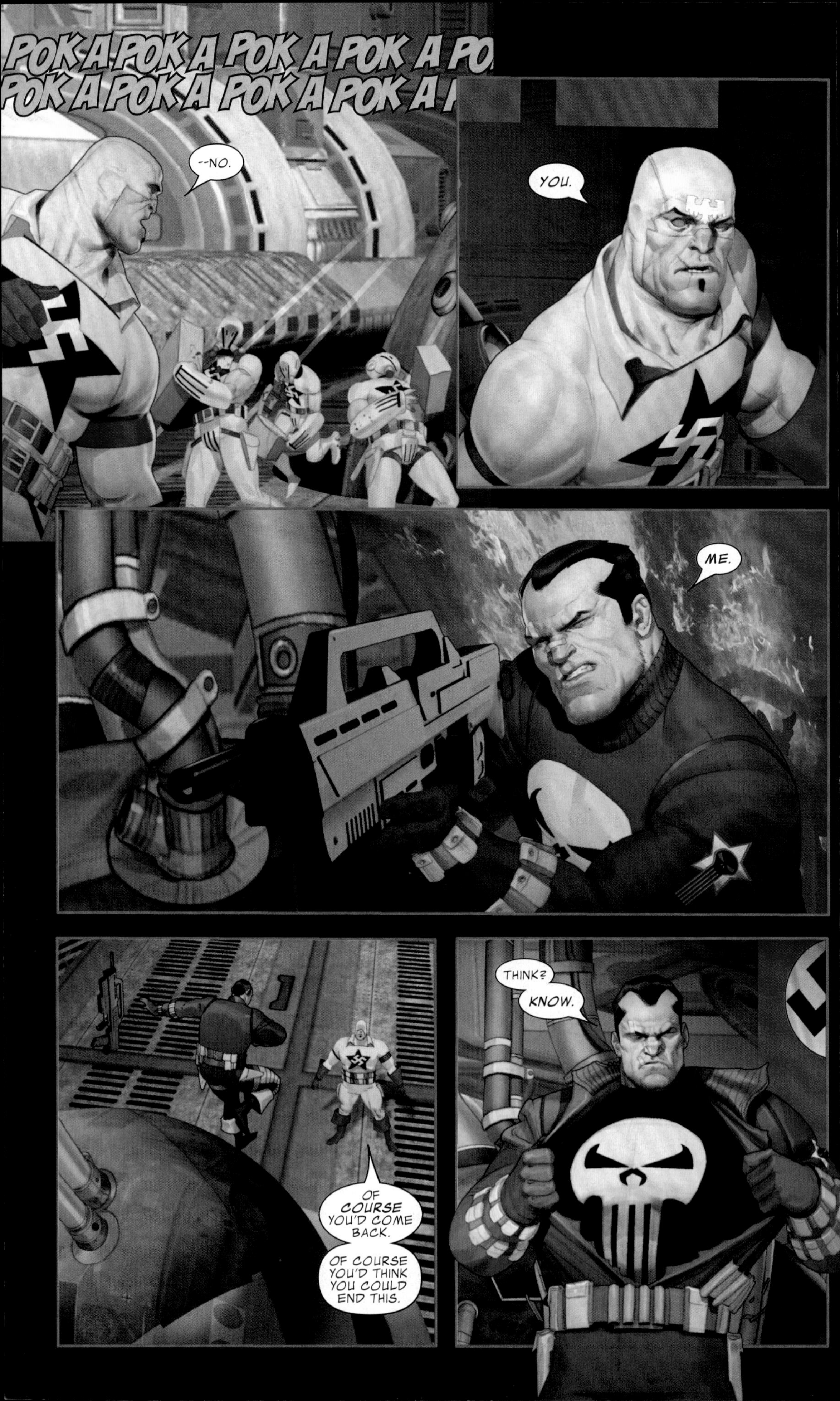
POK A POK A POK A POK A PO
POK A POK A POK A POK A
--NO.
YOU.
ME.
OF COURSE YOU'D COME BACK.
OF COURSE YOU'D THINK YOU COULD END THIS.
THINK?
KNOW.

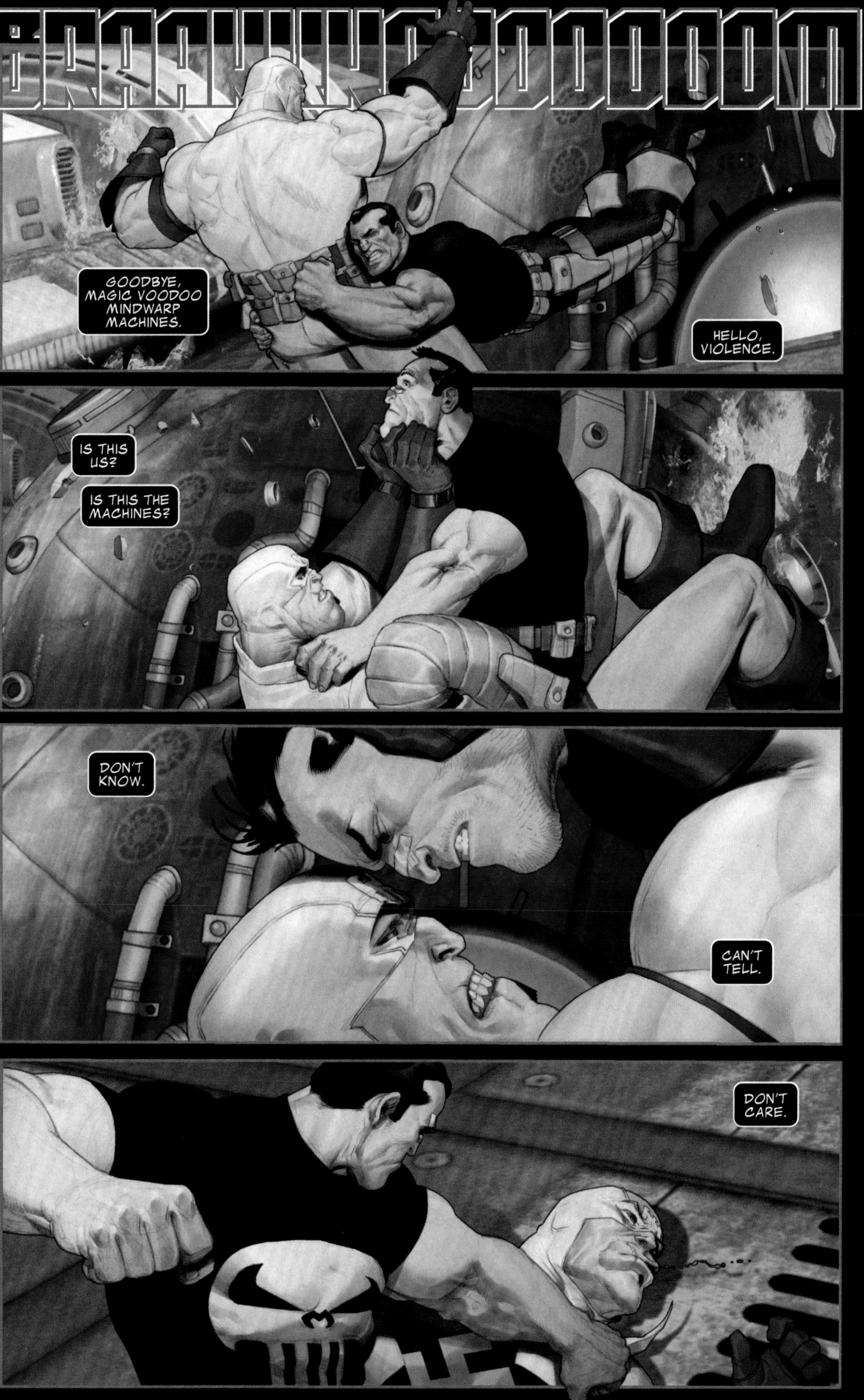
GOODBYE, MAGIC VOODOO MINDWARP MACHINES.
HELLO, VIOLENCE.
IS THIS US?
IS THIS THE MACHINES?
DON'T KNOW.
CAN'T TELL.
DON'T CARE.

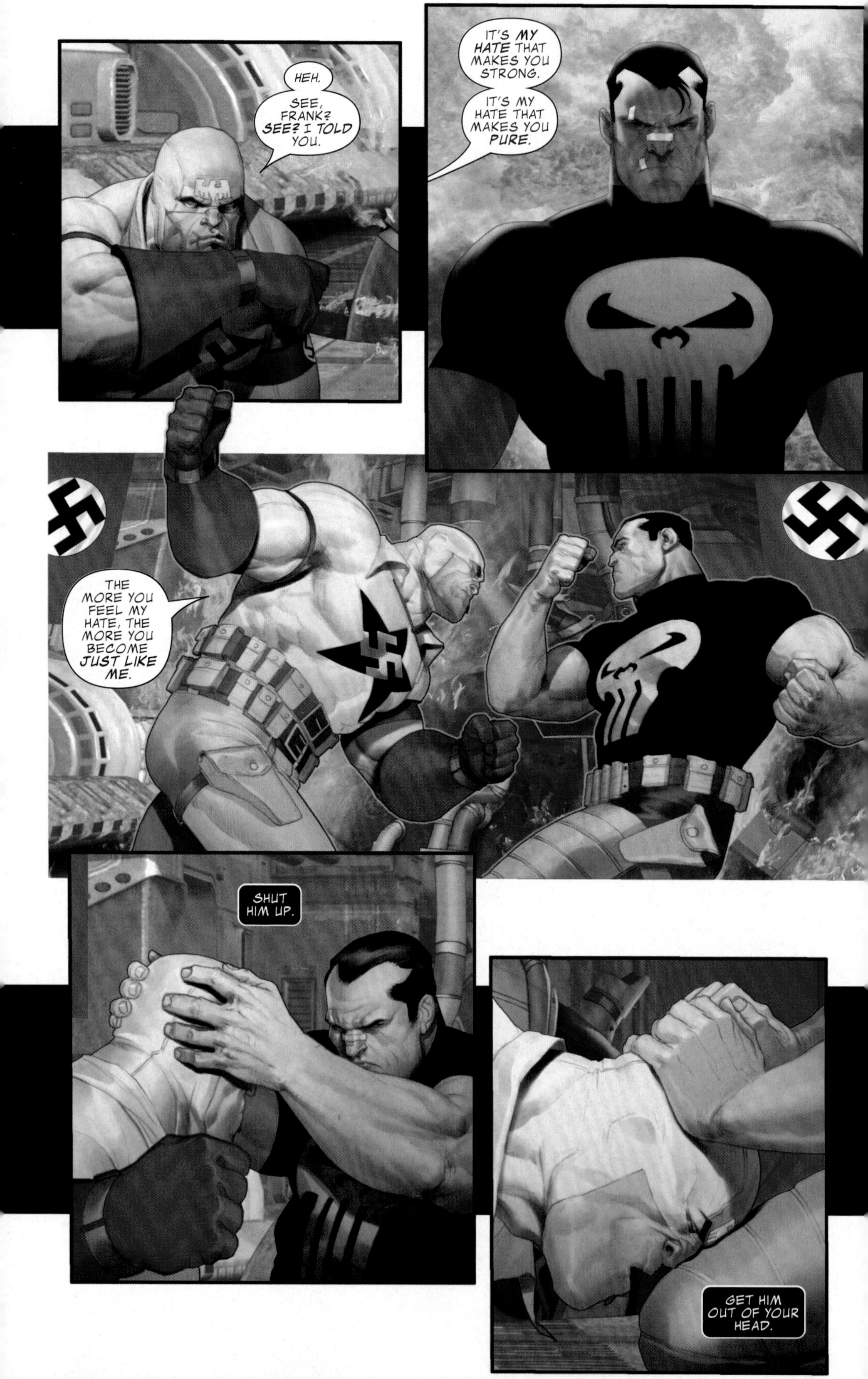
HEH.
SEE, FRANK? SEE? I TOLD YOU.
IT'S MY HATE THAT MAKES YOU STRONG.
IT'S MY HATE THAT MAKES YOU PURE.
THE MORE YOU FEEL MY HATE, THE MORE YOU BECOME JUST LIKE ME.
SHUT HIM UP.
GET HIM OUT OF YOUR HEAD.

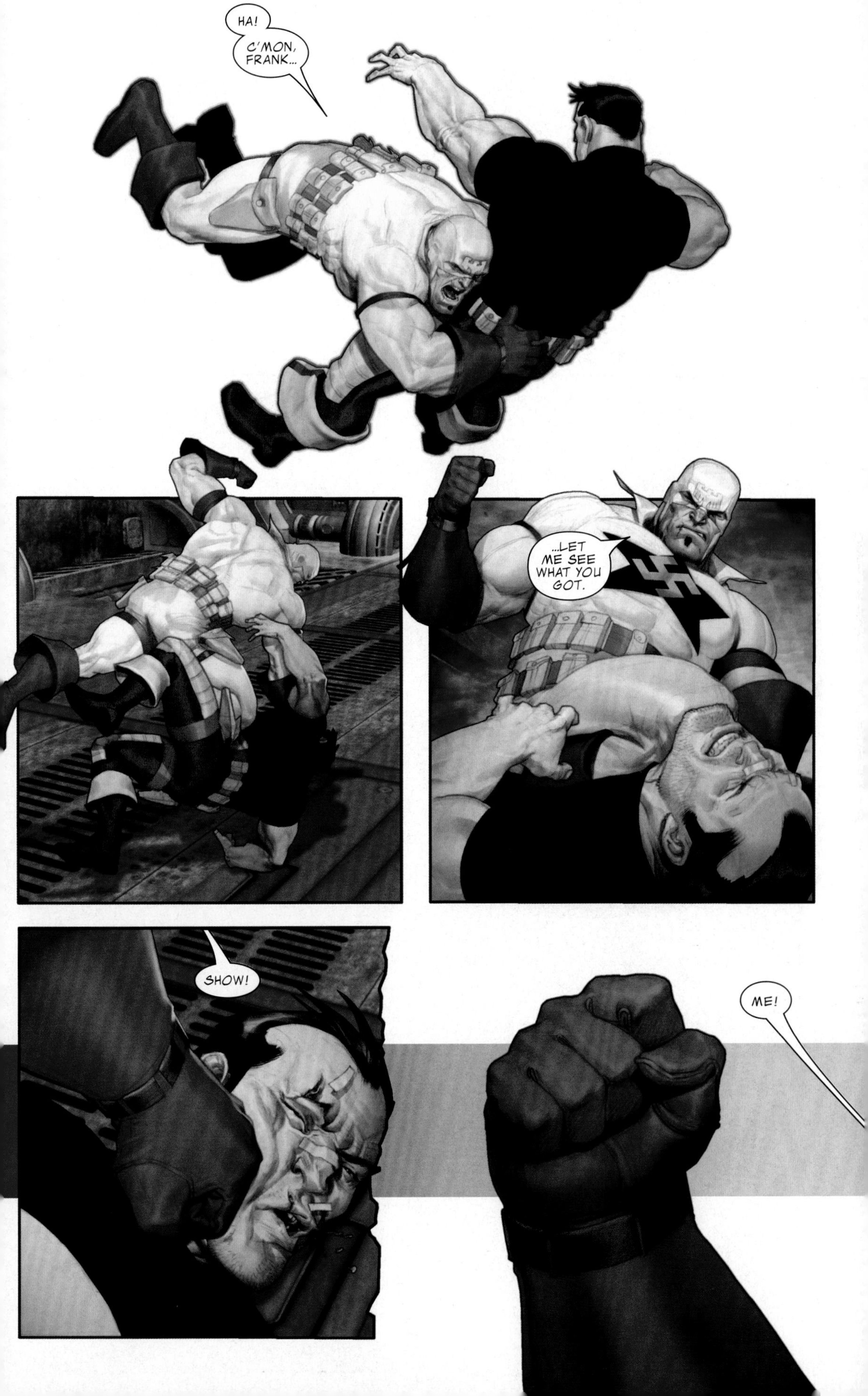
HA!
C'MON, FRANK...
...LET ME SEE WHAT YOU GOT.
SHOW!
ME!

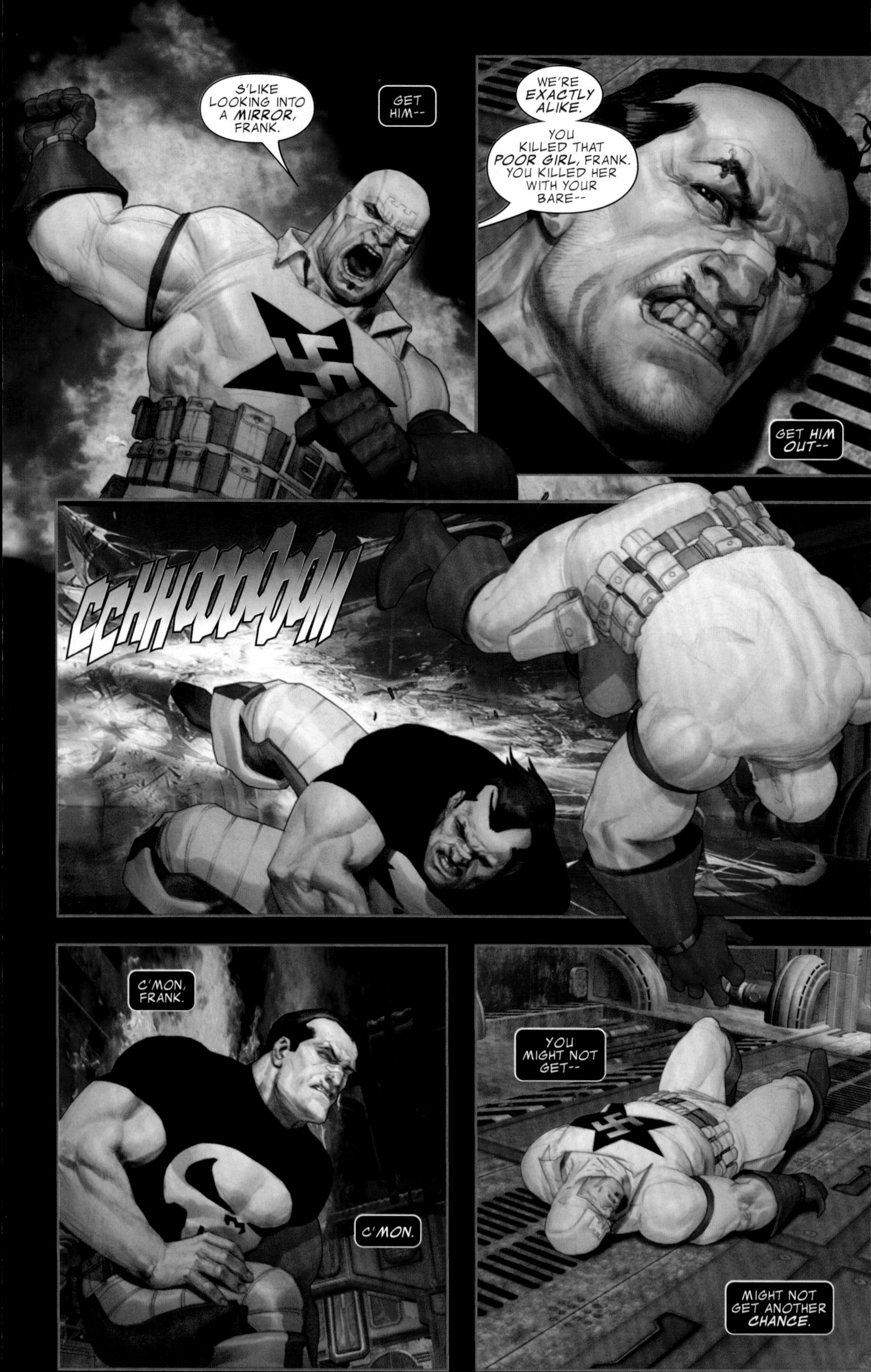
S'LIKE LOOKING INTO A MIRROR, FRANK.
GET HIM--
WE'RE EXACTLY ALIKE.
YOU KILLED THAT POOR GIRL, FRANK. YOU KILLED HER WITH YOUR BARE--
GET HIM OUT--
CCHHOOOOOOM
C'MON, FRANK.
C'MON.
YOU MIGHT NOT GET--
MIGHT NOT GET ANOTHER CHANCE.

:KAFF:
:KAFF KAFF:

LOOK AROUND.

GO AHEAD. TAKE A LOOK.

NO-- HEY, C'MON, DON'T--

YOUR LITTLE EMPIRE IS DEAD.

MY MASK.

YOUR MACHINES ARE ALL BROKEN.

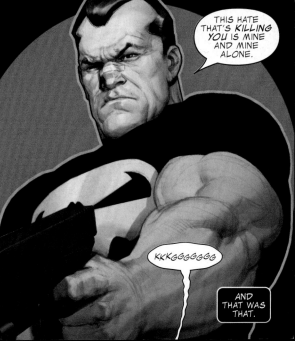

THIS HATE THAT'S KILLING YOU IS MINE AND MINE ALONE.

KKKGGGGGGG

AND THAT WAS THAT.

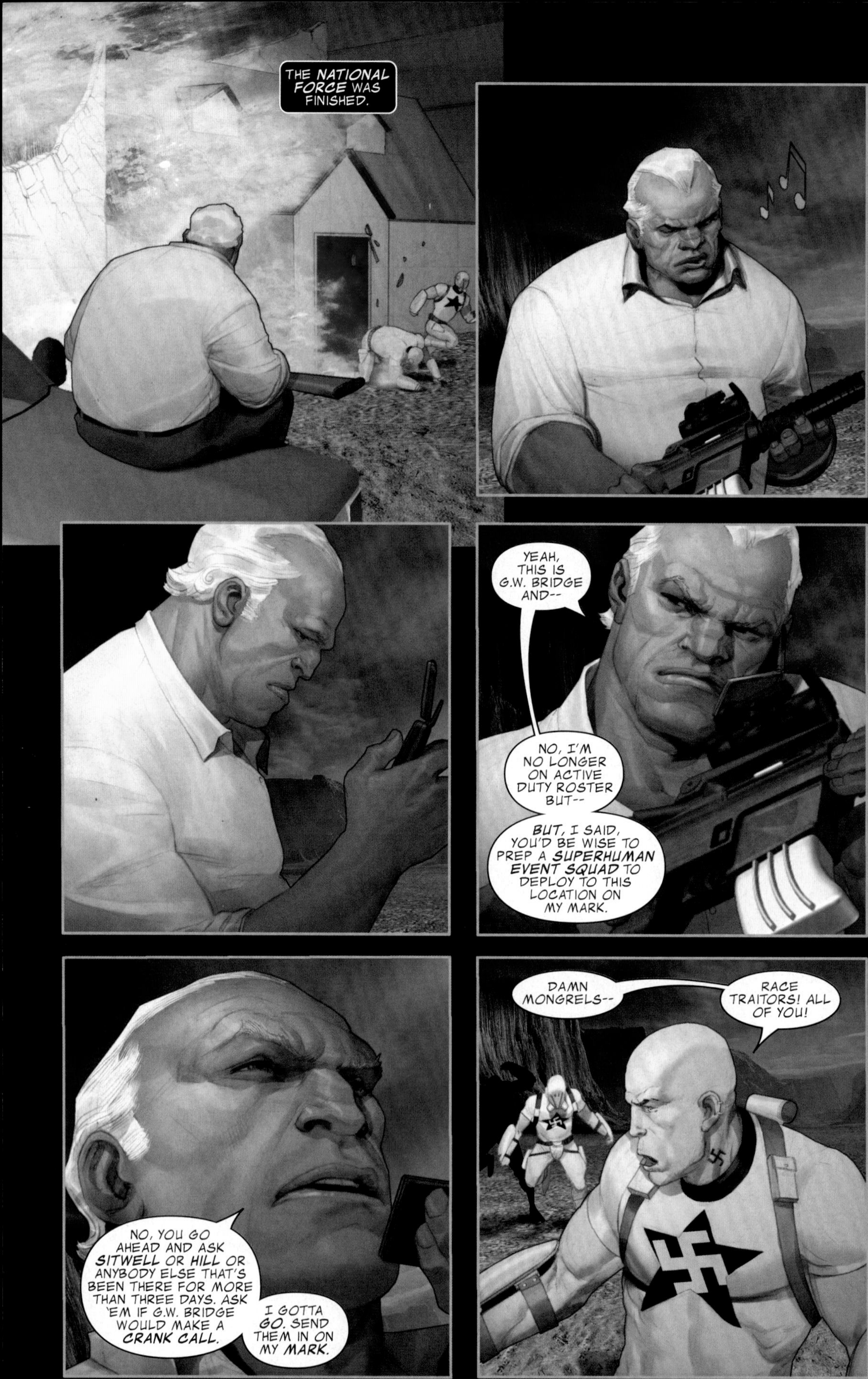
THE NATIONAL FORCE WAS FINISHED.
YEAH, THIS IS G.W. BRIDGE AND--
NO, I'M NO LONGER ON ACTIVE DUTY ROSTER BUT--
BUT, I SAID, YOU'D BE WISE TO PREP A SUPERHUMAN EVENT SQUAD TO DEPLOY TO THIS LOCATION ON MY MARK.
NO, YOU GO AHEAD AND ASK SITWELL OR HILL OR ANYBODY ELSE THAT'S BEEN THERE FOR MORE THAN THREE DAYS. ASK 'EM IF G.W. BRIDGE WOULD MAKE A CRANK CALL.
I GOTTA GO. SEND THEM IN ON MY MARK.
DAMN MONGRELS--
RACE TRAITORS! ALL OF YOU!

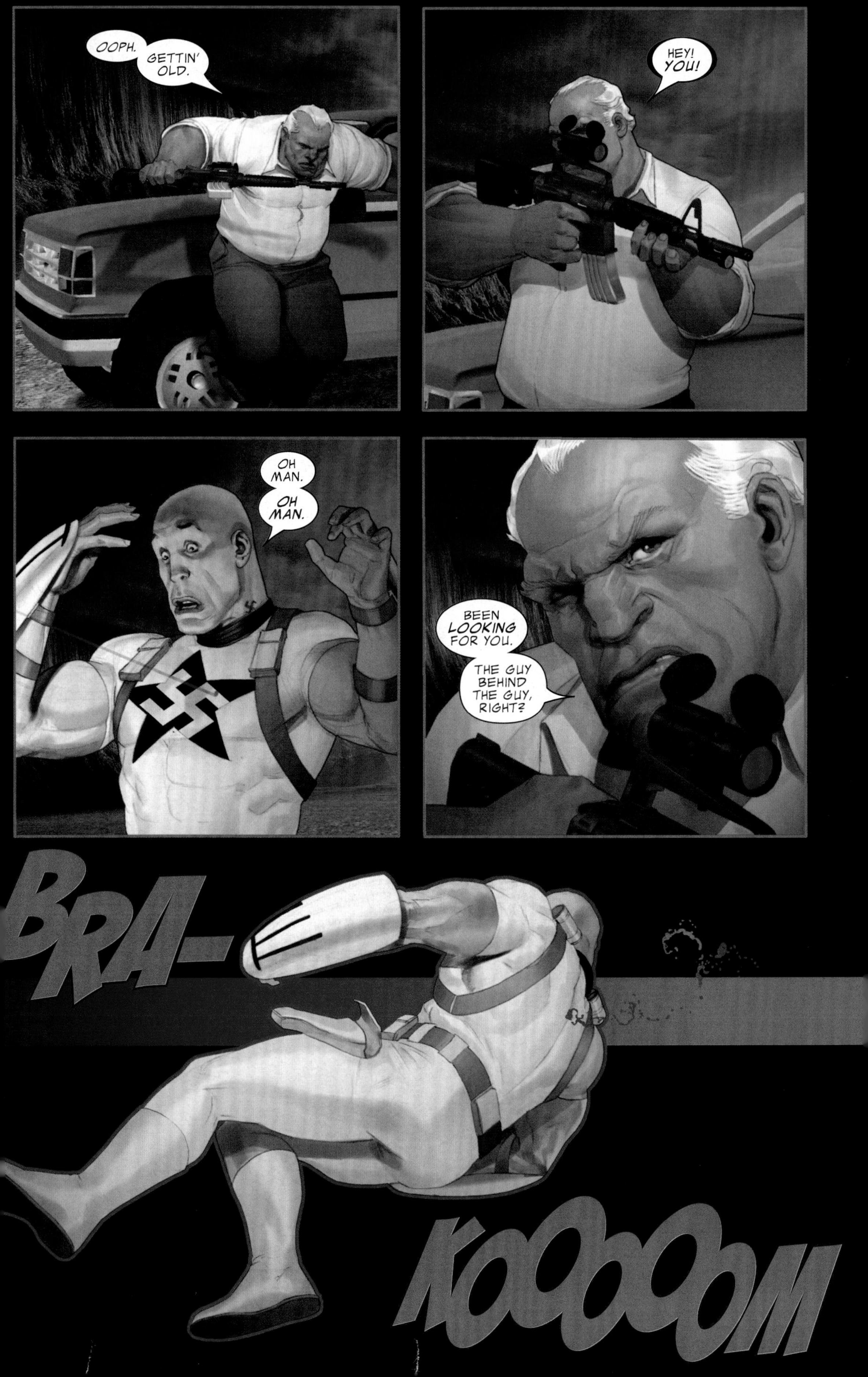
OOPH.
GETTIN' OLD.
HEY! YOU!
OH MAN.
OH MAN.
BEEN LOOKING FOR YOU.
THE GUY BEHIND THE GUY, RIGHT?
BRA-
KOOOOOM

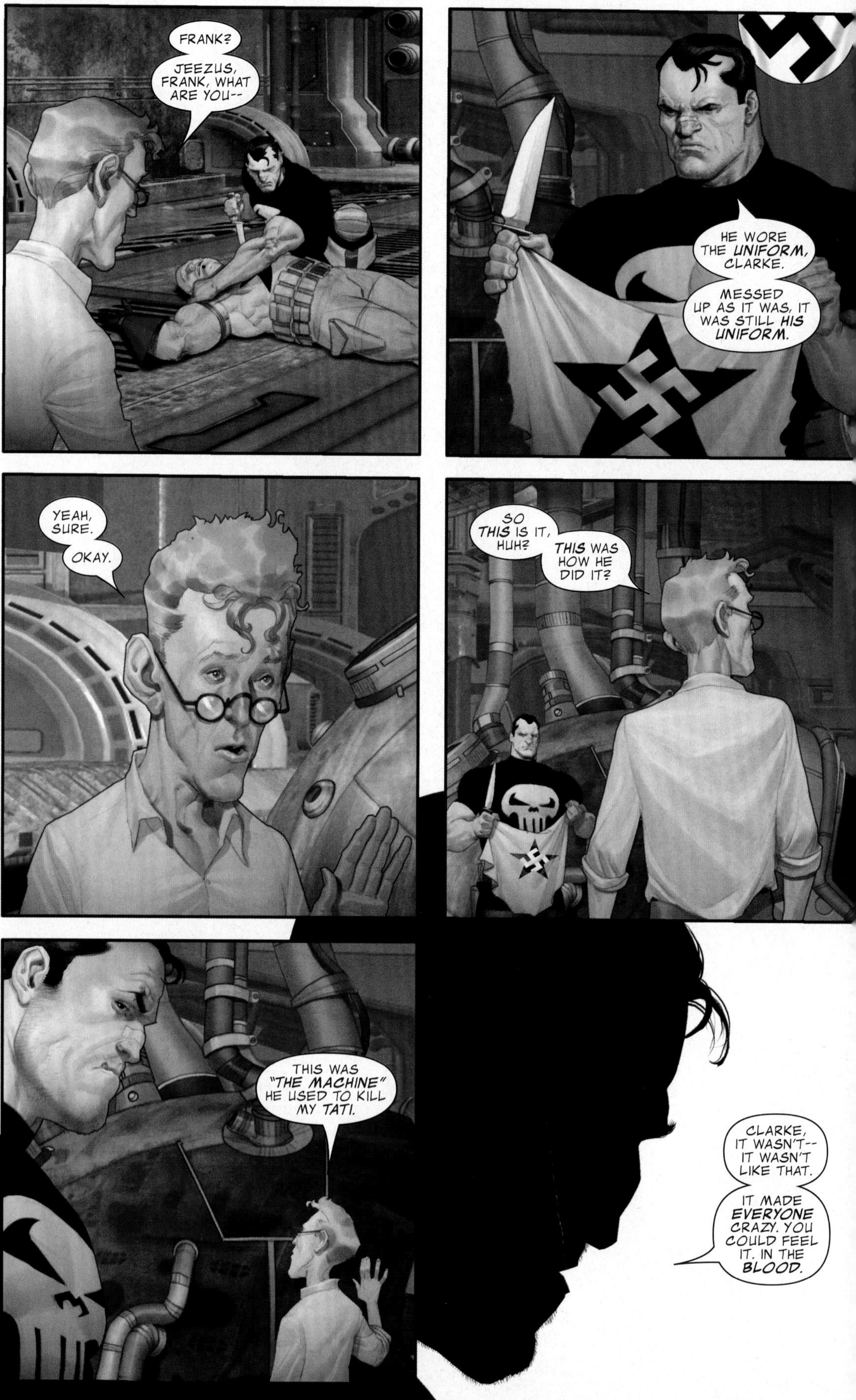
FRANK?
JEEZUS, FRANK, WHAT ARE YOU--
HE WORE THE UNIFORM, CLARKE.
MESSED UP AS IT WAS, IT WAS STILL HIS UNIFORM.
YEAH, SURE.
OKAY.
SO THIS IS IT, HUH?
THIS WAS HOW HE DID IT?
THIS WAS "THE MACHINE" HE USED TO KILL MY TATI.
CLARKE, IT WASN'T-- IT WASN'T LIKE THAT.
IT MADE EVERYONE CRAZY. YOU COULD FEEL IT. IN THE BLOOD.

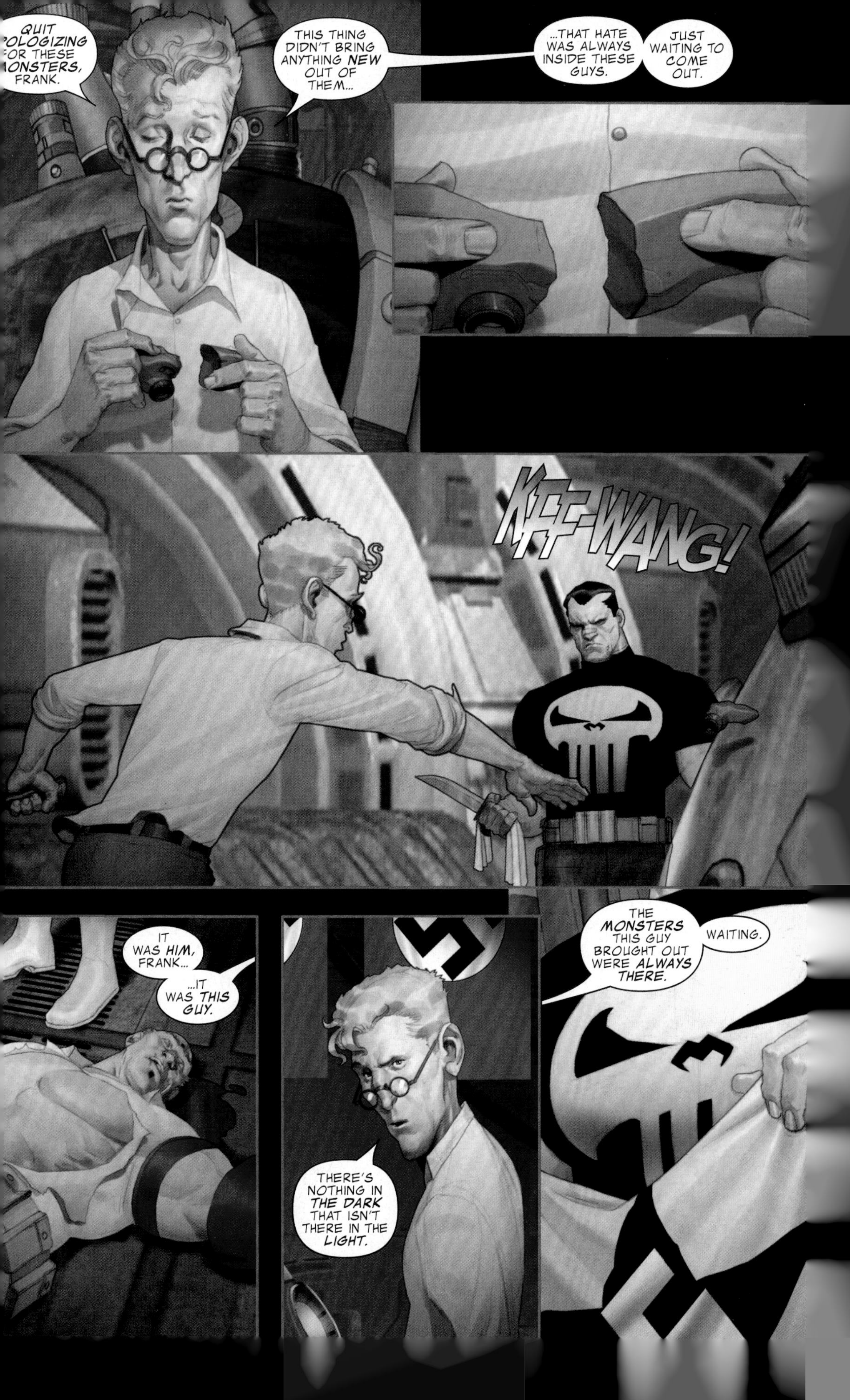
QUIT APOLOGIZING FOR THESE MONSTERS, FRANK.
THIS THING DIDN'T BRING ANYTHING NEW OUT OF THEM...
...THAT HATE WAS ALWAYS INSIDE THESE GUYS.
JUST WAITING TO COME OUT.
KIFF-WANG!
IT WAS HIM, FRANK...
...IT WAS THIS GUY.
THERE'S NOTHING IN THE DARK THAT ISN'T THERE IN THE LIGHT.
THE MONSTERS THIS GUY BROUGHT OUT WERE ALWAYS THERE.
WAITING.

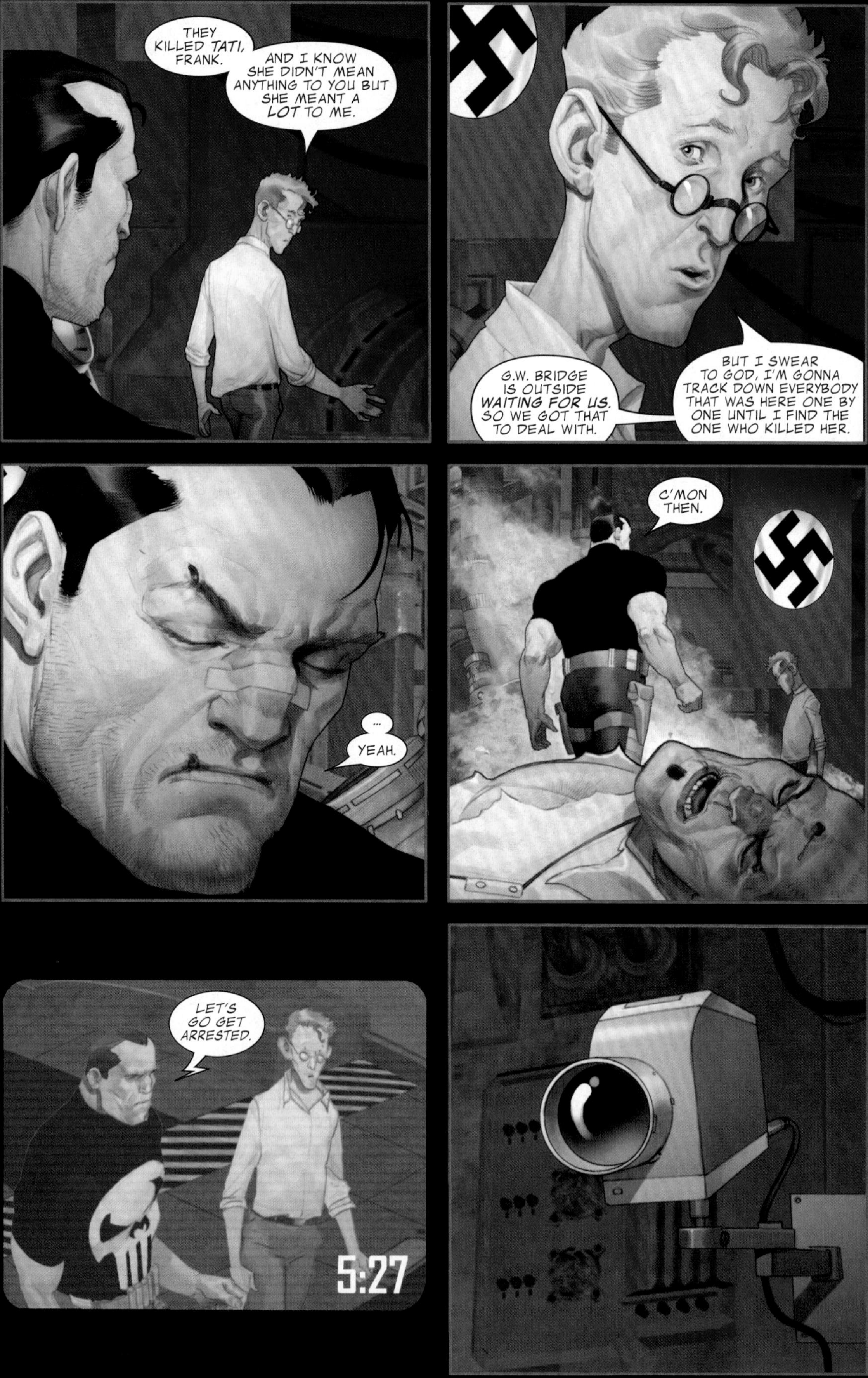
THEY KILLED *TATI*, FRANK.
AND I KNOW SHE DIDN'T MEAN ANYTHING TO YOU BUT SHE MEANT A *LOT* TO ME.
BUT I SWEAR TO GOD, I'M GONNA TRACK DOWN EVERYBODY THAT WAS HERE ONE BY ONE UNTIL I FIND THE ONE WHO KILLED HER.
G.W. BRIDGE IS OUTSIDE *WAITING FOR US.* SO WE GOT THAT TO DEAL WITH.
... YEAH.
C'MON THEN.
LET'S GO GET ARRESTED.
5:27

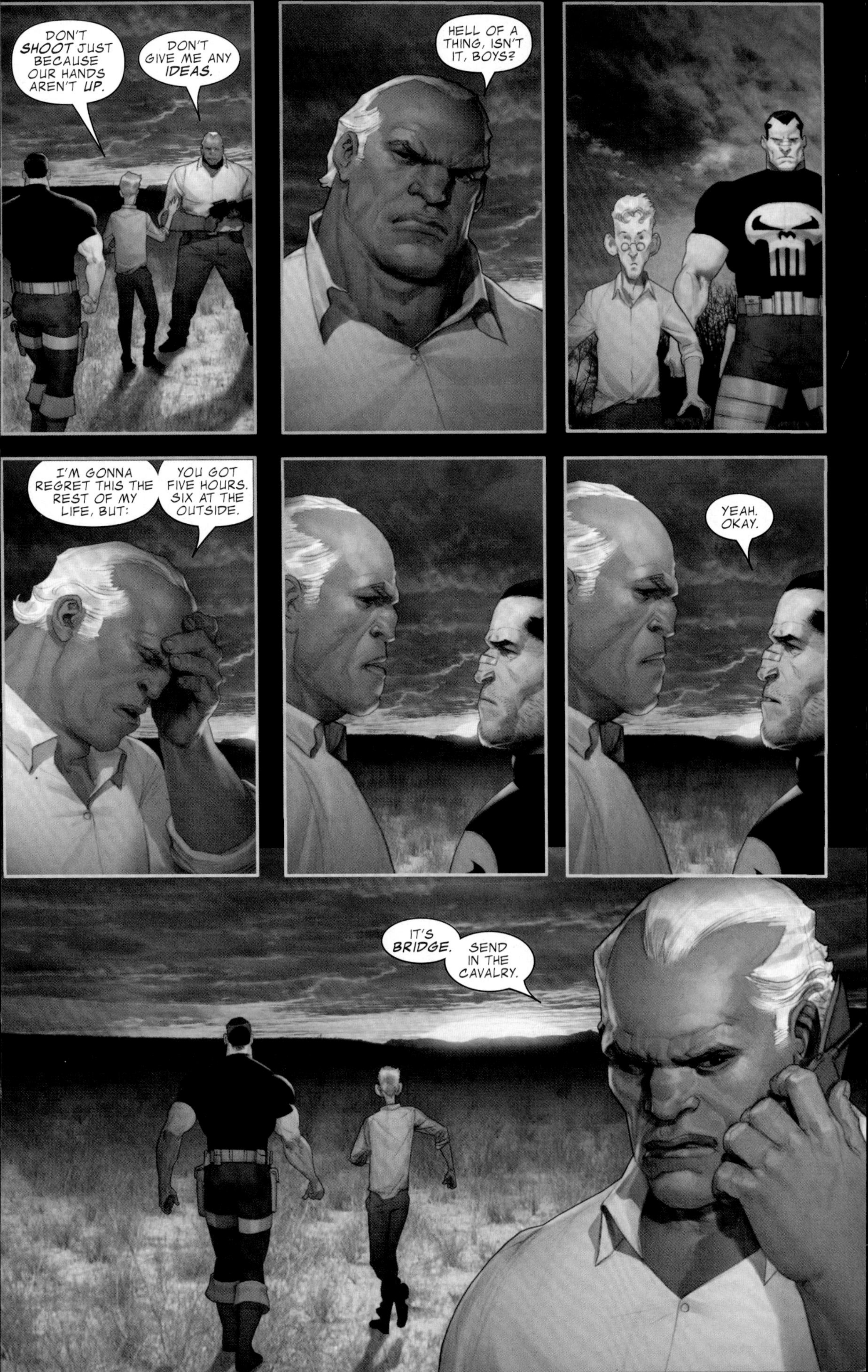

DON'T SHOOT JUST BECAUSE OUR HANDS AREN'T UP.
DON'T GIVE ME ANY IDEAS.
HELL OF A THING, ISN'T IT, BOYS?
I'M GONNA REGRET THIS THE REST OF MY LIFE, BUT:
YOU GOT FIVE HOURS. SIX AT THE OUTSIDE.
YEAH. OKAY.
IT'S BRIDGE.
SEND IN THE CAVALRY.

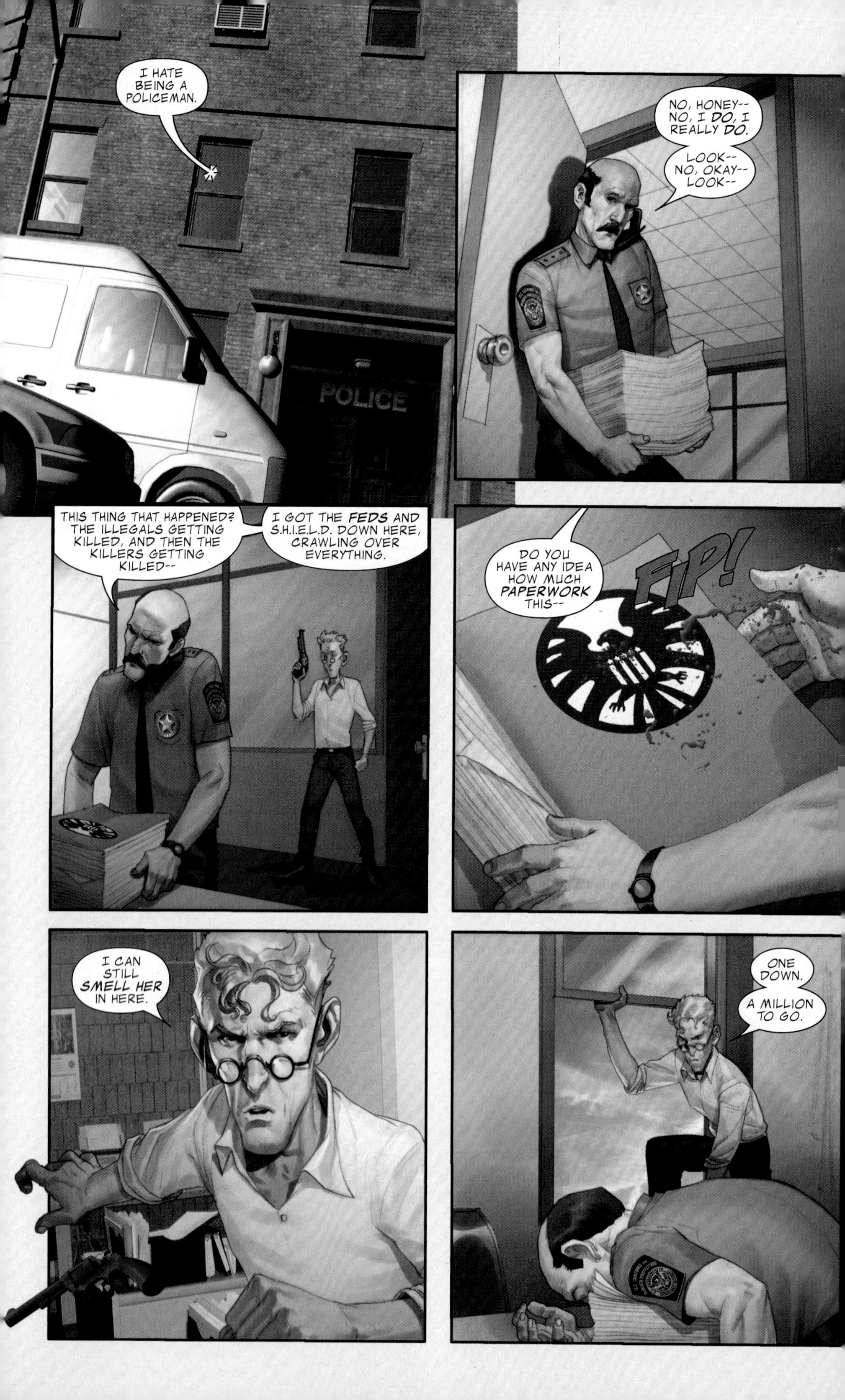
I HATE BEING A POLICEMAN.
POLICE
NO, HONEY-- NO, I DO, I REALLY DO.
LOOK-- NO, OKAY-- LOOK--
THIS THING THAT HAPPENED? THE ILLEGALS GETTING KILLED, AND THEN THE KILLERS GETTING KILLED--
I GOT THE FEDS AND S.H.I.E.L.D. DOWN HERE, CRAWLING OVER EVERYTHING.
DO YOU HAVE ANY IDEA HOW MUCH PAPERWORK THIS--
FIP!
I CAN STILL SMELL HER IN HERE.
ONE DOWN.
A MILLION TO GO.

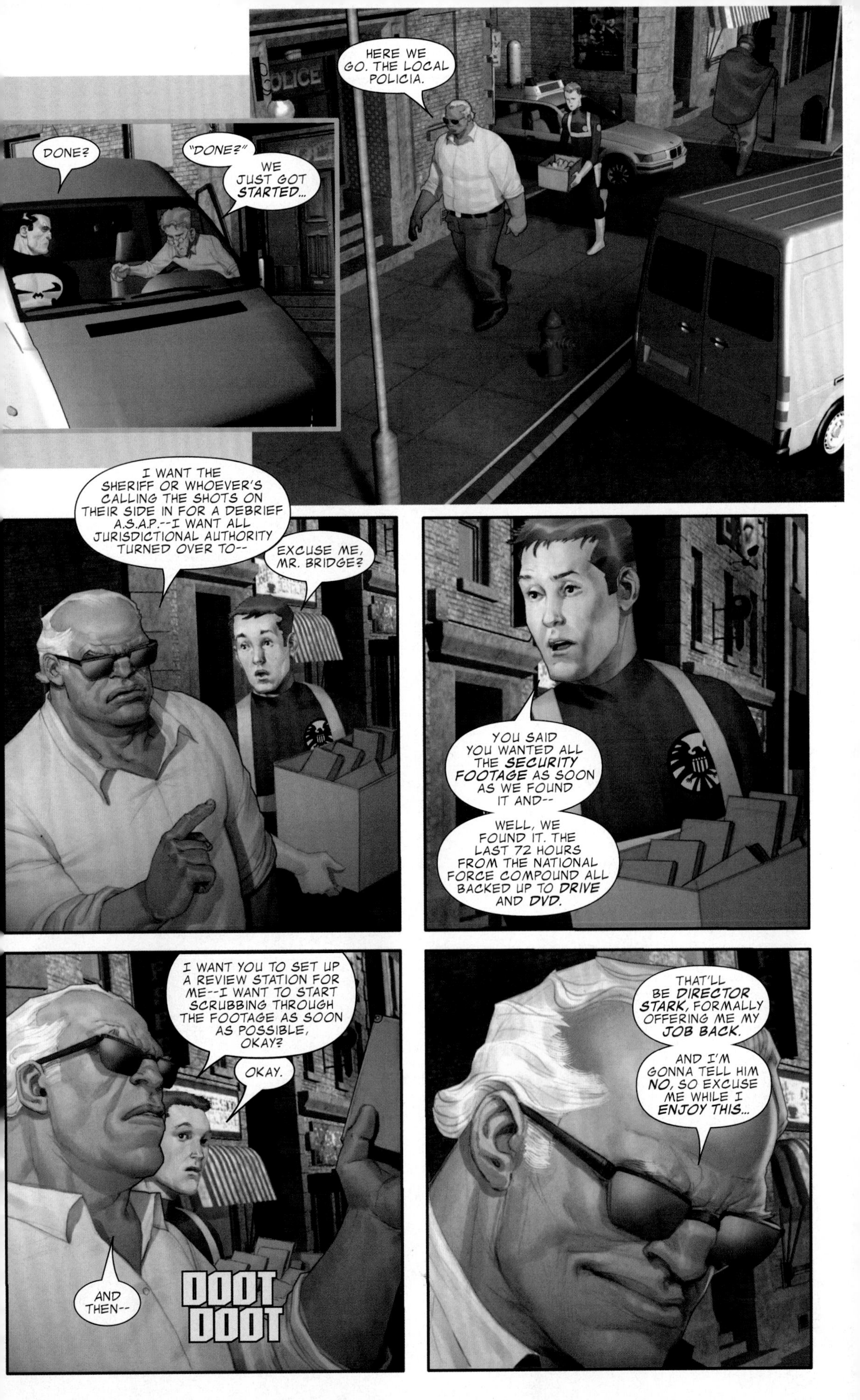

HERE WE GO. THE LOCAL POLICIA.
DONE?
"DONE?"
WE JUST GOT STARTED...
I WANT THE SHERIFF OR WHOEVER'S CALLING THE SHOTS ON THEIR SIDE IN FOR A DEBRIEF A.S.A.P.--I WANT ALL JURISDICTIONAL AUTHORITY TURNED OVER TO--
EXCUSE ME, MR. BRIDGE?
YOU SAID YOU WANTED ALL THE SECURITY FOOTAGE AS SOON AS WE FOUND IT AND--
WELL, WE FOUND IT. THE LAST 72 HOURS FROM THE NATIONAL FORCE COMPOUND ALL BACKED UP TO DRIVE AND DVD.
I WANT YOU TO SET UP A REVIEW STATION FOR ME--I WANT TO START SCRUBBING THROUGH THE FOOTAGE AS SOON AS POSSIBLE, OKAY?
OKAY.
AND THEN--
DOOT DOOT
THAT'LL BE DIRECTOR STARK, FORMALLY OFFERING ME MY JOB BACK.
AND I'M GONNA TELL HIM NO, SO EXCUSE ME WHILE I ENJOY THIS...

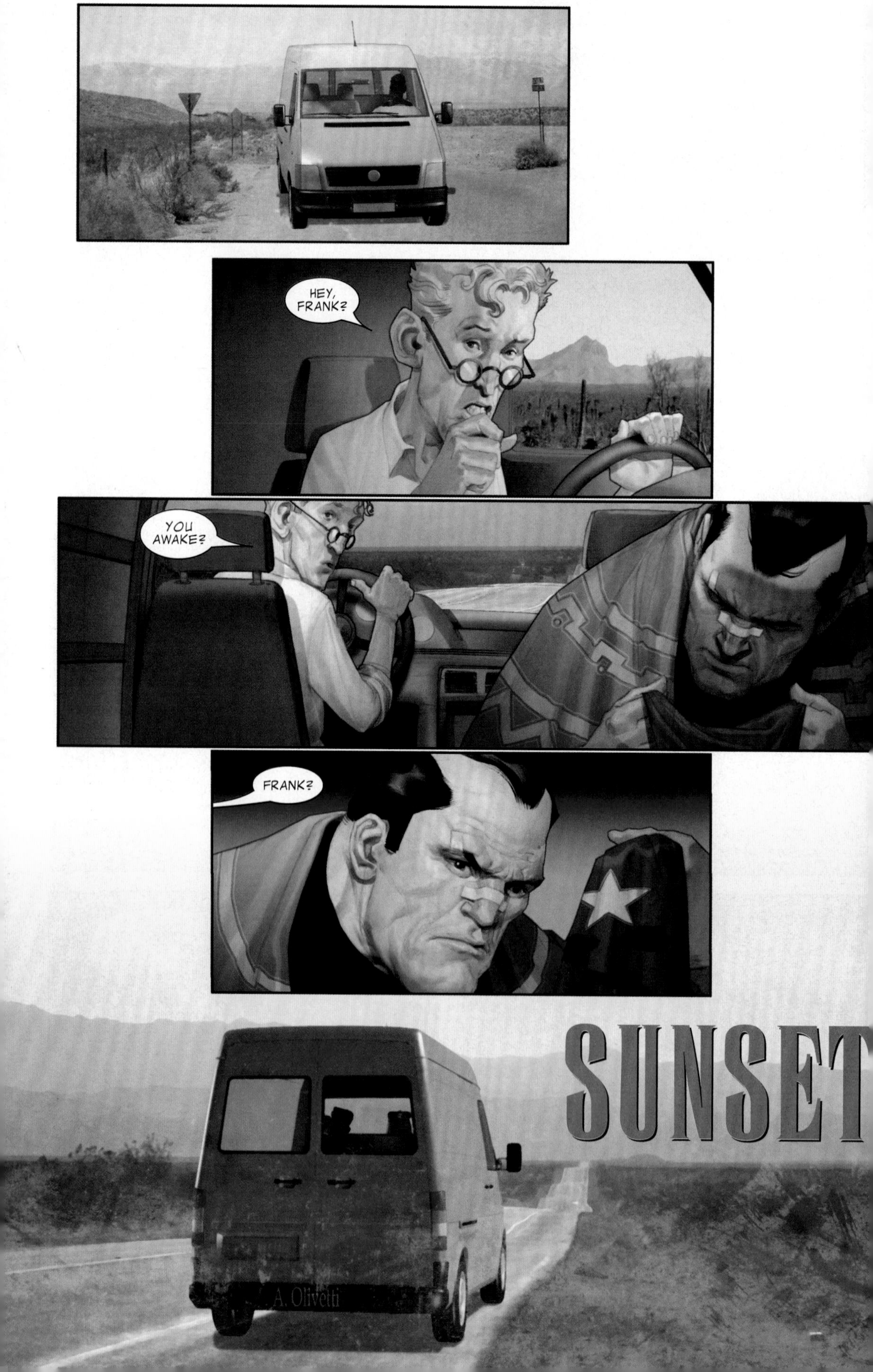
HEY, FRANK?
YOU AWAKE?
FRANK?
SUNSET
A. Olivetti

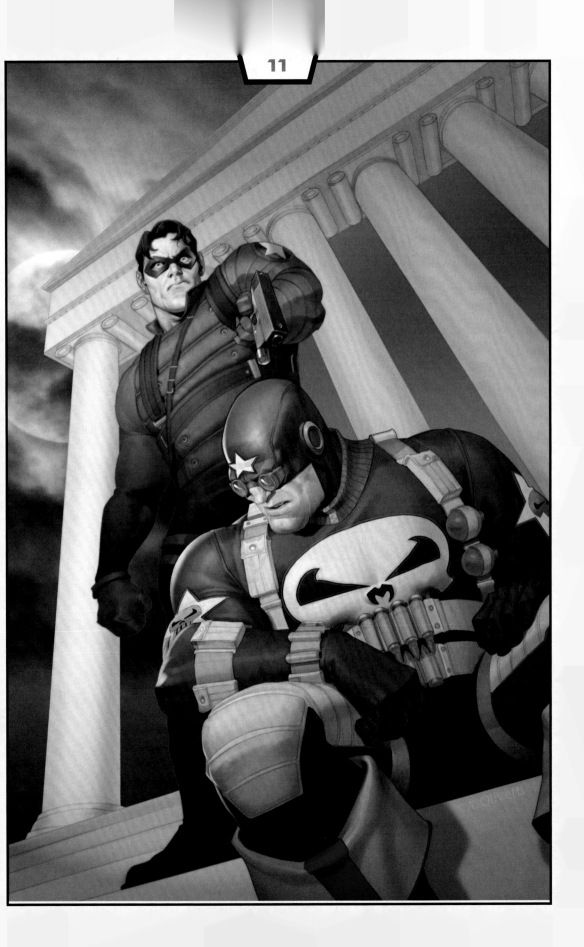

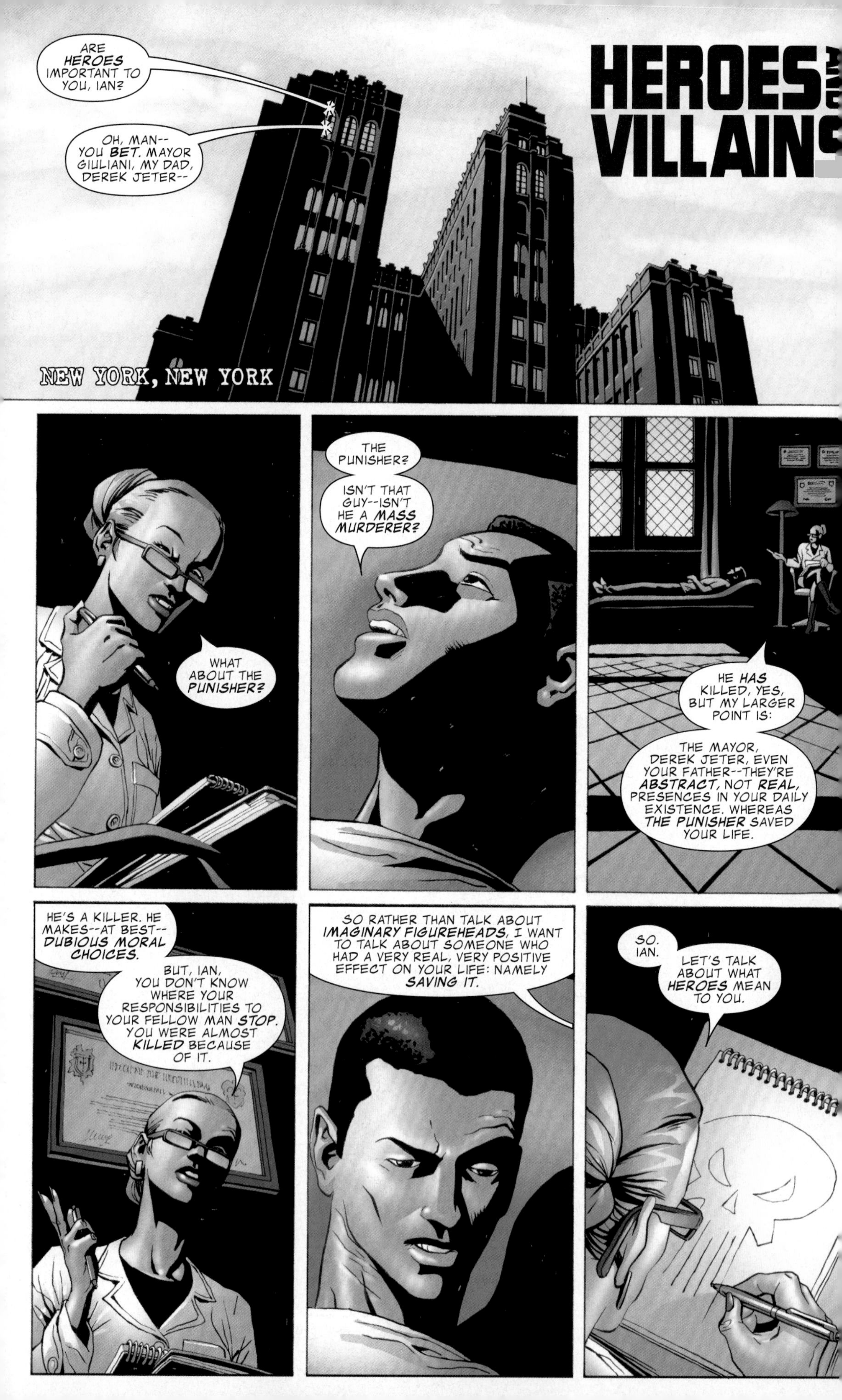

HEROES AND VILLAINS
ARE HEROES IMPORTANT TO YOU, IAN?
OH, MAN-- YOU BET. MAYOR GIULIANI, MY DAD, DEREK JETER--
NEW YORK, NEW YORK
WHAT ABOUT THE PUNISHER?
THE PUNISHER?
ISN'T THAT GUY--ISN'T HE A MASS MURDERER?
HE HAS KILLED, YES, BUT MY LARGER POINT IS:
THE MAYOR, DEREK JETER, EVEN YOUR FATHER--THEY'RE ABSTRACT, NOT REAL, PRESENCES IN YOUR DAILY EXISTENCE. WHEREAS THE PUNISHER SAVED YOUR LIFE.
HE'S A KILLER. HE MAKES--AT BEST--DUBIOUS MORAL CHOICES.
BUT, IAN, YOU DON'T KNOW WHERE YOUR RESPONSIBILITIES TO YOUR FELLOW MAN STOP. YOU WERE ALMOST KILLED BECAUSE OF IT.
SO RATHER THAN TALK ABOUT IMAGINARY FIGUREHEADS, I WANT TO TALK ABOUT SOMEONE WHO HAD A VERY REAL, VERY POSITIVE EFFECT ON YOUR LIFE: NAMELY SAVING IT.
SO. IAN.
LET'S TALK ABOUT WHAT HEROES MEAN TO YOU.

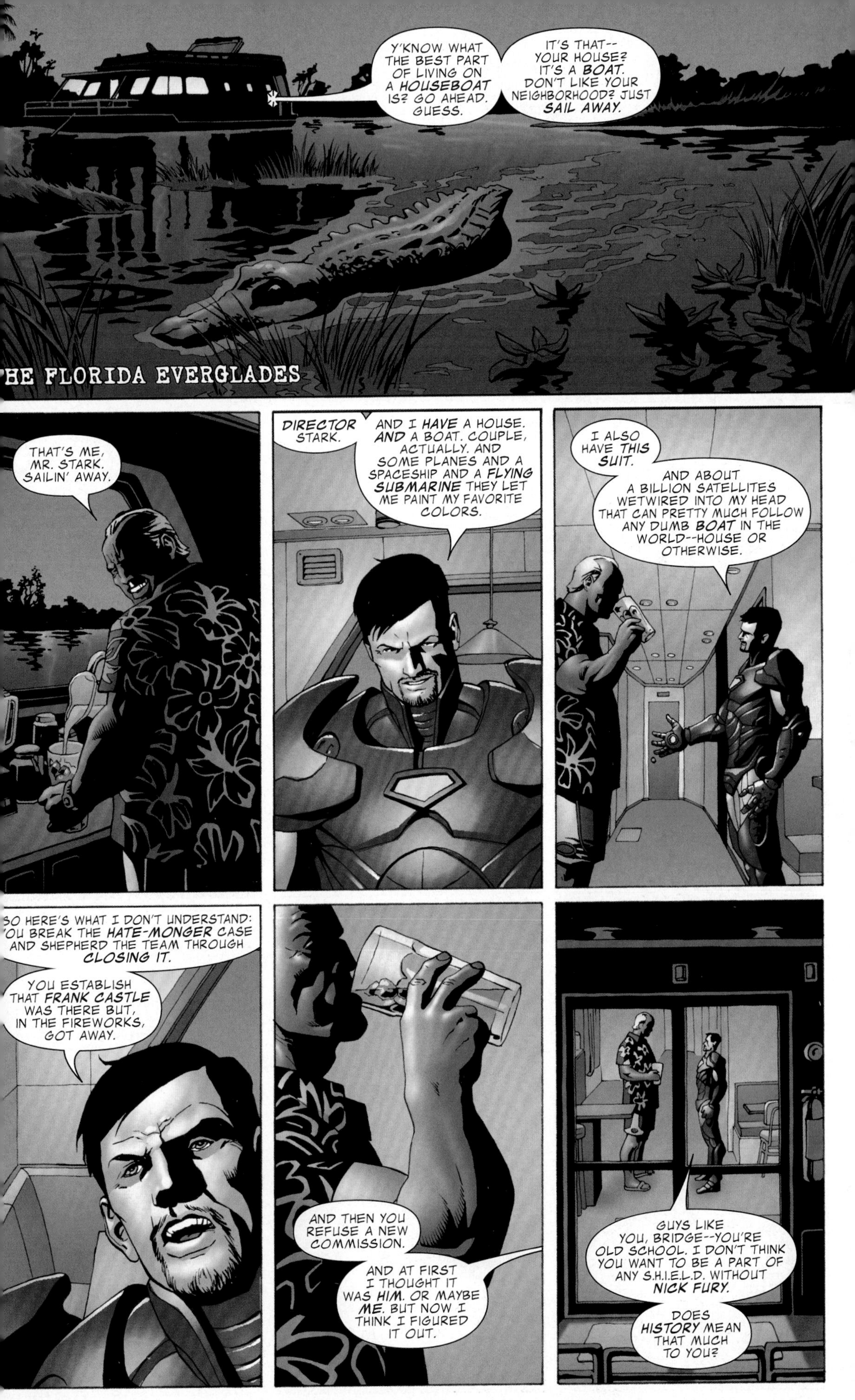
Y'KNOW WHAT THE BEST PART OF LIVING ON A HOUSEBOAT IS? GO AHEAD. GUESS.
IT'S THAT-- YOUR HOUSE? IT'S A BOAT. DON'T LIKE YOUR NEIGHBORHOOD? JUST SAIL AWAY.
HE FLORIDA EVERGLADES
THAT'S ME, MR. STARK. SAILIN' AWAY.
DIRECTOR STARK.
AND I HAVE A HOUSE. AND A BOAT. COUPLE, ACTUALLY. AND SOME PLANES AND A SPACESHIP AND A FLYING SUBMARINE THEY LET ME PAINT MY FAVORITE COLORS.
I ALSO HAVE THIS SUIT.
AND ABOUT A BILLION SATELLITES WETWIRED INTO MY HEAD THAT CAN PRETTY MUCH FOLLOW ANY DUMB BOAT IN THE WORLD--HOUSE OR OTHERWISE.
SO HERE'S WHAT I DON'T UNDERSTAND: YOU BREAK THE HATE-MONGER CASE AND SHEPHERD THE TEAM THROUGH CLOSING IT.
YOU ESTABLISH THAT FRANK CASTLE WAS THERE BUT, IN THE FIREWORKS, GOT AWAY.
AND THEN YOU REFUSE A NEW COMMISSION.
AND AT FIRST I THOUGHT IT WAS HIM. OR MAYBE ME. BUT NOW I THINK I FIGURED IT OUT.
GUYS LIKE YOU, BRIDGE--YOU'RE OLD SCHOOL. I DON'T THINK YOU WANT TO BE A PART OF ANY S.H.I.E.L.D. WITHOUT NICK FURY.
DOES HISTORY MEAN THAT MUCH TO YOU?

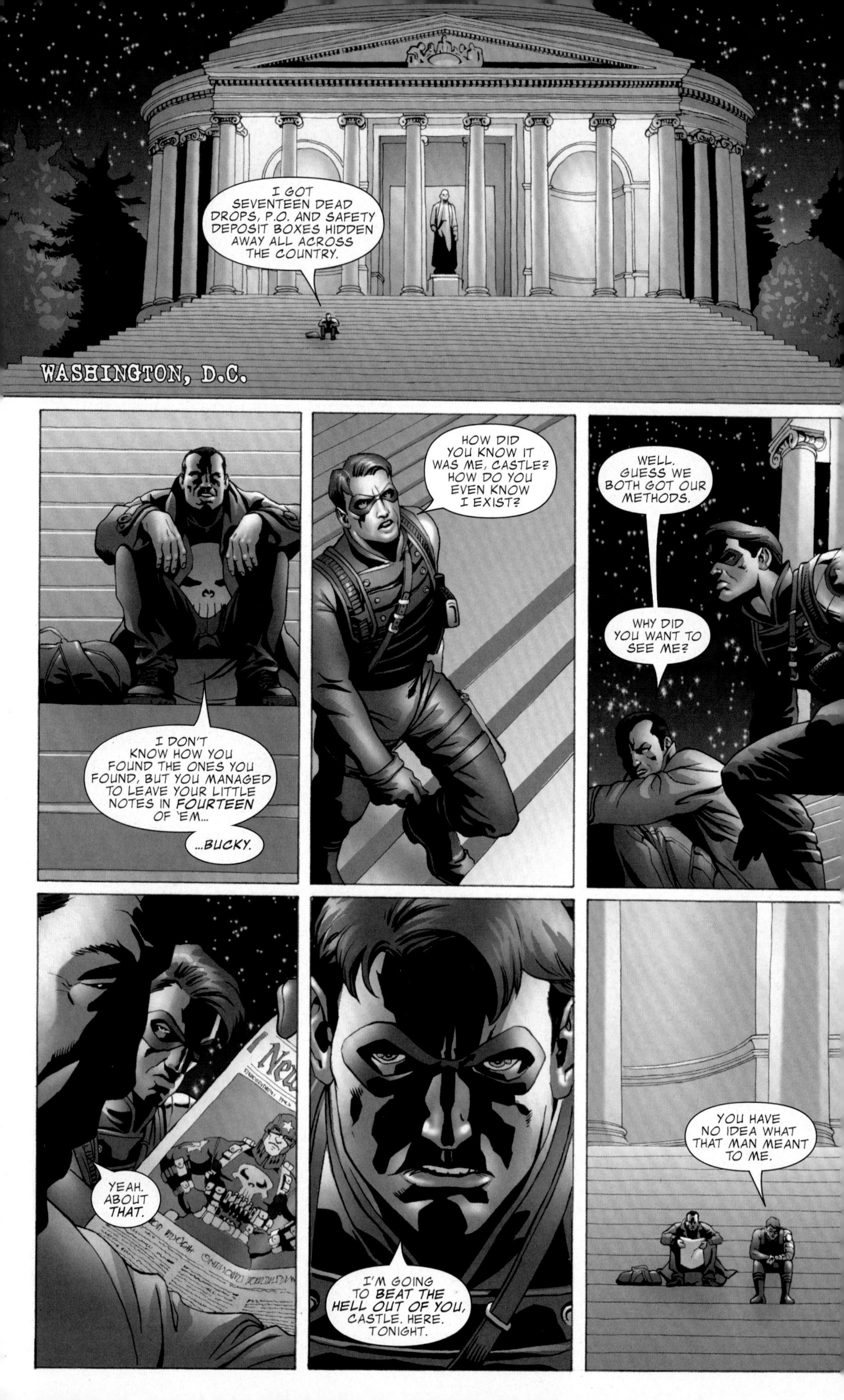
I GOT SEVENTEEN DEAD DROPS, P.O. AND SAFETY DEPOSIT BOXES HIDDEN AWAY ALL ACROSS THE COUNTRY.
WASHINGTON, D.C.
I DON'T KNOW HOW YOU FOUND THE ONES YOU FOUND, BUT YOU MANAGED TO LEAVE YOUR LITTLE NOTES IN FOURTEEN OF 'EM...
...BUCKY.
HOW DID YOU KNOW IT WAS ME, CASTLE? HOW DO YOU EVEN KNOW I EXIST?
WELL. GUESS WE BOTH GOT OUR METHODS.
WHY DID YOU WANT TO SEE ME?
YEAH. ABOUT THAT.
I'M GOING TO BEAT THE HELL OUT OF YOU, CASTLE. HERE. TONIGHT.
YOU HAVE NO IDEA WHAT THAT MAN MEANT TO ME.

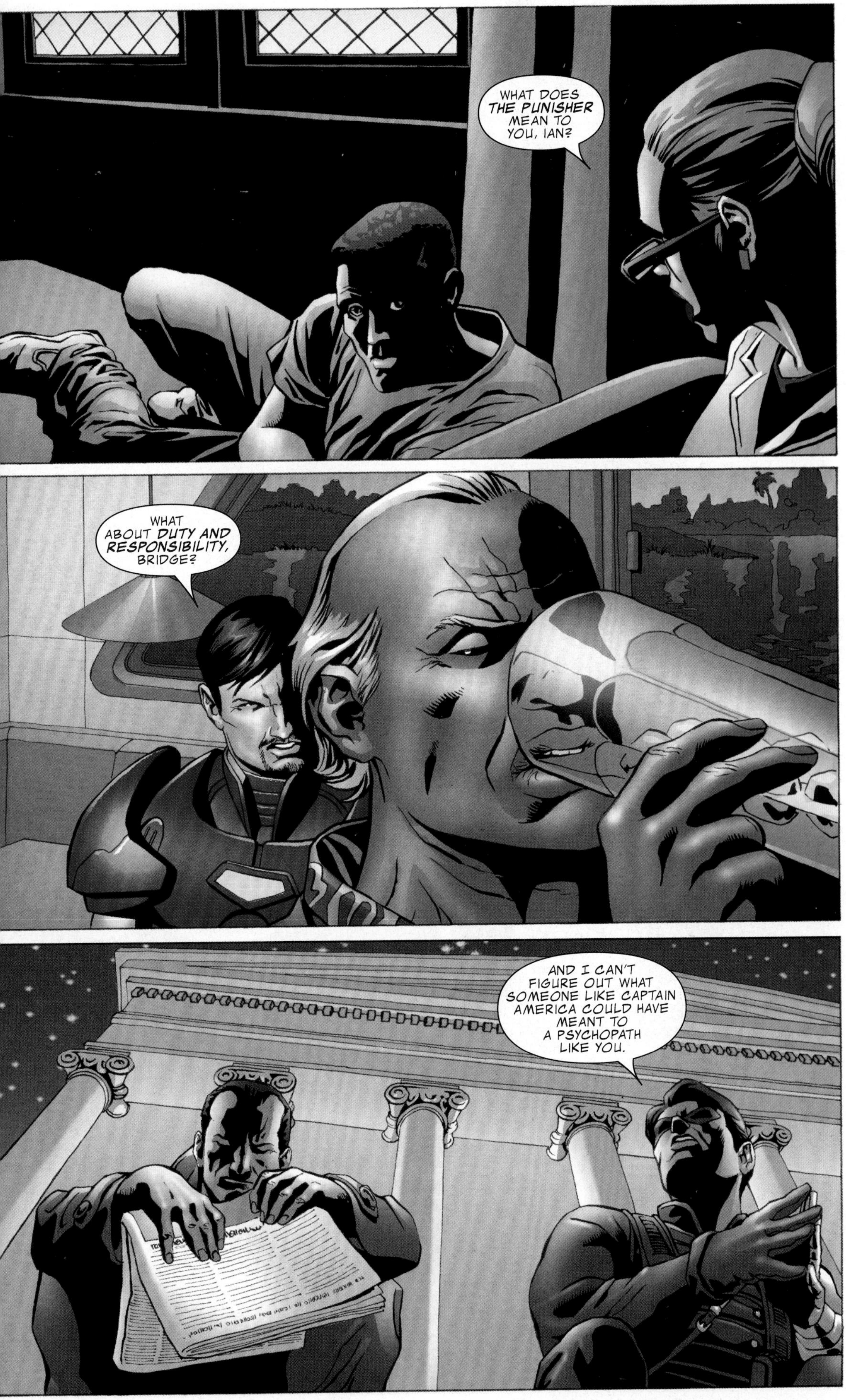
WHAT DOES THE PUNISHER MEAN TO YOU, IAN?
WHAT ABOUT DUTY AND RESPONSIBILITY, BRIDGE?
AND I CAN'T FIGURE OUT WHAT SOMEONE LIKE CAPTAIN AMERICA COULD HAVE MEANT TO A PSYCHOPATH LIKE YOU.

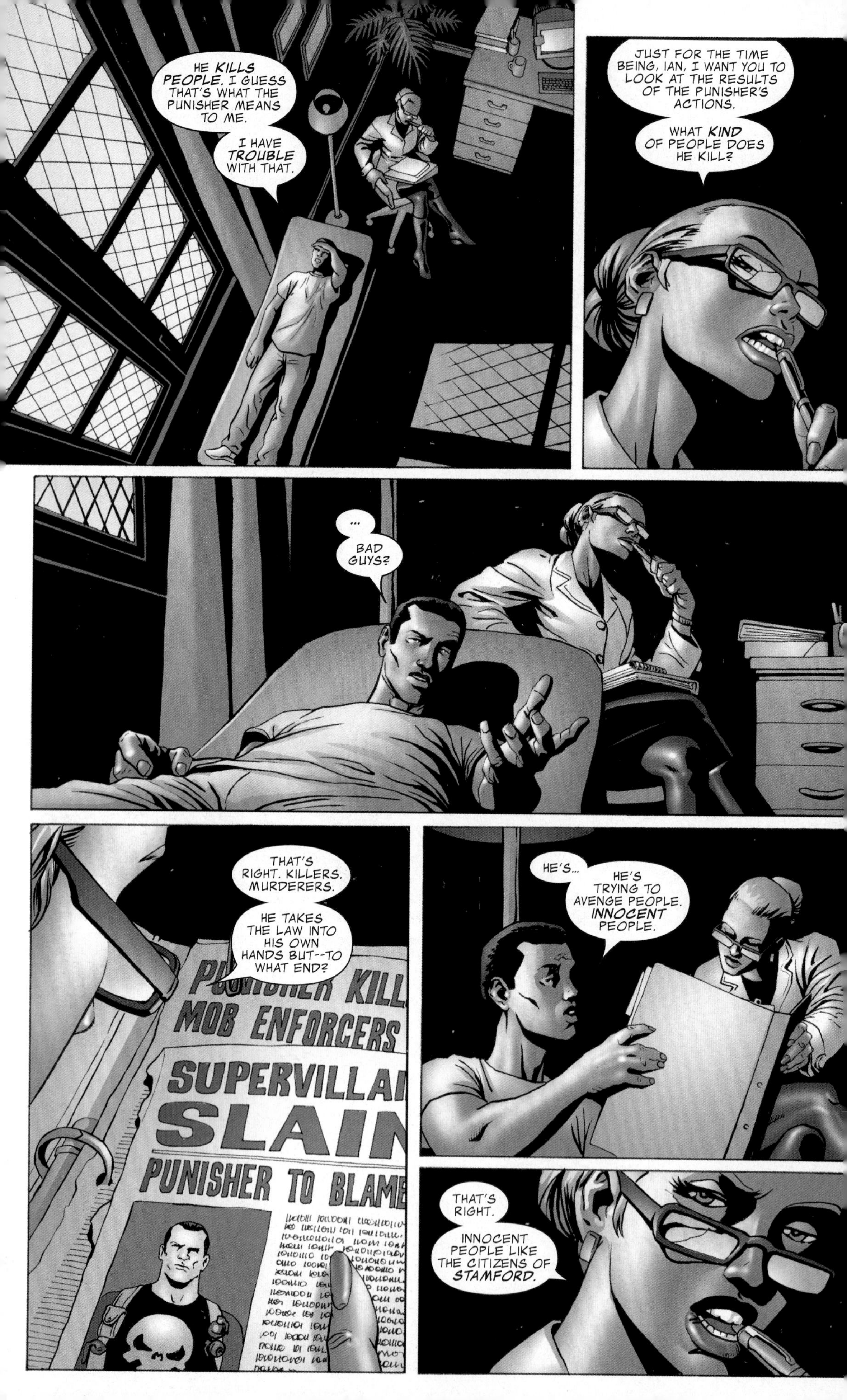

HE KILLS PEOPLE. I GUESS THAT'S WHAT THE PUNISHER MEANS TO ME.
I HAVE TROUBLE WITH THAT.
JUST FOR THE TIME BEING, IAN, I WANT YOU TO LOOK AT THE RESULTS OF THE PUNISHER'S ACTIONS.
WHAT KIND OF PEOPLE DOES HE KILL?
...
BAD GUYS?
THAT'S RIGHT. KILLERS. MURDERERS.
HE TAKES THE LAW INTO HIS OWN HANDS BUT--TO WHAT END?
MOB ENFORCERS
SUPERVILLAI
SLAIN
PUNISHER TO BLAME
HE'S...
HE'S TRYING TO AVENGE PEOPLE. INNOCENT PEOPLE.
THAT'S RIGHT.
INNOCENT PEOPLE LIKE THE CITIZENS OF STAMFORD.

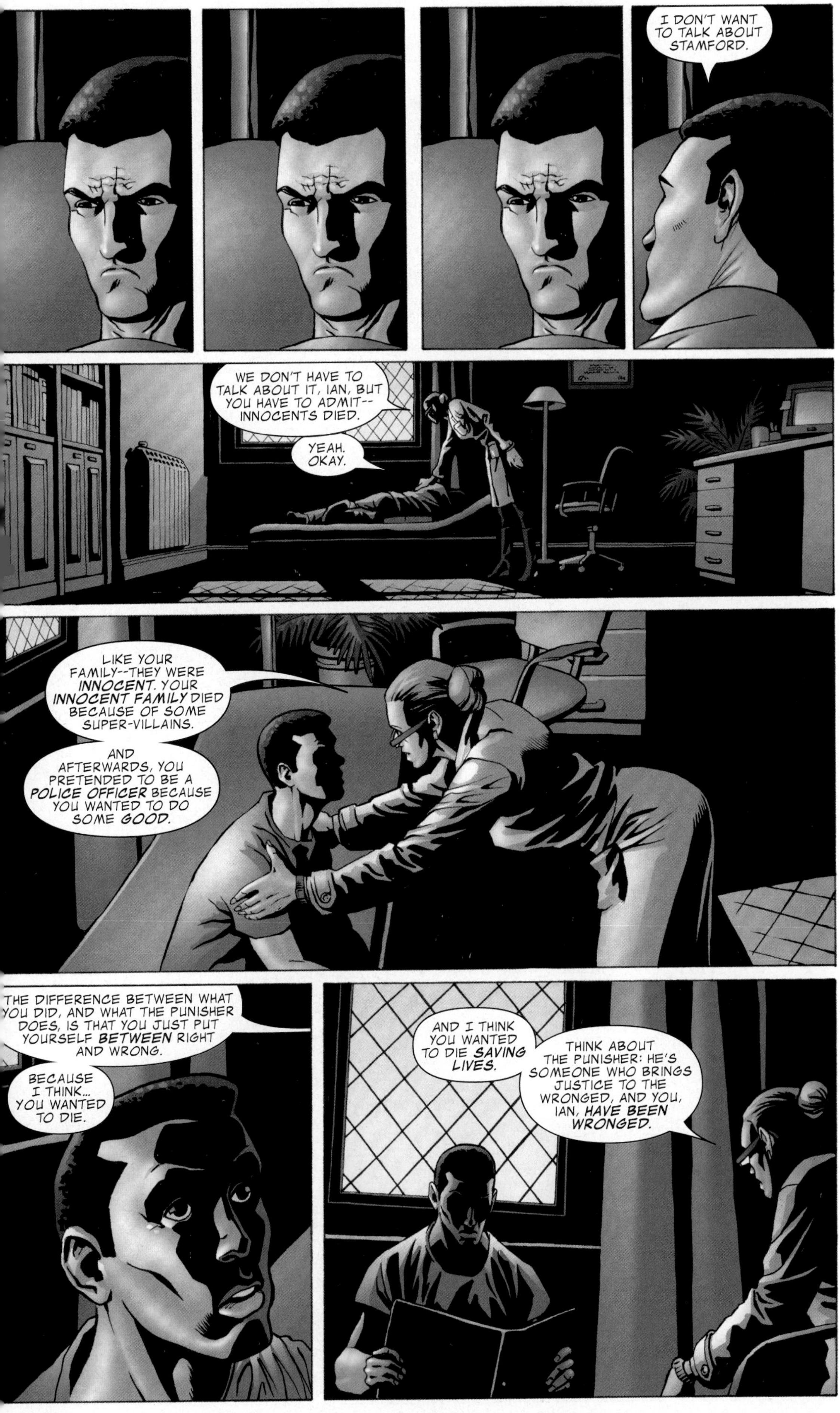
I DON'T WANT TO TALK ABOUT STAMFORD.
WE DON'T HAVE TO TALK ABOUT IT, IAN, BUT YOU HAVE TO ADMIT-- INNOCENTS DIED.
YEAH. OKAY.
LIKE YOUR FAMILY--THEY WERE INNOCENT. YOUR INNOCENT FAMILY DIED BECAUSE OF SOME SUPER-VILLAINS.
AND AFTERWARDS, YOU PRETENDED TO BE A POLICE OFFICER BECAUSE YOU WANTED TO DO SOME GOOD.
THE DIFFERENCE BETWEEN WHAT YOU DID, AND WHAT THE PUNISHER DOES, IS THAT YOU JUST PUT YOURSELF BETWEEN RIGHT AND WRONG.
BECAUSE I THINK... YOU WANTED TO DIE.
AND I THINK YOU WANTED TO DIE SAVING LIVES.
THINK ABOUT THE PUNISHER: HE'S SOMEONE WHO BRINGS JUSTICE TO THE WRONGED, AND YOU, IAN, HAVE BEEN WRONGED.

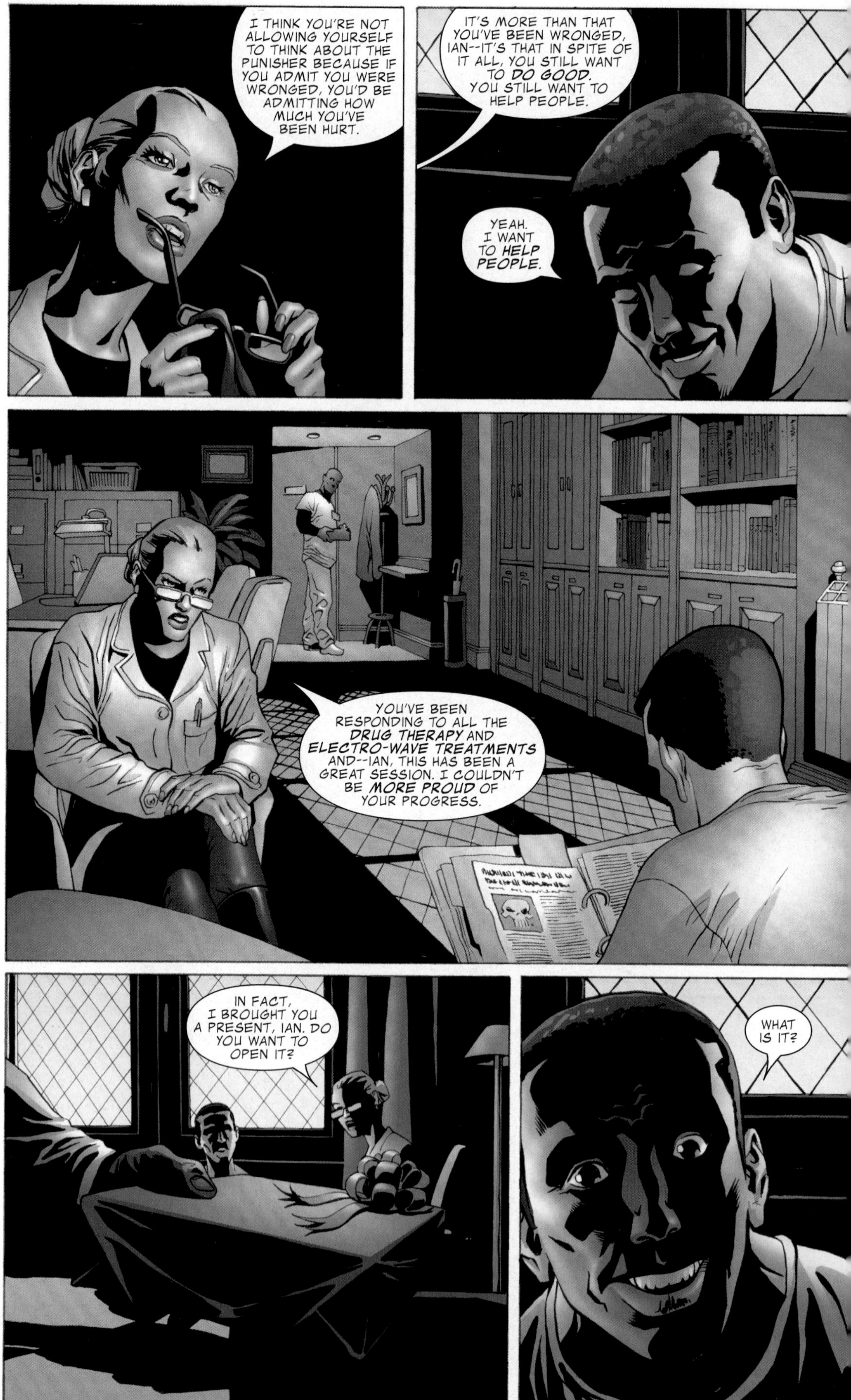

I THINK YOU'RE NOT ALLOWING YOURSELF TO THINK ABOUT THE PUNISHER BECAUSE IF YOU ADMIT YOU WERE WRONGED, YOU'D BE ADMITTING HOW MUCH YOU'VE BEEN HURT.
IT'S MORE THAN THAT YOU'VE BEEN WRONGED, IAN--IT'S THAT IN SPITE OF IT ALL, YOU STILL WANT TO DO GOOD. YOU STILL WANT TO HELP PEOPLE.
YEAH. I WANT TO HELP PEOPLE.
YOU'VE BEEN RESPONDING TO ALL THE DRUG THERAPY AND ELECTRO-WAVE TREATMENTS AND--IAN, THIS HAS BEEN A GREAT SESSION. I COULDN'T BE MORE PROUD OF YOUR PROGRESS.
IN FACT, I BROUGHT YOU A PRESENT, IAN. DO YOU WANT TO OPEN IT?
WHAT IS IT?

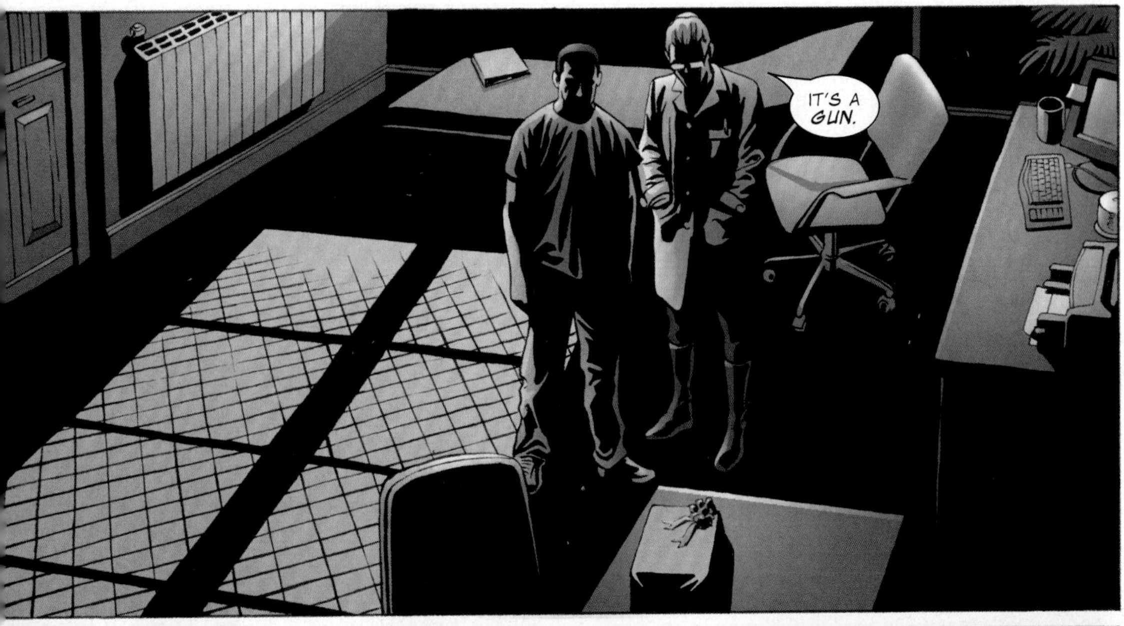
IT'S A GUN.

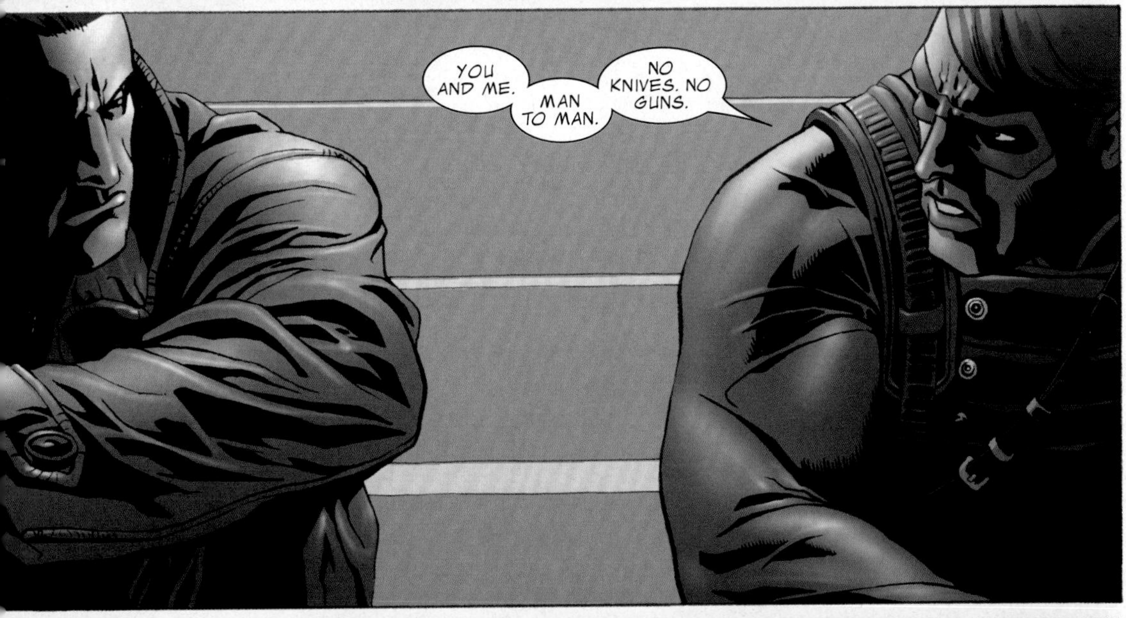
YOU AND ME.
MAN TO MAN.
NO KNIVES. NO GUNS.

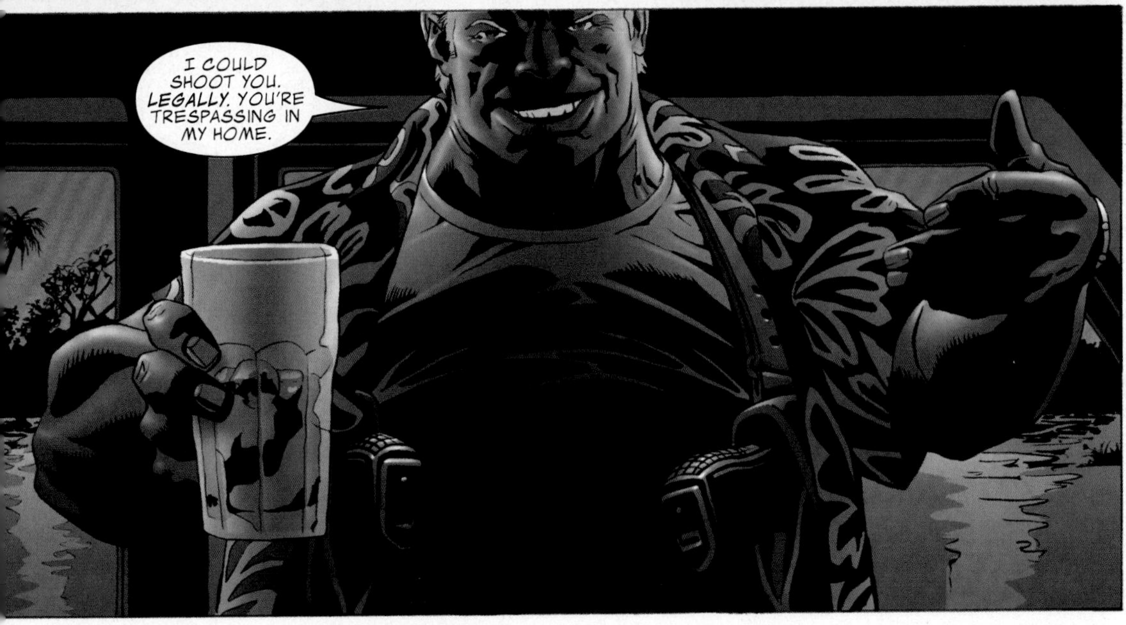
I COULD SHOOT YOU. LEGALLY. YOU'RE TRESPASSING IN MY HOME.

JEEZ, GEORGE. THAT WASN'T THE RESPONSE I WAS EXPECTING.

AND YOU'RE NOT *THE BOSS* I WAS EXPECTING.

THIS ISN'T *THE JOB* I WAS--

ARE YOU *ACTUALLY TWEAKED* THAT THINGS AREN'T THE WAY THEY *WERE* TWENTY YEARS AGO?

THAT THE WORLD HAS MAYBE MOVED ON A LITTLE BIT?

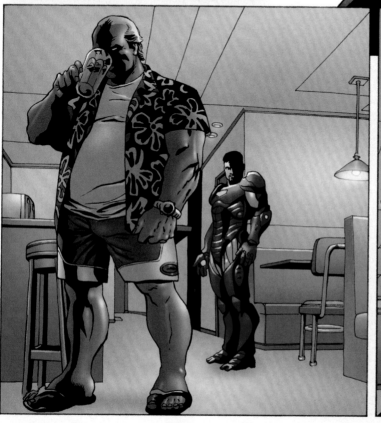

I'M "TWEAKED" BY A *TERRORIST* THAT I CAN'T EQUALLY MATCH IN METHODS PROFESSIONALLY OR MORALLY.

I'M "TWEAKED" THAT, SOMETIMES, HE GOES AFTER GUYS LIKE *HATE-MONGER* BY TAKING HEADSHOTS I CAN'T--AND *WON'T*--TAKE.

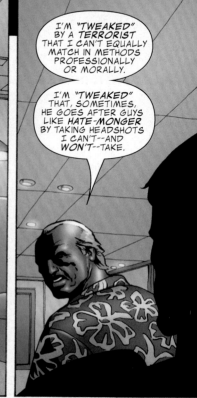

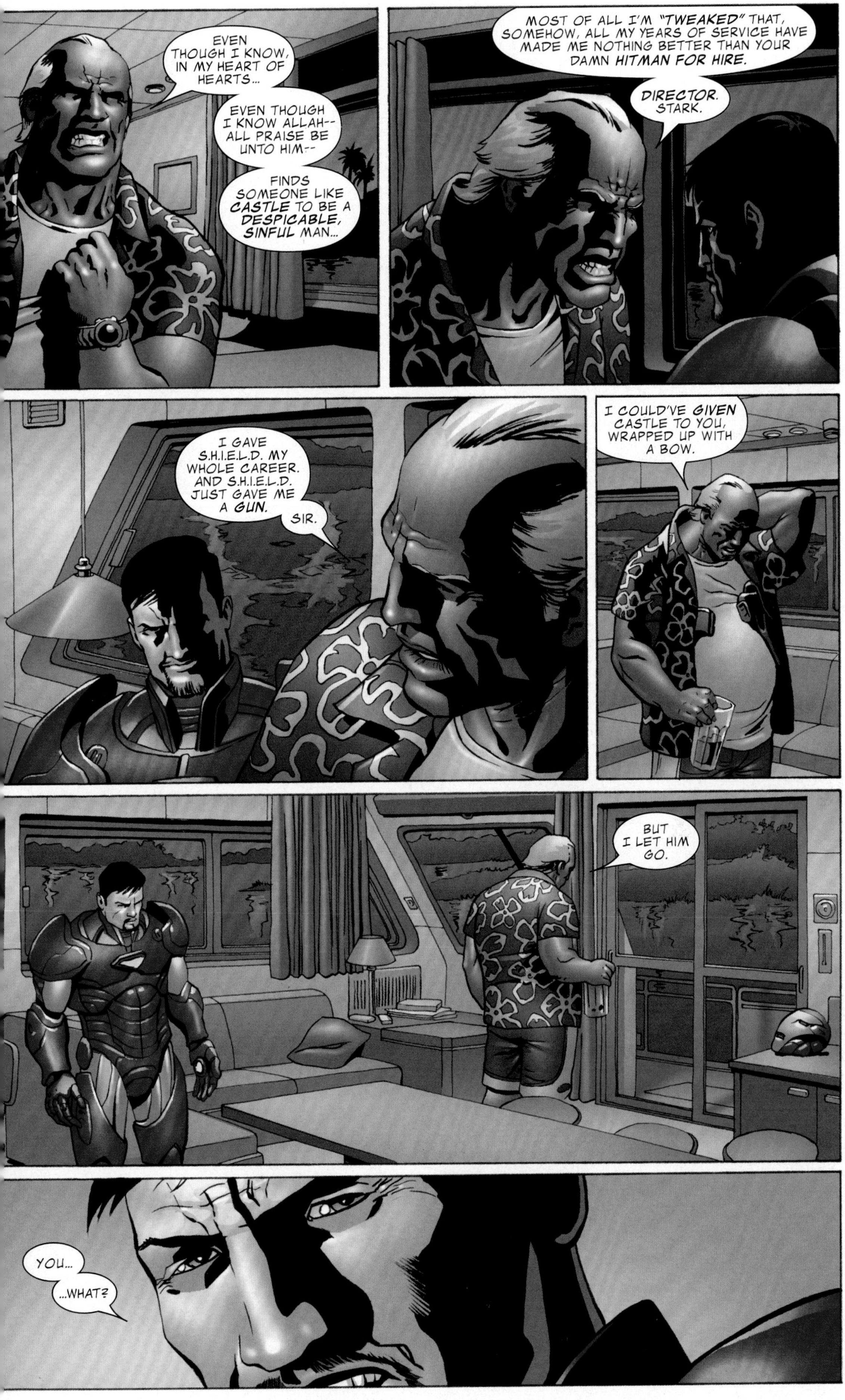
EVEN THOUGH I KNOW, IN MY HEART OF HEARTS...
EVEN THOUGH I KNOW ALLAH-- ALL PRAISE BE UNTO HIM--
FINDS SOMEONE LIKE CASTLE TO BE A DESPICABLE, SINFUL MAN...
MOST OF ALL I'M "TWEAKED" THAT, SOMEHOW, ALL MY YEARS OF SERVICE HAVE MADE ME NOTHING BETTER THAN YOUR DAMN HITMAN FOR HIRE.
DIRECTOR. STARK.
I GAVE S.H.I.E.L.D. MY WHOLE CAREER. AND S.H.I.E.L.D. JUST GAVE ME A GUN.
SIR.
I COULD'VE GIVEN CASTLE TO YOU, WRAPPED UP WITH A BOW.
BUT I LET HIM GO.
YOU...
...WHAT?

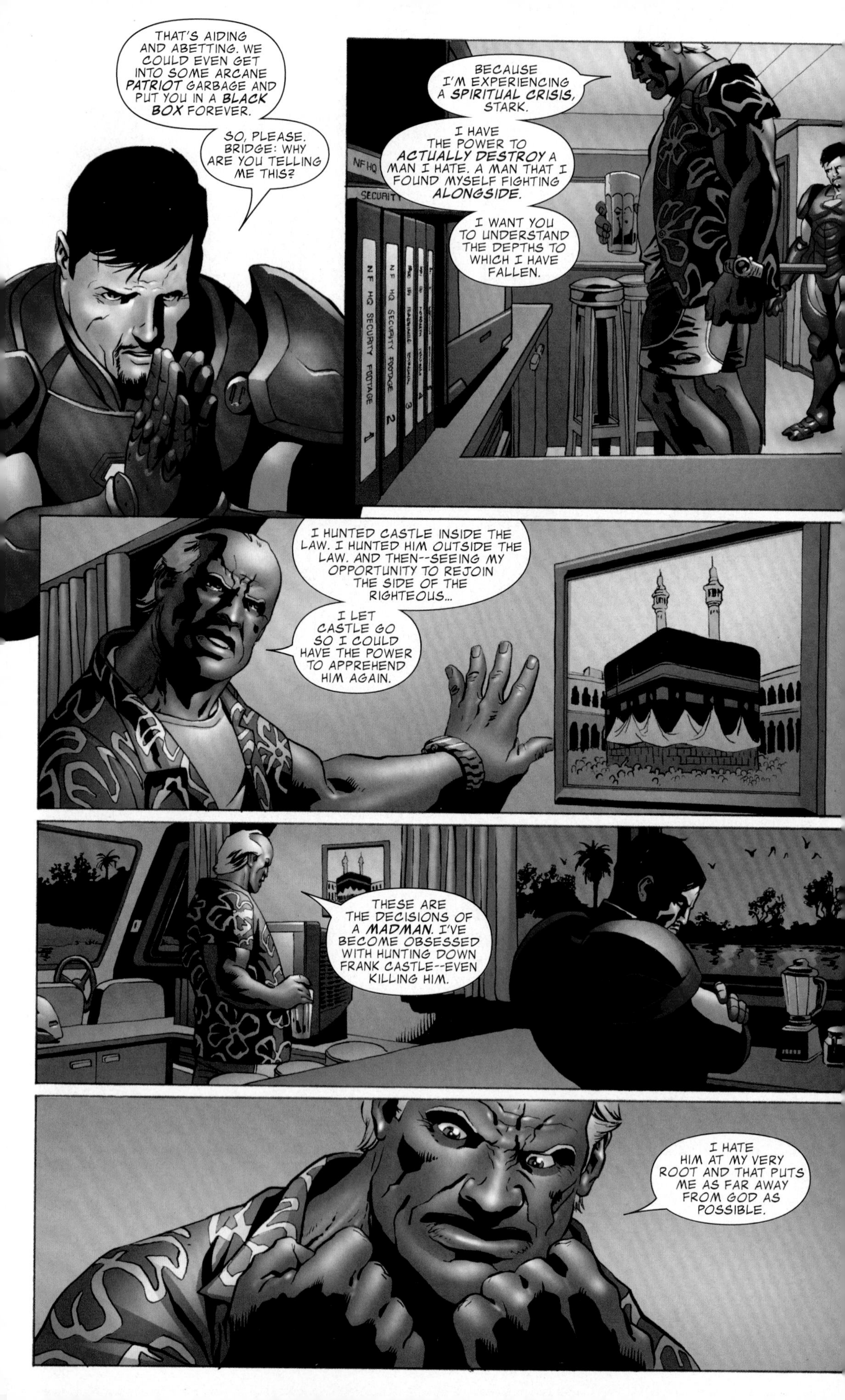
THAT'S AIDING AND ABETTING. WE COULD EVEN GET INTO SOME ARCANE PATRIOT GARBAGE AND PUT YOU IN A BLACK BOX FOREVER.
SO, PLEASE. BRIDGE: WHY ARE YOU TELLING ME THIS?
NF HQ
NF HQ SECURITY FOOTAGE 1
NF HQ SECURITY FOOTAGE 2
BECAUSE I'M EXPERIENCING A SPIRITUAL CRISIS, STARK.
I HAVE THE POWER TO ACTUALLY DESTROY A MAN I HATE. A MAN THAT I FOUND MYSELF FIGHTING ALONGSIDE.
I WANT YOU TO UNDERSTAND THE DEPTHS TO WHICH I HAVE FALLEN.
I HUNTED CASTLE INSIDE THE LAW. I HUNTED HIM OUTSIDE THE LAW. AND THEN--SEEING MY OPPORTUNITY TO REJOIN THE SIDE OF THE RIGHTEOUS...
I LET CASTLE GO SO I COULD HAVE THE POWER TO APPREHEND HIM AGAIN.
THESE ARE THE DECISIONS OF A MADMAN. I'VE BECOME OBSESSED WITH HUNTING DOWN FRANK CASTLE--EVEN KILLING HIM.
I HATE HIM AT MY VERY ROOT AND THAT PUTS ME AS FAR AWAY FROM GOD AS POSSIBLE.

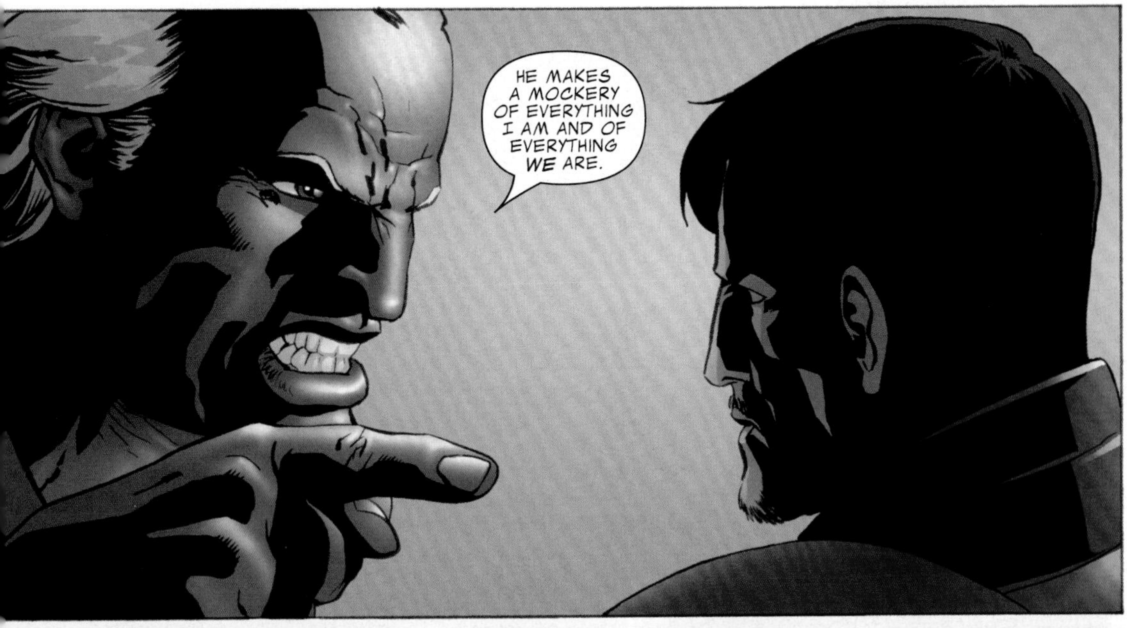
HE MAKES A MOCKERY OF EVERYTHING I AM AND OF EVERYTHING WE ARE.

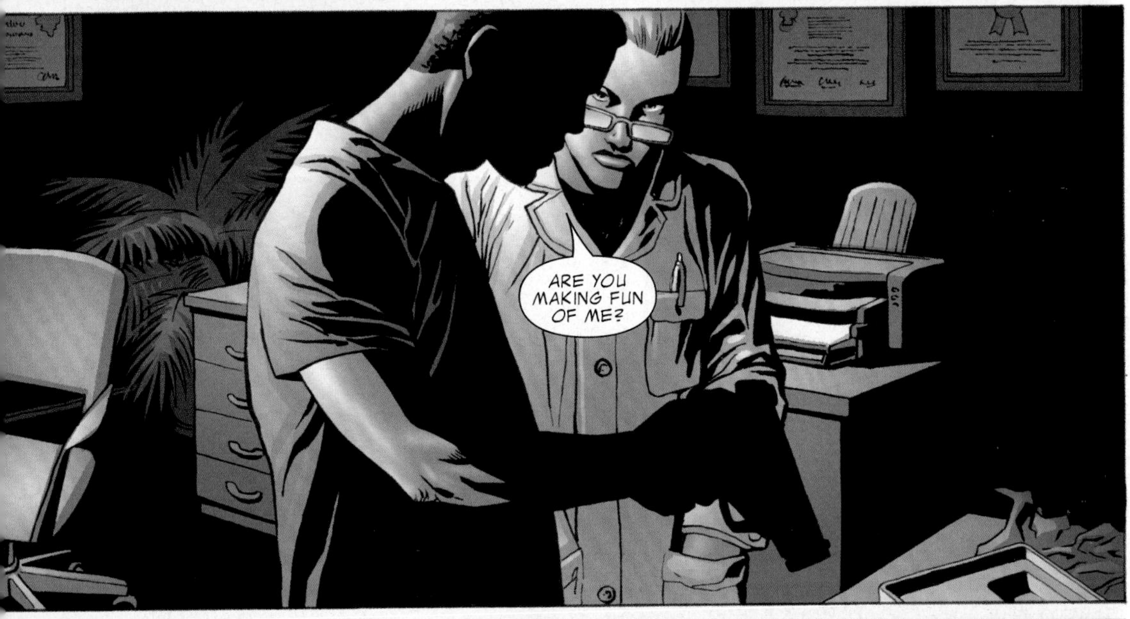
ARE YOU MAKING FUN OF ME?

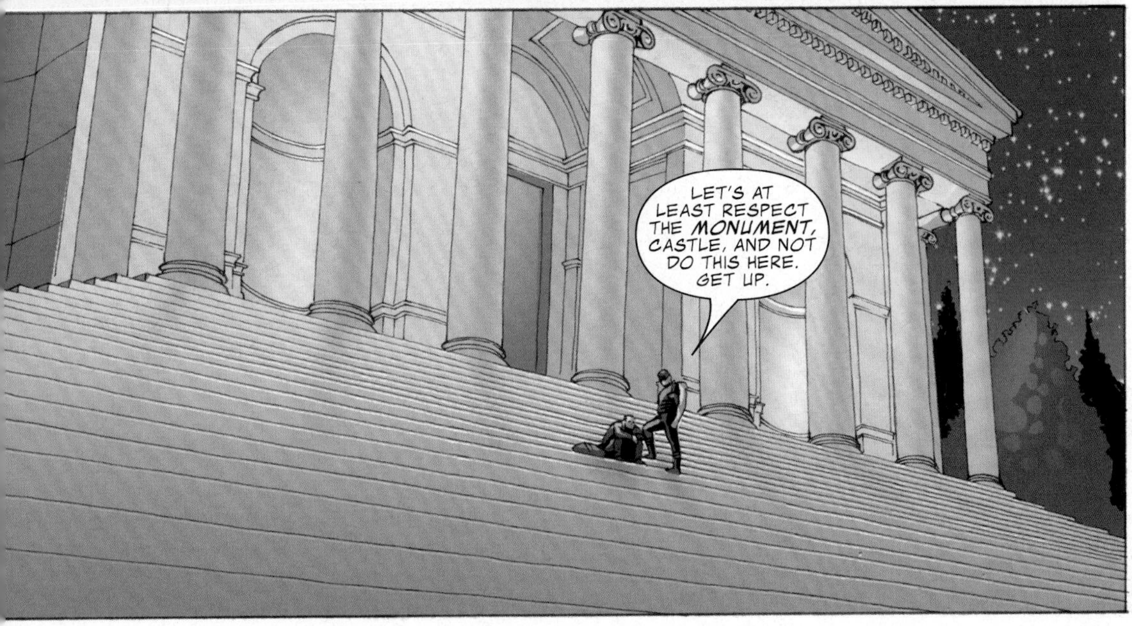
LET'S AT LEAST RESPECT THE MONUMENT, CASTLE, AND NOT DO THIS HERE. GET UP.

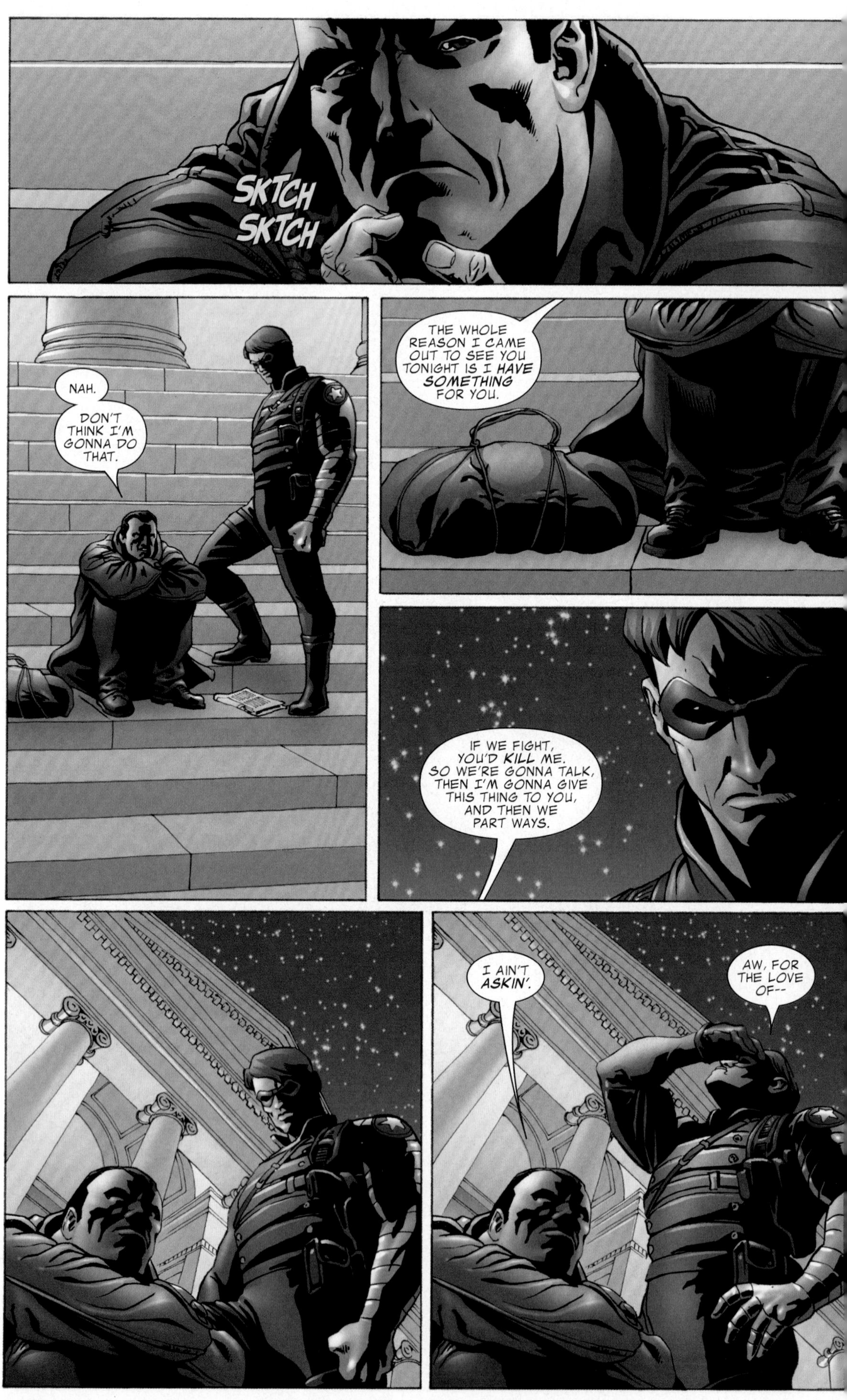
SKTCH SKTCH
NAH.
DON'T THINK I'M GONNA DO THAT.
THE WHOLE REASON I CAME OUT TO SEE YOU TONIGHT IS I HAVE SOMETHING FOR YOU.
IF WE FIGHT, YOU'D KILL ME. SO WE'RE GONNA TALK, THEN I'M GONNA GIVE THIS THING TO YOU, AND THEN WE PART WAYS.
I AIN'T ASKIN'.
AW, FOR THE LOVE OF--

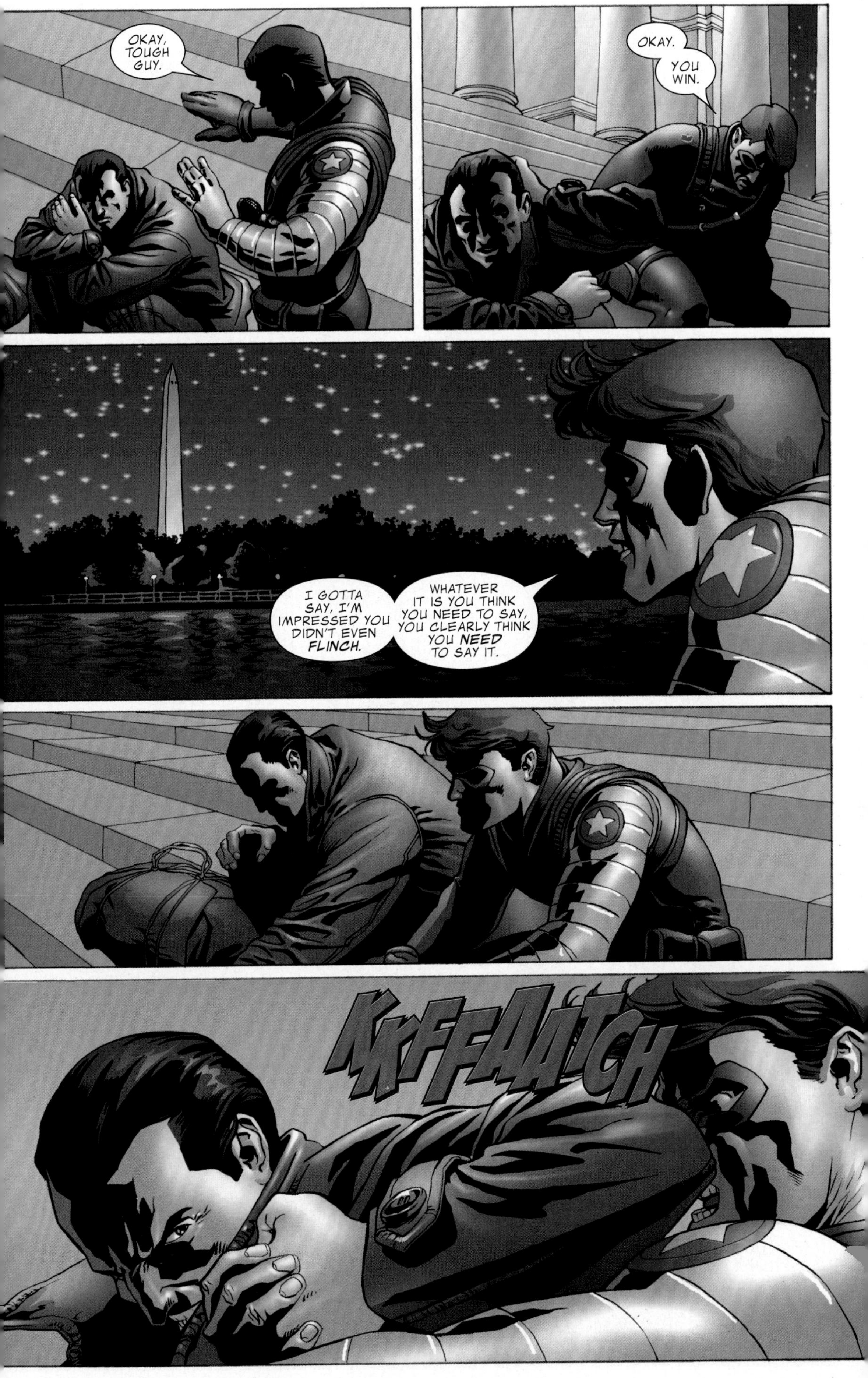
OKAY, TOUGH GUY.
OKAY.
YOU WIN.
WHATEVER IT IS YOU THINK YOU NEED TO SAY, YOU CLEARLY THINK YOU NEED TO SAY IT.
I GOTTA SAY, I'M IMPRESSED YOU DIDN'T EVEN FLINCH.
KKFFAATCH

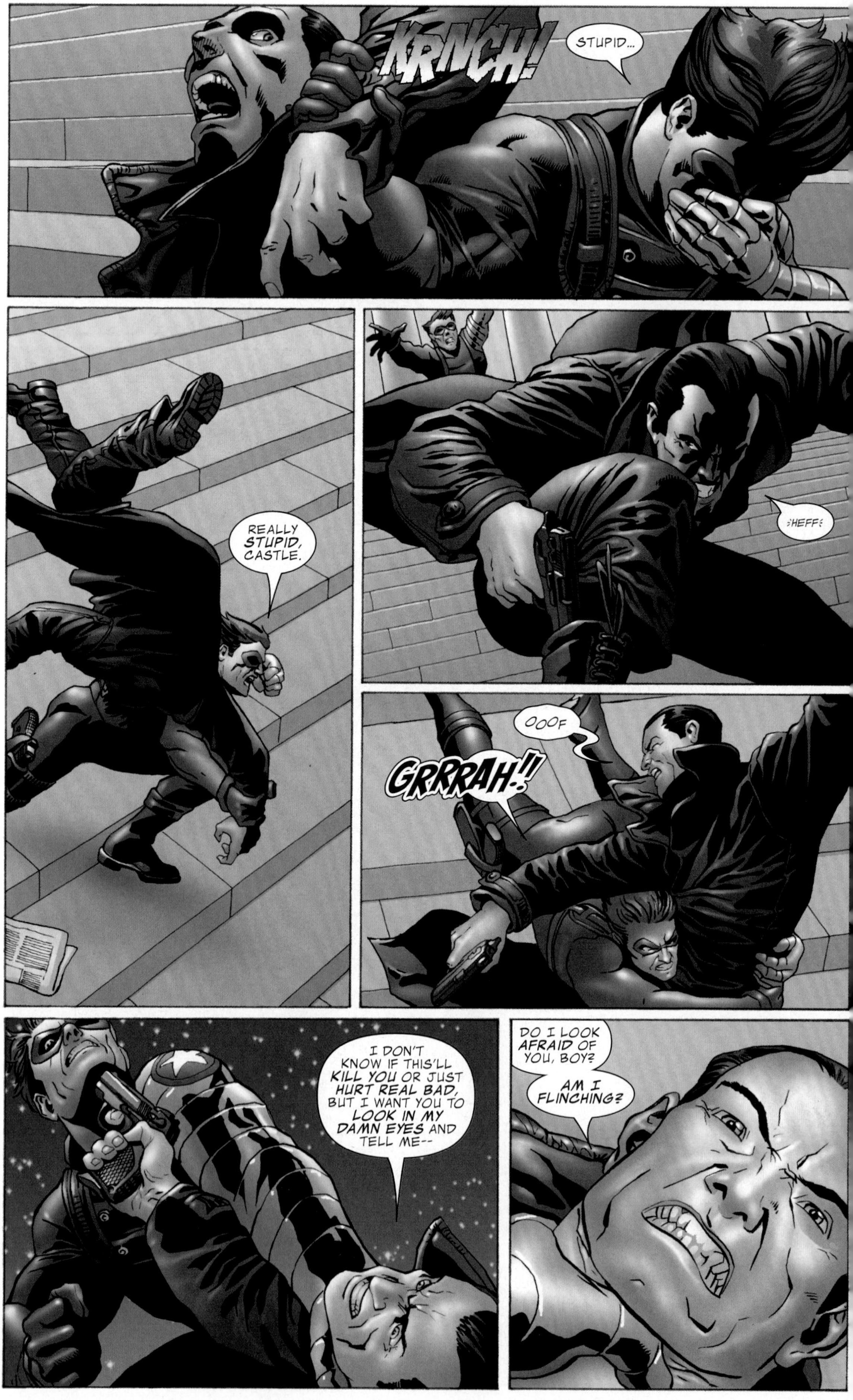
KRINCH!
STUPID...
REALLY STUPID, CASTLE.
HEFF
OOOF
GRRRAH!!
I DON'T KNOW IF THIS'LL KILL YOU OR JUST HURT REAL BAD, BUT I WANT YOU TO LOOK IN MY DAMN EYES AND TELL ME--
DO I LOOK AFRAID OF YOU, BOY?
AM I FLINCHING?

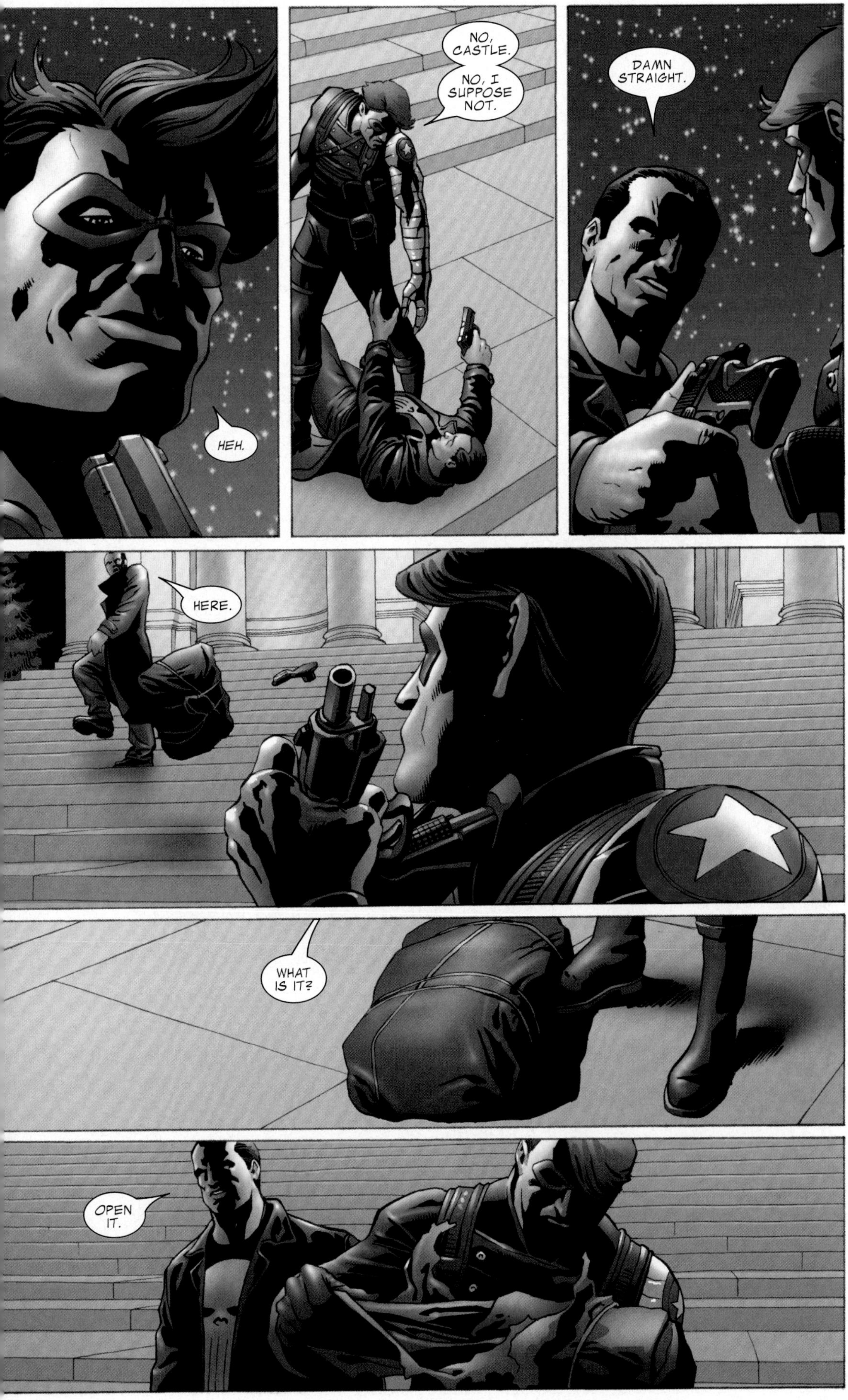
HEH.
NO, CASTLE.
NO, I SUPPOSE NOT.
DAMN STRAIGHT.
HERE.
WHAT IS IT?
OPEN IT.

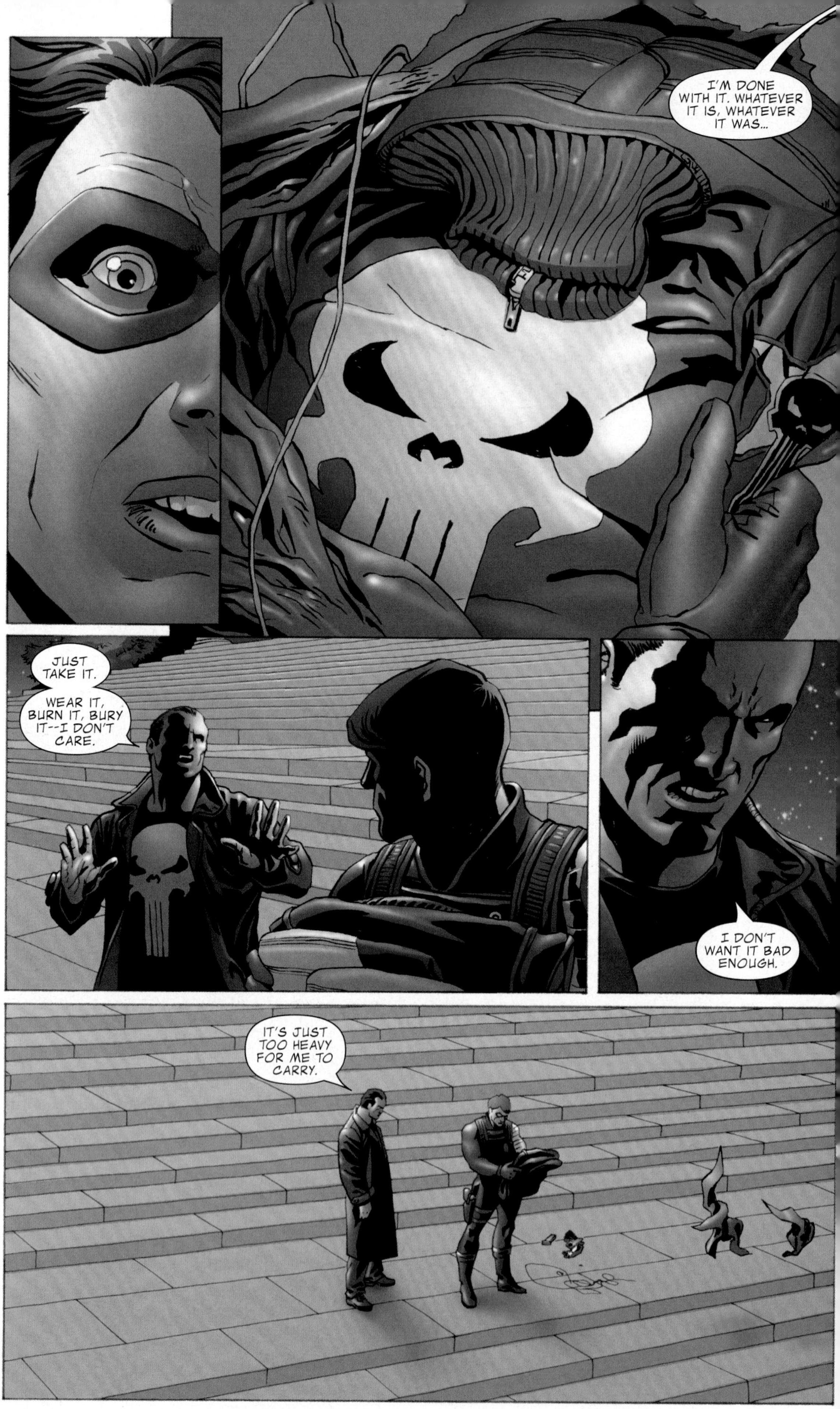
I'M DONE WITH IT. WHATEVER IT IS, WHATEVER IT WAS...
JUST TAKE IT.
WEAR IT, BURN IT, BURY IT--I DON'T CARE.
I DON'T WANT IT BAD ENOUGH.
IT'S JUST TOO HEAVY FOR ME TO CARRY.

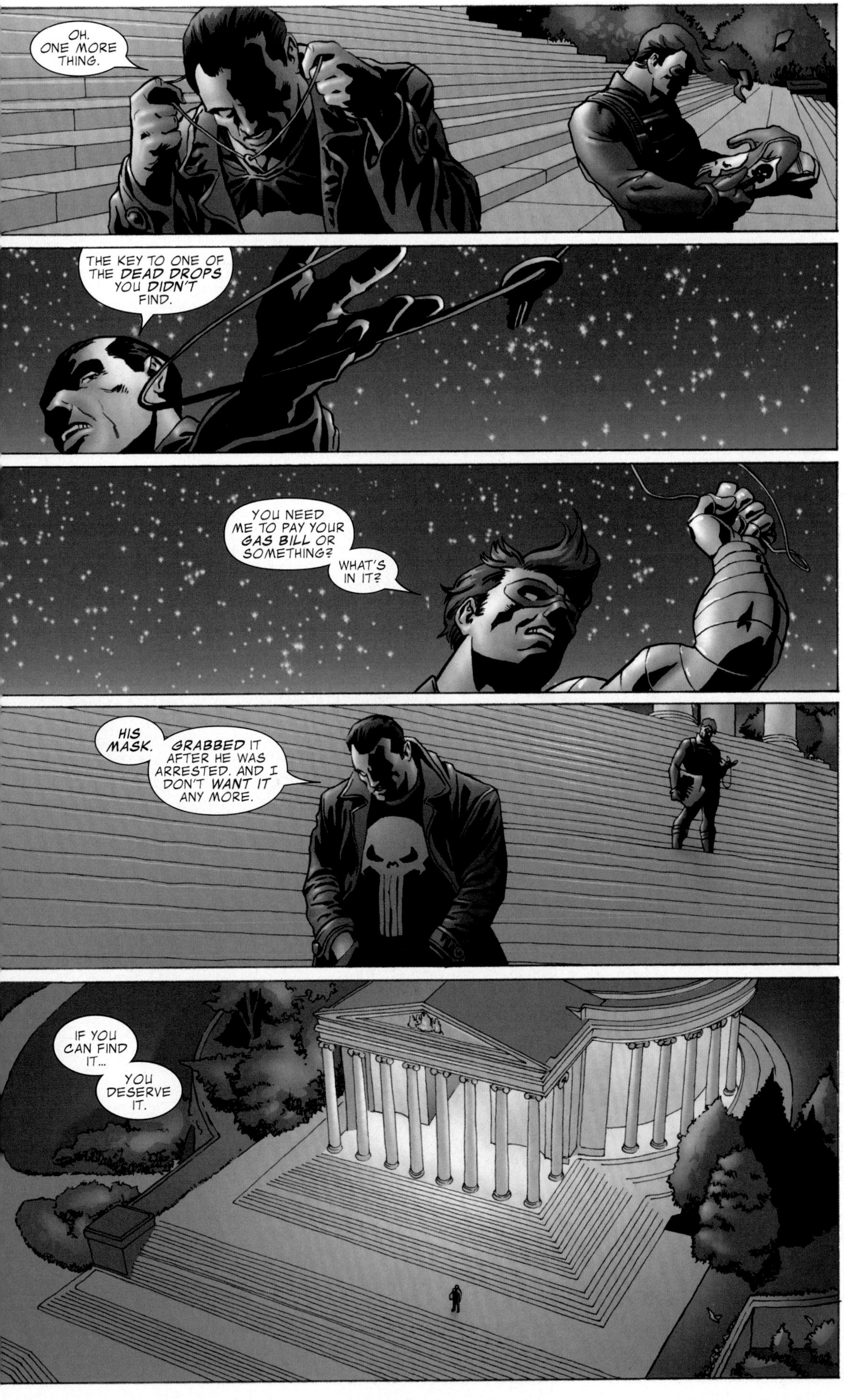
OH. ONE MORE THING.
THE KEY TO ONE OF THE DEAD DROPS YOU DIDN'T FIND.
YOU NEED ME TO PAY YOUR GAS BILL OR SOMETHING?
WHAT'S IN IT?
HIS MASK.
GRABBED IT AFTER HE WAS ARRESTED. AND I DON'T WANT IT ANY MORE.
IF YOU CAN FIND IT...
YOU DESERVE IT.

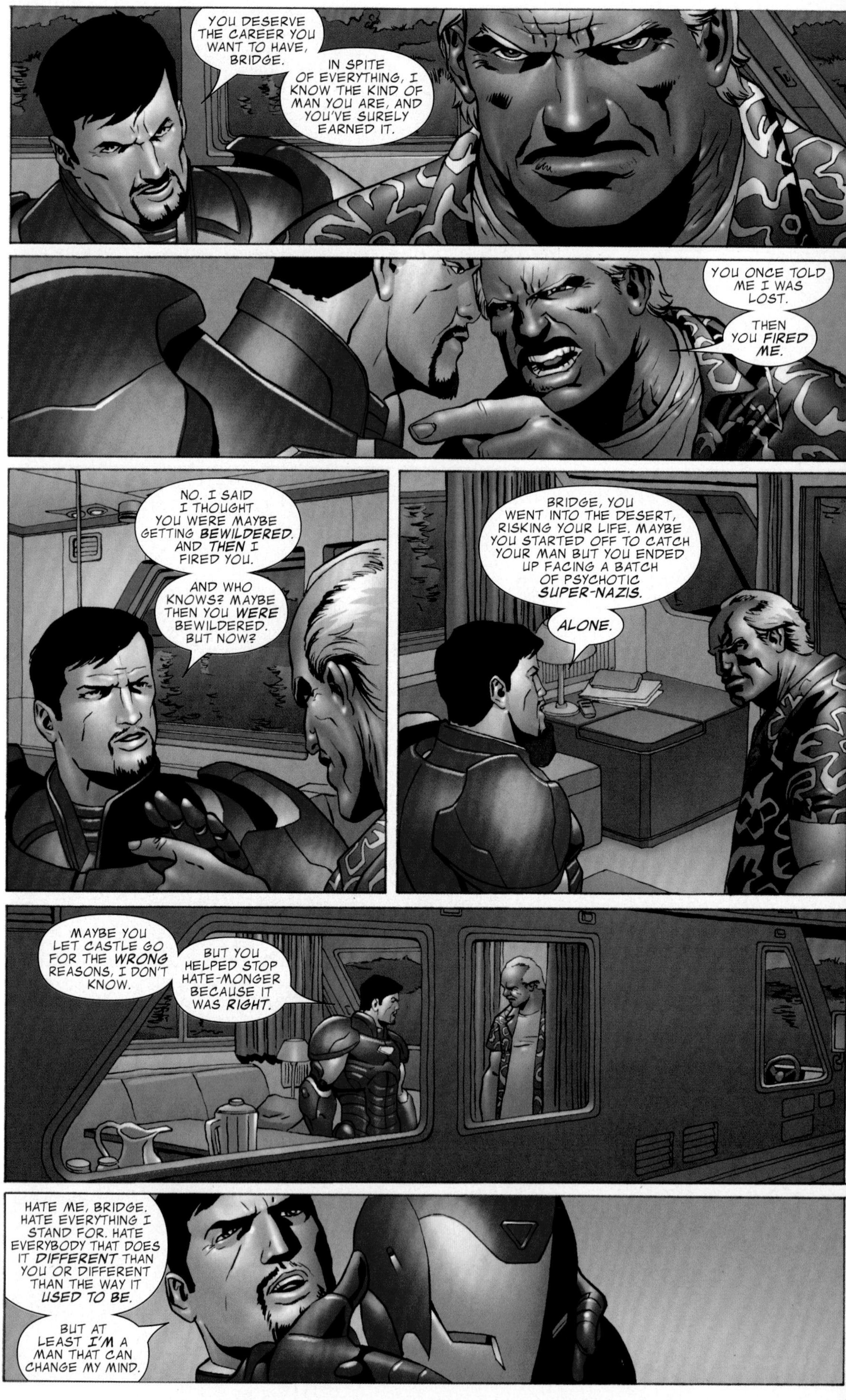

YOU DESERVE THE CAREER YOU WANT TO HAVE, BRIDGE.
IN SPITE OF EVERYTHING, I KNOW THE KIND OF MAN YOU ARE, AND YOU'VE SURELY EARNED IT.
YOU ONCE TOLD ME I WAS LOST.
THEN YOU FIRED ME.
NO. I SAID I THOUGHT YOU WERE MAYBE GETTING BEWILDERED. AND THEN I FIRED YOU.
AND WHO KNOWS? MAYBE THEN YOU WERE BEWILDERED. BUT NOW?
BRIDGE, YOU WENT INTO THE DESERT, RISKING YOUR LIFE. MAYBE YOU STARTED OFF TO CATCH YOUR MAN BUT YOU ENDED UP FACING A BATCH OF PSYCHOTIC SUPER-NAZIS.
ALONE.
MAYBE YOU LET CASTLE GO FOR THE WRONG REASONS, I DON'T KNOW.
BUT YOU HELPED STOP HATE-MONGER BECAUSE IT WAS RIGHT.
HATE ME, BRIDGE. HATE EVERYTHING I STAND FOR. HATE EVERYBODY THAT DOES IT DIFFERENT THAN YOU OR DIFFERENT THAN THE WAY IT USED TO BE.
BUT AT LEAST I'M A MAN THAT CAN CHANGE MY MIND.

I LIKE CHANGE. I LIKE IT WHEN THINGS *EVOLVE*.

I MAY HAVE THOUGHT YOU WERE WASHED UP AND SLOPPY ONCE, BUT, DAMMIT, MAN...

YOU WERE A ONE-MAN CAVALRY OUT THERE. THE GOOD GUYS COULD USE ANOTHER *DOZEN* LIKE YOU.

GUYS LIKE YOU-- OLD SCHOOL, DISCIPLINED, HARDCORE-- ARE HEROES TO GUYS LIKE ME.

TAKE IT, LEAVE IT, I DON'T CARE. BUT I'M SAYING:

I KNOW YOU STILL GOT IT IN YOU, BRIDGE.

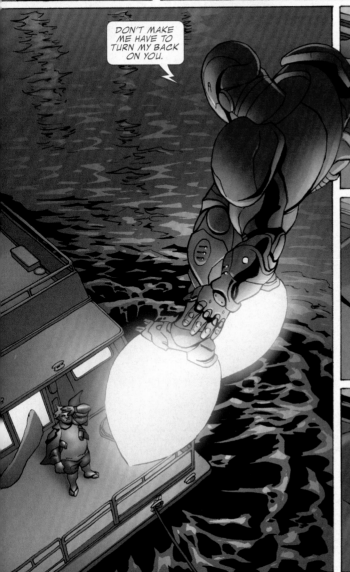

DON'T MAKE ME HAVE TO TURN MY BACK ON YOU.

...

...

I'M GONNA NEED *MY* CREW.

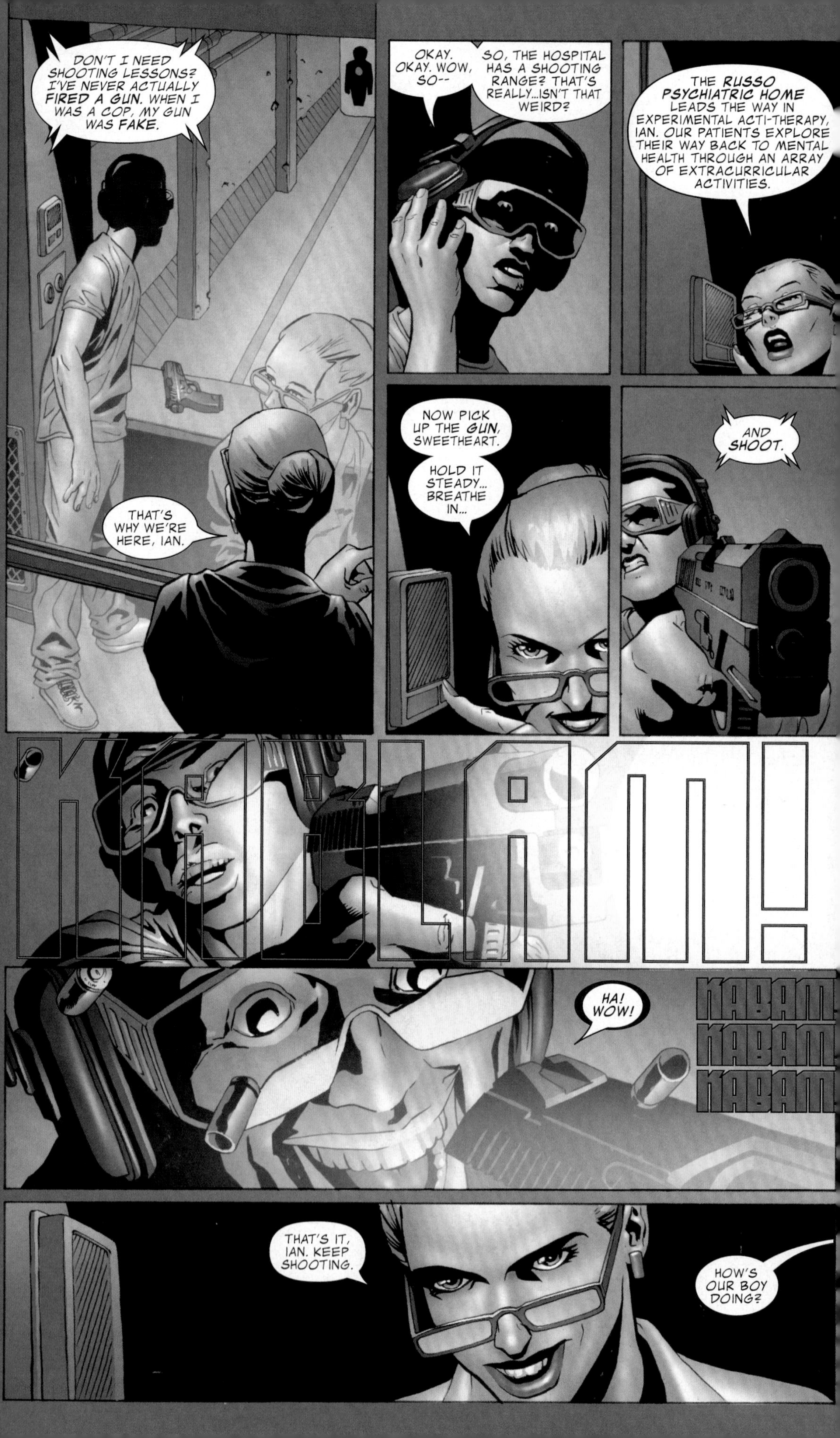
DON'T I NEED SHOOTING LESSONS? I'VE NEVER ACTUALLY FIRED A GUN. WHEN I WAS A COP, MY GUN WAS FAKE.
THAT'S WHY WE'RE HERE, IAN.
OKAY. OKAY. WOW, SO--
SO, THE HOSPITAL HAS A SHOOTING RANGE? THAT'S REALLY...ISN'T THAT WEIRD?
THE RUSSO PSYCHIATRIC HOME LEADS THE WAY IN EXPERIMENTAL ACTI-THERAPY, IAN. OUR PATIENTS EXPLORE THEIR WAY BACK TO MENTAL HEALTH THROUGH AN ARRAY OF EXTRACURRICULAR ACTIVITIES.
NOW PICK UP THE GUN, SWEETHEART.
HOLD IT STEADY... BREATHE IN...
AND SHOOT.
KABLAM!
HA! WOW!
KABAM. KABAM. KABAM.
THAT'S IT, IAN. KEEP SHOOTING.
HOW'S OUR BOY DOING?

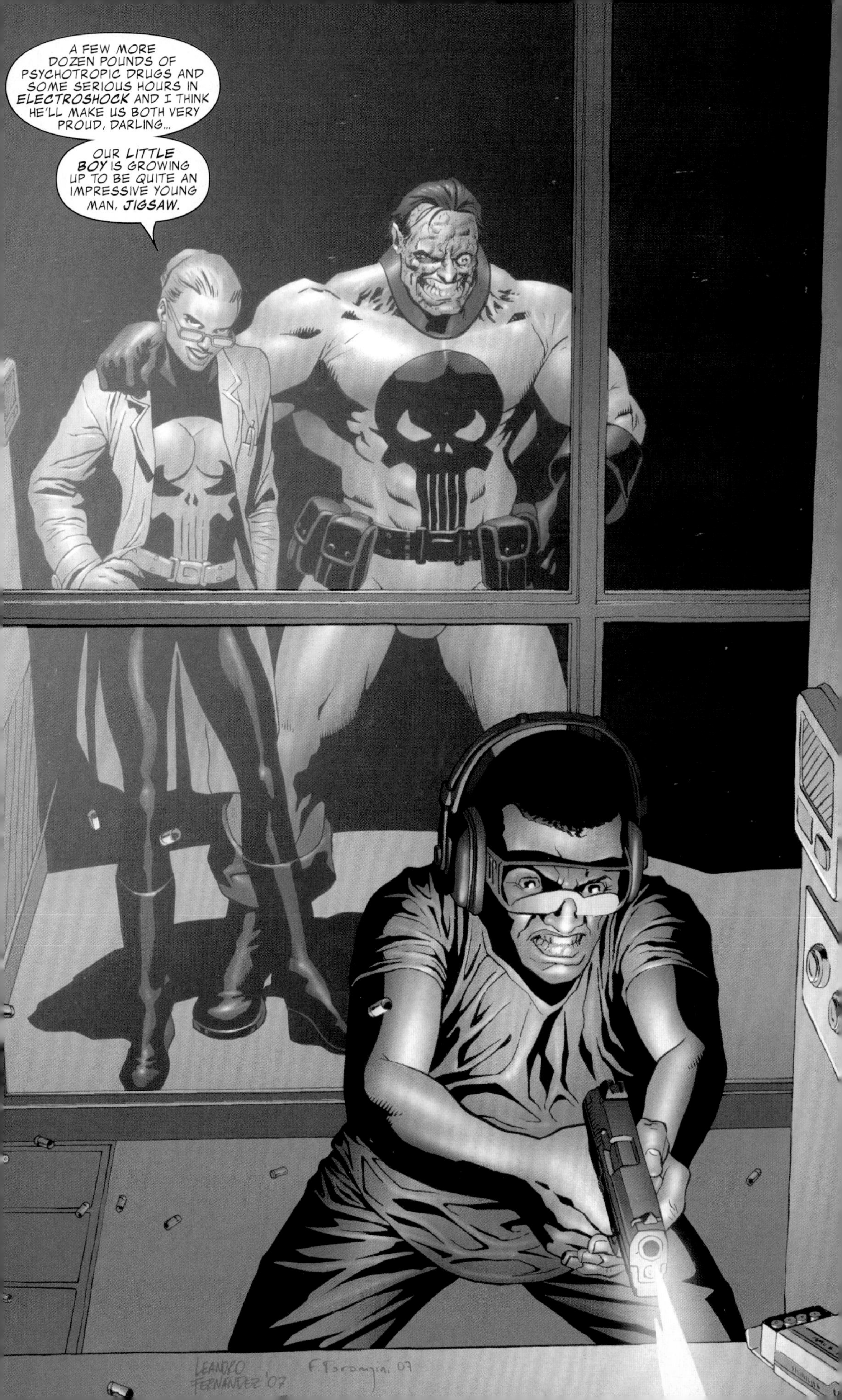

A FEW MORE DOZEN POUNDS OF PSYCHOTROPIC DRUGS AND SOME SERIOUS HOURS IN ELECTROSHOCK AND I THINK HE'LL MAKE US BOTH VERY PROUD, DARLING...
OUR LITTLE BOY IS GROWING UP TO BE QUITE AN IMPRESSIVE YOUNG MAN, JIGSAW.
LEANDRO FERNANDEZ '07
F. Parangini '07

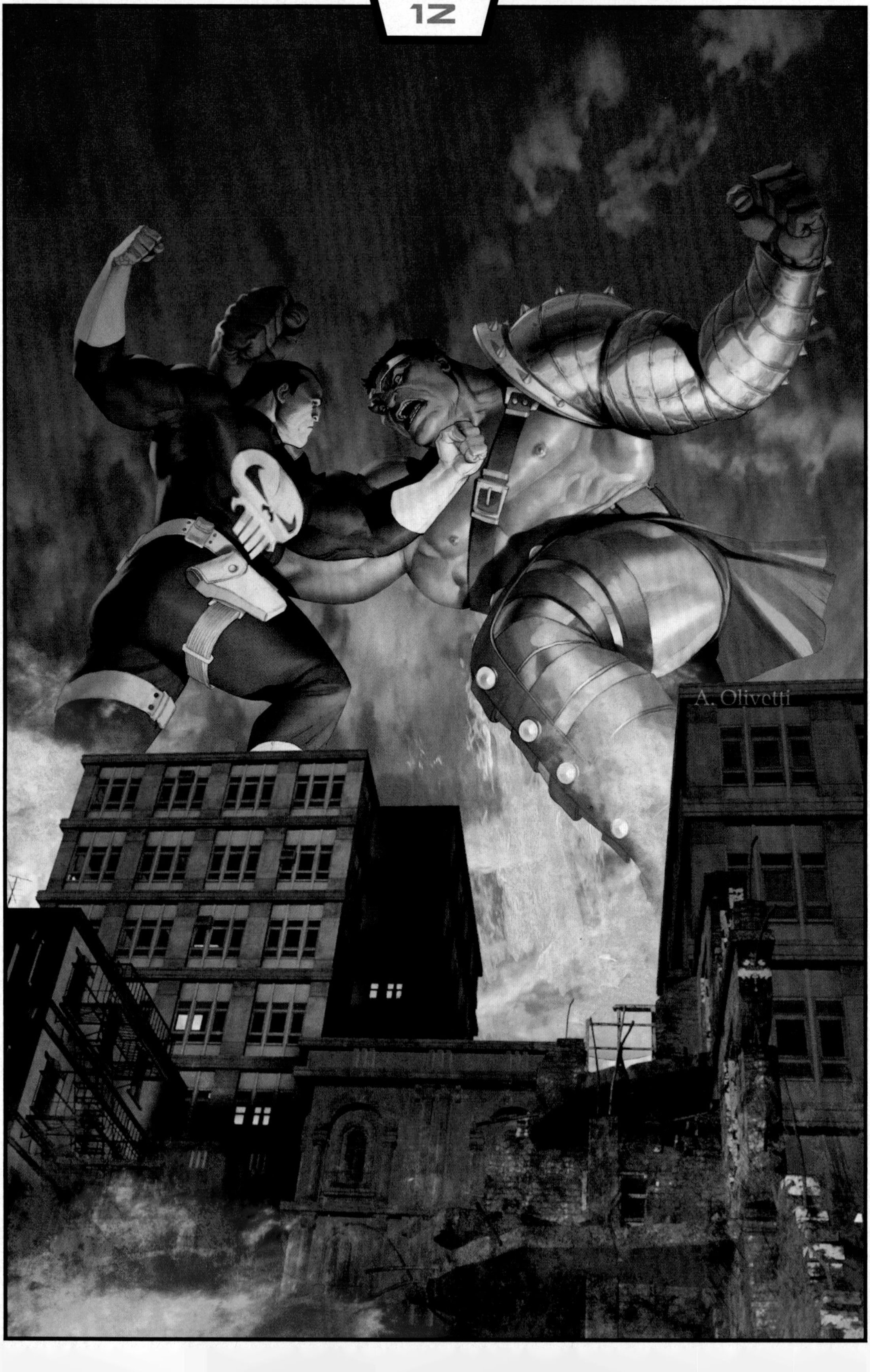
A. Olivetti

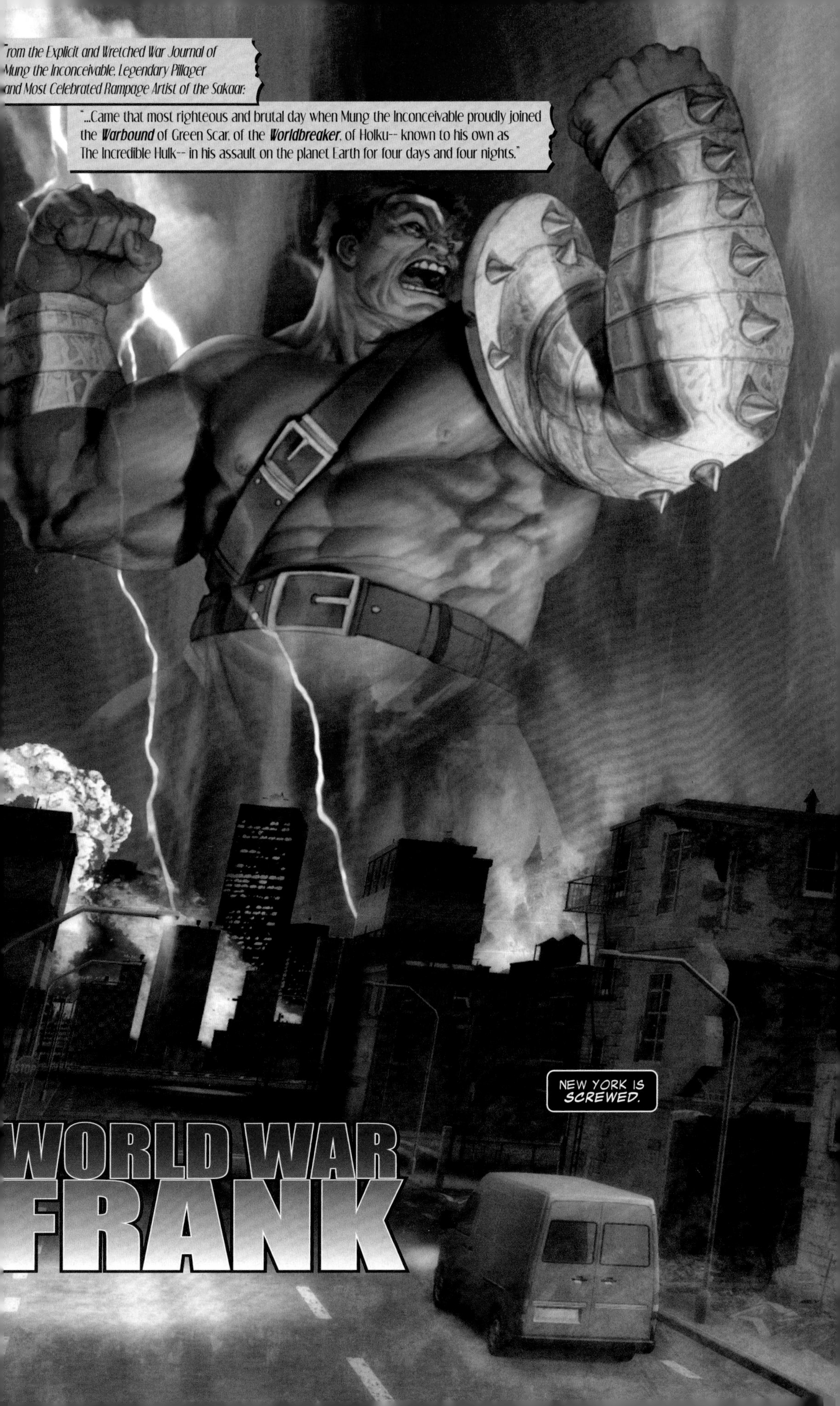
rom the Explicit and Wretched War Journal of Mung the Inconceivable, Legendary Pillager and Most Celebrated Rampage Artist of the Sakaar:
"...Came that most righteous and brutal day when Mung the Inconceivable proudly joined the *Warbound* of Green Scar, of the *Worldbreaker*, of Holku-- known to his own as The Incredible Hulk-- in his assault on the planet Earth for four days and four nights."
NEW YORK IS SCREWED.
WORLD WAR FRANK

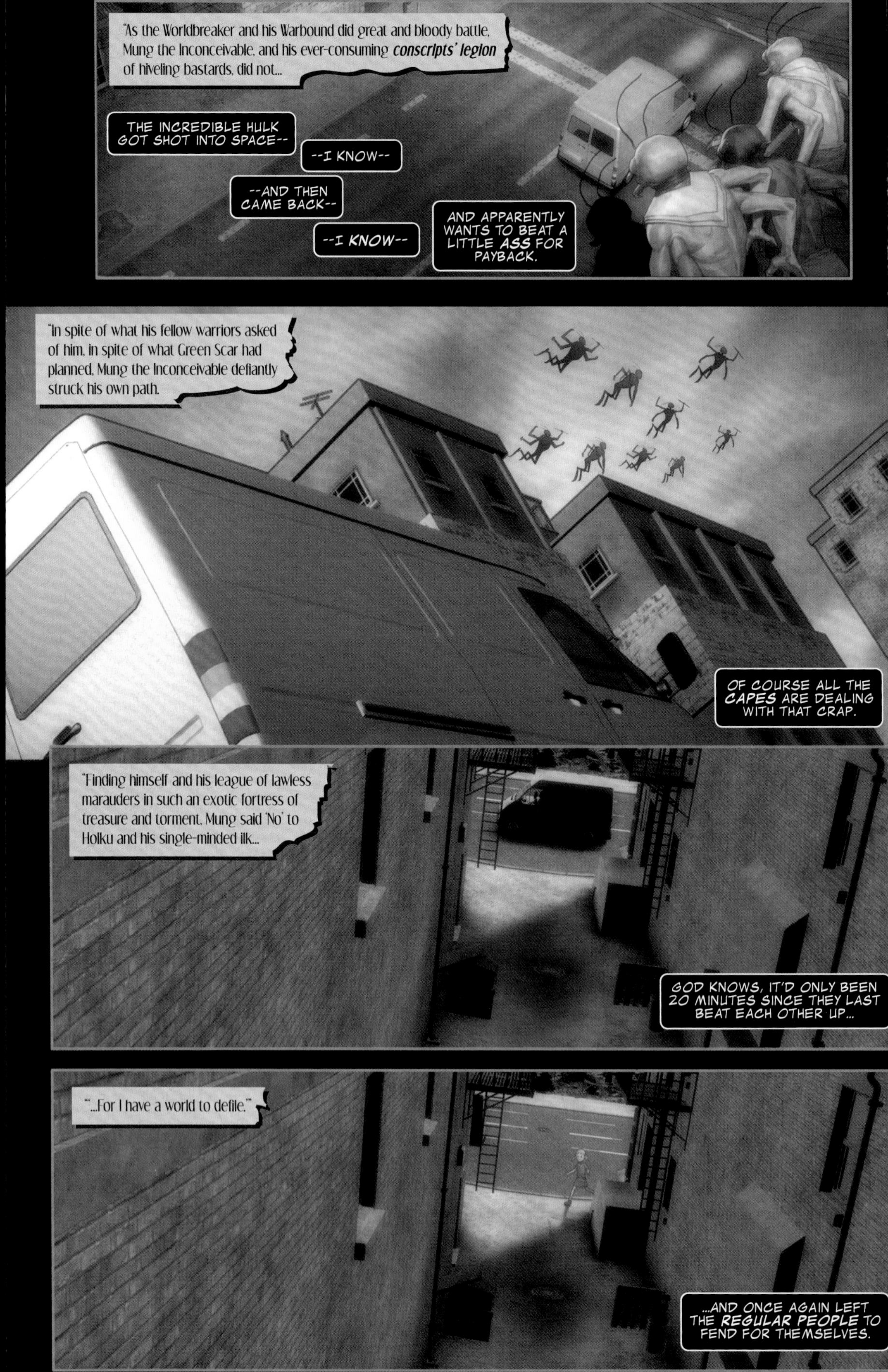
"As the Worldbreaker and his Warbound did great and bloody battle, Mung the Inconceivable, and his ever-consuming conscripts' legion of hiveling bastards, did not...
THE INCREDIBLE HULK GOT SHOT INTO SPACE--
--I KNOW--
--AND THEN CAME BACK--
--I KNOW--
AND APPARENTLY WANTS TO BEAT A LITTLE ASS FOR PAYBACK.
"In spite of what his fellow warriors asked of him, in spite of what Green Scar had planned, Mung the Inconceivable defiantly struck his own path.
OF COURSE ALL THE CAPES ARE DEALING WITH THAT CRAP.
"Finding himself and his league of lawless marauders in such an exotic fortress of treasure and torment, Mung said 'No' to Holku and his single-minded ilk...
GOD KNOWS, IT'D ONLY BEEN 20 MINUTES SINCE THEY LAST BEAT EACH OTHER UP...
"'...For I have a world to defile.'"
...AND ONCE AGAIN LEFT THE REGULAR PEOPLE TO FEND FOR THEMSELVES.

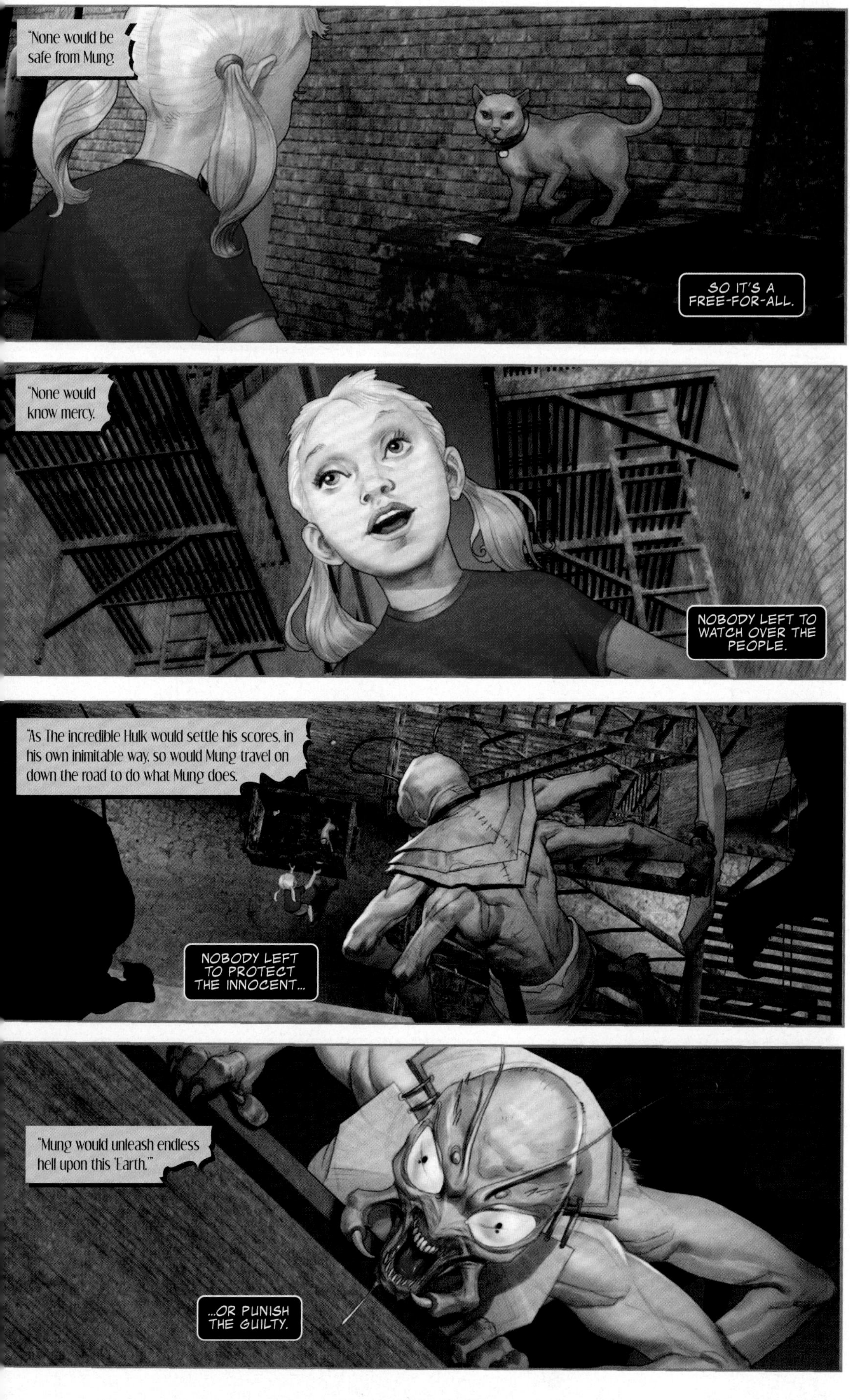
"None would be safe from Mung.
SO IT'S A FREE-FOR-ALL.
"None would know mercy.
NOBODY LEFT TO WATCH OVER THE PEOPLE.
"As The incredible Hulk would settle his scores, in his own inimitable way, so would Mung travel on down the road to do what Mung does.
NOBODY LEFT TO PROTECT THE INNOCENT...
"Mung would unleash endless hell upon this 'Earth.'"
...OR PUNISH THE GUILTY.

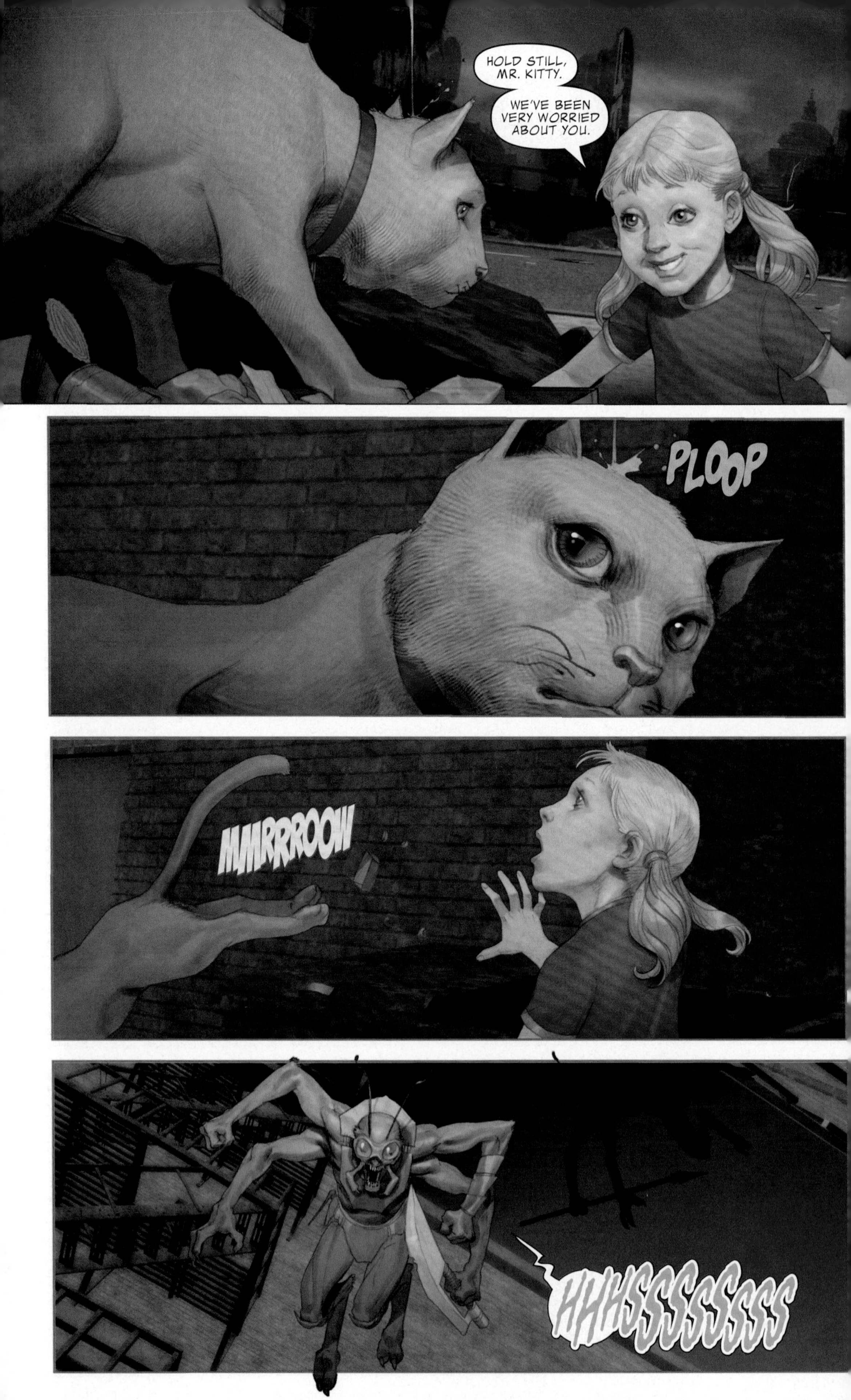
HOLD STILL, MR. KITTY.
WE'VE BEEN VERY WORRIED ABOUT YOU.
PLOOP
MMRRROOW
HHHSSSSSSSS

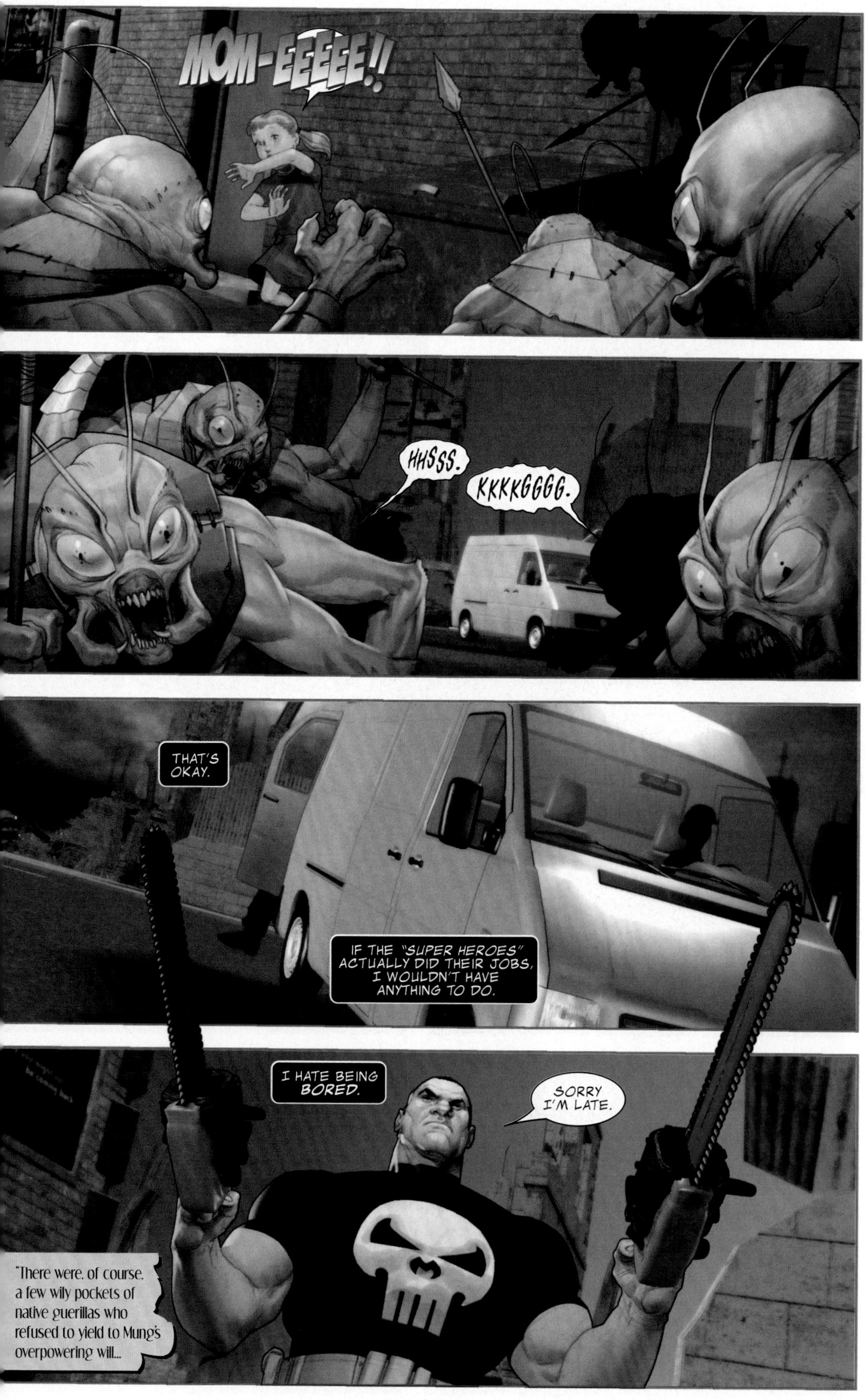
MOM-EEEEE!!
HHSSS.
KKKKGGGG.
THAT'S OKAY.
IF THE "SUPER HEROES" ACTUALLY DID THEIR JOBS, I WOULDN'T HAVE ANYTHING TO DO.
I HATE BEING BORED.
SORRY I'M LATE.
"There were, of course, a few wily pockets of native guerillas who refused to yield to Mung's overpowering will...

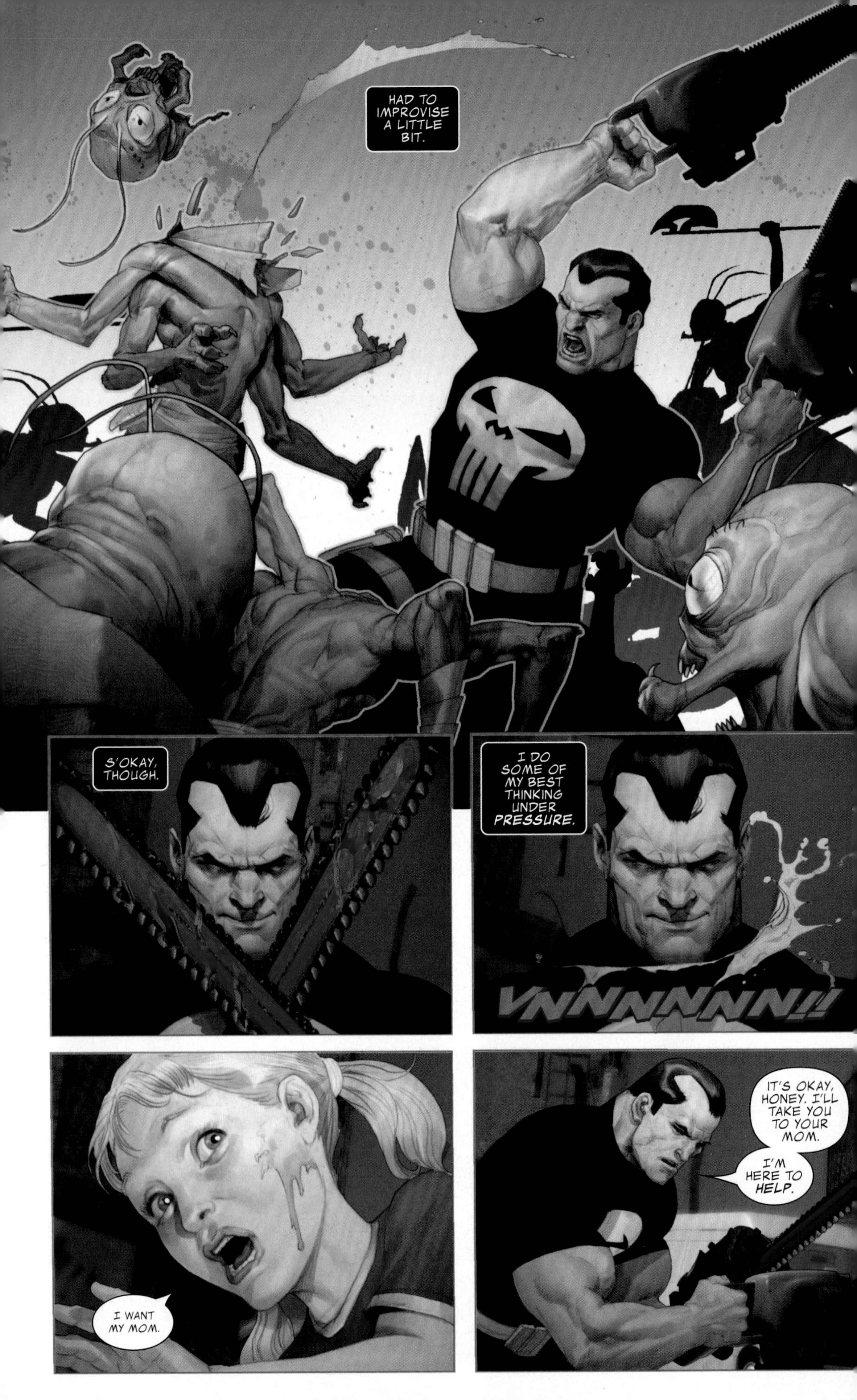
HAD TO IMPROVISE A LITTLE BIT.
S'OKAY, THOUGH.
I DO SOME OF MY BEST THINKING UNDER PRESSURE.
VNNNNNN!!
I WANT MY MOM.
IT'S OKAY, HONEY. I'LL TAKE YOU TO YOUR MOM.
I'M HERE TO HELP.

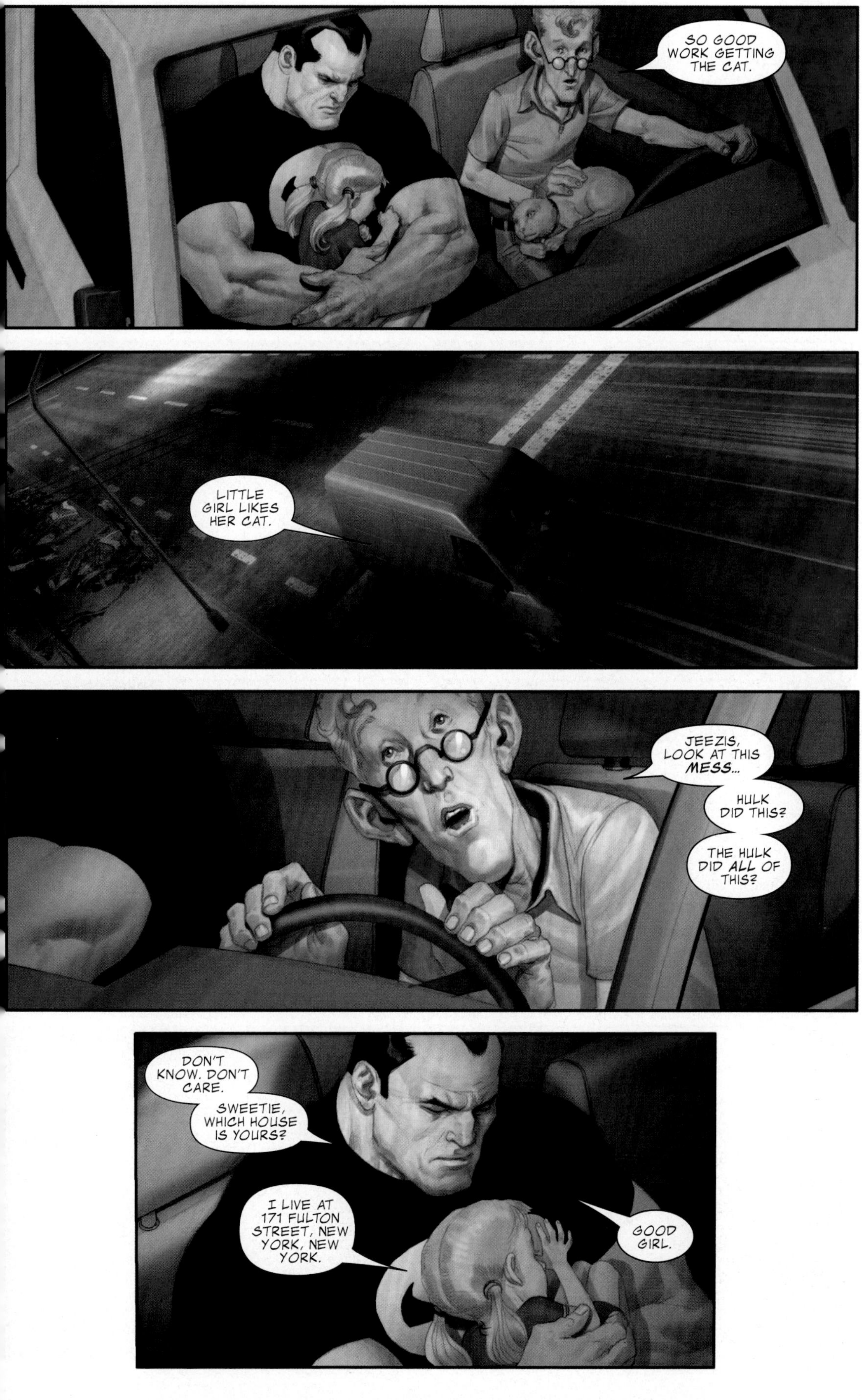
SO GOOD WORK GETTING THE CAT.
LITTLE GIRL LIKES HER CAT.
JEEZIS, LOOK AT THIS MESS...
HULK DID THIS?
THE HULK DID ALL OF THIS?
DON'T KNOW. DON'T CARE.
SWEETIE, WHICH HOUSE IS YOURS?
I LIVE AT 171 FULTON STREET, NEW YORK, NEW YORK.
GOOD GIRL.

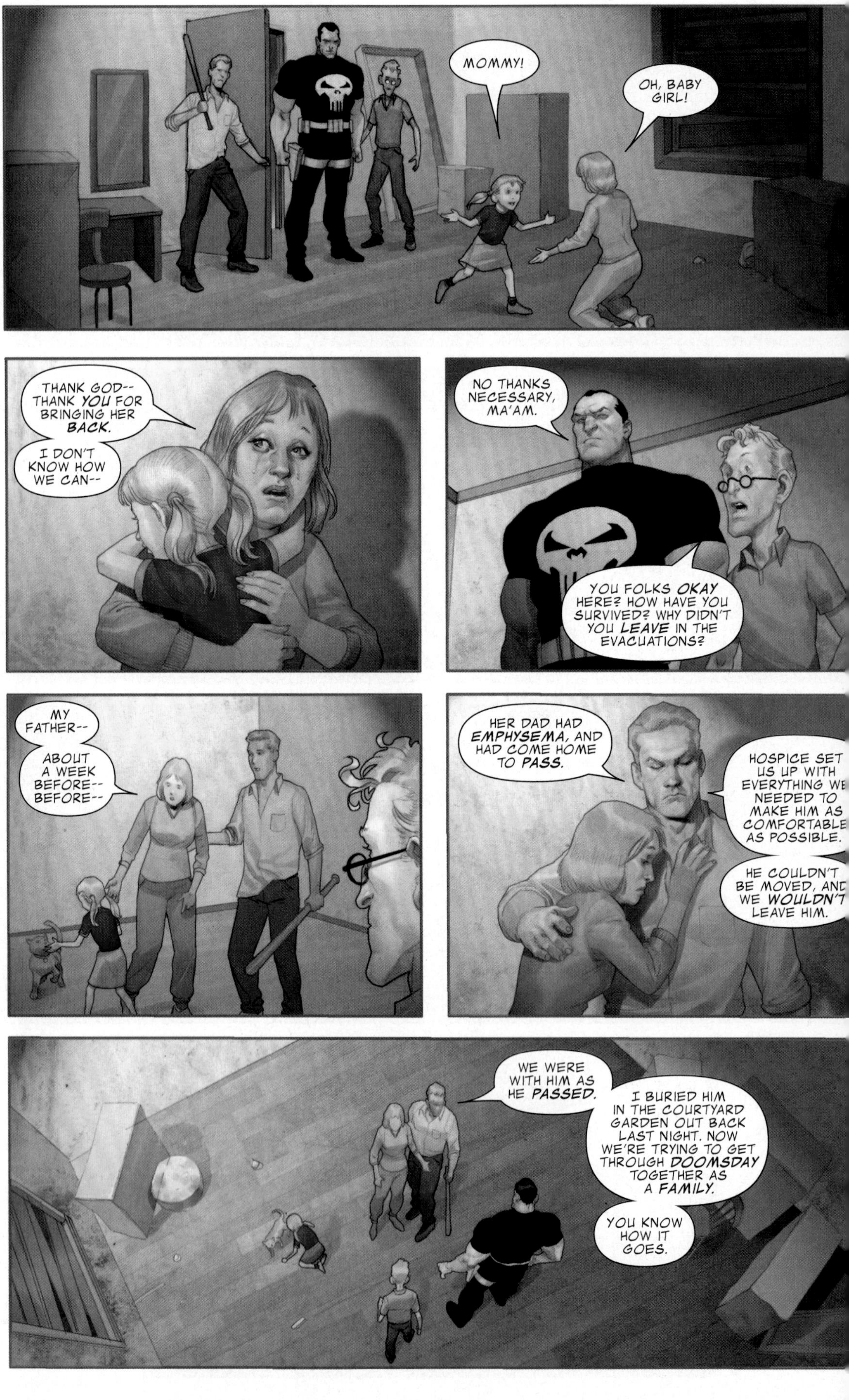

MOMMY!
OH, BABY GIRL!
THANK GOD-- THANK YOU FOR BRINGING HER BACK.
I DON'T KNOW HOW WE CAN--
NO THANKS NECESSARY, MA'AM.
YOU FOLKS OKAY HERE? HOW HAVE YOU SURVIVED? WHY DIDN'T YOU LEAVE IN THE EVACUATIONS?
MY FATHER--
ABOUT A WEEK BEFORE-- BEFORE--
HER DAD HAD EMPHYSEMA, AND HAD COME HOME TO PASS.
HOSPICE SET US UP WITH EVERYTHING WE NEEDED TO MAKE HIM AS COMFORTABLE AS POSSIBLE.
HE COULDN'T BE MOVED, AND WE WOULDN'T LEAVE HIM.
WE WERE WITH HIM AS HE PASSED.
I BURIED HIM IN THE COURTYARD GARDEN OUT BACK LAST NIGHT. NOW WE'RE TRYING TO GET THROUGH DOOMSDAY TOGETHER AS A FAMILY.
YOU KNOW HOW IT GOES.

THEY NEVER--

THE HEROES, OR S.H.I.E.L.D. OR THE ARMY OR ANYBODY-- NOBODY CAME BACK.

WE HOLED UP AND HOPED WE'D BE SAFE...

WE'RE NOT.

THERE ARE... HORDES...OUT THERE. PICKING THE NEIGHBORHOOD CLEAN.

I DON'T THINK THEY'RE... "FROM"... HERE. YOU KNOW?

ARE THEY FROM NEW JERSEY, DADDY?

YES, SWEETIE.

THEY CAME FROM NEW JERSEY.

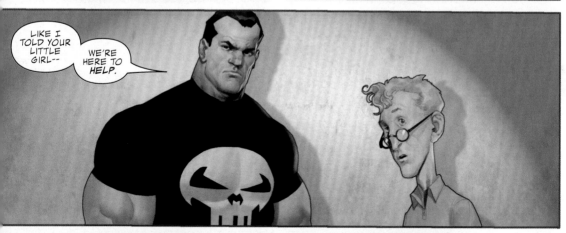

LIKE I TOLD YOUR LITTLE GIRL--

WE'RE HERE TO HELP.

YOU'RE NOT GOING BACK OUT THERE, ARE YOU?

IT'S OKAY. I LEFT SOME STUFF AT THE OFFICE.

DON'T WORRY. WE'RE PROFESSIONALS

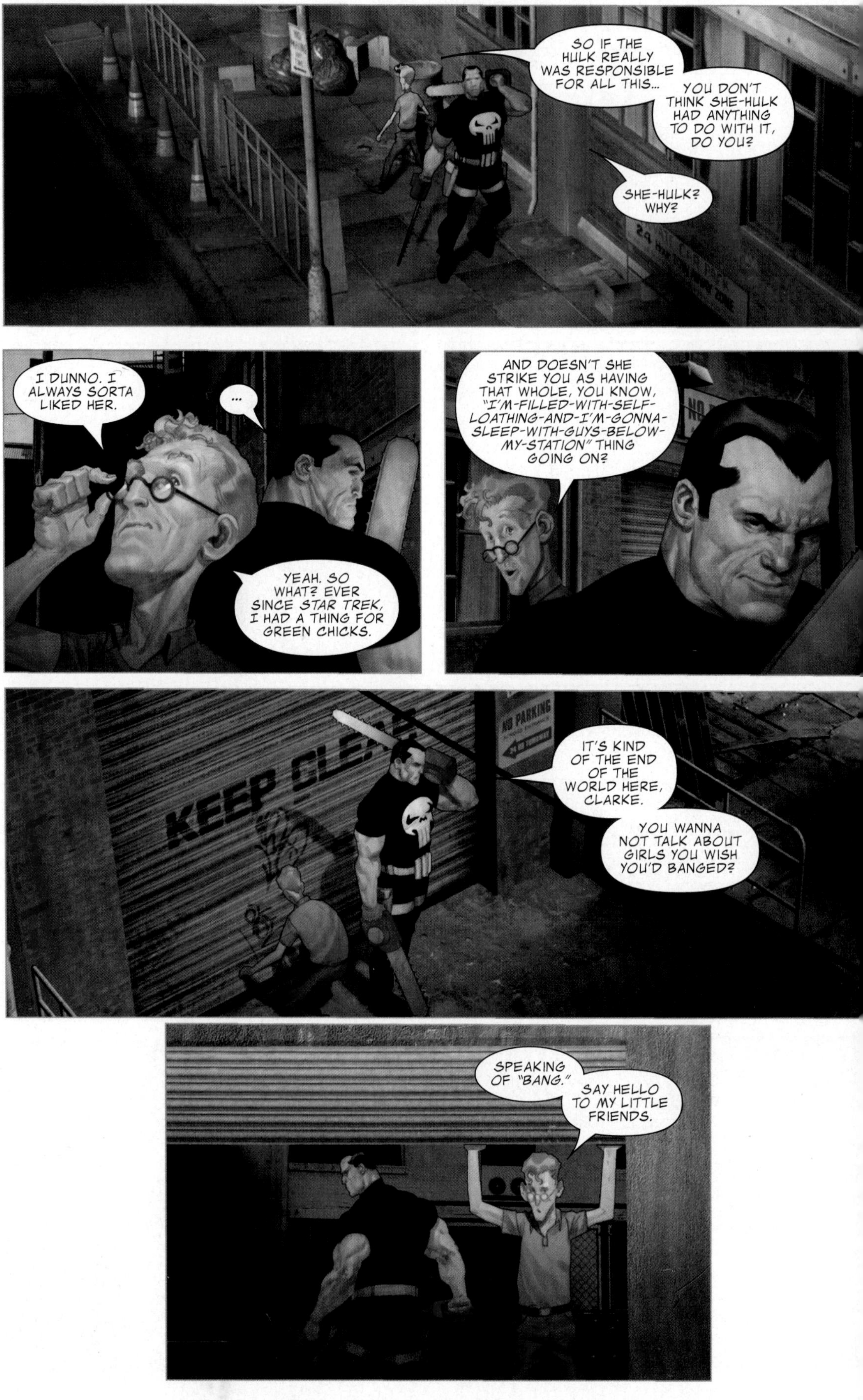
SO IF THE HULK REALLY WAS RESPONSIBLE FOR ALL THIS...
YOU DON'T THINK SHE-HULK HAD ANYTHING TO DO WITH IT, DO YOU?
SHE-HULK? WHY?
I DUNNO. I ALWAYS SORTA LIKED HER.
...
YEAH. SO WHAT? EVER SINCE *STAR TREK*, I HAD A THING FOR GREEN CHICKS.
AND DOESN'T SHE STRIKE YOU AS HAVING THAT WHOLE, YOU KNOW, *"I'M-FILLED-WITH-SELF-LOATHING-AND-I'M-GONNA-SLEEP-WITH-GUYS-BELOW-MY-STATION"* THING GOING ON?
NO PARKING
IT'S KIND OF THE END OF THE WORLD HERE, CLARKE.
YOU WANNA NOT TALK ABOUT GIRLS YOU WISH YOU'D BANGED?
SPEAKING OF *"BANG."*
SAY HELLO TO MY LITTLE FRIENDS.

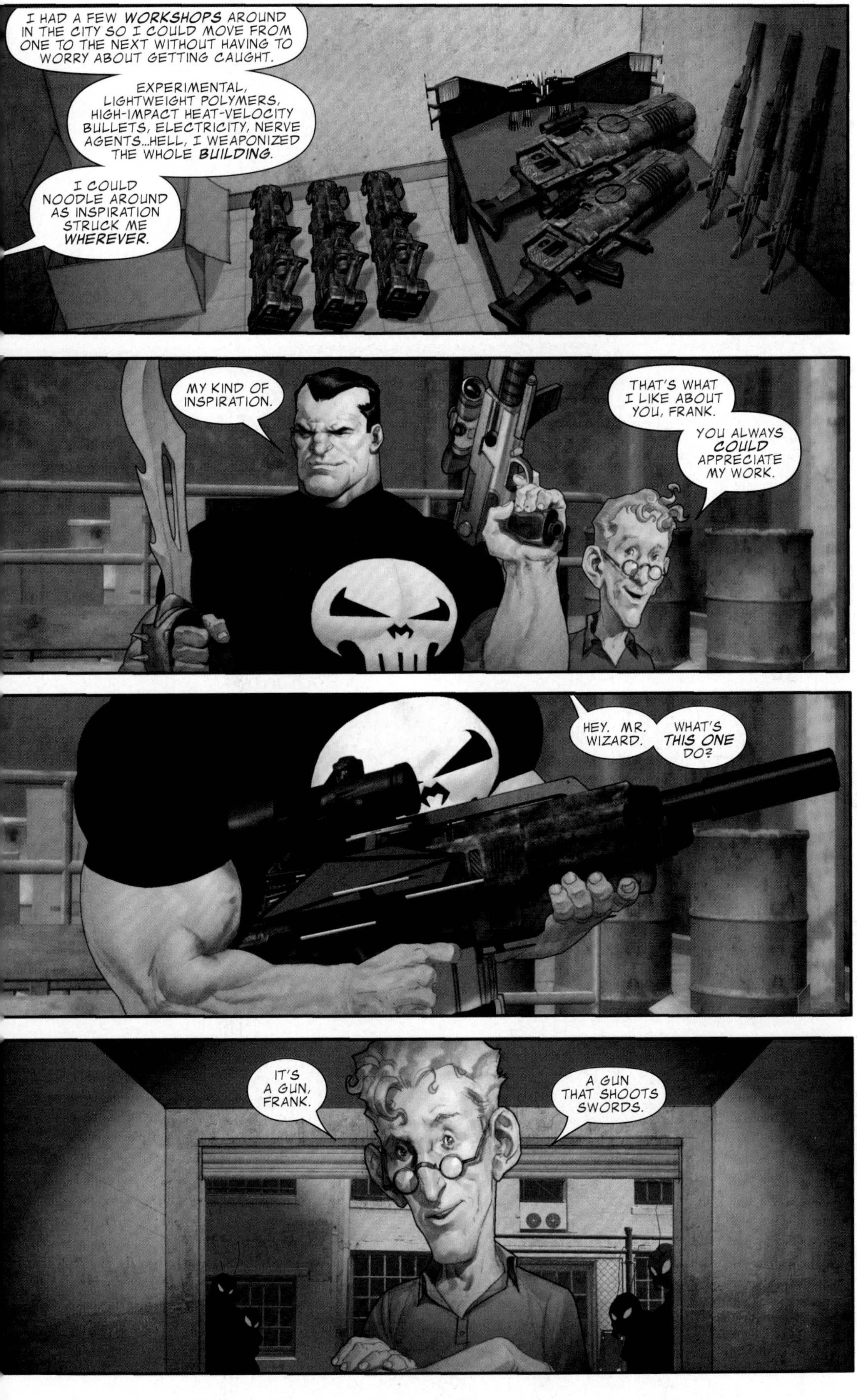
I HAD A FEW WORKSHOPS AROUND IN THE CITY SO I COULD MOVE FROM ONE TO THE NEXT WITHOUT HAVING TO WORRY ABOUT GETTING CAUGHT.
EXPERIMENTAL, LIGHTWEIGHT POLYMERS, HIGH-IMPACT HEAT-VELOCITY BULLETS, ELECTRICITY, NERVE AGENTS...HELL, I WEAPONIZED THE WHOLE BUILDING.
I COULD NOODLE AROUND AS INSPIRATION STRUCK ME WHEREVER.
MY KIND OF INSPIRATION.
THAT'S WHAT I LIKE ABOUT YOU, FRANK.
YOU ALWAYS COULD APPRECIATE MY WORK.
HEY. MR. WIZARD.
WHAT'S THIS ONE DO?
IT'S A GUN, FRANK.
A GUN THAT SHOOTS SWORDS.

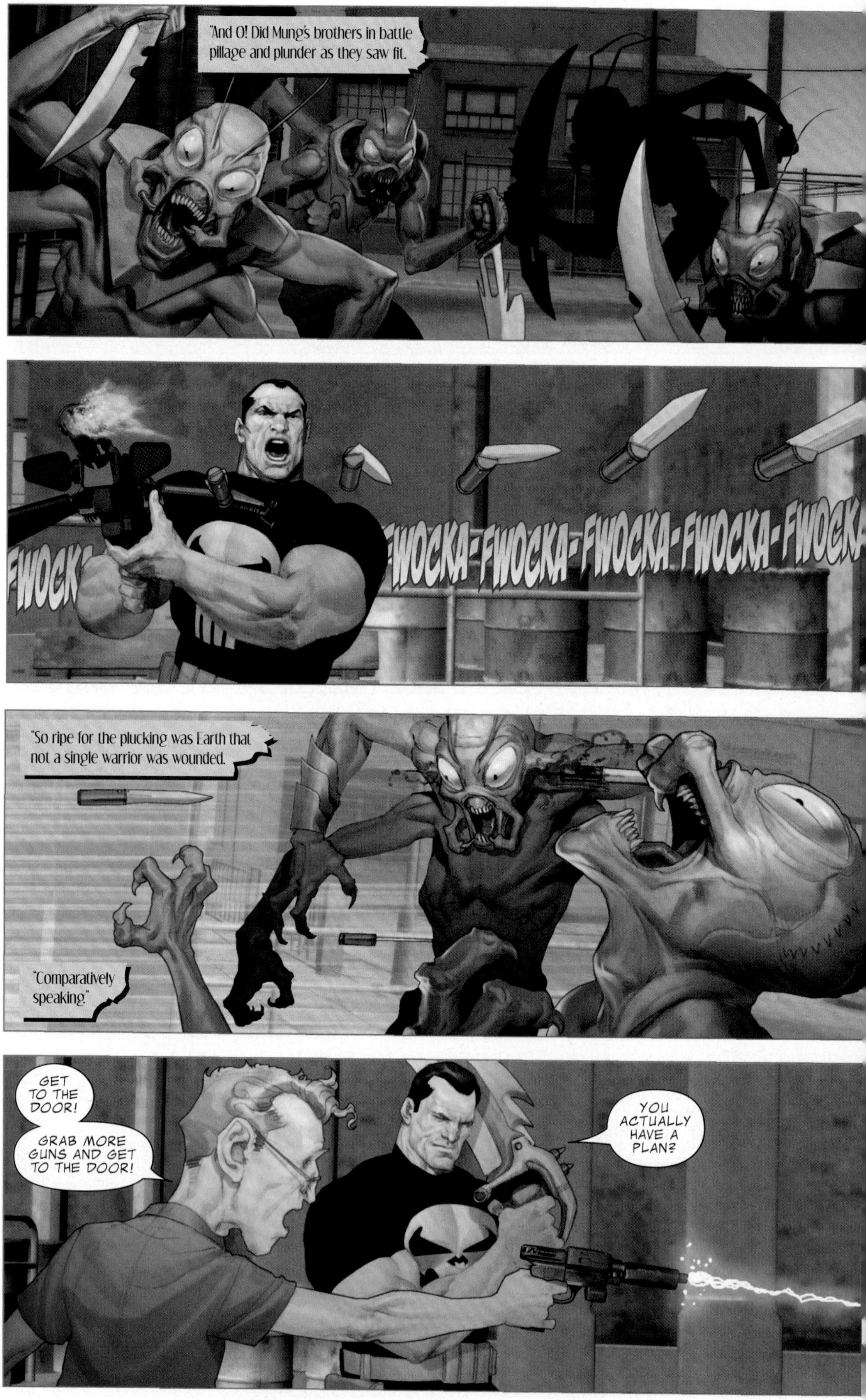
"And O! Did Mung's brothers in battle pillage and plunder as they saw fit.
FWOCKA-FWOCKA-FWOCKA-FWOCKA-FWOCKA-FWOCKA
"So ripe for the plucking was Earth that not a single warrior was wounded.
"Comparatively speaking."
GET TO THE DOOR!
GRAB MORE GUNS AND GET TO THE DOOR!
YOU ACTUALLY HAVE A PLAN?

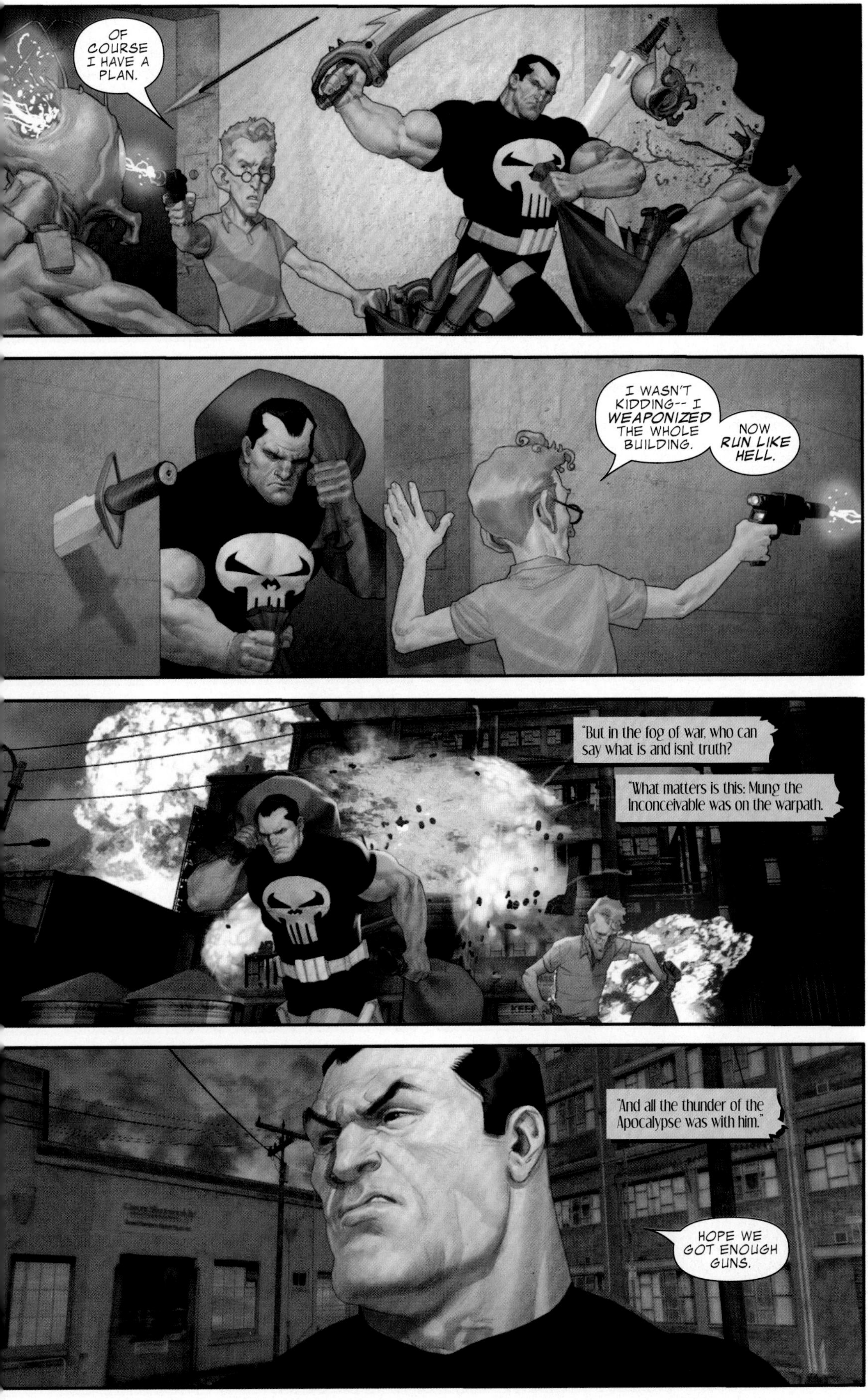
OF COURSE I HAVE A PLAN.
I WASN'T KIDDING-- I WEAPONIZED THE WHOLE BUILDING.
NOW RUN LIKE HELL.
"But in the fog of war, who can say what is and isn't truth?
"What matters is this: Mung the Inconceivable was on the warpath.
"And all the thunder of the Apocalypse was with him."
HOPE WE GOT ENOUGH GUNS.

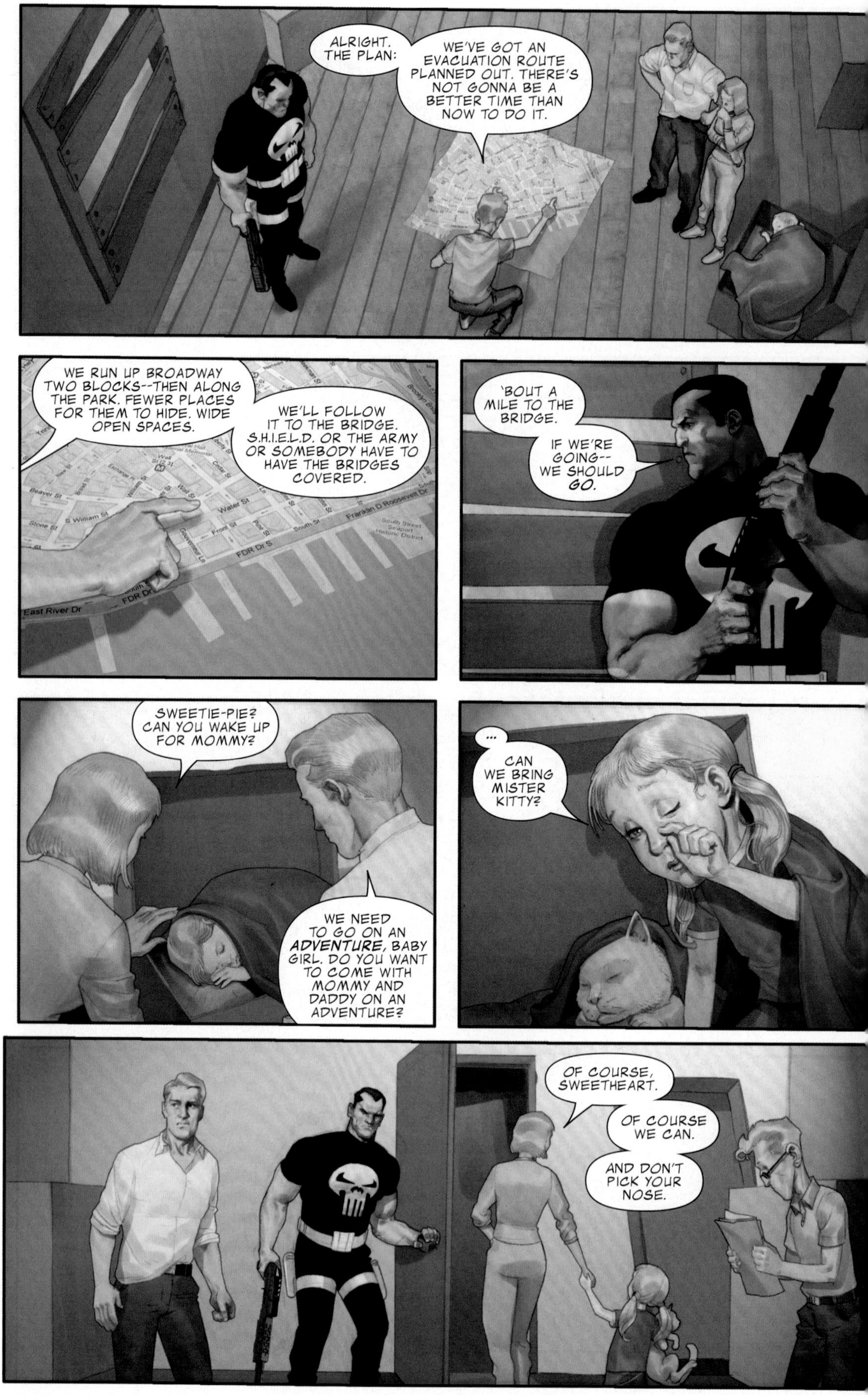
ALRIGHT. THE PLAN:
WE'VE GOT AN EVACUATION ROUTE PLANNED OUT. THERE'S NOT GONNA BE A BETTER TIME THAN NOW TO DO IT.
WE RUN UP BROADWAY TWO BLOCKS--THEN ALONG THE PARK. FEWER PLACES FOR THEM TO HIDE. WIDE OPEN SPACES.
WE'LL FOLLOW IT TO THE BRIDGE. S.H.I.E.L.D. OR THE ARMY OR SOMEBODY HAVE TO HAVE THE BRIDGES COVERED.
'BOUT A MILE TO THE BRIDGE.
IF WE'RE GOING-- WE SHOULD GO.
SWEETIE-PIE? CAN YOU WAKE UP FOR MOMMY?
WE NEED TO GO ON AN ADVENTURE, BABY GIRL. DO YOU WANT TO COME WITH MOMMY AND DADDY ON AN ADVENTURE?
...
CAN WE BRING MISTER KITTY?
OF COURSE, SWEETHEART.
OF COURSE WE CAN.
AND DON'T PICK YOUR NOSE.

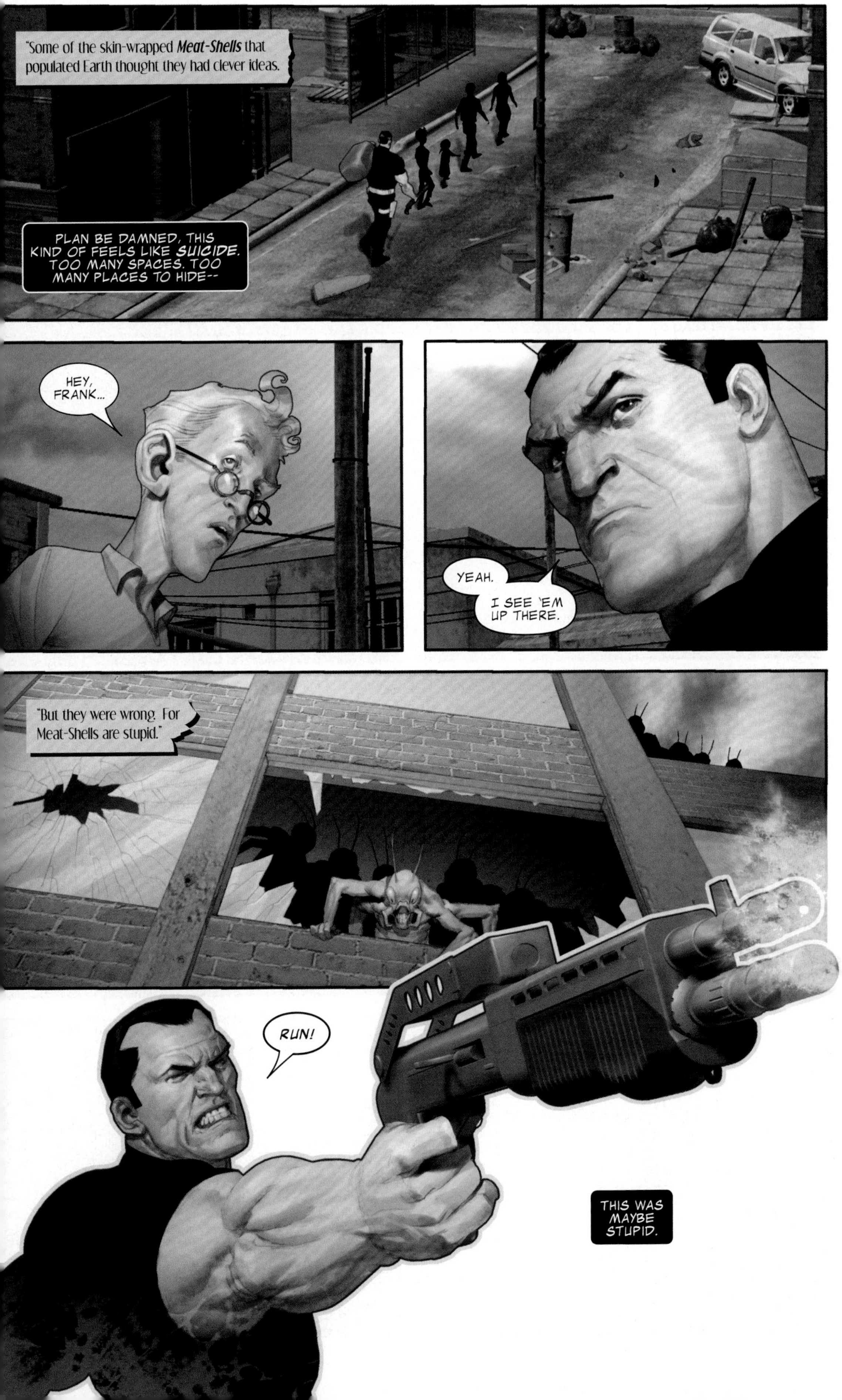
"Some of the skin-wrapped Meat-Shells that populated Earth thought they had clever ideas.
PLAN BE DAMNED, THIS KIND OF FEELS LIKE SUICIDE. TOO MANY SPACES. TOO MANY PLACES TO HIDE--
HEY, FRANK...
YEAH.
I SEE 'EM UP THERE.
"But they were wrong. For Meat-Shells are stupid."
RUN!
THIS WAS MAYBE STUPID.

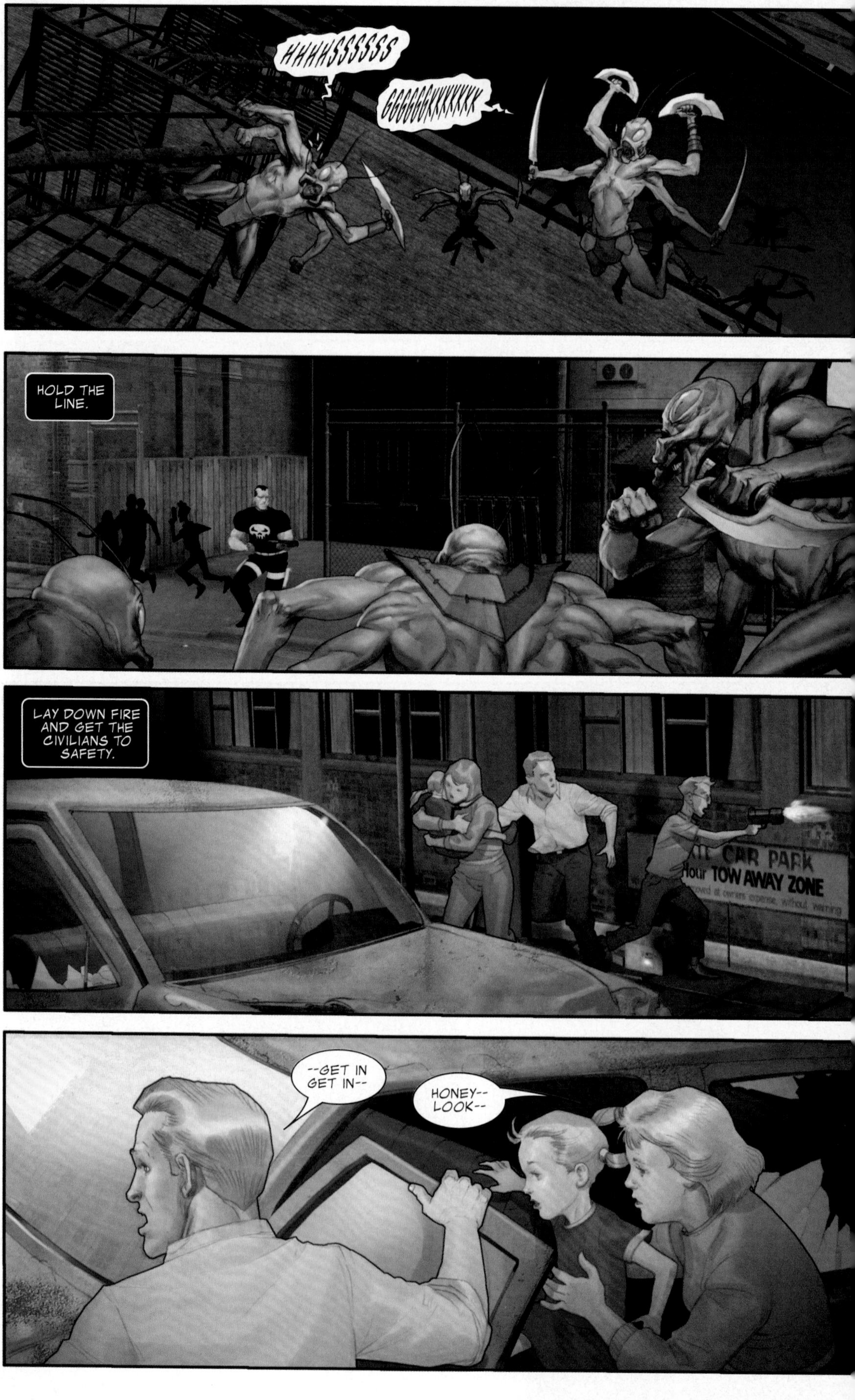
HHHHSSSSSSS
GGGGGKKKKKKK
HOLD THE LINE.
LAY DOWN FIRE AND GET THE CIVILIANS TO SAFETY.
CAR PARK
Hour TOW AWAY ZONE
--GET IN GET IN--
HONEY-- LOOK--

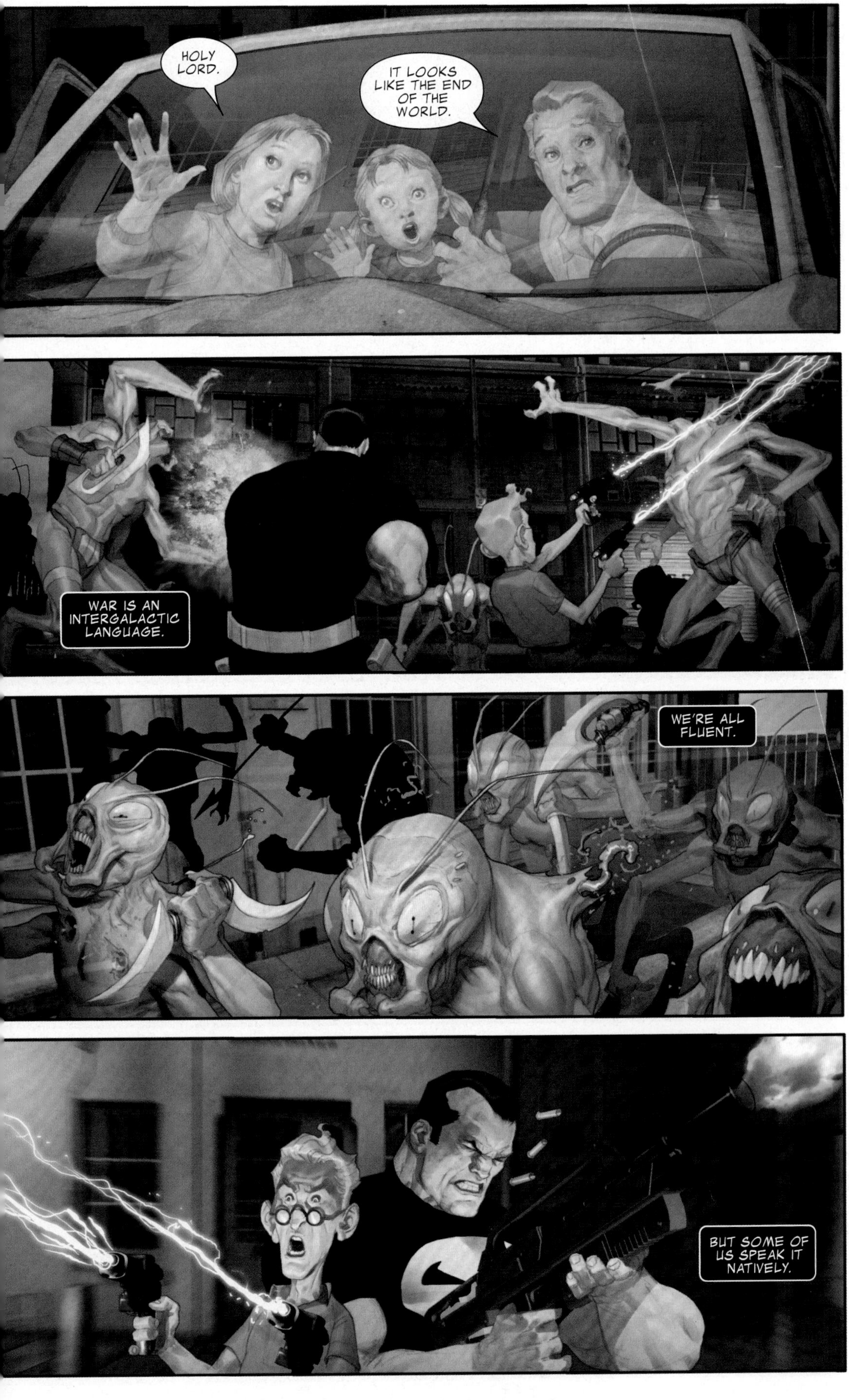
HOLY LORD.
IT LOOKS LIKE THE END OF THE WORLD.
WAR IS AN INTERGALACTIC LANGUAGE.
WE'RE ALL FLUENT.
BUT SOME OF US SPEAK IT NATIVELY.

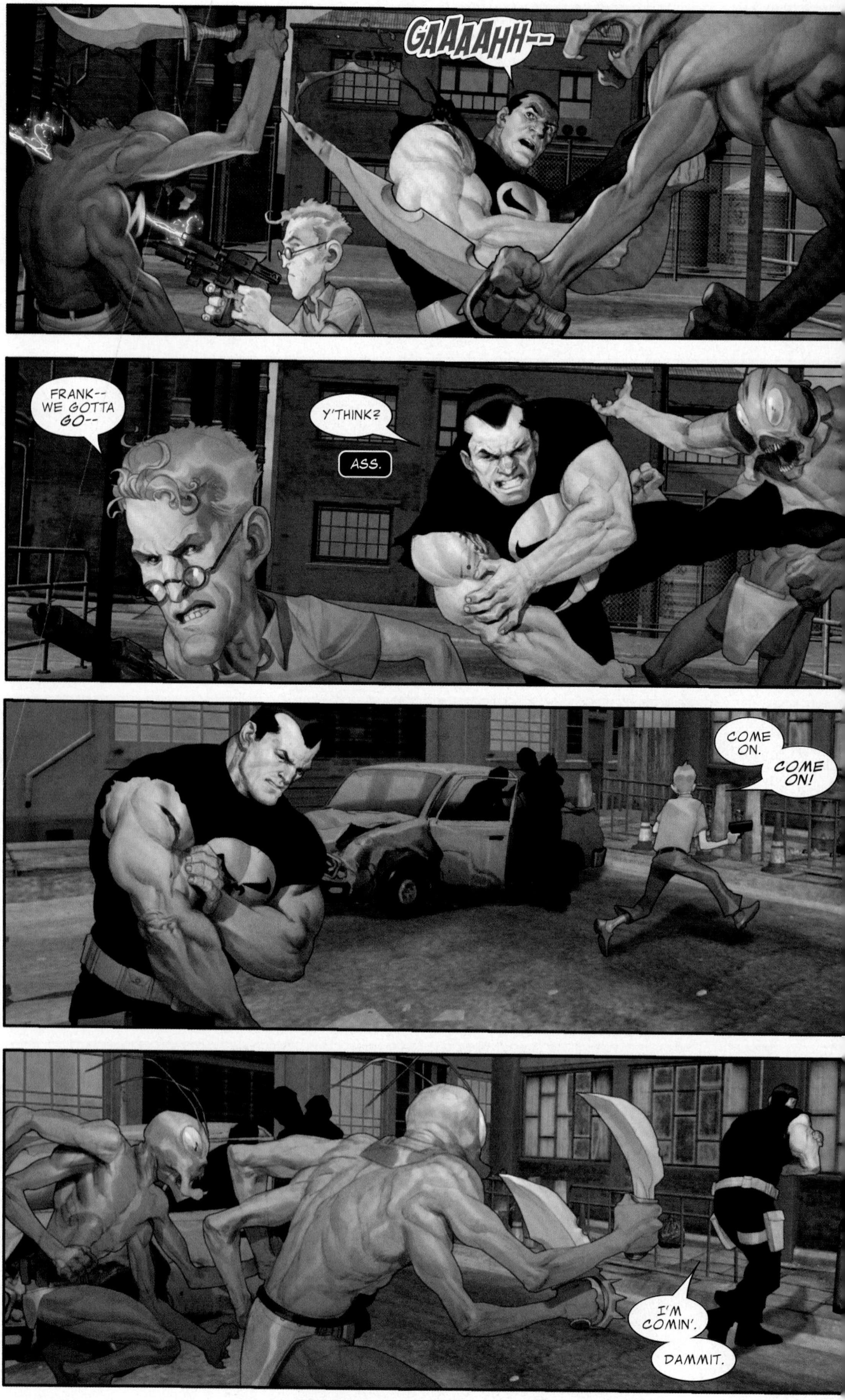
GAAAAHH--
FRANK-- WE GOTTA GO--
Y'THINK?
ASS.
COME ON.
COME ON!
I'M COMIN'.
DAMMIT.

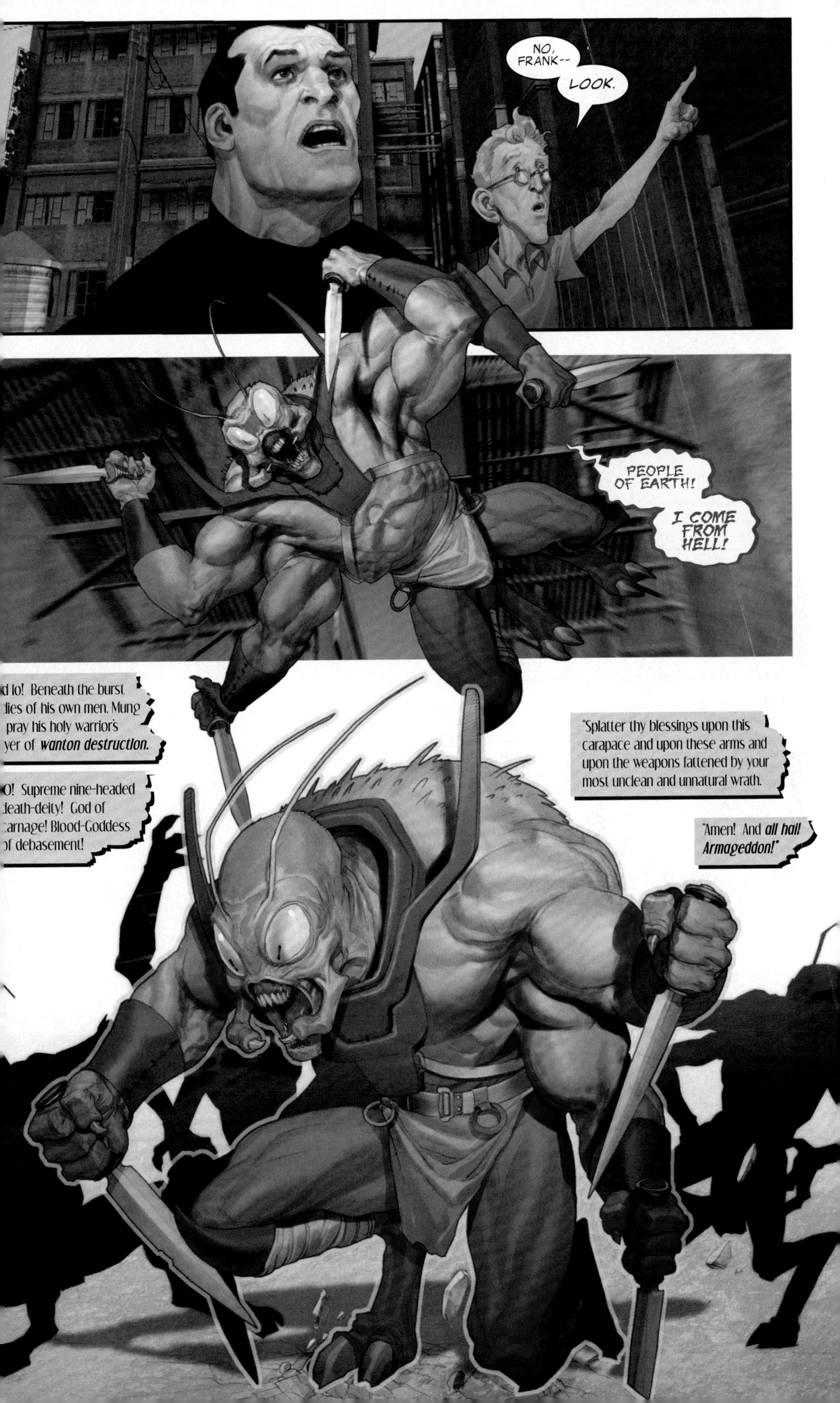

NO, FRANK--
LOOK.
PEOPLE OF EARTH!
I COME FROM HELL!
d lo! Beneath the burst dies of his own men, Mung pray his holy warrior's yer of *wanton destruction.*
O! Supreme nine-headed death-deity! God of carnage! Blood-Goddess of debasement!
"Splatter thy blessings upon this carapace and upon these arms and upon the weapons fattened by your most unclean and unnatural wrath.
"Amen! And *all hail Armageddon!*"

GOOD.

GOD.

I HAVE BEEN KNOWN... FROM TIME TO TIME...

...TO ANSWER TO THAT NAME, TOO. ALTHOUGH I AM A GOD FAR REMOVED FROM THE CONCEPT OF "GOOD."

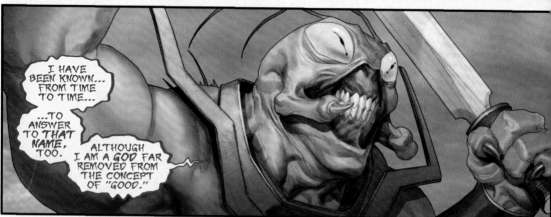

AIAAAAACCKKKKK!!!

WE DID THE ONLY SANE THINGS WE COULD.

WE PRAYED...

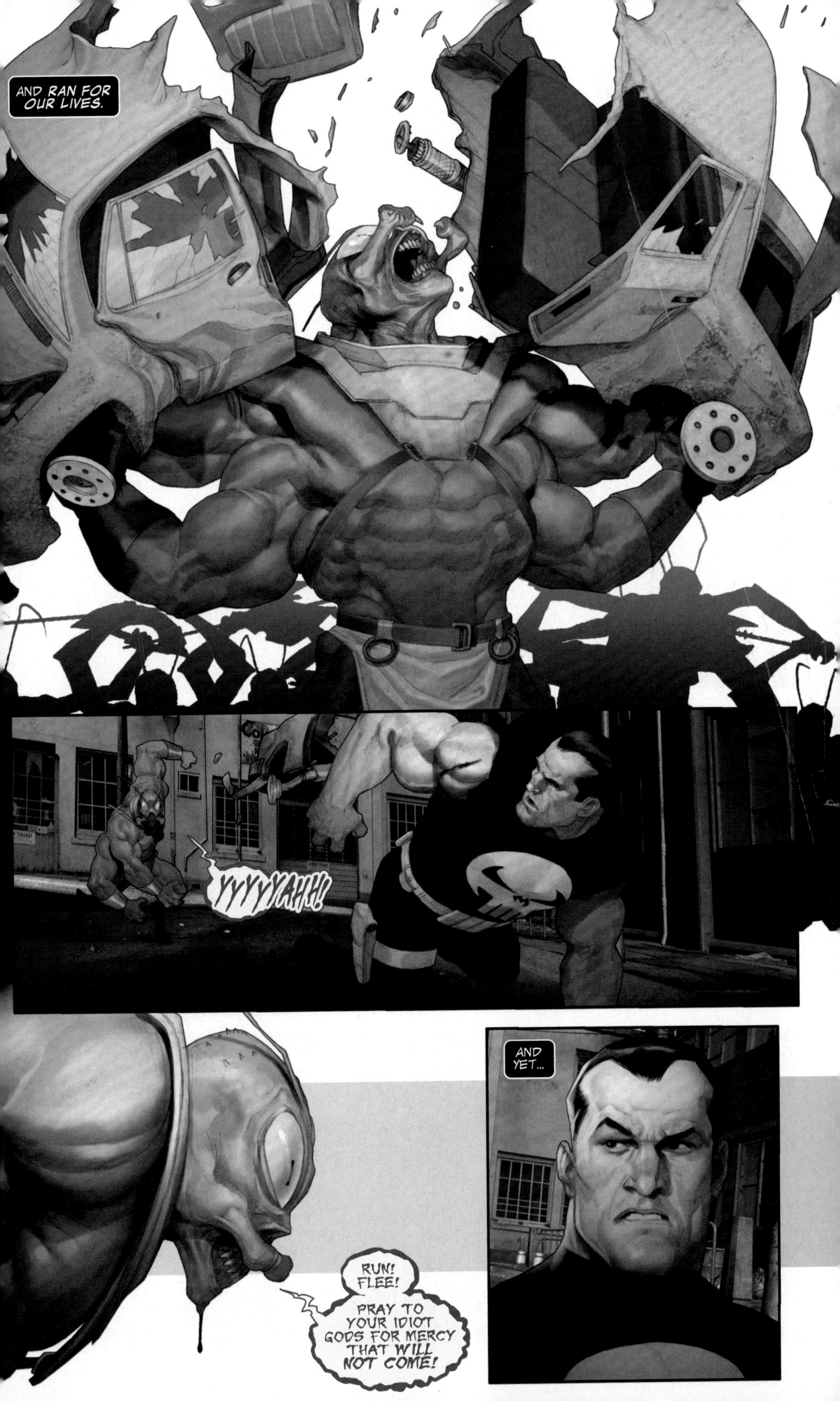
AND RAN FOR OUR LIVES.
YYYYYAHH!
AND YET...
RUN! FLEE!
PRAY TO YOUR IDIOT GODS FOR MERCY THAT WILL NOT COME!

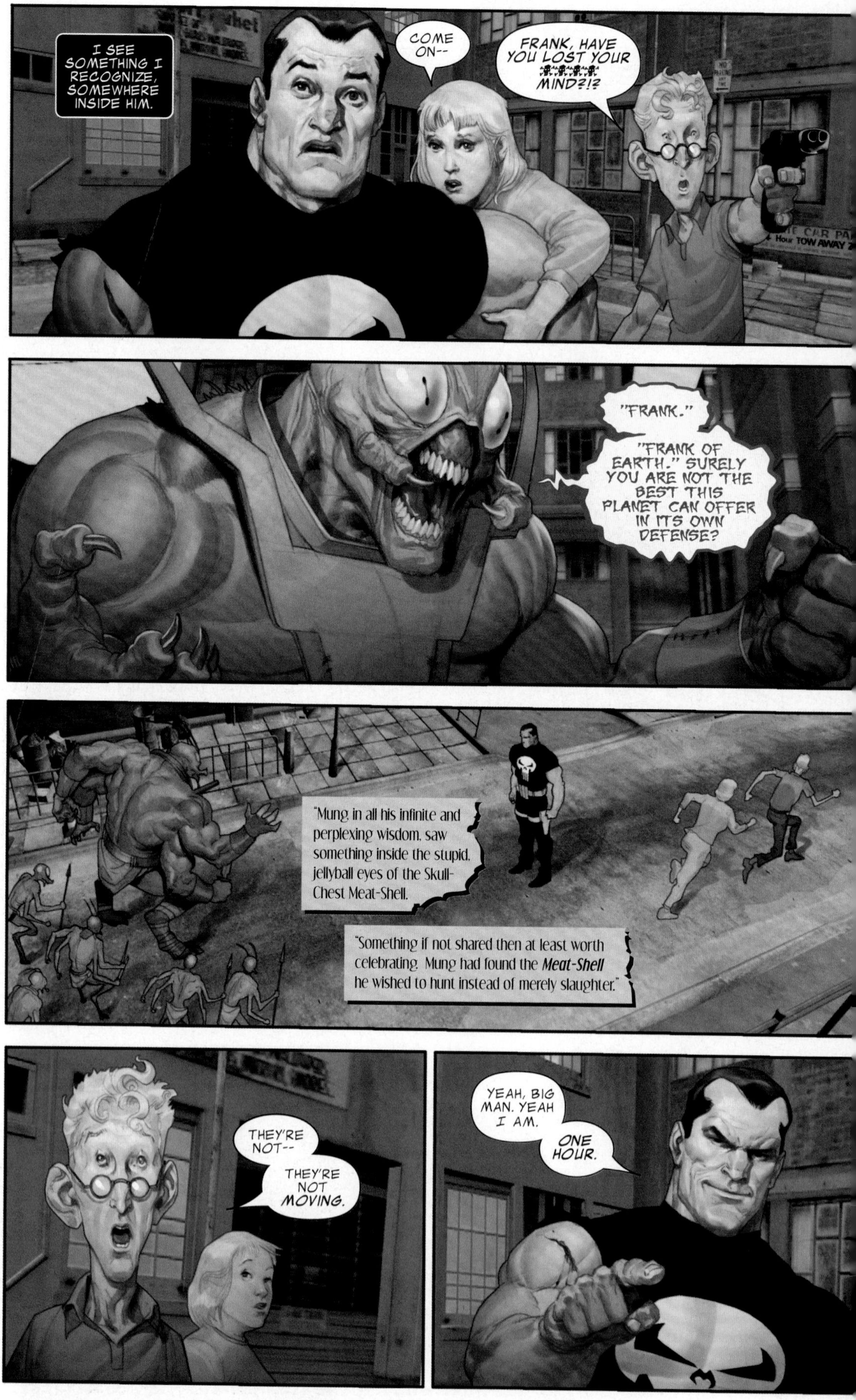
I SEE SOMETHING I RECOGNIZE, SOMEWHERE INSIDE HIM.
COME ON--
FRANK, HAVE YOU LOST YOUR MIND?!?
"FRANK."
"FRANK OF EARTH." SURELY YOU ARE NOT THE BEST THIS PLANET CAN OFFER IN ITS OWN DEFENSE?
"Mung in all his infinite and perplexing wisdom, saw something inside the stupid, jellyball eyes of the Skull-Chest Meat-Shell.
"Something if not shared then at least worth celebrating. Mung had found the *Meat-Shell* he wished to hunt instead of merely slaughter."
THEY'RE NOT--
THEY'RE NOT *MOVING.*
YEAH, BIG MAN. YEAH I AM.
ONE HOUR.

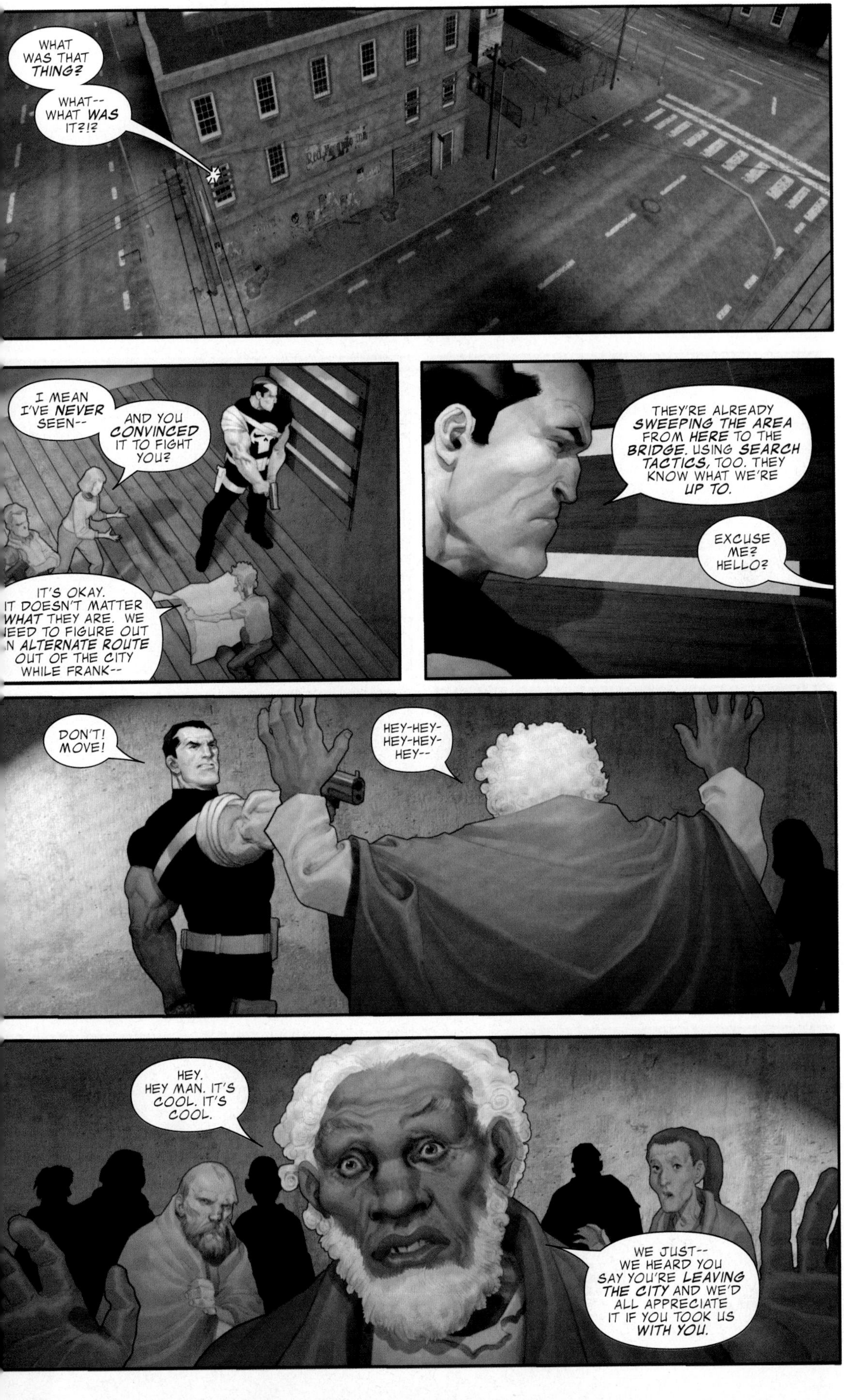
WHAT WAS THAT THING?
WHAT-- WHAT WAS IT?!?
I MEAN I'VE NEVER SEEN--
AND YOU CONVINCED IT TO FIGHT YOU?
IT'S OKAY. IT DOESN'T MATTER WHAT THEY ARE. WE NEED TO FIGURE OUT AN ALTERNATE ROUTE OUT OF THE CITY WHILE FRANK--
THEY'RE ALREADY SWEEPING THE AREA FROM HERE TO THE BRIDGE. USING SEARCH TACTICS, TOO. THEY KNOW WHAT WE'RE UP TO.
EXCUSE ME? HELLO?
DON'T! MOVE!
HEY-HEY-HEY-HEY-HEY--
HEY. HEY MAN. IT'S COOL. IT'S COOL.
WE JUST-- WE HEARD YOU SAY YOU'RE LEAVING THE CITY AND WE'D ALL APPRECIATE IT IF YOU TOOK US WITH YOU.

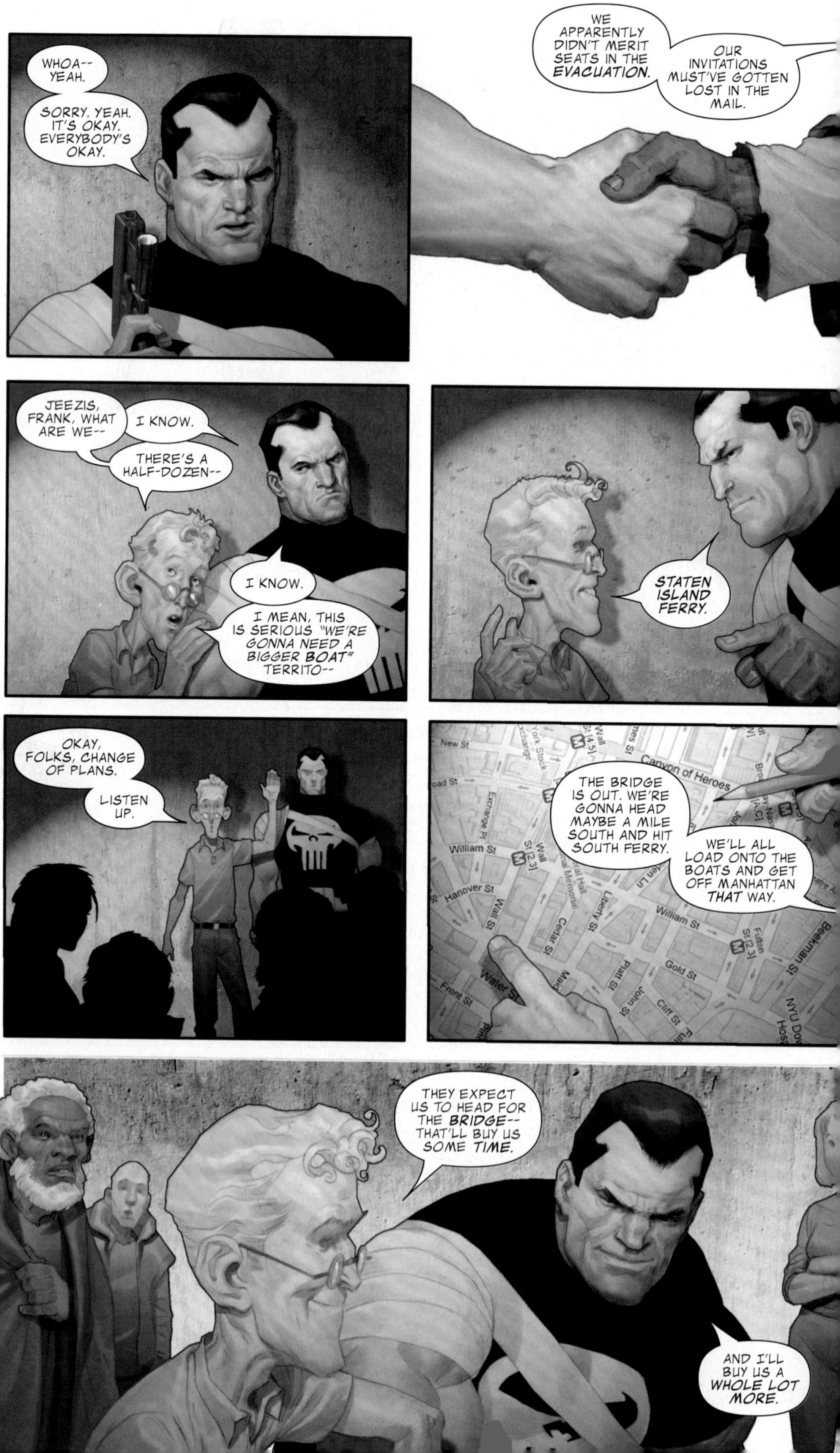
WHOA-- YEAH.
SORRY. YEAH. IT'S OKAY. EVERYBODY'S OKAY.
WE APPARENTLY DIDN'T MERIT SEATS IN THE EVACUATION.
OUR INVITATIONS MUST'VE GOTTEN LOST IN THE MAIL.
JEEZIS, FRANK, WHAT ARE WE--
I KNOW.
THERE'S A HALF-DOZEN--
I KNOW.
I MEAN, THIS IS SERIOUS "WE'RE GONNA NEED A BIGGER BOAT" TERRITO--
STATEN ISLAND FERRY.
OKAY, FOLKS, CHANGE OF PLANS.
LISTEN UP.
THE BRIDGE IS OUT. WE'RE GONNA HEAD MAYBE A MILE SOUTH AND HIT SOUTH FERRY.
WE'LL ALL LOAD ONTO THE BOATS AND GET OFF MANHATTAN THAT WAY.
New St
Canyon of Heroes
Exchange Pl
William St
Hanover St
Liberty St
Cedar St
William St
Gold St
Platt St
John St
Cliff St
Water St
Front St
Beekman St
THEY EXPECT US TO HEAD FOR THE BRIDGE-- THAT'LL BUY US SOME TIME.
AND I'LL BUY US A WHOLE LOT MORE.

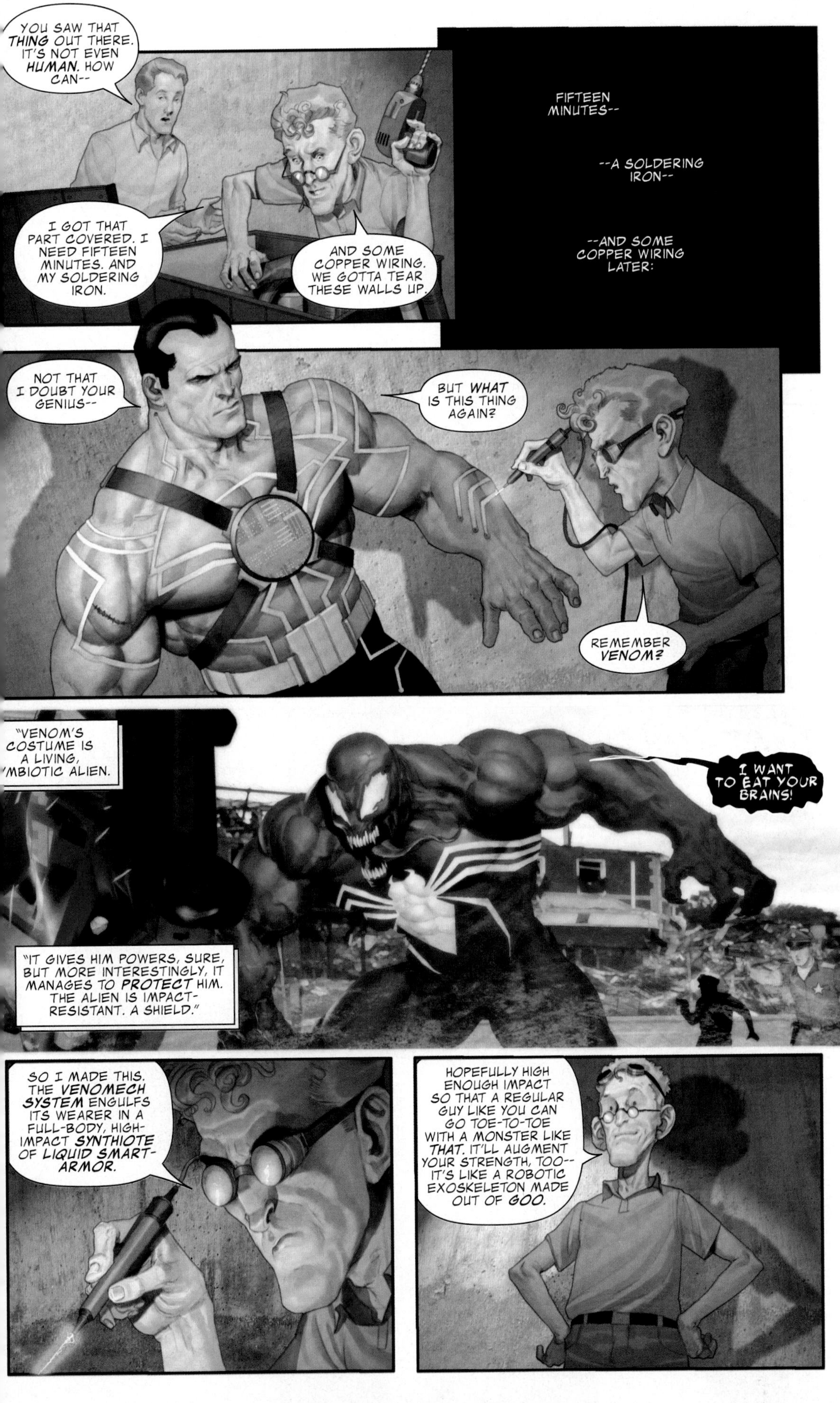
YOU SAW THAT THING OUT THERE. IT'S NOT EVEN HUMAN. HOW CAN--
I GOT THAT PART COVERED. I NEED FIFTEEN MINUTES. AND MY SOLDERING IRON.
AND SOME COPPER WIRING. WE GOTTA TEAR THESE WALLS UP.
FIFTEEN MINUTES--
--A SOLDERING IRON--
--AND SOME COPPER WIRING LATER:
NOT THAT I DOUBT YOUR GENIUS--
BUT WHAT IS THIS THING AGAIN?
REMEMBER VENOM?
"VENOM'S COSTUME IS A LIVING, YMBIOTIC ALIEN.
I WANT TO EAT YOUR BRAINS!
"IT GIVES HIM POWERS, SURE, BUT MORE INTERESTINGLY, IT MANAGES TO PROTECT HIM. THE ALIEN IS IMPACT-RESISTANT. A SHIELD."
SO I MADE THIS. THE VENOMECH SYSTEM ENGULFS ITS WEARER IN A FULL-BODY, HIGH-IMPACT SYNTHIOTE OF LIQUID SMART-ARMOR.
HOPEFULLY HIGH ENOUGH IMPACT SO THAT A REGULAR GUY LIKE YOU CAN GO TOE-TO-TOE WITH A MONSTER LIKE THAT. IT'LL AUGMENT YOUR STRENGTH, TOO-- IT'S LIKE A ROBOTIC EXOSKELETON MADE OUT OF GOO.

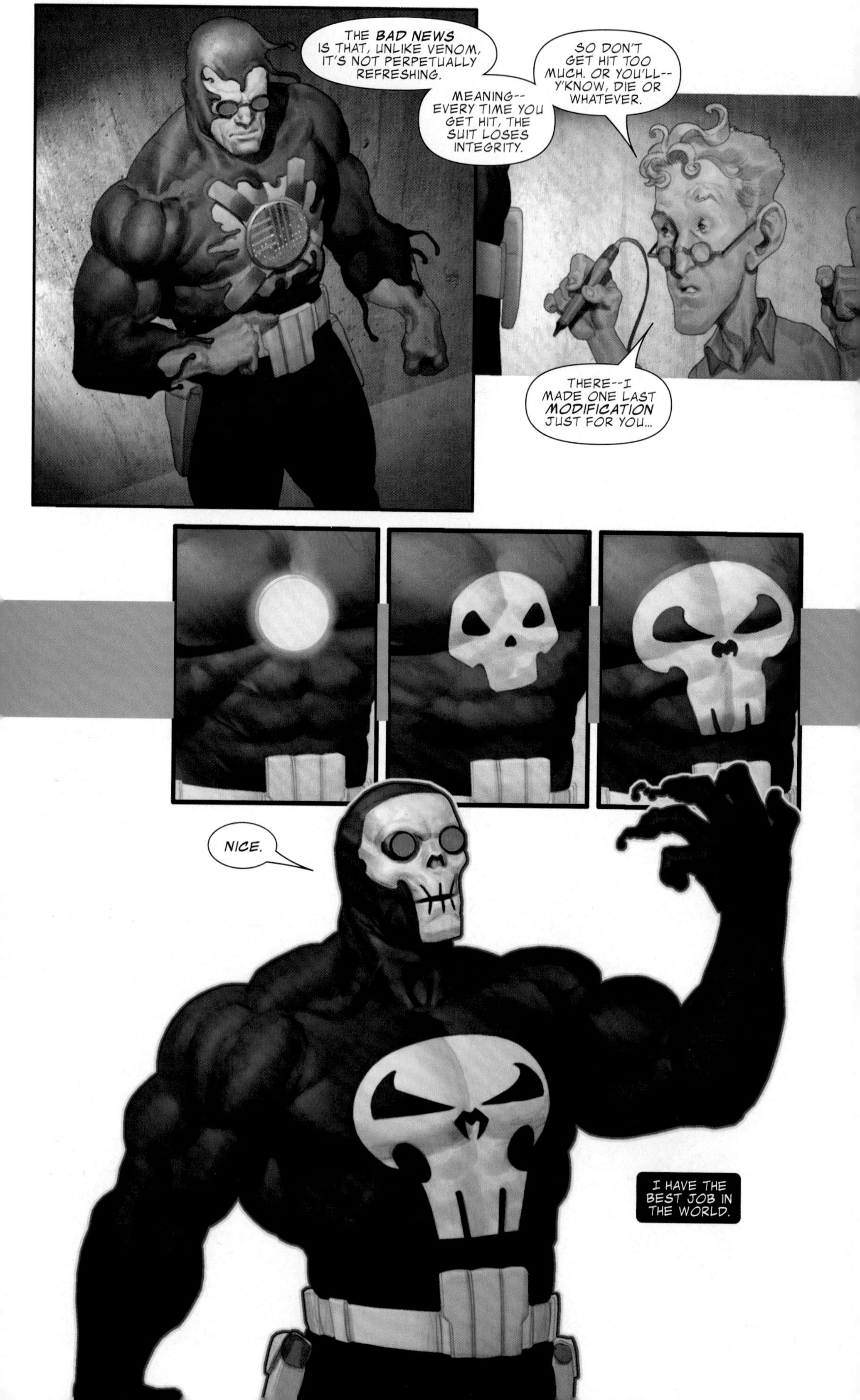
THE BAD NEWS IS THAT, UNLIKE VENOM, IT'S NOT PERPETUALLY REFRESHING.
MEANING-- EVERY TIME YOU GET HIT, THE SUIT LOSES INTEGRITY.
SO DON'T GET HIT TOO MUCH. OR YOU'LL-- Y'KNOW, DIE OR WHATEVER.
THERE--I MADE ONE LAST MODIFICATION JUST FOR YOU...
NICE.
I HAVE THE BEST JOB IN THE WORLD.

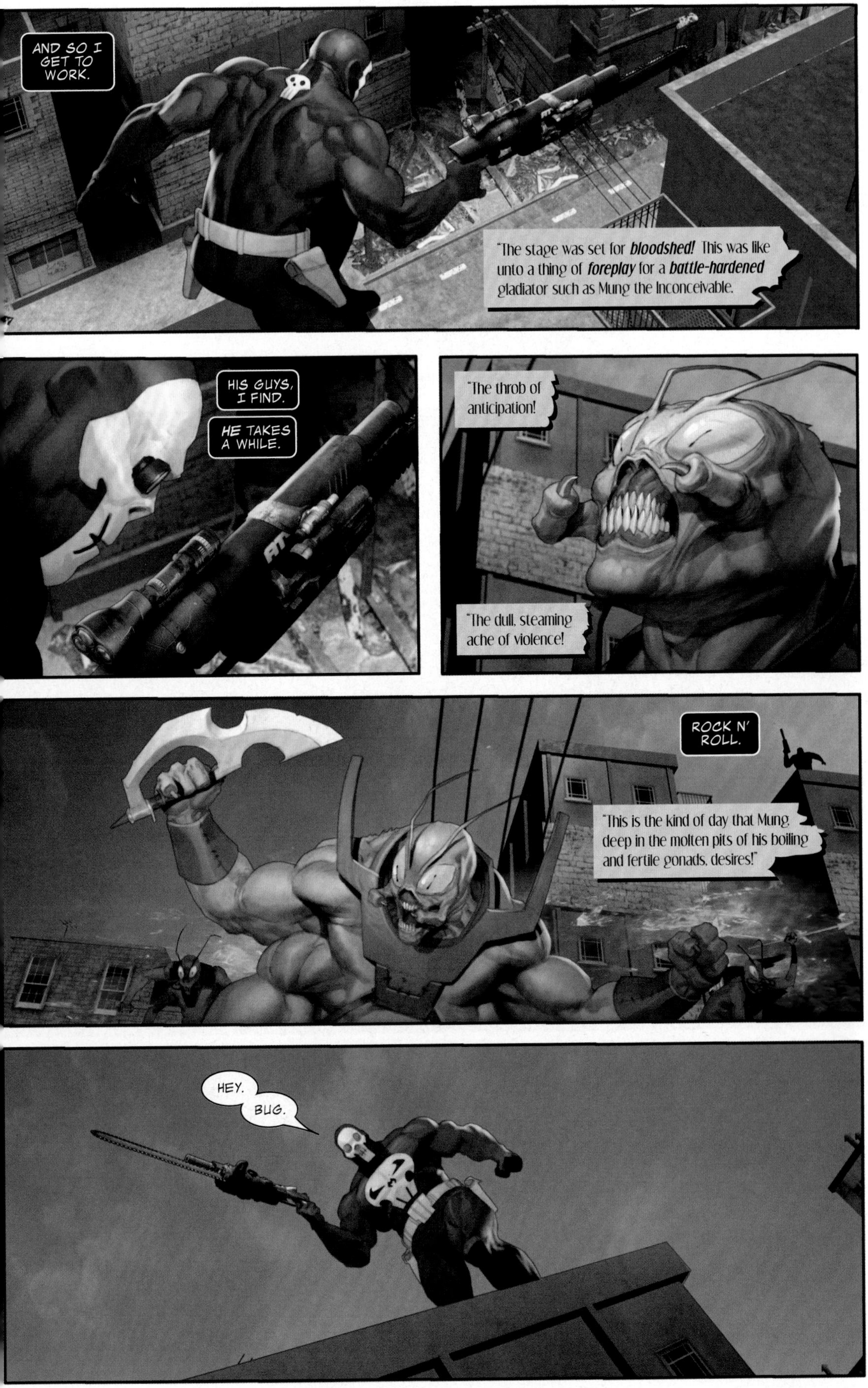
AND SO I GET TO WORK.
"The stage was set for bloodshed! This was like unto a thing of foreplay for a battle-hardened gladiator such as Mung the Inconceivable.
HIS GUYS, I FIND.
HE TAKES A WHILE.
"The throb of anticipation!
"The dull, steaming ache of violence!
ROCK N' ROLL.
"This is the kind of day that Mung, deep in the molten pits of his boiling and fertile gonads, desires!"
HEY.
BUG.

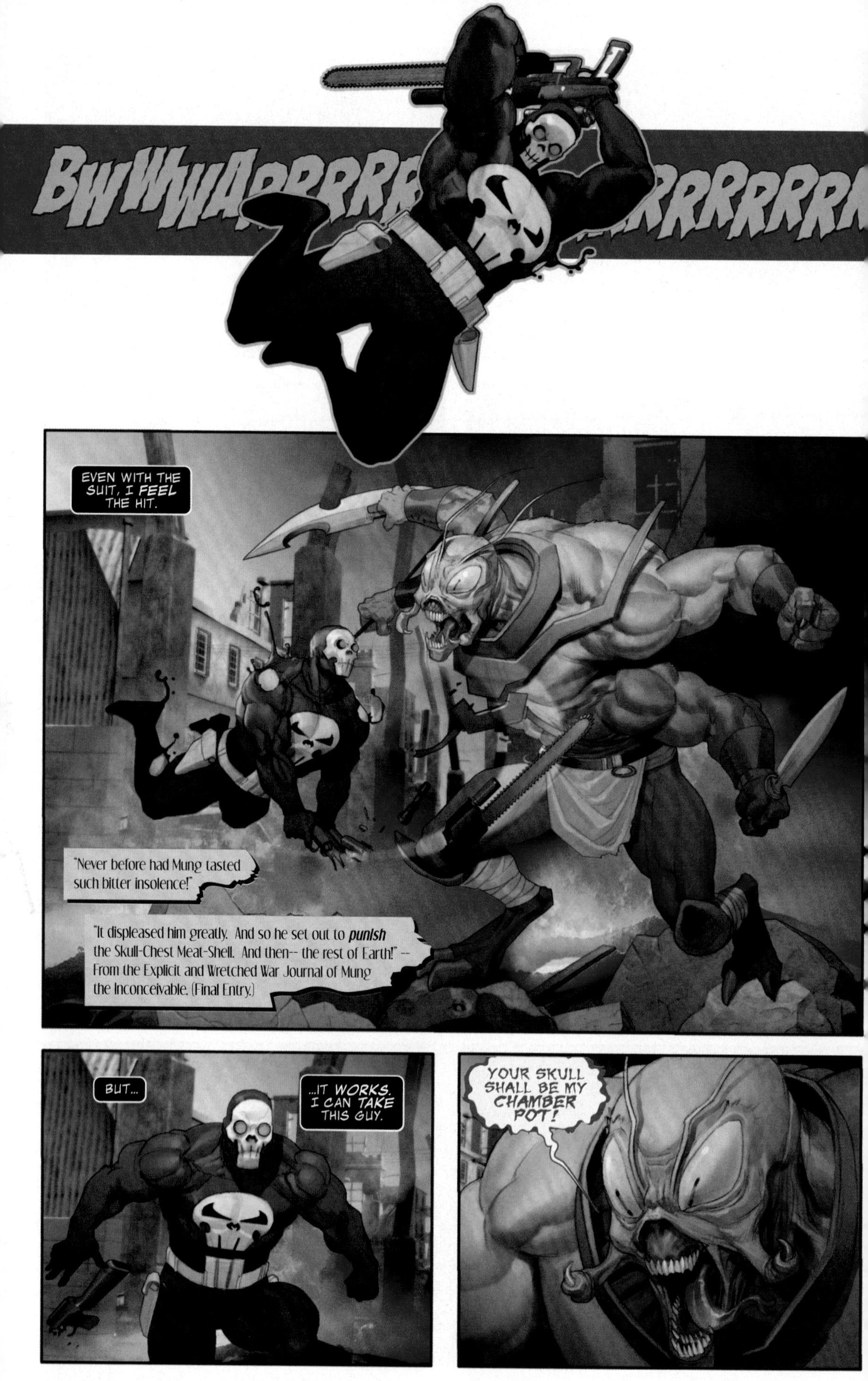

BWWWARRRR
RRRRRRR
EVEN WITH THE SUIT, I FEEL THE HIT.
"Never before had Mung tasted such bitter insolence!"
"It displeased him greatly. And so he set out to punish the Skull-Chest Meat-Shell. And then-- the rest of Earth!" --From the Explicit and Wretched War Journal of Mung the Inconceivable. (Final Entry.)
BUT...
...IT WORKS. I CAN TAKE THIS GUY.
YOUR SKULL SHALL BE MY CHAMBER POT!

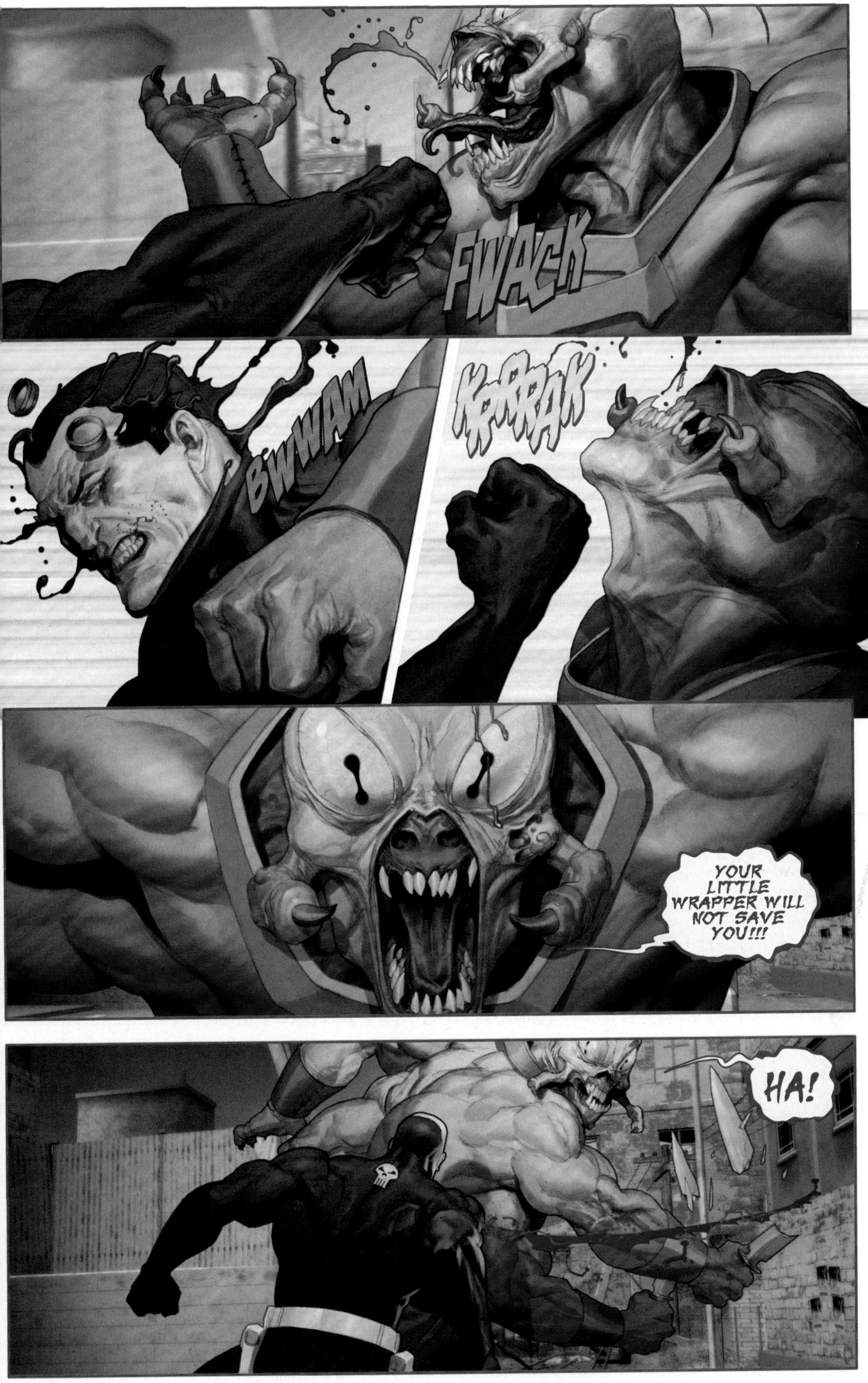
FWACK
BWWAM
KRRAK
YOUR LITTLE WRAPPER WILL NOT SAVE YOU!!!
HA!

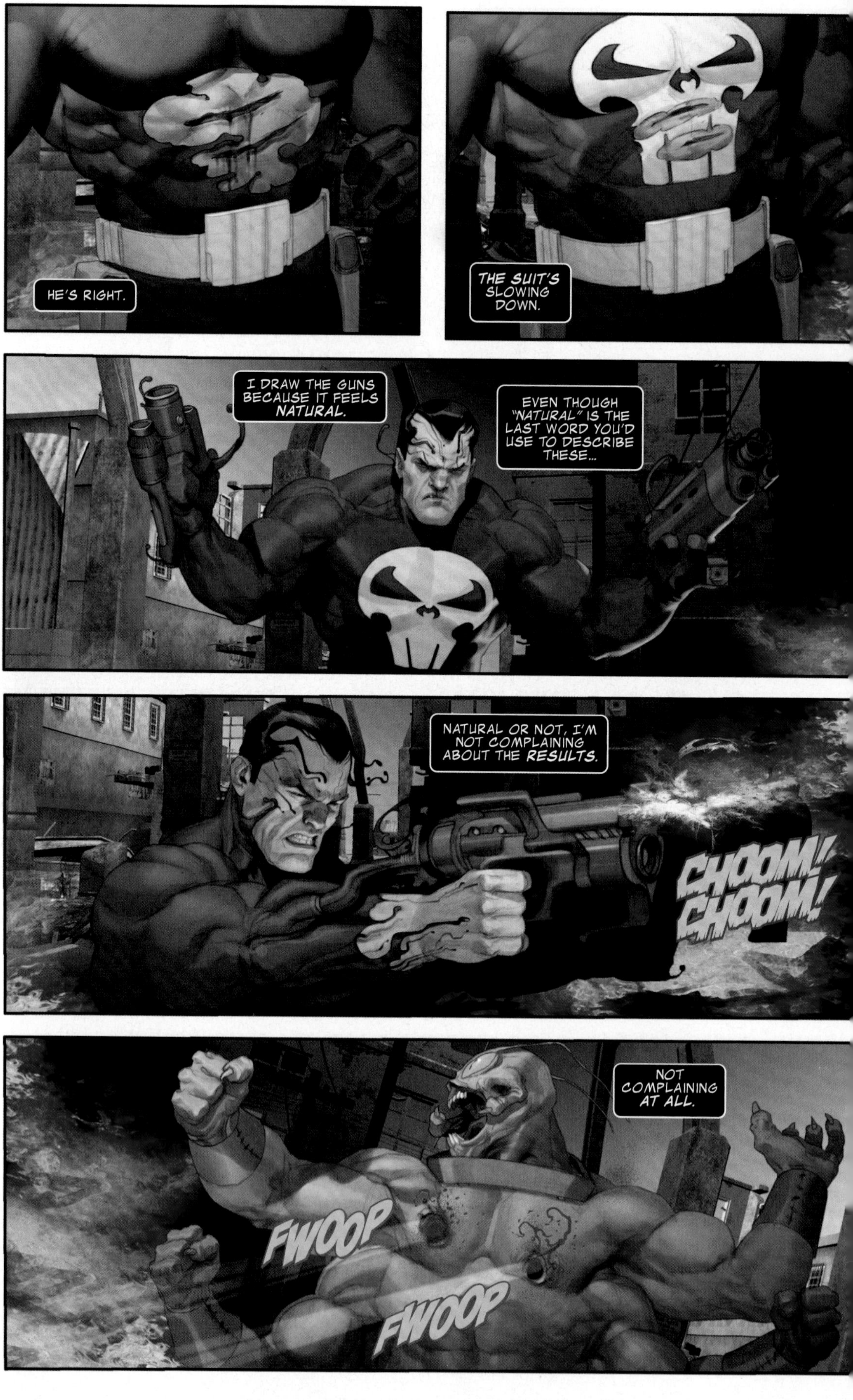
HE'S RIGHT.
THE SUIT'S SLOWING DOWN.
I DRAW THE GUNS BECAUSE IT FEELS NATURAL.
EVEN THOUGH "NATURAL" IS THE LAST WORD YOU'D USE TO DESCRIBE THESE...
NATURAL OR NOT, I'M NOT COMPLAINING ABOUT THE RESULTS.
CHOOM! CHOOM!
NOT COMPLAINING AT ALL.
FWOOP
FWOOP

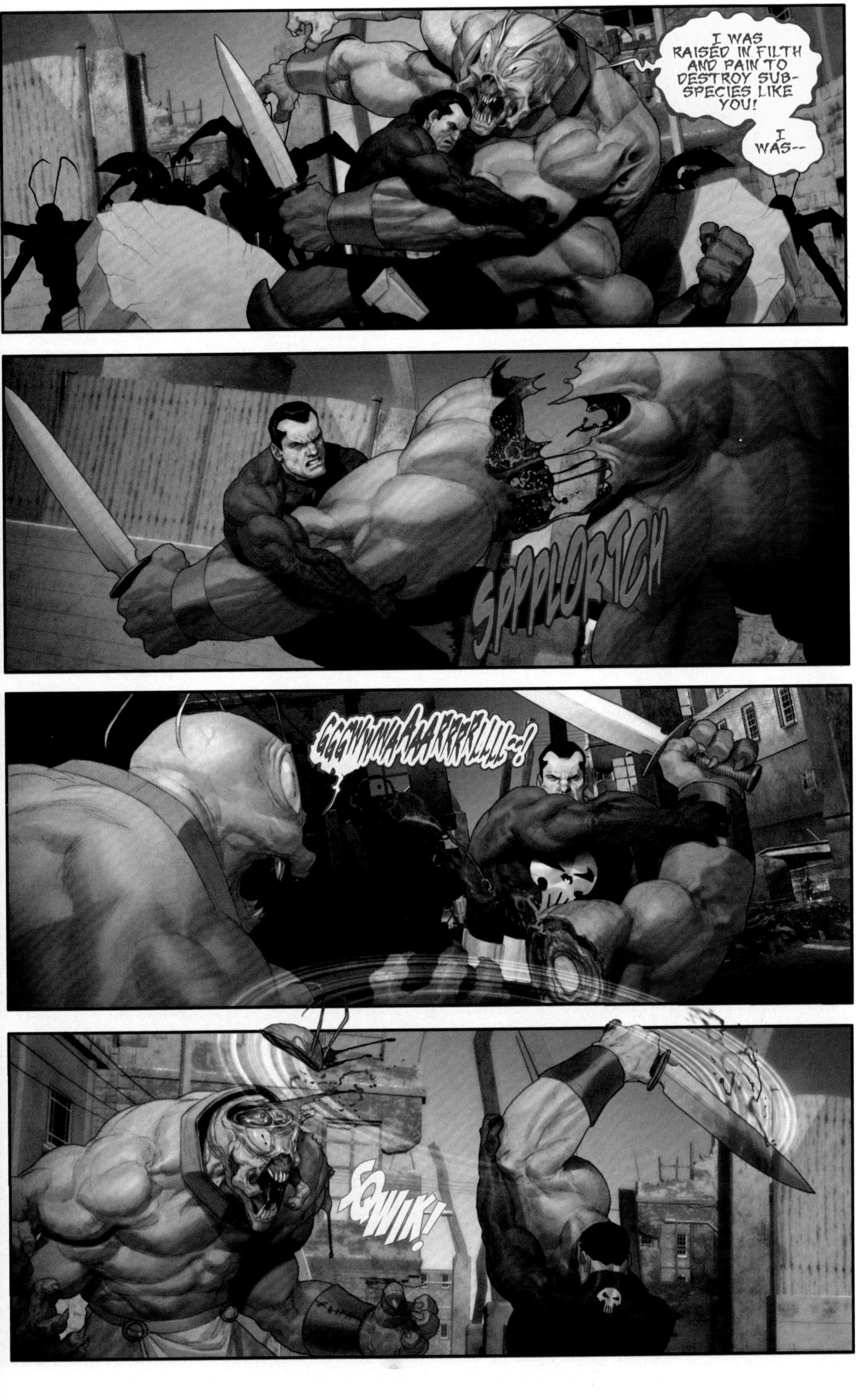
I WAS RAISED IN FILTH AND PAIN TO DESTROY SUB-SPECIES LIKE YOU!
I WAS--
SPPPLORTCH
GGGWWWAAARRRRLLLL--!
SQWIK!

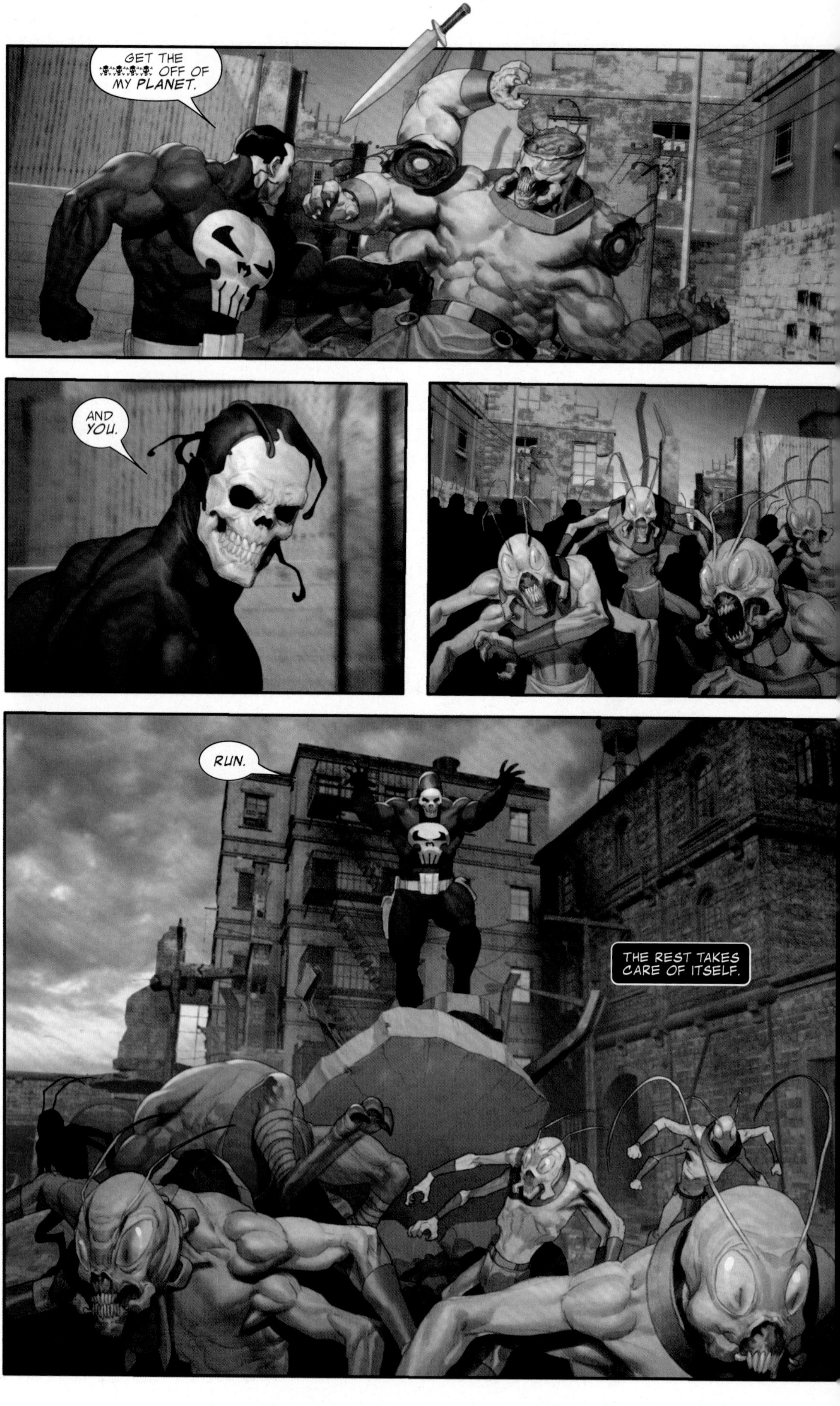
GET THE ☠☠☠☠ OFF OF MY PLANET.
AND YOU.
RUN.
THE REST TAKES CARE OF ITSELF.

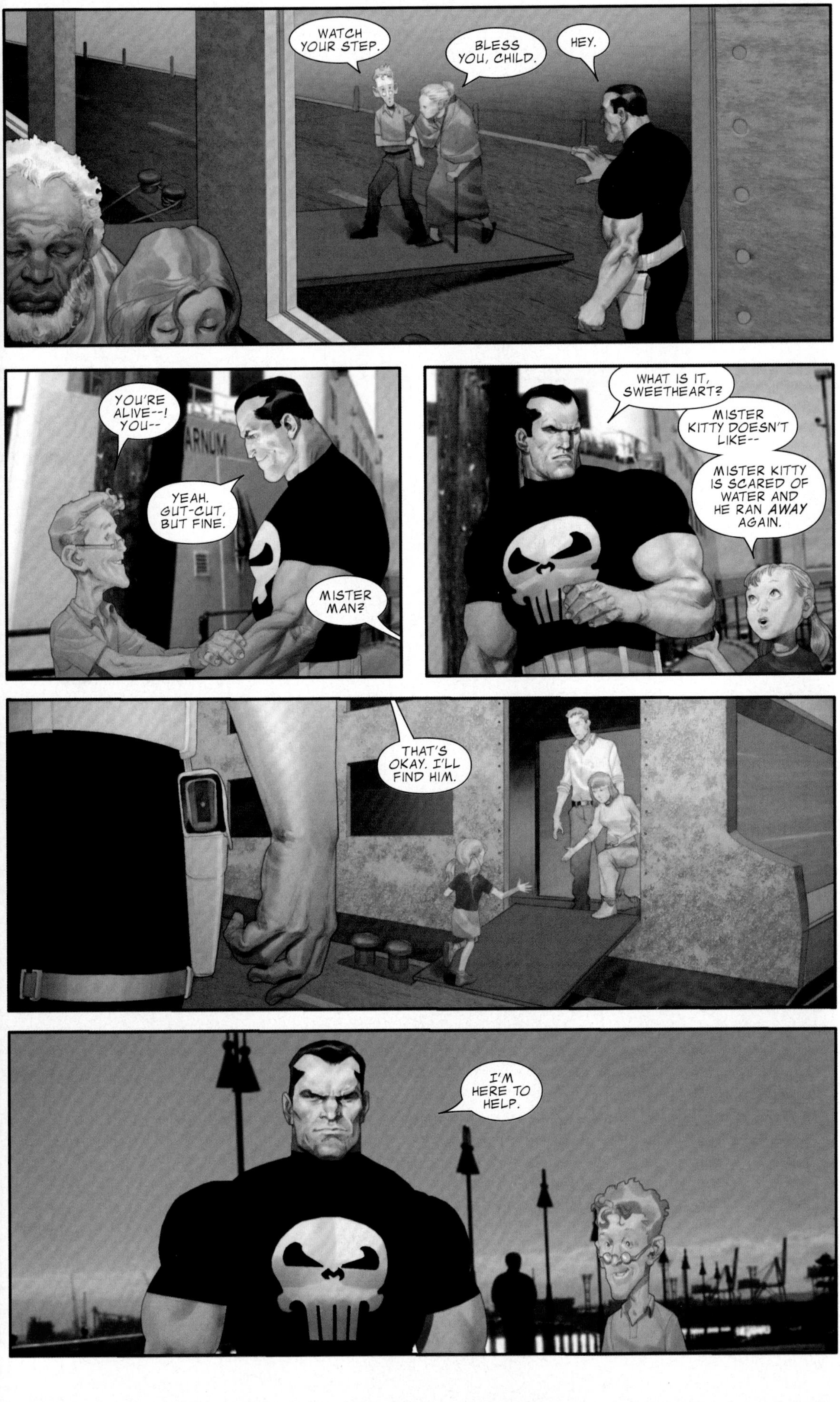
WATCH YOUR STEP.
BLESS YOU, CHILD.
HEY.
YOU'RE ALIVE--! YOU--
ARNUM
YEAH. GUT-CUT, BUT FINE.
MISTER MAN?
WHAT IS IT, SWEETHEART?
MISTER KITTY DOESN'T LIKE--
MISTER KITTY IS SCARED OF WATER AND HE RAN *AWAY* AGAIN.
THAT'S OKAY. I'LL FIND HIM.
I'M HERE TO HELP.

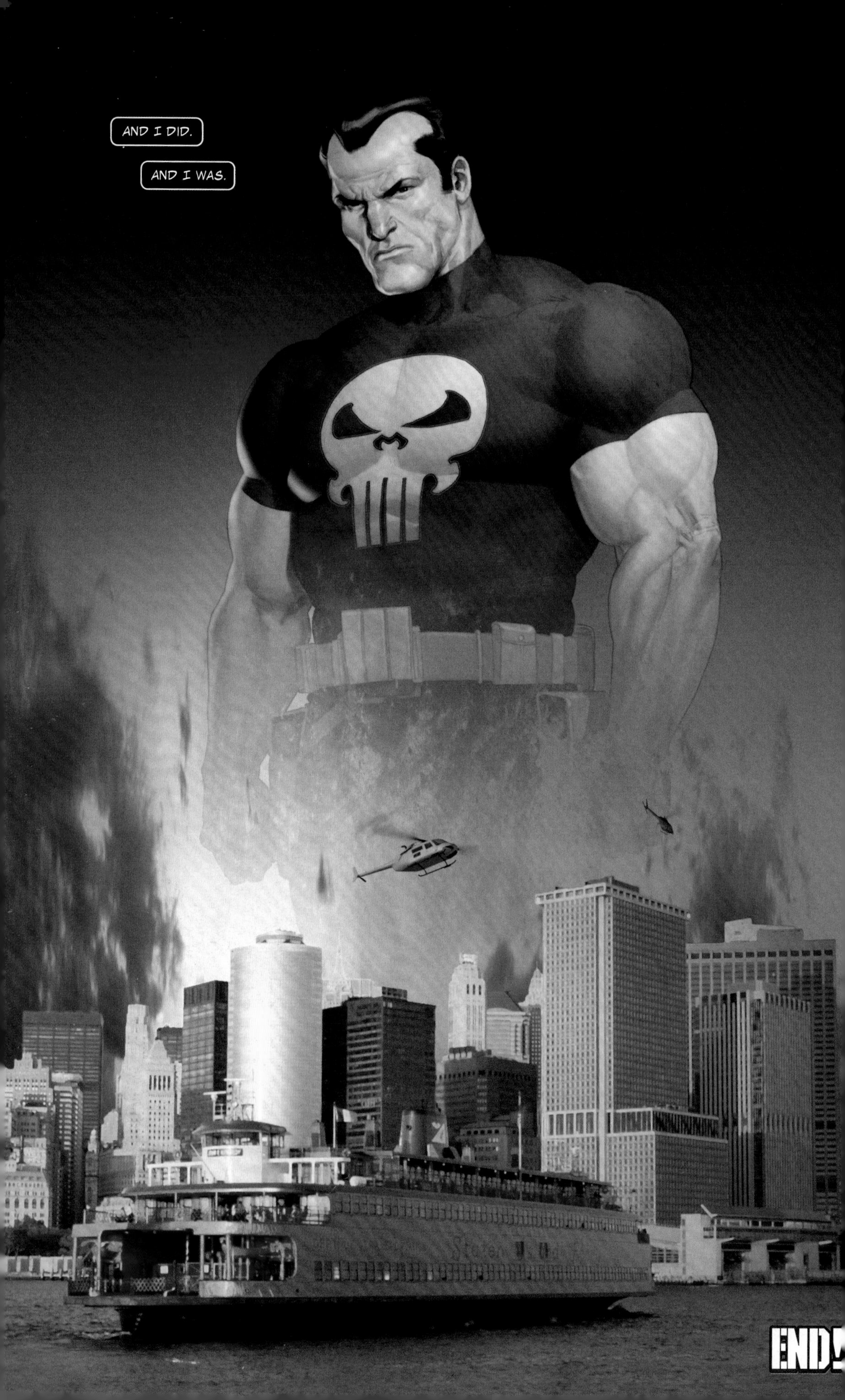
AND I DID.
AND I WAS.
END!

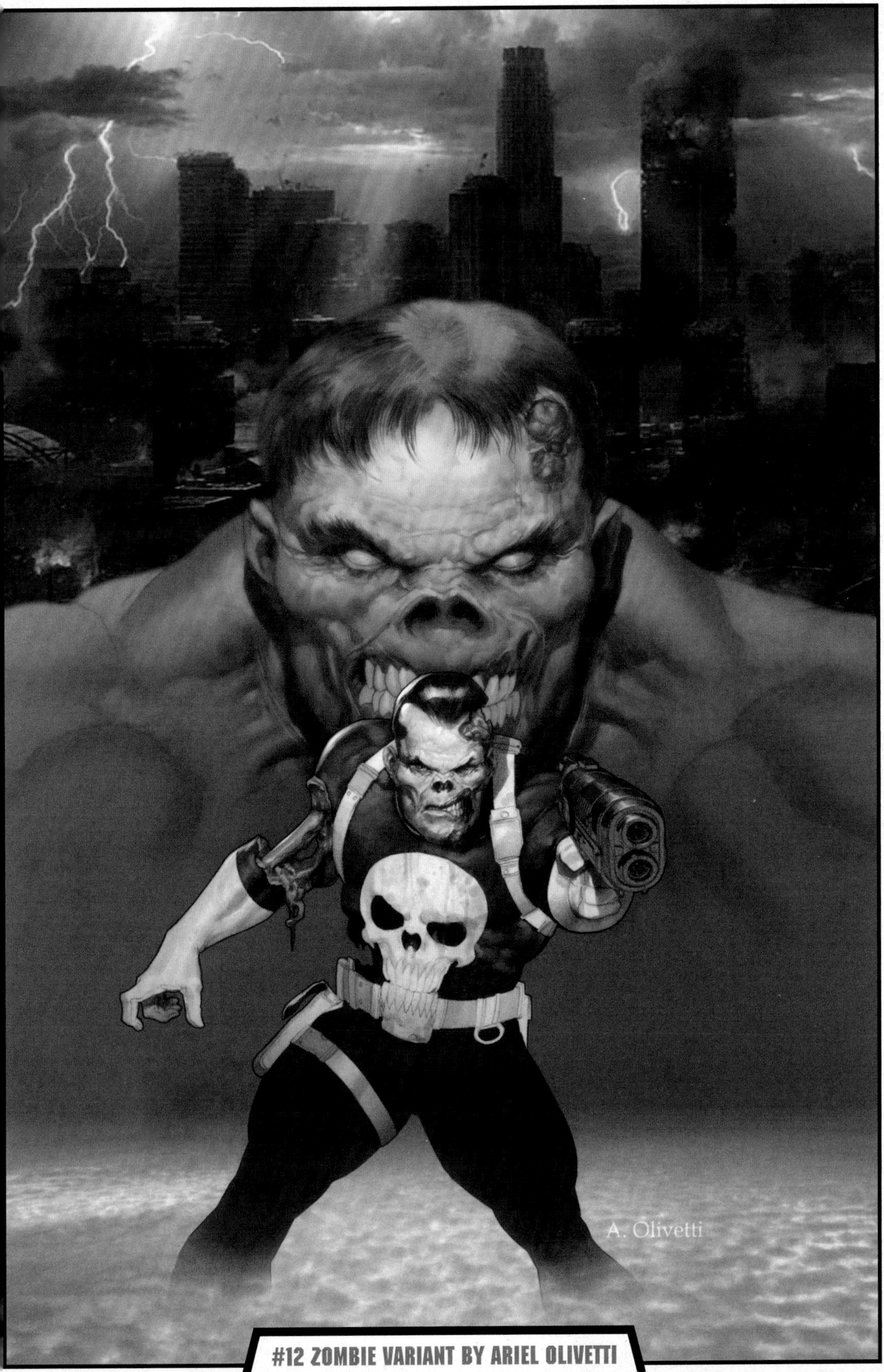
A. Olivetti

#12 ZOMBIE VARIANT BY ARIEL OLIVETTI

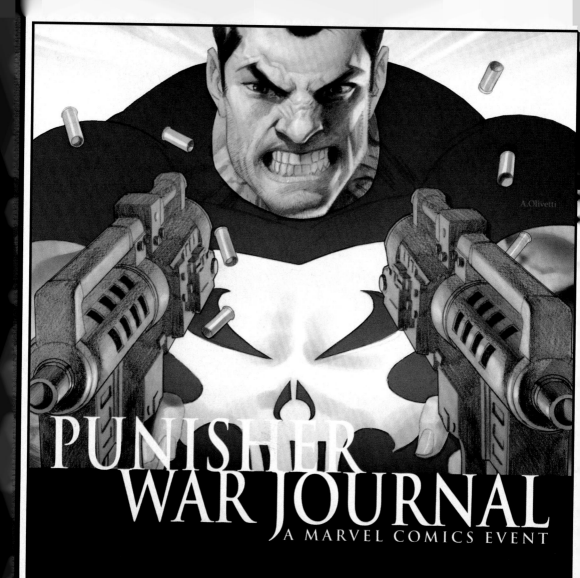

PUNISHER
WAR JOURNAL
A MARVEL COMICS EVENT

A.Olivetti

CIVIL
WAR

#1 BLACK & WHITE EDITION

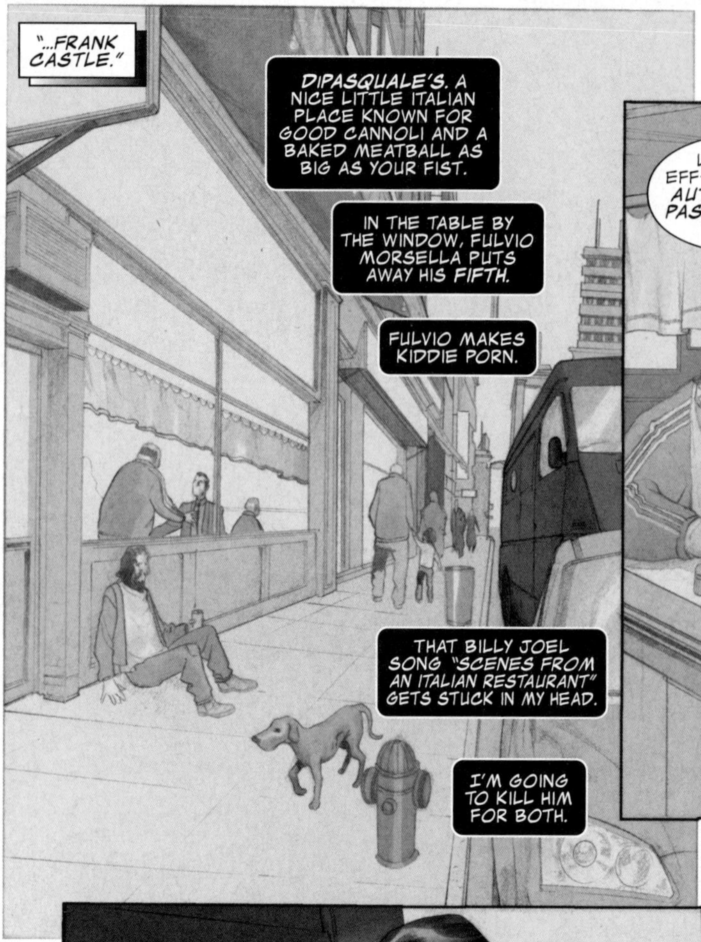
"...FRANK CASTLE."
DIPASQUALE'S. A NICE LITTLE ITALIAN PLACE KNOWN FOR GOOD CANNOLI AND A BAKED MEATBALL AS BIG AS YOUR FIST.
IN THE TABLE BY THE WINDOW, FULVIO MORSELLA PUTS AWAY HIS FIFTH.
FULVIO MAKES KIDDIE PORN.
THAT BILLY JOEL SONG "SCENES FROM AN ITALIAN RESTAURANT" GETS STUCK IN MY HEAD.
I'M GOING TO KILL HIM FOR BOTH.

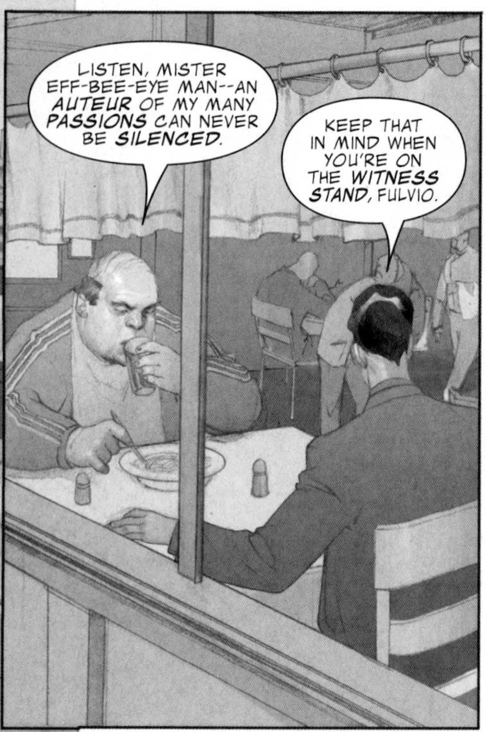
LISTEN, MISTER EFF-BEE-EYE MAN--AN AUTEUR OF MY MANY PASSIONS CAN NEVER BE SILENCED.
KEEP THAT IN MIND WHEN YOU'RE ON THE WITNESS STAND, FULVIO.

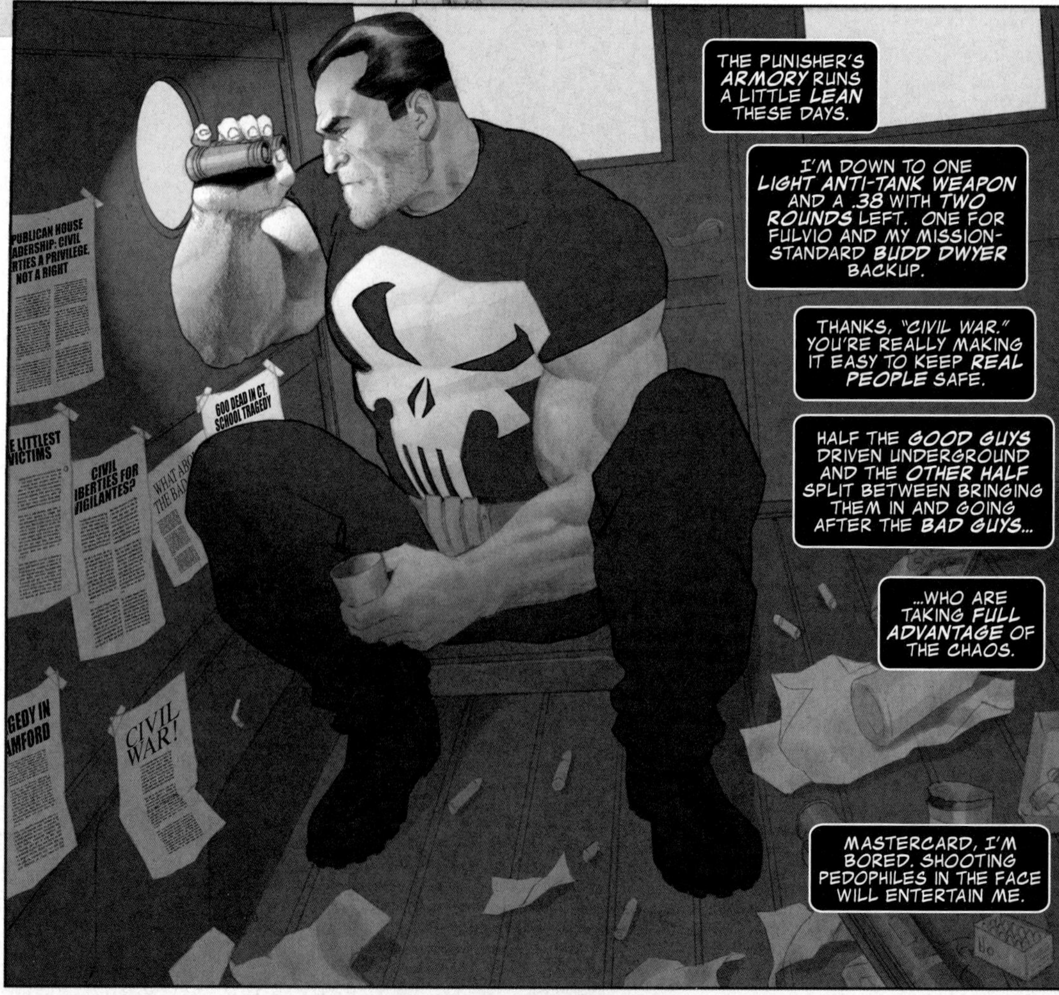
THE PUNISHER'S ARMORY RUNS A LITTLE LEAN THESE DAYS.
I'M DOWN TO ONE LIGHT ANTI-TANK WEAPON AND A .38 WITH TWO ROUNDS LEFT. ONE FOR FULVIO AND MY MISSION-STANDARD BUDD DWYER BACKUP.
THANKS, "CIVIL WAR." YOU'RE REALLY MAKING IT EASY TO KEEP REAL PEOPLE SAFE.
HALF THE GOOD GUYS DRIVEN UNDERGROUND AND THE OTHER HALF SPLIT BETWEEN BRINGING THEM IN AND GOING AFTER THE BAD GUYS...
...WHO ARE TAKING FULL ADVANTAGE OF THE CHAOS.
MASTERCARD, I'M BORED. SHOOTING PEDOPHILES IN THE FACE WILL ENTERTAIN ME.
600 DEAD IN CT. SCHOOL TRAGEDY
CIVIL LIBERTIES FOR VIGILANTES?
CIVIL WAR!

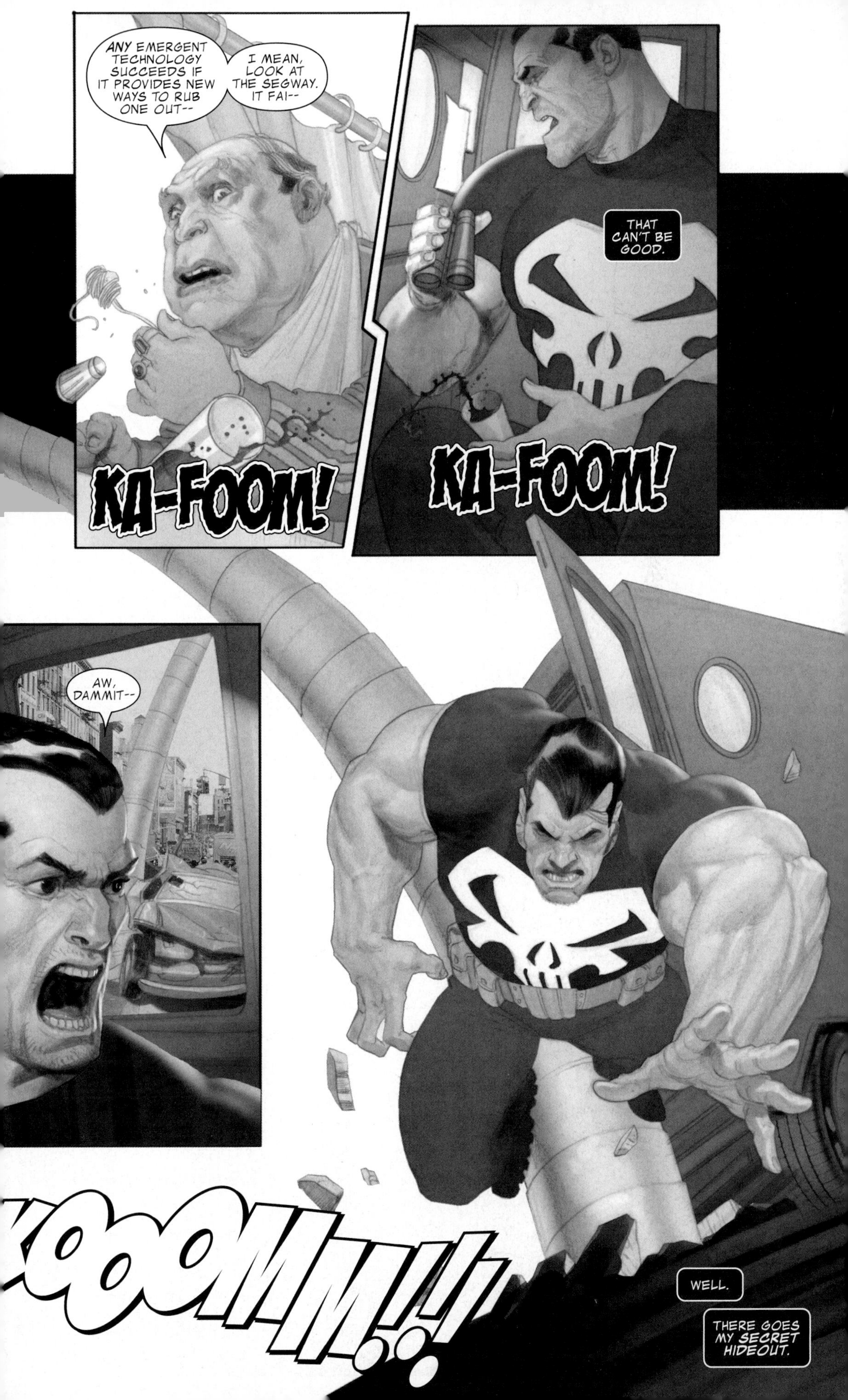
ANY EMERGENT TECHNOLOGY SUCCEEDS IF IT PROVIDES NEW WAYS TO RUB ONE OUT--
I MEAN, LOOK AT THE SEGWAY. IT FAI--
KA-FOOM!
THAT CAN'T BE GOOD.
KA-FOOM!
AW, DAMMIT--
WELL.
THERE GOES MY SECRET HIDEOUT.

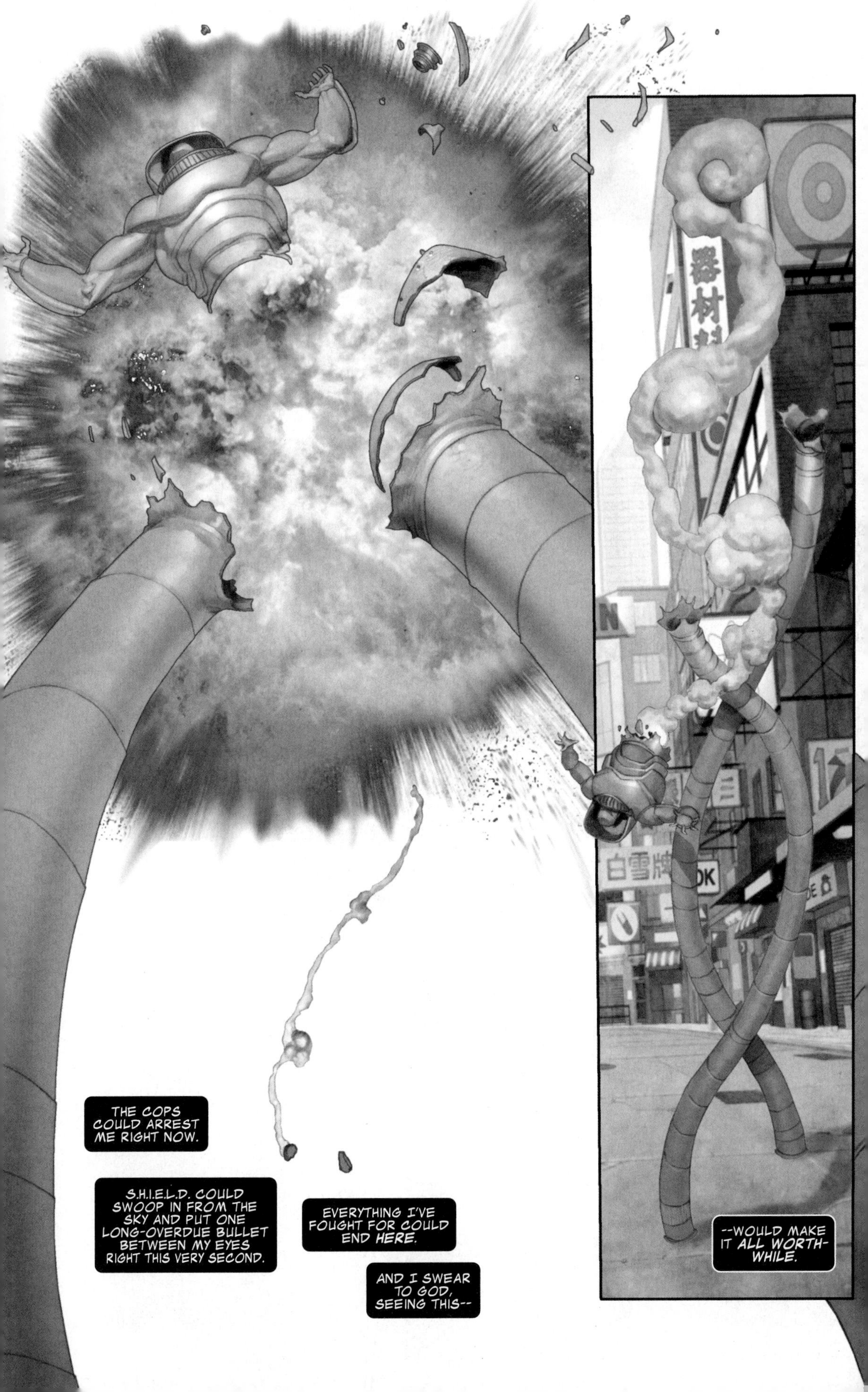
THE COPS COULD ARREST ME RIGHT NOW.
S.H.I.E.L.D. COULD SWOOP IN FROM THE SKY AND PUT ONE LONG-OVERDUE BULLET BETWEEN MY EYES RIGHT THIS VERY SECOND.
EVERYTHING I'VE FOUGHT FOR COULD END HERE.
AND I SWEAR TO GOD, SEEING THIS--
--WOULD MAKE IT ALL WORTH-WHILE.

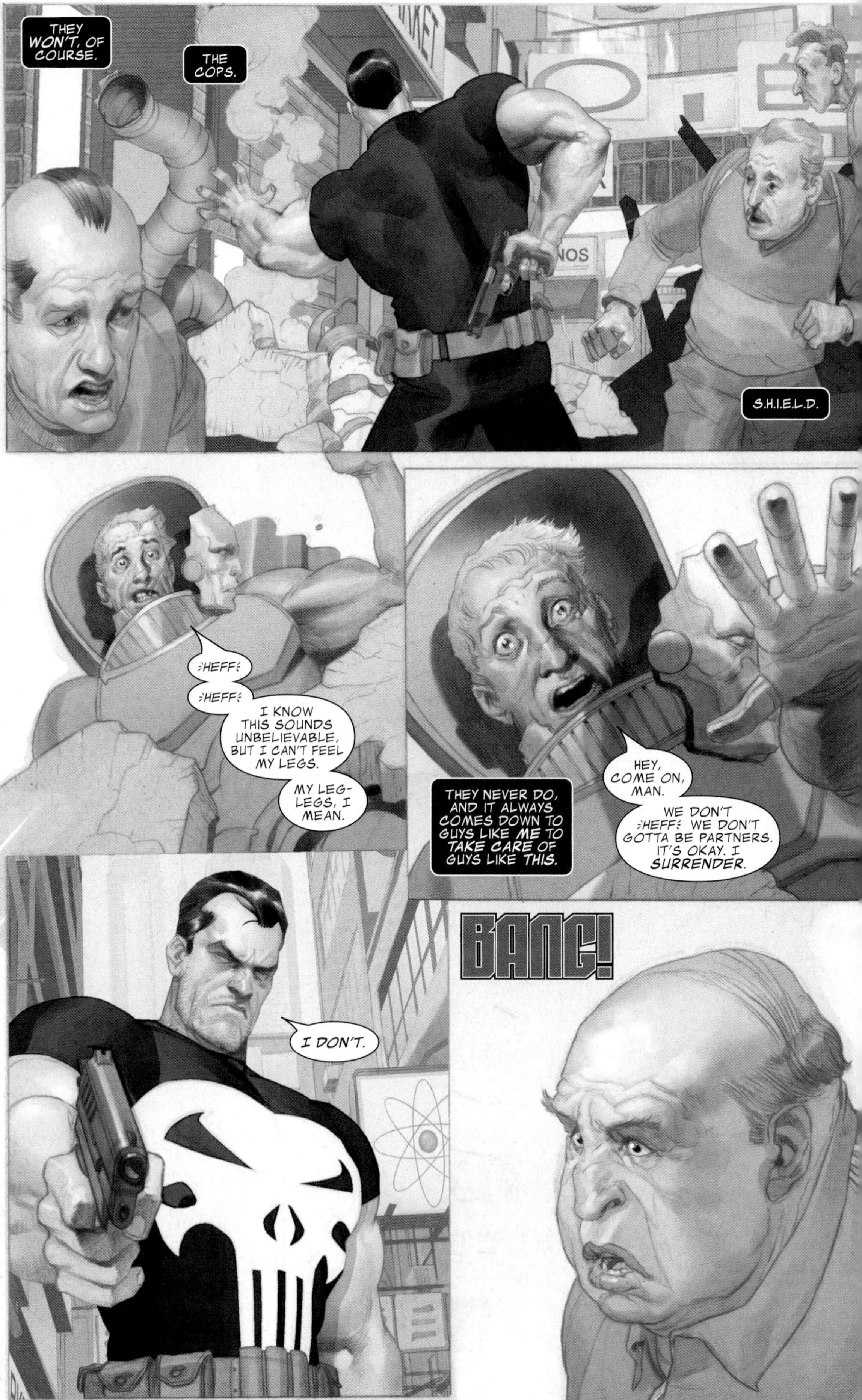
THEY WON'T, OF COURSE.
THE COPS.
S.H.I.E.L.D.
⚡HEFF⚡
⚡HEFF⚡
I KNOW THIS SOUNDS UNBELIEVABLE, BUT I CAN'T FEEL MY LEGS.
MY LEG-LEGS, I MEAN.
THEY NEVER DO, AND IT ALWAYS COMES DOWN TO GUYS LIKE ME TO TAKE CARE OF GUYS LIKE THIS.
HEY, COME ON, MAN.
WE DON'T ⚡HEFF⚡ WE DON'T GOTTA BE PARTNERS. IT'S OKAY. I SURRENDER.
I DON'T.
BANG!

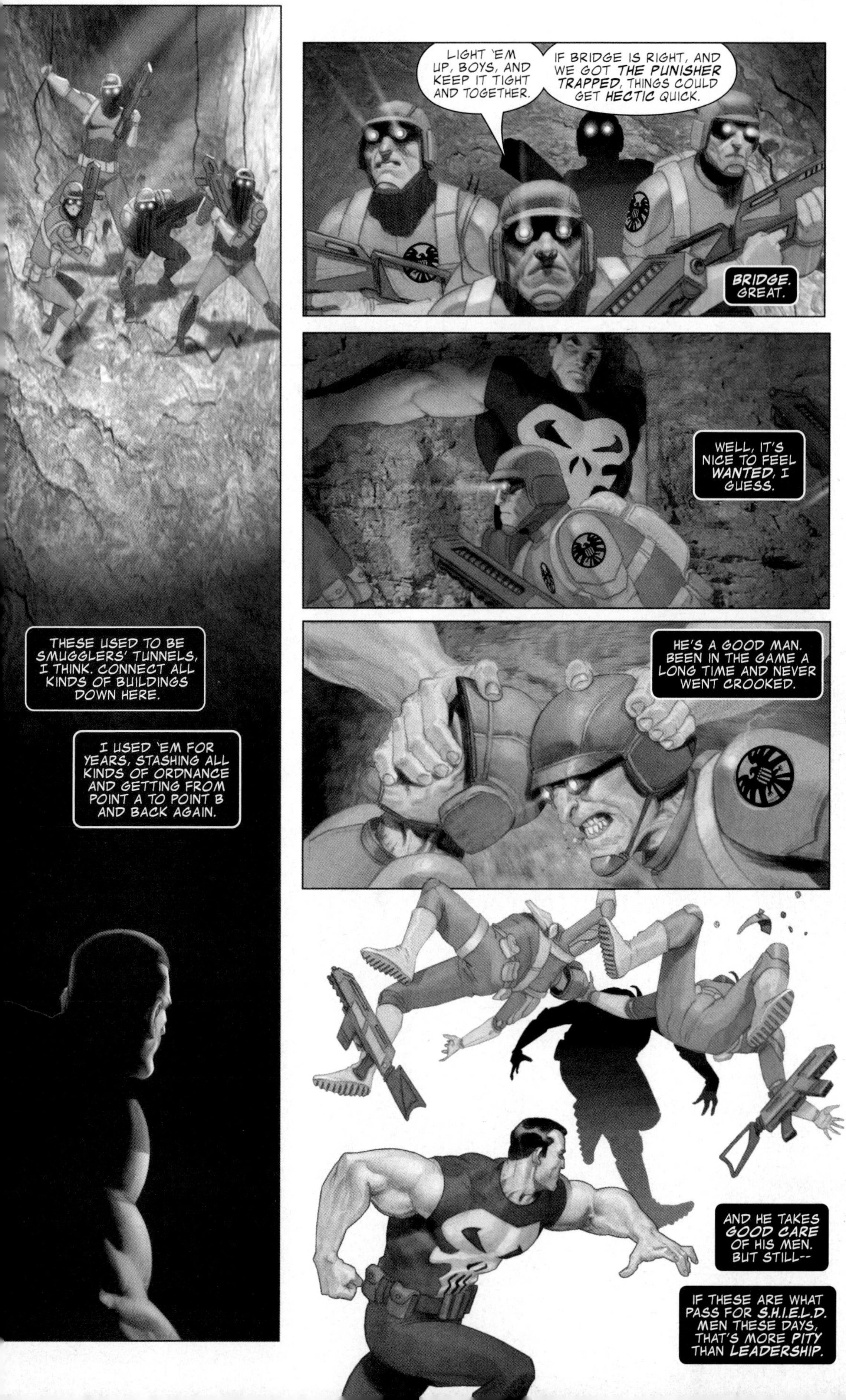
LIGHT 'EM UP, BOYS, AND KEEP IT TIGHT AND TOGETHER.
IF BRIDGE IS RIGHT, AND WE GOT THE PUNISHER TRAPPED, THINGS COULD GET HECTIC QUICK.
BRIDGE. GREAT.
WELL, IT'S NICE TO FEEL WANTED, I GUESS.
THESE USED TO BE SMUGGLERS' TUNNELS, I THINK. CONNECT ALL KINDS OF BUILDINGS DOWN HERE.
I USED 'EM FOR YEARS, STASHING ALL KINDS OF ORDNANCE AND GETTING FROM POINT A TO POINT B AND BACK AGAIN.
HE'S A GOOD MAN. BEEN IN THE GAME A LONG TIME AND NEVER WENT CROOKED.
AND HE TAKES GOOD CARE OF HIS MEN. BUT STILL--
IF THESE ARE WHAT PASS FOR S.H.I.E.L.D. MEN THESE DAYS, THAT'S MORE PITY THAN LEADERSHIP.

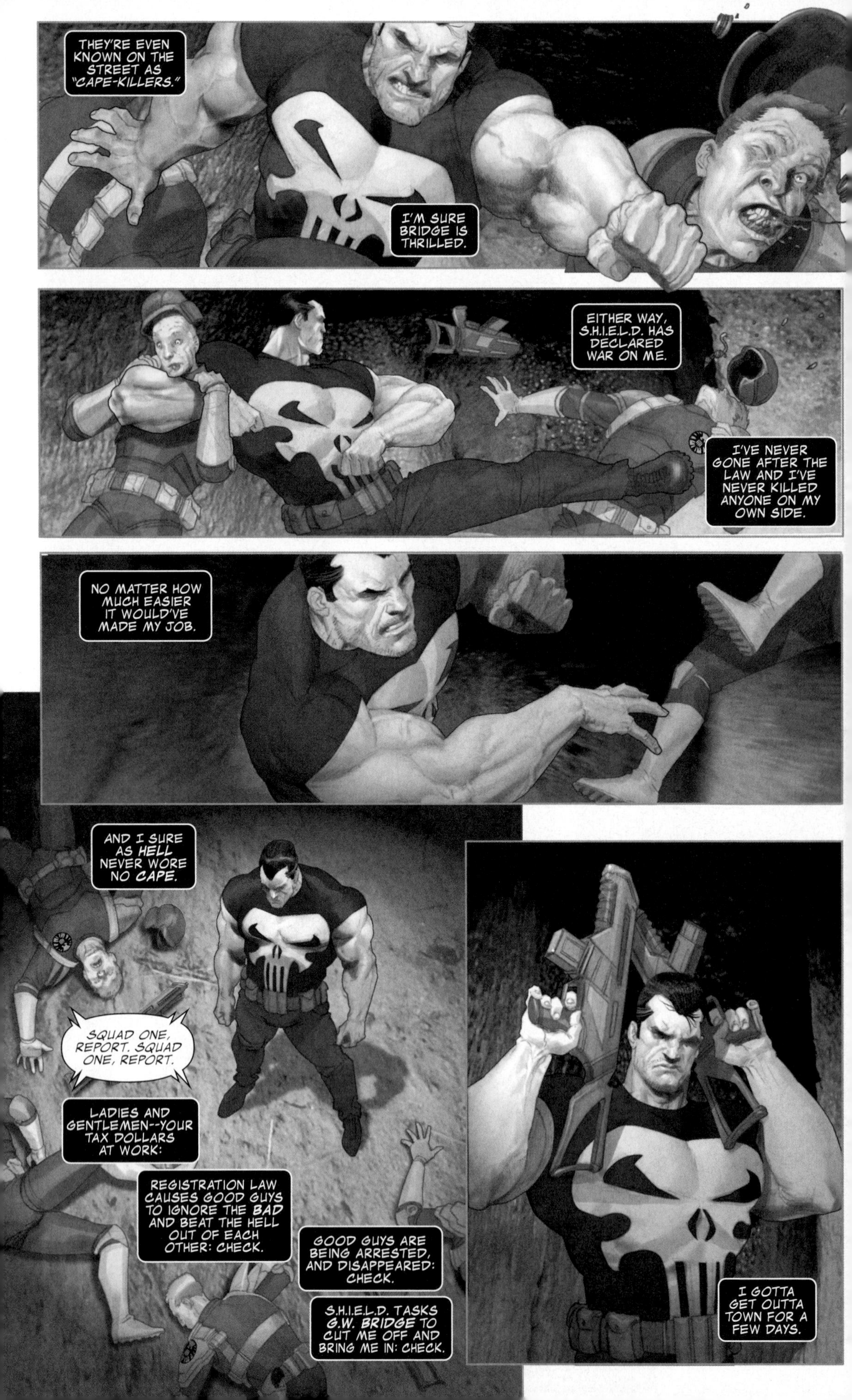
THEY'RE EVEN KNOWN ON THE STREET AS "CAPE-KILLERS."
I'M SURE BRIDGE IS THRILLED.
EITHER WAY, S.H.I.E.L.D. HAS DECLARED WAR ON ME.
I'VE NEVER GONE AFTER THE LAW AND I'VE NEVER KILLED ANYONE ON MY OWN SIDE.
NO MATTER HOW MUCH EASIER IT WOULD'VE MADE MY JOB.
AND I SURE AS HELL NEVER WORE NO CAPE.
SQUAD ONE, REPORT. SQUAD ONE, REPORT.
LADIES AND GENTLEMEN--YOUR TAX DOLLARS AT WORK:
REGISTRATION LAW CAUSES GOOD GUYS TO IGNORE THE BAD AND BEAT THE HELL OUT OF EACH OTHER: CHECK.
GOOD GUYS ARE BEING ARRESTED, AND DISAPPEARED: CHECK.
S.H.I.E.L.D. TASKS G.W. BRIDGE TO CUT ME OFF AND BRING ME IN: CHECK.
I GOTTA GET OUTTA TOWN FOR A FEW DAYS.

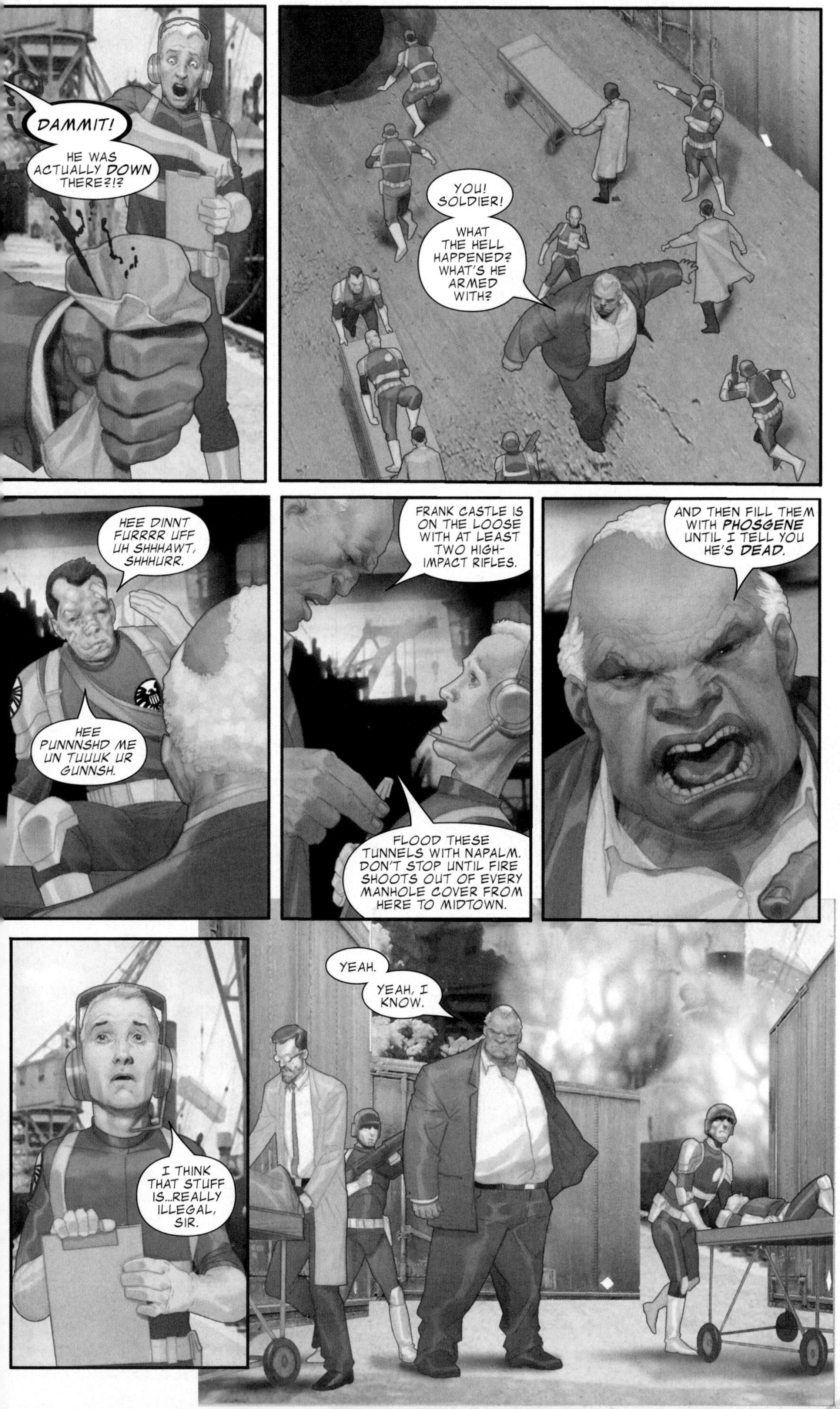
DAMMIT!
HE WAS ACTUALLY DOWN THERE?!?
YOU! SOLDIER!
WHAT THE HELL HAPPENED? WHAT'S HE ARMED WITH?
HEE DINNT FURRRR UFF UH SHHHAWT, SHHHURR.
HEE PUNNNSHD ME UN TUUUK UR GUNNSH.
FRANK CASTLE IS ON THE LOOSE WITH AT LEAST TWO HIGH-IMPACT RIFLES.
FLOOD THESE TUNNELS WITH NAPALM. DON'T STOP UNTIL FIRE SHOOTS OUT OF EVERY MANHOLE COVER FROM HERE TO MIDTOWN.
AND THEN FILL THEM WITH PHOSGENE UNTIL I TELL YOU HE'S DEAD.
I THINK THAT STUFF IS...REALLY ILLEGAL, SIR.
YEAH.
YEAH, I KNOW.

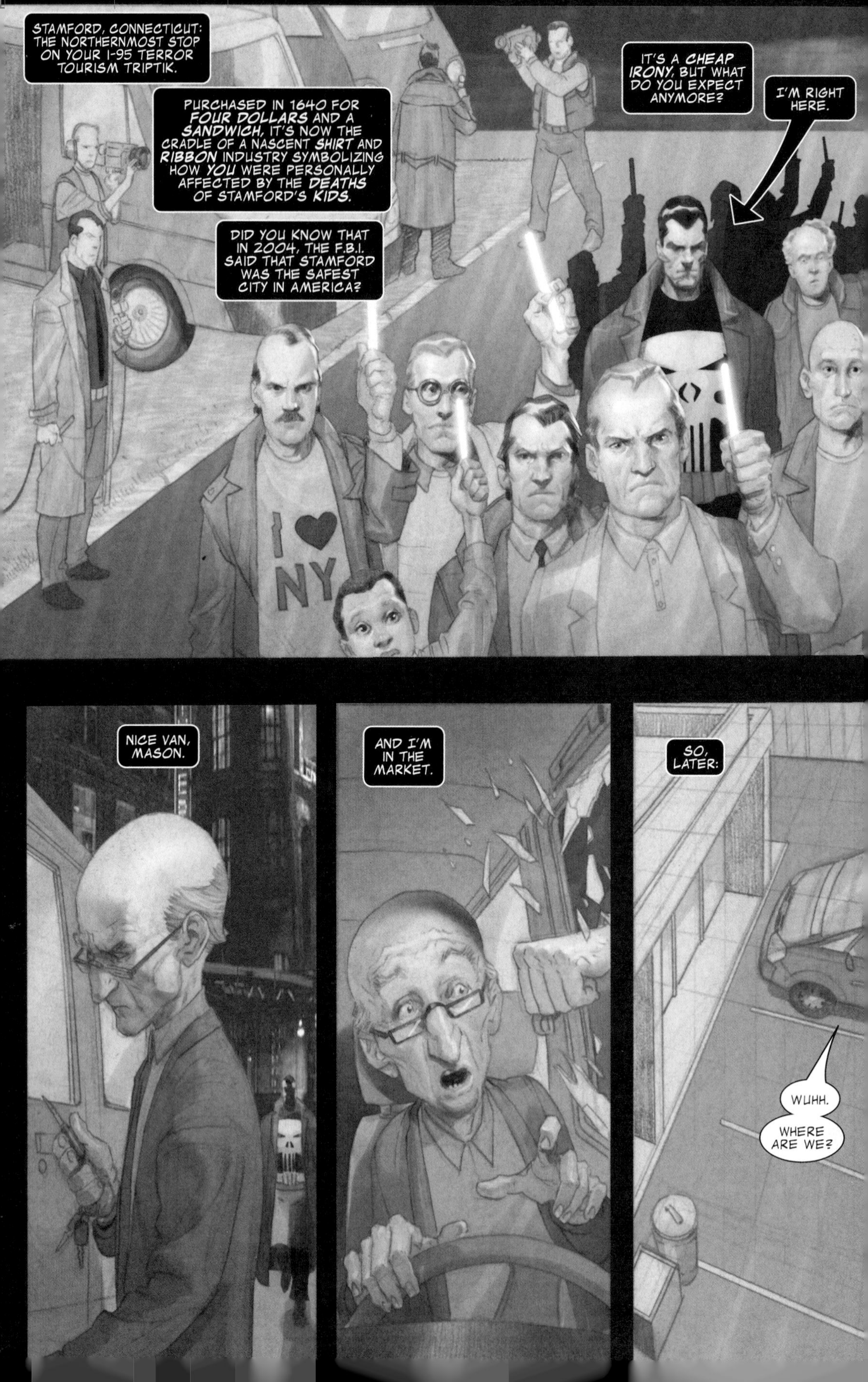
STAMFORD, CONNECTICUT: THE NORTHERNMOST STOP ON YOUR I-95 TERROR TOURISM TRIPTIK.
PURCHASED IN 1640 FOR FOUR DOLLARS AND A SANDWICH, IT'S NOW THE CRADLE OF A NASCENT SHIRT AND RIBBON INDUSTRY SYMBOLIZING HOW YOU WERE PERSONALLY AFFECTED BY THE DEATHS OF STAMFORD'S KIDS.
DID YOU KNOW THAT IN 2004, THE F.B.I. SAID THAT STAMFORD WAS THE SAFEST CITY IN AMERICA?
IT'S A CHEAP IRONY, BUT WHAT DO YOU EXPECT ANYMORE?
I'M RIGHT HERE.
I ♥ NY
NICE VAN, MASON.
AND I'M IN THE MARKET.
SO, LATER:
WUHH.
WHERE ARE WE?

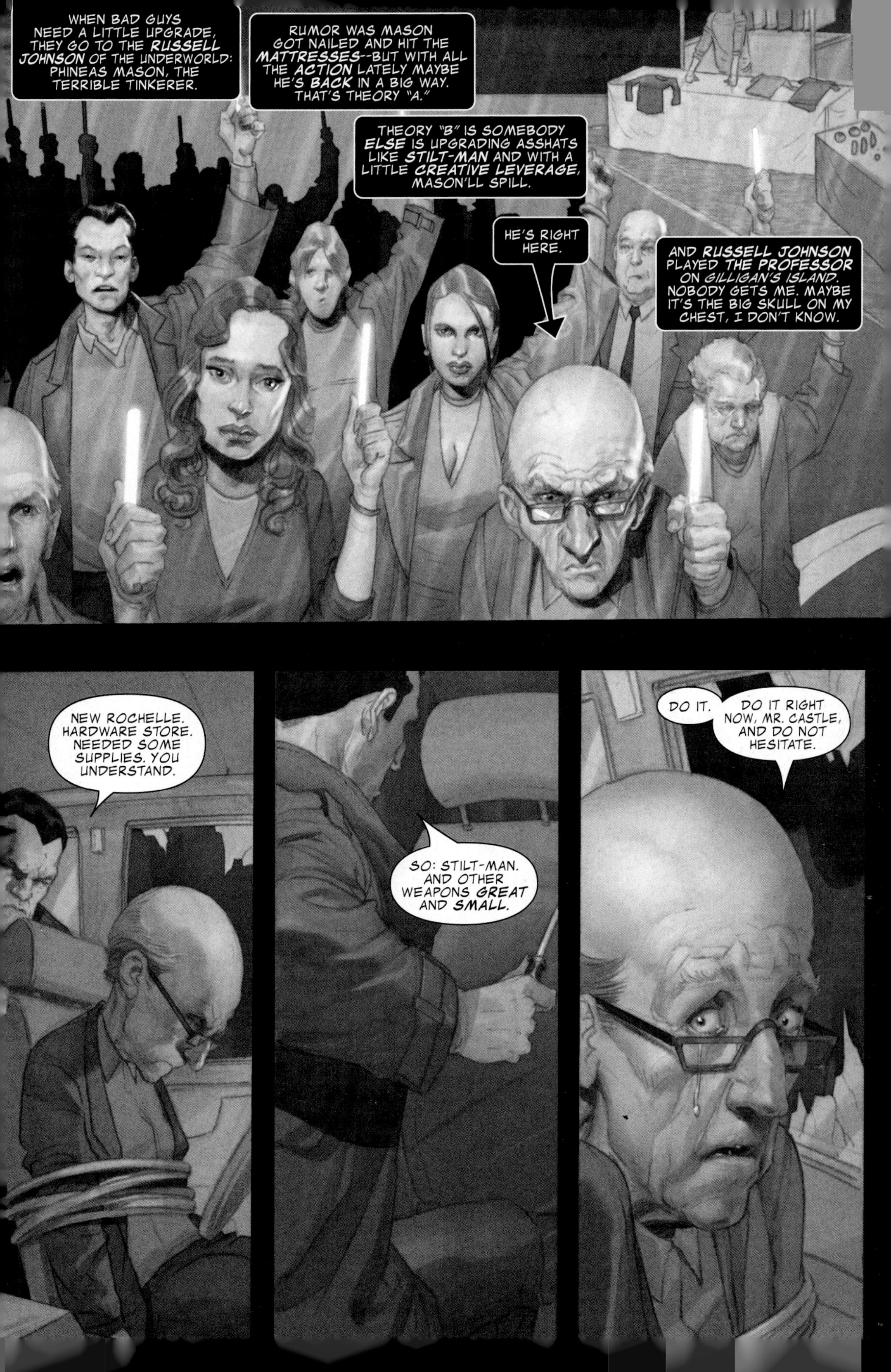
WHEN BAD GUYS NEED A LITTLE UPGRADE, THEY GO TO THE RUSSELL JOHNSON OF THE UNDERWORLD: PHINEAS MASON, THE TERRIBLE TINKERER.
RUMOR WAS MASON GOT NAILED AND HIT THE MATTRESSES--BUT WITH ALL THE ACTION LATELY MAYBE HE'S BACK IN A BIG WAY. THAT'S THEORY "A."
THEORY "B" IS SOMEBODY ELSE IS UPGRADING ASSHATS LIKE STILT-MAN AND WITH A LITTLE CREATIVE LEVERAGE, MASON'LL SPILL.
HE'S RIGHT HERE.
AND RUSSELL JOHNSON PLAYED THE PROFESSOR ON GILLIGAN'S ISLAND. NOBODY GETS ME. MAYBE IT'S THE BIG SKULL ON MY CHEST, I DON'T KNOW.
NEW ROCHELLE. HARDWARE STORE. NEEDED SOME SUPPLIES. YOU UNDERSTAND.
SO: STILT-MAN. AND OTHER WEAPONS GREAT AND SMALL.
DO IT.
DO IT RIGHT NOW, MR. CASTLE, AND DO NOT HESITATE.

I ASSURE YOU I HAVE NOTHING LEFT TO LIVE FOR.

STILT-MAN CAME TO ME. SAID HE COULD *TURN OVER A NEW LEAF.* HE WANTED NEW WEAPONRY.

I THOUGHT, MAYBE. MAYBE A *MORON* LIKE HIM WOULD GET OTHER *MORONS LIKE HIM* KILLED. MY *FIRST JOB* IN A YEAR. MAYBE MORE.

MY SON DIED. HE WAS-- HE WAS IN THE *BUSINESS.*

HIS SON, MY GRANDSON. *HE* WAS IN THE FIFTH GRADE.

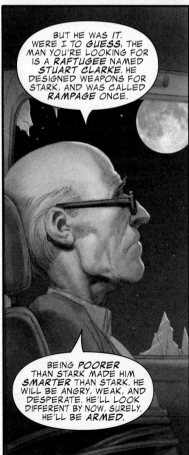

BUT HE WAS IT. WERE I TO *GUESS,* THE MAN YOU'RE LOOKING FOR IS A *RAFTUGEE* NAMED *STUART CLARKE.* HE DESIGNED WEAPONS FOR STARK, AND WAS CALLED *RAMPAGE* ONCE.

BEING *POORER* THAN STARK MADE HIM *SMARTER* THAN STARK. HE WILL BE ANGRY, WEAK, AND DESPERATE. HE'LL LOOK DIFFERENT BY NOW, SURELY. HE'LL BE *ARMED.*

ARE YOU GOING TO KILL MMNNGGHGH'KKK

THAT *AWL* JUST SLID BETWEEN YOUR FOURTH AND FIFTH VERTEBRAE.

TINKER WITH *THAT* FOR AWHILE.

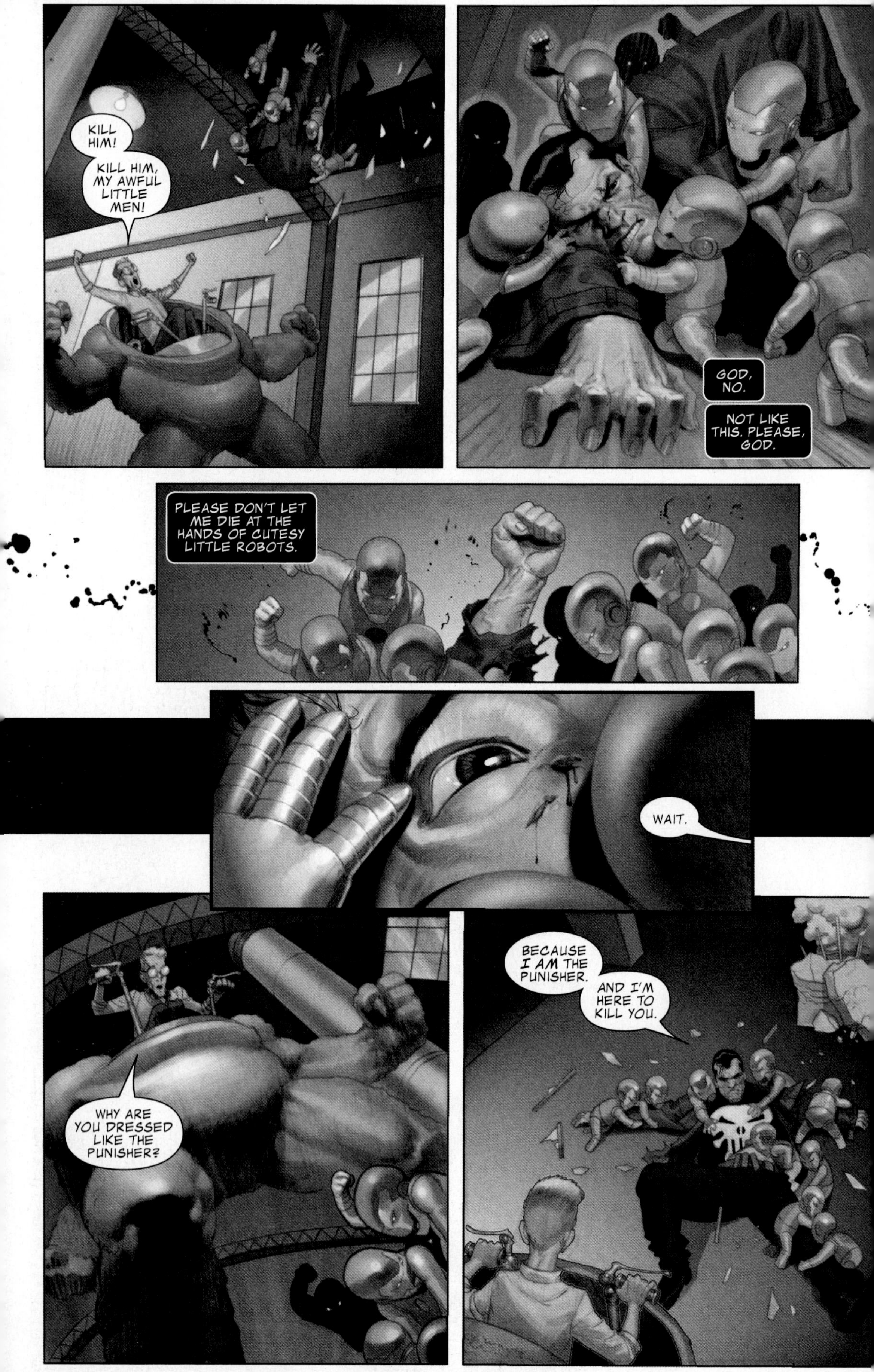
KILL HIM!
KILL HIM, MY AWFUL LITTLE MEN!
GOD, NO.
NOT LIKE THIS. PLEASE, GOD.
PLEASE DON'T LET ME DIE AT THE HANDS OF CUTESY LITTLE ROBOTS.
WAIT.
WHY ARE YOU DRESSED LIKE THE PUNISHER?
BECAUSE I AM THE PUNISHER.
AND I'M HERE TO KILL YOU.

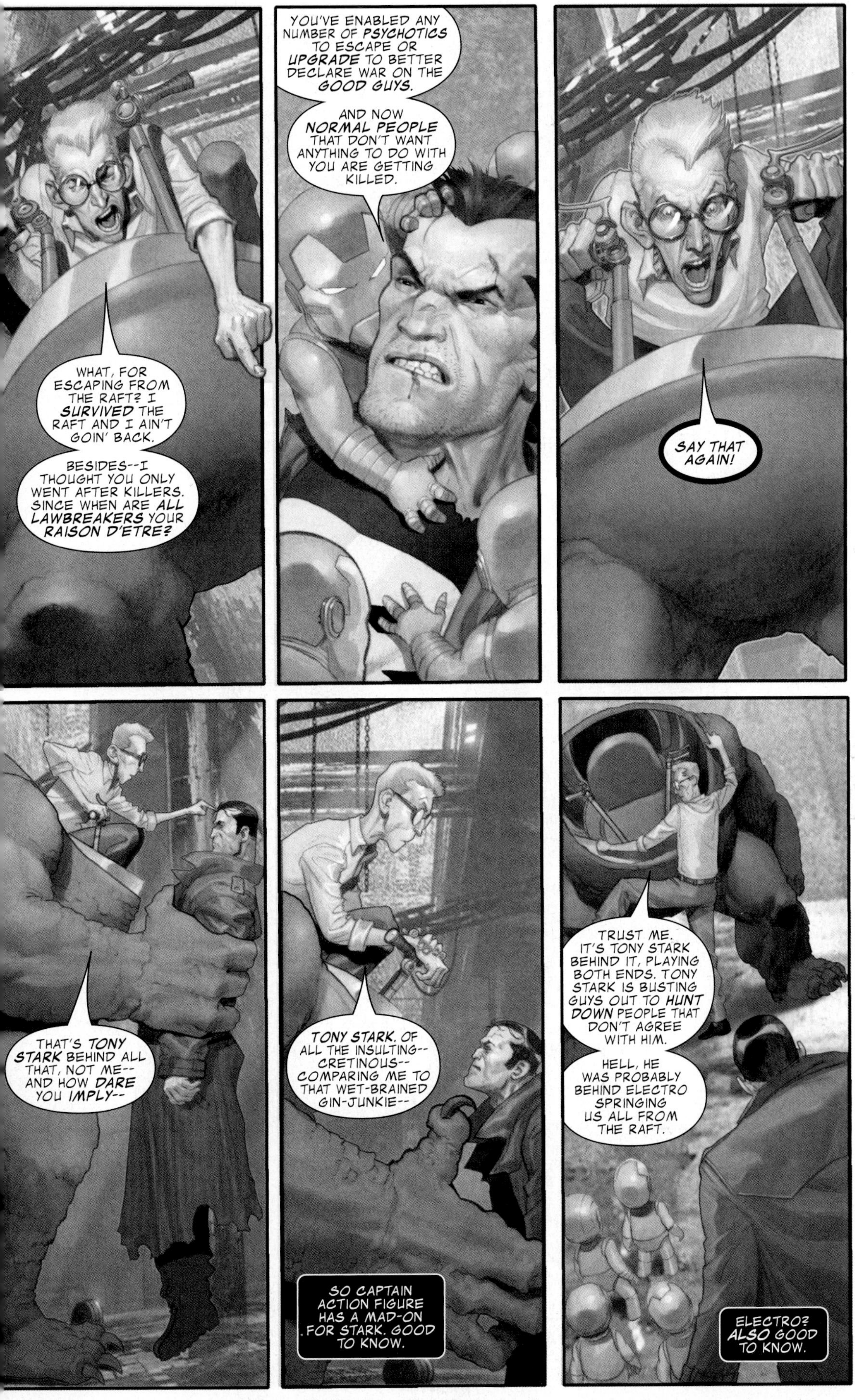
WHAT, FOR ESCAPING FROM THE RAFT? I SURVIVED THE RAFT AND I AIN'T GOIN' BACK.
BESIDES--I THOUGHT YOU ONLY WENT AFTER KILLERS. SINCE WHEN ARE ALL LAWBREAKERS YOUR RAISON D'ETRE?
YOU'VE ENABLED ANY NUMBER OF PSYCHOTICS TO ESCAPE OR UPGRADE TO BETTER DECLARE WAR ON THE GOOD GUYS.
AND NOW NORMAL PEOPLE THAT DON'T WANT ANYTHING TO DO WITH YOU ARE GETTING KILLED.
SAY THAT AGAIN!
THAT'S TONY STARK BEHIND ALL THAT, NOT ME--AND HOW DARE YOU IMPLY--
TONY STARK. OF ALL THE INSULTING--CRETINOUS--COMPARING ME TO THAT WET-BRAINED GIN-JUNKIE--
SO CAPTAIN ACTION FIGURE HAS A MAD-ON FOR STARK. GOOD TO KNOW.
TRUST ME. IT'S TONY STARK BEHIND IT, PLAYING BOTH ENDS. TONY STARK IS BUSTING GUYS OUT TO HUNT DOWN PEOPLE THAT DON'T AGREE WITH HIM.
HELL, HE WAS PROBABLY BEHIND ELECTRO SPRINGING US ALL FROM THE RAFT.
ELECTRO? ALSO GOOD TO KNOW.

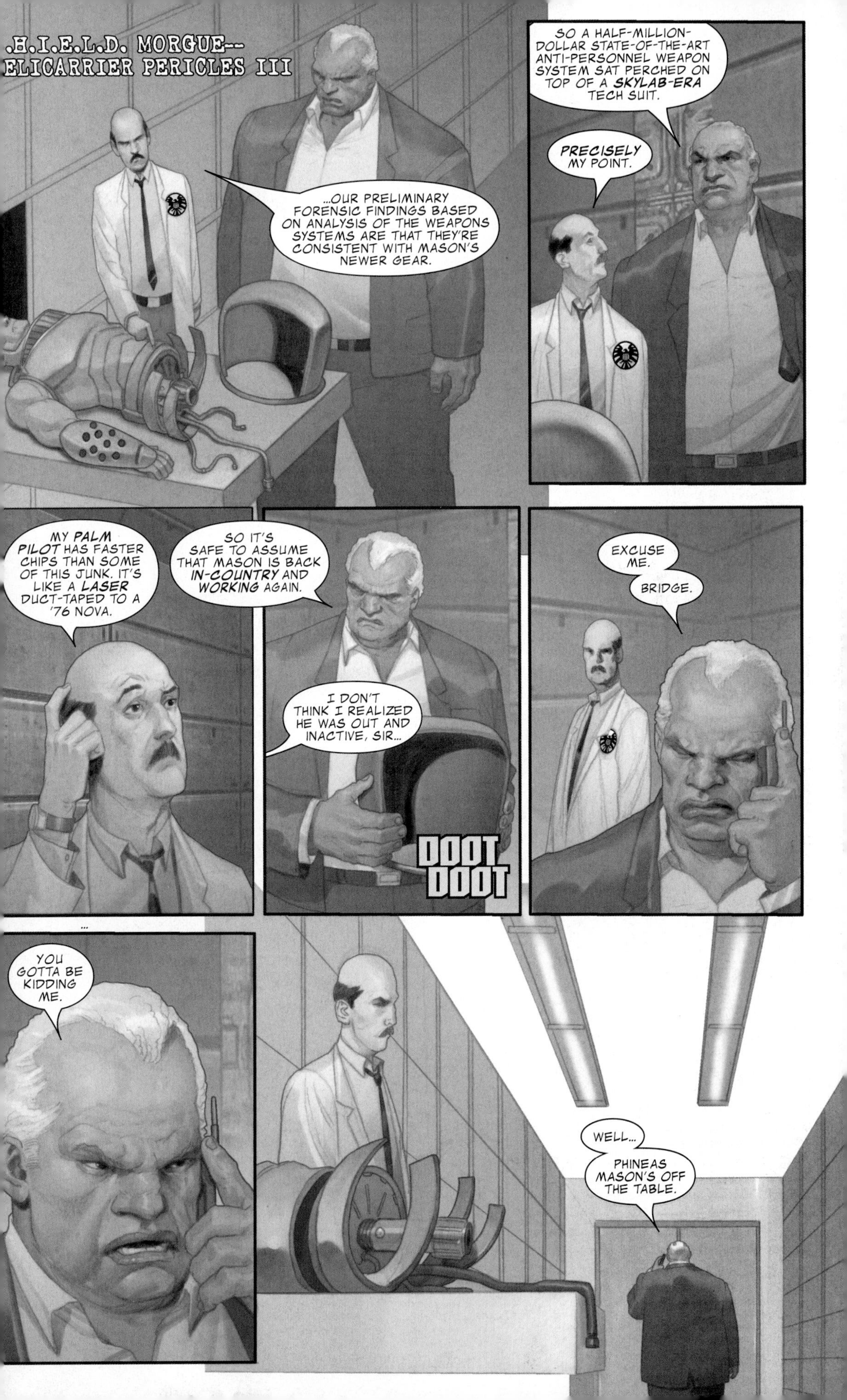

.H.I.E.L.D. MORGUE--
ELICARRIER PERICLES III
...OUR PRELIMINARY FORENSIC FINDINGS BASED ON ANALYSIS OF THE WEAPONS SYSTEMS ARE THAT THEY'RE CONSISTENT WITH MASON'S NEWER GEAR.
SO A HALF-MILLION-DOLLAR STATE-OF-THE-ART ANTI-PERSONNEL WEAPON SYSTEM SAT PERCHED ON TOP OF A SKYLAB-ERA TECH SUIT.
PRECISELY MY POINT.
MY PALM PILOT HAS FASTER CHIPS THAN SOME OF THIS JUNK. IT'S LIKE A LASER DUCT-TAPED TO A '76 NOVA.
SO IT'S SAFE TO ASSUME THAT MASON IS BACK IN-COUNTRY AND WORKING AGAIN.
I DON'T THINK I REALIZED HE WAS OUT AND INACTIVE, SIR...
DOOT DOOT
EXCUSE ME.
BRIDGE.
...
YOU GOTTA BE KIDDING ME.
WELL...
PHINEAS MASON'S OFF THE TABLE.

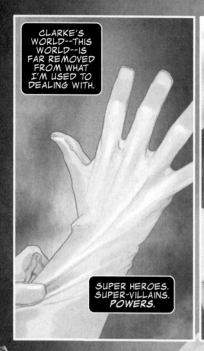

CLARKE'S WORLD--THIS WORLD--IS FAR REMOVED FROM WHAT I'M USED TO DEALING WITH.

SUPER HEROES. SUPER-VILLAINS. POWERS.

I MEAN, DID YOU *SEE* THAT GUY? WITH HIS FIN-FANG-FEET AND LITTLE IRON MAN TOYS?

THESE GUYS, THE SUPER-POWERS--THAT *TWEAKED BLOOD* GETS INTO THE *BRAIN* AND ALL THAT POWER MAKES 'EM BELIEVE THEY HAVE THE RIGHT TO TELL ANYONE HOW TO LIVE.

AND PEOPLE SAY I'M CRAZY.

I'M THE *SANEST GUY* THIS TOWN HAS EVER SEEN.

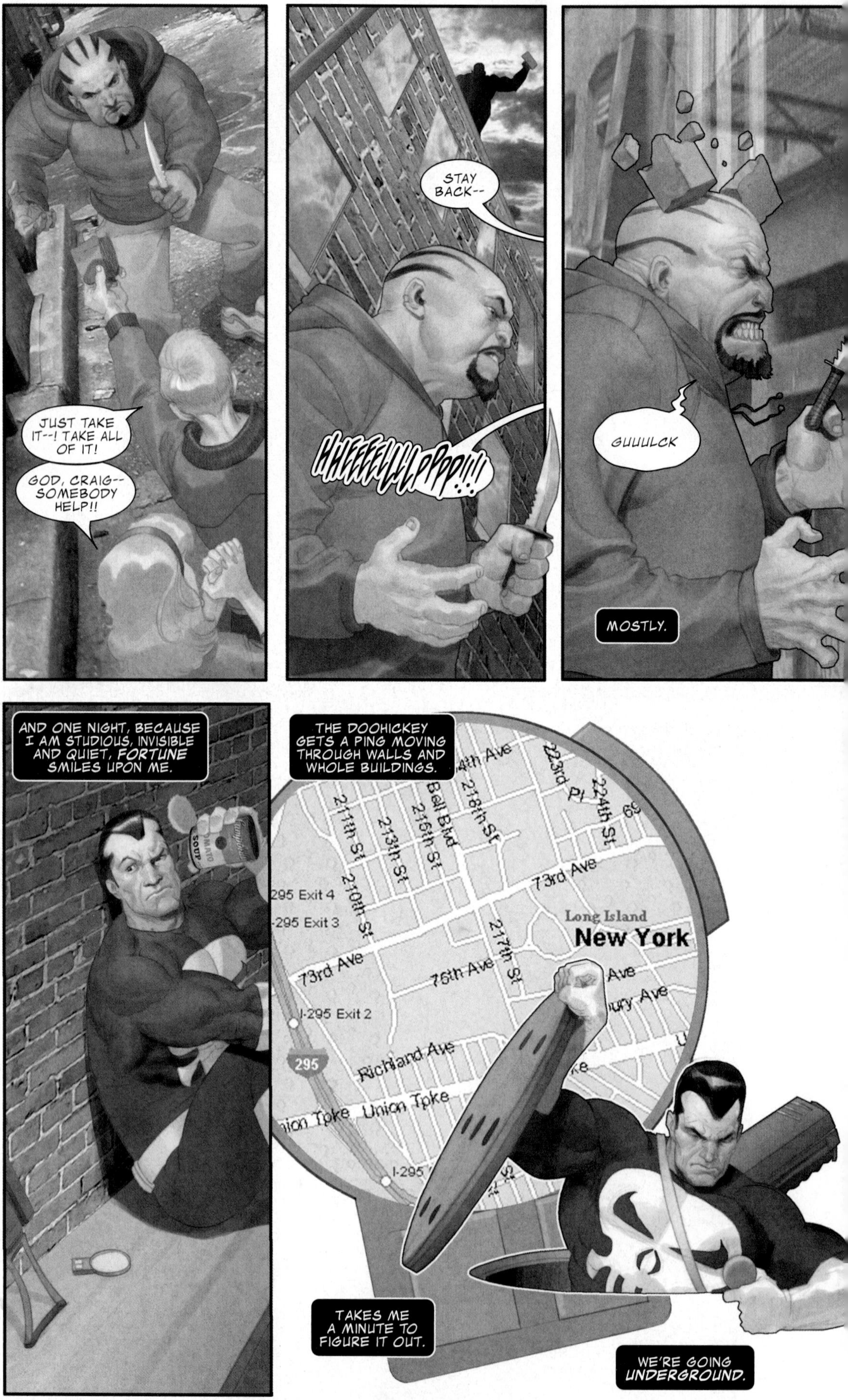
JUST TAKE IT--! TAKE ALL OF IT!
GOD, CRAIG-- SOMEBODY HELP!!
STAY BACK--
HHEEEELLLPPPP!!!
GUUULCK
MOSTLY.
AND ONE NIGHT, BECAUSE I AM STUDIOUS, INVISIBLE AND QUIET, FORTUNE SMILES UPON ME.
THE DOOHICKEY GETS A PING MOVING THROUGH WALLS AND WHOLE BUILDINGS.
Long Island
New York
TAKES ME A MINUTE TO FIGURE IT OUT.
WE'RE GOING UNDERGROUND.

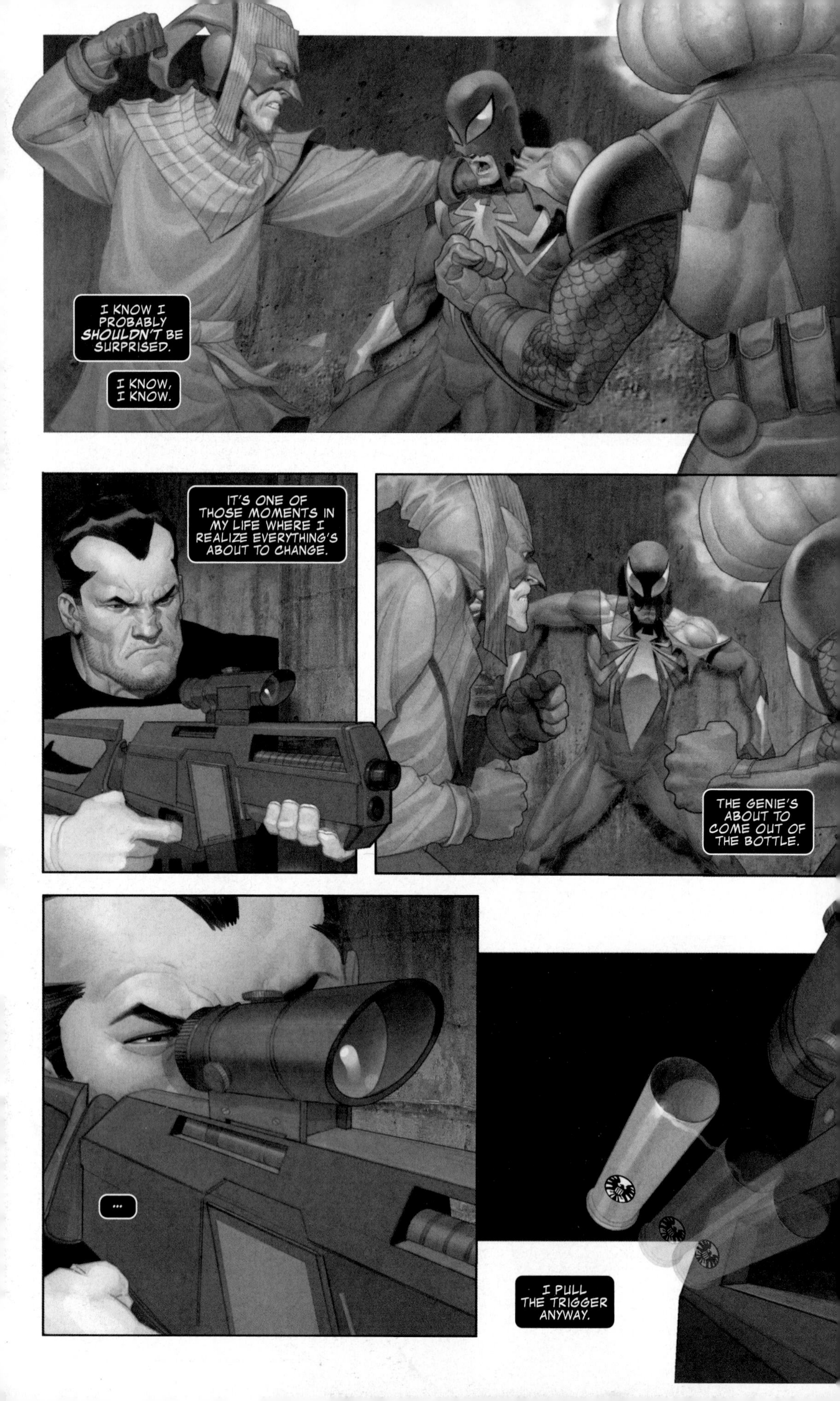
I KNOW I PROBABLY SHOULDN'T BE SURPRISED.
I KNOW, I KNOW.
IT'S ONE OF THOSE MOMENTS IN MY LIFE WHERE I REALIZE EVERYTHING'S ABOUT TO CHANGE.
THE GENIE'S ABOUT TO COME OUT OF THE BOTTLE.
...
I PULL THE TRIGGER ANYWAY.

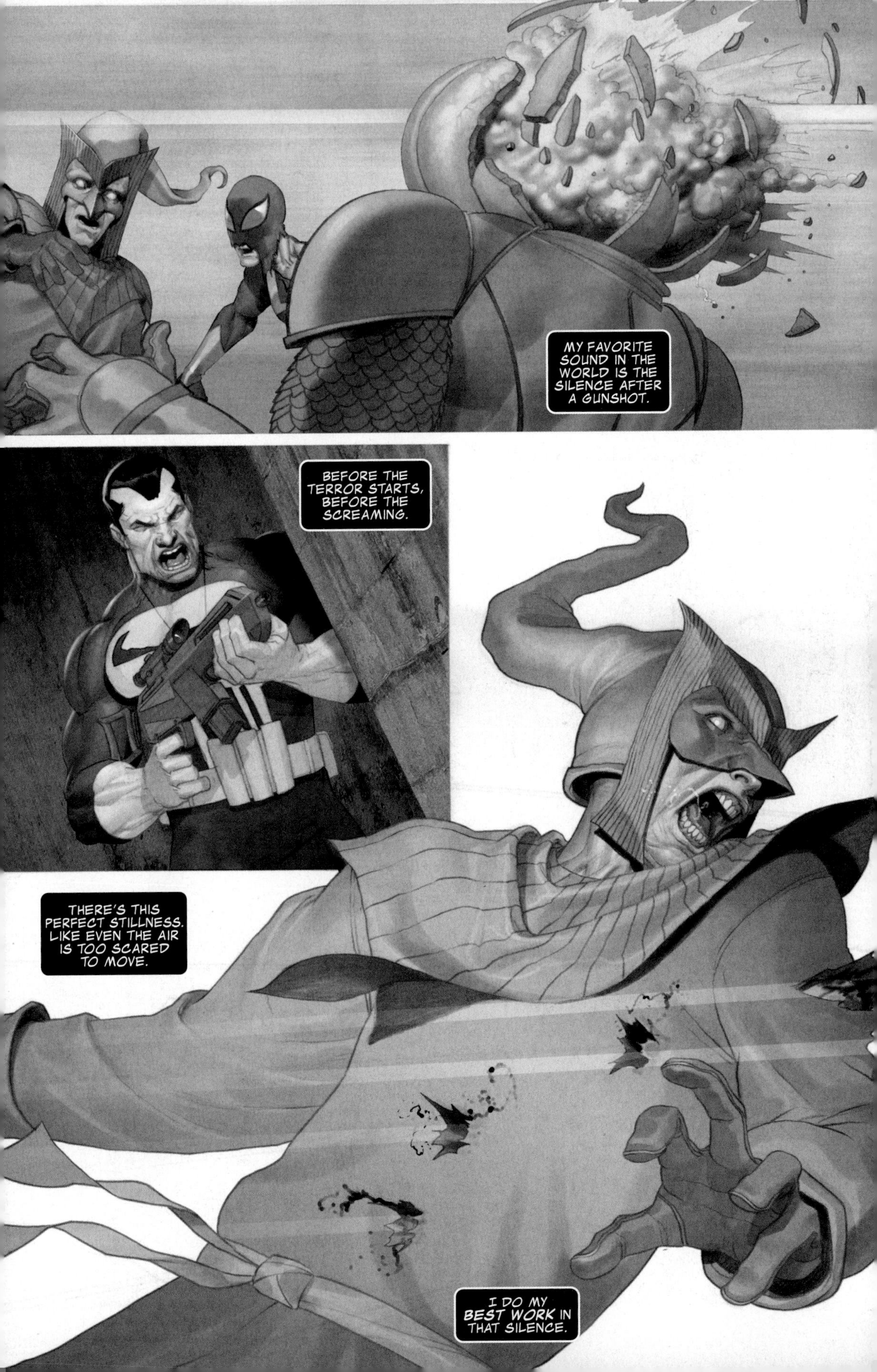
MY FAVORITE SOUND IN THE WORLD IS THE SILENCE AFTER A GUNSHOT.
BEFORE THE TERROR STARTS, BEFORE THE SCREAMING.
THERE'S THIS PERFECT STILLNESS. LIKE EVEN THE AIR IS TOO SCARED TO MOVE.
I DO MY **BEST WORK** IN THAT SILENCE.

KNOCK IT OFF.

DAMMIT. I THINK MY GOVERNMENT SPACE-GUN IS EMPTY.

YOU SUPER-TYPES. IT'S A WHOLE 'NOTHER WORLD WITH YOU GUYS, Y'KNOW?

WAIT. SO YOU'RE NOT HERE TO KILL ME?

I CAN'T KILL YOU.

I JUST SAID MY GUN IS EMPTY.

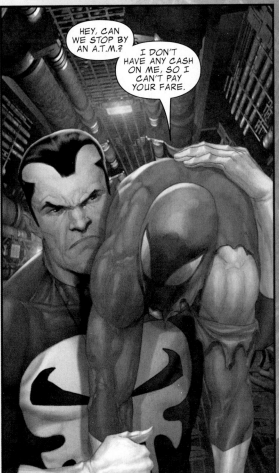

HEY, CAN WE STOP BY AN A.T.M.? I DON'T HAVE ANY CASH ON ME, SO I CAN'T PAY YOUR FARE.

YOU DON'T HAVE TO PAY ME, JACKASS.

OH, AWESOME.

ACTION IS MY REWARD, TOO.

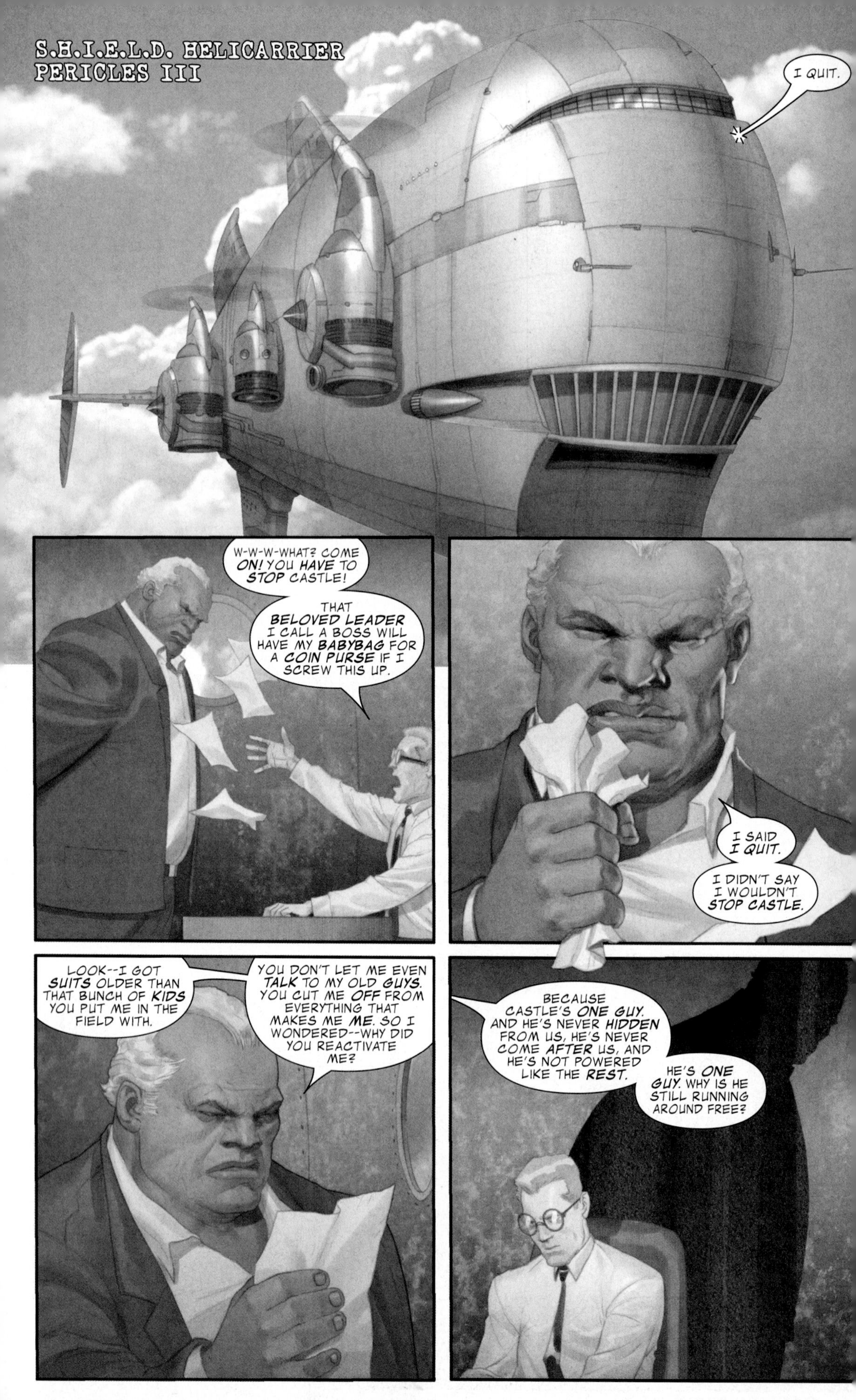
S.H.I.E.L.D. HELICARRIER
PERICLES III
I QUIT.
W-W-W-WHAT? COME ON! YOU HAVE TO STOP CASTLE!
THAT BELOVED LEADER I CALL A BOSS WILL HAVE MY BABYBAG FOR A COIN PURSE IF I SCREW THIS UP.
I SAID I QUIT.
I DIDN'T SAY I WOULDN'T STOP CASTLE.
LOOK--I GOT SUITS OLDER THAN THAT BUNCH OF KIDS YOU PUT ME IN THE FIELD WITH.
YOU DON'T LET ME EVEN TALK TO MY OLD GUYS. YOU CUT ME OFF FROM EVERYTHING THAT MAKES ME ME. SO I WONDERED--WHY DID YOU REACTIVATE ME?
BECAUSE CASTLE'S ONE GUY. AND HE'S NEVER HIDDEN FROM US, HE'S NEVER COME AFTER US, AND HE'S NOT POWERED LIKE THE REST.
HE'S ONE GUY. WHY IS HE STILL RUNNING AROUND FREE?

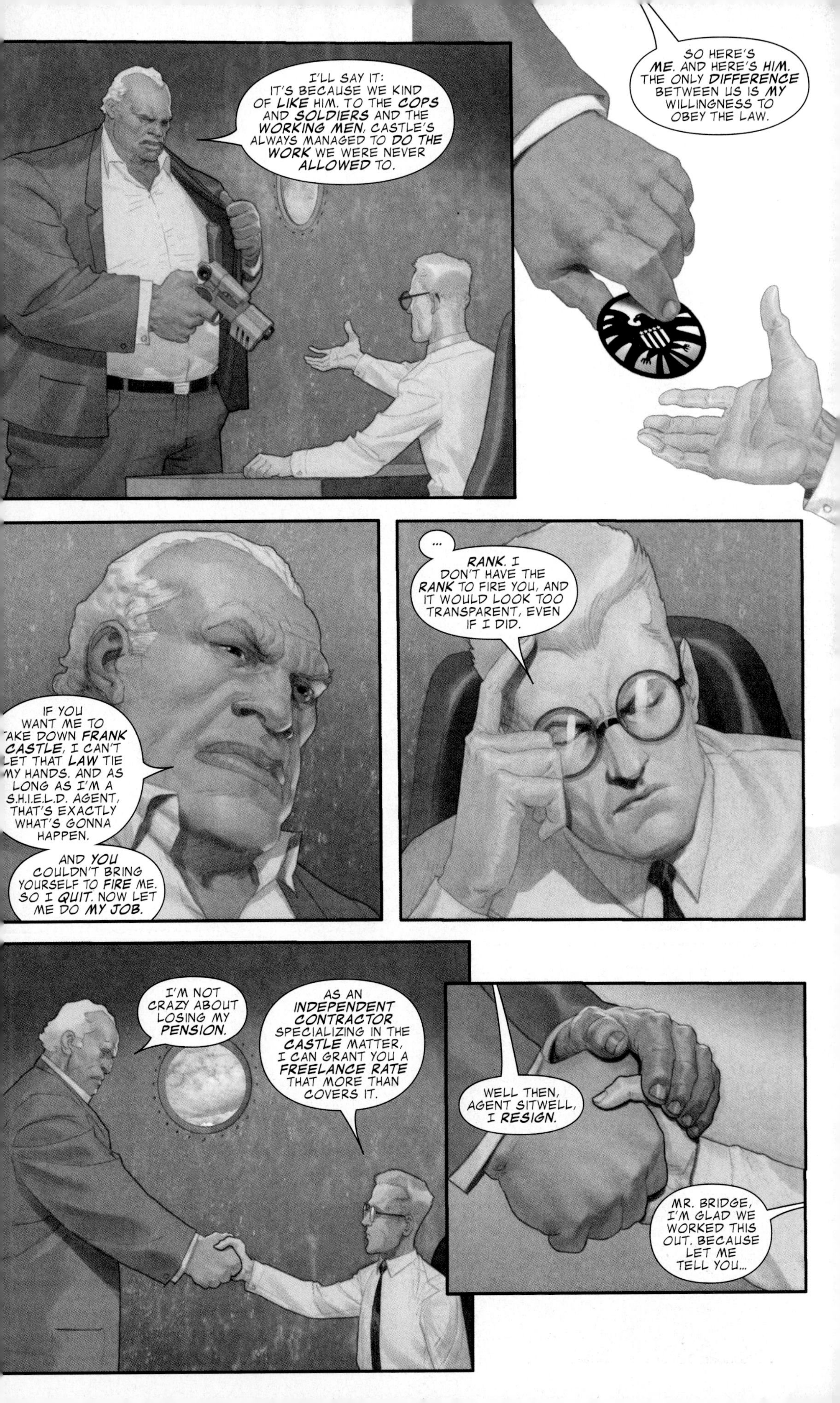

I'LL SAY IT: IT'S BECAUSE WE KIND OF LIKE HIM. TO THE COPS AND SOLDIERS AND THE WORKING MEN, CASTLE'S ALWAYS MANAGED TO DO THE WORK WE WERE NEVER ALLOWED TO.
SO HERE'S ME. AND HERE'S HIM. THE ONLY DIFFERENCE BETWEEN US IS MY WILLINGNESS TO OBEY THE LAW.
IF YOU WANT ME TO TAKE DOWN FRANK CASTLE, I CAN'T LET THAT LAW TIE MY HANDS. AND AS LONG AS I'M A S.H.I.E.L.D. AGENT, THAT'S EXACTLY WHAT'S GONNA HAPPEN.
AND YOU COULDN'T BRING YOURSELF TO FIRE ME. SO I QUIT. NOW LET ME DO MY JOB.
...
RANK. I DON'T HAVE THE RANK TO FIRE YOU, AND IT WOULD LOOK TOO TRANSPARENT, EVEN IF I DID.
I'M NOT CRAZY ABOUT LOSING MY PENSION.
AS AN INDEPENDENT CONTRACTOR SPECIALIZING IN THE CASTLE MATTER, I CAN GRANT YOU A FREELANCE RATE THAT MORE THAN COVERS IT.
WELL THEN, AGENT SITWELL, I RESIGN.
MR. BRIDGE, I'M GLAD WE WORKED THIS OUT. BECAUSE LET ME TELL YOU...

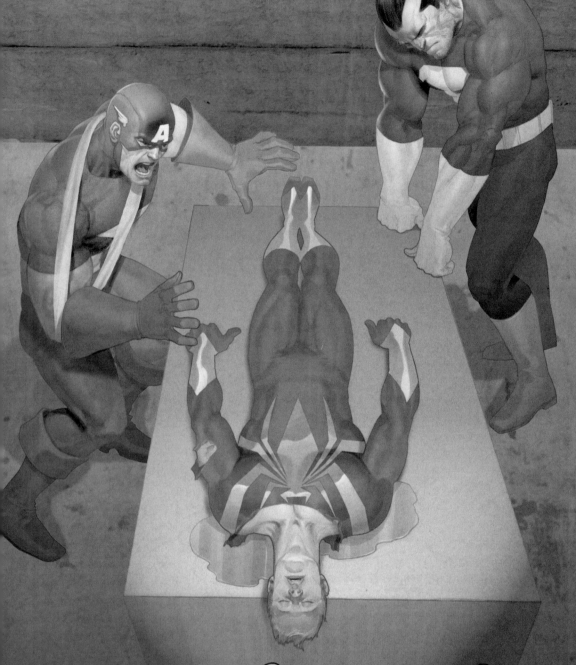

How I Won The War
PART 1: BRING ON THE BAD GUYS

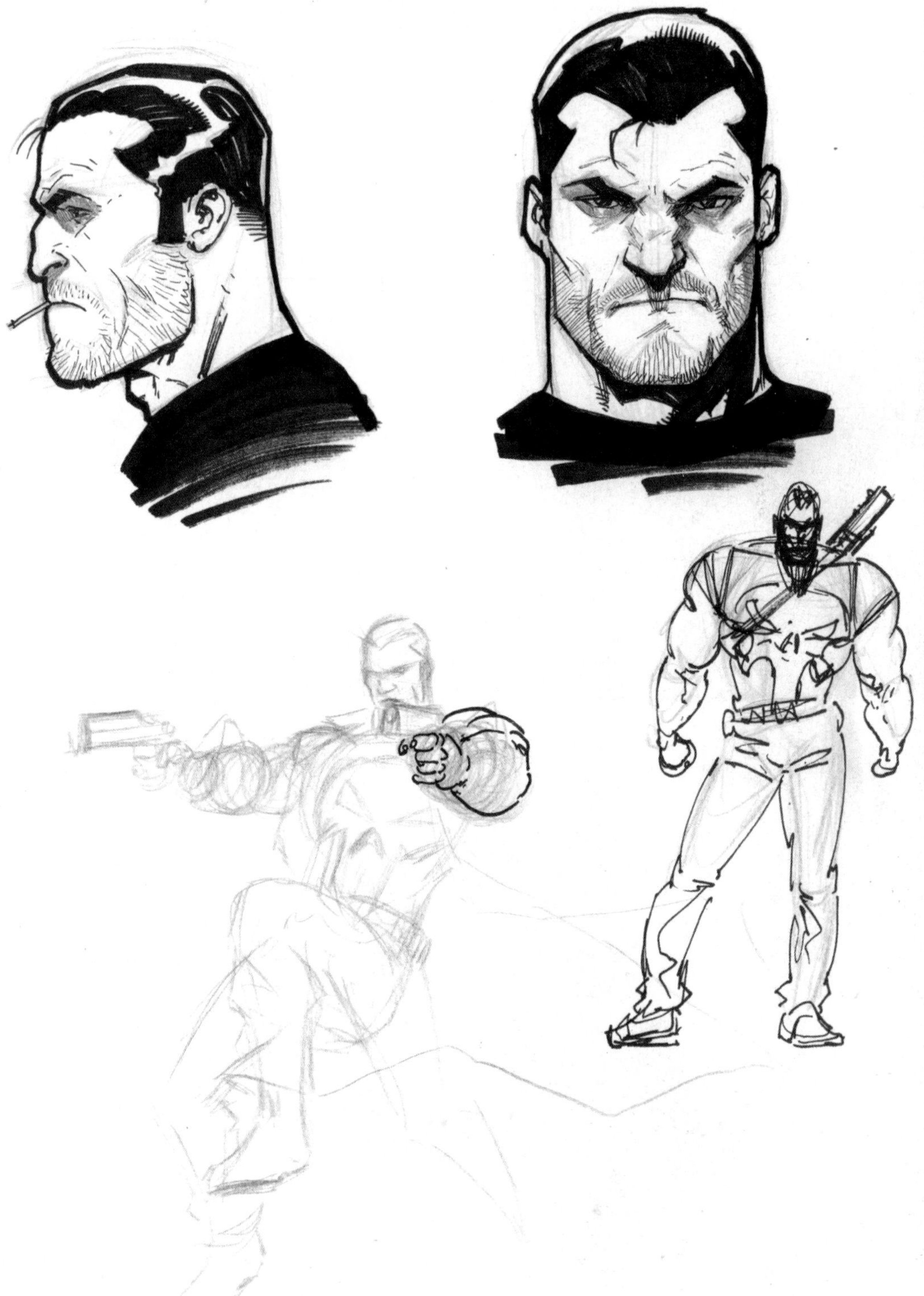

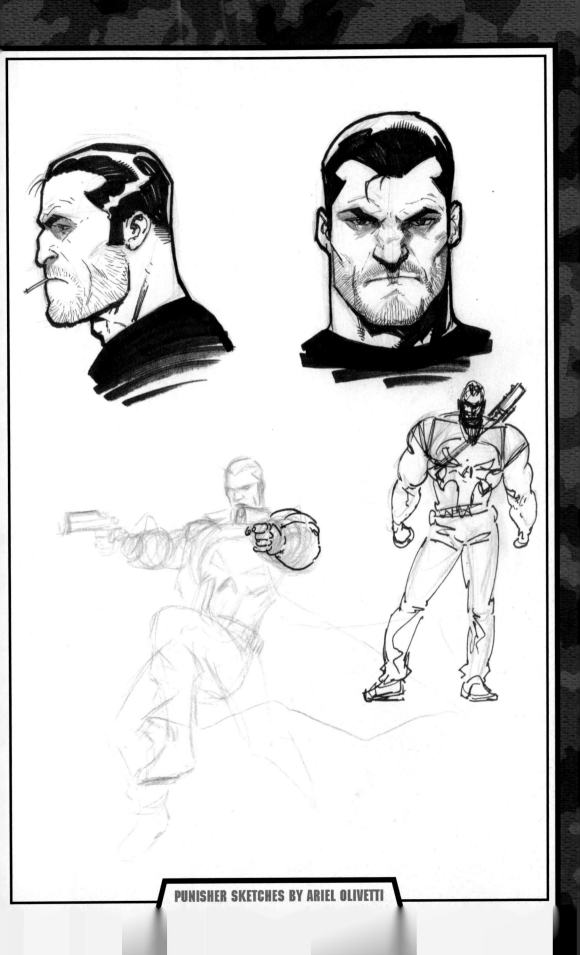

PUNISHER SKETCHES BY ARIEL OLIVETTI

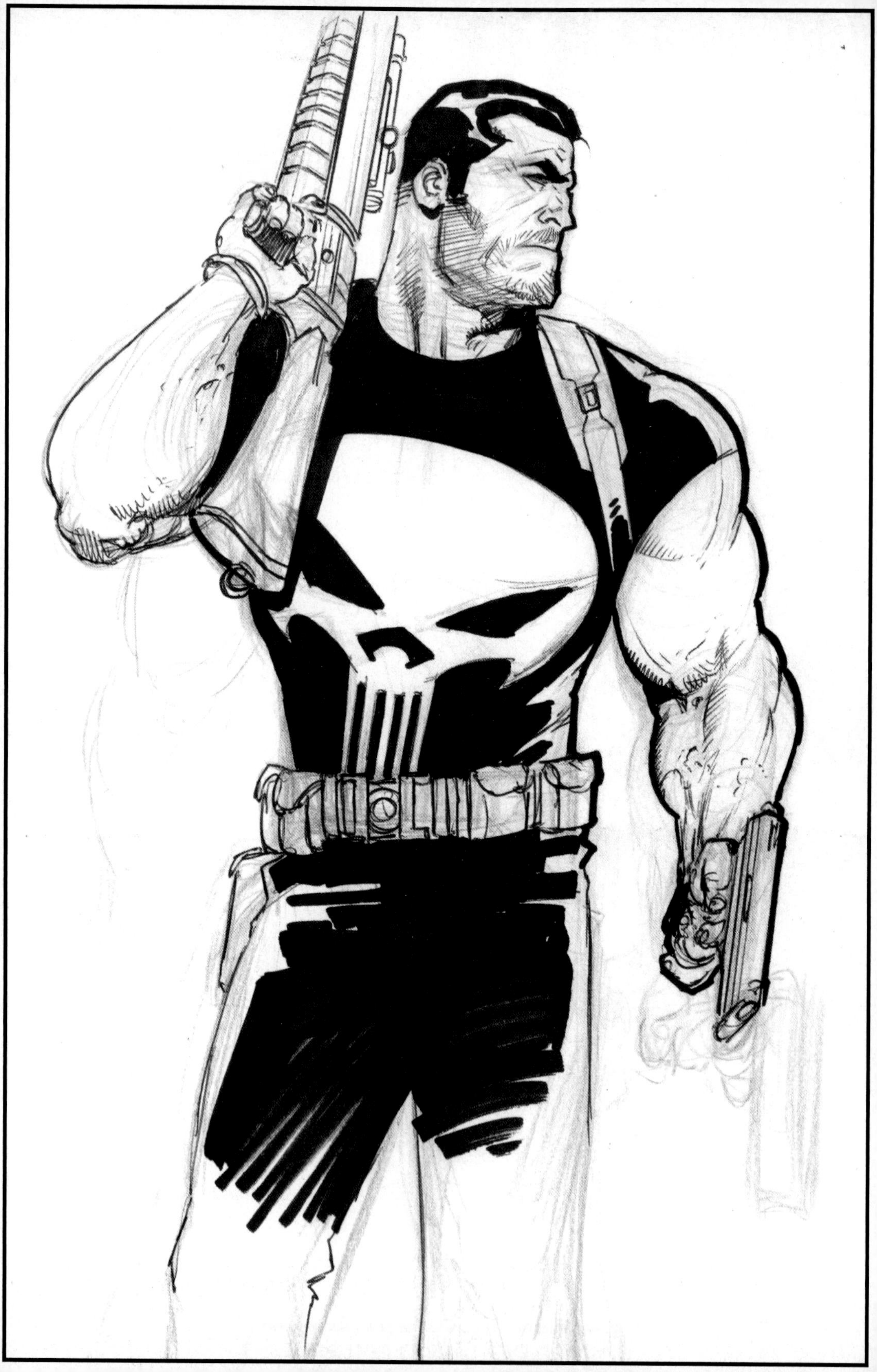

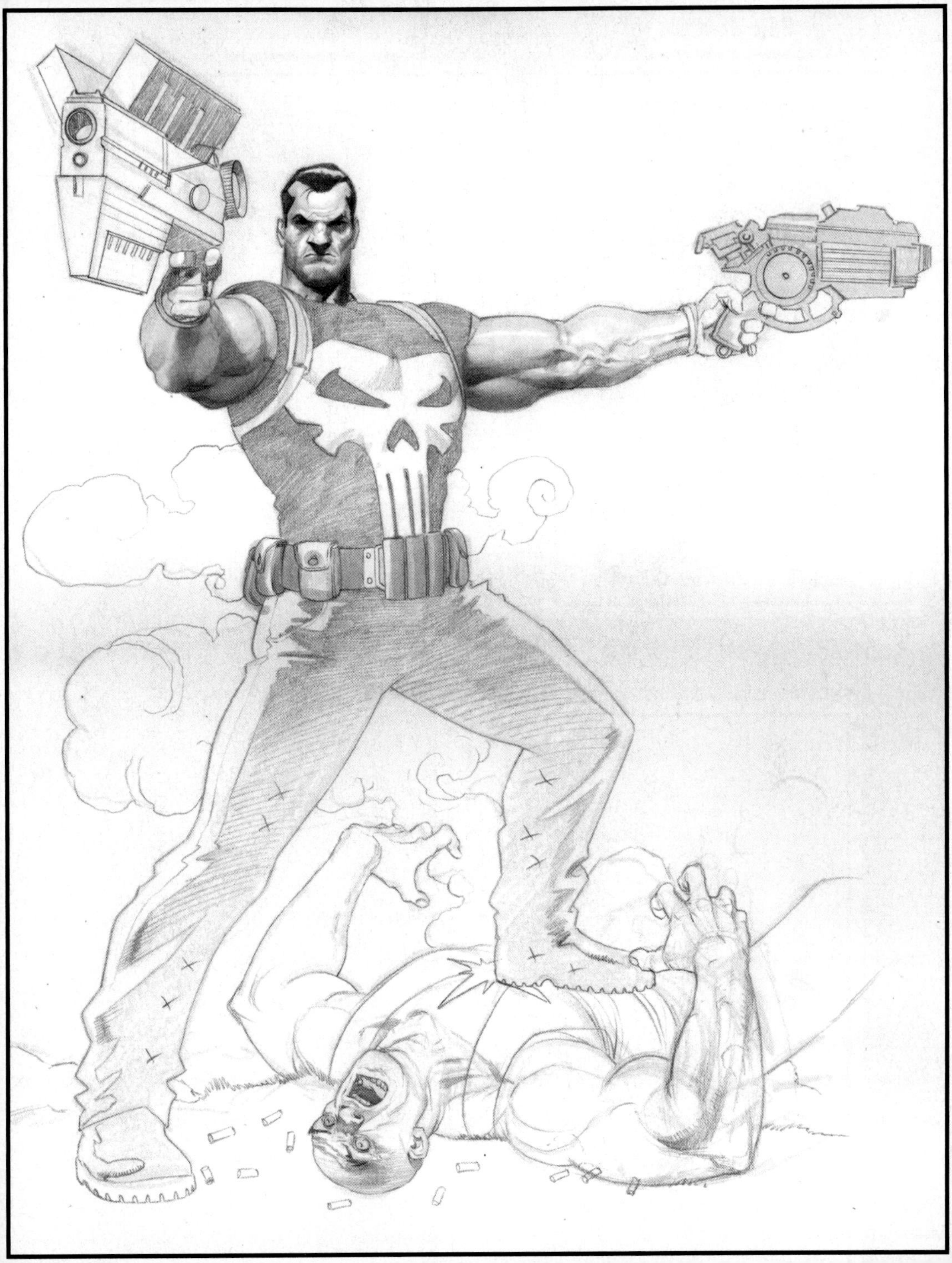

CHARACTER SKETCHES
BY ARIEL OLIVETTI

HATE-MONGER

BUSHWHACKER

ISSUE #7 VARIANT
PENCILS BY ARIEL OLIVETTI

PUNISHER'S
CAPTAIN AMERICA COSTUME
SKETCH BY ARIEL OLIVETTI

ISSUE #7 COVER
PENCILS BY ARIEL OLIVETTI

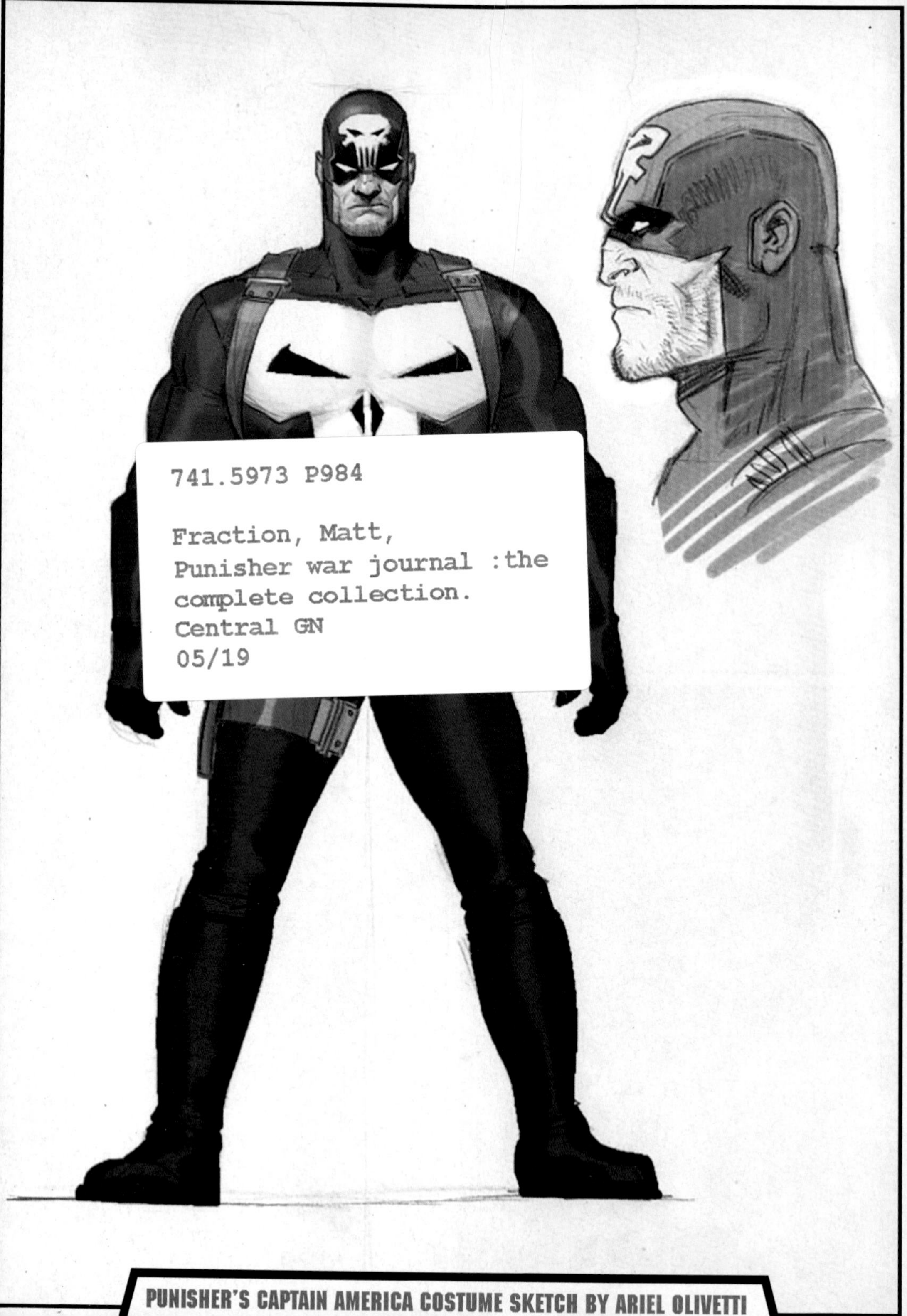

PUNISHER'S CAPTAIN AMERICA COSTUME SKETCH BY ARIEL OLIVETTI